The European Union – A Global Actor?

Sven Gareis
Gunther Hauser
Franz Kernic (eds.)

The European Union –
A Global Actor?

Language consultant: Cathryn Backhaus

Barbara Budrich Publishers
Opladen • Berlin • Toronto 2013

A CIP catalogue record for this book is available from
Die Deutsche Bibliothek (The German Library)

© 2013 by Barbara Budrich Publishers, Opladen, Berlin & Toronto
         www.barbara-budrich.net
         ISBN   978-3-8474-0040-0
         eISBN   978-3-86649-520-3 (eBook)

Das Werk einschließlich aller seiner Teile ist urheberrechtlich geschützt. Jede Verwertung außerhalb der engen Grenzen des Urheberrechtsgesetzes ist ohne Zustimmung des Verlages unzulässig und strafbar. Das gilt insbesondere für Vervielfältigungen, Übersetzungen, Mikroverfilmungen und die Einspeicherung und Verarbeitung in elektronischen Systemen.

Die Deutsche Bibliothek – CIP-Einheitsaufnahme
Ein Titeldatensatz für die Publikation ist bei Der Deutschen Bibliothek erhältlich.

Verlag Barbara Budrich 🅑 Barbara Budrich Publishers
Stauffenbergstr. 7. D-51379 Leverkusen Opladen, Germany

86 Delma Drive. Toronto, ON M8W 4P6 Canada
www.barbara-budrich.net

Jacket illustration by disegno, Wuppertal, Germany – www.disenjo.de
Editing: Cathryn Backhaus, Münster, Germany
Typesetting: R + S, Redaktion + Satz Beate Glaubitz, Leverkusen, Germany
Printed in Europe on acid-free paper by paper & tinta, Warsaw, Poland

Table of Contents

Introduction

Sven Bernhard Gareis/Gunther Hauser/Franz Kernic

Being the world's largest economic power the European Union is still struggling to find its role as a political actor that successfully contributes to the shaping of a peaceful and stable global order conducive to free trade and commerce.
Without doubt, twenty years after its creation by the Maastricht Treaty signed
in February of 1992 the European Union has made remarkable progress in the
field of its Common Foreign and Security Policy (CFSP) and its Common Security and Defence Policy (CSDP). The Union is actively engaged in establishing stable relationships with other international organisations and alliances,
regions and countries around the globe and it is in its vital interest to maintain a
peaceful global order conducive to free trade and commerce.

The European Union's new roles and ambitions in global politics and international relations have attracted much public and scholarly attention: it can
be viewed as a unique and remarkable experiment in regional integration and
cooperation, in which a community of twenty-seven sovereign states tries to
perform as a unified actor in the pursuit of common policies and goals on the
international stage. Looking at the various practical difficulties of this ambitious endeavour, however, the question remains open whether this project
will in the end lead to long-term political success.

The emergence of the European Community and later the European Union
in international relations has also stimulated new thoughts and approaches in International Relations theory. The established mainstream theoretical approaches
of the Cold War era were suddenly confronted with a new political reality, i.e.
the fact that a new type of political entity has emerged and gradually taken over
a number of roles and policies that were previously solely attached to a sovereign state. Consequently new questions were raised and discussed: Do we still
need to see the individual EU member states as the primary actors in global
politics? How can we adequately describe the relationship between the EU and
its member states with respect to the wide field of external relations, including
the dimensions of foreign economic relations, global trade and foreign and security policy? What kind of an "actor" is the EU in international relations?

A wide array of answers has been given to these or similar questions in the
social and political sciences and numerous scholars continue to struggle with

the problem to properly explain certain peculiarities of the European Union and its external relations. One difficulty emanates from the fact that the EU is neither a "super-state" nor a political entity totally subordinated to sovereign states. Consequently, the interplay between *intergovernmental* and *supranational* cooperation within the EU framework has attracted particular attention among both political practitioners and scholars. Other important aspects to be addressed in this context have been the status as a legal personality (which the Union gave to itself in Article 47 of the Lisbon Treaty) and the question of a minimum capacity for autonomous action in the sphere of global politics. From this special nature of the European Union result a number of theoretical and practical challenges when studying and analyzing EU external relations.

In 2012 and in the years to come the European Union and its established mechanisms are being put to the test, particularly due to the challenge of tackling Europe's current severe economic and monetary crisis. There can be no doubt that those recent developments have weakened the Union's position also in global politics and foreign affairs. But on the other hand this process has also contributed to an increased awareness about today's interdependences and interconnections in a globalised world. Thus, it suddenly appears even more crucial than ever before to deepen the European structures in the field of finance and economics by enhancing intra-union solidarity as well as the responsibility and accountability of every single member state for its budget and fiscal politics. Furthermore, it becomes necessary to improve the Union's external relations with other global powers in order to tackle the present economic crisis, that is not confined to the European realm but also affects other regions like the US or Asia.

Considering these challenges, one can even argue that this severe crisis puts additional pressure on the European Union to further develop its capacities to act more efficiently on the global stage both in terms of economics and politics. But though considerable progress has been made in the build-up of common institutions and procedures for collective external action, the European Union's foreign, security and defence policies continue to be strictly guided by the principles of intergovernmental coordination and unanimity. Of course this limits the Union's capacity for autonomous foreign policy action and it raises the old question of whether or not consensus can be achieved when crucial and maybe controversial foreign policy issues come to the table. So the current crisis may productively contribute to revitalizing the debate on the finality of the European integration process: Shall there emerge a strong political Union that pursues its common interests in international relations or shall Europe appear as a loose association of self-interested states that can easily be divided by powerful actors like the US or China?

In the Union's real politics of today those superior questions, however, are somewhat insignificant. "Stabilisation" has become one of the key words in the EU vocabulary. Strategic partnerships and joint action plans are supposed to prepare the ground and to safeguard common interests and values. The European Union and NATO share common interests in stabilizing Europe, particularly by means of integrating Russia, Ukraine, Central Asia as well as the Mediterranean countries in North Africa and in the Middle East into a wider Euro-Atlantic zone of stability. But how lasting and sustainable have those efforts been?

After all, in recent years the EU has developed its own set of foreign policy instruments which are now at its disposal with respect to conducting foreign and security policy. These instruments include diplomacy, development cooperation and partnership agreements. By signing pre-accession agreements with candidate countries, the EU also aims at exporting the *acquis communautaire* – the collection of treaties, legislation, agreements, court decisions and principles that constitute the law of the European Union – beyond its borders. In addition, it is also noteworthy to mention that the EU has been seen by other regions and countries as a potential role-model for their own regional integration projects. Especially in the case of the African Union (AU) and the Union of South American Nations (UNASUR), the EU has served as such a role-model, thus indirectly also exporting certain European values, norms and ideas.

Furthermore, the European Union has established comprehensive relationships and frameworks of cooperation with all major global players and concluded strategic partnerships with political actors of all continents. The closest ties, however, have been developed with the US, thus giving transatlantic relations a very high priority on the foreign policy agenda. In this context it must also be mentioned that 21 out of today's 27 EU states are members of NATO. Since the establishment of its Common Security and Defence Policy (CSDP) after 1999 the EU has taken some advantage of NATO's and the United Nations' rules and lessons learned to strengthen the readiness of European autonomous capabilities to plan and conduct military operations in the field of international crisis management and peacekeeping. Over the last decade, the Union has been coordinating comprehensively civilian and military crisis management together with UN, OSCE, NATO, but also with the African Union (AU) and ASEAN. The EU has become a major sponsor for AU-led peace operations and a key supporter of African security organisations (Sicurelli 2010: 33). Finally, it is also important to mention the EU engagement in the field of international law, where the Union's foreign policy clearly aims at promoting human rights and international law and "the pursuit of CFSP objectives through diplomatic and economic means" (Terzi 2010: 3).

It has become quite common to see the European Union "as a model of how states and their citizens can work together in peace and in freedom" (Mkrtchyan/Huseynov/Gogolashvili 2009: 6). Of course there are also differences in how the European Union is perceived internally and externally. These perceptions are shifting; they are frequently linked to how successful the EU appears to be in economic, political and social terms. But regardless of its limitations and weaknesses: there can be no doubt that the EU is being perceived as being increasingly active on the international scene.

At the same time, however, it also has to be stated that the Union obviously lacks internal coherence with respect to many foreign policy issues, e.g. Turkish accession to the EU, recognition of Kosovo as a state. In the Iraq crisis of 2002/3 CFSP mechanisms were paralyzed when EU members were split over the question of joining the US in their war against Saddam Hussein; in 2011 again approaches to national ambitions prevailed over common procedures when Europe was confronted with the 'Arab Spring' and the war against the Qaddafi regime in Libya. Even in the relationship with NATO, overlaps in responsibilities and controversies over strategic interests as in the crisis over Iraq (2002/3) as well as disputes between the EU and NATO countries like Turkey and Cyprus result in factual stalemates in inter-agency relations of these two most important Western institutions. Furthermore, it is very common to criticise the Union for not having a clear strategic vision for regions such as the Caucasus, the Middle East and other regions critical of world politics. In addition, it sometimes appears very difficult to evaluate the long-term impact of certain strategic partnerships concluded between the EU and other countries, particularly when it comes to the questions of a potential "payoff" for Europe and mutual benefits on both sides. A good example is the strategic partnership that the EU established with China in 2003, and which is characterised by strong trade relations on the one hand and continuing debates on intellectual property rights and import quota as well as on political issues like human rights and the Union's arms embargo against the People's Republic (see Men 2007).

Up to now, the EU primarily continues to be a "civilian power" regarding its means to exert influence in international relations. Therefore, it is frequently referred to as a "normative power", a promoter of norms such as peace, liberty, democracy, the rule of law, and respect for human rights (Terzi 2010: 3). From this perspective, the European Union again appears to be a different kind of global actor that particularly with respect to the use of military force in international politics differs significantly from the United States of America. This fact may also contribute to the globally prevailing image of the Union according to which it constantly tries – with limited success – "to appear as a unitary and effective actor in the international arena" (Sicurelli 2010: 1).

Before this background, the present volume in its 24 chapters comprehensively analyses the EU's external relations, its Common Foreign and Security Policy, institutions, procedures and fields of action and critically discusses the Union's capability to pursue its vital interests as a unified actor in world politics. Hereto the book is structured in three main parts: The first part contains a number of contributions which focus on institutions, policy frameworks and the history of the EU's common foreign and security policy. The second part aims at studying the EU's external relations with important international institutions and organisations as well as major regional powers and states. The third and final part resembles articles which address key issues of the Union's external activities and analyze specific foreign policy areas in detail. The book's general approach is an inter-disciplinary one: Many contributions come from political science and international law but clearly put an emphasis on practical foreign policy issues rather than on theory-building. They all aim at increasing our understanding of the EU's specific profile as an actor in global politics.

References

Men, Jing (2007): The EU-China Strategic Partnership. Achievements and Challenges. Policy paper no 12. University Center of International Studies, Pittsburg PA: Pittsburg University.

Mkrtchyan, Tigran/Huseynov, Tabib/Gogolashvili, Kakha (2009): The European Union and the South Caucasus. Three Perspectives on the Future of the European Project from the Caucasus, Europe in Dialog 2009/01, Gütersloh: Bertelsmann Stiftung.

Sicurelli, Daniela (2010): The European Union's Africa Policies. Norms, Interests and Impact. Farnham (UK) and Burlington (Vt): Ashgate Publishing.

Terzi, Özlem (2010): The Influence of the European Union on Turkish Foreign Policy. Ashgate Publishing: Farnham (UK) and Burlington (Vt).

Part 1: History and Institutions

The EU's Institutional Structure Involved in Shaping Foreign and Security Policy

Gunther Hauser

Introduction

This article aims at elaborating and analyzing the main institutions involved in shaping CFSP/CSDP policy, taking into account the institutional key changes in the EU's external action after the Lisbon Treaty. When the Lisbon Treaty entered into force on December 1, 2009 the Treaty on European Union (TEU) kept the same name, and the treaty establishing the European Community became the Treaty on the Functioning of the European Union (TFEU). The Union's institutions in general shall be (Article 13 TEU): The European Parliament; the European Council; the Council; the European Commission; the Court of Justice of the European Union; the European Central Bank; and the Court of Auditors. The following institutions are involved in shaping policy in the framework of the Common Foreign and Security Policy (CFSP) and the Common Security and Defence Policy (CSDP): the European Council; the Council; the European Commission/High Representative of the Union for Foreign Affairs and Security Policy; and the European Parliament.

Relating to Article 15 (1) TEU the "*European Council* shall provide the Union with the necessary impetus for its development and shall define the general political directions and priorities thereof. It shall not exercise legislative functions." As Article 15 (2) TEU states, the "European Council shall consist of the Heads of State or Government of the Member States, together with its President and the President of the Commission. The High Representative of the Union for Foreign Affairs and Security Policy shall take part in its work." According to Article 15 (3) TEU

> "The European Council shall meet twice every six months, convened by its President. When the agenda so requires, the members of the European Council may decide each to be assisted by a minister and, in the case of the President of the Commission, by a member of the Commission. When the situation so requires, the President shall convene a special meeting of the European Council."

Under the Lisbon Treaty, the European Council became an institution which is assisted by the General Secretariat of the Council. The staff of the General Secretariat is therefore at the President's disposal, including the Directorate for general political questions, the Legal Service, policy Directorate-Generals

(Ecofin, Environment, Justice and Home Affairs, etc.), translation services, protocol, press office, etc.

In the Lisbon Treaty, the General Affairs Council (GAC) and the Foreign Affairs Council (FAC) are the only Council formations which are laid down. The *Foreign Affairs Council* elaborates "the Union's external action on the basis of strategic guidelines laid down by the European Council and ensure that the Union's action is consistent" (Article 16 (6) TEU, third sentence). There is only one *Council* of the EU, it can meet in ten different formations. The Council formations can be extended or limited in numbers by the heads of state or government. The *High Representative of the Union for Foreign Affairs and Security Policy* who is also one of the Vice-Presidents of the European Commission chairs the Foreign Affairs Council, contributes through proposals towards the preparation of the CFSP and ensures implementation of the decisions adopted by the European Council and the Council.

Article 16 (7) TEU states: "A *Committee of Permanent Representatives of the Governments of the Member States* shall be responsible for preparing the work of the Council."

A new political figure has come on the scene since the entry into force of the Lisbon Treaty: the fixed full-time *President of the European Council*. At their informal meeting in Brussels on November 19, 2009, ahead of the entry into force of the Lisbon Treaty, EU heads of state or government agreed on the election of Mr Herman van Rompuy as the elect President. According to Article 15 (6) of the Treaty on the European Union, the President of the European Council:

- chairs it and drives forward its work;
- ensures the preparation and continuity of the work of the European Council in cooperation with the President of the Commission, and on the basis of the work of the General Affairs Council;
- endeavours to facilitate cohesion and consensus within the European Council;
- presents a report to the European Parliament after each of the meetings of the European Council.

The President shall also, "at his/her level and in that capacity, ensure the external representation of the Union on issues concerning its common foreign and security policy, without prejudice to the powers of the High Representative of the Union for Foreign Affairs and Security Policy." According to Article 15 (5) TEU

> "The European Council shall elect its President, by a qualified majority, for a term of two and a half years, renewable once. In the event of an impediment or

serious misconduct, the European Council can end the President's term of office in accordance with the same procedure."

As Article 42 (1) TEU states, the CSDP is an integral part of CSFP. It shall provide the Union with an operational capacity drawing on civilian and military assets. The Union may use them on missions outside the Union for peacekeeping, conflict prevention and strengthening international security in accordance with the principles of the UN Charter. Relating to CSDP operations and missions, a "*constructive abstention*" could be used by the Member States as follows in Article 31 TEU (1):

> "Decisions under this Chapter shall be taken by the European Council and the Council acting unanimously, except where this Chapter provides otherwise. The adoption of legislative acts shall be excluded.
>
> When abstaining in a vote, any member of the Council may qualify its abstention by making a formal declaration under the present subparagraph. In that case, it shall not be obliged to apply the decision, but shall accept that the decision commits the Union. In a spirit of mutual solidarity, the Member State concerned shall refrain from any action likely to conflict with or impede Union action based on that decision and the other Member States shall respect its position. If the members of the Council qualifying their abstention in this way represent at least one third of the Member States comprising at least one third of the population of the Union, the decision shall not be adopted."

The formal role of the *European Parliament* in relation to the CFSP stems from its two main roles as stipulated in the Treaties i.e. that of political scrutiny and budgetary authority. The High Representative has a central role in ensuring the consistent and effective formulation of CSFP/CSDP. In this respect, the Lisbon Treaty tasks the High Representative to work with the European Parliament (Article 36 TEU).

The High Representative and the European External Action Service (EEAS)

At the informal meeting in Brussels on November 19, 2009, EU heads of state or government agreed on the appointment of Ms Catherine Ashton as the High Representative of the Union for Foreign Affairs and Security Policy. Ms Ashton has been appointed by the European Council with the agreement of the President of the Commission. Her term of office (five years) coincides with the Commission's term of office.

The High Representative exercises, in foreign affairs, the functions which, so far, were exercised by the six-monthly rotating Presidency, the High Representative for CFSP and the Commissioner for External Relations.

According to Articles 18 and 27 of the Treaty on the European Union, the High Representative:

- conducts the Union's common foreign and security policy (Article 18 (2) TEU);
- contributes by her proposals to the development of that policy, which she will carry out as mandated by the Council, and ensures implementation of the decisions adopted in this field (Article 18 (2) TEU);
- presides over the Foreign Affairs Council (Article 18 (3) TEU and Article 27 (1) TEU);
- is one of the Vice-Presidents of the Commission. She ensures the consistency of the Union's external action. She is responsible within the Commission for responsibilities incumbent on it in external relations and for coordinating other aspects of the Union's external action (Article 18 (4) TEU);
- represents the Union for matters relating to the CFSP, conducts political dialogue with third parties on the Union's behalf and expresses the Union's position in international organisations and at international conferences (Article 27 (2) TEU);
- exercises authority over the European External Action Service and over the Union delegations in third countries and at international organisations (General Secretariat of the Council of the EU 2009).

Article 18 (1) TEU states as follows:

> "The European Council, acting by a qualified majority, with the agreement of the President of the Commission, shall appoint the High Representative of the Union for Foreign Affairs and Security Policy. The European Council may end his term of office by the same procedure."

The High Representative is subject, together with the President of the Commission and the other members of the Commission, to a vote of consent by the European Parliament. In fulfilling her mandate, the High Representative is assisted by a European External Action Service (EEAS) and has authority over some 130 delegations of the Union in third countries and to international organisations. Article 27 (3) TEU constitutes the legal basis for the Council decision on the organisation and functioning of the EEAS.

The EEAS helps the High Representative ensure the consistency and coordination of the Union's external action as well as prepare policy proposals and implement them after their approval by Council. It also assists the President of the European Council and the President as well as the Members of the Commission in their respective functions in the area of external relations and shall ensure close cooperation with the Member States.

The EEAS is a service of a *sui generis* nature, separate from the Commission and the Council Secretariat (Council of the European Union 2009: 6). The EEAS has its own section in the EU budget, to which the usual budgetary and control rules will apply. 60 percent of the EEAS personnel originate from the European Commission and the Council Secretariat.

The Commission's delegations became Union delegations under the authority of the High Representative and as part of the EEAS structure. Delegations contain both regular EEAS staff (including Heads of Delegation) and staff from relevant Commission services. EU delegations work in close co-operation with diplomatic services of the Member States. They shall play a supporting role as regards diplomatic and consular protection of Union citizens in third countries. In order to enable the High Representative to conduct the CSDP, the EEAS includes the Crisis Management and Planning Directorate (CMPD), the Civilian Planning and Conduct Capability (CPCC) and the EU Military Staff (EUMS) and the Situation Centre (SitCen) (Council of the European Union 2009: 3, Hynek 2010: 4). Consultation procedures have been established between the EEAS and the services of the European Commission with external responsibilities, including those in charge of internal policies with significant external dimensions. The EU Special Representatives (EUSR) or their tasks became also part of the EEAS (ibid: 5).

According to Article 33 TEU

> "The Council may, on a proposal from the High Representative of the Union for Foreign Affairs and Security Policy, appoint a special representative with a mandate in relation to particular policy issues. The special representative shall carry out his mandate under the authority of the High Representative."

With regard to CFSP/CSDP, the High Representative's core responsibility is to oversee the implementation of decisions taken by the ministerial Council of the European Union and the European Council (Article 43 (2) TEU) – the Heads of State or Government. Tasks and functions of the High Representative are: International representation of the EU, appointment of EU Special Representatives, head of the European Defence Agency, the European Union Satellite Centre, chair of the board of the European Union Institute for Security Studies (EU ISS) and of the European Security and Defence College (ESDC).

The previous office of High Representative of the CFSP was introduced on October 18, 1999 by the Amsterdam Treaty. The former NATO Secretary General Javier Solana has been the EU High Representative for CFSP since then. Solana played an important role in the establishment of the European Security and Defence Policy (ESDP), amongst others by promoting the integration of structures and resources of the Western European Union (WEU). Nevertheless, the High Representative was and remains dependent on the census of the Member States in the Council. In June 2003, the European

Council of Thessaloniki tasked Javier Solana to develop a European Security Strategy (ESS), which was adopted by the Brussels European Council in December 2003. Javier Solana was re-appointed Secretary-General (SG) of the Council in 2004. The SG assisted the Council in foreign policy matters, through contributing to the formulation, preparation and implementation of policy decisions. He acted on behalf of the Council in conducting political dialogue with third parties and helped coordinate the EU's action on the world stage. The six-monthly rotating Presidency has been in charge of chairing the External Relations Council, representing the Union in CFSP matters, implementing the decisions taken and for expressing the EU position internationally.

Council Role in CSDP

The Council is assisted in military CSDP operations by the Political and Security Committee (PSC); the European Union Military Committee (EUMC); and the European Union Military Staff (EUMS), composed of military experts seconded to the Council Secretariat by the Member States. These three political and military bodies within the Council were established by the Helsinki European Council in December 1999.

The European Council (Nice, December 7-10, 2000) decided to establish these permanent political and military structures within the Council of the European Union "in order to provide political control and strategic direction in a crisis" (Perruche 2006: 6). The PSC meets at the ambassadorial level as a preparatory body for the Council of the EU. Its main functions are keeping track of the international situation and helping to define policies within the CSDP. The PSC "prepares a coherent EU response to a crisis and exercises political control and strategic direction", however, the PSC is the linchpin of the CSDP (ibid). As the highest military body set up in the Council, the EUMC is composed of the Chiefs of Defence of the Member States, who are regularly represented by their permanent military representatives. The EUMC provides the PSC with advice and recommendations on all military matters within the EU. In parallel with the EUMC, the PSC is advised by a Committee for Civilian Aspects of Crisis Management (CIVCOM). This committee provides information, drafts and recommendations, and also expresses its opinion on civilian aspects of crisis management to the PSC (Perruche 2006: 6). The EUMS is to perform early warning, situational awareness and strategic planning within the framework of crisis management outside of the EU Member States territories. It is responsible e.g. for peacekeeping tasks, tasks of combat forces in crisis management (including peacemaking), and also for joint disarmament operations, support for third countries in combating terrorism and security sector reform (SSR). "The mission of EUMS also includes identifying European and multinational forces as well as implementing policies and decisions as directed by the European Union Military Committee" (Perruche 2006: 6). The role and tasks of the EUMS have some unique characteristics. On the one hand the EUMS is an integral part of the General Secretariat of the Council and directly attached to the High Representative of the Union for Foreign Affairs and Security Policy. On the other hand the EUMS operates under the military direction of the EUMC, by which it is assisted and to which it reports. The EUMS ensures all the necessary military expertise for the internal work within the EU, providing an early warning capability to that end. It also supports the EUMC with regard to situation assessment and military aspects of strategic planning over the full range of EU-led military operations (Perruche 2006: 6 and 7). As part of the General Secretariat, the EUMS has established relations with the Department for Peacekeeping Operations (DPKO) of the United Nations (UN). Twice a year, a joint steering committee (EU/UN) meets in either Brussels or New York to discuss points of common interests and decide on future cooperation (Perruche 2006: 9). An EU Military Staff's liaison officer was established at the UN Headquarters in December 2008 which has already been "an interesting step in coordination of communication" for the EUFOR Tchad/RCA and EU NAVFOR Somalia missions (Hynek 2010: 2). Additionally, a permanent EU liaison cell has been created at NATO's Supreme Headquarters Allied Powers Europe (SHAPE), and a SHAPE liaison team was situated within the EUMS in the Brussels Kortenbergh building (Perruche 2006: 9, Hynek 2010: 6). The EUMS, along with Member States, also helped for some months, had been supporting their African Union counterparts by working on the AU's military mission in the Sudanese province of Darfur (Perruche 2006: 9).

According to Article 42 (3) TEU, Member States shall make civilian and military capabilities available to the Union for the implementation of CSDP, to contribute to the objectives defined by the Council. Those Member States which together establish multinational forces may also make them available to the CSDP. As Article 42 (4) TEU states, decisions relating to CSDP

"shall be adopted by the Council acting unanimously on a proposal from the High Representative of the Union for Foreign Affairs and Security Policy or an initiative from a Member State. The High Representative may propose the use of both national resources and Union instruments, together with the Commission where appropriate."

In order to operate, the Council "may entrust the execution of a task, within the Union framework, to a group of Member States in order to protect the Union's values and serve its interests" (Article 42 (5) TEU). Those member States "whose military capabilities fulfil higher criteria and which have made more binding commitments to one another in this area with a view to the most demanding missions shall establish permanent structured cooperation within the Union framework. Such cooperation shall be governed by Article 46. .."

The tasks

"in the course of which the Union may use civilian and military means, shall include joint disarmament operations, humanitarian and rescue tasks, military advice and assistance tasks, conflict prevention and peace-keeping tasks, tasks of combat forces in crisis management, including peace-making and post-conflict stabilisation. All these tasks may contribute to the fight against terrorism, including by supporting third countries in combating terrorism in their countries" (Article 43 (1) TEU).

Relating to these tasks, the

"Council shall adopt decisions ..., defining their objectives and scope and the general conditions for their implementation. The High Representative of the Union for Foreign Affairs and Security Policy, acting under the authority of the Council and in close and constant contact with the Political and Security Committee, shall ensure coordination of the civilian and military aspects of such tasks" (Article 43 (2) TEU).

The Council also

"may entrust the implementation of a task to a group of Member States which are willing and have the necessary capability for such a task. Those Member States, in association with the High Representative of the Union for Foreign Affairs and Security Policy, shall agree among themselves on the management of the task" Article 44 (1) TEU.

Those Member States which are participating in the task are obliged to keep the Council regularly informed of its progress on their own initiative or at the request of another Member State. Those states shall inform the Council immediately should the completion of the task entail major consequences or require amendment of the objective, scope and conditions determined for the task in the decisions referred to in paragraph 1. In such cases, the Council shall adopt the necessary decisions.

Those Member States which wish to participate in the Permanent Structured Cooperation (PESCO) and which fulfil the criteria and have made the commitments on military capabilities set out in the protocol on Permanent Structured Cooperation, "shall notify their intention to the Council and to the High Representative of the Union for Foreign Affairs and Security Policy" (Article 46 (1) TEU). Within three months "the Council shall adopt a decision establishing permanent structured cooperation and determining the list of participating Member States. The Council shall act by qualified majority after consulting the High Representative" (Article 46 (2) TEU).

"Any participating Member State which wishes to withdraw from permanent structured cooperation shall notify its intention to the Council, which shall take note that the Member State in question has ceased to participate" (Article 46 (5) TEU).

EC Co-Ordinated External Activities

The European Commission (EC) is fully associated within CFSP and to an extent within CSDP. Together with the respective Council bodies, the Commission is involved in the planning of CSDP missions. Currently the Commission has RELEX (external relations) representatives in the PSC, EUMC, CIVCOM, the Crisis Response Coordination Team and the Civilian-Military Cell (Civ/Mil Cell) located within the EUMS which ensures a real civilian-military cooperation from the planning phase:

"The Civ/Mil Cell including its inherent Operations Centre capacity is the first standing EU body that fully integrates military and civilian expertise. ... The Cell has significantly contributed to the planning and preparation of the ACEH Monitoring Mission, the EU Border Assistance Mission in RAFAH/GAZA, and the EU Support Action to the AU/AMIS in Darfur/Sudan..." (Brauss and Zinzius 2007).

This cell was tasked to set up an Operations Centre[1] "able to plan and to run a particular operation, in particular where a joint civil/military response is required and where no national HQ is identified" (EU Council Secretariat 2007).

The Commission is responsible for the CFSP budget financing the common administrative costs of each CSDP mission not related to defence.

Article 21 (3) TEU emphasises the role of the Council and the Commission in order to ensure consistency in the field of external actions as follows:

"The Union shall ensure consistency between the different areas of its external action and between these and its other policies. The Council and the Commission, assisted by the High Representative of the Union for Foreign Affairs and Security Policy, shall ensure that consistency and shall cooperate to that effect."

---

1 The Operations Centre is non-standing. The UK together with other EU Member States strongly opposes the creation of a standing structure to provide for autonomous planning. The compromise was to create a core staff unit, the Operations Centre, which would be activated in cases where neither the recourse to NATO command and control (C2) structures nor national Operation Headquarters (OHQ) would be available options (Gebhard 2009: 12).

The Commission itself is completely independent of national governments, so the Members of the Commission are committed to acting in the interests of the Union and not taking instructions from national governments. A new Commission is appointed every five years.

The European Commission has four main roles:

- to propose new laws to Parliament and the Council;
- to manage the EU's budget and allocate funding;
- to enforce EU law (jointly with the Court of Justice);
- to represent the EU on the international stage, "for example by negotiating agreements between the EU and other countries" (European Commission 2011a).

Officials of the Commission are participating at the European External Action Service (EEAS). On October 30, 2009 the European Council agreed on guidelines for the new European External Action Service – EEAS (doc. 14930/09). According to the guidelines, the EEAS will be a single service under the authority of the High Representative of the European Union for Foreign Affairs and Security Policy, who is one of the Vice-Presidents of the European Commission (General Secretariat of the Council of the EU 2009). The High Representative conducts the Union's CFSP and contributes to the development of that policy and ensures implementation of the decisions adopted in this field.

The European Commission is divided into several departments known as Directorates-General (DGs), so five DGs are involved in external relations: Enlargement (ELARG), EuropeAid Development & Cooperation (DEVCO), Foreign Policy Instruments Service (EEAS), Humanitarian Aid (ECHO) and Trade (TRADE).

On January 3, 2011 *DG Development and Cooperation Directorate General – EuropeAid* (DEVCO) started work in order to design European development policy and to deliver aid throughout the world. DEVCO brought together the two former DGs Development and EuropeAid and

> "reinforces the ability of the EU to design state-of-the-art development policy for all developing countries, and enhances policy coherence for development while further improving implementation and delivery mechanisms. It also defines the future development policy drawing from the objectives of the EU's Green Paper on development policy and contributes to global challenges ahead. ... It acts as the single contact point for stakeholders both inside and outside the EU, but also for the European External Action Service (EEAS), and for all sectoral DGs of the European Commission" (European Commission 2011b).

DEVCO works with international organisations like the United Nations, the Organisation for Economic Cooperation and Development (OECD) and the World Bank, among others. Valued partners of DEVCO are civil society organisations, "they also help boost citizen participation and good governance" (European Commission 2011c). DEVCO is also heading coordination of its activities with national parliaments of the EU Member States "because they play an important role in shaping and overseeing EU development policy and funding. This ensures that activities at the EU and national level complement each other" (ibid).

In the context of citizen participation in third countries, the Commission runs the *European Instrument for Democracy and Human Rights* (EIDHR). EIDHR was launched in 2006 and builds upon the European Initiative (2000-2006); its "aim is to provide support for the promotion of democracy and human rights in non-EU countries" (European Commission 2011e). The key objectives of the EIDHR (budget: 1,104 million euro 2007-2013) are: strengthening the role of civil society in promoting human rights and democratic reform, in supporting the peaceful conciliation of group interests and in consolidating political participation and representation; supporting and strengthening the international and regional framework for the protection of human rights, justice, the rule of law and the promotion of democracy (ibid). The EIDHR "can grant aid where no established development cooperation exists, and can intervene without the agreement of the governments of third countries. It can support groups or individuals within civil society defending democracy as well as intergovernmental organisations that implement the international mechanisms for the protection of human rights" (ibid).

Through *DG ECHO* which was established in 1992, the European Commission spends on average 640 million euro per year on humanitarian aid. The EU's mandate to ECHO (Regulation (CE) no 1257/96) is to provide emergency assistance and relief to the victims of natural disasters or armed conflict outside the EU. The Humanitarian Aid and civil protection department of the European Commission's (ECHO) task is to ensure goods and services get to crisis zones fast. Goods and services reach disaster areas via ECHO partners. DG ECHO is the only publicly financed department in the world solely devoted to funding the delivery of humanitarian aid and civil protection. Humanitarian action occupies a key position in the EU's external action. ECHO is the world's main player in this field. ECHO operations are financed under the budget headings specifically devoted to humanitarian aid: the EC budget Title 23 for humanitarian aid and the allocation to ACP countries for humanitarian and emergency assistance under the European Development Fund. The Commission may also ask the budgetary authority (Parliament and Council) to increase its funding by mobilising the reserve for emergency aid (tile 40), introduced by the 1992 Edinburgh European Council. Over the past years, DG ECHO's budget was systematically reinforced, either through use of the Emergency Aid Reserve (EAR), through transfers from other budget lines within the External Aid heading or, in respect of ACP countries, by using resources from the European Development Fund (B-envelope) for amounts ranging from 71 million euro in 2001 to 177 million euro in 2008. Through ECHO funding, some 18 million people are helped each year through 200 partners (NGOs, ICRC, and UN agencies like the UNHCR and the WFP) (European Commission 2011f).

The *DG for Trade* aims at defining the trade interests of the European Union *"in both defensive and offensive terms"* (European Commission 2011d), also at monitoring and ensuring the implementation of international agreements by using the WTO dispute settlement system and the instruments for trade promotion or defence adopted by the Community (the anti-dumping and anti-subsidy rules and the trade barriers regulation (TBR)). DG for Trade shall also ensure consistency within the RELEX group between commercial policy and the Union's general external relations policy on the one hand and the contribution of the EU to global economic governance on the other (ibid).

EP Role in Co-Decision, Overseeing and its Own Activity in CFSP/CSDP

The European Parliament consists of 751 Members of the European Parliament (MEPs) including the President of the European Parliament. The number of MEPs cannot exceed 751 and the breakdown of parliamentary seats between Member States will be degressively proportional. The Lisbon Treaty also stipulates that no Member State can have fewer than 6 or more than 96 seats:

> "The European Parliament shall be composed of representatives of the Union's citizens. They shall not exceed seven hundred and fifty in number, plus the President. Representation of citizens shall be degressively proportional, with a minimum threshold of six members per Member State. No Member State shall be allocated more than ninety-six seats.
>
> The European Council shall adopt by unanimity, on the initiative of the European Parliament and with its consent, a decision establishing the composition of the European Parliament, respecting the principles referred to in the first subparagraph" (Article 14 (2) TEU).

According to Article 14 (1) TEU, "The European Parliament shall, jointly with the Council, exercise legislative and budgetary functions. It shall exercise functions of political control and consultation as laid down in the Treaties. It shall elect the President of the Commission." As Article 14 (3) TEU states, "The members of the European Parliament shall be elected for a term of five years by direct universal suffrage in a free and secret ballot." According to Article 14 (4) TEU: "The European Parliament shall elect its President and its officers from among its members."

In particular the European Commission, the European Parliament and the Council of the European Union are involved in the decision-making process at EU level. New legislation is generally proposed by the European Commission, but it is the Council and the European Parliament that pass the laws. Directives and regulations are the main forms of EU law.

The co-decision procedure which was introduced by the Maastricht Treaty increased the influence of the European Parliament significantly. In this procedure, the Parliament shares legislative power equally with the Council. In the meantime the co-decision procedure has been used for most EU law-making. This procedure gives the European Parliament the opportunity to negotiate directly with the Council in a conciliation committee, composed of equal numbers of Council and Parliament representatives. This only happens in the event of lack of agreement on a proposal. Once this committee has reached an agreement (time limit six weeks), the text is sent once again to Parliament and the Council so that they can finally adopt it as law. The Council and the European Parliament have six weeks to adopt the bill (Folketinget 2011). The Council of Ministers (e.g. agriculture, economy, transportation, justice and home affairs) generally takes a decision by qualified majority, while the European Parliament has to approve the bill by a majority of the votes cast (ibid). However, if neither the Council nor the European Parliament can approve the bill within the time limit of six weeks, the proposal is automatically rejected (ibid). Conciliation is becoming increasingly rare. Most laws passed in co-decision are, in fact, adopted either at the first or second reading. The co-decision procedure is divided into three phases. Whether final adoption takes place during the first or second reading, or whether the proposal must go through a third reading depends on the parties' willingness to negotiate (ibid).

Foreign policy, security and defence are matters over which the national governments retain independent control. However, they did not pool their national sovereignty in these areas, therefore the European Parliament and the Commission play only a limited role here. The CFSP

> "shall be put into effect by the High Representative of the Union for Foreign Affairs and Security Policy and by Member States. ... The specific role of the European Parliament and of the Commission in this area is defined by the Treaties. ..." (Article 24 (1) TEU).

According to Article 36 TEU

> "The High Representative of the Union for Foreign Affairs and Security Policy shall regularly consult the European Parliament on the main aspects and the basic choices of the common foreign and security policy and the common security and

defence policy and inform it of how those policies evolve. He shall ensure that the views of the European Parliament are duly taken into consideration. Special representatives may be involved in briefing the European Parliament.

The European Parliament may ask questions of the Council or make recommendations to it and to the High Representative. Twice a year it shall hold a debate on progress in implementing the common foreign and security policy, including the common security and defence policy."

Relating to the European External Action Service (EEAS), the European Parliament may exercise budgetary control in all questions not related to the responsibilities of the Member States. European "diplomats" could be invited to contribute hearings by the Members of the European Parliament (MEPs).

Financing CSDP

The Union's annual budget is decided jointly by the Council and the European Parliament. According to Article 41 (2) TEU

"Operating expenditure to which the implementation of this Chapter gives rise shall … be charged to the Union budget, except for such expenditure arising from operations having military or defence implications and cases where the Council acting unanimously decides otherwise.

In cases where expenditure is not charged to the Union budget, it shall be charged to the Member States in accordance with the gross national product scale, unless the Council acting unanimously decides otherwise. As for expenditure arising from operations having military or defence implications, Member States whose representatives in the Council have made a formal declaration under Article 31 (31), second subparagraph, shall not be obliged to contribute to the financing thereof."

Relating to Article (3) TEU,

"The Council shall adopt a decision establishing the specific procedures for guaranteeing rapid access to appropriations in the Union budget for urgent financing of initiatives in the framework of the common foreign and security policy, and in particular for preparatory activities for the tasks referred to Article 42 (1) and Article 43. It shall act after consulting the European Parliament."

Civilian crisis-management operations are funded from the CFSP budget which is established following the budgetary procedure laid down for the Community budget. The Union's CFSP budget was growing from approx. 35 million euros prior to 2004 to approx 280 million euros in 2010 (Quille 2010: 6).

Operations with military implications or defence operations cannot be financed from Community funds. For the common costs of such operations, the Council of the EU has set up a special mechanism (ATHENA) that was established on March 1, 2004 (EU Council Secretariat 2006: 1). ATHENA administers "the financing of common costs of EU operations having military or defence implications" (ibid). A review is foreseen after every operation and at least every 18 months respectively. ATHENA is managed by a Special Committee (SC) composed of representatives of EU States (contributors). The European Commission attends the SC meetings (ibid: 3).

The Operations Commander "is the authorising officer for the operation he commands. Where there is no Operations Commander, ATHENA's administrator becomes the authority officer" (ibid: 2). Member States have the choice either to pay contributions in anticipation of a possible rapid reaction operation or to pay within five days.

The Council shall adopt by a qualified majority, on a proposal from the High Representative of the Union for Foreign Affairs and Security Policy, decisions establishing:

- the procedures for setting up and financing the start-up fund, in particular the amounts allocated to the fund;
- the procedures for administering the start-up fund;
- the financial control procedures (Assembly of the Western European Union 2008: 31).

The High Representative shall report to the Council on the implementation of this remit (ibid). If expenditure is not charged to the Union budget, it will be generally charged to the Member States in accordance with their gross national product (unless the Council unanimously decides otherwise). The rather new aspect, which was introduced by the TEU (Lisbon) is the creation of a so-called start-up fund. Preparatory activities for the tasks referred to Article 42 (1) and 43 TEU which are not charged to the Union budget will be financed by a start-up fund made up of Member States' contributions. The Council will then authorise the High Representative to use the fund (ibid).

Conclusions

More than one decade after the inception of the Common European Security and Defence Policy, the CSDP "presents itself as highly institutionalised and considerably matured" (Gebhard 2009: 8). However, since the first EU civilian missions and military operations, launched in 2003, the institutional development "has very often lagged behind actual operational requirements" (ibid). With the entry into force of the Lisbon Treaty in early December

2009, the EU partly renewed the chain-of-command in crisis-management in order to reduce institutional duplication and competition within the CFSP and CSDP. Particularly in the field of EU foreign and security policy, the Lisbon Treaty established the High Representative of the Union for Foreign Affairs and Security Policy which combined the former functions of the High Representative for the CFSP and of the External Affairs Commissioner, thereby reducing the possibility of inter-institutional conflict (Sicuelli 2010: 17). The office of the Presidency of the European Council has become a full-time position with an extended term of two and a half years. Policy areas that previously belonged to the second pillar remain bound by unanimity voting. But through the Lisbon Treaty, there still remains space for competition between the High Representative of the Union for Foreign Affairs and Security Policy, the President of the Commission and the strengthened President of the Council (ibid). However, the development from the European Security and Defence Policy (ESDP) to the Common Security and Defence Policy (CSDP) in the Lisbon Treaty is desirable to increase coherence in the EU's external action, including the EU crisis management efforts.

Bibliography

Assembly of Western European Union (2008): Treaty of Lisbon. Amending the Treaty on European Union and the Treaty Establishing the European Community. Paris, 31 January 2008.

Brauss, Heinrich/Zinzius, Roland (2007): Remarks to the European Parliament Sub-Committee on Security and Defence. Brussels, 01 March 2007.

Council of the European Union (2009): Presidency report to the European Council on the European External Action Service. Doc. 14930/09, Brussels, 23 October 2009.

EU Council Secretariat (2006): Financing ESDP operations, Factsheet, Brussels, June 2006.

EU Council Secretariat (2007): The EU Operations Centre. Background, Brussels.

Gebhard, Carmen (2009): The Crisis Management and Planning Directorate: Recalibrating ESDP Planning and Conduct Capabilities. In: CFSP Forum, Vol. 7, No. 4, pp. 8-14, July 2009.

General Secretariat of the Council of the EU (2009): The High Representative for Foreign Affairs and Security Policy/The European External Action Service, Brussels, November 2009.

Hynek, Nik (2010): Consolidating the EU's Crisis Management Structures: Civil-Military Coordination and the Future of EU OHQ. Directorate-General for External Policies, Policy Department, European Parliament.

Perruche, Jean-Paul (2006): The European Union Military Staff on Its Way Ahead. In: Truppendienst 1/2006, pp. 6-9.

Quille, Gerrard (2010): The European Parliament and the Common Security and Defence Policy. Policy Briefing, Brussels, 24 August 2010.

Sicurelli, Daniela (2010): The European Union's Africa Policies. Norms, Interests and Impact. Farnham (UK) and Burlington (Vt): Ashgate Publishing.

Treaty on European Union

Consolidated Version of the Treaty on European Union, Official Journal of the European Union, C83/13, 30 March 2010.
Consolidated Version of the Treaty on the Functioning of the European Union, Official Journal of the European Union, C83/47, 30 March 2010.

Internet links:

European Commission (2011a): http://europa.eu/about-eu/institutions-bodies/european-commission, accessed on August 8, 2011.
European Commission (2011b): About Development and Cooperation – EuropeAid, http://ec.europa.eu/europeaid/who/about/index_en.htm, accessed on August 8, 2011.
European Commission (2011c): Partners in Development, http://ec.europa.eu/europeaid/who/partners/index_en.htm, accessed on August 8, 2011.
European Commission (2011d): Directorate-General for Trade – Mission, http://ec.europa.eu/trade/about/mission/, accessed on August 8, 2011.
European Commission (2011e): European Instrument for Democracy & Human Rights (EIDHR), http://ec.europa.eu/europeaid/how/fiance/eidhr_en.htm, accessed on August 8, 2011.
European Commission (2011f): ECHO's finances, http://ec.europa.eu/echo/funding/finances_en.htm, and European Commission, ECHO Background & mandate, http://ec.europa.eu/echo/about/what/history_en.htm, accessed on August 8, 2011.
Folketinget (2011): How does the codecision procedure work? http://www.eu-oplysningen.dk/euo_en/spsv/all/69/?print=1, accessed on August 10, 2011.

The Common Security and Defence Policy (CSDP) – Challenges after "Lisbon"

Gunther Hauser

Introduction

With the entry into force of the Treaty on European Union (TEU) on November 1, 1993 (the Maastricht Treaty), the Common Foreign and Security Policy (CFSP) became an essential part of the European Union as an intergovernmental pillar. In the Lisbon Treaty, Article 21 (1) TEU sets out its main principles of the common foreign and security policy (CFSP):

> "The Union's action on the international scene shall be guided by the principles which have inspired its own creation, development and enlargement, and which it seeks to advance in the wider world: democracy, the rule of law, the universality and indivisibility of human rights and fundamental freedoms, respect for human dignity, the principles of equality and solidarity, and respect for the principles of the United Nations Charter and international law."

Furthermore, the EU

> "shall seek to develop relations and build partnerships with third countries, and international, regional or global organisations which share the principles referred to in the first paragraph. It shall promote multilateral solutions to common problems, in particular in the framework of the United Nations."

According to Article 21 (2) of the Lisbon Treaty on European Union (TEU), the EU shall define and implement a CFSP covering all areas of foreign and security policy, the objectives of which shall be:

- to safeguard its values, fundamental interests, security, independence and integrity;
- to consolidate and support democracy, the rule of law, human rights and the principles of international law;
- to preserve peace, prevent conflicts and strengthen international security, in accordance with the purposes and principles of the United Nations Charter, with the principles of the Helsinki Final Act and with the aims of the Charter of Paris, including those relating to external borders;
- to foster the sustainable economic, social and environmental development of developing countries, with the primary aim of eradicating poverty;

- to encourage the integration of all countries into the world economy, including through the progressive abolition of restrictions on international trade;
- to help develop international measures to preserve and improve the quality of the environment and the sustainable management of global natural resources, in order to ensure sustainable development;
- to assist populations, countries and regions confronting natural or manmade disaster; and
- to promote an international system based on stronger multilateral cooperation and good global governance.

On the basis of these principles and objectives, "the European Council shall identify the strategic interests and objectives of the Union" (Article 22 (1) TEU, first sentence). However, decisions of the European Council relating to EU strategic interests and objectives

> "may concern the relations of the Union with a specific country or region or may be thematic in approach. They shall define their duration, and the means to be made available by the Union and the Member States." (Article 22 (1) TEU, second sentence).

According to Article 42 (1) TEU, the Common Security and Defence Policy (CSDP)

> "shall be an integral part of the common foreign and security policy. It shall provide the Union with an operational capacity drawing on civilian and military assets. The Union may use them on missions outside the Union for peacekeeping, conflict prevention and strengthening international security…"

When the European Council decides unanimously, the CSDP will lead to a "common defence" (Article 42 (2) TEU).

Both – CFSP and CSDP – serve to fulfil the EU's foreign policy objectives. CSDP is subsumed under the wider umbrella of the CFSP. CFSP and CSDP serve to complement each other. The CFSP concentrates on foreign policy objectives at the strategic level, while the CSDP enables the EU to execute crisis management operations on the ground. CSDP also covers civilian missions. This article intends to analyse and discuss the impacts of the Lisbon Treaty on CSDP as well as the main challenges for the CSDP in the near future.

Toward a Common Security and Defence Policy (CSDP)

The Franco-British meeting in Saint Malo (December 4, 1998), and subsequently the Cologne European Council summit (June 3-4, 1999), set out the guidelines required for the strengthening of the European Security and Defence Policy (ESDP). In Cologne, European governments declared that "the Union must have the capability for autonomous action, backed up by credible military forces, the means to decide to use them, and a readiness to do so, in order to respond to international crisis without prejudice to actions by NATO" (European Council 1999, Annex III, point 1).

The lack of European autonomous action and capacity

"was clearly demonstrated during the War on Kosovo in 1999. Operation *Allied Force* underlined the conclusion that Europe had no capability for autonomous action and should develop a force projection capability for operations in an out-of-area environment" (de Wijk 2004: 11).

This war showed that EU nations are largely dependent on the US for carrying out large-scale military operations. The US carried out 65 percent of all flights and, within that figure, 80 percent of all combat missions (ibid). EU leaders saw the need to strengthen European capabilities in the fields of intelligence, strategic transport, and command and control (C2), which implies efforts to adapt, exercise, and bring together national and multinational European forces.

In 1997, the former Petersberg tasks that were adopted by the Western European Union (WEU)[1] on June 19, 1992 were incorporated into Title V of the Treaty on European Union (the Amsterdam Treaty). This was a crucial step forward at a time when there had been a resurgence of local conflicts posing a real threat to European security, even though the risk of large-scale conflicts had fallen significantly compared to those of the Cold War period. The Petersberg tasks represent a very fitting response by the Union, and embody the member states' shared determination to safeguard security through operations such as humanitarian and rescue tasks; peacekeeping tasks; tasks of combat forces in crisis management, including peacemaking; and peace enforcement. In 1998, US State Secretary Madeleine Albright's "three Ds" summed up the US conditions for the possibility of the EU building its own functions:

- no duplication of existing NATO structure;
- no discrimination against non-EU-NATO members; and
- no decoupling from Alliance structures (Reichard 2006: 354).

---

1   The WEU was created by the Treaty on Economic, Social and Cultural Collaboration and Collective Self-Defence signed at Brussels on March 17, 1948 (the Brussels Treaty), as amended by the Protocol signed in Paris on October 23, 1954, which modified and completed it. The Brussels Treaty was signed by Belgium, France, Luxembourg, the Netherlands and the UK. Its main feature was the commitment to mutual defence should any of the signatories be the victim of an armed attack in Europe (Western European Union 2011).

A fourth condition was added by the US Congress: that NATO should have a "right of first refusal" versus the EU on any peacekeeping activity. These four conditions duly reflected US interests in Europe in 1998 (ibid).

After the lack of action and coordination during the conflicts and secession wars in former Yugoslavia in the 1990s which were a challenge to European security structures (Institute "Clingendael" 2010: 8), in June 1999 the Cologne European Council placed crisis management at the core of the process of strengthening the CFSP. This action led to priority being given to conflict prevention two years later at the Gothenburg Summit. Conflict prevention not only means preventing the initial outbreak of violence, but also its escalation and later recurrence (International Crisis Group 2001: 2). Major efforts were underway to assess and improve the EU's capability to act, as evidenced, for example, by the joint report on conflict prevention presented to the Nice European Council on December 10, 2000 by the Secretary-General (who is also the High Representative and so called *Mr. CFSP*) and Commission, and the endorsement at the Gothenburg European Council on June 16, 2001. This report outlined the EU program for the prevention of violent conflicts. Yet, conflict management also deals with how to respond to a crisis that has crossed the threshold into armed conflict, to prevent it from escalating and to bring it to a conclusion.

On the basis of the declaration at the NATO summit held in Washington on April 23-25, 1999 the Union should be able to conduct operations with recourse to NATO resources and capabilities. To implement this category of operations, specific arrangements were agreed upon with the Alliance. At the Helsinki European Council meeting of December 10-11, 1999 the heads of state and government confirmed that they intended to give the European Union autonomous capacity to make decisions and made clear their intention, where NATO as a whole was not engaged, to launch and conduct EU-led military operations in response to international crises worldwide (Hauser 2006: 44). In Helsinki, the EU nations also decided rapidly to develop collective capability goals, particularly in the field of command and control (C2), intelligence and strategic transport. NATO obligations of EU member states are not in contradiction with engagement in EU security and defence issues according to Article 42 (2) TEU (the Lisbon Treaty):

> "The policy of the Union [. . .] shall not prejudice the specific character of the security and defence policy of certain Member States and shall respect the obligations of certain Member States, which see their common defence realised in the North Atlantic Treaty Organisation (NATO), under the North Atlantic Treaty and be compatible with the common security and defence policy established within that framework."

At the Cologne and Helsinki European Council Summits in 1999, heads of state decided that the European Rapid Reaction Forces (EU RRF) – 60,000 troops – should have the capacity to undertake autonomous actions until 2003 so the European Union "can take decisions and approve military action where the Alliance as a whole is not engaged" (North Atlantic Council 1999: para. 9a). The EU RRF of 60,000 servicemen shall constitute a pool of more than 100,000 persons and 400 combat aircraft and 100 warships (de Wijk 2004: 12). To fulfil the whole spectrum of EU Petersberg tasks – from peacekeeping to peace enforcement actions – the European Union will need advanced military capabilities to close capability gaps between the United States and the European allies.

The military component was introduced by the Helsinki (December 10-11, 1999) and Nice (December 7-10, 2000) European Councils. First, Helsinki established the *headline goal* for the EU Rapid Reaction Force to be deployable within sixty days and to sustain for at least one year (Hauser 2006: 44; Perruche 2006: 8). This headline goal was the logical outcome of lessons learned during the conflicts in former Yugoslavia of the 1990s. The EU RRF does not intend to establish a European army. The commitment and deployment of national troops are based on sovereign decisions taken by member states. The primary task for the European Union is now to increase and coordinate capabilities both for its own security and for the stabilisation of the European area.

The headline goal was accompanied by a European Capabilities Action Plan (ECAP) launched on December 15, 2001. This plan

> "was designed to meet the capability requirements identified under the four military scenarios developed by the EU Military Staff (EUMS) and approved by the then fifteen Member States: the prevention of conflicts, the evacuation of nationals, the forced separation of belligerents and humanitarian aid" (Perruche 2006: 8).

ECAP was launched

> "to address known shortfalls in military capabilities across the spectrum of capabilities from procurement issues such as air to air refuelling, and to qualitative issues such as headquarters, where with five OHQs [Operation Headquarters], four FHQs [Force Headquarters] and sixteen Component Commands, the shortfall was clearly not quantitative" (Dunn 2006: 130).

Much of the work of ECAP has already been transferred to the European Defence Agency that was founded in 2004 (ibid). The initial Helsinki Headline Goal 2003 prepared the way for the Headline Goal 2010 (HHG 2010) adding qualitative criteria for achieving capability improvements. However, the member states should be able *"to deploy smaller rapid response elements with very high readiness.* These forces must be self-sustaining, with the necessary command, control, and intelligence capabilities, logistics, other combat support services and, additionally as appropriate, air and naval elements" (Assembly of Western European Union 2003: 7).

In order to increase high readiness capabilities, the development of rapid response battle groups was launched in 2004 at the Noordwijk Defence Ministers summit. During this informal meeting, defence ministers agreed to create battlegroups based on a French/British/German initiative, beginning with the Initial Operational Capability (IOC) in January 2005 (at least one battlegroup on standby) and the initial commitments on the Full Operational Capability (FOC) from January 2007 onwards (Dutch EU Presidency 2004a). The EU Military Staff (EUMS) developed the Battlegroup Concept, in June 2004, and the EU Military Committee (EUMC) agreed this concept. Since 2007, the EU shall be able to fulfil its ambition of having the capacity to undertake two concurrent single battlegroup-sized rapid response operations, including the ability to launch both such operations nearly simultaneously: (General Secretariat of the Council of the European Union 2007: 1).

"The battlegroup is the minimum militarily effective, credible, rapidly deployable, coherent force package capable of stand-alone operations, or of being used for the initial force phase of larger operations. It is based on a combined armed, battalion-sized force and reinforced with combat support and combat service support elements. In its generic composition, but depending on the mission, the battlegroups are about 1,500 personnel strong. A battlegroup is associated with a deployable force headquarters and pre-identified operational and strategic enablers, such as strategic lift and logistics. ... The battlegroups are sustainable for 30 days in initial operations, extendable to 120 days, if re-supplied appropriately (ibid).

Defence Ministers also agreed to consider the possibility of third countries participating in EU battlegroups and to harmonise the EU battlegroups and the NATO Response Force (NRF) that became operable in late 2006. As a part of the Headline Goal 2010, the objective was to have integrated forces based on a reinforced infantry battalion (about 1,500 troops) by January 2007, that are able to start an operation on the ground within ten days after an EU decision to launch an operation (Perruche 2006: 8 and 9).

The civilian component, developed at the Feira European Council (June 19-20, 2000) and Gothenburg European Council (June 15-16, 2001) with extensive contributions by the Commission, aimed to improve actions in a field where the international community has shown itself to be lacking. In order to provide added value, the European Union intended to establish, before 2003, four main instruments that are mutually dependent:

- police cooperation which would provide up to 5,000 policemen, including 1,000 within thirty days, for tasks ranging from restoring order in cooperation with a military force to the training of local police (candidate countries and NATO members Iceland and Norway participate in this cooperation by providing police capacities);
- strengthening the rule of law by providing up to 200 judges, prosecutors, and other experts in the field;
- civilian administration which would provide a team to establish or guarantee elections, taxation, education, water provision, and perform similar functions; and
- civil protection which would assist humanitarian efforts in emergency and other operations and would require the European Union be capable, within three to seven hours, of providing two to three assessment teams consisting of ten experts as well as intervention teams consisting of 2,000 people (Hauser 2006).

The Ministers of Defence of France, Italy, Spain, Portugal and the Netherlands signed a Declaration of Intent on September 17, 2004 concerning the establishment of a European Gendarmerie Force (EGF) during the informal meeting of Ministers of Defence of the EU in Noordwijk. The EGF is a police force with military status and might be excellently suited to deployment during or immediately after a military operation for maintaining public order and safety and in situations where local police forces are not (sufficiently) deployable. For the rapidly-deployable EGF it should be possible to conduct operations in support of the fight against organised crime and the protection of participants in civil missions. The EGF is a multinational unit that is not only allocated to the EU, but also to the UN, the OSCE and NATO. The initiative for establishing the EGF was taken in 2003 by the Minister of Defence of France, Michèle Alliot-Marie. The force headquarters in Vicenza / Italy was established in early 2005, the EGF became operational at the end of 2005 (Dutch EU Presidency 2004c). Romania joined the EGF in 2007.

The European Convention decided in its draft constitution in Article III-309 to adapt the Petersberg tasks to the new challenges and threats in security policy. The tasks in the performance of which the EU may use civilian and military means

> "include joint disarmament operations, humanitarian and rescue tasks, military advice and assistance tasks, conflict prevention and peace-keeping tasks, tasks of combat forces in crisis management, including peace-making and post-conflict stabilisation. All these tasks may contribute to the fight against terrorism, including by supporting third countries in combating terrorism in their territories."

The European Convention Working Group VIII on Defence recommended this new definition of Petersberg tasks. However, this new definition was completely incorporated into Article 43 of the EU Lisbon Treaty. Relating to the fight against terrorism, the European Council reaffirmed in 2002 "that terrorism is a real challenge for Europe and the world and poses a threat to our security and our stability". However, the extraordinary European Council meeting on September 21, 2001

> "decided to step up the action of the Union against terrorism through a coordinated and inter-disciplinary approach embracing all Union policies, including by developing the Common Foreign and Security Policy (CFSP) and by making the European Security and Defence Policy (ESDP) operational" (European Council 2002a, point 1).

Thus, the "fight against terrorism will continue to be a priority objective of the European Union and a key plank of its external relations policy" (ibid, point 2).

The European Defence Agency (EDA)

As the EU Lisbon Treaty states, member states shall improve their military capabilities. The establishment of an agency in the field of defence capabilities development, research, acquisition and armaments (European Defence Agency, EDA) has been foreseen to identify operational requirements, to promote measures to satisfy those requirements, to contribute to identifying and, where appropriate, implementing any measure needed to strengthen the industrial and technological base of the defence sector, to participate in defining a European capabilities and armaments policy, and to assist the Council in evaluating the improvement of military capabilities (Art. 42 (3) TEU). In detail, the EDA has as its task to

- contribute to identifying the Member States´ military capability objectives and evaluating observance of the capability commitments given by the Member States;
- promote harmonisation of operational needs and adoption of effective, compatible procurement methods;
- propose multilateral projects to fulfil the objectives in terms of military capabilities, ensure coordination of the programmes implemented by the Member States and management of specific cooperation programmes;
- support defence technology research, and coordinate and plan joint research activities and the study of technical solutions meeting future operational needs;

- contribute to identifying and, if necessary, implementing any useful measure for strengthening the industrial and technological base of the defence sector and for improving the effectiveness of military expenditure (Article 45 (1) TEU).

The EDA was established on July 12, 2004, its steering board met for the first time on September 17, 2004 in Noordwijk, the Netherlands, under the chairmanship of the first High Representative of the EU, Javier Solana. (Dutch EU Presidency 2004b).

Mainly EU states cooperate within the framework of OCCAR (France, Great Britain, Germany, Italy) – *Organisation Conjointe de Coopération en matière d'Armement* – and in the "Letter of Intent (LoI) Group" (France, Germany, Italy, Spain, Sweden and the UK). There is no interest by LoI countries in including EU states that have less clout in terms of their armaments industry. In view of the establishment of the EDA, European armaments cooperation takes place within the EU, so there was no longer need for activities in the framework of the Western European Armaments Group (WEAG) within the Western European Union (WEU). The Ministers of Defence of the 19 WEAG nations held their last meeting in Brussels on November 22, 2004.

The EDA shall be open to all Member States wishing to be part of it. Military and civilian capabilities should be made available to the CFSP. Those Member States which together establish multinational forces may also make those forces available to the CSDP (Art. 42 (3) TEU). These are the multinational military units which have already been created by Member States, and which have headquarters or general staff. This is the case with Eurocorps (land forces: Belgium, France, Germany, Luxembourg, Spain); Eurofor (land forces: France, Italy, Portugal, Spain); Euromarfor (maritime forces: France, Italy, Portugal, Spain); European Air Group (Belgium, France, Germany, Italy, the Netherlands, Spain, United Kingdom); Multinational Division (Centre) (Belgium, Germany, Netherlands, United Kingdom); and the General Staff of the German-Netherlands First Corps. There are also other multinational forces established between EU Member States (for example the British-Netherlands Landing Force and the Spanish-Italian Amphibious Force) and multinational military units (like the Scandinavian NORDCAPS, with the participation of three EU Member States – Denmark, Finland and Sweden – and also of Norway).

The "Solidarity Clause" and the "Mutual Assistance Clause"

A "solidarity clause" will enable member states to mobilise all the necessary military and civilian instruments within the Union to prevent terrorist threats. Article 222 (1) TFEU (Treaty on the Functioning of the European Union) reads,

> "The Union and its Member States shall act jointly in a spirit of solidarity if a Member State is the object of a terrorist attack or the victim of a natural or man-made disaster. The Union shall mobilise all the instruments at its disposal, including the military resources made available by the Member States, to:

- prevent the terrorist threat in the territory of the Member States;
- protect democratic institutions and the civilian population from any terrorist attack;
- assist a Member State in its territory at the request of its political authorities, in the event of a terrorist attack;
- assist a Member State in its territory, at the request of its political authorities, in the event of a natural or man-made disaster".

However, the Union shall mobilise all the instruments at its disposal, including the military resources made available by the EU Member States. Article 222 TFEU follows directly from the EU Convention Working Group VIII on Defence Issues' recommendations for the inclusion of a solidarity clause in the Constitution. As regards assistance to a Member State following a terrorist attack, states need to take action immediately after the event. Accordingly, the second paragraph provides that assistance should be triggered automatically at the request of the Member State in question. The affected Member State will need to specify its requirements, and the other states, meeting in Council, will co-ordinate the action and resources needed to remedy the situation.

In the Union framework, limited mutual assistance is given in case of armed aggression:

> "If a Member State is the victim of armed aggression on its territory, the other Member States shall have toward it an obligation of aid and assistance by all the means in their power, in accordance with Article 51 of the United Nations Charter. This shall not prejudice the specific character of the security and defence policy of certain Member States" (Art. 42 (7) TEU).

The second part of this sentence continued to be effective due to the role of Austria, Finland, Ireland and Sweden to be neutral or non-aligned states. Austria proposed in 2000 to introduce a mutual assistance defence clause into the EU Treaty; this proposal was rejected by all EU states – during a time when fourteen EU member states supported political sanctions against the

Austrian government. The reason for the sanctions was the participation of the nationalist *Freiheitliche Partei Österreichs* (FPÖ) in the coalition government with the conservative *Österreichische Volkspartei* (ÖVP). The sanctions started on February 4, 2000 and ended on September 12, 2000. Only France could entertain the idea of introducing a mutual assistance clause in the EU Treaty during this time. After British political leadership started to support the idea of introducing mutual assistance in the EU Constitution in October 2003 together with France and Germany, the Italian EU presidency submitted a proposal for mutual military assistance to be included in the EU Constitution during the EU summit in Naples/Italy on November 28, 2003 – along with the idea of replacing the WEU Treaty's policy of robust mutual military commitment. Suddenly, the Austrian government began to oppose this project by emphasizing Austria's neutral status (Hauser 2005: 210-215). The then Foreign Minister Benita Ferrero-Waldner underscored the necessity of coordination with the governments of the other neutral and non-aligned countries: Finland, Ireland, and Sweden. The compromise of the EU Summit on December 12, 2003 was to agree to mutual assistance, but with consideration given to "the specific character of the security and defence policy of certain Member States." That's why then Austrian Chancellor Wolfgang Schüssel, the then Foreign Minister Benita Ferrero-Waldner and the then Minister of Defence Günther Platter emphasised compatibility of neutral status and mutual military commitment (ibid). As Austrian President Heinz Fischer declared, EU security policy has to take into account the specific constitutional characters of Austria, Finland, Sweden, and Ireland (Interview with Heinz Fischer, Wiener Zeitung, September 4, 2004). In Article 42 (7) TEU, on comparison with Article V of the Western European Union (WEU) Treaty, military means are no longer explicitly mentioned as an element of that aid and assistance. There is again uncertainty about the manner in which the security of the six EU member states which are not NATO members – Austria, Cyprus, Finland, Ireland, Malta, and Sweden – is to be guaranteed (Hauser 2005: 210-215).

In spring 2011, ten of the EU's Member States were members of the WEU and were, therefore, bound by a robust mutual defence commitment under Article V of the Brussels Treaty. On June 30, 2011 the WEU was closed "following the termination of the Modified Brussels Treaty of 1954" (Council of the European Union 2011), as was stated by the WEU presidency on March 31, 2010. A mutual assistance clause was already incorporated in the EU Lisbon Treaty in Article 42 (7), the Lisbon Treaty entered into force on December 1, 2009: "The WEU has therefore accomplished its historical role" (WEU 2010). Since the "cessation of WEU activities" (Council of the Western European Union 2011), mutual assistance in defence matters in Europe can only be guaranteed effectively by NATO (Article 5 of the NATO

Treaty). Similar defence assistance could be invoked within the EU frame-work, but only, if neutral and non-aligned EU Member States agree. How-ever, these states would loose their neutral and non-aligned status when joining a defence alliance.

The Permanent Structured Cooperation (PESCO)

A new mechanism that could make capability development more efficient and coherent was introduced by the Lisbon Treaty: the Permanent Structured Cooperation (PESCO) (Biscop and Coelmont 2011: 1). Relating to Article 42 (6), those

> "Member States whose military capabilities fulfil higher criteria and which have made more binding commitments to one another in this area with a view to the most demanding missions shall establish permanent structured cooperation within the Union framework. Such cooperation shall be governed by Article 46. ..."

These states should notify their intention to the Council and to the High Rep-resentative of the Union Minister for Foreign Affairs and Security Policy (Article 46 (1) TEU). The Council acts by a qualified majority after consult-ing the High Representative of the Union Minister for Foreign Affairs and Security Policy (Article 46 (2) TEU), but only members of the Council repre-senting the participating Member States take part in the vote. By 2014, this qualified majority is defined as at least 55 percent of the members of the Council representing the participating Member States, comprising at least 65 percent of the population of these states. A blocking minority must include at least the minimum number of Council members representing more than 35 percent of the population of the participating Member States, plus one mem-ber, failing which the qualified majority shall be deemed attained (Article 238 (3) TFEU). Participating Member States could also make use of Union structures such as the Political and Security Committee (PSC) and the EU Military Committee (EUMC). However, operations undertaken by that group of member states would not be Union operations. Article 2 of the Protocol on PESCO attached to the Lisbon Treaty states how PESCO objectives are to be achieved. The Member States to take part in PESCO should commit to agree on objectives for the level of investment in defence equipment, to "bring their defence apparatus into line with each other as far as possible", by har-monizing military needs, pooling, and, "where appropriate", specialisation, to enhance their forces' availability, interoperability, flexibility and deployabil-ity, notably by setting "common objectives regarding the commitment of forces"; to address the shortfalls identified by the Capability Development Mechanism (CDM), including through multinational approaches; to take part, "where appropriate", in equipment programmes in the context of the European Defence Agency (EDA). The final Article 3 states that the EDA "shall contribute to" a regular assessment of participating Member States' contributions (Biscop 2008: 2).

In spite of the lack of common understanding of PESCO, the Ministers of Defence of the EU nations urged on by the financial and debt crisis, on December 9, 2010 agreed on potentially far-reaching conclusions: the so-called Ghent Framework,

> "aiming at measures to increase interoperability for capabilities to be maintained on national level, at exploring which capabilities offer potential for pooling, and at intensifying cooperation regarding capabilities, at supporting structures and tasks which could be addressed on the basis of role-and-task sharing (pooling and sharing)" (Biscop and Coelmont 2011: 1).

On December 9, 2010 the first formal Foreign Affairs Council for Ministers of Defence also took place.

The Challenge of 'Pooling and Sharing'

Some EU Member States remain reluctant to commit themselves to a common defence policy: Denmark "is not in favour of the EU having a defence role or any kind of engagement in common military activities" (Institute "Clingendael" 2010: 11). As for Ireland, it is not willing to risk its neutrality status, nor is Austria. Finland and Sweden emphasise their non-aligned status, although all neutral and non-aligned EU Member States are engaged in EU crisis management operations, but remain excluded in EU defence matters. However, the new mutual assistance clause based on Article 42 (7) TEU does not encompass the neutral and non-aligned EU nations in defence matters. By international law, neutral countries are responsible for their own defence. Relating to the EU-NATO security cooperation, neutrality as an EU member is not the way to strengthen comprehensive trans-Atlantic and common EU security initiatives. Nevertheless, all neutral states in the world have pledged to support the goals and resolutions of the United Nations, up to and including military actions. Therefore, coordinated force planning in the EU and trans-Atlantic contexts are based on the Headline Goal Catalogue 2010, the EU Framework Nation Concept, and the criteria of force planning within the NATO Partnership for Peace. Particularly in times of heavy defence expenditure cuts, European nations tend to pool and share resources to plug looming gaps, e.g. in transport and tanking capabilities (Chuter, Tran 2010: 11). Twelve nations own 150 C-130 Hercules transportation aircraft, six nations plan to buy 180 Airbus A400M aircraft and seven nations own 420 F-

16 fighter jets (Keohane and Blommestijn 2009: 4). The strength of the EU armed forces is in total 1.8 million servicemen. For more than a decade, European militaries have been struggling with shrinking defence budgets as they face new procurement and political challenges, so many EU member countries are already cutting procurement programs (Kington 2010: 3). NATO General Secretary Anders Fogh Rasmussen asks "how to avoid having the economic crisis degenerate into a security crisis" (Rasmussen 2011: 3). European forces have to improve their performance in respect of availability, deployability, sustainability and interoperability in the framework of crisis management. A coordinated development of the CSDP will strengthen the Union´s contribution to international peace and security in accordance with the principles of U.N. Charter. However, the Ghent Framework not only has to be long-term, it also has to create a platform to launch new capability initiatives and to coordinate defence planning (Biscop and Coelmont 2011: 2). Member States national defence planning is still in "splendid isolation", without really taking into account either EU or NATO guidelines (ibid). By the Ghent Framework, Member States can safely decide not to expand or even to disinvest in national capabilities of which at the EU-level there is already overcapacity (ibid: 3). Rising costs of participation on foreign military and peacekeeping operations are driving Nordic governments to create a joint system that is more cost-efficient and optimises the available logistical resources of militaries in Denmark, Finland, Norway and Sweden. NORDEFCO was created as a chief vehicle for interstate military collaboration; it has proposed the establishment of a Nordic Joint Logistic Support System (NJLSS), primarily for use in international operations but also with a parallel national defence function. The Battalion Task Force 2020 project is based on the potential establishment of a Nordic rapid-deployment force (O´Dwyer 2011: 10). In general, logistics has been identified as an area of pan-Nordic collaboration, with great potential to improve international operations and reduce costs by coordinating troops and equipment transits while pooling assets such as heavy transport aircraft.

On September 1, 2010 the European Air Transport Command (EATC) was inaugurated in Eindhoven/the Netherlands. The four participating nations – Belgium, France, Germany and the Netherlands – have put most of their air transport and air-to-air refuelling assets under the command of the EATC. The missions of almost 160 aircraft are planned, tasked and controlled in Eindhoven. The Initial Operating Capability (IOC) was declared on May 11, 2011 by the Military Air Transport Committee (MATraC) under the chairmanship of Lt. Gen. Jacques Jansen (NLD Air Chief). A very important task of the EATC is the harmonisation and standardisation of regulations, procedures and the national logistical employment in theatre. The A400M will be the backbone of the EATC, this plane will also be used as tanker (Both 2011: 8-14).

The UK and France launched a wide-ranging bilateral cooperation treaty on November 2, 2010 in order to pool their requirements for a new medium-altitude long endurance (MALE) UAV, to share capabilities (perhaps British aerial tankers, French Atlantique 2 spy planes, or maintenance crews for the Airbus A400M airlifters) and to combine certain aspects of their nuclear-weapon efforts (Tran and Chuter 2011: 14). The programme is delivered through an overarching Defence Cooperation Treaty, a subordinate treaty relating to a joint nuclear facility, a letter of intent signed by defence ministers and a package of joint defence initiatives. The measures agreed between France and the UK include jointly developing a Combined Joint Expeditionary Force (CJEF) as a non-standing bilateral capability able to carry out a range of operations in the future whether acting bilaterally or through NATO, the EU or other coalition agreements; the UK and France will aim to have, by the early 2020s, the ability to deploy a UK-French integrated carrier strike group incorporating assets owned by both countries; developing joint military doctrine and training programmes (British Ministry of Defence 2010). The pressure to cut defence spending on both sides of the channel has driven the two governments together, so therefore the UK and France also plan to coordinate aspects of nuclear submarine systems design (Tran and Chuter 2011: 14).

European Shortfalls Strain Transatlantic Ties

The air war against Libya in 2011 has stalled EU efforts to craft an independent military identity, vaulting the Anglo-French partnership launched on November 2, 2010 to the fore as a potential new hub of regional defence cooperation. While France and the UK has been bolstering military engagement in Libya, Germany abstained from the March 17, 2011 vote on the UN Security Council resolution 1973, which approved military force to protect civilians and to enforce the no-fly zone. French aircraft opened the military campaign two days later. The then French president Nicolas Sarkozy proposed that the EU take command of the UN-backed naval embargo on arms shipments to Libya. The EU has been doing a similar job in coordinating the anti-piracy effort off the Somali coast. But the suggestion found no favour at the EU (Tran and Chuter 2011: 1). In the run-up to the initial air strikes by US, British and French aircraft and naval vessels, it became obvious that the EU lacked the planning and command and control (C2) capacity to run such a relatively limited campaign. The Libyan experience has shown the need for a permanent European planning and C2 function. The NATO operation Unified Protector in Libya also revealed "that NATO allies do not lack military capabilities. Any shortfalls have been primarily due to political, rather than military, constraints" (Rasmussen 2011: 2). However, Europe still struggles to deploy more than 4 percent of its 1.8 million troops (Biscop and Coelmont 2010).

> "Downward trends in European defence budgets raise some legitimate concerns. At the current pace of cuts, it is hard to see how Europe could maintain enough military capabilities to sustain similar operations in the future" (Rasmussen 2011: 2).

The primary challenge is to provide the EU with more effective military capabilities to mount crisis management operations. European defence should be coordinated, pooled and shared, output-oriented and cost-effective. So the EU approach to defence "is down in Paris and out in London", says Daniel Keohane from the European Union Institute for Security Studies (EUISS) in Paris. That leaves the UK and France, partners in a bilateral cooperation treaty since November 2, 2010 as the military leaders in Europe (ibid: 14). In 2004, Dutch security analyst Rob de Wijk stated:

> "While EU nations have a collective gross national product similar to the US, they spend only 65 percent of what Washington spends on its armed forces. Due to poor coordination and basically Cold War force structures, Europeans get a disproportional low return from their budgets in key areas such as procurement and research and development. In some areas, the European allies have collectively only 10 to 15 percent of the assets of the Americans" (de Wijk 2004: 11).

This situation has not significantly changed since 2004. As European countries have become richer, they have spent less on defence:

> "Since the end of the Cold War, defence spending by the European NATO countries has fallen by almost 20 percent. Over the same period, their combined GDP grew by around 55 percent. ... By the end of the Cold War, in 1991, defence expenditures in European countries represented almost 34 percent of NATO's total, with the United States and Canada covering the remaining 66 percent. Since then, the share of NATO's security burden shouldered by European countries has fallen to 21 percent" (Rasmussen 2011: 3).

The 27 EU governments spent just over € 160 billion on defence in 1999, which has since risen to almost € 210 billion in 2008. However, this apparent rise is misleading, since defence expenditure as a percentage of GDP has fallen between 1999 and 2009, from 2.1 percent in 1997 to 1.7 percent in 2007. The figures for defence budgets – which should not be confused with defence expenditure – are even lower, having fallen from 1.8 percent of GDP in 1998 to 1.4 percent of GDP in 2008 (Keohane and Blommestijn 2009: 3). Furthermore, four countries provide roughly 70 percent of EU defence spending – the UK and France (43 percent) and Germany and Italy. Add the Dutch and Spanish defence budgets to the four bigger countries, and those six account for around 80 percent of EU defence spending. Add Greece, Poland, Sweden and Belgium, and only ten countries account for 90 percent of EU defence spending (ibid). In 1999 the 27 EU governments had almost 2.5 million personnel in their collective armed forces, including more than 1.1 million conscripts, which are costly and much less preferable for international peacekeeping operations than professional soldiers. In 2008, the 27 EU governments had reduced their armed forces to 2 million personnel, and just over 200,000 conscripts. According to the European Defence Agency (EDA), the 26 Member States of the EDA (Denmark is not a member) could deploy 444,000 soldiers in 2007, but could only sustain 110,000 on international operations – which nevertheless represents an increase of 10 percent on the previous year. This looks like progress, but according to a 2008 report from the European Council on Foreign Relations, a massive 70 percent of Europe's land forces remain unusable outside national territory (Keohane and Blommestijn 2009: 3).

If "European defence spending cuts continue, Europe's ability to be a stabilizing force even in its neighborhood will rapidly disappear. This, in turn, risks turning the United States away from Europe" (Rasmussen 2011: 4). Rasmussen suggests for Europe to pursue a "smart defence" approach: "Smart defence is about building security for less money by working together and being more flexible" (Rasmussen 2011: 5). "Uncoordinated defence cuts could jeopardise the continent's future security" (Rasmussen 2011: 6).

> "Keeping a deployable army, a powerful navy, and a strong air force costs money, however, and not all European countries can afford to have a bit of everything. So they should set their priorities on the basis of threats, cost-effectiveness, and performance – not budgetary considerations or prestige alone" (Rasmussen 2011: 5).

Conclusion

A comparison of EU military capabilities in 1999 and 2009 shows that progress has been made, especially in cutting conscripted personnel and inventories of outdated equipment. But there are still a number of key capability weaknesses within CSDP, such as strategic transport assets. In 2005, security analyst Karl-Heinz Kamp stated that the build-up of a true European Security and Defence Policy (ESDP) "will take longer than expected, since the EU member states are not prepared to bolster their ambitious political goals with adequate financial means" (Kamp 2005: 10). EU defence expenditure has been low, inefficient and uncoordinated for decades. EU governments should "tackle the decline of European military capabilities by raising defence budgets, by integrating and coordinating their spending and by reducing waste and duplication" (Gilli 2011: 52). The good news is that in the coming years, based on their procurement plans, EU nations should have a number of new strategic capabilities such as: A400M and more C-17 transport planes; A330 air tankers; Eurofighter, Rafale and Joint-Strike-Fighter jets; and France-British aircraft carriers. EU defence ministers will also be able to use Galileo – a satellite navigation system – to guide their equipment and define their positions. All this equipment will greatly add to the military prowess of Europe's armies in the future.

The main objective of CSDP is to achieve a coordinated approach to crisis management and to strengthen civilian/military cooperation (CMCO). EU crisis-management missions and operations are mainly focused on civilian missions: in 24 operations since 2003, only 7 were typically military. Missions and operations have been conducted with partners like Argentina, Canada, Chile, Morocco, South Africa, Turkey and the United Arab Emirates and also with ASEAN Member States. EULEX Kosovo became the largest ever conducted civilian mission. Within EULEX Kosovo, US police officers participated in an EU mission the first time. However, NATO is a relevant security partner by supporting EU crisis management operations with military and civilian assets. The EU can be therefore considered "an emerging peacekeeping actor" (Sicurelli 2010: 1). In fact, as of 2011, the majority of CSDP missions have been civilian in nature, but since 2003 the EU has strengthened its efforts in the civil-military coordination of crisis-management. The EU's strong emphasis on civil-military coordination relates to the recognition that the new security threats cannot be addressed through military means alone. The EU needs to define and guarantee security interests; protect citizens and defend human rights; redefine security strategy every five years at the start of each new European legislative term, including drafting a long-term document and a white paper; and own capabilities and equipment for defence and security, such as satellite navigation and intelligence, UAVs, helicopters, telecommunications, and air and sea transport assets (Tran 2008: 32). The EU governments must spend more money on defence and explain the reasons to their publics. With modern and coordinated military and civilian capabilities, the European Union and its Member States would be more able to guarantee security to EU citizens and to export stability beyond borders.

Bibliography

Assembly of Western European Union (2003): The EU headline goal and the NATO Response Force (NRF) – reply to the annual report of the Council. Report submitted on behalf of the Defence Committee by Mr. Rivolta, Rapporteur, Forty-ninth Session, Document A/1825, 3 June 2003.

Biscop, Sven (2008): Permanent Structured Cooperation and the Future of ESDP: Transformation and Integration. Presented at the 3rd Seminar in the EUISS-coordinated series on the European Security Strategy: Strengthening ESDP: The EU's Approach to International Security, Helsinki, 18-19 September 2008. Brussels: Egmont Royal Institute for International Relations.

Biscop, Sven/Coelmont, Jo (2010): Permanent Structured Cooperation In Defence of the Obvious. Security Policy Brief No. 11, June 2010. Brussels: Egmont Royal Institute for International Relations.

Biscop, Sven/Coelmont, Jo (2011): Pooling & Sharing: From Slow March to Quick March? Security Policy Brief No. 23, May 2011, Brussels: Egmont Royal Institute for International Relations.

Both, Jochen (2011): The European Air Transport Command. A Blueprint of European Integration. In: Luftwaffe 2011, CPM-forum, pp. 8-14.

British Ministry of Defence (2010): UK-France Defence Co-operation Treaty announced, November 2, 2010.

Chuter, Andrew/Tran, Pierre (2010): Budget Pressures Push U.K., French Cooperation. Special Report European Defence. In: Defence News, June 7, p. 11.

Clarke, Jack (2011): The Death of European Defence? In: Defence News, March 7, p. 21.

Council of the European Union (2011): Council Decision 2011/297/CFSP of 23 May 2011 amending Joint Action 2001/555/CFSP on the establishment of a European Union Satellite Centre.

Council of the Western European Union (2011): Decision of the Council of the Western European Union on the Residual Rights and Obligations of the WEU, 27 May 2011.

Dunn, Rob (2006): Developing Command and Control for EU Operations. In: Truppendienst 2/2006, pp. 127-131.

Dutch EU Presidency (2004a): Informal Meeting Ministers of Defence in Noordwijk, 17-09-2004/Press releases / General Affairs and External Relations, Ministerie van Buitenlandse Zaken, http://www.eu2004.nl , accessed on 18 September, 2004.

Dutch EU Presidency (2004b): Steering board of the European Defence Agency meets for the first time, 17-09-2004/Press releases/General Affairs and External Relations, Ministerie van Buitenlandse Zaken, http://www.eu2004.nl , accessed on 18 September, 2004.

Dutch EU Presidency (2004c): Signature of Declaration of Intent for a European Gendarmerie Force, 17-09-2004/Press releases/General Affairs and External Relations, Ministerie van Buitenlandse Zaken, http://www.eu2004.nl , accessed on September 18, 2004.

European Council (1999): European Council Declaration on Strengthening the Common European Policy on Security and Defence, Annex III, European Council Presidency Conclusions, Cologne, June 3-4, 1999.

European Council (2002a): Declaration of the European Council, on the contribution of the CFSP, including the ESDP, in the fight against terrorism, Seville European Council, 21-22 June 2002.

European Council Presidency Conclusions (2002b): Annex II, ESDP: Implementation of the Nice Provisions on the Involvement of the Non-EU European Allies, paragraph 2, Brussels, 24 and 25 October 2002.

General Secretariat of the Council of the European Union (2007): The European Union Battlegroups, January 2007.

Gilli, Andrea (2011): EU's Military Decline. In: Defence News, June 20, p. 52.

Hauser, Gunther (2005): ESDP and Austria: Security Policy between Engagement and Neutrality. In: Bischof, G., Pelinka, A., and Gehler, M. (eds.), Austrian Foreign Policy in Historical Context, Contemporary Austrian Studies, Volume No. 14. New Brunswick, New Jersey: Transaction Publishing, pp. 207-245.

Hauser, Gunther (2006): The ESDP: The European Security Pillar. In: Hauser, Gunther/Kernic, Franz (eds.), European Security in Transition. Aldershot/UK and Burlington (Vt): Ashgate Publishing, pp. 39-62.

Institute "Clingendael" (2010): Mapping Research on European Peace Missions, Netherlands Institute of International Relations "Clingendael", The Hague, November 2010.

International Crisis Group (ICG) (2001): EU Crisis Response Capability: Institutions and Processes for Conflict Prevention and Management, ICG Issues Report No. 2, Brussels, 26 June 2001.

Kamp, Karl-Heinz (2005): The Need to adapt NATO's Strategic Concept. In: NATO Defence College, Security Strategies and their Implications for NATO's Strategic Concept, NDC Occasional Paper No. 9, Rome, November 2005, pp. 7-14.

Keohane, Daniel/Blommestijn, Charlotte (2009): Strength in numbers? Comparing EU military capabilities in 2009 with 1999. ISS Policy Brief No 5. Paris: EU Institute for Security Studies, December 2009.

Kington, Tom (2010): Italy Cuts Eurofighter, Frigate Programs; Ponders JSF's Future. In: Defence News, June 21, p. 3.

Mkrtchyan, Tigran/Huseynov, Tabib/Gogolashvili, Kakha (2009): The European Union and the South Caucasus. Three Perspectives on the Future of the European Project from the Caucasus. Europe in Dialog 2009/01. Gütersloh: Bertelsmann Stiftung.

North Atlantic Council (1999): Washington Summit Communiqué, issued by the heads of state and government participating in the meeting of the North Atlantic Council, Press Release NAC-S(99)64, 24 April 1999.

O'Dwyer, Gerard (2011): Nordic Countries Seek To Pool Logistics Resources. In: Defence News, April 25, p. 10.

Perruche, Jean-Paul (2006): The European Union Military Staff on Its Way Ahead. In: Truppendienst 1/2006, pp. 6-9.

Rasmussen, Anders Fogh (2011): NATO After Libya. The Atlantic Alliance in Austere Times. In: Foreign Affairs, July/August, pp. 2-6.

Reichard, Martin (2006): The EU-NATO Relationship. A Legal and Political Perspective. Aldershot (UK) and Burlington (Vt): Ashgate Publishing.

Sicurelli, Daniela (2010): The European Union's Africa Policies. Norms, Interests and Impact. Farnham (UK) and Burlington (Vt): Ashgate Publishing.

Tran, Pierre (2008): Lawmakers Want European Defence. In: Defence News, September 15, p. 32.

Tran, Pierre/Chuter, Andrew (2011): U.K., France Vault to Center of European Defence. In: Defence News, April 11, pp. 1 and 14.

Western European Union (2010): Statement of the Presidency of the Permanent Council of the WEU on behalf of the High Contracting Parties to the Modified Brussels Treaty – Belgium, France, Germany, Greece, Italy, Luxembourg, The Netherlands, Portugal, Spain and the United Kingdom. Brussels, 31 March 2010.

Western European Union (2011): History of WEU, http://www.weu.int/History.htm, accessed on July 22, 2011.

de Wijk, Rob (2004): The European Union's Foreign, Security and Defence Policies and Austria's Ambitions. Strategische Analysen, Büro für Sicherheitspolitik, Bundesministerium für Landesverteidigung (Austrian Ministry of Defence), Wien, March 2004.

Treaty on European Union

Consolidated Version of the Treaty on European Union, Official Journal of the European Union, C83/13, 30 March 2010.

Consolidated Version of the Treaty on the Functioning of the European Union, Official Journal of the European Union, C83/47, 30 March 2010.

The European Security Strategy – The Way Ahead

Gustav Lindstrom

Introduction

In December 2013, the European Security Strategy (ESS) will celebrate its tenth anniversary. As the date nears, two pre-existing camps will become increasingly vocal concerning the future of the ESS. One side will highlight the continued relevance of the ESS, underscoring how it has effectively navigated a turbulent decade where threats frequently blurred the lines between internal and external security. Eager to preserve the ESS, they will seek to largely maintain the ESS in its current form. At most, periodic updates can be achieved via specific conferences and review documents – such as the 2008 "Report on the Implementation of the European Security Strategy".

A second camp will extol the need for a new security strategy. They will argue that although many elements of the existing ESS are still relevant, there is a need for a new strategy to help transform the EU into a successful global actor in a multi-polar world. A new strategy that engages all relevant stakeholders and provides greater clarity regarding priority regions and issues would be a step in this direction. While both camps share many views; for example the types of threats and challenges facing the EU, the fundamental dividing point is whether a new strategy is needed or not.

This chapter aims to explore the way ahead for the ESS. Specifically, it considers how the ESS might evolve in the future. To do so, the chapter first examines the principal achievements and limitations of the ESS, including recent developments. It then identifies the principal trends that are likely to impact the future evolution of the ESS. With this in mind, the chapter concludes with three recommendations for the way ahead.

What are the Key Achievements and Limitations of the European Security Strategy?

At least three principal achievements can be associated with the ESS. First, the formulation of the strategy and its release in 2003 was an achievement in itself. At the time, EU Member States were deeply divided over the war in Iraq, bringing the EU's Common Foreign and Security Policy to a virtual standstill. It was during this time that a small team of officials in the Council General Secretariat, consulting with EU national capitals and other EU agencies, started the process of drafting a European Security Strategy. The draft was completed in the early summer of 2003 and was then reviewed across EU capitals and in three seminars organised by the EU Institute for Security Studies in Rome, Paris, and Stockholm. Discussions covered all aspects of the draft, including whether reference should be made to the use of force, the role of pre-emption, and the need for UN Security Council resolutions in support of EU action. Based on the input received, changes were made and a final draft was adopted at the 2003 December European Council. Its release came as a surprise to many, especially given ongoing divisions over Iraq. In many ways, though, it was precisely these divisions that had encouraged its creation and rapid adoption.

A second achievement of the ESS is its identification of the key threats and global challenges facing Europe. Prior to the ESS, no EU official document of importance contained such information due to national divergences. Prior to the ESS, such a document would try to summarise the collection of threats facing individual EU Member States. These could range from illegal immigration in the south to energy security in the north. With the 2003 ESS, five key threats are singled out: terrorism, the proliferation of weapons of mass destruction, regional conflicts, state failure, and organised crime. A set of longer term global challenges such as poverty, pandemics, and competition for natural resources are also acknowledged. The 2008 Report on the Implementation of the ESS builds on these sets of threats and challenges, including new issues such as cyber security and energy security. By identifying these threats and related strategic objectives, the 2003 ESS led to the release of four follow-on strategies or tracks, such as the 2005 Counter-Terrorism Strategy, that provide greater detail on EU action and priorities. The identification of a select number of threats has also encouraged a more focused use of limited resources with respect to future capability acquisitions. The push for new ways to pool or share existing crisis management assets to lower defence expenditures is frequently traced back to the ESS which calls for a more active, capable, and coherent European Union.

Third, and relating to the previous point, the ESS crystallises key concepts that help explain and guide EU action. Examples include the concept of "effective multilateralism" and the centrality of civilian-military cooperation (frequently called the "comprehensive approach") to address new security threats. Beyond communicating EU concepts to an internal and external audience, their inclusion helps define which tools the EU is likely to employ or promote in response to security challenges. For example with respect to effective multilateralism, the strategy highlights the importance of a "stronger international society, well-functioning international institutions and a rule-based international order" (ESS 2003: 19) to enhance security and prosperity. In practical terms, effective multilateralism seeks to support international organisations such as the United Nations as the international community responds to challenges such as proliferation, terrorism, and global warming (ESS 2003:21).

With respect to shortcomings, at least four issues stand out. First, the ESS is amorphous when it comes to identifying EU-level strategic interests. Unlike most national security strategies which identify vital or important national interests at the outset, the ESS goes directly into an examination of the key threats and challenges facing Europe. However, this does not come as a complete surprise given the EU's special status as an international organisation with substantial supranational powers composed of twenty seven Member States with varying security interests. Nonetheless, the lack of a clear set of vital interests at the EU level complicates the ESS' ability to prioritise among the identified threats and challenges as well as the priority regions for possible EU action. This is one of the reasons why some analysts question why the EU launched a monitoring mission in Aceh in 2005. Located in South East Asia some 10,000 kilometres from Brussels, many did not see the EU's interest in operating so far away from its neighbourhood.

While the need to link the strategy to EU-level interests has been raised before, for example in one of the four conferences (Helsinki) organised in 2008 to discuss the future Report on the Implementation of the ESS, no attempt was made to include such interests in the ensuing 2008 implementation report. Two principal reasons may explain why: 1) a belief that a discussion on interests would be futile as EU Member States would express diverging viewpoints, 2) a desire to focus the implementation report on how well the 2003 European Security Strategy had been implemented rather than presenting a new strategy.

A second shortcoming of the ESS is its release date. When it came out in December 2003, the Common Security and Defence Policy (CSDP) – then known as the European Security and Defence Policy or ESDP – was still in its infancy. The first missions and operations were initiated only months earlier in 2003 and EU crisis management institutions such as the Civilian Planning and Conduct Capability were years from existence. While the ten countries that were to join the EU in May 2004 were consulted and involved in the formulation of the ESS, the release of the strategy only a few months prior to their formal inclusion may have inadvertently lead to an underrepresentation of their strategic concerns. Moreover, with the Treaty of Lisbon entering into force in December 2009, the ESS is increasingly out of touch with recent EU developments of significance such as the establishment of a European External Action Service. The 2008 implementation report, which includes some new threats to reinforce the ESS, does not analyze how intra-EU

developments may have impacted the ESS, focusing rather on implementation levels as mandated.

Third, there is no mechanism for updating or launching a new ESS. Currently, the ESS is a stand-alone document which is reinforced by the 2008
implementation report. It is up to the EU Member States to decide for how
long the two documents will remain strategically relevant and whether follow-up is needed. The lack of an automated process has already led to some
confusion. It was clearly apparent in 2008, when the ESS turned five and
there were calls for a new ESS. Some EU Member States, such as France and
Sweden signalled the need for a new/updated strategy. In Brussels, officials
were gravitating towards an implementation report to gauge the degree to
which the 2003 strategy had been successfully implemented rather than releasing an updated or new version. The diverging goals were apparent during
the four seminars organised in 2008 (Rome, Warsaw, Helsinki, and Paris) to
discuss the ESS. On multiple occasions, participants provided suggestions
for the content of a new strategy, only to be reminded that the goal was to
discuss the degree to which the 2003 ESS had been implemented. The structure of the 2008 implementation report reflects this duality: the first part of
the document covers old security threats described in the 2003 ESS and provides new additions to the list. The remaining portion of the report gauges
the implementation of the 2003 ESS and provides recommendations for continued progress. With no formal review of the update mechanism, this methodology may be repeated in the future. Over time, this may result in an ESS
with limited strategic relevance.

Fourth, the 2003 ESS has limited links to other strategic EU documents,
many of which were released after the ESS came out. Although reference to
the ESS is made in several of these documents, such as the Headline Goal
2010, the links tend to be superficial and there are limited efforts to ensure
consistency. While the ESS has a privileged position as the strategic reference document, it also needs to fit with other strategic reference documents
such as the Long Term Vision which examines the types of security threats
the EU is likely to face around 2025 and the implications it has for CSDP
missions and operations as well as for capability development. Although this
is less of a challenge to the ESS than the follow-on documents, the presence
of feeble links weakens the strategic value of the ESS over time.

What Trends will Impact the Future of the European Security Strategy?

There are at least five trends that impact the future of the ESS. First, any follow-on work on the ESS will need to take into account the new security
strategies released by EU Member States since 2003. In some cases, these
represent the first release of a national security strategy. Among the better
known are:

- France's 2008 White Paper on defence and national security ("Livre
  blanc sur la Défense et la Sécurité nationale")
- Germany's 2006 White Book ("Weißbuch 2006 zur Sicherheitspolitik
  Deutschlands und zur Zukunft der Bundeswehr)
- The UK's 2010 "National Security Strategy: A Strong Britain in an Age
  of Uncertainty".

With respect to the documents listed above, it is interesting to note that there
are substantial parallels vis-à-vis threat assessments and the need for international collaboration. The findings are consistent with those in the ESS which
reinforces its principal messages. However, looking ahead, a new or updated
ESS would need to carefully consider the nuances present in the different
strategies to minimise potential divergences. In other words, some form of
bottom-up process may be needed to ensure that nation-specific elements are
either captured or acknowledged in future variations of the ESS. Table 1 provides an overview of select EU Member State white books and security
strategies. As shown in the table, some strategies contain country specific
elements that are not detailed extensively in the ESS.

A second trend that will impact a future ESS is the growing link between
internal and external security. When the ESS was released in 2003, there was
limited reference to internal security. While the ESS notes that "the post Cold
War environment is one of increasingly open borders in which the internal
and external aspects of security are indissolubly linked" (ESS 2003: 7), there
is no specific reference to such threats or the measures needed to address
them. To some extent, the 2008 implementation report seeks to fill this void
by referencing the 2005 Strategy for the External Dimension of Justice and
Home Affairs. On behalf of the 2003 ESS, there were – and still are – strong
forces that limit the discussion of internal security at the EU level. Internal
security is considered an EU Member State competency in which the EU
should have a limited role, e.g. information sharing and coordination. In addition, the Common Foreign and Security Policy should be implemented outside the borders of the EU.

Table 1:   Comparison of Threats and Vulnerabilities: Select EU Member
             States Security Strategies / White Books

Country	Document type	Year	Examples of Threats / Vulnerabilities
France	White Paper	2008	Weapons of mass destruction (WMD) terrorism; ballistic missile proliferation; cyber-attacks; espionage; criminal networks; health risks; citizens abroad in vulnerable areas
Germany	White Book	2006	International terrorism; proliferation and military build-up; regional conflicts; illegal arms trade; fragile statehood; transportation routes; energy security; uncontrolled migration; epidemics and pandemics
Hungary	Security Strategy	2012	Terrorism; proliferation of WMD; unstable regions/failed states; illegal migration; economic instability; challenges to information society; global natural, man-made and medical sources of danger; regional challenges; internal challenges
Netherlands	Security Strategy	2007	Breaches of international peace and security; CBRN (chemical, biological, radiological, nuclear); terrorism; international organised crime; social vulnerability; lack of digital security; lack of economic security; climate change and natural disasters; infectious diseases and animal diseases
Poland	Security Strategy	2007	Organised international terrorism; organised international crime; energy security; illegal migration; weakened transatlantic links; frozen and regional conflicts; weak levels of integration of economic life and financial markets; environmental threats; internal challenges (e.g. population changes, infrastructure, energy storage)
Spain	Security Strategy	2011	Armed conflicts; terrorism; organised crime; financial and economic insecurity; energy vulnerability; proliferation of weapons of mass destruction; cyber threats; uncontrolled migratory flows; emergencies and disasters; critical infrastructures; supplies and services
United Kingdom	Security Strategy	2010	International terrorism affecting the UK or its interests (including the use of WMD); hostile attacks upon UK cyber space; a major accident or natural hazard; an international military crisis between states, drawing in the UK; an attack on the UK or its Overseas Territories by another state or proxy using chemical, biological, radiological, and nuclear (CBRN); risk of major instability, insurgency or civil war overseas; organised crime; severe disruption to information received, transmitted or collected by satellites; disruption to oil or gas supplies to the UK; short to medium term disruption to international supplies of resources (e.g. food, minerals) essential to the UK

With the entry into force of the Lisbon Treaty, these limitations are weaker.
For example, the introduction of a Solidarity Clause allows the Union and its
Member States to assist each other if one is the victim of a terrorist attack or

natural/man-made disaster. The clause notes that all available instruments, including "military resources", may be used to prevent, protect, and assist under such circumstances (Treaty of Lisbon 2009: 131). The fact that Member States still may have varying views on how the Solidarity Clause might be operationalised, demonstrates that the boundaries for how resources may be used in response to such trans-boundary threats is unclear. From a different vantage point, the establishment of a Standing Committee on Operational Cooperation on Internal Security (COSI) in 2009 and the release of an Internal Security Strategy 2010 underscore the increased visibility of internal security within the EU.

This trend has several implications for the ESS. Any future changes or updates in the strategy would need to give greater consideration to internal security matters and how they might be addressed. The strategy would also need to take into account the Internal Security Strategy and ensure that there is consistency and complementarity between both documents.

Third, there is a growing recognition that the EU should do more with fewer resources. This trend is exacerbated by the weak economic performance felt in several EU Member States. As such, the need to find synergies and other mechanisms to save resources is likely to remain strong over the short- to medium-term. For a future ESS, this translates into finding greater coherence across instruments. Such synergies would go beyond the defence industry and extend to the entire range of economic, diplomatic, and military tools at the disposal of the EU. Rather than acknowledge the need for a more active, capable, and coherent EU, a future strategy would need to outline more precisely how such goals would be achieved.

Fourth, and related to the point above, there is a growing appreciation of the link between traditional security policies, development cooperation policies, and economic tools at large to promote security and development. This trend is already recognised within the EU, where concepts such as the comprehensive approach recognise that there often is a need to combine military and civilian tools to achieve desired ends on the ground. Even at the institutional level, the EU has taken measures that reflect this reality. To illustrate, the new Foreign Affairs Council (FAC) includes EU Member State ministers responsible for Foreign Affairs, Defence and Development. Already in late 2007, defence and development ministers met together in a joint session under the auspices of a European Council summit held in Brussels.

In response to this trend, a future ESS would need to take a broader perspective that devotes greater attention to issues pertaining to development and economic growth. While some aspects of this will be difficult to agree on at the EU level, for example the types of economic and development tools that are best suited to promote stability in an area of tension, it is indispensable to enable and guide future complex operations. The 2003 ESS already laid the ground work by identifying the need for a more coherent Common Foreign and Security Policy and CSDP that takes into account different instruments and capabilities such as the "European assistance programmes and the European Development Fund, military and civilian capabilities from Member States and other instruments" (ESS 2003: 26).

Fifth, the trend towards an increasingly multi-polar world will impact the formulation of a future ESS. Some EU foreign ministers' meetings have already included discussions on how to develop the EU's existing strategic partnerships with countries such as Russia, India, and China. The last such meeting was a Gymnich-style meeting of the EU foreign ministers held on September 2-3, 2011 in Sopot (Poland) to discuss, among others, how the EU can strengthen its external relations with strategic partners. The need for such discussion and reflections in strategy will only grow as countries forming part of the BRICS (Brazil, Russia, India, China, South Africa) and Next Eleven (N-11 or Bangladesh, Egypt, Indonesia, Iran, Mexico, Nigeria, Pakistan, Philippines, South Korea, Turkey, and Vietnam) develop and strengthen their foreign and economic policies.

What is the Way Ahead?

With these weaknesses, strengths, and trends in mind, what is the way ahead for the ESS? Policymakers should take into account at least three elements as they consider future or new iterations of a European security strategy. The three recommendations examined below are by no means exhaustive; their aim is to identify areas which will require careful consideration by officials in Brussels and in EU Member State capitals as they consider follow-on work for the ESS.

1. *The ESS needs to include EU-level interests.* While the ESS does not clearly specify EU-level interests and discussions to date have not led to their inclusion, there is a need to incorporate EU-level interests in a future strategy. These would form the bedrock from which policies and priority areas for action are derived, an increasingly important function as the EU tries to do more with less resources. It should be noted that the discussion of European security interests predates the establishment of a Common Foreign and Security Policy. An example is the Hague Platform on European Security Interests, which was adopted by the Western European Union Council of October 1987. It outlines priorities in areas such as territorial integrity, arms control and disarmament, and East-West dialogue and cooperation.

   A possible way ahead is to identify vital interests of a general nature – those that are likely to be of interest to a majority of EU Member States and their populations. Thus, rather than combining the security interests of the EU-27, the goal would be to highlight a select number of EU-level vital interests. Examples of such interests are offered in a 2010 study by Biscop and Coelmont who identify interests such as "defence against any military threat to the territory of the Union; open lines of communication and trade; a secure supply of energy and other vital natural resources; a sustainable environment; manageable migration flows; the maintenance of international law and universally agreed rights; preserving the autonomy of the decision-making of the EU and its Member States" (Biscop and Coelmont 2010: 13). By ranking some of these interests and those identified in individual EU Member States' security strategies and the ESS, an initial matrix of EU-level interests can be produced. A general outline is illustrated in Table 2.

Table 2:   Sample Illustration of EU-level Interests

Interest level	Interest description
1st tier-vital interests	Ensure the territorial integrity of the EU
	Ensure stability in the EU's neighbourhood
	Promote EU economic security, including access to vital resources and lines of communication
	Promote EU energy security
	Strengthen and promote international law ; uphold human rights
2nd tier-very important interests	Establish productive relations with partners and nations that could become strategic adversaries or competitors
	Promote disarmament and curb the proliferation of weapons of mass destruction (WMD)
	Support a sustainable environment
	Manage large-scale migration flows to the EU
	Fight terrorism, organised crime, and trafficking
	Strengthen institutional relations with regional security organisations that have acted/may act in the same geographic space

While the interests listed in Table 2 are illustrative and could be complemented and/or exchanged for others, it is worthwhile noting that they tend to be broad and wide ranging. For example, the goal of energy security would most likely be shared by most of the EU-27, especially in the aftermath of the gas disputes between Russia and the Ukraine that affected several EU Member States. As energy dependence increases, this interest is likely to become more acute, especially if the EU continues to rely on countries that do not always share EU goals and values for its energy. Under such a scenario, EU Member States would have great incentives to find joint solutions and approaches to ensure a steady and reliable access to energy resources.

The inclusion of EU-wide interests in a future update or iteration of the ESS would encourage greater coherence between EU Member States' means and ends. It would also help policymakers prioritise among competing goals that are either functional (e.g. curbing the proliferation of WMD) or geographic (e.g. the region in which to launch a CSDP mission or operation). While choices on EU action will ultimately hinge on political will, the availability of pre-established interests should facilitate policy choices and decisions. This may be particularly useful when the EU has limited resources to spare or needs guidance concerning the procurement of future capabilities and assets.

2. *The ESS needs a review/release mechanism.* As noted, there is no formal system for reviewing or updating the ESS. This is not sustainable over the long run as it may lead to an outdated ESS or a document that is updated only when it is politically expedient. The confusion which surfaced in 2008 on whether or not a new ESS would come out should be avoided and a system is needed to guide updates or re-releases. Since the ESS is owned collectively by the EU Member States and does not represent the political priorities of a single government, there is no "natural" review system that appears when a government administration is replaced by another. The EU, like NATO and its Strategic Concept, do not have a mechanism for deciding when it is time to revise or renew their strategies. Ideally, a system needs to be created to guide the review process. Two alternatives seem plausible. One option would be to introduce a time limit for the ESS, after which it is either updated or a new strategy is released. With respect to the length of the time limit, a suitable option might be five years to adequately reflect global trends and changes. The decision to either update or release a new strategy would rest with decision-makers in EU capitals who would agree on a course of action at least a year in advance of the expiration date.

An alternative option would be to review or re-release a security strategy when a new High Representative for Foreign Affairs and Security Policy (FASP)/Vice President for the European Commission is selected. With term lengths of five years, this would ensure a periodic review of the strategy. It would also give the incoming High Representative / Vice-President an opportunity to set his or her imprint on the strategy, effectively making it a roadmap for EU external action during his or her term in office. Input would likewise be solicited from EU capitals to ensure political buy-in and support. Additional input for the strategy could be gathered from the discussions stemming from informal meetings of foreign affairs ministers (e.g. Gymnich meetings). Under both scenarios, the European External Action Service and relevant stakeholders in the General Secretariat of the Council would be responsible for spearheading the updating or renewal process.

The establishment of a review or update process would make the ESS a more "living document" that can adapt more effectively to global trends and changes. It would also give the strategy greater credence as periodic reviews would ensure that the content is relevant over time. Finally, it would open the door for a more systematised system further down the road for how a strategy is best updated or renewed.

3. *The ESS needs stronger links to existing and follow-on "sub-strategies".* To maintain the relevance of the European Security Strategy, there is a need to continue linking the ESS with "sub-strategies" that detail how the ESS will be practically implemented. As noted earlier, the 2003 ESS was associated with four follow-on tracks in areas such as counter-terrorism and effective multilateralism. The purpose of these sub-strategies is to provide guidance on how the EU will address such challenges. The 2005 EU Counter-Terrorism Strategy, for instance, identifies policies across four different pillars – prevent, protect, pursue, and respond – to combat terrorism. For example in the area of protection, the strategy notes the importance of introducing a "Visa Information System (VIS) and the second generation Schengen Information System (SISII)" to avert potential attacks (The European Union Counter-Terrorism Strategy 2005:11).

An updated or new security strategy would also need to be consistent with already existing EU sub-strategies, policies and partnerships such as the new 2011 European Neighbourhood Policy, Euro-Mediterranean Partnership, and the Eastern Partnership. The ESS would also need to be consistent with CSDP-related strategy documents such as the Headline Goal 2010 and the Civilian Headline Goal 2010. Updated or new versions of the ESS should ideally also take account of more recent European strategy documents, examples include:

- "A Strategy for the External Dimension of JHA : Global Freedom, Security and Justice" (2005)
- "Europe in the World – Some Practical Proposals for Greater Coherence, Effectiveness and Visibility" (2006)
- "Internal Security Strategy for the European Union" (2010)

Lastly, the strategy should be consistent with relevant sections of forward-looking documents such as the "Long Term Vision" and "Europe 2020" which outlines the EU's growth strategy for the coming decade in areas such as innovation, climate, and energy. This would help establish consistency across strategic documents which consider the medium- and long-term. Also, by creating a link between an updated or new ESS with already existing EU strategy documents the EU would achieve greater coherence and consistency vis-à-vis its strategic objectives and its wider security interests.

Conclusion

The adoption of a European Security Strategy in 2003 was a significant step forward for the European Union. It marked the first time EU Member States put forward a strategic document outlining key threats and challenges, strategic objectives, and the policy implications for Europe. Its concise and clear language set it apart from many previous EU documents, further boosting its popularity and relevance.

However, the ESS' initial success may also prove to be a weakness in the long-run. After five years, a decision was made to maintain the ESS in its current form, based on the argument that it remained relevant and that opening up a review or renewal process among the EU-27 would be too cumbersome. Instead, an implementation report was released in 2008 to reinforce the ESS, highlighting new threats and how EU foreign policy is addressing current challenges. While this indirectly served to "update" the ESS, the question over its future remains.

Looking ahead, it is increasingly clear that the ESS will need to be updated or re-released to remain strategically relevant. Given enough political will, such a venture is feasible. The recent initiative of four European think tanks to develop a concept for a European Global Strategy is a step in the right direction. Should policymakers consider a future ESS, consideration should be given to EU-level interests and how they might fit into a future strategy, how to link it with existing "sub-strategies", and devising a periodic review of update mechanisms to ensure its relevance over time.

References

"A Strong Britain in an Age of Uncertainty: The National Security Strategy", London, October 2010. Paper Reference: Command 7953, Session 2010.

Biscop, Sven/Coelmont, Jo (2010): A Strategy for CSDP: Europe's Ambitions as a Global Security Provider. Brussels: Royal Institute for International Relations, Egmont Papers No. 37, October 2010.

Biscop, Sven/Coelmont, Jo (eds.) (2011): Europe Deploys: Towards a Civil-Military Strategy for CSDP. Brussels: Royal Institute for International Relations, Egmont Papers No. 49, June 2011.

Council of the European Union (2008): Report on the Implementation of the European Security Strategy - Providing Security in a Changing World. S407/08, Brussels, 11 December 2008.

Communication from the Commission to the European Council, COM(2006) 278 final: Europe in the World – Some Practical Proposals for Greater Coherence, Effectiveness, and Visibility. Brussels, 8 June 2006.

European Security Strategy (2003): A secure Europe in a better world. Adopted by the European Council of Brussels on 13 December 2003.

Government of Spain (2011): Spanish Security Strategy: Everyone's responsibility. Madrid.

National Security Strategy (2010), The White House, May 2010.

National Security Strategy of the Republic of Poland, Warsaw 2007.

National Security Strategy and Work Programme 2007-2008, Ministry of the Interior and Kingdom Relations, The Hague, May 2007.

The European Union Counter-Terrorism Strategy, Brussels, Council of the European Union, document 14469/4/05 REV 4, 30 November 2005.

The French White Paper on defence and national security, Présidence de la République, Paris, 2008.

The National Security Strategy of the Republic of Hungary, Resolution No. 2073/2004 (III.31.), 15 April 2004.

Treaty of Lisbon Amending the Treaty on European Union and the Treaty Establishing the European Community, 2007/C 306/01, 13 December 2007.

Western European Union (1987): Platform on European Security Interests. The Hague, 27 October 1987.

The European External Action Service (EEAS): Reality, Potential and Challenges

Doris Dialer, Anja Opitz

The 2009 Lisbon Treaty raised high hopes concerning the European Union's role as a global actor. Europe should no longer be a silent partner not employing its strength[1], its instruments and its institutions to assert its interest and those of its citizens on the world stage. Those hopes are contrasted by the fact that the financial crisis and controversial national foreign policies of its member states seriously damaged the image of the EU as a "normative power" (Wright 2011; Manners 2000) in world politics and led to a fundamental loss of standing in international relations. Some scholars even identify a slow process of a de-Europeanisation (Schmid 2012). For the US, Europe went from being an underperforming partner in solving global challenges to being one of those challenges itself. However, every challenge throws up new opportunities. Foreign and security policy in the future will increasingly have to address new forms of conflict and crisis, such as the shortage of resources. Therefore, the US wants the EU to be the backup, reaching other regions of geostrategic interest and assuming responsibility (Bell 2012).

Fit for the Purpose?

In order to develop a more coherent, effective and visible EU foreign policy, changes at two levels have been introduced: Firstly, the objectives of the EU's external policies, from security over development to trade and environment, were merged in Art. 21 TEU. Secondly, on a structural level, the institutional architecture and procedural framework for EU external action were fundamentally amended. The most relevant institutional change, however, relates to the creation of the position of a High Representative of the Union for Foreign Affairs and Security Policy (HR). To enhance coordina-

---

1   With its 27 Member States the EU represents 491 million people, i.e. 8 % of the world's population. Thanks to domestic markets' revenues these 8 % hold one third of the world's wealth and achieve around 31 % of the world GDP. The EU provides around 60 % of the world's development aid (Brok 2011: 2).

tion and cooperation and to ensure "consistency between the different areas of its external action"[2] (Lindstrom 2010: 2), the HR has to take part in the work of the European Council (Art. 15(2) TEU), preside over the Foreign Affairs Council (Art. 18(2) TEU) and hold the post of Vice-President of the European Commission (VP) (Blockmans 2011: 7f.). This seems to be a rather impossible job, because as a Vice President, the newly installed grand coordinator of external policy draws on Community method; while as a High Representative, he/she carries out decisions negotiated among the member states at the intergovernmental level. This complex construct is called "double hat" or HR/VP.

To assist the HR/VP the Lisbon Treaty provides for the establishment of a new diplomatic service, the European External Action Service (EEAS). Article 27(3) TEU, the only Treaty basis, remains vague in respect to the structure and duties of this service, merely stating that it

> "shall work in cooperation with the diplomatic services of the Member States and shall comprise officials from relevant departments of the General Secretariat of the Council and of the Commission as well as staff seconded from national diplomatic services of the Member States. The organisation and functioning of the EEAS shall be established by a decision of the Council. The Council shall act on a proposal from the High Representative after consulting the European Parliament and after obtaining the consent of the Commission."

Its hybrid role and final functioning was of course up to further interinstitutional negotiations. Thus, the July 26, 2010 Council decision is more precise and makes clear that the EEAS will support the HR/VP in her triplehatted – and not double-hatted – capacity by specially mentioning the Foreign Affairs Council. In Article 2(2) it states, that 'the EEAS shall assist the President of the European Council, the President of the Commission, and the Commission in the exercise of their respective functions in the area of external relations'[3].

The aim of this contribution is to challenge two common but contrasting assumptions: Supporters of the EEAS say that such a body is long overdue and will be a success story in the long run. The more the EEAS evolves towards a pro-active EU foreign policy, the greater would be its added value (Lloveras Soler 2011: 25). Opponents say the EEAS will mean a new layer of EU bureaucracy, competing with national diplomatic services and "demonstrating an ever-refined mode of 'rationalised intergovernmentalism'" (Wessels/Bopp 2008). Hence the article starts with a short reflection on the

---

2   Treaty of Lisbon Amending the Treaty on European Union and the Treaty Establishing the
    European Community, Article 10A(3), December 2009.
3   Council Decision on the organisation and functioning of the EEAS, 2010/427/EU, 26 July
    2010, L 201/30, Official Journal of the European Union (3 Aug. 2010).

key institutional elements of the EEAS. After a critical discussion of the main challenges of the body, mainly focusing on leadership and strategy, the authors will reflect on the imperative of coherence and continuity in EU foreign policy. This analysis will show the "symbolic character" (Lindstrom 2010: 5) of the EEAS as *the* institutionalised answer to the EU's efforts towards a more active, more coherent and more capable global role of the Union.

A Pan-European Diplomatic Corps

The final creation of the EEAS has to be seen as the outcome of a power struggle between the three main EU institutions: the European Commission, the Council of Ministers and the European Parliament (EP). Especially, the latter has consistently called for the setting-up of a diplomatic service that is *sui generis* from an organisational and budgetary point of view, but incorporated into the Commission's administrative structure, as this would ensure full transparency (European Parliament 2009: 7). By its procedural involvement, the European Parliament's role has gradually evolved along legislative, supervisory and budgetary powers (Dialer/Lichtenberger/Neisser 2010). For example the EP is able to scrutinise the HR/VP and the EEAS by acquiring more access to information on Common Foreign and Security Policy (CFSP)/Common Security and Defence Policy (CSDP), by holding staff and the HR/VP accountable and by controlling the budget of the EEAS (Lefebvre/Hillion 2010: 4-5).

From an organisational point of view, the EEAS seems to be a 'work in progress'. For the time being the EEAS is suffering from a continuing deficit of staff and tools. Therefore Council and European Parliament agreed to increase the EEAS budget for 2012 by 23.5 million euro (5 % more than 2011), to build a modern, flexible and service-oriented diplomatic service. This is quite an achievement, given the general freeze in the EU's administrative expenditure.

In general, one has to distinguish between cabinet members and EEAS staff. Ashton's cabinet is a relatively young one, with many officials under the age of 40. Almost half of its members came straight from Ashton's office as former Commissioner for Trade. On October 25, 2010 Pierre Vimont was appointed EEAS Executive Secretary-General. Previously, Vimont was France's ambassador to the US and a top diplomat in Brussels for four years. Significant responsibilities have been delegated to Vimont paying tribute to the illusion that the HR/VP can indeed master three jobs. Below the secretary-general there are two deputy secretaries-general, one for Political Affairs and one for Inter-Institutional Affairs. Together with the Irish career diplomat David O'Sullivan, who was appointed EEAS Chief Operating Officer, the Secretary General and the two deputies belong to the EEAS Corporate Board. At full capacity, the EEAS will employ a total staff[4] of almost 4,000 people, with approximately 1,600 staff in Brussels and the remainder based at about 140 overseas posts. An additional 2,000-3,000 staff from the Commission will also be based at these EU delegations (Hemra/Raines/Whitman 2011: 3).

All in all, the EEAS is not such a new concept given the fact that most of its staff came from the Commission. It is building on existing structures and intergovernmental practices in external relations, with the only difference that the former delegations (about 140) which mainly administered trade and aid policies, have been transformed into diplomatic missions staffed by officials from the EU and national governments. Previously, the Commission Delegations (now EU Delegations) dealt with trade and aid only, now they also deal with foreign and security policy, coordinating and representing the positions of the EU in third countries. They are indeed the "external action" part of the EEAS and need to be fully integrated into policy shaping, as well as policy implementation. Given the budgetary constraints facing national diplomatic corps, the Delegations provide an excellent opportunity to reduce duplication and enhance cooperation (Balfour/Bailes/Kenna 2012: 47).

Coherence, Strategy and Leadership

The overall political objective of the EEAS – "to give the EU a coherent voice in the foreign policy realm" (Lindstrom 2010:2) – reflects on both the EU's performance in crisis management and conflict prevention. Currently, Europe's response towards the Arab transitions, especially the incoherent reaction towards the Libyan crisis has shown, that the "post-Lisbon institutional structure has done little to compensate for these internal divisions" (Koenig 2011: 1). In fact, in contrast to actors like China, the Arab States of the Gulf or the US, the EU is a unique international actor and a unique neighbour of the North African countries combining political, security and economic interests as well as interests for development policy.

Coherence, according to Koenig (2011: 6-7), can be measured in four dimensions: Horizontal coherence asks for the coherence of different approaches for EU conflict management; institutional coherence analyses the

---

4   At least 60% of EEAS staff is made up of permanent EU officials. Officials from national diplomatic services – one third of the staff – will be temporary agents for a term of up to eight years with a possible extension of two years. Recruitment will be "based on merit whilst ensuring adequate geographical and gender balance" (European Parliament 2009).

interaction of different institutions involved and sharing responsibility for the EU crisis response; vertical coherence measures the "degree to which member states' national policies are in line with and reinforce the EU-level crisis response". Finally, multilateral coherence addresses the positive contribution of the EU response with those of other international actors, like the United Nations (UN), the North Atlantic Treaty Organisation (NATO) and in the African case the African Union (AU).

In her paper, Koenig locates incoherence in the EU response towards Libya in all four categories, which is a critical finding considering the fact that the "Libyan crisis was the first major security-related crisis after the ratification of the Lisbon Treaty" (Koenig 2011: 7). Indeed, there was no one voice European response which vice versa would have been a chance for the EU to show unity in its foreign policy. Rather, the performance proved an existing elitism of the main EU institutions. The HR/VR responded first on behalf of the EU. Then her declaration was followed by declarations by the president of the European Parliament, the president of the European Commission and the president of the European Council. Had there been large discrepancies between the different actors and their statements, the credibility of the EU as a strong and unified global actor would have suffered even more (Koenig 2011: 8). This finding is subsequently getting worse, if European elites and member state officials state different aims for measures of EU crisis management. This has been the case regarding a possible military operation EUFOR Libya – the purpose of the operation was on the one hand seen in a regime change and on the other hand as a support to ensure the implementation of humanitarian aid.

The "institutional lens" takes into account Treaty prerogatives, organisational roles and responsibilities, standard operating procedures as well as formal and informal relationships among such entities. In contrast, the "people lens" examines the individuals who occupy these bodies, generally those who are on the tops of the organisational charts. It might be that Europe finally has the *"the single phone line"* once so ardently wished for by Henry Kissinger, but does the HR/VP really have the means to be the power broker in EU foreign policy?

The driving ethos behind the institutional set-up of HR/VP and the EEAS was to ensure more coordination between the EU external actions. But coordination failings are only one reason for the weakness of the EU's foreign policy. A lack of political vision, leadership and strategic orientation is the deeper reason for Europe's low performance on the global foreign policy stage. In sophisticated debate, this lack of ability is often described as a problem of coordinating 27 separate national foreign policies. Indeed, as Biava, Drent and Herd analyse in their paper, "until the EU develops a supranational federal state, rather than an arena for intergovernmental bargaining, it cannot forge a strategic culture – the state being the *sine qua non* of strategic actor status" (Biava/Drent/Herd 2011: 1234; Göler 2012: 6). As already mentioned, the EEAS does not significantly affect the distribution of competences between the Member States and the EU and the decision-making procedures – remaining largely intergovernmental and based on unanimity, at least in CFSP – relating to the EU. For Reuter (2011: 31) the EEAS can be considered an explicitly autonomous body of an inter-institutional nature, aimed at establishing structures for the inter-institutional coordination in EU foreign policy-making. Coordination and pooling of competences is therefore essential for enhancing the EU's credibility as a negotiator who is supposed to deliver one message. Thus the focus of the debate should be less on fragmentation and more on the EEAS fully utilizing the diplomatic expertise available across the Member States.

The Lisbon Treaty offers no guide to the EU's general leadership gap[5] although it clearly mentions those actors who should represent the EU externally: the European Commission on non-CSFP matters (Art. 17(1) TEU), the President of the European Council and the HR/VP on CSFP issues (Art. 15(6) TEU and Art. 27(2) TEU respectively), and EU Delegations on both CFSP and non CFSP issues (Art. 221(1) TEU).

Perhaps the most undefined element of the post will be 'cohabitation' with the President of the European Council. What is additionally leading to lengthy discussions is a clear definition of the role of the rotating Presidency in external representation. The foreign minister of the country holding the six-month EU rotating Presidency is one of the HR/VP four Deputies together with the Commissioners for Enlargement and European Neighbourhood Policy (ENP), for Development and Cooperation – Europeaid – and for International Cooperation, Humanitarian Aid and Crisis Response.

The horizontal dimension of coherence refers to the compatibility of different EU crisis response measures with one another. In general and as the European Security Strategy calls for, the EU follows a comprehensive understanding of conflict resolution. Ideally, different approaches are geared to the different phases of a conflict. That leads to a civil-military approach from conflict prevention (mostly civil) via crisis management (mostly military and civil-military) to the point of post-conflict resolution.

A situation of incoherence arises, when different opinions regarding the aim and termination of specific measures are expressed by the member states

---

5   The ongoing financial crisis has pulled the Commission out of the front-line leadership and constrained Europe's ability to react to the revolutions in the Middle East and North Africa. EU leadership and priority-setting has shifted to the European Central Bank (ECB), to summit diplomacy and to Berlin and Paris. Increasingly Germany is using economic means to force France but also the UK and Poland – a new player within the EU 27 – into a follower role in their foreign-policy goals.

and different institutions like the Commission or the HR/VR or the European Parliament. That has been the case in many missions and operations running under the CSFP (Opitz 2012) and again under the Libyan crisis (Koenig 2011). The negative effect here is that incoherence does not lead to sustainability. On the contrary – as seen for example in the case of Bosnia and Herzegovina – it counteracts regional stability. But regional stability can only be achieved by ensuring state sustainability (Tocci 2011: 2). The conditions for state sustainability can first and foremost be expressed in two criteria: (1) social economic – referring to the engagement of the civil society and (2) political – meaning the quality of political institutions and not only their existence. The transitions in the Arab world impressively showed, that stagnation erroneously understood as the stability of political systems is highly unstable.

Challenges Ahead

Given the current situation, the HR/VP is clearly both undermined by a general leadership fragmentation and overwhelmed by the sheer workload of her/his job. Yet, there is still a great confusion about the job description. The lack of precision, however, provides the HR/VP and the EEAS with an opportunity to be innovative and entrepreneurial. For Hemra, Raines and Whitman (2011: 12 and 21) this involves a clear commitment to sophisticated leadership, creative foreign policy implementation and innovative communication. Thus, the HR/VP, and the EEAS respectively will have to consider the integration of new tools of communications, in particular social media, into its diplomacy.

The first two and a half years of the EEAS were filled with efforts to shape a team and to act and react to acute international conflicts. Now the focus is placed on communication and on a first full assessment during the mid-term review in 2013, which will give some answers to the question whether it was worth establishing.[6] The ongoing debate about design and responsibilities of the EEAS has been following a bureaucratic logic rather than a strategic ambition and is driven by improvisation and re-nationalistic attempts. The creation and communication of a clear medium and long term vision for the service is indeed overdue.

The international system faces a transformation process itself, global security changes will expand by a strategic dimension: the access to strategic

---

6   The decision opens the door to early adaptation by establishing that the HR/VP will provide a review of the organisation and functioning of the service by mid-2013 that may lead to a revision (Art. 13.3) (Lloveras Soler 2011: 10).

areas. Global resources are highly interlinked, the scarcity of resources like water contains a rising potential for conflict and crisis. The security and foreign policy of the EU must have to address these changes and challenges. Even more since the US needs Europe as a backup because resources for US-external (re)action are becoming scare and the country will not be able to globally act as a crisis manager. The EU itself will then not be able to access the variety of capabilities of the US.

Against this background it becomes evident that the EU needs a clear strategic aim in its external relations and a gradually increased "leadership for coherence". Therefore, the HR/VP should "increase the output of policy analysis, providing the member states with different options for coherent crisis management" (Koenig 2011: 14). On the inter-institutional level, the EU member states should bring forward the setup of a Strategic Policy Planning Department. This body will play a "key role for facilitating coherence and identifying forward looking foreign and security policies" (Lindstrom 2010: 5). Therefore, Koenig calls for staffing with the experience in "drafting political concepts" because this "could provide the strategic guidance that currently seems to be lacking" (Koenig 2011: 14).

Of course, an organisational culture combined with strategic ambitions takes longer to work out. It is indeed a challenge to build an *esprit de corps* among people of 27 nationalities coming from various diplomatic cultures. It will also take time to effectively integrate different instruments and tools: diplomacy, political engagement, development assistance, economic cooperation, civil and military crisis management capabilities in support of conflict prevention and poverty reduction, security and stability, and the promotion of human rights worldwide. The EEAS also needs to be properly plugged in to the institutional and policy-making system, working in close cooperation with the Commission and the Council to develop joined-up policy (Ashton 2011: 25).

A clear idea about the EEAS's medium- and long-term direction would be needed to frame a more pro-active Diplomatic and Foreign Policy. The EEAS needs to focus its energies to give greater room to coordination tasks. Blockmans (2011: 12) is right when they stipulate that the potential for the EEAS lies in becoming a 'decision-shaping' body or in other words a 'European External Policy Coordination Service'. Also practical cooperation between the EEAS and the Commission and the Council Secretariat (meeting premises, infrastructure) should be reviewed to maximise the EEAS' effectiveness.

Balfour/Balies and Kenna (2012: 4) argue in their paper that the EEAS has to ensure that information is conveyed horizontally (between institutions, agencies and bodies) and vertically (from the Delegations to the EEAS, and from the EU institutions to the Member States) in order to develop more efficient policies and more engagement with the European public. This focuses also on the debate regarding the impact of public opinion on EU foreign policy. How do Europeans perceive the world and their place in it? When it comes to legitimacy, the European people and their views have to be considered important in the formation of policy. Hence, the EEAS and its HR/VP should better promote its triumphs, simply put: the EEAS must "sell" itself better. For instance, on May 3, 2011, a resolution[7] was passed in the UN General Assembly, granting the EU delegation at the UN the right to speak on behalf of the EU.

Finally, another vital aspect of the EU's diplomacy today should be public diplomacy. Philip Seib (2009), for example, calls for "reaching out directly to foreign publics rather than foreign governments". Public diplomacy is even more important because of its association with "soft power". In this sense, the effectiveness of public diplomacy in conveying the EU's soft power to the world seems to be crucial for advancing the EEAS broader diplomatic tasks and aims. Communication methods and channels have to be improved. The EEAS's added value has to be more visible both from within and from outside.

Literature

Ashton, Catherine (2011): Coherence in a Changing World, E!Sharp, March/April 2011. 24-25.

Balfour, Rosa/Bailes, Alyson/Kenna, Megan (2012): The European External Action Service at work. How to improve EU foreign policy, EPC Issue Paper no 67, Jan. 2012.

Bell, Robert G. (2012): Geopolitische Relevanz Europas im asiatisch-pazifischen Jahrhundert – trotz der inneren Verwerfungen? Berliner Colloquium 2012 der Clausewitz Gesellschaft e.V.: Europas Platz im asiatisch-pazifischen Jahrhundert – Ziele, Strategien, Handlungsoptionen.

Biava, Alessia/Drent, Margriet/Herd, Graeme P. (2011): Characterizing the European Union's Strategic Culture. An Analytical Framework. In: Journal of Common Market Studies 6, 1227-1248.

Blockmans, Steven (2011): Beyond Conferral: The Role of the European External Action Service in Decision-Shaping. In: Moraru, Madalina/Larik, Joris (2011): Ever-Closer in Brussels – Ever-Closer in the World? EU External Action after the Lisbon Treaty, European University Institute (EUI) Working Paper on Law 2010/2011, 5-17.

Brok, Elmar (2011): Prejudices, Challenges and Potential: an Impartial Analysis of the European External Action Service. In: Fondation Robert Schuman, Policy Paper, European Issue, no 199, 21.3.2011.

Dialer, Doris/Lichtenberger, Eva/Neisser, Heinrich (2010): Das Europäische Parlament. Institution, Vision und Wirklichkeit, Europawissenschaftliche Reihe Bd. 2, innsbruck university press.

---

7   Resolution a/65/L.64/Rev.1

74 Doris Dialer, Anja Opitz

European Parliament (2009): Report on the institutional aspects of setting up the European External Action Service (2009/2133(INI)), Committee on Constitutional Affairs, Rapporteur: Elmar Brok, A7-0041/2009.

Göler, Daniel (2012): Die Europäische Union in der Libyen-Krise: Die "responsibility to protect" als Herausforderung für die strategischen Kulturen in Europa. In: integration 35(1), 3-18.

Hemra, Staffan/Raines, Thomas/Whitman, Richard (2011): A Diplomatic Entrepreneur. Making the Most of the European Action Service. A Chatham House Report, December 2011.

Koenig, Nicole (2011): The EU and the Libyan Crisis: In Quest of Coherence? July 2011, IAI Working Papers, no 11.

Lefebvre, Maxime/Hillion, Christophe (2010): The European External Action Service: Towards a Common Diplomacy. Issue 6 (European Policy Analysis), June 1010, SIEPS (Swedish Institute for European Policy Studies).

Lindstrom, Gustav (2010): The European External Action Service: Implications and Challenges. GCSP Policy Paper 8, November 2010.

Llovares Solar, Josep M. (2011): The new EU Diplomacy: Learning to Add Value. EUI Working Papers RSCAS 2011/05.

Manners, Ian (2000): Normative Power Europe: A Contradiction in Terms? Working Paper 38/2000, Copenhagen Peace Research Institute.

Moraru, Madalina/Larik, Joris (2011): Ever-Closer in Brussels – Ever-closer in the World? EU External Action Service after the Lisbon Treaty. EUJ Working Paper on Law 2010/11.

Opitz, Anja (2012): Politische Vision oder praktische Option? Herausforderung eines zivil-militärischen Krisenmanagementansatzes im Rahmen der GSVP. Baden-Baden: Nomos.

Reuter, Kirstin (2011): Restraints on Member States' Powers Within the EEAS: A Duty to Form a Common Position? In: Moraru, Madalina/Larik, Joris (2011): Ever-Closer in Brussels - Ever-Closer in the World? EU External Action after the Lisbon Treaty, European University Institute (EUI) Working Paper on Law 2010/2011, 29-40.

Schmid, Gunther (2012): Von der Weltwirtschaftskrise zur Weltordnungskrise? Veränderungen in der globalen und regionalen Sicherheitsarchitektur in der 1. Hälfte des 21. Jahrhunderts. Berliner Colloquium 2012 der Clausewitz Gesellschaft e.V.: Europas Platz im asiatisch-pazifischen Jahrhundert – Ziele, Strategien, Handlungsoptionen.

Seib, Philip (ed.) (2009): Toward a New Public Diplomacy: Redirecting U.S. Foreign Policy. New York: Palgrave Macmillan.

Tocci, Nathalie (2011): State (un)Sustainability in the Southern Mediterranean and Scenarios to 2030: The EU´s Response. August 2011, MEDPRO Policy Paper no 1.

Wessels, Wolfgang/Bopp, Franziska (2008): The Institutional Architecture of CFSP after the Lisbon Treaty – Constitutional breakthrough or challenges ahead? June 2008, Challenge Liberty & Security, Research Paper no 10.

Wright, Nick (2011): The European Union: What Kind of International Actor? Political Perspectives 5(2), 8-32.

Military Transitions in the CSDP

Bastian Giegerich[1]

Is the CSDP out of Steam in its Second Decade?

After ten years of rapid development, the EU's Common Security and Defence Policy (CSDP) hit a rough patch in 2011, in particular in the military sphere. Institutions have been set up and have gained practical experience running operations. EU civilian missions and military operations have developed considerable geographical reach and functional scope even though they have not yet strayed into the upper end of the operational spectrum the EU defined for itself. By and large, the operations have fulfilled their objectives within the narrow parameters set by politicians and have thus proven to be marginally useful. A narrative, promoted by both scholars and practitioners, that praises the EU's potential as a comprehensive actor, well equipped to confront the wicked security challenges of today's world, has spread throughout Brussels and has infected member state capitals and external actors alike.

And yet the buzz is gone. Currently, neither France, Germany nor the United Kingdom seem to pursue a coherent vision for how to shift the CSDP to a level where it can truly accomplish its aspirations. With the big three vacating, for the moment, their seats as policy innovators, the next tier of defence players, like Poland during its turn at the wheel in the second half of 2011, struggled to advance the discussion and create the necessary impetus.

The push towards greater effectiveness in the CSDP, expected to flow from the Lisbon Treaty, was halted in the North African sands when EU leaders were unable to agree what the Arab Spring was about and what to do in response. Other actors did not necessarily fare better, but the debilitating disunity and lack of leadership was most profound in the EU. NATO, equally affected by divisions among its members and adjusting with some difficulty to the US decision to provide crucial enabling military capability but leave the frontline to others, demonstrated that, at the very least, it can be a coordinating command and control toolbox for member states and partners to conduct complex operations like Unified Protector in Libya. In contrast, an EU

---

1   The author is writing in a personal capacity and his views do not necessarily represent the position of the Bundeswehr Institute of Social Sciences or the German Ministry of Defence.

operation, EUFOR Libya, offered to the UN in April 2011 and designed to lend support to humanitarian assistance was neither deemed necessary by the UN's Office for the Coordination of Humanitarian Affairs (OCHA) nor did it receive more than lukewarm support from key EU member states. As a result, the offer was not taken up and EUFOR Libya was abandoned without being activated.

At first the CSDP's lack of dynamism seems highly paradoxical. Events in the Middle East and North Africa have yet again underlined the need for crisis management capability. The capability gaps persisting in Europe are well understood and often rehearsed. Member state governments, reeling from the financial and economic crisis, are looking to make their scarce defence euros work harder. Surely this triangle of push factors should lead to the conclusion that more cooperation is needed and that only by working together through instruments such as the CSDP, do EU governments stand a chance of playing a significant role on the global security stage.

This essay suggests that, as far as the military side of the CSDP is concerned, two main factors stand in the way of such a development. First, the national strategic cultures of EU member states are still very different. No matter how much an EU strategic culture might be deemed desirable, it does not yet exist – governments, and their electorates, throughout the EU still think very differently about core questions, such as what the military is for, under which circumstances it should be used and for what purposes. Second, and in part a consequence of these ideational divisions, there is disillusionment regarding the CSDP's ability to generate improved capabilities for force projection and international crisis management operations. Together, these factors lead to the often chastised but rarely scrutinised lack of political will.

The remainder of this essay will briefly expand on this background by firstly giving a quick review of the strategic culture debate to illustrate its potential to either facilitate or hinder EU level security and defence policy. It will, secondly, and very briefly because this ground has been covered extensively before (see for example Asseburg and Kempin 2009; Grevi et al. 2009), examine the military footprint of CSDP operations and the CSDP military capability development process. Thirdly, this chapter will discuss recent CSDP initiatives launched under the impression of the economic and financial crisis to explore whether the lack of money might finally produce a push towards a more effective CSDP and shed some light on how EU member states are trying to cope with the budget crunch.

The Problem of Strategic Cultures

In the wake of Europe's hapless response to the Arab Spring, the preoccupation of European leaders with matters of financial and economic governance and shrinking defence budgets, any discussion exploring the extent to which the EU is living up to its aspiration of becoming a global security actor will sooner or later touch upon strategic culture. For some, the EU needs a strategic culture in order to become a strategic actor in its own right. Witness the European Security Strategy (ESS) which explains "we need to develop a strategic culture that fosters early, rapid, and when necessary, robust intervention" (European Union 2003: 11). It is clear that the assumption in the ESS was that such a strategic culture would make the EU into a more active player and that a more active player would carry "greater political weight" (Ibid.). Others have argued that "similarity of [national] strategic cultures" is one vital precondition for successful European military pooling and sharing arrangements, which in turn look like one of the few solutions on offer for dealing with the defence budget crunch (Valasek 2011: 21). Yet others suggest that a European strategic culture might be the result of the CSDP because, in the long-term, the shared experience of continuous interaction will eventually be a driver of convergence and bring national strategic cultures into close alignment. Finally, some have argued that national strategic cultures are in fact so different and so persistent that they serve as a convincing explanation for why the EU will not become a strategic actor anytime soon, and will fail to generate capabilities commensurate with its aspirations.

Culture, as an ideational construct shared by a society, helps to understand policy preferences and expectations for appropriate behaviour in different policy areas. Strategic culture, then, focuses on security and defence policy and in particular on issues relating to the use of armed force (Giegerich 2006: 36–37; 40). It should not be understood, however, to determine particular outcomes or policy decisions. Rather, it can be expected to structure what kind of options are considered appropriate and are judged to be possible. National strategic cultures, if they are aligned, can enable or at least facilitate the implementation of EU-level goals, including in the areas of capability development and operational activity. The flipside is that, if they are not aligned, they will continue to be a major disruptive factor, likely to make the EU look incoherent, confused and unable to live up to its aspirations.

While scholars will have different conceptions of which features make up strategic culture, four issue areas do stand out as dimensions in which an alignment of national preferences would seem to be an important condition for cooperation in security and defence policy (Jonas and Giegerich 2011): Member states differ on the level of ambition they pursue in international security policy and correspondingly on the means they seek to make available to meet this ambition. Second, their formal and informal procedures afford their executives, to varying degrees, decision-making freedom. Third, differences in foreign policy outlook mean that member states regard different available frameworks for cooperation, for example the EU's CSDP and NATO, to have different comparative advantages. Finally, the respective attitudes towards the use of military force and the place of this instrument within the toolbox of all available means, as seen by member states, leaves much room for disagreement.

Assuming that the different EU member states have different national strategic cultures, the key question becomes one of convergence. Are national strategic cultures converging and if so in what way? Scholars approaching the issue from a constructivist theoretical base line by and large find support for the convergence thesis, although that convergence remains limited (Meyer 2005; Giegerich 2006). These findings stand in contrast to the work of realists who judge differences among member states to remain so significant that anything that might emerge on the EU level will not amount to a coherent set of norms guiding the use of force (Lindley-French 2002; Rynning 2003).

To show that convergence is taking place, whatever the pace, constructivists had to unpack strategic culture in order to come up with analytical dimensions that can actually be empirically observed if properly operationalised. To provide just one example, Meyer used four scalable norms to do this, which showed different degrees of activism in the use of force. They were (Meyer 2005: 530): "goals for the use of force", "way in which force is used", "preferred mode of cooperation", and "threshold for domestic international authorisation". On the issue of goals, for example, countries could pursue territorial defence, displaying a low degree of activism or, at the other end of the scale, extra-territorial expansion with a high degree of activism. Meyer's findings correspondingly allow for a nuanced understanding of convergence and the shape it takes. Meyer characterised normative convergence as spanning a shift away from territorial defence towards humanitarian intervention, the need for a UN-mandate to legitimise the use of force, and a growing appreciation of the role the EU might play in this policy arena. Persisting differences were noteworthy regarding the perceived legitimacy of pre-emptive action, the role of NATO and the US, as well as the casualty averseness of countries. While he noted a convergence effect of some form on all countries under study, it was most pronounced for those countries that had strategic cultures with low levels of activism regarding the different norms in the use of force: "Convergence is thus not simply the process of approximating the British or French strategic mind-set, but a process of hybridisation of strategic cultures, a gradual ironing out of differences, but on a higher level of activism" (Ibid.: 545).

Even this relatively modest position – which essentially suggests a European strategic culture might in time emerge out of national level convergence – is not shared by other important contributions. To simplify Rynning's (2003) position somewhat, the EU might have a vision for its strategic role as actor, but it will not be able to implement this vision unless it becomes a state. In the absence of such a development, the best the EU can hope for is issue specific leadership by changing coalitions of the willing and able member states. The EU's vision, as outlined by Rynning, would essentially be to remake the world in its own image: "In short, the EU believes that progress in world politics is possible, just as the Union purports to represent progress in Europe. The external ambition translates into a policy of resolving other peoples' conflicts by military means if necessary, but without violating international law" (Ibid.: 486). While one can certainly argue with the realist premise that only nation states can be actors of consequence, Rynning is clearly on to something. Lindley-French, focussing his analysis on Britain, France, Germany and Italy comes to a similar assessment, arguing "uncertainty over the means and ends of security…render the development of a European transnational strategic concept almost impossible" (Lindley-French 2002: 790). His recommendation is somewhat more drastic than Rynning's: "What is needed is a new concert of Europe" as only a consensus among the big powers in the EU can have any hope of propelling the Union towards coherence (Ibid.: 810).

On one level the two schools of thought come to incompatible conclusions: whereas constructivists see a weak but emerging and growing level of compatibility between national strategic cultures, realists suggest that the core states in the realm of defence must provide a strategic vision that other member states should adopt. Thus, the prospects of the CSDP look very different to the respective authors. On another level, however, both strands of literature help to explain why EU leaders have found it difficult to translate commonly agreed ambitions into action. What is to be achieved, by what means and under which circumstances has by and large escaped consensus and remains defined by national considerations – of course, this important piece is exactly what has been missing from the CSDP's edifice: an actual multinational strategy for this policy arena. National strategic cultures will make this difficult to achieve, but nonetheless, the outlines of what such a strategy might look like have been put forward (Biscop and Coelmont 2011). For the time being, the operational record of the CSDP and its inability to generate capabilities point to the strategic void and are an important source of disillusionment.

The Operational Record and Capability Development[2]

When EU member states initiated the CSDP in 1999, then known as the European Security and Defence Policy (ESDP), a major goal was to improve capabilities for crisis management missions in order to fulfil the ambition to provide capacities for autonomous EU action. This in turn would help the EU to live up to its self-declared aspiration of being a global security actor. France and the United Kingdom, whose agreement at St. Malo in 1998 paved the way for the CSDP, had fierce disagreements about the degree of the CSDP's autonomy from the US and NATO and the way to run it, but they agreed on two fundamental points: the CSDP was supposed to generate improved European capabilities and it was meant to conduct demanding operations.

Over more than a decade of trying, these goals have only been partially met. This is surprising since they were the very essence of the Anglo-French bargain, which was significant not least because it was entered into by the two militarily most capable EU member states traditionally pursuing opposed visions for European security. Considerable military capability gaps continue to exist if judged against the spectrum of operations the EU wants to be able to conduct. The former EU high representative for Common Foreign and Security Policy (CFSP), Javier Solana, remarked: "Our ambitions are growing, not diminishing. However, there is a gap between our ambitions and the reality of our capabilities" (Solana 2009).

The processes for military capability development starts with the definition of illustrative scenarios which, on the basis of parameters – such as the duration of a mission, rotation requirements, required readiness levels and distance to the theatre of operation – describe the different types of missions that fall within the CSDP's competence. On the basis of these planning assumptions, one then defines which capabilities would be necessary to conduct a certain operation. All of this planning work leads to the so-called Requirements Catalogue. Once this catalogue is defined, EU member states are invited to pledge their contributions according to the list of capabilities contained in the Requirements Catalogue. These pledges from member-state governments are then combined in a so-called Force Catalogue, which defines and describes what has been pledged by member states. If one then compares the two catalogues, it is possible to identify the capability gaps or shortfalls. These exist either because member states do not possess the necessary capabilities, or because they do not make them available to the EU. The list of capability gaps and their implications for potential CSDP operations are then brought together in yet another catalogue misleadingly called the Progress Catalogue.

---

2   This section draws on Giegerich 2010.

The core capability gaps in the areas of strategic and tactical air lift; intelligence and reconnaissance, as well as force protection, persist since the CSDP's inception. To revive this topic, the French EU presidency in the second half of 2008 initiated a Declaration on Strengthening Capabilities (European Union 2008). The declaration was noteworthy in that it set out in relatively clear terms what the EU's level of ambition would be for civilian and military crisis-management missions. The paper argued that the EU should be able to conduct simultaneously two major stabilisation and reconstruction operations involving up to 10,000 troops plus a civilian contingent for at least two years; two rapid response operations using EU battle groups; an evacuation operation in less than ten days; a maritime or air surveillance/interdiction operation; a civil–military humanitarian assistance operation of up to 90 days' duration, or around a dozen civilian missions including one major operation involving up to 3,000 personnel for several years. Notably absent from this list is an operation dealing with a 'separation of parties by force' scenario. Even though such an operation falls within the EU's ambitions, persistent capabilities shortfalls seem to have precluded its inclusion.

Overview of CSDP Military Operations 2003-2011:

Operation	Area of Operations	Duration
Concordia	Former Yugoslav Republic of Macedonia	2003
Artemis	Democratic Republic of Congo	2003
EUFOR Althea	Bosnia – Herzegovina	Since 2004 (on-going)
EUFOR RD Congo	Democratic Republic of Congo	2006
EUFOR Tchad/RCA	Tchad / Central African Republic	2008-2009
EUNAVFOR Atalanta	Coast of Somalia	Since 2008 (on-going)
EUTM Somalia	Somalia/Uganda	Since 2010 (on-going)
EUFOR Libya	Libya	NOT ACTIVATED

Source: http://consilium.europa.eu/eeas/security-defence/eu-operations.aspx?lang=en (September 2011).

Since 2003 the EU has launched 24 CSDP operations and missions.[3] While these endeavours demonstrate a certain shared will to engage, the flurry of activity should not be mistaken for progress. CSDP operations cover an increasing geographical and functional scope but they are often rather limited in size and their impact on the crisis situation at hand is often unclear. Furthermore, it is not possible to discern clear criteria upon which decisions to launch an operation are based. Most of the time the EU is reactive rather than

---

3   On overview is available at: http://consilium.europa.eu/eeas/security-defence/eu-operations.aspx?lang=en.

proactive, driven by either external demands, specific interests of a member state, or the sheer desire to demonstrate a capacity for action. The fact that five of the EU's missions took place in the Democratic Republic of the Congo (DRC), for example, seems to be due to French interests, UN requests and the desire to show that the CSDP had entered the real, operational world. None of those are bad reasons for engagement per se, but they fall short of the preventive character the EU aspires to and demonstrate a lack of strategic planning. Some governments within the EU resent the impression that an EU-label is attached to what are essentially priorities of a single member state; whereas actors outside the EU question the neutrality of EU action in cases where postcolonial ties are perceived to be among the reasons for engagement. The results are tightly defined and risk averse EU mandates because of the need to balance different member states' interests and the desire to maintain international legitimacy.

The core problems remain the ever-increasing operational demands on military and civilian personnel on operations, the persistent gaps as yet not filled by the capability development processes in the EU, and the enormous cost pressure. In the future there will even be less money available, in particular with regard to defence. To be sure, many of the operations the EU wants to be able to conduct could be undertaken on the basis of existing capabilities if EU member states chose to make them available. However, to fulfil the self-defined aspiration of being a global security actor, the gap has to be closed. If it is not, those countries that saw the CSDP only ever as a partial reflection of their national level of ambition but without whom the CSDP will not be credible – in particular France and the UK – are likely to lose interest and will increasingly turn to pragmatic cooperation, designed to solve a particular problem, with a few select partners.

Lack of Money: A Driving Force?

The financial and economic crisis could theoretically be both a blessing and a curse for European defence capabilities. On the one hand, shrinking resources for defence might force European governments into greater levels of cooperation and in the process see them spend their money more efficiently and on the capabilities needed for modern operations. On the other hand, governments might retrench to the national level trying to implement defence cuts with neither a clear understanding of what their partners are doing nor an attempt to coordinate their actions, leading to degraded capabilities across the board. In fact, the severity of the budget crunch varies greatly from country to country and, at this stage, no clear pattern has emerged. Some countries have long begun to implement cuts, others seem set to lower their ambitions whereas yet others are working hard to identify opportunities for greater co-operation (Mölling and Brune 2011).

The big three are in the middle of, or are about to begin, an important re-form and restructuring process in the security and defence realm. Germany has suspended conscription, published new defence policy guidelines in May 2011 and is set to announce important steps to create a smaller but more ca-pable Bundeswehr. The United Kingdom has completed a Strategic Defence and Security Review in 2010 which amounted to a frantic attempt to align ambitions with the reality of diminishing resources. In 2011 further cuts were announced suggesting that the 2010 review failed to provide a sustainable basis. France, having completed a major review in 2008, which saw the pub-lication of a defence and security policy whitepaper, has embarked on an up-date of this document and will make an explicit effort to analyze the implications of the changing financial parameters during 2012. None of these processes has benefitted from sustained and coherent conversations with key partner countries and all are driven by a sense of urgency that – as avoidable as it is given the external pressures – is unlikely to improve the quality of analysis.

In any event, how to manage the unabated pressure on defence budgets remained a question at the forefront of many defence ministers' minds across Europe. At an informal meeting of EU defence ministers on September 23-24, 2010 in the Belgian city of Ghent, the EU's High Representative for For-eign Affairs and Security Policy, Baroness Catherine Ashton, argued that EU member governments should cooperate more in order to deliver defence ca-pability and focus "spending on our agreed priorities. We need to explore ways of pooling and sharing. Our existing resources need to better fit our needs" (European Union 2010a). Then German defence minister Karl Theo-dor zu Guttenberg (2010) suggested member states should evaluate three core questions: Which capabilities would have to remain outside of pooling and sharing arrangements for national security reasons? For which capability areas could member states envision pooling arrangements? And, finally, where would member governments be willing to consider task and role shar-ing with other EU partners?

Pooling and sharing is not a new idea as such for European defence es-tablishments. It has been discussed on and off over the years against the background of declining resources, both financially and in manpower, and growing operational demand in crisis management deployments. But now the budget pressure that most EU member states feel in the defence realm has created a window of opportunity that should, in theory, propel governments toward closer European cooperation in defence. In the words of Javier So-lana, "out of the necessity for higher efficiency and cooperation might grow benefits" (Solana 2011).

Germany, this time joined by Sweden, thought to further advance the pooling and sharing agenda by providing a food for thought paper outlining a methodology for EU member states to determine where they would want to engage. The CSDP council conclusions from December 9, 2010 called on EU member states to "seize all opportunities to cooperate in the area of capability development" and in particular think about pooling and sharing (European Union 2010b). The initiative is meant to preserve and enhance national operational capabilities with improved effect, sustainability, interoperability and cost efficiency as a result. Member states, between themselves, have initially identified more than 300 possible areas for pooling and sharing, essentially by answering zu Guttenberg's three questions. However, that was the easy part. Now, member states will have to prove that they are willing to move from ideas to action. In November 2011, the European Defence Agency presented 11 concrete projects to its steering board of defence ministers. Member states have to accept that pooling and sharing is likely to yield benefits, but only at the price of somewhat reduced national autonomy. To strike the balance between autonomy and capability is a difficult political task but unavoidable.

Many of the areas for closer cooperation identified by member states fall into the fields of education, training, logistical support and maintenance. These are not frontline capabilities, which shows that member states feel pooled and shared capability create a level of mutual dependency that they are uncomfortable with if it stretches to actual fighting. Furthermore, most identified capability areas seem to be foreseen for pooling, but not sharing with the latter creating much higher levels of mutual dependence. Thus, for the time being member states are going for the quick wins that will have a relatively small impact on national autonomy. Plucking the low hanging fruits can by itself save money and create the same or improved capability at lower cost and furthermore help create a mindset that makes cooperation the default position. However, this logic will still need to be complemented by a coherent long term approach that firmly anchors pooling and sharing in national defence planning processes and focuses on those capabilities relevant for the likely tasks European armed forces will be called upon to achieve. Member states should avoid the temptation to feed projects into pooling and sharing initiatives that would be redundant otherwise. Multinational cooperation on capability must not become a way to upload obsolete assets to the European level in order to avoid cutting them.

For the time being, the role of EU level institutions in this process is likely to remain limited. They are service providers to the member states and are supposed to reduce the transaction costs of member states engaging in pooling and sharing. They can do this best by creating visibility of the different ideas, by ensuring information exchange, and by mapping the activities of member states with a possible view to identify best practices.

The discussion about pooling and sharing has developed into one of the central themes in European defence. Governments have tried to focus it on the pragmatic goal of saving money and at the same time protecting – possibly even improving – capability. However, keeping in mind structural limitations extrapolated from past performance will be very helpful in selecting and identifying concrete new projects and partners. Valasek has convincingly argued that countries need to have similar strategic cultures, have to share a sense of mutual trust and solidarity, have to command forces of similar size and quality, and need compatible defence industrial policies for pooling and sharing in order to work. Given that these factors have to fall into place more or less simultaneously, Valasek concludes that successful pooling and sharing, despite its promises, might continue to be a rare animal (Valasek 2011).

Chief among these limitations is that EU member states still have very heterogeneous strategic cultures. As has been argued above, there is little convergence on fundamental questions, such as what kind of armed forces do nations want and for what purpose. In addition, member states have vastly different legal and constitutional frameworks for the external deployment of their armed forces in place. These factors contribute to diverse levels of ambition across EU member states and also affect trust among countries. Such political factors will become even more important if pooling and sharing includes deployable front-line capabilities. On the industrial side, pooling and sharing could lead to losses of jobs and skills in member states that do have a defence industrial and technology base. Hence, defence industrial interests may stand in the way of successful pooling and sharing as well. Pooling and sharing increases mutual dependence and reduces national autonomy. Therefore, it raises the question whether EU member states can really rely on each other to make pooled capabilities available when needed. The necessary trust does not seem to extend across the EU yet.

Conclusion

The often cited bicycle theory of European cooperation suggests that when cooperation stops moving forward, the whole enterprise will fall over. CSDP has not moved forward lately. The new crisis management structures and institutions created by the Lisbon Treaty have disappointed when confronted with the Arab Spring. Yet, this test might have come too soon, in particular for the European External Action Service, and the EU still has a chance to play a constructive and useful long-term role in supporting the transition processes in the Middle East and North Africa. More worryingly for CSDP and the question of whether it will shift to a new level of achievement in its second decade, is that there are no signs of EU member governments, hampered by different strategic cultures, overcoming the central problem: the CSDP does not seem to be very good at generating much needed capability for crisis management tasks and the operations conducted through CSDP, while useful and by and large successful, are not of strategic importance. Member states vital to a credible CSDP, including France, have become disillusioned as a result.

The impact of the financial crisis on European security and defence is still unfolding. It is clear, however, that further fragmentation and decline of national capabilities is a real danger. Such a development, which would further undermine the CSDP, becomes more likely if EU member governments treat cooperation as an afterthought, only to be contemplated when gaps and holes created by national defence cuts need to be filled through the capabilities of partners. It would be pure coincidence if uncoordinated national adjustments led to a coherent and useable European capability. Pooling and sharing, despite the inherent difficulty of balancing potential benefits (savings and capability gains) and potential costs (loss in political and operational autonomy), will be one important element of the solution. Without leadership from key defence powers, the CSDP will not simply fall over – the wheels might come off the bicycle.

Literature

Asseburg, M. and R. Kempin (eds.) (2009): Die EU als strategischer Akteur in der Sicherheits- und Verteidigungspolitik? Eine systematische Bestandsaufnahme von ESVP Missionen und -Operationen. SWP Studie 2009/S32. SWP, Berlin.

Biscop, S. and J. Coelmont (eds.) (2011): Europe Deploys: Towards a Civil-Military Strategy for CSDP. Egmont Paper No. 49. Egmont Institute, Brussels.

European Union (2003): A Secure Europe in a Better World: European Security Strategy, December 12, 2003.

European Union (2008): Declaration on Strengthening Capabilities, December 12, 2008, www.consilium.europa.eu/ueDocs/cms_Data/docs/pressData/en/esdp/104676.pdf.

European Union (2010a): Remarks by High Representative Catherine Ashton at the informal meeting of EU Defence Ministers, Ghent, September 23 and 24, 2010, http://www.consilium.europa.eu/uedocs/cms_data/docs/pressdata/EN/foraff/116710.pdf.

European Union (2010b): Council Conclusions on Military Capability Development. 3055th Foreign Affairs (Defence) Council Meeting, Brussels, December 9, 2010, http://www.eutrio.be/files/bveu/118347.pdf.

Giegerich, Bastian (2006): European Security and Strategic Culture: National Responses to the EU's Security and Defence Policy. Baden-Baden: Nomos.

Giegerich, Bastian (2010): Military and Civilian Capabilities for EU-led Crisis Management Operations, in: Giegerich, Bastian (ed.): Europe and Global Security. Abingdon: Routledge, pp. 41-57.

Grevi, Giovanni/Helly, Damien/Keohane, Daniel (eds.) (2009): ESDP: The First 10 Years. Paris: EUISS.

Guttenberg, Karl-Theodor zu (2010): Die Stunde Europas, in: Frankfurter Allgemeine Zeitung, 09.12.10, p. 10.

Jonas, Alexandra/Giegerich, Bastian (2011): After Libya: Time to bury the EU's foreign and security policy? http://www.sicherheitskultur.org/de/blog.html.

Lindley-French, Julian (2002): In the Shade of Locarno? Why European Defence is Failing, in: International Affairs 78(4), pp. 789-811.

Meyer, Christoph O. (2005): Convergence Towards a European Strategic Culture? A Constructivist Framework for Explaining Changing Norms, in: European Journal of International Relations 11(4), pp. 523-549.

Mölling, Christian/Brune, Sophie-Charlotte (2011): The Impact of the Financial Crisis on European Defence. Study for the European Parliament's Subcommittee on Security and Defence. Brussels: European Parliament.

Rynning, Sten (2003): The European Union: Towards a Strategic Culture?, in: Security Dialogue 34(4), pp. 479-496.

Solana, Javier (2009): ESDP@10: What Lessons for the Future?, Document No. S195/09, Brussels, http://www.consilium.europa.eu/uedocs/cms_data/docs/pressdata/en/discours/109453.pdf.

Solana, Javier (2011): Für ein wehrhaftes Europa, in: Handelsblatt, 05.01.11, p. 56.

Valasek, T. (2011): Surviving Austerity: The Case for a New Approach to EU Military Collaboration. Centre for European Reform, London.

EU Military Operations

Structures, Capabilities and Shortfalls

Lisa Karlborg

Introduction

The European Union (EU) is an increasingly visible actor in international crisis and conflict management (Johansson *et al*. 2010: 30). After a decade in the business of international crisis and military operations, the EU has to-date launched 24 missions in Africa, Asia, Europe, and the Middle East (EEAS, 2011a). With the ratification of the Lisbon Treaty and the launch of the European Common Security and Defence Policy, CSDP[1] in 2010, the EU made strides towards solidifying a comprehensive institutional framework guiding collective military action. However, this new phase in the development of the EU has raised important issues pertaining to the *raison d'être* of the Union, and its role in international crisis and conflict management in particular. Although few predict that the EU is turning into a new military superpower, many take a critical stance on its progressive process of converging national military capabilities within an overarching EU framework. A key criticism put forward identifies the Union's emerging military persona as a potential threat to EU diplomacy, which historically has been rooted in the identity of a peaceful and –first and foremost– political and economic actor.

In the following chapter, I address the new military role of the EU in international conflict management, examining more precisely the Union's implementation of collective military operations. The undertaking of military interventions is an important litmus test of the EU's collective military capabilities because it represents the Union's most robust security policy instrument (Missiroli 2003: 496). In my analysis, I juxtapose the EU's current legal and strategic framework for collective military action against its practical experiences of collective military interventions, integrating analysis on the EU's, to-date, seven military operations. I argue that there is still a gap between the organisation's strategic ambition and operative capabilities to promote a more visible and coherent European approach to military intervention. I conclude the chapter by identifying remaining challenges to European military capabilities illustrated with the present 'non-case' of Libya.

---

1   Previously, the European Security and Defence Policy, ESDP.

There are different conceptualisations of what constitutes an EU military operation. In the following chapter, I refer to operations classified as "military operations" by the European External Action Service (EEAS 2011d), namely EUFOR Concordia, EUFOR Artemis, EUFOR Althea, EUFOR RD Congo, EUFOR Chad/Central African Republic, EU NAVFOR Somalia and EUTM Somalia. I thus exclude civilian election monitoring missions and assistance projects, as well as civil-military missions in support of Security Sector Reform from the analysis (EU Support for the African Union Mission in Darfur/Sudan, EUSEC DR Congo, and EU SSR Guinea-Bissau). However, a military operation may still refer to a mission where the EU employs a "comprehensive approach", and parallel to its military engagements also supports the judicial, economic or social sectors of the host state.

The Rise of EU Military Capabilities

European states have widely participated in peace operations under the auspices of the UN, NATO and the Organisation for Security and Co-operation in Europe (OSCE) since long before the launch of the European Security and Defence Policy (ESDP). Also, joint action by European states in crises and conflicts predates ESDP with initiatives such as a military monitoring mission to Croatia and Slovenia in 1991[2] (Johansson et al. 2010: 26). Furthermore, the EU is the largest financial contributor to the UN peacekeeping enterprise, funding more than two-fifths of all UN operations (EEAS 2011e). However, the Petersberg Declaration issued by the Western European Union (WEU) in 1992 marked an important event in the nascent development of a European framework for joint military action. With it, the notion of the collective use of force moved beyond the existent principle of self-defence to include a wide range of responsibilities, spanning from the enactment of humanitarian and rescue tasks to peacekeeping and the deployment of combat forces in crisis management or peace-making missions (later referred to by the EU as the "Petersberg Tasks", WEU 1992: Article 2.4). The envisioned role of the WEU as a capable stabilizing regional actor was however quickly challenged by the apparent failure to act rapidly and decisively to halt the deteriorating situation in the Balkans. European inability to autonomously – without intervention by the United States or the North Atlantic Treaty Organisation (NATO) – manage conflict and crisis playing out on its own soil spurred the beginning of a sequence of events aimed at strengthening European collective security, defence, and military capabilities. In December 1998, the two leading EU military powers, Great Britain and France, called

---

2   European Community Monitoring Mission, ECMM.

for the establishment of autonomous EU capabilities to collectively react "rapidly to [...] new risks" and international crises "backed up by credible military forces". Thus, at a time when the political and strategic context was deeply coloured by the recent experiences of European failure to collectively and decisively respond to crises and conflicts in the Balkans, the two states paved the way for the birth of the ESDP with the Franco–British St. Malo Declaration (1998).

From the start, the development of ESDP had clear restrictions relating to the role of NATO, which had already been stipulated in the Treaty on European Union (1992): the framing of a common defence policy "shall not prejudice the specific character of the security and defence policy of certain Member States and shall respect the obligations of certain Member States under the North Atlantic Treaty and be compatible with the common security and defence policy established within that framework" (Article J 4.4). In early 1999, at NATO's Washington Summit, the *Berlin Plus* agreements formalised EU access to NATO operational planning, capabilities, common assets, and command options (Hauser 2006: 50). However, disagreements between Greece and Turkey "over the use of NATO assets and possible deployments in the Aegean Sea and Cyprus" delayed the signing of the agreements until 2003 (ibid: 50). The *Berlin Plus* agreements were an important development in the relationship between NATO and the EU because it recognised the Union's nascent military and security identity as separate from NATO. At the same time, it also formalised the EU's close cooperation with NATO in the field of crisis and conflict management (Oswald 2006: 127). The relationship with NATO is still a major influence on the development of European capabilities, with NATO still shouldering the role of primary security guarantor of its twenty-one European Member States (Keohane 2009a: 127).

In June, the European Council asserted that the EU would be equipped with the "necessary means and capabilities to assume its responsibilities regarding a common European policy on security and defence" (Cologne European Council 1999: Article 1) in line with the envisioned Petersberg Tasks. In so doing, it formalised the strategic vision of the development of a collective defence as part of the EU's Common Foreign and Security Policy, CFSP. In December, marking the end of an eventful year in the development of EU military capabilities, the European Council followed the guiding principles agreed upon in Cologne and operationalised the strategic framework of ESDP into a set of military goals referred to as the Helsinki Headline Goal (Helsinki European Council 1999). With a view to covering the full range of the Petersberg Tasks (currently comprised in the TEU 2010: Articles 42 and 43), it stated that the EU would, no later than 2003, establish autonomous operational capabilities to authorise and deploy a rapid reaction and stabilisation force consisting of 50,000 to 60,000 troops within 60 days (sustainable for at least a year) (EEAS 2011a). Over the course of only a couple of years, the EU thus set out to develop the capacity to independently respond to situations of crisis and conflict with, if deemed necessary, the use of military means.

EU Military Operations: Past and Present

When the 2003 deadline arrived, and it was time for the EU to demonstrate its military operational capabilities, relations between some Member States were tense over an internal rift on the US intervention in Iraq. In spite of this fact, the EU managed to launch four operations during 2003 in accordance with its new security and defence policy, two of which were military operations. Although both military operations were deemed successful (Solana 2003a, 2003b), they also illustrated the necessity of further developing and strengthening the EU's rapid military response capabilities, and thus, in many ways, these two missions became blueprints for future EU military operations. In the following section, I briefly present the Union's, to-date, seven military operations, and discern a few lessons learned from these first attempts at EU military diplomacy.

EUFOR Concordia

When the EU's operational military structure was still in its infancy, the Union launched its first military operation. Not only a crucial first test of EU military capabilities, the recent experiences from the Balkan situation put additional symbolic weight on this first military operation *EUFOR Concordia* (March–December, 2003) deployed to the former Yugoslav Republic of Macedonia, FYROM (Council of the European Union 2003b). Being one of the most capable military Member States, France shouldered the role of *framework nation* for the mission, which translated into providing the operational mission leadership of a Force Commander, as well as deploying the largest military contingent to the field. The relatively benign security situation in FYROM was deemed to require only a light military footprint consisting of 350 mission staff tasked with surveillance, reporting, reconnaissance, and patrolling. Despite the mission's relatively limited scope, EU military engagements in FYROM would demonstrate several areas in need of improvement. One key challenge to the mission was EU cooperation with NATO. Prior to deployment, Turkey delayed the inter-organisational *Berlin Plus* agreements and, in effect, blocked the EU's ability to deploy a mission with the planning and logistical support from NATO. Throughout deployment, the less than ideal inter-organisational structures for cooperation and communication seemed to blur the image of the EU as the political and military head of the mission; a negative image that was further enhanced due to a lack of internal coordination between the Union's military engagements and the broader political spectrum of EU commitments and activities in the Balkans (Gross 2009).

EUFOR Artemis

With the military operation in FYROM underway, the EU launched its second military mission, *EUFOR Artemis* (June–September, 2003), to the Democratic Republic of the Congo, DRC (Council of the European Union 2003c). The deployment of this first autonomous military operation put coordination within the ESDP framework of military and political structures[3] to the test. However, the exercise demonstrated that the EU successfully managed to carry out a peace enforcement mission mandated by the UN to deploy to an area outside of Europe without the support of NATO or the "Berlin Plus" agreements (Helly 2009a). The mission was indeed a learning experience for the nascent European military power. On one hand, *Artemis* was used as a blueprint for European stand-alone forces. A main feature of the "Headline Goal 2010" (2004) was the ambition to increase the quality of the EU's autonomous military capabilities in terms of rapid deployment, sustainability and interoperability through the operationalisation of Battlegroups (Directorate-General for External Policies of the Union 2006a). EU Battlegroups consist of battalion-size formations (1500 soldiers each), which are deployable to "crisis areas" and "extremely hostile environments" within 15 days after authorisation, and are able to maintain autonomous sustainability for at least 30 days (ibid). Since January 1, 2007, there have been two EU Battlegroups on stand-by "able to undertake if so decided by the Council two concurrent single Battlegroup-sized rapid response operations" (EU Council Secretariat 2009). On the other hand, the military operation also raised a few concerns. Although 14 Member States participated in the operation, France was again the acting framework nation. France provided the force commander and deployed the majority of troops, and was thus granted considerable flexibility in the operative and tactical implementation of the mission (Hendrickson 2008; Council of the European Union 2003c). With the dominant role played by a single Member State in a region that is of such specific historical national interest, some questioned if Operation *Artemis* was in fact a *European* military mission, or the product of lingering French strategic interests in the area (Helly 2009a).

---

3   The Political Security Council, PSC, the EU Military Committee, EUMC, and EU Military
    Staff, EUMS.

Concluding its first year of ESDP operations, the EU and former High Representative Javier Solana launched a new strategic framework aimed at strengthening *European* foreign security and defence: the European Security Strategy (ESS) (Council of the European Union 2003a, for a revised version, see Council of the European Union 2009). This was the first official document in which the EU presented a joint threat assessment and "set clear objectives for advancing its security interests" (Council of the European Union 2009, Foreword). As part of the strategy, the EU proclaimed a "convergence of European interests and the strengthening of mutual solidarity" as means of making the Union into a unified, "more credible and effective actor" (Council of the European Union 2003a, 1). Although the strategy emphasises the importance of political, economic and humanitarian tools of conflict management, it also refers to mandated instruments of force: "[i]n failed states, military instruments may be needed to restore order" (ibid, 7). The strategy further stipulates the collective ambition to "share […] the responsibility for global security" and to "defend its [European] security and to promote its values" (ibid, 1, 6). These strategic objectives have not yet been translated into full-scale defence planning procedures, however, with the adoption of the Lisbon Treaty (see below), several key concepts and political guidelines steering a common defence planning have been introduced.

EUFOR Althea

A year after the conclusion of *EUFOR Concordia*, the EU launched its third, and still on-going, military operation, *EUFOR Althea*, in Bosnia Herzegovina in December 2004. With over 7000 troops deployed (approximately 1600 in January, 2011), *Althea* is the largest and longest running EU military mission to-date. The operation is mandated under UN chapter VII and carried out with recourse to the "Berlin Plus" agreements (Council of the European Union 2004). Initially, it replaced the NATO-led Stabilisation Force (SFOR) mission, and during its first years of deployment the main military task of the operation was to assure compliance with the Dayton-Paris peace agreement and, if so required, use force to meet this objective. In addition, the mission acted in support of Bosnian authorities in their efforts to detain war criminals and combat organised crime (EEAS 2011b; Keohane 2009b). In late 2010, after a renewed UN mandate, the Council of the EU announced a continued commitment to lead the military mission in support of Bosnian authorities (EEAS 2011b). *EUFOR Althea* presented another set of challenges to the EU-NATO relationship. Prior to deployment, the Union's recourse to the "Berlin Plus" agreements had again delayed the implementation of the mission. The Union announced its willingness to replace SFOR already in late 2002 but due to the unfinished status of the agreement, the mission was postponed for a year and a half (Keohane 2009b). Also, the strategic planning concerning the handover from SFOR turned into a lengthy six-months process, mainly because of "political disagreements over the precise meaning of EU access to NATO assets and capabilities" (ibid: 213). Another aspect of EU-NATO relations that proved challenging for the EU was the perceived need, to strike a balace between establishing credibility amongst the local population as a capable replacement of NATO forces, and to distance the EU mission from previous NATO engagements in order to reinforce the Union's self-image as a military actor that is capable of making a *European* contribution (ibid).

EUFOR RD Congo

In April 2006 the UN authorised the EU to deploy a military operation to the Democratic Republic of the Congo (DRC) in support of the ongoing UN operation MONUC and its mandate to safeguard the upcoming democratic elections (UN Security Council 2006). After a lengthy force-generation process, prolonged due to a lack of interest amongst Member States to contribute to the operation, the EU finally launched its fourth military operation *EUFOR RD Congo* at the end of July 2006. In total, the EU deployed approximately 2400 troops from 21 Member States (together with Turkey and Switzerland) to the Congo (Council of the European Union 2006). Germany headed the Operational Headquarter and France provided the Force Headquarter and again supplied the largest military contingent of over 1000 troops (Major 2009). In short, operation *RD Congo* was hardly the ultimate test case for the ESDP framework. It was the EU's second military mission in Africa and the Congo, and it was not a rapidly deployed autonomous mission. However, the operation offered important initial insights to military coordination and organisational relations with the UN, and thus provided the Union with vital lessons for future EU-UN cooperation in the implementation of military operations (ibid 2009). In theatre, the mission was hampered by internal restrictions and inconsistencies, such as national caveats and a lack of resources from member states, but also from a lack of overall communication and coordination of logistics between the two missions. Similar to their experiences from *Althea*, EU forces worked actively in the field towards clarifying their role and purpose in relation to UN troops, but also sought to demonstrate to the local population their capacity to provide support to the MONUC mission and the overall security situation (ibid 2009). Within the framework of its limited mandate, *RD Congo* fulfilled its purpose and has been deemed a successful mission. In retrospect, however, the presence of EU forces had a merely temporary stabilisation effect indicated by a rapidly deteriorating security situation following the return of EU troops from the Congo.

EUFOR Tchad/RCA

The deployment of *EUFOR Tchad/RCA* to the Central African Republic, CAR, and Chad (January 2008 – March 2009) was a key step forward in the Union's longstanding interest in managing the crisis in Darfur (Assembly of WEU 2008: 25). The mission was intended as a "bridging" or "hybrid" mission implemented in support of the UN operation MINURCAT. Its main task was to improve the level of security and the delivery of humanitarian aid in the area of operation, as well as protecting civilians, UN staff and humanitarian personnel (Council of the European Union 2007). Overall, this fifth military mission represents the Union's logistically most complex military operation to-date. The area of operations was remote and inaccessible, which made it difficult to guarantee the Headline Goal of *deployability* ("the ability to move personnel and material to the theatre of operations") and *sustainability* (the "mutual logistic support between the deployed forces") (*Headline Goal 2010* 2004: footnote 1). Similar to previous missions, the internal structures of coordination proved insufficient, especially due to a lack of strategic coordination between the Commission and the Council. Furthermore, Member States employed national caveats on the activities of their deployed troops, which complicated the implementation of the mission in the field (Helly 2009b). In regard to the EU-UN relations, the operation experienced similar difficulty as *RD Congo* in reaching the expected synergy effects of inter-organisational cooperation (ibid 2009b). Furthermore, the mission provoked a debate on the impartiality of force. Due to its past military involvement as a colonial power in the Central African region (Ayissi 1999), France sought to limit its participation in the EU mission. However, the lack of troop contributions from other Member States resulted in the fact that France, once again, shouldered the responsibility of framework nation, deploying half of all troops as well as the mission Force Commander. The dominant role of France not only raised the issue of impartiality, but also generated valid concerns regarding the implementation of the ESDP's strategic aspirations without heavy reliance on French involvement or deployment to conflicts far beyond the European context.

EU NAVFOR Atalanta

The two most recent EU military operations have both been deployed to Somalia as part of the Union's wider support of the Transitional Federal Government of Somalia and its TFG, work to rebuild security and stability on the Somali mainland and off the Somali Coast (EEAS 2011c). *EU NAVFOR Atalanta* is the EU's first naval military operation (December 2008 – on-going) and it is tasked with providing "security in the maritime zone off the coast of Somalia and protect humanitarian convoys heading towards that country". In particular, this refers to "the deterrence, prevention and repression of acts of piracy and armed robbery" (Assembly of WEU 2008: 29-30). In December 2008, NATO's *Operation Allied Provider* handed over the responsibility of protecting the World Food Program's assistance shipments to the EU (Ploch *et al.* 2009: 15). The EU is merely one of many actors operating off the coast of Somalia and in the Gulf of Aden as the area has become a virtual "laboratory for international military naval coordination". This development reflects the increased geostrategic interest in the region for actors such as the US, China, India, Russia, Japan and South Korea (Helly 2009c: 399; McGivern 2010: 3), which all adhere to different mandates and mission objectives (EU NAVFOR Somalia). Also, NATO has remained in the area with the deployment of two consecutive anti-piracy missions, *Operation Allied Protector* (2009) now replaced by *Operation Ocean Shield* (mandated to run until the end of 2012) (McGivern 2010: 3; Ploch *et al.* 2009: 15). It was initially feared that the presence of both EU and NATO military missions in the same theatre of operations would lead to a duplication of efforts. Since the beginning of ESDP, the EU has gone through a phase of identification, contextualisation and positioning of its military capabilities in relation to those of NATO, and the outcome of inter-organisational cooperation has been mixed at best. In the last few years, however, developments have signalled a more constructive approach to inter-organisational relations (Keohane 2009a: 127), which appears to be reflected in a satisfactory coordination of efforts in Somalia (McGivern 2010: 3). With the absence of a clear-cut international legal framework guiding maritime operations, participating EU Member States are able to switch from EU to national operational command at their own choosing. Although Member States are encouraged to follow a coherent set of operative military measures, the possibility to revert to national command has resulted in variation in national approaches to the use of force within the scope of the mission mandate (Helly 2009c: 397). The lack of a coherent operative framework is a potentially controversial issue. Considering that the Lisbon Treaty transformed the EU into a single legal body, what are the collective ramifications if military actions employed in the field by a single Member State would generate international criticism?

EUTM Somalia

On April 7, 2010, the EU launched *EUTM Somalia* in conjunction with *Operation Atalanta*, which is the Union's seventh military mission, but its first military training mission. Under the shared leadership of Spain and France as acting framework nations, approximately 150 EU troops are stationed in Uganda where they train Somali forces. In Uganda, the EU is partnering with principal actors such as the African Union and its military mission AMI-SOM, the UN, the US, and the humanitarian assistance provided by the

World Food Programme (EEAS 2011c; McGivern 2010: 2). The mission's main challenges are innate to the current fragile state of government institutions in Somalia and the limited military skills of Somali recruits, which are in apparent need of greater assistance than current EU operations are able to provide. However, the Council deemed the mission successful at generating significant progress in the Somali security track, and iterated its commitment to the security situation in the country Somali by extending the mandate of *EUTM Somalia* for two additional 6-month training periods (terminating in 2012) (Council of the European Union 2011a).

The Lisbon Treaty: New Strategic and Institutional Frameworks for Military Action

After a lengthy ratification process that was prolonged by political debates in Member States throughout Europe, the Lisbon Treaty finally entered into force in December 2009. With its abolishment of the European Community and removal of the pillar structure, the Treaty reformed the EU into a single organisation and legal personality (TEU 2010). In the realm of security and defence, the Treaty introduced the Common Security and Defence Policy, CSDP, which aims to consolidate the image of a unified EU equipped with a coherent institutional framework that helps Member States to act jointly and swiftly on matters of common security and defence. In the following section, I briefly discuss the impact of the Lisbon Treaty on the Union's current strategic and institutional capacity to implement joint military operations.

Strategic Vision

The Lisbon Treaty broadened the scope of the envisioned role of the EU in the maintenance of international security. Besides the enactment of humanitarian, peacekeeping, crisis management and peace-making missions, the Petersberg Tasks were stretched to include disarmament operations, military advice and assistance tasks, and the deployment of combat forces to support post-conflict stabilisation. In addition, these responsibilities extend to include the support of "third countries in combating terrorism in their territories" (TEU 2010, Article 43.1). These additional tasks reflect the Union's willingness to implement CSDP operations along a more comprehensive continuum of security related concerns. The new tasks indicate that the Union seeks to progress towards shouldering more complex situations. In particular, this refers to activities that border the military, police and judiciary spheres of influence, such as combating terrorism or disarming former combatants in post-conflict societies. In line with this new scope of CSDP operations, the

Lisbon Treaty establishes a Solidarity Clause, which makes it possible for Member States to use the CSDP framework to implement – if deemed necessary – a military mission in the European region, "if a Member State is the object of a terrorist attack or the victim of a natural or man-made disaster". In such a case, the Union "shall mobilise all the instruments at its disposal, including the military resources made available by the Member States, to: ... assist a Member State in its territory" (TFEU 2010: Article 222.3). However, the inclusion of 'lighter' forms of CSDP interventions (advising and assistance oriented tasks) demonstrates that the EU does not seek to forsake its past frequent task of shouldering a 'reinforcing' or complementary military role to other organisations in the field, such as it did to the UN in the DRC in 2006 (Johansson *et al.* 2010).

Furthermore, the Lisbon Treaty iterates the Union's commitment to developing a progressive common defence policy, which "will lead to a common defence, when the European Council, acting unanimously, so decides" (TEU 2010: Article 42.2). Building on this vision, the Treaty stipulates a Mutual Assistance Clause (also referred to as a *mutual defence clause*), which states that "if a Member State is the victim of armed aggression on its territory, the other Member States shall have towards it an obligation of aid and assistance by all the means in their power" (ibid: Article 42.7). Member States, however, choose the means by which they help a fellow member, which is a consequence of the Union's continuing commitment not to "prejudice the specific character of the security and defence policy of certain Member States" (TEU 2010: Article 42.7). Thus, there are still no fixed operative resources at the EU's disposal, which may be tapped in case of an attack on a fellow Member State.

Institutions, Joint Resources and Collective Decision-Making

The Lisbon Treaty does not radically alter the EU's institutional framework and decision-making surrounding the process of implementing a military mission. The decision to deploy a EU military operation still requires a unanimous vote in the Council following a formal mission request by either a Member State or the High Representative (with the exception of Denmark that due to a defence opt-out does not participate in any decision-making with defence implications, TEU 2010: Article 42.4). Thus, Member States preserve the right to veto a collective decision to deploy a military operation, or refrain from participating in a Council vote. When abstaining in a vote, a Member State is not obliged "to apply the decision, but shall accept that the decision commits the Union" (TEU 2010: Article 31). If a vote fails to generate support amongst at least two thirds of all Member States, the proposed decision is not adopted. However, in order to promote a 'common' approach to foreign and security policy, a new leadership post has been established: High Representative of the Union for Foreign Affairs and Security Policy, currently held by Catherine Ashton. The High Representative is tasked with steering EU external action "on the basis of strategic guidelines laid down by the European Council and ensure that the Union's action is consistent" (TEU 2010: Article 16.6). To be able to efficiently coordinate the Council of Ministers, European Commission, and the Foreign Affairs Council, Ashton chairs the Foreign Affairs Council and is Vice-President of the Commission (ibid). The High Representative is assisted by the European External Action Service, EEAS, which is comprised of diplomats from Member States, previous staff with the European Commission and the Council of Ministers (in equal proportion).

Although the EU does not have any permanent military resources, or a European army by any means, the Lisbon Treaty does demonstrate that the Union intends to proceed with the development of joint defence capabilities. Furthermore, it solidifies the Union's intention to put institutional functions into place that allow for joint military resources to become both available and deployable, and thus, the Union works towards establishing more usable and flexible Battlegroups through an increased "pooling and sharing of resources" (Biscop and Coelmont 2010; Council of the European Union 2009). The establishment of the European Defence Agency, EDA, in 2004 was an important initial step forward in this respect as it is tasked with overseeing the bridging of the military "capabilities-expectations gap" in the EU security and defence organisation (Blockmans and Wessel 2009: 272). The Lisbon Treaty introduces two institutional amendments that aim to enhance collaboration between Member States on defence arrangements: permanent structured cooperation between these Member States "whose military capabilities fulfil higher criteria" (TEU 2010: Article 42.6) and 'coalition of the willing' operations carried out by willing and able Member States within the framework of CSDP (ibid: Article 44). The focus on enhanced cooperation between 'able' states intends to contribute to more efficient force-generating processes. In this vein, the EU can delegate to a group of Member States the task of implementing an operation within the framework of the CSDP. In such a case, the participating Member States "agree among themselves on the management of the task" in association with the High Representative (ibid: Article 44.1). A newly established forum for cooperation in this respect is the Defence and Security Cooperation Treaty launched by France and Great Britain in November 2010. This act affirmed the two states' intention to work more closely within the area of defence either "through mutual dependence on each other's industrial base and armed forces, or through pooling and sharing capability" (Jones 2011: 5).

The institutional changes introduced with the ratification of the Lisbon Treaty, which have an impact on the organisation's ability to deploy military operations, are indeed important steps towards making European military co-operation more efficient and deployable. However, the treaty and its new institutional measures for enhancing cooperation in the field of security and defence also raise several concerns. One such concern relates to the status of inclusiveness of European defence policies. Great Britain and France together currently finance around half of all European defence spending, figures that are expected to increase further over the next couple of years (ibid: 11). The use of permanent structured cooperation is perceived by some as potentially reinforcing the concentrated influence (power) of militarily strong Member States within the sphere of CSDP at the cost of excluding the majority of Member States. If permanent structured cooperation ends up strengthening the dominance of a few Member States in the realisation of CSDP and, in particular, the implementation of military missions, this will have a negative impact on both the internal understanding of CSDP as built on representativeness and coherency in the promotion of wider European interests, as well as it will challenge the international image of the CSDP as a pan-European endeavour (Jones 2011).

Lingering Challenges to EU Military Operations: the 'Non-Case' of Libya

When juxtaposing the EU's new strategic and operational framework for collective military action with its actual experiences of military operations, there are indeed several lessons to be learned in order to increase the fruitfulness of future military operations and provide guidance to upcoming developments within the overall security and defence framework. In the following section, I illustrate some of the remaining pitfalls of the EU's military machinery with the recent 'non-case' of an EU military operation: the Union's response to the Gaddafi regime's brutal suppression of political protests by the Libyan people in 2011.

When faced with the unfolding crisis in Libya, the EU took several collective measures to curb the deteriorating situation. After the UN Security Council had imposed an arms embargo and mandated targeted sanction against the country (UN SC Resolution 1970 2011), the EU not only implemented these sanctions but also imposed additional sanctions (Council of the European Union 2011d). When the UN later authorised the use of all necessary means for the purpose of protecting Libyan civilians (UN SC Resolution 1973 2011),[4] the

---

4   Including a no-fly zone, but excluding the deployment of an occupation force.

EU activated two of its key crisis management tools under CFSP: the European civil protection mechanism and humanitarian assistance. Being the single largest contributor to humanitarian assistance in the country, the EU aimed to strengthen civil protection in Libya (Koenig 2011) and implemented the civil protection mechanism to facilitate the evacuation of EU citizens from troubled areas (European Commission 2012). In March 2011, a US-led coalition of UN member states launched *Operation Odyssey Dawn* in an effort to enforce the UN SC Resolutions on Libya (US Department of Defense 2011). At the same time, the Council of the European Union declared its intention to deploy a military operation (*EUFOR Libya*) for the purpose of providing humanitarian assistance in the region *if requested* to do so by the UN Office for the Coordination of Humanitarian Affairs (OCHA) (Council of the European Union 2011b: Article 1). In case of such a 'humanitarian' military operation, the EU had already appointed a mission commander (Italy), provided operational headquarters (Rome, Italy), and decided on the duration of the mission (a maximum of four months deployment) (ibid: Article 2, 3, 13, Council of the European Union 2011c: Article 4). However, the EU was never called upon to deploy *EUFOR Libya*. Instead, NATO took the lead of all international military efforts in Libya with *Operation Unified Protector* (OUP). The mission was deployed to Libya on March 31, where it was successfully concluded seven months later after the Libyan opposition had overthrown remnants of the Gaddafi regime following the death of Colonel Gaddafi (NATO 2012).

Despite the fact that the EU implemented numerous collective efforts in Libya under the CFSP, it was criticised for having acted "too slow, too weak, too divided, and essentially incoherent" (Koenig 2011, 3), and for not having taken the lead of a military intervention that was carried out in its own backyard. To some, the EU's lack of resolve represents the abrupt ending to the *illusion* that was the CSDP (Menon 2011). Considering the leading role shouldered by European countries in Libya under the NATO flag, why did the EU not instead intervene with its own CSDP operation in Libya? The EU had access to all necessary institutional capabilities, such as rapid reaction forces, which are well suited for launching a military operation of this kind at short notice, and had even prepared and adopted a decision mandating a military operation. Furthermore, only a few months prior to the Libyan uprising, the EU had reaffirmed its regional ties with North Africa in the *Tripoli Declaration*[5], which reads: "we attach utmost importance to all efforts of conflict prevention, reconciliation, justice and post conflict reconstruction and development for the sake of people undergoing conflict. [...] Peace and security remain a cornerstone of our cooperation" (2010, 2).

---

5   The Declaration was issued at the Africa EU Summit, which was ironically held in the city of Tripoli.

Although the reasons behind non-intervention may be numerous, the EU's response to the Libyan crisis illustrates at least two factors, which appear to represent generic pitfalls to EU military missions, namely the *dynamics of political incoherence* and the *lack of military capabilities*. During the Libyan crisis an internal split unfolded between the EU's three 'military' powers when France and Great Britain –the two main advocates of European defence cooperation– lobbied for a military intervention in Libya, whilst Germany demonstrated its reluctance to support such a mission by abstaining from voting in the UN SC Council on Resolution 1973. In so doing, Germany deviated from the EU's collective stance on the issue, namely to (if requested) deploy *EUFOR Libya*. This led the Franco-British coalition to bypass EU military structures and instead make a formal request within the NATO alliance. Germany's conflicting standpoint thus demonstrates that in spite of the joint strategy and institutional capabilities comprised in the Lisbon Treaty, a single Member State still holds the power to significantly alter the course of EU collective military action.

On top of the political incoherence on display amongst EU Member States in the case of Libya, experiences from previous military operations have made it apparent that EU military capabilities lack credibility in comparison to other military actors in the field of international crisis and conflict management. Being a fairly new military actor, and having deployed quite small missions with limited scope and few troops, the EU has struggled with establishing credibility as a deterrent military presence. Although the Union is becoming increasingly more visible in crisis and conflict management, and by now has partnered with many different organisations and actors in the field, there appears to linger a hesitance regarding the military capabilities of the EU compared to other actors in the field, primarily the US and NATO. A key reason for this is that previous military operations have made it clear that force-generating processes may turn into lengthy procedures that, in the end, will fall short without the substantial involvement and support by France or Great Britain. In Libya, European states did implement the majority of air strikes and enforcements of the arms embargo, but again relied heavily on military contributions by France and Great Britain. Furthermore, it is doubtful that the mission would have been a success without US assistance. The lack of European 'essential military capabilities' during *Operation Unified Protector* (National Public Radio 2012) was perhaps not surprising considering the strained economy of many EU Member States (topped off with the current crisis situation in Greece), and costly European military contributions in support of NATO activities in Afghanistan (Biscop 2008; Biscop and Coelmont 2010; Johansson *et al.* 2010; Gowan 2011).

The lack of political coherence and deployable military capabilities in the case of Libya are interrelated and illustrate a key current tension within the

EU, namely that between the EU's traditional role as a soft power, in which it mainly provides support within areas of humanitarian assistance and economic/political development, and its recent steps towards acquiring the capabilities of a hard power that, if necessary, is both willing and able to use military force. Although Libya was a disappointing 'test case' for the still young CSDP structures, it does not mean that the CSDP is doomed to fail if once again faced with a similar challenge (such as the current crisis in Syria). However, it is clear that the mere existence of the Lisbon Treaty and new institutional structures *per se* are not sufficient means to maintain the persona of a credible international military actor. Despite the impressive transformation of the EU that has taken place over the last decade, the Union is still left with tackling a lingering key challenge: to generate the willingness of each and every EU Member State to collectively *contribute* to the realisation of the Union's joint ambitions.

References

Assembly of WEU (2008): Milestones along the Road to European Defence (1984-2008). Available at http://www.assembly-weu.org/documents/MilestonesEN_Dec2008.pdf (2011-09-08).

Ayissi, Anatole N. (1999): Powershift and Strategic Adjustment in French Military Engagement in Central Africa. African Journal of Political Science 4(2), pp. 16-45.

Biscop, Sven (2008). Permanent Structured Cooperation and the Future of ESDP. Egmont Paper 20. Brussels: The Royal Institute for International Relations. Available at http://www.egmontinstitute.be/paperegm/ep20.pdf (2011-09-19).

Biscop, Sven and Coelmont, Jo (2010): Permanent Structured Cooperation: In Defence of the Obvious. ISS Opinion. European Union Institute for Security Studies. Available at http://www.iss.europa.eu/uploads/media/Permanent_structured_cooperation.pdf (2011-09-13).

Blockmans, Steven/Wessel, Ramses A. (2009): The European Union and Crisis Management: Will the Lisbon Treaty Make the EU More Effective?, Journal of Conflict & Security Law 14(2), pp. 265-30.

Cologne European Council (1999): Annex III: European Council Declaration on Strengthening the Common European Policy on Security and Defence, Cologne European Council Declaration on the Common Policy on Security and Defence 3 and 4 June 1999. Available at http://www.esdp-course.ethz.ch/content/ref/199906Cologne_ Excerpt.htm (2011-09-29).

Council of the European Union (2003a): The European Security Strategy ESS: A Secure Europe in a Better World. Available at http://www.consilium.europa.eu/uedocs/cms Upload/ 78367.pdf (2011-09-02).

Council of the European Union (2003b): Council Decision relating to the launch of the EU Military Operation in the former Yugoslav Republic of Macedonia. Brussels. Available at http://www.consilium.europa.eu/uedocs/cmsUpload/Council%20Decision%20 launch%20of%20the%20EU%20Military%20Operation.pdf (2011-09-15).

Council of the European Union (2003c): Council Joint Action 2003/423/CFSP of 5 June 2003 on the European Union Military Operation in the Democratic Republic of Congo.

Available at http://www.consilium.europa.eu/uedocs/cmsUpload/Joint%20action% 205.6.03.pdf (2011-08-09).

Council of the European Union (2004): Council Joint Action 2004/570/CFSP of 12 July 2004 on the European Union Military Operation in Bosnia and Herzegovina. Available at http://eur-lex.europa.eu/LexUriServ/LexUriServ.do?uri=OJ:L:2004:252:0010:0014: EN:PDF (2011-09-09).

Council of the European Union (2006): Council Joint Action 2006/319/CFSP of 27 April 2006 on the European Union Military Operation in Support of the United Nations Organisation Mission in the Democratic Republic of the Congo (MONUC) during the Election Process. Available at http://eur-lex.europa.eu/LexUriServ/LexUriServ.do?uri =OJ:L:2006:116:0098:0101:EN:PDF (2011-09-10).

Council of the European Union (2007): Council Joint Action 2007/677/CFSP of 15 October 2007 on the European Union Military Operation in the Republic of Chad and in the Central African Republic. Available at http://eur-lex.europa.eu/LexUriServ/site/en/oj/ 2007/l_279/l_27920071023en00210024.pdf (2011-09-09).

Council of the European Union (2009): Ministerial Declaration: ESDP Ten Years – Challenges and Opportunities. Available at http://www.consilium.europa.eu/uedocs/cms_ Data/docs/pressdata/en/gena/111253.pdf (2011-09-25).

Council of the European Union (2011a): Council Decision 2011/483/CFSP of 28 July 2011 Amending and Extending Decision 2010/96/CFSP on a European Union Military Mission to Contribute to the Training of Somali Security Forces (EUTM Somalia). Available at http://eur-lex.europa.eu/LexUriServ/LexUriServ.do?uri=OJ:L:2011:198: 0037:0038:EN:PDF (2011-09-12).

Council of the European Union (2011b): Council Decision 2011/210/CFSP of 1 April 2011 Decides on a European Union Military Operation in Support of Humanitarian Assistance Operations in Response to the Crisis Situation in Libya. Available at http://eur-lex.europa.eu/LexUriServ/LexUriServ.do?uri=OJ:L:2011:089:0017:0020:en   :PDF (2011-10-01).

Council of the European Union (2011c): Council Conclusions on Libya. Available at http://www.consilium.europa.eu/uedocs/cms_Data/docs/pressdata/EN/foraff/122923. pdf (2011-10-01).

Council of the European Union (2011d): Council Decision 2011/178/CFSP of 23 March 2011 Amending Decision 2011/137/CFSP Concerning Restrictive Measures in View of the Situation in Libya. Available at http://eur-lex.europa.eu/LexUriServ /LexUriServ. do?uri=OJ:L:2011:078:0024:0036:EN: PDF (2012-05-12).

EEAS (European External Action Service) (2011a): Military Capabilities. Available at http:// www.consilium.europa.eu/showPage.aspx?id=1349&lang=en (2011-09-03).

EEAS (2011b): EU Military Operation in Bosnia and Herzegovina. Available at http://www. consilium.europa.eu/uedocs/cms_data/docs/missionPress/files/110106%20Factsheet% 20EUFOR%20Althea%20-%20version%2023_EN.pdf (2011-09-30).

EEAS (2011c): EUTM Somalia: European Union Military Mission to Contribute to the Training of Somali Security Forces. Available at http://www.consilium.europa.eu/eeas/security-defence/eu-operations/eu-somalia-training-mission.aspx?lang=en (2011-09-10).

EEAS (2011d): Overview of the Missions and Operations of the European Union February 2011. Available at http://www.consilium.europa.eu/eeas/security-defence/eu-operations. aspx?lang=en (2011-09-25).

EEAS (2011e): About the EU at the UN. Available at http://europa-eu-un.org/articles/en/ article_9389_en.htm (2011-09-28). Directorate-General for External Policies of the Union

(2006): The European Security and Defence Policy: from the Helsinki Headline Goal to the EU Battlegroups. Available at http://www.europarl.europa.eu/meetdocs/2009_2014/ documents/sede/dv/sede030909noteesdp_/sede030909noteesdp_en.pdf (2011-09-20).

Engberg, Katarina (2011): The EU's Collective Use of Force: Exploring the Factors behind its First Military Operations. PhD diss., Uppsala University.

EU Council Secretariat (2009): EU Battlegroups. Available at http://www.consilium. europa.eu/uedocs/cmsUpload/090720-Factsheet-Battlegroups_EN.pdf (2011-09-20).

EUNAFOR Somalia (2011): Mission. Available at http://www.eunavfor.eu/about-us/mission/ (2011-09-10).

European Commission (2012): Humanitarian Aid and Civil Protection: Libyan Crisis. Available at http://ec.europa.eu/echo/files/aid/countries/factsheets/libya_en.pdf (2012-05-30).

Franco–British St. Malo Declaration (1998): Available at http://www.ena.lu/francobritish_ st_malo_declaration_december_1998-020008195.html (2011-09-02).

Gowan, Richard (2011): Does Libya Really Need EU Peacekeepers? European Council on Foreign Relations. Available at http://ecfr.eu/content/entry/commentary_gowan_eu_ peacekeepers_for_libya (2011-10-01).

Gross, Eva (2009): EU Military Operation in the Former Yugoslav Republic of Macedonia. In: Grevi, Giovanni/Helly, Damien/Keohane, Daniel, (eds.) (2009): European Security and Defence Policy: The First Ten Years (1999-2009), Institute for Security Studies.

Hauser, Gunther (2006): The ESDP: The European Security Pillar. In: Hauser, Gunther/ Kernic, Franz, (eds.): European Security in Transition. Burlington, US: Ashgate Publishing Limited.

Headline Goal 2010 (2004): Available at http://consilium.europa.eu/uedocs/cmsUpload/ 2010%20Headline%20Goal.pdf (2011-09-09).

Hendrickson, Ryan C./Strand, Jonathan R./Raney, Kyle L. (2008): Operation ARTEMIS and Javier Solana: EU Prospects for a Stronger Common Foreign and Security Policy. Available at http://www.journal.dnd.ca/vo8/no1/hendrick-eng.asp (2011-10-02).

Helsinki European Council (1999): Annex IV of the Presidency Conclusions 10 and 11 December 1999. Available at http://www.consilium.europa.eu/uedocs/cmsUpload/ Helsinki%20European%20Council%20%20Annex%20IV%20of%20the%20 Presidency%20Conclusions.pdf (2011-09-28).

Helly, Damien (2009a): The Military Operation in DR Congo (Artemis). In: Grevi, Giovanni/Helly, Damien/Keohane, Daniel (eds.): European Security and Defence Policy: The First Ten Years (1999-2009), Institute for Security Studies.

Helly, Damien (2009b): The EU Military Operation in the Republic of Chad and in the Central African Republic (Operation EUFOR Tchad/RCA). Grevi, Giovanni/Helly, Damien/Keohane, Daniel (eds.): European Security and Defence Policy: The First Ten Years (1999-2009), Institute for Security Studies.

Helly, Damien (2009c): The EU Military Operation Atalanta. Grevi, Giovanni/Helly, Damien/Keohane, Daniel (eds.): European Security and Defence Policy: The First Ten Years (1999-2009), Institute for Security Studies.

Johansson, Emma/Kreutz, Joakim/Wallensteen, Peter/Altpeter, Christian/Lindberg, Sara/ Lindgren, Mathilda/Padskocimait, Ausra (eds.) (2010): A New Start for EU Peacemaking? Past Record and Future Potential. UCDP Paper no. 7. Available at http://www. pcr.uu.se/digitalAssets/22/22054_UCDP_paper_7.pdf (2011-09-25).

Jones, Ben (2011): Franco-British Military Cooperation: A New Engine for European Defence? Occasional Paper 88. February 2011. Available at http://www.iss.europa.eu/

uploads/media/op88--Franco-British_military_cooperation--a_new_engine_for_ European_defence.pdf (2011-09-30).

Keohane, Daniel (2009a): ESDP and NATO. Grevi, Giovanni/Helly, Damien/Keohane, Daniel (eds.): European Security and Defence Policy: The First Ten Years (1999-2009), Institute for Security Studies.

Keohane, Daniel (2009b): The European Union Military Operations in Bosnia and Herzegovina (Althea). In: Grevi, Giovanni/Helly, Damien/Keohane, Daniel (eds.): European Security and Defence Policy: The First Ten Years (1999-2009), Institute for Security Studies.

Koenig, Nicole (2011): The EU and the Libyan Crisis: In Quest of Coherence? Istituto Affari Internazionali (IAI) working papers 11, 19 (July, 2011). Available at http://www.iai.it/pdf/DocIAI/iaiwp1119.pdf (2012-05-30).

Major, Claudia (2009): The Military Operation EUFOR RD Congo. In: Grevi, Giovanni/Helly, Damien/Keohane, Daniel (eds.): European Security and Defence Policy: The First Ten Years (1999-2009), Institute for Security Studies.

McGivern, Laurence (2010): The European Union as an International Actor: Has Operation Atalanta Changed Global Perceptions of the EU as a Military Force?. Available at http://www.atlantic-community.org/app/webroot/files/articlepdf/McGivern-Operation %20Atalanta.pdf (2011-09-20).

Menon, Anand (2011): European Defence Policy from Lisbon to Libya. Survival: Global Politics and Strategy 53, 3, pp. 75-90.

Missiroli, Antonio (2003): The European Union: Just a Regional Peacekeeper?. European Foreign Affairs Review 8: pp. 493–503.

National Public Radio (NPR) (12 September 2012): NATO's Intervention In Libya: A New Model? Available at http://www.npr.org/2011/09/12/140292920/natos-intervention-in-libya-a-new-model (2012-05-12).

NATO (2012): NATO and Libya. Available at http://www.nato.int/cps/en/natolive/ topics_71652.htm (2012-05-28).

Oswald, Franz (2006): Europe and the US: the Emerging Security Partnership. Westport: Praeger Security International Publishers.

Ploch, Lauren/Blanchard, Christopher M./O'Rourke, Ronald/Mason, R. Chuck/King, Rawle O. (2009): Piracy off the Horn of Africa. CRS Report for Congress. Available at http://www.nps.edu/research/mdsr/Docs/R40528.pdf (2011-09-29).

Solana, Javier (2003a): Remarks by Javier Solana at the Ceremony Marking the End of the EU-led Operation Concordia. Available at http://www.consilium.europa.eu/uedocs/ cmsUpload/Solana%20-%20ceremonies%20for%20termination%20of%20Operation %20Concordia%20and%20launch%20of%20Mission%20Proxima%2015.12.2003.pdf (2011-09-20).

Solana, Javier (2003b): Remarques de Javier SOLANA, Haut Représentant de l'UE pour la PESC, à l'Occasion de la Fin de l'Opération Artémis à Bunia (République Démocratique du Congo). Available at http://www.consilium.europa.eu/uedocs/cmsUpload/ Remarques%20SOLANA%20fin.pdf (2011-09-01).

TEU (Consolidated Version of the Treaty on The European Union) (2010): Available at http://eurlex.europa.eu/LexUriServ/LexUriServ.do?uri=OJ:C:2010:083:0013:0046:EN :PDF (2011-09-11).

TFEU (Consolidated Version of the Treaty on the Functioning of the European Union) (2010): Available at http://eur-lex.europa.eu/LexUriServ/LexUriServ.do?uri=OJ:C: 2010:083:0047:0200:en:PDF (2011-09-11).

Treaty of Nice (Amending the Treaty on European Union, the Treaties Establishing the European Communities and Certain Related Acts (2001/C 80/01) (2001): Available at http://eur-l ex.europa.eu/en/treaties/dat/12001C/pdf/12001C_EN.pdf (2011-09-05).

Treaty on European Union (1992): Available at http://eur-lex.europa.eu/en/treaties/dat/11992M/htm/11992M.html (2011-09-07).

Tripoli Declaration (3rd Africa EU Summit) (29/30 November 2010): Tripoli: Available at http://www.africa-eu-partnership.org/sites/default/files/doc_tripoli_declaration_en.pdf (2012-05-14).

UN Security Council (2011): S/RES/1671 2011. New York. Available at http://daccess-dds-ny.un.org/doc/UNDOC/GEN/N06/326/70/PDF/N0632670.pdf?OpenElement (2011-10-01).

UN Security Council (2011): S/RES/1970 2011. New York. Available at http://www.securitycouncilreport.org/atf/cf/%7B65BFCF9B-6D27-4E9C-8CD3-CF6E4FF96FF9%7D/Libya%20S%20RES%201970.pdf (2012-05-12).

UN Security Council (2011): S/RES/1973 2011. New York. Available at http://www.securitycouncilreport.org/atf/cf/%7B65BFCF9B-6D27-4E9C-8CD3-CF6E4FF96FF9%7D/Libya%20S%20RES%201973.pdf (2012-05-12).

U.S. Department of Defence (March 19, 2011): Coalition Launches Operation Odyssey Dawn. Available at http://www.defense.gov/news/newsarticle.aspx?id=63225 (2012-05-12).

WEU (Western European Union) (1992): Petersberg Declaration. Bonn. Available at http://www.weu.int/documents/920619peten.pdf (2011-10-01).

Part 2:
EU Foreign Relations: Organisations, Regions and Countries

The European Union at the United Nations
Partners in a Multilateral World?

Sven Bernhard Gareis

Based on a broad set of shared values and interests the European Union (EU) and the United Nations (UN) have established a close cooperation in many important fields of world politics. Both organisations put into the centre of their political efforts a peaceful and stable world order, the respect of human rights and the protection of the environment as well as the preservation of the natural living conditions in the world. The EU and UN agree in the assessment of global challenges and threats to international peace and security, reaching from wide-spread underdevelopment, environmental degradation and climate change over terrorism and proliferation of weapons of mass destruction to violent conflict and wars. Those problems can no longer be tackled by single states but require an enhanced and energetic international cooperation. In confronting those challenges both institutions prefer preventive and peaceful strategies, multilateral balance of interests as well as an increasing role of international law and legal regimes in the practice of international relations.

Beyond those values and maxims, however, interaction between the EU and UN is based on a number of common or complementary objectives and interests. The EU needs an effective global organisation to foster a stable international order conducive to its economic interests as well as to the further advancement of principles like democracy, rule of law, or human rights that inspired the EU's own creation and development (Art 21 (1) Treaty on European Union-Lisbon (TEU-L)). In turn, especially after the end of the East-West Antagonism 1989/90, the UN has become increasingly dependent on strong regional organisations supporting the organisation in fulfilling its main tasks for international peace and security, not just through solemn declarations but also through practical measures (see Griep 2008: 147f.).

However, despite a substantive amount of common views on the world and though their cooperation is close and advanced, the EU and UN remain to be two clearly distinct organisations with very different internal structures and procedures as well as differing perceptions of multilateralism and inter-agency cooperation. Both organisations cannot perform on the global stage as independent actors; they appear instead as multilateral institutions whose international conduct is fully under the control of their respective member states, their guidance and rules. In this system of 'intersecting multilateralisms' (Laatikainen/Smith 2006) specific challenges arise that often constrain the practical interaction between the EU and the UN.

This chapter examines the role of the EU at the UN by analyzing the opportunities and the limits of EU-UN cooperation in central fields like the maintenance of peace and international crisis management. Before doing so, however, it appears to be helpful to shed some light on the politico-legal fundaments of this specific cooperation as well as to have a closer look at the procedures of policy coordination amongst the EU members that strongly impact the Union's performance as a sometimes more and sometimes less unified actor in the global arena provided by the UN.

EU and UN: The Political and Legal Framework of Cooperation

In their institutional cooperation the EU (as well as its predecessors) and the UN can look back at a long history, which started as early as 1964, when the Commission of the European Economic Community (EEC) opened an information office at the seat of the UN in New York. In 1974 the General Assembly (Res. 3208 (XXIX) of 11 October 1974) granted to the then European Community (EC), as the first international organisation ever, the status of an observer at the General Assembly and the Economic and Social Council (ECOSOC), allowing the EC to establish a permanent diplomatic mission to the UN Headquarters. Even after the creation of the European Union in 1994, the observer status and the diplomatic representation stayed with the European Commission and remained focused on policy fields in the realm of the Treaty on European Community (Pillar 1 of the EU). The Lisbon Treaty that entered into force on December 1, 2009 gave a legal entity to the EU as a whole (Art. 47 TEU-L) thus yielding the observer status to the Union. The diplomatic representation at the UN was moved to the 'Delegation of the European Union to the United Nations' which belongs to the Union's newly created External Action Service (EAS) under the authority of the High Representative of the Union for Foreign Affairs and Security Policy. The EU is also accredited with delegations to UN secretariats and bodies in Geneva, Nairobi, Paris, Rome and Vienna. In return, the UN system is represented in Brussels by twenty-six specialized agencies, funds and programs. The director of the Brussels-based United Nations Development Programme (UNDP) office also serves as the UN Secretary General's special representative to the European institutions.

All 27 EU member states and all accession candidates are members of the United Nations, many of them belonged to the world organisation's fifty-one founding nations in 1945. Amongst the ten largest contributors to the UN's regular budget are five EU members (Germany, United Kingdom, France, Italy and Spain); the EU as a whole finances approximately 40 per cent of both the regular budget and the expenses for UN-led peace missions. The work of the various UN funds and programs (e.g. UNHCR, UNICEF, WFP etc.) largely depends on voluntary contributions by the UN members. In this vast field the European Commission and the Union's member states provide for roughly fifty per cent of the needed resources. (For more information see: www.europa-eu-un.org).

Indeed, there is hardly another international institution whose members give greater support to the norms and values of the UN Charter as well as to the principles and mechanisms of multilateral cooperation epitomized by the world organisation than the European Union (see Commission 2003). No major European text or position paper would miss a strong reference to the UN Charter and the UN Security Council's (SC) primary responsibility for peace and international security. In its European Security Strategy of 2003 the EU called for an 'international order based on effective multilateralism' and expressed its support for an eminent role of the United Nations in world politics: 'The fundamental framework for international relations is the United Nations Charter. Strengthening the United Nations, equipping it to fulfil its responsibilities and to act effectively must be an European priority' (European Institute for Security Studies 2003: 9).

The Lisbon Treaty also refers to the UN and its specific significance to the EU when it states, that the Union 'shall promote multilateral solutions to common problems, in particular in the framework of the United Nations' (Art. 21 TEU-L). The UN General Assembly in return passed a resolution that upgraded the Union's observer status by permitting EU representatives 'to present positions of the European Union and its Member States as agreed by them' (A/RES/65/276 of 3 May 2011). Though still lacking a right to vote the EU is thus represented in the General Assembly alongside its 27 member states; its increased scope of action comprising the oral articulation of political views, the circulation of papers, or the proposals for changes in draft documents distinguishes the EU from other observers like the Holy See, the International Committee of the Red Cross or the Palestinian Authority. Furthermore, the EU as the only non-state actor is member or participant in a number of international agreements, subsidiary organs and specialized agencies of the UN, such as the Food and Agricultural Organisation (FAO), the Commission on Sustainable Development (CSD), the Peacebuilding Commission or the conferences of parties to the UN Framework Convention on Climate Change (UNFCCC).

The EU forms a Regional Arrangement according to Chapter VIII of the Charter of the United Nations that carry special responsibility for the maintenance of peace and the pacific settlement of disputes (Art. 52 UN Charter).

Under Art 53 of the UN Charter regional arrangements can be utilized by the Security Council for collective enforcement action against perpetrators when appropriate. In the political practice, however, the UN and regional arrangements have been practicing cooperation in partnership rather than utilisation under the authority of the SC. This is especially true for the EU and its contributions in the framework of the maintenance of peace (see section 3).

EU Policy Coordination at the UN

As already mentioned, the EU's performance at the UN is in many fields that of a multinational actor whose role is directed by 27 governments – coordination and harmonisation of national views and approaches are therefore essential for a coherent articulation of European policies at the world organisation. Before the Lisbon Treaty became functional the Delegation of the European Commission was responsible for supranational 'Pillar 1-policies' like international commerce, food and agriculture or development cooperation, whilst the coordination of foreign and security issues (Pillar 2) was supported by a European Council Liaison Office. To 'ensure the consistency of the Union's external action', Article 18 (4) TEU-L determines that the High Representative is one of the Vice-Presidents of the Commission, being 'responsible within the Commission for responsibilities incumbent on it in external relations and for coordinating other aspects of the Union's external action.' In New York the Delegation of the European Union consequently absorbed both the European Commission Delegation and the Council Liaison Office; when exercising the responsibilities of the Commission, however, the High Representative and his envoys are bound by Commission procedures (Art. 18 (4) TEU-L).

All EU policies relevant to the UN outside those responsibilities of the Commission, however, are being coordinated within the framework of the Union's Common Foreign and Security Policy (CFSP) that was established in 1992 by the Maastricht Treaty and that received its actual shape – including the Common Security and Defence Policy (CSDP) created in 1999 – by the follow-up treaties of Amsterdam, Nice and Lisbon. Both CFSP and CSDP continue to be submitted to strictly intergovernmental procedures, being 'defined and implemented by the European Council and the Council acting unanimously' (Art. 4 (1) TEU-L). Any of the numerous statements made by the President of the Council, the High Representative or the Head of the EU Delegation at the General Assembly or the Security Council therefore also reflects the positions of the Union's member states – as the UK representative made clear in 2011, when he insisted that statements by EU representatives should be delivered on behalf of the EU and its member states, rather than on behalf of the EU alone (see Borger 2011).

In Brussels the general guidelines of the Union's UN policies are being mapped by the Working Party on UN affairs (CONUN) under the Council's Political and Security Committee (PSC) which forwards them to the Council of Ministers for approval. However, CONUN which holds monthly meetings is often considered to be too far away from the political realities in New York (see Rasch 2008: 131f.); the predominant part of concerting EU member states national policies therefore has to be done by the missions in situ.

In this regard Article 34 TEU-L plays a pivotal role: In its Paragraph 1 it obliges the EU member states to 'coordinate their action in international organisations and at international conferences' where they also 'shall uphold the Union's positions (...)'. It also stipulates that the High Representative is in charge of this coordination. Paragraph 2 determines that

> 'Member States represented in international organisations or international conferences where not all the Member States participate shall keep the other Member States and the High Representative informed of any matter of common interest. Member States which are also members of the United Nations Security Council will concert and keep the other Member States and the High Representative fully informed. Member States which are members of the Security Council will, in the execution of their functions, defend the positions and the interests of the Union, without prejudice to their responsibilities under the provisions of the United Nations Charter. When the Union has defined a position on a subject which is on the United Nations Security Council agenda, those Member States which sit on the Security Council shall request that the High Representative be invited to present the Union's position.'

A closer look to this article reveals three different levels of EU member states' obligations to coordinate their policies at the UN. First, Art. 34 (1) generally requires all member states to participate in the coordination process and to support common policies. In the General Assembly EU members continuously show a strong coherence of around ninety-five per cent of concurring votes (see in detail Luif 2003, Delcourt 2011). On invitation by and under the chair of the respective EU presidency, the Union's member states meet once a week on the level of the Heads of Missions (HoM) as well as on the level of the experts on special matters. The work of the General Assembly and its six Main Committees can be compared to a permanent conference whose compromises and consensus procedures are too often just intermediate steps or transitory solutions to keep the interaction between 193 member states ongoing. Thus, the active involvement in these perpetuated procedures requires daily meetings of diplomats and experts from all twenty-seven EU member states in New York totalling more than seven-hundred within the six months of a presidency; similar figures are reported from Geneva and Vienna.

Second, the members of the Security Council are exempted from this general obligation to coordinate with their fellow Europeans as far as their work in the SC is concerned. The EU regularly holds four to five seats in this most powerful UN body: France and the United Kingdom as Permanent Members (often referred to as P2) and two to three non-permanent members elected for a two-year term from the Western European and Others or rather the Eastern European regional group (in 2012 Germany and Portugal). Art 34 (2) solely demands from the SC members to concert and then to keep the other EU member 'fully informed'. To a certain extent this provision is adequate to the working procedures of the Security Council that often require fast and discrete (not to say intransparent) negotiations and decisions that can frequently be subject to lengthy harmonisation processes in the format of EU 27. Furthermore, permanent as well as non-permanent members are chosen or elected into the Security Council in their capacity as sovereign states rather than as representatives of a regional organisation – and Article 103 of the UN Charter determines that the obligations under the Charter prevail over those under any other international agreement thus constraining an external coordination or decision-making system to formulate requests to an SC member (see Winkelmann 2000: 415.f). At the same time those provisions are creating welcome pretexts for the SC members to show strict limits of how much information they are willing to share with their fellow Europeans (Rasch 2008: 84).

Third, though no longer mentioned expressively in the Lisbon Treaty, France and the United Kingdom form a special pair amongst the EU members in the Security Council. They belong to the exclusive club of the Permanent Five (P5) who regularly convene meetings of their own to discuss and – if possible – harmonize their views on salient issues of world politics. Both France and the United Kingdom are also obliged to 'defend the positions and the interests of the Union', but the formula 'without prejudice to their responsibilities under the provisions of the United Nations Charter' in connection with the aforementioned Art. 103 offer them a wide range for the interpretation of their duties towards CFSP harmonisation. Especially with regard to the hard issues dealt with in the Security Council, the obligations the Treaty on European Union imposes on EU member states to concert within the framework of CFSP or CSDP have to be considered as fairly moderate.

In essence, it is not surprising that concurring votes are mostly achieved on the 'soft issues' being handled and decided upon in the General Assembly. The likelihood of dissolution of European unity and an increase of split votes is growing as soon as vital national interests are at stake in the Security Council. In the Iraq crisis of 2002-3 not only the Security Council but also the EU and its member states were divided between the supporters and the opponents of a US-led military campaign against Saddam Hussein and his regime. More recently, when the UN Security Council convened its 6498th meeting on March 17, 2011 to adopt the landmark Resolution 1973 on the

use of force against Libya, the abstention of Germany again led to a split vote
of the four EU member states represented in the SC. While France, Portugal,
the United Kingdom and another seven Council members voted in favour of
the authorisation of the use of military force to protect the civilian population
in Libya from large-scale violence by Muammar al-Khadafy's militias, Germany stood alongside Brazil, China, Russia and India expressing its
scepticism over the appropriateness of forceful measures by an abstention.

The German vote in the Security Council, however, was the most prominent but by all means not the only indication that in the Libya case national
interests prevailed over strategies and actions harmonized on the European
level. The French and British lobbying for military action against Khadafy as
well as the early French recognition of the newly formed National Transitional Council (NTC) as the legitimate government of Libya on March 10,
2011 also followed national agendas without too much consideration of the
mechanisms of EU's Common Foreign and Security Policy. As before in the
split over Iraq, the Libya case again remorselessly discloses the weaknesses
of EU foreign policy making on the UN stage and raises serious questions
not only about the coherence of EU's external actions but also about the Union's aptitude to play at all the role of a real global actor.

The EU as an Actor at the UN

The EU activities at the UN cover a wide range of policy fields – reaching
from its traditional focus on development cooperation over protection of the
environment and measures against climate change to efforts on the enhancement of human rights. In the following section, however, the EU's role in the
framework of UN peace maintenance is considered in more depth. In this
relatively new area the Union's opportunities and constraints in effectively
performing as a collective actor can exemplarily be examined.

International crisis management is one area in which cooperation between
the EU and UN has developed dynamically over the last two decades. The
beginnings of this relationship date back to 1992, when the Council of Ministers of the Western European Union (WEU) adopted the 'Petersberg
Declaration' by which they declared their preparedness to support the UN in
the field of international peace maintenance in a broad range of military tasks
including combat missions (see Western European Union 1992). However, it
took the EU as a traditional economic power another eleven years to integrate those new and unfamiliar tasks into its treaties and to establish in the
frameworks of CFSP and CSDP, the structures and bodies necessary for the
conduct of peace missions under the umbrella of the UN. Following the first
deployment of an EU military force to Macedonia in 2003 the Union's en-

gagement in military and civilian support of international peace missions increased considerably with regard both to quantity and quality.

This was made necessary by a growing number of requests to the UN to respond to more and more complex scenarios in global crisis management since the early 1990s. As the result of a persistent surge in peacekeeping operations in March 2012 around 121 000 peacekeepers – soldiers, police and civilian experts – were deployed in 16 UN-led peace missions world-wide consuming a budget of US dollars 7.84 trillion. Other than in the classical period of blue-helmet peacekeeping those new missions are tasked with peacebuilding efforts in post-conflict scenarios. They are complex and multi-facetted by nature, requiring – besides the creation of a secure environment – the build-up of state institutions, the establishment of a rule of law as well as the creation of administrative and economic structures, schools, media or any other kind of infrastructure. Facing those challenges the EU with its military and civilian CSDP capabilities (see Gareis et al. 2008: 91f.) must appear to the UN as an attractive partner.

However, from the side of the EU, any direct support of UN-led missions falls under the responsibility of single member states that have to negotiate their contributions bilaterally with the UN Department of Peacekeeping Operations (DPKO). But EU member states are more than reluctant to provide for the UN substantive contributions: With France (ranking 18) there is only one EU member state amongst the top twenty of 118 states contributing to UN peace operations.

EU member states prefer missions that are mandated by the Security Council but conducted solely under the supervision of European institutions. Also, any other EU support to UN missions has to remain under the full control and strategic guidance by the (Political and Security Committee (PSC) – as prescribed by Article 38 TEU-L. Any kind of subordination of EU forces under the command and control of the United Nations is being excluded hereby.

This provision is also reflected in the basic documents on EU-UN cooperation in the area of peacekeeping. In September 2003 then UN Secretary General, Kofi Annan and Italian Prime Minister, Silvio Berlusconi in his capacity as President of the European Council, signed a first 'Joint Declaration on UN-EU Co-operation in Crisis Management' establishing a common steering committee to examine ways and means to enhance mutual coordination and compatibility in the areas of mission planning, training of staff and personnel, communication between the two organisations including the establishment of liaison elements, and the development of best practices from shared lessons-learned (see Council of the European Union 2003: on the implementation of this declaration see Thardy 2005). A second Joint Statement signed in June 2007 under the German EU presidency aimed at fostering the mechanisms of inter-organisational cooperation through enhanced dialogue on the level of EU-Troika and the UN Secretary General, regular exchange of views of experts both from EU and UN Secretariats or coordination mechanisms in theatres where both organisations are engaged (Council of the European Union 2007), without however making even slightest changes on the principle of exclusive PSC control over EU forces deployed.

On the basis of those declarations the UN and EU developed three models of cooperation in international crisis management:

- In stand-alone missions like 'Concordia' in Macedonia (2003), EUFOR Althea in Bosnia-Herzegovina (since 2004) or the anti-piracy operation ATALANTA off-shore Somalia (since 2008) the EU takes a mandate from the UN to conduct an autonomous operation based on a Security Council resolution.
- The 'bridging model' is a form of support of UN missions in which the EU provides for a limited time capacities the UN is not yet able to generate. In the framework of the UN Mission in Congo (MONUC) with its ARTEMIS operation in 2003, the EU thus filled a gap between the withdrawal of Uruguayan blue helmets and the deployment of the UN-led Ituri Brigade in Bunia/DR Congo. The Union's largest military operation so far, the EUFOR Chad/Central African Republic, also worked according to the bridging model by maintaining stability in the region of deployment during the build-up of the UN's MINURCAT mission in 2008/09.
- The stand-by (or support) model implies the availability of a strong force that can be called for in case of a perilous deterioration of the security situation of the supported UN mission. The most prominent example for this model is the EUFOR DR Congo's support to MONUC during the presidential election process in the DR Congo in 2006 (on the most important EU missions in the UN framework see table 1).

Though the EU forces interact closely with the UN mission both in the bridging and the stand-by model, a direct access of UN authorities to the EU forces is prohibited; the EU deployment forms a separate mission with its own mandate and rules of procedure.

The fact that EU missions are conducted under the strict control of the PSC does by no means guarantee the participation of all EU member states – on the contrary. EU missions are Joint Actions under the provisions of CFSP, which require a unanimous vote in the Council of the European Union. The contribution of national forces or other assets, however, lies with every single EU member. In political practice, EU missions are staffed and financed by a smaller number of countries, whilst the majority opts out of deployments or confines its contribution e.g. to a small numbers of officers serving in the Operational Headquarters (OHQ) of such a mission. Regularly, the mission mandate is a compromise on the smallest common denominator between sometimes conflicting interests of the contributing member states. These circumstances often make EU missions more symbolic interventions with a very limited scope of action and fixed exit dates without reference to the situation in the theatre (see Gareis 2009). The biggest EU missions in support of the UN, the EUFOR DR Congo (2006) and the EUFOR Chad/CAR (2008-9), were limited in their duration to six and twelve months respectively. The Chad/CAR mission that reached its full operational capability only in its last four months was terminated before the build-up UN's MINURCAT mission was completed. To avoid a dangerous vacuum, countries like Austria, France or Ireland left their national contingents under UN command on a bilateral basis.

Table 1: Important EU missions within the UN framework

Name	Country/Region	Mandate	Start	End	Type	Category
EUPM/BiH	Bosnia and Herzegovina	S/RES/1396 (2002)	1 Jan 2003	ongoing	Police	Stand-alone
CONCORDIA	Former Yugoslav Republic of Macedonia	S/RES/1371 (2003)	31 Mar 2003	15 Dec 2003	Military	Stand-alone
ARTEMIS	Democratic Republic of Congo	S/RES/1484 (2003)	16 Jun 2003	1 Sept 2003	Military	Bridging
EUFOR ALTHEA	Bosnia and Herzegovina	S/RES/1575 (2004)	2 Dec 2004	Ongoing	Military	Stand-alone
EUFOR RD Congo	Democratic Republic of Congo	S/RES/1671 (2006)	30 Jul 2006	30 Nov 2006	Military	Stand-by
EUFOR Chad/CAR	Chad/Central African Republic	S/RES/1778 (2007)	28 Jan 2008	15 Mar 2009	Military	Bridging
EUNAVFOR (ATALANTA)	Somali Coastal Waters and Indian Ocean	S/RES/1814 (2008)	8 Dec 2008	Onging	Military	Stand-alone
EULEX Kosovo	Kosovo	S/RES/1244 (1999)	9 Dec 2008	Ongoing	Rule of Law	Stand-alone
EUTM Somalia	Somalia	S/RES/1872 (2009)	7 Apr 2010	Ongoing	Military	Stand-alone

Source: Author's own compilation

This kind of cooperation continuously creates dilemmas for the UN: On the one hand mandated stand-alone missions and widely autonomous bridging or stand-by deployments make available valuable and expensive capacities and assets needed in complex peace missions. Furthermore, EU member states cover all costs related to those missions thus freeing the UN from enormous financial burdens. On the other hand, with the industrialized countries reserving their high-value assets for mandated missions conducted in their particular national or regional interests a two-tier system of international maintenance of peace has come into being: Here the high-tech deployments of EU (and NATO) and there the often ill-equipped and overcharged UN operations which become increasingly 'third world forces for third world conflicts' prone to high numbers of casualties and eventual failure (Gareis/Varwick 2007).

A Permanent Seat for the EU on the UN Security Council?

Besides the European Union's policies at the UN, the question of a European Permanent Seat on the Security Council is an issue that keeps coming up on the political and academic agendas. It therefore needs to be discussed here as well.

Here is not the space for an in-depth consideration of the different approaches to UN Security Council reform. So it should be mentioned only that the discussion on the reform of the UN Security Council, its size, composition and working procedures has been ongoing since 1992. A vast majority of UN member states agrees on the need for reform without, however, having been able to pursue a common reform approach so far. In the preparation of the 2005 World Summit a high-level panel on UN reform presented two different models for reform – one with new permanent seats (Model A) and one with an increased number of non-permanent members (Model B; on SC reform see detailed Gareis 2012: 253f.). In this context special emphasis is laid on the question whether a Permanent Seat on the Security Council for the EU is a realistic option that could help to mitigate the difficulties resulting from the different status of the Union's permanent and non-permanent members of the SC and the great majority of the other EU member states.

Indeed, the idea of a common European seat on the Security Council seems fascinating: the Union speaking with one voice and being represented by a single EU ambassador to the United Nations. But is it achievable and – even more importantly – is this a desirable approach?

With regard to legal and political realism the answer appears to be simple: Articles 3 and 4 of the UN Charter declare that only states are eligible for membership in the organisation. A union of states like the EU, even a confederation would first have to shape its internal constitution in a way that would correspond to the postulate of statehood the UN is asking from its members. But even after the Lisbon Treaty the EU is still far from being prepared to fulfil this requirement. The opposite way of enabling the membership of unions of states does not seem very promising either. Any change of the UN Charter is a difficult endeavour that would drag on such a reform for decades. Any amendment to the Charter requires not only a two-thirds majority of member states in the General Assembly but also the ratification of that new Charter by the same majority – including all five permanent members of the SC (Art. 108 and 109 UN Charter). It is more than questionable that France and the United Kingdom would be willing to support such a change that they consider as being to the detriment of their national interest and prestige.

But even in the unlikely situation that France and the United Kingdom were prepared to support a European Permanent Seat – would such a step make sense? For the time being, the EU is represented in the Security Council by its two permanent and by up to three non-permanent members. At best, the EU has a third of the votes in the SC, including two (potential) veto powers. Why should the Union give up that strong position by reducing its voice from four or five to one? Such a loss of influence cannot lie in the EU's interest since its members have so many national channels to impact decision-making in their partner countries (Winkelmann 2003: 250). And would the Europeans be able to formulate a common view without having reformed their CFSP/CSDP procedures? In the current situation the presence of up to five EU member states at the SC allows – even at the price of split votes – some flexibility that would be sacrificed to the request for unanimity according to CFSP/CSDP procedures. Without the possibility of a majority vote in CFSP/CSDP issues, the common EU seat on the SC most probably would be subject to ongoing blockade in all significant questions and abstention would become the dominant voting pattern of the EU. If at all, a Permanent Seat for the EU is imaginable only as a final step in a successful and deep integration in CFSP structures and mechanisms.

Furthermore, a single permanent seat on the Security Council would also imply a single EU membership in the UN that would impact the Union's overall influence within the organisation. With its 27 member states the EU holds around 15 per cent of the votes in the General Assembly – plus some other forty to fifty states that orientate their voting on the example of their European partners. This constitutes a significant impact on the decision-making procedures in the United Nations that the EU should not give up in its own interest.

Instead of reducing the number of European seats on the Security Council an additional permanent seat for an integration-willing EU member might be a solution – that is very much favoured by Germany and other supporters of Model A. Since there is no consent amongst the European countries which of its members should take that position, another kind of representation might be imaginable: Non-permanent but re-eligible seats for two or three European countries – an approach that shows some similarities with Model B – and that is heralded by a group of states around Italy. Given a very limited prospect for a successful and comprehensive SC reform in general and a lack of consent of the Europeans on new forms of representation in the UN's top body, the most realistic outcome of the discussion on the European Union's participation in the SC, however, might be the strengthening of the role of the High Representative. HR Catherine Ashton and her future successors could be given more space to speak on behalf of the Union, explaining to the Council Members European views and Joint Actions (considered to be) taken. In its aforementioned Resolution 276 the General Assembly has opened this option – the onus is on the EU member states to adopt it.

Conclusions and Prospects of EU-UN Cooperation

As shown above, the EU and the UN established a fairly efficient infrastructure for communication and cooperation that has been continuously developed and extended over the course of time. The Union's overall appearance at the UN is that of a considerably coherent organisation – as long as there are no vital national interests at stake in the Security Council or with regard to deployments in support of UN peace missions. The latter areas, however, are of major significance for the EU's performance as a convincing actor on the global stage provided by the UN. Any increase in the Union's political weight in global politics therefore largely depends on its willingness and preparedness to postpone national views and agendas in favour of common interests and matters of concern.

EU-UN cooperation, however, clearly reflects the internal difficulties EU members face in the process of shaping their common foreign policies and effectively using the instruments they created in recent years. Even twenty years after the establishment of CFSP the Union's members are still sticking to a rather purist form of inter-governmentalism that results from deeply rooted fears of transferring national sovereign rights to the European level – especially with regard to such important policy fields like security or external relations. Decisions on Joint Actions in the framework of international crisis management or on the rationale, the composition and the appropriate mandate of an EU-led operation are delicate endeavours that may rapidly reach the limits of EU-internal multilateralism.

A union of states, however, that has to make great effort to play its role as a global actor is hardly inclined to yield further competencies to an even more fuzzy organisation like the UN that would be allowed to impose far-reaching obligations in the field of peace maintenance. Despite often-uttered mutual appreciation and recognizable progress EU-UN cooperation will continue to face clear constraints.

This trend could only be reversed if the EU and its member states resolved to give more effective support to the UN. With regard to the still disparate constitution of CFSP this is easier said than done. But the Europeans will have to accept that the principle of multilateralism will only work on the global level if strong and integrated regional organisations are serving as successful role models. As long as EU members compromise their vociferously heralded commitment to effective multilateralism by persistently falling back into their national behaviour, this principle will hardly be implemented effectively on the level of the UN.

There are various overlaps in the policies of the EU and UN, which demand even more intensified cooperation especially in the field of international security. Not only does the UN framework not impose any limitations on the EU members in the enhancement of their multilateral cooperation in GASP and CSDP, the global stage of the UN actually offers the Europeans various opportunities to reach common views and follow joint strategies in tackling challenges and problems differing in significance and complexity. By continued efforts on speaking with one single voice and subsequently acting in a unified manner the European Union might well increase its role as a global actor in many fields of world politics, thus serving its own interests as well as those of the UN.

Bibliography

Algieri, Franco/Lang, Sibylle/Staack, Michael (eds.)(2008): Militärische Aspekte der Europäischen Sicherheits- und Verteidigungspolitik im Lichte der deutschen EU-Ratspräsidentschaft. Bremen.

Borger, Julian (2011): EU anger over British stance on EU statement. In: The Guardian, 20 October 2011. online: http://www.guardian.co.uk/world/2011/oct/20/uk-eu-un-statements-wording

Commission of the European Communities 2003: The European Union and the United Nations: The choice of multilateralism. Draft communication from the commission to the Council and the European Parliament. Brussels.

Council of the European Union (2003): Joint Declaration on UN-EU Co-operation in Crisis Management. online: http://www.consilium.europa.eu/uedocs/cmsUpload/st12730.en03.pdf

Council of the European Union (2007): Joint Statement on UN-EU Cooperation in Crisis Management. online: http://www.consilium.europa.eu/uedocs/cmsUpload/EU-UNstatmntoncrsmngmnt.pdf

Delcourt, Barbara (2011): The EU at the UNGA. online: http://halshs.archives-ouvertes.fr/docs/00/63/83/79/PDF/EWP_politics_ideology_EU_at_the_UN.pdf

Council of the European Union (2011): EU Priorities for the 66th Session of the General Assembly of the United Nations online: http://register.consilium.europa.eu/pdf/en/11/st11/st11298.en11.pdf

European Institute for Security Studies (2003): A more Secure Europe in a Better World. European Security Strategy. Paris.

European Union (2010): Consolidated Treaties. Consolidated Versions of the Treaty on European Union and of the Treaty on the Functioning of the European Union. Luxembourg.

Frowein, Jochen Abr./Scharioth, Klaus/Winkelmann, Ingo/Wolfrum, Rüdiger (eds.) (2003): Verhandeln für den Frieden. Berlin, Heidelberg.

Gareis, Sven Bernhard (2012): The United Nations. An Introduction. 2nd edition: Pallgrave Macmillan: Basingstoke.

Gareis, Sven Bernhard (2009): Nachhaltigkeit statt Symbolik: Zum fragwürdigen Nutzen der EUFOR Chad/CAR. In: Vereinte Nationen (4) 2009: 153.

Gareis, Sven Bernhard/Lang, Sibylle/Varwick, Johannes (2008): Militärische Aspekte der Zusammenarbeit zwischen Europäischer Union und Vereinten Nationen im Krisenmanagement. In: Algieri/Lang/Staack (2008): pp. 87-101.

Gareis, Sven Bernhard/Varwick, Johannes (2007): Frieden erster und zweiter Klasse. Die Industriestaaten lassen die Vereinten Nationen bei Peacekeeping-Einsätzen im Stich. In: Internationale Politik (5): pp. 68-74.

Griep, Ekkehard (2008): Tendenz: Steigend. Die Zusammenarbeit der Vereinten Nationen mit Regionalorganisationen in der Friedenssicherung. In: Vereinte Nationen (4): pp. 147-152.

Laatikainen, Katie Verlin/ Smith, Karen E. (eds.) (2006): The European Union at the United Nations. Intersecting Multilateralisms. Basingstoke: Wiley Blackwell.

Luif, Paul (2003): EU Cohesion in the General Assembly. Paris (Chaillot Paper 49)

Ortega, Martin (ed.) (2005): The European Union and the United Nations. Partners in Effective Multilateralism? Paris (Chaillot Paper 78)

Rasch, Maximilian B. (2008): The European Union at the United Nations. The Functioning and Coherence of EU External Representation in a State-centric Environment. Leiden.

Tardy, Thierry (2005): EU-UN Cooperation in Peacekeeping. A Promising Relationship in a Restrained Environment. In: Ortega, Martin (2005): The EU and the UN: implementing effective multilateralism, pp. 49-68.

Western European Union (1992): Petersberg Declaration. online: http://www.weu.int/documents/920619peten.pdf

Wewers, Ariane (2009): Die Pflicht der EU-Partner zur Koordinierung in internationalen Organisationen und auf internationalen Konferenzen (Art. 19 EUV). Die Praxis der GASP dargestellt am Beispiel der Vereinten Nationen. Frankfurt am Main.

Winkelmann, Ingo 2000: Europäische und mitgliedstaatliche Interessenvertretung in den Vereinten Nationen. In: Zeitschrift für ausländisches Öffentliches Recht und Völkerrecht (2): pp. 413-445.

Winkelmann, Ingo (2003): Das Postulat einer stärkeren Beteiligung des Südens am Sicherheitsrat der Vereinten Nationen. In: Frowein/Scharioth/Winkelmann/Wolfrum (2003), pp. 229-252.

The Relationship between the EU and NATO: Complementary Co-operation or Institutional Rivalry?

Sven Bernhard Gareis

It would have been a major clash on the diplomatic parquet: In anticipation of the NATO Summit held in Chicago in May 2012 Turkey had threatened to veto an invitation to the President of the European Council, Herman van Rompuy and the President of the European Commission, José Manuel Barroso, unless the Organisation of Islamic Conference (OIC), whose contributions to the peace process in Afghanistan exceeded the European efforts, would be invited as well (Yanatma 2012). Though the Turkish side eventually gave in and accepted the two top EU representatives to address the delegations from 28 NATO member states and another thirteen partner countries, the incident provided further evidence of how difficult interaction between the two most important Western organisations still is.

Indeed, despite a shared membership of 21 states (out of 27 EU and 28 NATO members) and despite an established mechanism for EU-NATO co-operation in the field of international peace operations (the 'Berlin Plus' agreement; see below) the relationship between the two Brussels-based institutions is still lacking a coherent conceptual framework that would clarify which tasks and responsibilities should be shouldered by either NATO or the EU. This deficit reflects the old and ongoing debate between 'Atlanticists' and 'Europeans', whether enhanced European security efforts should take place within the framework of US-led NATO or should lead to more autonomous European security arrangements. Furthermore, in its ongoing disputes with Greece and Cyprus as well as in negotiations with the EU, Turkey continues to use EU-NATO relations as a bargaining chip (Ahmed 2012) in the pursuit of its national interests. Both the conceptual deficits as well as conflicts between single states thus led to a factual stalemate in the bilateral relations that is often referred to as a 'frozen conflict' (Hofmann/Reynolds 2007).

However, the urgent need to find a solution to this problem can no longer be overlooked. The US, whose global dominance is increasingly being challenged by rising powers like China or India, is rebalancing its security interests as well as the capacities needed to pursue them. The US' ongoing pivot toward Asia-Pacific requires a partial withdrawal from Europe, thus challenging the Europeans to undertake more efforts in maintaining their own security and to redefine their role within NATO – and in world politics. As Johannes Varwick (2011: 128) has put it correctly: The future relations between Europe and the US will largely depend on the institutional arrangements between EU and NATO.

Against this background the present chapter examines the delicate relationship between EU and NATO as well as its possible development in the foreseeable future. It hereto looks at the achievements and the state of the art of the inter-institutional co-operation, analyses problems and challenges such as structural conflicts or different organisational cultures, and discusses possible future scenarios in terms of complementarity or competition.

EU-NATO Co-operation: Origins, Development, and Mechanisms

Throughout the period of the Cold War there existed a clear and well accepted complementary division of labour between European and transatlantic institutions: The European Economic Community (EEC) efficiently organized the integration of national economies into a common market thus creating the basis for wealth and welfare in the Western European realm. NATO was responsible for providing the security umbrella, in particular by keeping the US – with its conventional and nuclear deterrents – engaged against the Soviet threat.

While being highly successful in the field of economics, the European countries had been failing for decades in creating effective forms of co-operation – not to mention integration – in areas like foreign or security policies. Ambitious projects in the early 1950s when France and Germany jointly developed the ideas of a European Defence Community (EDC) and a European Political Community (EPC) died a sudden death in the French Assemblée Nationale after the French lost interest in establishing institutions curbing sovereignty in such crucial fields as national security. The Western European Union (WEU) that was founded in 1955 as a European defence arrangement never went operational and remained the sleeping beauty of European security policy for nearly four decades. The European Political Co-operation (EPC) established in 1970 also never became more than a fairly loose format for consultation between the members of the European Community (EC) on external affairs. Only in the 1980s did security policy issues once again appear on the European agenda when the European Single Act (ESA) of 1986 formally codified structures and procedures for (intergovernmentally organised) foreign policy coordination amongst the members of the EC. Even within NATO itself efforts to strengthen the 'European Pillar' by an enhanced co-operation in arrangements like the EUROGROUP only had very limited effect. European security lasted depending on the US-led North Atlantic Alliance.

New Strategic Requirements

In 1989/90 the fall of the Iron Curtain, the German reunification and other new dramatic developments required comprehensive European responses. Internally, substantial steps toward a political union had to be taken to appease 'realist reflexes' (Sebastian Harnisch) in Paris and London, where the prospect of Germany's reunification raised fears of a re-emergence of Germany as the dominant European power. So the increasing weight of Germany had to be balanced out by a deepened integration that would confine its scope for powerful action. Externally, the collapse of Yugoslavia remorselessly displayed the European inability to counter severe security challenges in its immediate vicinity. It became clear that the new European Union (EU) would have to create appropriate instruments for external action – one answer found in the Maastricht Treaty on European Union (TEU) of 1992 was the establishment of a Common Foreign and Security Policy (CFSP) with the revived WEU as its power tool for security and defence. The follow-ups to the Maastricht Treaty signed in Amsterdam (1997), Nice (2000) and eventually in Lisbon (2009) further refined the provisions on CFSP and CSDP giving the Union a remarkable set of norms, procedures and institutions for a foreign and security policy of its own (see Gunther Hauser's chapter in this volume).

From the very beginning – and parallel to NATO's transformation from a defence alliance into a provider of stability for a politically volatile Europe – the Europeans declared themselves willing and prepared to take on more responsibilities for the security of their own continent. In its 'Petersberg Declaration' of June 1992 the WEU members pledged to take a wide array of military tasks – reaching from humanitarian and rescue tasks to combat tasks – in order to support the maintenance of peace in Europe and beyond (WEU 1992: II, 4).

The new European efforts in the field of security policy, however, created new political and organisational questions on how those commitments could be put into practice. In political terms the debate went on between the advocates of a more emancipated and autonomous Europe and those of a stronger European pillar within NATO. France envisaged a new European power built on forces like the German-French Brigade and the EUROCORPS that had been brought into being previously. In contrast, the US and the United Kingdom, fearing a split of the Alliance, were calling for a larger and more coherent European contribution to the common transatlantic efforts. Germany, traditionally torn between its two closest allies, France and the US, eventually was in favour of a

NATO-first approach that constrained the operational role of the WEU and preferred a build-up of European security and defence capacities in close cooperation with NATO (see Dembinski 2005: 68f.).

But also with regard to organisation there was not much room for manoeuvre for an exclusive European security force. The start of the EU/WEU
ambitions coincided with substantial cuts in the defence budgets and considerable force reductions in practically all European countries as a result of the
improved security situation after the end of the East-West antagonism. Additional resources for new European forces were thus never a realistic option –
on the contrary: Though WEU member states reported large numbers of
'Forces Answerable to the Western European Union' (FAWEU), this organisation never had at its disposal any kind of headquarters, command and
control or logistics infrastructure enabling it to lead a major military operation. If the Europeans wanted to establish some military capabilities of their
own this had to be done within the existing structures of NATO.

New Mechanisms: 'Berlin' and 'Berlin Plus'

At their Brussels Summit of January 1994 NATO's heads of state and government offered to the Europeans the Alliance's full support in the
development of a European Security and Defence Identity (ESDI) 'which, as
called for in the Maastricht Treaty, in the longer term perspective of a common defence policy within the European Union, might in time lead to a
common defence compatible with that of the Atlantic Alliance. The emergence of a European Security and Defence Identity will strengthen the
European pillar of the Alliance while reinforcing the transatlantic link and
will enable European Allies to take greater responsibility for their common
security and defence. The Alliance and the European Union share common
strategic interests' (NATO 1994: para 4). As a key concept for the future cooperation with the WEU in the framework of the emerging European Security and Defence Identity (ESDI), NATO endorsed the principle of
Combined Joint Task Forces (CJTF) as a means to facilitate the conduct of
complex military operations tailored to a certain mission under participation
of states outside the alliance (ibid: para 9). Furthermore, the Alliance promised to support the 'development of separable but not separate capabilities
which could respond to European requirements and contribute to Alliance
security' (ibid: para 6), thus recognizing that there existed just a single set of
forces to be employed by NATO and EU member states.

The Declaration, however, unmistakably insisted on NATO's supremacy
in European Security affairs – a pattern that is also to be found in the Final
Communiqué of the North Atlantic Ministerial Meeting in Berlin of 3 June
1996, a landmark document that marked the starting point of the 'Berlin-

Process': In supporting ESDI, NATO proposed identifying those 'types of separable but not separate capabilities, assets and support assets, as well as, in order to prepare for WEU-led operations, separable but not separate HQs, HQ elements and command positions, that would be required to command and conduct WEU-led operations and which could be made available' (NATO 1996: para 7). In practice this and other provisions in the Communiqué allowed the Europeans access to NATO-owned HQ structures and capacities for the planning and conduct of WEU-led exercises and operations; so-called 'double-hatted' positions were created for regular NATO staff members who could be activated on call for the conduct of a European operation. All those support offers, however, remained subject to case-by-case decision by the North Atlantic Council – thus keeping the US the most influential player in European security affairs. This again frustrated France who – after its failed bid for the lead position of NATO's Southern Headquarters (AFSOUTH) – raised serious doubts over an equal righted relationship across the Atlantic. The 'Berlin-Process' thus remained an unfinished business for more than two years, until the Kosovo crisis of 1998/99 revealed the fundamental weaknesses of the European military capacities in comparison to those of the US and, in return, to influence the strategic and operational decision-making within the Alliance.

Though the US administration under President Bill Clinton had indicated its willingness to give the Europeans an assured access to NATO assets, a new initiative toward a more distinct European security policy with its own structures and capabilities was launched by France and – astonishingly enough – the UK. In their Joint Declaration on European Defence published on a bilateral summit in St. Malo on 4 December 1998, President Jacques Chirac and Prime Minister Toni Blair claimed the European Union's 'capacity for autonomous action, backed up by credible military forces, the means to decide to use them and a readiness to do so, in order to respond to international crises' (Franco-British Summit 1998: para 2), questioning for the first time an exclusive NATO/US supremacy in European security matters.

In her reaction to this new development instigated by the St. Malo declaration, US Secretary of State Madeleine Albright thwarted plans for an enhanced European security policy: 'The key to a successful initiative is to focus on practical military capabilities. Any initiative must avoid pre-empting Alliance decision-making by de-linking ESDI from NATO, avoid duplicating existing efforts, and avoid discriminating against non-EU members' (Albright 1998; quoted in Hunter 2002: 33f.). However, on its meeting in Cologne in June 1999 – and still under the influence of the ongoing war over Kosovo – the European Council decided on the creation of common European Security and Defence Policy (ESDP) that would enable the EU to play its full role on the international stage' (Consilium 1999: Annex III, para.

1). In order to fulfil the 'Petersberg Tasks' that had been integrated into the TEU in Amsterdam, the Union needed 'the capacity for autonomous action, backed up by credible military forces, the means to decide to use them, and a readiness to do so, in order to respond to international crises without prejudice to actions by NATO' (ibid., para. 2). In its Presidency Report the German Government also outlined a first set of common institutions and mechanisms for decision-making, including a permanent Political and Security Committee, a Military Committee and a Military Staff (Consilium 1999: Annex III). According to the Report, NATO should remain the foundation of the collective defence of its members; for the implementation of operations under the umbrella of ESDP the paper called for two options: missions using NATO assets and capabilities and those without recourse to capacities provided by the Alliance.

In the following negotiations on an assured access to NATO capabilities ('Berlin Plus') EU members accepted the US insistence on NATO's primary role in the planning and the conduct of European military operations. On their Council meeting in Helsinki in December 1999 EU member states confirmed the conduct of military operations only, 'where NATO as a whole is not engaged' and to avoid unnecessary duplication of EU-led military operations in response to international crises (Consilium 1999a: para. 27). The EU also provided modalities to include the non-EU European NATO members in EU-led operations. On this basis both sides ended up in Copenhagen in December 2002 signing a joint declaration according to which NATO 'is giving the European Union, inter alia and in particular, assured access to NATO's planning capabilities' (EU-NATO Declaration 2002). In March 2003 the Berlin Plus arrangements entered into force. The EU's second option, to conduct military operations on its own without relying on Alliance assets appeared to be subject to a number of strict constraints resulting from the primary role of NATO (see Meiers 2005: 126). Over the course of the transatlantic disputes over the war on Iraq 2003, however, autonomous European planning and command capabilities like a civil-military planning cell were discussed and eventually implemented (see below).

The Current Framework of EU-NATO Relations

The Berlin Plus arrangements built the framework for EU-NATO consultation and co-operation in international crisis management. In particular there are three major elements, that can be employed by both sides, once they agreed on giving the lead of a mission to the EU.

First, NATO is giving the EU assured access to its planning capabilities so that even in an early stage the EU Military Staff can ask for NATO expertise for the outline of different courses of action. Once a mission is decided upon under recourse of NATO assets, the Alliance will provide the operational planning. Second, for the conduct of a mission the EU can ask NATO to provide an Operational Headquarters. In this case, the Deputy Supreme Allied Commander Europe (who is always a European four star general) is activated as the EU operational commander. Beneath that level, Forces Headquarters, force commanders and all relevant capabilities can be provided either by NATO or by the EU and its member states. Third, NATO declares itself willing to give the Europeans those collective assets (e.g. logistics, command and control infrastructure, or reconnaissance) essential for the successful conduct of the mission. Those assets, however, could be recalled by the Alliance when needed for operations of its own.

On the basis of the Berlin Plus arrangement the EU launched its first military mission in Macedonia from March to December 2003. 'Operation Concordia's' objective was to secure a safe environment for the implementation of the Ohrid Agreement balancing the interests and rights of Macedonian and Albanian ethnicities in the country (for further information see consilium.europa.eu). A second mission under the umbrella of Berlin Plus is the ongoing 'EUFOR Althea' in Bosnia-Herzegovina that the EU took over from NATO in December of 2004 to maintain peace in the country. The Berlin Plus arrangements cemented NATO's supremacy in European security affairs – at least on paper. In political practice, however, those two missions have been the only examples for the employment of that agreement so far. All other operations, including with EUFOR Congo (2006), EUFOR Chad/Central African Republic (2008-9), the naval mission ATALANTA offshore Somalia, and EULEX in Kosovo (since 2008) the largest CSDP engagements so far, were conducted under exclusive recourse on EU and member states' assets.

Conceptual Deficits and Challenges

At first glance, EU-NATO relations developed logically as co-operative and complementary institutional structures formed by two like-minded organisations. A closer look, however, reveals an establishment of widely parallel security policies of two Western institutions that never succeeded in consistently defining their roles and functions in European security matters and consequently never reached a sustainable agreement on its mutual relationship and division of labour. This finding is the more astonishing when considering the major overlaps in membership as well as their vital security interests, which exist between the EU and NATO. In the EU-NATO negotiations, 21 countries are jointly discussing how to best serve their common security needs. As a result, the EU created with themselves – both in terms of function and in organisation – some parallel structures like the Political and Se-

curity Committee (PSC) as the top steering committees, the EU Military Committee (EUMC), the EU Military Staff (EUMS), the EU Battlegroups as rapid
reaction forces etc. Those bodies are much smaller and more constrained than
their counterparts in NATO but they are unavoidable because they allow the
EU to conduct autonomous operations (see also Fröhlich 2008: 196).

The reasons for that parallelism in security policies are multi-fold. First
and foremost, the role of the US has to be considered. At no time since World
War II have the Europeans been able to guarantee their regional security by
their own means. As Josef Joffe once put it, the US served as the 'European
pacifier', securing the Western European post-war integration process, protecting its European allies against the Soviet threat by its nuclear umbrella,
and eventually contributing significantly to the Eastern European transformation process and regional crisis management after the end of the East-West
antagonism. This unique commitment made the US the dominant power in
Europe – a role that it sought to maintain, but that persistently sparked am-
bivalent perceptions and disputes among the Europeans. While France, and to
a certain extent Germany, heralded a more autonomous European security policy, 'Atlanticists' like the UK or some of the new NATO members from the
former Soviet bloc preferred a strong role of the Alliance under US leadership
– not least to have a counterweight to a sometimes too powerful Franco-
German directorate on the old continent. But also the US view on European
security efforts has constantly been ambiguous: On the one hand Washington
urged its European allies to take more responsibility for their own security –
but then warily observed – and tried to curb – any serious initiative of the
Europeans to organize their own capacities. In the end, the emergence of parallel security structures can be considered as a tacit agreement: the
'Atlanticists' accept that Europe needs – for the sake of its political identity –
some room for manoeuvre in its security policy affairs. The 'Europeans' again
have learned from the split over the Iraq war that any attempt to contain the
US was counter-productive to European coherence. The Libya case in 2011,
when Europeans around France and the UK drew the US into a coalition war,
gave another enlightening example of the European dependence on US capabilities, when the European forces simply ran out of ammunition shortly after
the start of the campaign. Given the fact, that both 'camps' accept each other,
the unsolved problem, however, remains in the field of a proper distinction of
the roles and functions that either the EU or NATO should take over.

In this regard, the different organisational cultures come into play – both
as a problem and as a part of its solution: Though NATO is a political organisation by nature, its overall performance and global perception is that of
a military alliance and a protagonist in the field of classical hard power, conducting robust missions such as in former Yugoslavia or in Afghanistan. In
contrast, the EU, traditionally an economy-oriented organisation, is focusing

its security policy efforts more on stabilisation and peace-building scenarios, explicitly emphasizing the civilian dimensions of those engagements. Whilst NATO missions are increasingly involved in war-like theatres suffering considerable losses, EU missions so far did not count any fatalities in combat. The civilian dimension in CSDP is well established and founded by appropriate means. The EUPOL missions in Bosnia and Afghanistan as well as the EULEX mission in Kosovo or the Security Sector Reform (EUSEC) mission in the DR Congo usually are smaller and less spectacular than the Union's military operations. But whilst the latter mission (with the exception of ALTHEA and ATALANTA) mostly are subject to strict time limits and limited mandates often making their deployment more symbolic rather than effective (see Gareis 2009), the civilian missions are long-term engagements committed to a higher degree of sustainability. In this functional area, a more consistent division of labour might be found – with the EU responsible for the 'softer' stabilisation and civilian missions, and NATO for the more robust enforcement and combat tasks. So far, however, both organisations claim responsibilities for the full range of possible missions, a conceptual clarification of the respective responsibilities has not yet been undertaken.

Though power issues and unclear functional responsibilities contribute substantially to the EU-NATO conundrum, the biggest challenge for the present and the future of co-operation between the two organisations lies in the field of internal conflicts between member states. As shown above the question of non-discrimination of non-EU NATO partners has been a major point of discussion from the onset of European security policy efforts. Whilst most of the countries initially concerned have become EU members (like the Baltic states, Bulgaria and Romania) or have a clear accession perspective (like Croatia), the problems culminated with regard to Turkey. The Turkish accession process has been kept on hold since the county signed its association agreement with the EEC in 1963; problems escalated after the EU had accepted the Republic of Cyprus as a full member in 2004, although the Greek part of the country – other than the Turkish – had rejected a reunification, which the EU had postulated as a precondition for Cyprian membership before. Turkey refused to recognize Cyprus with the effect of a kind of double veto for EU-NATO relationship in the field of military operations. Turkey does not allow EU recourse on NATO assets; the EU refuses to negotiate security issues with a country that does not recognize one of its members. As a consequence the Berlin Plus mechanism is on ice; EUFOR Althea in Bosnia-Herzegovina is still being run under that mechanism but no further EU-NATO mission has been launched so far, nor will this presumably be happening in the foreseeable future.

What may be the outcome of this 'frozen conflict'? Johannes Varwick (2011: 132) offers two possible scenarios: The first one is characterized by

an enhanced co-operation between the two organisations, putting into practice the old idea of an Atlantic bridge built on two strong pillars in North
America and in Europe. In this scenario EU member states and the US would
closely consult each other and harmonize their policies based on a clearly defined distribution of tasks and responsibilities. To this end, the Europeans
were requested to accept a stronger commitment to carrying their share of efforts for regional and global security and the US needed to recognize the EU
as an equal partner. In his second, more pessimistic scenario, Varwick envisaged a collapse of the transatlantic relations as a result of diverging interests
and different perceptions of threats and risks. This might end up in a strategic
rivalry between the US and the EU – a vision that admittedly is not very
likely for the near future. But in the case of a progressing alienation between
the US and the EU, with the US losing interest in the EU and the Europeans
transforming their economic power into political impact, such a scenario
might become a reality in a multi-polar world.

Consequences for Europe's Future Role

The US shift of interest to the Asia-Pacific region creates a new momentum for transatlantic relations and for the interaction between the EU and
NATO. The US' means and capabilities to exert its role as a sole world
power are shrinking and need to be refocused in that region of the world
that poses the most significant challenge to American global leadership.
The partial withdrawal of the US from Europe will force the Europeans to
do more in tackling their security challenges in the region but also in safe-
guarding their vital interests on the global stage. For example: It is not in
the European interest to passively observe a possible power conflict between the US and China in Asia-Pacific, a region where Europe has a lot at
stake in terms of economic exchange and trade. The US pivot to Asia-
Pacific requests from the EU to think more globally with regard to international relations and power politics.

For the years to come, Europe's interest will be in maintaining NATO as
an effective organisation – and keeping the US involved in Europe. The US
and EU members share a wide array of values and political objectives preparing a stable basis for the continuation of a preferred partnership. In this
regard the EU needs to become more unified and consistent to remain an attractive partner to the US. A deeper integration in the field of CFSP and
CSDP will be unavoidable if the Union wants to play a bigger role within
transatlantic relations as well as on the global stage.

The main purpose of a more coherent European security policy, however,
is not to please the US, but to serve the EU's own security interests. With its

shift to Asia, the US made clear that it is going to prioritize its engagements primarily according to its national preferences. For the Europeans the message of this turn is twofold: First, the US mission in Europe has been accomplished; the continent can stand on its own. Second, Europe is no challenge for US global supremacy – so that in the future stronger engagements on the Asian theatre could result in a weaker commitment to Europe. In the European capitals political leaders should therefore anticipate that the old continent might be declining within the hierarchy of significant partners to the US. Indeed, despite the utterances of common defence in the Alliance's strategic concepts, NATO increasingly has become a tool box for ad hoc coalitions for specific tasks, with nations opting in and out according to their national decisions. Even in terms of collective defence the new provisions of the Lisbon Treaty on mutual defence assistance (Art 42 (7) TEU-L) can be considered stronger than Article 5 of the Washington Treaty.

From a European perspective the relationship with NATO continues to be a walk on the tightrope: On the one hand the EU countries should carry on trying to keep the US a European power, but at the same time they should be preparing for a future without US leadership and strong security guarantees on the continent. The answer to both possible scenarios is an EU enabled to perform on the global stage as a unified actor. Within a continuously successful Alliance the Europeans will have to harmonize their security and defence policies, combine their efforts and gain more efficiency and effectiveness by pooling and sharing their capabilities under the headline of 'smart defence'. In the case of a significant US drawdown, NATO would not survive as an effective organisation. A stronger and more coherent EU would then need to fulfil many tasks that were traditionally in the area of responsibility of NATO. The Europeans should therefore be prepared for either outcome. In the long run the EU-NATO relationship, with its inherent dominance of the US, might be replaced by a more equal Euro-Atlantic partnership between the EU and the US with NATO as a forum rather than an operational organisation.

Bibliography

Ahmed, Muddassar (2012): Turkey risks walking off the NATO tightrope. In: The Telegraph, 24 May 2012. online: http://www.telegraph.co.uk/news/worldnews/europe/turkey/9287849/Turkey-risks-walking-off-the-Nato-tightrope.html

Consilium (1999): Presidency Conclusions. Cologne European Council 3 and 4 June 1999. online: http://www.consilium.europa.eu/ueDocs/cms_Data/docs/pressData/en/ec/kolnen.htm

Consilium (1999a): Presidency Conclusions. Helsinki European Council 11 and 12 December 1999. online: http://www.europarl.europa.eu/summits/hel1_en.htm

Dembinski, Matthias (2005): Die Beziehungen zwischen NATO und EU von ‚Berlin' zu ‚Berlin Plus': Konzepte und Konfliktlinien. In: Varwick (2005): pp. 61-80.

EU-NATO Declaration on ESDP of 16 December 2002. online: http://www.nato.int/cps/en/natolive/official_texts_19544.htm

Franco-British Summit (1998): Joint Declaration on European Defence. St. Malo 4 December 1998. online: http://www.atlanticcommunity.org/Saint-Malo%20Declaration%20Text.html

Fröhlich, Stefan (2008): Die Europäische Union als Globaler Akteur. Wiesbaden.

Gareis, Sven Bernhard (2009): Nachhaltigkeit statt Symbolik: Zum fragwürdigen Nutzen der EUFOR Chad/CAR. In: Vereinte Nationen (4) 2009: 153.

Hofmann, Stephanie/Reynolds, Christopher (2007): EU-NATO Relations: Time to Thaw the 'Frozen Conflict'. Berlin: SWP-Comments 12.

Hunter, Robert E. (2002): The European Security and Defense Policy: NATO's Companion – or Competitor? Washington D.C. (Rand Monograph Reports 1463)

Kaldrack, Gerd F./Pöttering, Hans-Gert (eds.)(2011): Eine einsatzfähige Armee für Europa. Die Zukunft der Gemeinsamen Sicherheits- und Verteidigungspolitik nach Lissabon. Baden-Baden

Meiers, Franz-Josef (2005): Die ‚NATO Response Force' und die ‚European Rapid Reaction Force': Kooperationspartner oder Konkurrenten? In: Varwick (2005): pp. 119-138.

NATO (1994): Ministerial Meeting of the North Atlantic Council/North Atlantic Cooperation Council, NATO Headquarters, Brussels, 10-11 January 1994. Declaration of the Heads of State and Government. online: http://www.nato.int/docu/comm/49-95/c940111a.htm

NATO (1996): Ministerial Meeting of the North Atlantic Council Berlin 3 June 1996. Final Communiqué. Online: http://www.nato.int/docu/pr/1996/p96-063e.htm

Varwick, Johannes (ed.)(2005): Die Beziehungen zwischen NATO und EU. Partnerschaft, Konkurrenz, Rivalität? Opladen.

Varwick, Johannes (2008): Die NATO. Vom Verteidigungsbündnis zur Weltpolizei? München: C.H.Beck.

Varwick, Johannes (2011): EU und NATO – kein Gegensatz? In: Kaldrack/Pöttering (2011): pp. 127-134.

Western European Union (1992): Petersberg Declaration. online: http://www.weu.int/documents/920619peten.pdf

Yanatma, Servet (2012): Turkey blocks EU from NATO summit unless OIC also attends. In: Today's Zaman, online: http://www.todayszaman.com/news-278979-turkey-blocks-eu-from-nato-summit-unless-oic-also-attends.html

The EU and ASEAN – The Interregional Relationship Between Europe and Asia

Gerald Brettner-Messler

Introduction

Over more than five decades the European Union has proved a successful model of regional integration. Ten years after signing the Rome treaties ASEAN was founded. In South-East Asia the level of integration had not reached European dimensions but the development of Europe attracted interest in the region and provided its political leaders with inputs for framing their own regional affairs. The official relations which go back to 1972 became "the perhaps most advanced interregional relationship" (Rüland 2001: 4). This article describes the comprehensive ties between EU and ASEAN with a focus on security related matters. Concentrating on this particular aspect is vindicated by the fact that the foundation of ASEAN was motivated by the pursuit of security and stability in the region. Due to the ever increasing interconnections of countries and regions, creating security and stability has gained more and more prominence in the relations between EU and ASEAN. Therefore it is worth tracing the role of this issue in shaping the cooperation agenda between these entities. As primary sources for this analysis official documents were used; secondary literature supplements the work.

The Structures of ASEAN

The Association of South-East Asian Nations was founded in 1967 in Bangkok by Indonesia, Malaysia, the Philippines, Singapore and Thailand (ASEAN or Bangkok Declaration). Brunei Darussalam joined in 1984, Vietnam became a member in 1995, Laos and Myanmar in 1997. The latest accession to the treaty was by Cambodia in 1999. Aims and purposes of the organisation were defined in a broad manner. Economic growth, social progress and cultural development lead in a list of seven areas of cooperation. Regional peace and stability come second. In principle the Declaration encompasses all fields of human life. The "machinery" established to make the treaty work referred the new organisation to the sphere of foreign policy. The Annual Meeting brought together the foreign ministers; the Standing Committee consisted of ambassadors of the member countries under the chairmanship of the foreign minister of the host country (ASEAN Declaration 1967).

In fact it was a rather slow take-off. South-East Asia was divided by various conflicts and integration was not the priority of the participants. It was more about overcoming these conflicts and in doing so strengthening the role of the states. But ASEAN got a prominent function in transporting common interests of its members through dialogues with partners in Asia and on other continents (Yeo 2009: 46).

In 1976 the founding members of ASEAN signed the Treaty of Amity and Cooperation (TAC, also: Bali Treaty). Its provisions had been enshrined in the Kuala Lumpur Declaration and the aim was to create a legally binding conduct for the relations between Southeast Asian states (Politics and Security of ASEAN; Text of the TAC). Later all other members of the organisation acceded plus fifteen states outside ASEAN. In this treaty the fundamental principles of ASEAN are laid down. Article I states: "The purpose of this Treaty is to promote perpetual peace, everlasting amity and cooperation among their peoples ..." (TAC 1976: Art. 1). Any conflict should be solved by peaceful means but without any interference in internal affairs of the participating countries. The treaty upholds non-interference and territorial integrity as a precondition for all activities in accordance with its purpose. In case of disputes a High Council of representatives at ministerial level shall act as advisory body or even as "committee of mediation, inquiry or conciliation" (TAC 1976: Art. 15). Chapter III stipulates cooperation in a wide range of fields but puts special focus on the economy in order to raise the economic level and the living standards of the people. This is where the EU comes in: In order to achieve these aims the treaty requests the participants to cooperate "... with other States as well as international and regional organisations outside the region" (TAC 1976: Art. 6). But it was only possible for states to become a member of TAC, not for organisations. To support ASEAN and the regional integration in South-East Asia the EU intends to join the TAC and so the treaty had to be amended. This process started in 2007. Two years later the European Union declared its intent to join the treaty upon entry of force of an appropriate amendment. In 2010 the Third Protocol Amending the TAC was signed by the participants. It allows (after ratification) the accession of regional organisations consisting of sovereign states like the EU (TAC 1976; International treaty examination 2010: 5, 6; Declaration on Accession to the TAC 2009).

During the initial nine years ASEAN had only national secretariats in each of the member countries, when in 1977 the need was felt to establish a permanent institution for coordination and administration. That was the birth of the ASEAN Secretariat, located in Jakarta, Indonesia, with the Secretary-General as its head. The Secretariat and the Secretary-General is the hub of ASEAN. They take part in all meetings, broker relevant information between the various levels of ASEAN and initiate and supervise its activities. The Agreement on the Establishment of the ASEAN Secretariat further provided for the Directors of the Economic, the Science and Technology and the Social and Cultural Bureau. Over the years the Secretariat's dimension was raised. In 1986 the tenure of the Secretary-General was extended from two to three years (Agreement on the Establishment 1976: Art. 3, 5; Protocol Amending the Agreement 1985). In 1989 the positions of a Deputy Secretary-General and nine Assistant Directors were created. Since 1992 the General-Secretary is appointed by and responsible to the heads of government whose meeting(s) they attend (and to all meetings of ASEAN ministers when in session and to the Chairman of the Standing Committee at all other times). He/She has ministerial status; the tenure is now five years. Raising the number of Bureau Directors and Assistant Directors added to the strength of the Secretariat (Protocol Amending the Agreement 1989: Art. 4; Protocol Amending the Agreement 1992: Art. 3, 4).

The ASEAN Summit 2003 agreed on establishing the ASEAN Community, consisting of the three pillars "Political and Security Community", "Economic Community" and "Socio-Cultural Community. In January 2007 ASEAN decided to accelerate the establishment of the ASEAN Community by 2015 instead of 2020 (Cebu Declaration 2007). In a communication after the conference one could read: "The community is expected to be like the European Union." This was a bit of a simplification and General-Secretary Ong Keng Yong described the situation in a lecture in July 2007 more accurately. The EU could not serve as a model for ASEAN because this union organizes itself on an intergovernmental basis, but it could provide the people of ASEAN with experiences and conceptions. Ong named three challenges where this was especially true. ASEAN wants to become a ruled-base organisation. In drafting the ASEAN Charter the experts looked at how the EU ensures compliance with laws and regulations. The second challenge was the narrowing of the development gap between member states where establishing an ASEAN version of the European Bank of Reconstruction and Development, or the Structural Fund was deliberated. The third challenge was the lack of a distinct ASEAN identity that confers a sense of unity on the people of the member states. Youth rail travel or sporting events like a football championship were named by the Secretary-General as possible contributions to generating such an identity. Ong lauded the willingness of the EU to support ASEAN integration, especially through programmes like the EU-sponsored ASEAN Programme for Regional Integration Support (APRIS) which ran out in December 2010 (ASEAN-EU Programme for Regional Integration Support homepage) and is followed by the ASEAN Economic Integration Support Programme (AEISP), and the activities under the Trans Regional EU-ASEAN Trade Initiative (TREATI) and the Regional EU-ASEAN Dialogue Instrument (READI), (Forty Years of ASEAN 2007).

When in 2007 the ASEAN Charter was signed the organisation and its members had gone quite a long way from a cooperation network to the project of an ASEAN Community. According to the wording of the Charter, ASEAN aspires to become a Community which is "politically cohesive, economically integrated and socially responsible". Maintaining and enhancing peace, security and stability is now the primary goal. In this respect the Charter goes even further – it aims at a zone free of nuclear weapons (like the 1995 Southeast Asia Nuclear-Weapon-Free Zone or Bangkok Treaty, see: Hauser 2010: 125) and weapons of mass destruction. The economic concept for ASEAN is a single market which is economically integrated with a free flow of goods, services and investment. In the end all barriers towards economic integration shall be removed. Amongst ASEAN's principles, independence, sovereignty, equality, territorial integrity come first. These principles are combined with a commitment to non-interference in internal affairs and a national existence free from external interference, subversion and coercion, so that all members enjoy a high degree of autonomy foreclosing any meddling with internal affairs. The members share commitment and collective responsibility for prosperity, peace and security and rely on the peaceful settlement of disputes and renounce any use of force.

Top organ of the organisation which has legal personality is the ASEAN Summit by the heads of state or government. The foreign ministers now form the ASEAN Coordinating Council which is responsible for coordinating the implementation of decisions and agreements of ASEAN and for the coordination of the ASEAN Community Councils. There are three of these councils: the Political-Security Community Council, the Economic Community Council and the Socio-Cultural Community Council. Each council works in the respective field of its responsibility. Furthermore there is a selection of sectoral ministerial bodies with various mandates. Ministers with certain portfolios form such bodies (defence ministers, law ministers) but there were also bodies established concerned with certain aspects like the Commission on the South-East Asia Nuclear Weapon-Free Zone, the ASEAN Regional Forum or the ASEAN Centre for Energy. Moreover there is a list of entities which support ASEAN: it comprises such diverse organisations like the Inter-Parliamentary Assembly, the Kite Council or the Rheumatism Association of ASEAN. To broaden the representation of the member states in the Secretariat four Deputy Secretary-Generals from four different countries were installed. Each member state is represented in Jakarta by a Permanent Representative to ASEAN who all together form a Committee and ASEAN maintains a National Secretariat in every member state. The chair of ASEAN rotates annually in alphabetic order. The chairmanship presides the ASEAN Summit, the Coordinating Council, the Community Councils, the Committee of Permanent Representatives and where appropriate the Sectoral Ministerial

Bodies. ASEAN reaches decisions by consultation and consensus, so there are no majority votes. The principles of external relations are also regulated in the Charta. This document determines that "ASEAN shall develop friendly relations and mutually beneficial dialogue, cooperation and partnerships with countries and sub-regional, regional and international organisations and institutions." The Charter sets the fundament for the development of a common foreign policy. The members "shall (...) coordinate and endeavour to develop common positions and pursue joint actions." The ASEAN Summit gives the strategic directions and the ASEAN Foreign Ministers Meeting ensures coherence and consistency. The Charta provides also for the conclusion of agreements with countries and sub-regional, regional and international organisations and institutions. ASEAN may confer on external partners the status of Dialogue Partner (ASEAN Charter 2007).

The ASEAN Regional Forum

The ASEAN Regional Forum (ARF) as the only inter-governmental forum aimed at promoting peace and security through dialogue and cooperation in Asia Pacific was launched in 1993, the first meeting took place the following year. The ARF is not limited to the ASEAN member countries, which automatically participate, but shall function as a forum for the whole Asia-Pacific region. To prevent an overstretch, participation is restricted to states that influence peace and security in East Asia and Oceania. The EU participates together with Australia, Bangladesh, Canada, China, India, Japan, both Koreas, Mongolia, New Zealand, Pakistan, Papua New Guinea, Russia, Sri Lanka, Timor Leste and the USA. The value of the forum lies in the opportunity to discuss a broad range of issues, fostering transparency and trust between the participants through the network of ARF. An ARF unit is integrated in the ASEAN Secretariat to facilitate administration and support of the chair (ASEAN Regional Forum homepage). The chair of ASEAN also presides over ARF (Australian Government). European participation in the Forum resulted in co-chairing Inter-Sessional Meetings on Confidence Building Measures and Preventive Diplomacy. In 2004 the EU had the co-chair at the group's meeting in Cambodia. In 2005 Germany was the host of a meeting in Berlin. In 2006 the EU co-chaired a meeting in Batam, Indonesia and in 2007 the group met in Helsinki. In 2008 and 2011 a workshop was held in Berlin (ASEAN Regional Forum homepage).

The 17th ARF took place in July 2010 in Hanoi. It welcomed the commitment of the EU for its accession to the Treaty of Amity and Cooperation (TAC). The envisioned final state is that all ARF participants are parties to TAC. The EU suggested the possibility of financial assistance to the ARF

Unit through the European Commission-ASEAN Cooperation (Chairman's Statement, 17th ARF 2010: 6, 46).

EU and ASEAN – an ever closer relationship

The European Economic Community and in its succession the EU, is the oldest dialogue partner of ASEAN. It was in 1972 when the first informal meeting between ASEAN and the Commission of the then EC was held in Brussels. In the same year at the Paris Summit the Community had decided about a new development cooperation policy towards non-associated developing countries including ASEAN in order to "respond even more than in the past to the expectations of the developing countries." The focus of the relations between both organisations was put in those years on economic ties. A Special Coordinating Committee of ASEAN Nations was put up under the supervision of the Standing Committee to link ASEAN with Europe. Driving forces were Malaysia and Singapore that had lost trade preferences with the United Kingdom after its EC accession in 1973. A second factor was the intention to outbalance the economic clout of USA and Japan. ASEAN wanted less trade barriers for its export goods and a price stabilisation scheme for ASEAN primary commodities.

The soaring interdependence of the world economy made new ways and means of organizing it necessary. This insight provided the foundation for an ever increasing EC-ASEAN interconnection. According to the decision met by the conference of ASEAN Ministers and Vice President of the EC Commission, Christopher Soames, in Jakarta in 1974 the Joint ASEAN-European Commission Study Group was established in 1975 "to further the development and intensification of the continuing dialogue between ASEAN and the Commission of the European Community" (Yeo 2009: 46; Statement Paris Summit 1972; Joint Statement 1974; ASEAN. A Bibliography 1984: XVII; Rüland 2001: 9-10).

Formal relations between EC and ASEA go back to 1977, when the ASEAN foreign ministers agreed to make the step to a new level of cooperation. The world economy grew slowly in this year and the unemployment rate was high. Protectionism became a rising danger to international trade. Inflation added to those difficulties. The EC countries longed for a solution to this problem on a broad basis. To boost world trade the G7 decided in London "to strengthen the open international trading system" and rejected protectionism. German foreign minister Hans-Dietrich Genscher proposed to raise contacts between the EC and ASEAN to the ministerial level (Declaration 1977; ASEAN-European Dialogue).

The first ASEAN-EC Ministerial Meeting of the foreign ministers was held in Brussels in 1978. Spokespersons for the EU were Genscher and Roy

Jenkins, then President of the Commission, and on the ASEAN side Mochtar Kusumaatmadja, the Indonesian foreign minister. A range of regional and international topics was discussed. Cooperation projects according to the Joint Declaration were aimed at the expansion of trade. A success of the Conference on International Economic Co-operation (CIEC) was deemed necessary in pursuing this objective and the EC and ASEAN agreed on a quick implementation of the conference's agreements especially as far as commodity policy was concerned (ASEAN-EU Dialogue; Joint Declaration 1978; Downing Street Summit Conference 1977).

In 1978 talks over a Cooperation Agreement began (Joint Declaration 1978). This multilateral Agreement between ASEAN member states and the European Community was signed in 1980 and encompassed the fields of commerce, economy and development. After the enlargement of ASEAN the respective countries also joined the Agreement. Only an extension to Burma was rejected due to the gross violations of human rights there. Both parties guaranteed each other most-favoured-nation treatment. For the coordination of all activities a Joint Cooperation Committee was established (Cooperation Agreement 1980; Protocol on the Extension 1984). The Committee held its first meeting in the same year and adopted programmes for economic and commercial cooperation (Joint Press Statement 1980). Despite all those efforts the economic links between the EC and ASEAN remained weak. The European ministers attended the ministerial meetings only infrequently.

A few years after establishing relations international political developments caused a closing of ranks in the political arena. When the second ministerial meeting took place in 1980, ASEAN and the EC aligned in the rejection of the Soviet intervention in Afghanistan and the Vietnamese intervention in Cambodia. For ASEAN, Cambodia was the far more pressing case, because of the plight of the refugees. ASEAN and the EC rejected the intervention and called for the withdrawal of the foreign troops (Joint Statement 1980). Between 1979 and 1984 ASEAN and the EC stood united in the UN when it came to denouncing the occupation of these countries (Yeo 2009: 47). Nevertheless, the political relationship lacked substance and rested more on commitment than on common action (Rüland 2001: 12). Against the backdrop of the Cold War, stability of the pro-Western partners was the guiding line of European foreign policy. In this context values like democratic change and human rights were rather irrelevant (de Flers 2010: 3).

In 1994 the Commission presented a Communication "Towards A New Asia Strategy". The raised awareness for Asia was rooted in its economic growth in combination with the ongoing restructuring of international affairs after the end of the Cold War. The Commission described the appropriate course of European policy from its point of view as "to make a positive contribution to regional security dialogues and to follow closely developments in particular in the area of arms control and non-proliferation, regional disputes (Korea, Spratly, Kashmir) and the security of sea lanes." Two important clarifications were made. The term "Asia" stands for East-, South-East and South-Asia but not Central-Asia. The second point stresses the linkage between economy as the main focus of the EU in Asia and general political considerations: "However, this major component of the Union policy (i. e. economic matters, G. Brettner-Messler) has to be presented in the framework of the political and security balance of power in the region." Overall objectives were to strengthen the EU's economic presence in Asia, to contribute to stability in Asia and to promote the economic development of the less prosperous countries and regions in Asia. A list of priorities included the support of efforts of Asian countries to cooperate in the same way as the ARF and to strengthen relations "with regional groups such as ASEAN". The Communication stated that on the one hand Asian countries were interested in an intensified engagement of the EU in Asia, on the other hand were reluctant to formulate common endeavours. The Commission explained that with an uncertainty about the working mechanisms of the Union and a common notion in Asia that the EU is a difficult partner to negotiate with. This analysis resulted in the conclusion that the EU would have to raise interest in and knowledge of the Union and to show the Asian countries the European will and ability to contribute to the "peaceful development and stability of the region" (Towards a New Asia Strategy 1994: 10).

Thus the Commission suggested taking the relationship to a further level by getting away from merely discussing regional and global matters and substantiating it more through a higher degree of operationalisation. The idea was to prepare certain subjects for the various conferences, get results and transmit them to the next conference. A certain lack of direction was also detected in the relationship with ARF as the communication stated: "The Union must (…) develop ways for making its own particular contribution to the discussion of such matters" (Towards a New Asia Strategy 1994: 11). As "subjects for political discussion" the Commission proposed: arms control and non-proliferation, human rights and drugs. Special importance was attached to these three fields because of their impact on European interests. Given the fact of ASEAN's rising financial potential, various conflicts between the region's countries and a lack of multilateral organisations the danger of negative consequences on international relations loomed large. Human rights are a cornerstone of the Union and it supports all endeavours to raise their acceptance. The importance of human rights was not stressed only because of humanistic convictions but because of the insight that human rights lead to human development. A sound economic environment is a precondition for the existence of a civil society which is not devisable without human rights. The Union wanted to support reforms in this sector through technical training, scholarships, seminars and visits. The third field was the fight against drug trafficking – the greatest challenges in that respect are not the fatal consequences of drug abuse for the consumers' health but the devastating effects of organized drug crime on states and societies in Europe and Asia. Therefore the Commission deemed it as important that the EU requires the Asian states to do their best to counter drug trade and production. All EU strategies for the realisation of these objectives were directed at singular states and also regional groupings like ASEAN. ASEAN was called the "cornerstone of its (the EU, G. Brettner-Messler) dialogue with the region" (Towards a New Asia Strategy 1994: 19).

The 11th Ministerial Meeting that took place the same year, 1994, in Karlsruhe (Germany) reinforced the content of this Communication regarding ASEAN. It was seen as a significant step in promoting the EU-ASEAN relationship. An "ad hoc and informal eminent persons group" from both regions was created whose mission would be to contribute to the advancement of EU-ASEAN relations. According to the Joint Declaration of the Meeting "the ministers agreed that increased EU-ASEAN cooperation is a central element in relations between Europe and the Asia-Pacific region." It was stressed that the ASEAN and the EU had gained relevance and that both wanted to follow the successful path further down. The ASEAN ministers hoped that the Maastricht Treaty which had come into force in November 1993 and transformed the European Communities in the European Union would have a positive impact on ASEAN economies. The document also backed the promotion of disarmament and non-proliferation, reinforcement of the UN system and human rights (Joint Declaration 1994: 3, 4, 19, 22, 24, 25). But in contradiction to such declarations, the subjects of human rights and democracy caused frictions between the EU and ASEAN. ASEAN countries saw European insistence on democratisation and human rights as interference in inner affairs and rejected it strongly. Political relations weakened therefore but this trend had no impact on the economy. Controversial topics were excluded from conferences because Europeans did not want to be excluded from the booming Asian markets (de Flers 2010: 3-5).

In 1996 the Asia-Europe Meetings (ASEM) started. ASEM was an initiative by ASEAN and brings together the EU member states, the European Commission, the member states of ASEAN, the ASEAN Secretariat as well as Australia, China, India, Japan, (Republic of) Korea, Mongolia, New Zealand, Pakistan and Russia. Its informality is both its strength and its weakness. Here any topic can be discussed between heads of states and government, ministers and senior officials but also from people to people in an informal and unstructured manner. The ASEM Summit, i.e. the conference of the head of states/governments, the President of the European Commission and other top officials, takes place biannually. In the years in between, the foreign ministers hold their meetings. The economic ministers likewise convene every two years and the ministers of finance, environment, education and culture also hold separate meetings. The Asia-Europe Business Forum was established as a platform for business leaders of ASEM participants. ASEM command only one institution, the Asia-Europe Foundation for promoting intellectual, people-to-people and cultural contacts and there exist some cooperation programmes like the Trans-Eurasia Information Network for research and education communities across the Asia-Pacific. Beside the regular conferences, ministerial meetings on various topics like science and technology, migration and environment take place.

ASEM consists of three pillars: the political, the economic and the social, cultural and educational pillar. The political pillar chiefly comprises security policy, i.e. international crisis, security, multilateralism. Regional developments can be discussed as well as terrorism, proliferation, migration or human rights. Political dialogue is a key element of the ASEM process. On its homepage ASEM calls itself a "policy-making laboratory". So ASEM's role is not mainly about outcome but presentation of viewpoints, perspectives and intentions of all participants thus making it easier to find common ways and solutions for whatever problem when discussed later in the appropriate forum (ASEM InfoBoard; Communication 1996: 8).

1996 the Commission published a new Communication, this time focused on EU-ASEAN relations. *Creating a New Dynamic in EU-ASEAN relations* was intended as part of a "concerted effort" to strengthen the ties between both organisations. ASEAN was to take the position of a transmission belt for European interests in Asia. Particular importance was also assigned to ARF because the wide circle of its members set the best precondition for fulfilling a central function: stability and peace in Asia. The Commission proposed a stronger European engagement vis-à-vis the ASEAN states in order to make Europe more visible and perceivable in Asia. It felt that the lack of vision and a strong political impetus blocked the further development of relations. Since ASEM has started, the Commission has wanted more activities on the EU-ASEAN level. ASEM should function as a basis from where projects for a deepened EU-ASEAN cooperation could take off. The Commission underpinned the common features of EU and ASEAN: the tendency of regional integration, their contribution to regional peace and security and the planned admission of members in a process of political and economic change (the paper referred to Cambodia, Laos and Myanmar). This opened ample room for the exchange of experiences and knowledge for a better handling of a shifting political environment (Communication 1996: 1-11).

A permanent point of contention between the EU and ASEAN is Myanmar (Burma). In stark contrast to all commitments to democracy and human rights by both organisations, the Burmese government has constantly violated the rights of its citizens for many years. The country has been controlled by the military since 1962. Political dissent was quelled with violence, oppression, arbitrary detentions and censorship of the media. Reforms were rejected by the opposition as mere window dressing. Aung San Suu Kyi, who is the heart of the opposition, was awarded the Nobel Peace Prize in 1991. However allegations against the military go beyond the political sphere. Involvement in the prolific drug trade and the use of forced labour, including children, are the most abominable (BBC, Burma country profile, Profile: Aung San Suu Kyi). In 1997 the Europeans suspended the Ministerial Meetings as a protest against the admission of Burma to ASEAN. Three years later this course was changed and relations to ASEAN and Burma were separated from each other. EU sanctions against Burma were issued in 1996 and renewed several times (Council Common Positions). Over the years the position of ASEAN vis-à-vis Burma shifted from strict non-interference to mild pressure for reforms. This modification was partly due to external pressure and partly to the rising conviction that Burmese intransigence has negative repercussions on ASEAN itself because it adds to a negative image of ASEAN and so jeopardises regional integration (de Flers 2010: 7-8). The 18th ASEAN-EU Ministerial Meeting in May 2010 took on the cause. Both sides supported the establishment of a civil government and called on the Burmese government to ensure fair elections (the National League for Democracy, the largest opposition party, boycotted the November 2010 elections on the grounds of flawed party registrations and election laws). Nevertheless both sides agreed to respect sovereignty and territorial integrity of Burma – a clear hint to the limitations of a common effort to enforce reforms (18th ASEAN-EU Ministerial Meeting 2010; US Department of State, Background Note: Burma). In 2011 a reform process has been started by the Burmese government which raised hopes for a lasting improvement of the political and economic situation. Political prisoners were released, provisions against forced labour enacted, a peace process with the ethnic minorities has been introduced – and already resulted in a ceasefire with the Karen – and the rights of assembly and association are heeded now by the government to a previously unthinkable extent. Aung San Suu Kyi and other activists of the opposition were elected to the parliament in by-elections in the end of March 2012. In recognition of these positive developments and to encourage the government in its endeavours, the Council of the EU decided to suspend the sanctions against Burma (with exception of the arms embargo) in April 2012 (Council conclusions on Burma/Myanmar).

In 2003 the European Commission issued the Communication *A New Partnership with South-East Asia*. The Commission was led by the perception that international problems can only be addressed by international cooperation and that ASEAN countries are gaining more and more economic relevance. Furthermore the integration of the region and its diversity was seen as a common feature with the equally diverse EU that boded well for deepened cooperation, even if the situation in Burma is in stark contrast to the European notion of conducting a state's affairs. Six strategic priorities are listed in this Communication: regional stability and the fight against terrorism; human rights, democratic principles and good governance; justice and home affairs issues; regional trade and investment relations; development of less prosperous countries; dialogue and cooperation in specific strategic sectors. The desire for a rejuvenation of the relationship is rooted in the changed international environment since 09/11. Islamistic terrorists also hit South-East Asia. 202 people were killed in a bomb attack on a nightclub district in Bali in October 2002. In 2003 and 2004 two bomb attacks in Jakarta cost the lives of 12 and 11 people (Bali bombings timeline).

Stability in South-East Asia became a concern for Europe and paying attention to the region was a necessity in Europe's own interest. As a result of *A New Partnership with South-East Asia,* the Trans-Regional EU-ASEAN Trade Initiative (TREATI) was started. Trade between the EU and ASEAN had reached such an extent that such consideration was necessary. The EU was the second largest export market for ASEAN and the third largest market in 2004. To facilitate trade and investment to an even larger extent TREATI provided for consultation and regulatory cooperation (Trans-Regional EU-ASEAN Trade Initiative).

In March 2007, 30 years after starting their cooperation the EU and ASEAN signed the *Nuremberg Declaration on an EU-ASEAN Enhanced Partnership*. It reflected the long way both signatories had gone from a more loose cooperation to a comprehensive partnership. The preamble contains a commitment to regional integration "as a contribution to addressing regional and global security challenges" (Nuremberg Declaration 2007: 1). Trade and the economy add to the broader end of overcoming obstacles in international relations through integration in a way Europe has experienced since World War II. If such development is stable and permanent, a sound environment in regional and international relations is indispensable. The document underlines the role of ASEAN Regional Forum as "the main forum for regional dialogue and cooperation on political and security issues in the Asia Pacific" (Nuremberg Declaration 2007: 2) and presents the Aceh Monitoring Mission as an example for practical cooperation on the ground. Human rights and democratic values are accepted as the foundation of peace and stability.

The relevance of ASEAN for the EU lies in its integrative function for South-East Asia. Therefore it was very import for the EU to include a declaration of support for the realisation of the ASEAN Community in the agreement. In this context the EU serves as a blueprint for ASEAN and the "exchange of information and experience" (Nuremberg Declaration 2007: 2) between the EU and ASEAN has an important function in the creation of such a community. Because the EU-ASEAN relations had reached a state of high complexity, the Declaration lists only a few areas of cooperation without claiming to be complete.

The first area covers "Political and Security Cooperation". ASEAN and the EU commit themselves to internal and external cooperation to foster international peace and security. Security is conceived as a comprehensive concept – it has a political, human, social and economic dimension. Both partners want to counter a range of security challenges: terrorism, trafficking in human beings, drug trafficking, sea piracy, arms smuggling, money laundering, cyber-crime and related trans-national crime. Cooperation also extends to "disarmament, arms control and non-proliferation of weapons of mass destruction and their means of delivery". ASEAN and the EU pledge their allegiance to the existing disarmament and non-proliferation treaties and related accords.

The second area relates to "Economic Cooperation". Regional economic cooperation shall take place with TREATI as the basis. The conclusion of a Free Trade Agreement is envisaged (negotiations were stopped in 2009 (EU forciert Beziehungen)) as well as further integration through the ASEAN Economic Community. A logical consequence of these intentions is the strengthening of cooperation in multilateral frameworks like the World Trade Organisation and ASEM.

The third area addresses exclusively one of the big challenges of today's world: energy security and climate change/environment. Energy security, sustainable energy and multilateral measures for stable, effective and transparent global energy markets shall be reached through an EU-ASEAN policy dialogue. Renewable energy and energy efficiency shall be promoted to ensure energy security. EU and ASEAN commit themselves to the implementation of the UN Frame Convention on Climate Change and the Kyoto Protocol. Reduction of greenhouse gases, environmental conservation and protection, sustainable development and natural resources management, biodiversity and transboundary environmental control and management are additional measures ASEAN and the EU agreed on. They want to pave the way for negotiations on a global climate regime after 2012.

The fourth area is socio-cultural cooperation. Cooperation apart from trade and economy shall take place via the Regional EU-ASEAN Dialogue Instrument (READI). Achieving the Millennium Development Goal, sustainable development, the fight against ailments like AIDS and SARS, cooperation in disaster management, people-to-people contacts, interfaith dialogue and cultural exchange are elements of this chapter. The fifth area covers development cooperation to support the building of the ASEAN Community through various programmes (Nuremberg Declaration 2007: 3-6).

Eight months after the Declaration, in November 2007, a *Plan of Action to Implement the Nuremberg Declaration* was agreed. This plan has become the "master plan" for development of the relations between ASEAN and the EU till 2012. Both parties pledge continuing biennial ASEAN-EU Ministerial Meetings and the annual ASEAN Post Ministerial Conference with the EU (PMC +1). In years without a ministerial meeting, a senior officials' meeting shall take place. Cooperation and consultation in multilateral fora shall be developed – the United Nations and the Asia-Europe Meeting are named as such. Reinforcing ARF is an important goal of the plan. Seminars on human rights and seminars on confidence building measures and preventive diplomacy and a closer "dialogue and cooperation in crisis management in the form of knowledge transfer and exchange of best practices in civilian crisis management, building on the successful cooperation in the Aceh Monitoring Mission (AMM)" (Plan of Action 2007: 2) are concrete steps to a better adjustment of Europe and Asia in security cooperation. The participation of women in conflict prevention has proved to be a necessity the parties emphasize. A range of provisions for counter-terrorism and the fight against transnational crime is included in the plan. Some of those provisions contain merely the intention to implement already concluded agreements like the *ASEAN-EU Joint Declaration on Cooperation to Combat Terrorism*, the *ASEAN Convention on Counter Terrorism* and the *UN Global Counter Terrorism Strategy*. On a working level the *ASEAN Senior Officials Meeting on Transnational Crime (SOMTC) Plus EU Consultation* shall meet when necessary and related workshops shall take place. In addition to the aforementioned senior officials meeting, a ministerial meeting for the same purpose is planned. Linking ASEAN and EU law enforcement agencies to share experiences and best practice will be encouraged. Already existing engagement against human trafficking by ASEAN shall be supported and cooperation on the basis of relevant regulations like the *ASEAN Declaration against Trafficking in Persons particularly Women and Children* intensified. Both parties commit themselves to implementing treaties, conventions and instruments on arms control and non-proliferation. Dialogue, consultation, personal exchange and exchange of information in the combat against illegal drugs shall be encouraged. The EU will cooperate on effective national export control systems including through the EU export controls programme. The struggle against the dispersion of small arms, light weapons and anti-personnel mines is also part of the agenda. Assistance by the EU is especially required in technical assistance and through cooperation in information sharing, law enforcement, institutional capacity and legislative framework building with respect to countering all forms of transnational crime. The development of regional capacities for the prevention of illegal money transfers and the promotion of international standards to combat money laundering and terrorist financing complete the common endeavours in this field.

Likewise reflected in this plan is the comprehensive approach to security which also covers security related challenges outside the traditional canon.

Disaster management and emergency response require broad international cooperation. Risk reduction and management at regional and global level shall be advanced. To establish a regional emergency standby arrangement, the EU shall share its knowledge of disaster management. After the tsunami catastrophe of 2004 in which 230,000 people died, thousands of Europeans, the EU and its members pledged more than 2 billion Euros in disaster relief. Together with Sri Lanka and the Maldives, Indonesia was the biggest recipient of help (Post-Tsunami reconstruction). To ensure a proper reaction in the future, a national and regional network on information sharing and early warning systems shall be supported. The *ASEAN Agreement on Disaster Management and Emergency (AADMER)* and the *ASEAN Coordinating Centre for Humanitarian Assistance on Disaster Management (AHA Centre)* are two assets for ensuring a better preparedness in future catastrophes. Ensuring energy security is a part of the Economic Cooperation that shall guarantee the energy supply through functioning markets. Also related to security is the provision on transport which states that security and safety have to be brought in line with growing air traffic (Plan of Action 2007: 9, 13).

To further the intentions of the ASEAN Charter and the "Roadmap for ASEAN Community", the *Phnom Penh Agenda for the Implementation of the ASEAN-EU Plan of Action (2009-2010)* was agreed in May 2009. Priority in the relationship between the EU and ASEAN for these two years lay in supporting the implementation of the ASEAN Charter. So the input came chiefly from one side. The EU set the directions, while ASEAN followed. The activities listed include the possible participation in ESDP operations, sharing experiences of the EU in civilian capability planning and development, exchanges amongst officials and institutions in order to advocate European principles like human rights, rule of law and democracy. Border management and document security as well as non-proliferation and disarmament are also fields on which Europeans have rich experiences.

Other subjects concern the EU and ASEAN in equal measure. According to the Action Plan two seminars were held on *Measures to Enhance Maritime Security* and *International Security Implications of Climate-Related Events and Trends* in 2009. Cyber security and counter-terrorism are also fields of mutual interest. The "Activities to be considered in the 2011-2012 period" highlight once again that the focus of cooperation rests on CFSP related matters. Eight fields are mentioned, three of them refer to foreign and security policy: maritime security, search and rescue, drug enforcement and participation of ASEAN members in ESDP operations (Phnom Pen Agenda 2009).

The 18th EU-ASEAN Ministerial Meeting in May 2010 provided the chance to consider EU-ASEAN relations and to identify new goals. The EU supports ASEAN as a driving factor of regional cooperation especially in its approach to fostering external relations and internal integration. The European side is interested in adding the defence sector as a field of cooperation. Human rights are another field of intensified dialogue, especially in connection with the establishment of the *ASEAN Intergovernmental Commission on Human Rights (AICHR)* and the *ASEAN Commission on the Promotion and Protection of the Rights of Women and Children (ACWC)*. ASEM is deemed an important tool for securing peace and stability by mutually enforcing the EU-ASEAN dialogue. With respect to countering terrorism there are still elements of the *Joint Declaration on Co-operation to Combat International Terrorism* to implement. The review of ongoing cooperation indicated that for the years 2007-2013 the EU pledged 70 million euro to ASEAN and 1.3 billion euro to single member states. The ASEAN ministers asked their counterparts for support in ASEAN's ambitions for advanced regional integration. It was noted that the implementation of the *Regional EU-ASEAN Dialogue Instrument (READI)* for cooperation in non-trade areas is moving forward very well. A very important project under this instrument was the agreement by the ASEAN states to develop national laws against cyber-crime. Dialogues were launched in fields like information society, climate change, energy, science and technology and recently on disaster preparedness. The European initiative for a Chemical, Biological, Radiological and Nuclear (CBRN) Centre of Excellence in South-East Asia aims at countering the traffic of such materials. To bolster the struggle against non-traditional threats the EU supports ASEAN through the EU-ASEAN Migration and Border Management Programme which aims at a better protection of borders. The ASEAN Secretariat and the European Commission Humanitarian Office (ECHO) have intensified their cooperation for betterment of disaster management and humanitarian assistance capabilities. With European support for the AADMER Work Programme 2010-2015 this undertaking will be stepped up further (18th ASEAN-EU Ministerial Meeting 2010; APRIS II).

The 8th Asia-Europe Meeting (ASEM) summit took place in September 2010 in Brussels and brought together 46 heads of state and government, the President of the European Council, the President of the European Commission and the Secretary-General of ASEAN. This conference covered a broad range of topics from regional to global issues, in particular the economy and development (MEMO/10/458). Under the headline of "global issues" a range of security related issues was discussed: Piracy in the Gulf of Somalia concerns all parties because it threatens the freedom and security of the seas and in this respect the trade between Europe and Asia. Terrorism and organized crime are security threats but also have impact on trade, development and intellectual property rights. Disaster prevention and disaster relief is a humanitarian demand but also one of development due to the negative effects of catastrophes on development goals. Human rights and democracy as constant matters of concern were also part of the agenda. Nuclear non-proliferation and disarmament loomed large at the summit and the participants stressed their support for the NPT regime, the *Convention for the Suppression of Acts of Nuclear Terrorism*, the *Convention on the Physical Protection of Nuclear Material* and also for the *Comprehensive Nuclear Test Ban Treaty*. The reform of the UN system which is particularly directed at a better representation of developing countries and encouraging the dialogue of cultures and civilisations which serves as a tool for fostering peace and security through a better understanding of other cultures and religions are shared ambitions. In all those fields ASEM members rely mostly on other organisations and their activities, especially the United Nations, for the implementation of the various political objectives. Nevertheless there are some activities within ASEM itself. The fight against organized crime and illicit drug trade should be furthered through ASEM conferences in support of the *UN Global Counter-Terror Strategy*. Disaster prevention and relief requires increased cooperation between the ASEAN Secretariat and European Commission's Directorate-General on Humanitarian Aid & Civil Protection. Annual informal ASEM seminars on human rights are held on human rights and democracy. Various ASEM initiatives support the dialogue of cultures and civilisations (Asia-Europe Meeting 2010: 4-5).

Opportunities and Impediments for Cooperation

The structures of ASEAN are still very loose. The governments of the member states commit themselves in official documents to the realisation of ASEAN Community but "the governments, are, by and large, still grappling with the details of how they will implement the vision" (Constructive Engagement 2010: 3). Surin Pitsuwan, Secretary-General of the organisation, lamented that the Secretariat is mainly an organizing body for conferences and "has limited experience and expertise" (Constructive Engagement 2010: 4) on the ground. Only 260 persons are working there interacting mainly with the governments of the member states. The European Commission in comparison has 25,000 employees. ASEAN's operational budget is only 14 Million US dollars. Foreign contributions to build the ASEAN Community exceed those of the ASEAN governments. Most of ASEAN policies are a result of intergovernmental work; the private sector and NGOs are on the sidelines. The intention of the Secretary-General is to involve them and make them a driving force of South-East Asia's integration, for which the EU is a blueprint. Article 11 of the Treaty on the EU stipulates coordination and dialogue with the civil society. The European Economic and Social Committee and the Committee of the Regions act as voices of civil society. Much better

EU funding regulations in comparison to ASEAN allow the financing of various projects and organisations of the private sector (Constructive Engagement 2010: 4; EU-Beamte haben 2011 zwei Monate lang frei).

Despite all endeavours to overcome conflicts between ASEAN members, a decade long conflict between Cambodia and Thailand over the surroundings of an ancient Hindu temple escalated in February 2011. In stern contradiction to ASEAN principles the armies of these states exchanged fire. Secretary-General Pitsuwan characterized the events dully when he said that they are undermining the confidence in ASEAN. To restore confidence Pitsuwan intervened with both governments and suggested the support of ASEAN in brokering a peaceful solution. He feared that the conflict could have negative consequences on the economic development of the region. Indonesia tried to broker a temporary accord between the conflicting parties as a prerequisite for bilateral negotiations. ASEAN takes a rather cautious stance in the whole matter and a solution to the conflict lies primarily in the hands of the two states (Surin to Thailand and Cambodia). Indonesia helped in finding a solution and declared its willingness to send observers to the border zone to forestall new armed clashes. The Aceh Monitoring Mission served as a model for Indonesia's own observers (ASEAN Welcomes). Despite all efforts, the fights flared up again. Analysts warned that the conflict could become an obstacle for the realisation of the ASEAN Community (Thai, Cambodian Armies). In May 2011 Thailand and Cambodia accepted the offer (Cambodian, Thai border talks), but in April 2012 there were still no observers in the border region, even though a ceasefire was functioning (Cambodian, Thai disputed border situation).

The most significant undertaking in the field of security policy so far was the Aceh Monitoring Mission by the EU and some ASEAN member countries. The conflict in Aceh presented a permanent challenge for the integrity of conflict ridden Indonesia. Aceh has been a source of unrest since the independence of Indonesia. Root cause was the claim for autonomy by the political leaders of the province which was underpinned by the distinct Muslim orientation of its population. Neither autonomy nor a religious orientation of the new state was realized after Indonesia had gained independence. This resulted in political distance to Jakarta. In 1960 the exploitation of oil and gas in the province led to a further deterioration of the situation because nearly all profits flow out of Aceh. Finally the independence organisation Free Aceh Movement (FAM) started a guerrilla war against the government that resulted in the abolishment of the autonomy status and the declaration of the province as a military operation zone. A brutal civil war against the guerrilla movement and the population emerged (Heiduk 2004: 7-8).

The beginning of the peace process was marked by the Tsunami catastrophe in 2004. Aceh was among the hardest hit areas. This circumstance made it possible for all conflict parties to retreat from fixed positions without loosing face. Independence was given up as political aim and the government rescinded martial law. The compromises resulted in the Memorandum of Understanding by the Free Aceh Movement and the Indonesian government in August 2005 in Helsinki. The Aceh Monitoring Mission was launched in September 2005 and expired in December 2006. Its duty was to assist both former conflict parties in implementing the Memorandum and in this way to contribute to the peace process. In this context it has to be emphasized that its role was not an intermediating one. The EU and the ASEAN members Thailand, Singapore, Malaysia, Brunei and the Philippines together with Norway and Switzerland sent monitors to Aceh. At first the fighters of FAM were disarmed and parts of military and police forces redeployed. Political prisoners were released and together with former rebels had to be reintegrated into civil life. The protection of human rights was another important element of the peace process. For rapprochement in the long run, legislative measures decided upon in the agreement had to be implemented. The supervision of all this was entrusted to the Aceh Monitoring Mission (Aceh Monitoring Mission homepage). The Mission became a success, both conflict parties trusted in its impartiality. It also proved that the cooperation of two regional organisations can substantially contribute to conflict solution, whereas the EU provided expertise as a distant partner and the ASEAN members as partners closely related to regional affairs.

Peace, stability and security have become an important part of EU-ASEAN cooperation. In conferences and meetings the representatives of both organisations attach great importance to these fundamental values. Nevertheless the opinions about the quintessential factors for peace and stability differ. Especially human and civic rights do not have the same importance in some ASEAN member states as in Europe.

ASEAN consists of democratic (Philippines, Indonesia), semi democratic (Thailand, Malaysia, Singapore, Cambodia) and authoritarian ruled (Vietnam, Laos, Myanmar, Brunei Darussalam) states. These political disparities put a strain on EU-ASEAN relations because they impede closer connections. But progress has been made in recent years: Today ASEAN commits itself to the same values as the EU: democracy, good governance, the rule of law, human rights and fundamental freedoms. "In this regard, ASEAN's charter marks a significant turn in the organisation's normative and institutional history" (Kuhonta 2010: 6). The establishment of the ASEAN Intergovernmental Commission on Human Rights was an important step in the direction of a common understanding of human rights.

Constructive cooperation is far more fruitful in fields where both organisations and its members share the same interests and the same level of ambition like disaster relief or non-proliferation. Most of EU-ASEAN cooperation takes place on the intergovernmental level; the ASEAN Secretariat and Presidency do not have negotiation mandates. This means a legal restriction for direct co-operation between the organisations. Intergovernmental meetings provide the chance for politicians and officials to learn about the positions and perceptions of the other side. All in all one could say the relations have achieved considerable progress, but rather weak results leave room for improvement.

References

Official Documents

18th ASEAN-EU Ministerial Meeting Co-Chair's Statement, Madrid, 26 May 2010, http://www.aseansec.org, (06.04.2011).

43rd AMM/PMC/17th ARF, VIETNAM 2010, Chairman's Statement, 17th ASEAN Regional Forum, 23 July 2010, Ha Noi, Viet Nam, http://www.aseansec.org, (27.06.2011).

Agreement on the Establishment of the ASEAN Secretariat, Bali, 24 February 1976, http://www.aseansec.org, (08.02.2011).

ASEAN Declaration (Bangkok Declaration), 1967, http://www.aseansec.org, (07.02.2011).

Asia-Europe Meeting ASEM 8, Chair's Statement Of the Eighth Asia – Europe Meeting, Brussels, 4-5 October 2010, http://www.asem8.be, (01.06.2011).

Cebu Declaration on the Acceleration of the Establishment of an ASEAN Community by 2015, 2007, http://www.aseansec.org, (27.01.2011).

Charter of the Association of Southeast Asian Nations, 2007, http://www.aseansec.org, (14.02.2011).

Commission of the European Communities. Towards a New Asia Strategy. COM (94) 314 final, 13 July 1994, http://www.aei.pitt.edu, (23.02.2011).

Communication from the Commission to the Council, the European Parliament and the Economic and Social Committee, Creating a New Dynamic in EU-ASEAN relations. COM (96) 314 final, 03.07.1996, http://www.aei.pitt.edu, (28.03.2011).

Cooperation Agreement between Member Countries of ASEAN and European Community. Kuala Lumpur, 7 March 1980, http://www.aseansec.org, (27.06.2011)

Council Common Position 2009/615/CFSP, 2009/351/CFSP, 2006/318/CFSP, 2005/340/CFSP, 2004/423/CFSP, 2003/297/CFSP, 2002/831/CFSP, 1996/635/CFSP, http://eur-lex.europa.eu, (28.06.2011).

Council of the European Union. Council conclusions on Burma/Myanmar. 3159th Foreign Affairs Council meeting, Luxembourg, 23 April 2012, http://www.consilium.europa.eu, (25.04.2012).

Declaration on Accession to the Treaty of Amity and Cooperation in Southeast Asia by the European Union and European Community, 2009, http://www.aseansec.org, (15.02. 2011).

Declaration: Downing Street Summit Conference London, England, May 8, 1977, http://www.g7.utoronto.ca, (16.02.2011).

Joint Declaration of the 11th ASEAN-EU Ministerial Meeting, Karlsruhe, Germany, 22-23 September 1994, http://aseansec.org, 5 04 2011

Joint Declaration The ASEAN-EC Ministerial Meeting, Brussels, 21 November 1978, http://www.aseansec.org, (15.02.2011).

Joint Statement on Political Issues, Kuala Lumpur, 8 March 1980, http://www.aseansec.org, (27.06.2011).

Joint Statement The Informal Meeting of ASEAN Ministers and Vice-President and Commissioner of the EC Commission Jakarta, 24-25 September 1974, http://www.aseansec.org, (24.01.2011).

New Zealand, House of Representatives, International treaty examination of the Third Protocol Amending the Treaty of Amity and Cooperation in Southeast Asia. Report of the Foreign Affairs, Defence and Trade Committee, 2010, http://www.parliament.nz, (21.01.2011).

Nuremberg Declaration on an EU-ASEAN Enhanced Partnership, 2007, http://www.eeas.europa.eu, (01.02.2011).

Phnom Penh Agenda for the Implementation of the ASEAN-EU Plan of Action (2009-2010), 2009, http://www.aseansec.org, (20.04.2011).

Plan of Action to Implement the Nuremberg Declaration on an EU-ASEAN Enhanced Partnership, 2007, http://www.aseansec.org, (31.03.2011).

Protocol Amending the Agreement of the Establishment of the ASEAN Secretariat Bandar Seri Begawan, 4 July 1989, http://www.aseansec.org, 07 02 2011

Protocol Amending the Agreement on the Establishment of the ASEAN Secretariat (Term-of-Duty of the Secretary General) Kuala Lumpur, 9 July 1985, http://www.aseansec.org, 27 06 2011

Protocol Amending The Agreement On The Establishment Of The ASEAN Secretariat Manila, Philippines, 22 July 1992, http://www.aseansec.org, 27 06 2011

Protocol on the extension of the Cooperation Agreement between the European Economic Community and Indonesia, Malaysia, the Philippines, Singapore and Thailand, member countries of the Association of the South-East Asian Nations, to Brunei-Darussalam, 1984, http://ec.europa.eu, 04 04 2011

Statement from the Paris Summit (19 to 21 October 1972), http://www.ena.lu, 24 01 2011

Treaty of Amity and Cooperation in Southeast Asia Indonesia, 24 February 1976, http://www.asean.org, 21 01 2011

Articles, Research Papers, Publications

APRIS II, Promoting Mutual Understanding Through Enhanced dialogue, APRIS Support for TREATI and READI, http://www.aseansec.org, 07 04 2011

ASEAN Secretariat, Constructive Engagement. Building a People Oriented Community, Jakarta 2010, http://www.asean.org, 01 06 2011

ASEAN Secretariat, Text of the Treaty of Amity and Cooperation in Southeast Asia and related Information, Jakarta 2005, http://www.asean.org, 01 06 2011

de Flers, Nicole Alecu, EU-ASEAN Relations: The Importance of Values, Norms and Culture, EU Centre in Singapore, Working Paper, No. 1, June 2010, http://aei.pitt.edu, (21.04.2011).

Forty Years of ASEAN. Can the European Union Be a Model for Asia? Talk by the Secretary General of ASEAN at the Konrad Adenauer Foundation, Berlin, 16 July, 2007, http://www.aseansec.org, (07.04.2011).

Hauser, Gunther, Rüstungskontrollpolitik – rechtliche Aspekte und politische Herausforderungen, in: Werner Freistetter, Christian Wagnsonner (publ.), Raketen – Weltraum – Ethik, Beiträge zum Seminar "Ethik im Weltraum", 14.-16. April 2009, Hiller Kaserne Linz-Ebelsberg, Wien 2010.

Heiduk, Felix, Der Aceh-Konflikt und seine Auswirkungen auf die Stabilität Indonesiens und Südostasiens, SWP-Studie, Berlin 2004, http://www.swp-berlin.org, (25.03.2011).

Institute of Southeast Asian Studies (publ.), ASEAN. A Bibliography, Singapore 1984.

Kuhonta, Erik Martinez, Is ASEAN's illiberal peace a stable equilibrium, Paper presented at the Conference on "Issues and Trends in Southeast Asia," Center for Southeast Asian Studies, University of Michigan, Ann Arbor, 22 October 2010, http://www.umich.edu, (27.06. 2011).

Rüland, Jürgen, ASEAN and the European Union: A Bumpy International Relationship, ZEI Discussion Paper C 95, 2001, http://www.zei.de, (24.03.2011).

Yeo, Lay Hwee, Political Cooperation Between the EU and ASEAN. Searching for a Long-Time Agenda and Joint Projects, in: Paul J. J. Welfens, Cillian Ryan, Suthiphand Chirathivat, Franz Knipping, EU – ASEAN Facing Economic Globalisation, Berlin, Heidelberg 2009

Press Releases

ASEAN and EU: Family Matters, Jakarta, 1 March 2011, http://www.aseansec.org, (07.04.2011).

ASEAN Welcomes Cambodian-Thai Firm Commitment to Avoid Further Clashes, http://www.aseansec.org, (22.02.2011).

ASEM Summit (4-5 October), EU-Republic of Korea Summit (6 October), EU-China Summit (6 October), MEMO/10/458, Brussels, 29 September 2010, http://europa.eu, (27.06.2011).

Bali bombings timeline, http://www.rediff.com, (01.02.2011).

BBC, Burma country profile, http://news.bbc.co.uk; Profile: Aung San Suu Kyi, (04.04. 2011).

Cambodian, Thai border talks make headway: Cambodian official, http://khmerisation. blogspot.com, (21.05.2011).

Cambodian, Thai disputed border situation much improving: ASEAN chief, http://news. xinhuanet.com, (05.04.2012).

EU-Beamte haben 2011 zwei Monate lang frei, http://www.diepresse.at, (31.3.2011).

EU forciert Beziehungen zum ASEAN bei Wirtschaftsministertreffen, IP/10/1073, Brüssel, 27. August 2010, http://www.europa.eu, (30.03.2011).

Joint Press Statement The First ASEAN-EC Joint Cooperation Committee Meeting, Manila, 28-29 November 1980, http://www.aseansec.org, (27.01.2011).

Post-Tsunami reconstruction: 2 years on, MEMO/06/507, Date: 20/12/2006, http://europa. eu, (24.02.2011).

Surin to Thailand and Cambodia: "Let ASEAN help mediate soonest.", ASEAN Secretariat, 5 February 2011, http://www.aseansec.org, (10.02.2011).

Thai, Cambodian armies agree to ceasefire, borders opened for trade, http://hken.ibtimes. com, (05.05.2011).

Internet presentations, Homepages

Aceh Monitorin Mission, http://www.aceh-mm.org, (25.03.2011).

ASEAN-European Union Dialogue, http://www.aseansec.org, (15.02.2011).

ASEAN-EU Programmememe for Regional Integration Support (APRIS) – Phase II, http://www.aseansec.org, (07.04.2011).

ASEAN Regional Forum, About us, http://www.aseanregionalforum.org, (08.02.2011).

ASEM InfoBoard, About ASEM (Overview, Achievements, Main Pillars), ASEM Ministerial Meetings, http://www.aseminfoboard.org (28.03.2011).

Australian Government, Department of Foreign Affairs and Trade, ASEAN Regional Forum (ARF), http://www.dfat.gov.au, (09.02.2011).

Greater Mekong Subregion Agricultural Information Network, Politics and Security of
    ASEAN--Achievements in Political Collaboration, http://www.gms-ain.org, (01.07.
    2011).
Delegation of the EU to Malaysia, The Trans-Regional EU-ASEAN Trade Initiative,
    http://www.delmys.ec.europa.eu, (31.01.2011).
U.S. Department of State, Background Note: Burma, http://www.state.gov, (06.04.2011).

The Mediterranean Dialogue

Michele Brunelli

1. The Mediterranean Sea. "A machine producing civilisation"

The Mediterranean Sea is a liquid space which represented and still represents a clash/encounter environment for two leading hegemonies in a north-south dimension. Despite the many attempts to create a dialogue between the two opposite shores, wars prevailed for many centuries. In ancient times, a first period of peace was possible because of the unique rule over the whole Mediterranean and started with the end of the largest wars that had ever taken place: the Punic wars, when the Roman Empire defeated and destroyed Carthage (146 BC), scattering mounds of salt on its ashes, as a sign of destruction, but also to prevent anything from ever growing.

For the following four centuries the Sea become the *Mare Nostrum*, (Our Sea), constituting one of Roman Empire's main points of strength and wealth, but also a formidable vehicle to spread Latin civilisation all around the world as then known.

Mare Nostrum remained the toponym indicating "the Sea in the middle of the lands", (*Medius,* "in the middle", *Terraneus*, from *Terra, ae*, "land") until the XI century, when the Mediterranean Sea moved its centre of gravity on the southern shore, when a new civilisation arrived from the east.

With the Muslim conquest of Northern Africa, the Mediterranean Sea regained its ancient splendour and the southern shore started giving back part of the culture it received during the previous centuries. Through the Mediterranean Sea, Islam had a major influence on philosophy, arts, literature and medicine all over Europe. Frederick II of the Holy Roman Empire, called *al-inbiratur*, (the emperor) by the Muslims, was educated by Arab preceptors, and he always showed a deep interest and admiration not for the religion, but for the Arab political and cultural systems. Alfonso X of Castile, through the institutionalisation of the *escuela de traductores de Toledo*, supported the translation of the Jewish and Arab books into Latin and then into Castilian, favouring the spread of Arab/Muslim knowledge in Europe. Among the many translated works, the *Libros del Saber de Astronomia* (The Books of the Wisdom of Astronomy, 1276-77), containing studies about the movement of the stars, about astronomical and astrological instruments and the measurement of time or the *Liber Schalae Macometi*,[1] together with the Sufi mystic Ibn 'Arabī which had a greater influence over Dante Alighieri's structural conception of Hell in his *Comedy*.[2] Besides culture, maritime trade experienced a new golden age. Goods were shipped from Alexandria to Bergen, from Bukhara and Samarkand through Baghdad to Rome, Genoa, Paris and London. Overseas trade was so important for the development of the many different forms of states established in Europe, persuading Pope Innocent III, the caller of the fourth and fifth crusade, to grant Venice a temporary license to trade with the Saracens, because Venice "is not devoted to agriculture but rather to shipping and to commerce"[3] and so it must not suffer because of the Saracens and the religious rivalries. Innocent III and IV tried of course to maintain the political, financial and military support Venice could give to Papacy. The license, with its permission, but also with limitations (the license, in fact, banned Venice from trading in "iron, flax, pitch, pointed stakes, ropes, arms, helmets, ships, and boards, or unfinished wood"), give us a good picture of the political strain characterising the Mediterranean in that age. A state of good economic relations counterbalanced by tension and hostility among cultures, and therefore nations, which was described in the XVI century by the Spanish writer Don Juan Manuel (1282-1348) as a *guerra fria*, a cold war.

The Mediterranean turned into a *limes* between Christianity and Islamism and its main point of clash/encounter became the Ottoman Empire, until the XIX and the XX century, when its fall represented the "the last gasp of the extraordinary power of international Islam, and since then, Islam always tried to recreate its past greatness, but without success" (Fuller, Lesser, 1995).[4] The French Revolution, together with the ideological impact of its teaching, the European culture and in particular the spread of, first, Enlightenment and then Romanticism (as for political independence), the industrial and so the

---

1   It is an eighth-century Arabic text, translated into Castilian by Abraham Alfaquì, a translator, compiler and *capitulador*, at the court of Alfonso X the Wise, between 1264 and 1277. The book was then translated into Latin and French by Bonaventura of Siena. The journey of the prophet is fulfilled with the help of the Gabriel the archangel. Chapter 54 of the book describes the passage to hell, which lasts up to Ch. 79, when Muhammad receives the mandate to tell the people what he saw, so they can be saved from eternal damnation.

2   For the influence Islam had over Dante's thought, see Miguél Asin Palacios, *La Escatologia Musulmana en la Divina Comedia*, Impr. de E. Maestre, Madrid, 1919 and Enrico Cerulli, *Il «Libro della Scala» e la questione delle fonti arabo-spagnole della «Divina Commedia»*, Biblioteca Apostolica Vaticana, Città del Vaticano, 1949.

3   For the text in English see: Roy C. Cave & Herbert H. Coulson, *A Source Book for Medieval Economic History*, Milwaukee: The Bruce Publishing Co., 1936; reprint ed., New York: Biblo & Tannen, 1965, pp. 104-105. For the original text in Latin, see: Giulio Cipollone, *Cristianità – Islam cattività e liberazione in nome di Dio*, Editrice Pontificia Università Gregoriana, Roma, 2003, p. 63.

4   Graham E Fuller, Ian O Lesser, *A Sense of Siege. The Geopolitics of Islam and the West*, Westview Press, 1995, p. 28.

economic superiority showed by Europe, enhanced the role of the Mediterranean Sea as a new border, between colonizers and colonised people. Once more, Europe was giving its particular "cultural contribution" to the South Mediterranean, imposing a forced dialogue between two unbalanced civilisations.

If the main military goal of the French campaign in Egypt, in July 1798, was to undermine the British rule over the Mediterranean, cutting off the supply lines with India, from a broader point of view, the goal was to modernize the country. General Bonaparte, presenting himself to the Egyptians as the bearer of progress and enlightenment after the Battle of the Pyramids on July 21, 1798, issued a proclamation in Arabic, promising to liberate the country from foreign rule. He charged Joseph Fourier to publish a journal, *le Courrier de l'Egypte*, through which to report the military actions and the civilizer action of the expedition. L'*Institut d'Egypt* appeared a formidable tool promoting the European evolution and development in Egypt, trying to bring there all the goals attained by Enlightenment.

It is not a coincidence that, from the heritage left by the Bonaparte "cultural" campaign, a period of intellectual modernisation and reform, known as *al-Nahda*,[5] characterised Egyptian society in the second half of the XIX century. It was a real "awakening", as *al-Nahda* means. And the Egyptian awakening became a cultural archetype for the whole region, especially for the many different people living in the Ottoman Empire. The *al-Nahda* led to a new political dimension, passing over the "arabicity", moving into the universality. So Jamal al-Din al-Afghani (1838-97) was not only addressing the Egyptians, but all the "people of the Orient", and his innovative political thought had the pretension to build a new social and political order in the Arab-Islamic world. He also rejected the prevalent notion that Europeans were somehow innately superior to Muslims, but he accepted the validity of a scientific worldview: "the Islamic religion is the closest of religions to science and knowledge, and there is non incompatibility between science and knowledge and the foundation of the Islamic faith" (Keddie, 1983).

Rifa al-Tahtawi (1801-1874), another Arab reformist, brought Montesquieu principles into the Middle East political debate, underlying the importance of "nationalism". During the Egyptian awakening some new terms like *watan* ("homeland"/"nation"), *Hurriyya*, freedom (from *hurr*, "free") started to be introduced in the Arab political lexicon and through the elaboration of these two notions, came the development of Arab nationalism. He supported the formation of a national army, considered more than a military organisation, but a real school of nationalism. He was convinced that the

---

5   The term derives from the Arabic root *n-h-d*, which means "to rise, to wake up", in an active perspective and it indicates the renaissance of the literature and more in general of the Arabic thought, under the Western influence.

citizenship bonds were not religious in nature, but the cornerstones of the nation had to be the language, the territory, the morals, the traditions and the political education,[6] a discourse very close to the political debate which characterised Europe in the XVIII and XIX centuries.

2. Dialogue or Monologue?

An almost equal relationship between Europe and Middle East/Southern Mediterranean national states, only emerged more than a century later, at the beginning of the 1970s, since for such a dialogue there needs to be equality. In fact, after the First and the Second World Wars and the enormous bloody tribute their people gave, Europe accorded Near and Middle East states the right to be independent.

1973 was a year marking a meaningful development in the Western-Middle Eastern countries' relations. In that year, two main events occurred, leaving a deep legacy in contemporary history: the Yom Kippur War and the consequent oil crisis. The US decision to re-supply the Israeli army after the war, pushed the Arab oil-producing countries to proclaim an oil embargo aimed at pressuring the Western countries, specifically the US, into demanding the Israeli withdrawal from the Arab territories occupied since 1967. Within a few months, the price of oil climbed from around 10 to 40 US dollars a barrel.[7] It was a huge increase and the impact on the global economy was devastating. From a strategic point of view, Arab countries realized the strong influence that they had on the world through oil and that embargo could be used for economic means. Once they had resumed shipments of oil, they were able to keep the prices high and make a larger profit. Having gained a new international political weight, Arab countries were now taken into a deeper political consideration.

The nine countries composing the then European Economic Community (EEC) launched the first Euro-Arab dialogue during the Copenhagen Summit. The summit was organised on the demand of French President Georges Pompidou, who was trying to reaffirm France as a driving force not only for Europe, relaunching the European integration process "by taking advantage of the challenges raised by the new situation in the oil domain" (Beltran, 2010), but also a more active role of the nine in the Middle East policymaking. This was because the Kippur war had underlined, again, the in-

---

6   For a complete panorama on al-Tahtawi thought, see Rafa al-Tahtawi, *al-A'mal al-kamila*, M. 'Imarah, (Ed.) Markaz dirasat al-wahda al-'arabiyya, Beirut 1973.

7   Crude oil prices at 2008 US dollars. At current prices, in 1972, crude oil was about $3.00 per barrel. By the end of 1974, the price quadrupled to over $12.00. See: http://www.wtrg.com/prices.htm, consulted October 2nd, 2011.

consistency of the EEC in the Middle East policy and the minor weight it had in the conflict resolution. War ended thanks to the active engagement of the two superpowers, and to the Brezhnev-Kissinger talks on October 20th (Kumaraswamy, 2000) establishing the cease-fire called for in the UN Security Council Resolution 338. The French vision was manifestly and ruefully expressed by Michel Jobert, the Minister of Foreign Affairs, who stressed the complete inconsistency or a real European role towards the region. Jobert stated: "Traitée comme une «non-personne», humiliée dans son inexistence, l'Europe, dans sa dépendance énergétique, n'en est pas moins l'objet du deuxième combat de cette guerre du Proche-Orient" (Rucz, 1978).

On the basis of the successful memorandum which France signed a few weeks before (November 1973) with Saudi Arabia, President Pompidou succeeded in transforming the French policy towards the Middle East into a European policy, as the results of the Copenhagen Summit showed. For the first time, Europe – through France – expressed the idea of establishing a sacred union of partners so as to the initiate a Euro-Arab dialogue.

This was also because, after the first major oil shock, Arabs had a different political weight and in 1973, during the Summit, the EEC stated that:

> "The Community will implement its undertakings towards the Mediterranean and African countries in order to reinforce its long-standing links with these Countries. The Nine intend to preserve their historic links with the countries of the Middle East and to cooperate over the establishment and maintenance of peace, stability, and progress in the region".[8]

This was an important step not only for the dialogue, but especially in drawing a new role for EEC influence in the area.

Through the Copenhagen Summit, the EEC also adopted a common declaration fixing the Community's position towards the Arab-Israel conflict, trying to recover a new active role. The text dissipated any ambiguity of the resolution 242, asking the withdrawal of the Israeli army from "all the occupied territories", and reaffirmed that:

> "security of all states in the area, whether it be Israel or her Arab neighbours, can only be based on the full implementation of Security Council Resolution 242 in all its parts taking into account also the legitimate rights of the Palestinians (point 6)".

On these premises, the EEC reasserted the inadmissibility of territorial acquisition by force, the withdrawal of Israeli armed forces from territories occupied during the conflicts and the inclusion of the legitimate rights of the Palestinians in the peace process definition.

---

8   EEC, Meetings of the Heads of State or Government (Summit), Copenhagen, 14-15 December 1973, http://aei.pitt.edu/1439/1/copenhagen_1973.pdf

In a broader view, Europe was trying to introduce in its international relations system a new dimension of exchanges with the southern Mediterranean, but the premises, as history will show, were wrong. Once again Europe based its new strategy exclusively on its own interests, ignoring the single national interest of the southern Mediterranean countries. The goals were too different. Europeans were interested in the economic issues, especially after the oil shocks having damaged the western economies and hampered development. On the other hand, Arabs were more sensitive over the political issue, due to the high regional instability and insecurity, which led to four major conflicts in 25 years.

If the Copenhagen summit represented a first important step of a new dimension of the relations within the Mediterranean, the fundamental difference in the aims and attitudes reduced the efforts, and thereby the results, transforming dialogue into monologues.

Until the end of the 1980s, the Cold War got the upper hand in the EU policymaking and in the single international interest of each member, but after November 9, 1989 something changed. Before the formal implosion of the Soviet Union, new eastern European states regained their full sovereignty and became independent actors of the international relations context. This provoked great enthusiasm in the western government, but also a deep concern, with respect to risks and challenges emanating from the Southern and Eastern Mediterranean. The region, as many others, was now no more subdued in an "inactive" context generated by the Cold War, but there were now new actors, with their own national interests, strategies, policies and willingness to be active players. After 50 years of a frozen conflict, history seemed to set off again.

Ideological holes and new geopolitical and economic opportunities pushed Western countries to act and to profit from the "new world order" created with the fall of the USSR.

If Central and Eastern Europe did not pose any military threats, but in fact represented a potential enhancement of the Western defence system, with the NATO enlargement process, new states could represent a multi-dimensional/ structural (political, economic, social) and environmental risk for the EU's security.

However, the Iraq-Kuwait war, the Somali civil war, and first intifada (1987-1993) as a part of the long-lasting Arab-Israeli conflict, transformed the Bush's "new world order" into a "new world disorder", pushing western countries to be more and more engaged on the military side and the European Union to elaborate its own security doctrine. Eastern and southern flanks represented at the same time a source of instability, but also of wealth.

The EU started to see the need to render more secure and stable its neighbouring areas, so the importance of the Mediterranean area for the EU increased significantly. Rising regional political conflicts, once managed within the East-West confrontation, and socioeconomic problems, such as increasing unemployment and illiteracy rates, previously only considered a single national problem, now required a collective solution by those political actors more exposed to these potential threats. But this new strategy seemed to be limitedly addressed, from a geographical and from a substantial point of view. The need to establish, peace and development to reach human security and thus regional stability, for the sake of the EU's own security interests, entered into the political discourse only in the mid 1990's, with the UN Human Development Report on "new dimensions of human security". The geopolitical configuration of the dialogue radically changed, compared to the 1970's dialogue attempt. States of the Arab peninsula, together with Iraq, were now excluded, likewise some peripheral Arab states, such as Mauritania, Sudan and Somalia. This was because all these states have since been included in the US national interest. The first set of states "must" reward US effort in freeing Kuwait and in protecting Gulf emirates and kingdoms from Saddam Hussein's hegemonic aspirations, even if "Desert Storm Operation" (1991) was led by an international coalition. The second set, and especially Somalia, was considered a new area of conflict between the US and UN, the first trying to impose its own policy over the organisation, the latter attempting to regain a pragmatic and active political role, after 50 years of limitation, if not immobilisation. New fronts of action were opening and the US decreasing strategic interest in the Eastern Mediterranean, and the consequent growing interest for the Persian Gulf and Central Asia, together with the end of the Soviet support of Arab states, left the EU to act quite freely in a new Mediterranean neighbouring security policy.

The Enlarged Dialogue. The Mediterranean Dimension of the North Atlantic Organisation

Together with the EU, another supranational organisation started to put the accent on a dialogue dimension with the Mediterranean Sea: NATO. In 1994 the North Atlantic Council (NAC) decided to establish a specific partnership project for the region, aimed at linking NATO/European security with the security of the southern shores. As an integral part of NATO's adaptation to the post-Cold War security environment, the dialogue reflected (and still reflects) the Alliance's vision that security in Europe was closely linked to security and stability in the Mediterranean. The initiative initially involved seven non-NATO countries, such as Algeria, Egypt, Israel, Jordan, Mauritania, Morocco and Tunisia.

The dialogue was modelled in regard to some general principles which rendered the NATO initiative successful. These principles were:

- *Flexibility*, allowing the number of partners to grow, as the inclusion of Jordan (November 1995) and Algeria (March 2000) showed. The enlargement also contributed to extend the issues dealt with, and so the content of the dialogue itself;
- The possibility to organise meetings using a double model: *multilateral* (NATO+7) *and/or bilateral* (NATO+1), all on the regular basis;
- The principles of equality and non-discrimination, both of them considered essential features of the dialogue as a key to its successful establishment and subsequent development. Regarding *equality*, each participant was primus inter pares, erasing every or any presumed superiority, and each potential negative manipulation of the dialogue was avoided. With the *non-discriminatory* framework, countries were free to choose the extent and intensity of their participation (self-differentiation), including through the establishment of Individual Cooperation Programmes (ICP);[9]
- To complement the dialogue with other partnerships, whose object and objectives are related to the Mediterranean region. This would entail an enhanced cooperation with other supranational activities such as the Euro-Mediterranean Partnership and the Organisation for Security and Co-operation in Europe's Mediterranean Initiative (Partnership for the Mediterranean).

All these principles allowed the dialogue to develop towards different action lines and actively contributed to realizing a mutual confidence.

Ten years after the elaboration of the new Alliance's Strategic Concept, which placed the organisation in a post cold war context,[10] in June 2004, NATO elevated the Mediterranean dialogue to a genuine partnership. The process, known as the *Istanbul Cooperation Initiative*, aimed at "promoting essentially practical cooperation on a bilateral basis, with interested countries in the broader region of the Middle East, and opening to interested countries in the region which subscribe to the aim and content of this initiative, including the fight against terrorism and the proliferation of weapons of mass destruction. Each interested party, would be considered by the North Atlantic Council on a case-by-case basis and on its own merit".[11] The Initiative did not want to replace the dialogue, but enhance it, through the promotion of the bilateral cooperation with the Gulf Cooperation Countries (GCC), on a wide range of issues, such as defence, military-to-military cooperation, terrorism

---

9   The first ICP was established in October 2006, when Israel participated in the Active Endeavour Operation. See NATO Press Release http://www.nato.int/docu/pr/2006/p06-123e.htm, visited October 5th, 2011.

10 See: Summit Meeting in Washington, April 1999, http://www.nato.int/cps/en/natolive/official_texts_27433.htm, accessed, October 6th, 2011.

11 See: NATO Press Release http://www.nato.int/cps/en/natolive/topics_59419.htm, accessed, October 5th, 2011.

and the proliferation of Weapons of Mass Destruction (WMD), illicit trafficking and maritime cooperation.

From Helsinki to Budva: the Organisation for Security and Co-operation in Europe's Dialogue

Another intergovernmental organisation facing with the Mediterranean dialogue was the Organisation for Security and Co-operation in Europe (OSCE) which with the 1975 Helsinki Accords, declared its interest in cooperation with the Mediterranean Sea and in particular:

> "to promote the development of good-neighbourly relations with the non-participating Mediterranean States [...]; to increase mutual confidence, so as to promote security and stability in the Mediterranean area as a whole' [...]; to intensify their efforts and their co-operation on a bilateral and multilateral basis [...]directed towards the improvement of the environment of the Mediterranean..."[12]

These lines were reasserted in the 1990 Charter of Paris, in which the participating states maintained that they "will continue efforts to strengthen security and co-operation in the Mediterranean as an important factor for stability in Europe",[13] anticipating the ideas and the main concepts expressed later by NATO. However no meaningful progress has been made by OCSE in the dialogue and a renewed line of activity was launched in December 2003 when, during the OCSE Mediterranean Seminar held in Aqaba, the Organisation decided to involve new regional partners in the Mediterranean cooperation group.

Besides the number of potential participants, the Aqaba conference established the intensification of the dialogue aimed at translating the security in the Mediterranean region "into more concrete measures [...] through a comprehensive process of enhanced dialogue, economic co-operation and intercultural exchanges".[14] This was because "the need to address the new type of threats – originating from terrorism, organized crime, the existence of civic conflicts, xenophobia, racism, discrimination, illicit trafficking of human beings, of arms and drugs – unites the OSCE participating states and their partners from the Mediterranean".[15] Other seminars followed the Aqaba

---

12 See: Conference on Security on Co-operation in Europe, *Final Act*, Helsinki, 1975, http://www.osce.org/mc/39501, accessed, October 6th, 2011.

13 See: Conference on Security on Co-operation in Europe, *Charter of Paris for a new Europe*, Paris 1990, http://www.osce.org/mc/39516, accessed, October 6th, 2011.

14 See: *OSCE Press release*, OSCE's 2003 Mediterranean Seminar opens with calls for closer co-operation on security issues, http://www.osce.org/ec/55713, accessed October 9th, 2011.

15 See: *OSCE Press release*, ..., cit.

one, all characterised by the attempt to adapt the response to the multiple aspects of the threat. The instruments established during the 2008 Amman Seminar included the implementation of the international and trans-regional cooperation in fighting terrorism, through a multidisciplinary approach, which also entails the involvement of civil society, looking to a public-private partnership in order to enhance collaboration between state institutions and civil society, but also with the international organisations, such as the United Nations Office on Drugs and Crime (UNODC) and the Arab League, providing more than just a mere military approach.

The last Mediterranean Conference was held in Montenegro in October 2011,[16] and once again, it was an attempt to update the OSCE strategy to the new socio-political reality which started to characterise the southern Mediterranean since December 2010, with the so-called "Arab spring" or "Arab revolutions". In recognising the "structural lack of the desire for freedom" in the Arab world, OSCE states that it "cannot simply ignore what is happening in its neighbourhood [because] this would be foolish". An intervention must be realised, but "in engaging with Mediterranean partners, we have no ambition to 'teach' or 'lecture'. We would just seek to share with our partners what we have learned, and learn from them in return".[17] It is important to note the call for an indirect involvement, supporting the new potential regimes in elaborating their own path, presenting a successful experience (the western one), but not imposing it as a unique model.

3. The European Game: The Barcelona Process

As mentioned above, the changed strategic scenario, the new course of the US national interest and a revitalized European NATO members' strategy, allowed, if not favoured, the European Union to launch its own Mediterranean neighbouring security policy.

This was initially based on three strategic axes: i) establishing a Euro-Mediterranean framework based on cooperative security; ii) applying a multilateral relations framework with the aim of providing strength and cohesion to the Euro-Mediterranean area and iii) promoting domestic reforms in the Southern Mediterranean, in order to create an area of shared prosperity.

To be more precise, these three points promoted coordination and a regular consultation on political and security issues; an economic and financial

---

16   See: OSCE Summaries of seminars with Mediterranean Partners, http://www.osce.org/ec/66108, accessed June 1, 2012.

17   See: Address by Ambassador Janez Lenarčič, Director of the OSCE Office for Democratic Institutions and Human Rights (ODIHR) at the 2011 OSCE Mediterranean Partner Conference, http://www.osce.org/odihr/83890, accessed October 10th, 2011.

partnership which, in the long run, could entail a Mediterranean free-exchange area, but also a socio-cultural partnership addressed at enhancing the intercultural dialogue and common values.

This was a part of a broader strategy aimed at granting security and stability, in an era in which Europe was facing important territorial changes, with the first steps of an enlargement towards the north (Baltic States) and to the east, getting beyond the Iron Curtain. It was thus necessary to reach a new geopolitical equilibrium, and so the decision was taken to go south, to the heart of the Mediterranean.

These processes and strategies were embedded in the so-called "Barcelona Process", launched in November 1995 by the Ministers of Foreign Affairs of the then 15 EU members and 14 Mediterranean partners, as the framework to manage both bilateral and regional relations. On these premises a real dialogue with the two shores put on the same level was at last envisaged. Through the Barcelona Process, the Euro-Mediterranean Partnership wanted to link into the unique organisation of the whole Mediterranean region. According to the Declaration, this new strategy should represent the main tool for the Euro-Mediterranean relations, a strong instrument for promoting an "area of dialogue, exchange and cooperation guaranteeing peace, stability and prosperity".[18]

The development and the establishment (or the strengthening) of political, economic and social institutions were the main instruments chosen by the EU to foster a stable evolution of the area, and thus a real regional cohesion as was emerging in the 1950s. The EU tried to ensure a gradual convergence of the two shores of the Mediterranean Sea, around institutions capable of undertaking dialogue with each other, and able to manage the issues of public finance, a strong autonomy of the central banks, and a rigid monetary management. Once established or strengthened, the southern Mediterranean would have been able to implement some (Western driven and/or inspired) structural reforms.

These were all tools promoting and facilitating the establishment of a free trade area, the free movement of capital, but not of human beings. Even if from a theoretical point of view and according to the manifest policy of the Union, these instruments had created a convergence, which would have lead to an homogenisation of the unbalanced standards of living existing between the two shores, from a pragmatic point of view, it became clear that these instruments were fully to the advantage of the EU. In fact they wanted to create a market representing a fundamental support for EU goods. Furthermore, the

---

18 For the official text of the Barcelona Declaration, see: http://trade.ec.europa.eu/doclib/docs/2005/july/tradoc_124236.pdf, accessed, October 1, 2011.

EU tried to put immigration under its control, which was perceived (and still is) as a threat to the security and stability of the Union.

According to the Barcelona Process, the establishment of a peaceful Mediterranean also included the fulfilment of a cooperative security through the execution of a broader strategy, faced with two different levels of issues and so also goals.

The first level, easily shared with (and so potentially supported by) the US, because of its worldwide significance, envisaged fighting terrorism and the proliferation of weapons of mass destruction (WMD). A second level of issue was mainly concerned with European interests. In this case EU policy-makers established five main goals:

1. to counter illegal immigration, in order to hinder the recruitment capability of different terrorist groups operating in EU territory, but also to ease immigrants' pressure regarding the social fabric and the job market;
2. to control drug smuggling and illegal arms sales;
3. to protect the oil and gas routes, granting hydrocarbons supply to EU countries;
4. to solve disputes concerning fish resources;
5. to reduce the impact of environmental pollution.

The Process reached some positive results: it attained a certain degree of privatisation in the field of telecommunications; it brought to a stop a series of customs tariffs; it was successful in introducing VAT in different southern Mediterranean countries. But after the initial successes, mainly achieved in the economic and financial fields, the feeling of political failure began to emerge, and in fact the Process was unsuccessful.

Failure was due to several factors. Regional cohesion was not achieved. Some fundamental players involved in the Euro-Mediterranean Partnership were also entangled in some key regional conflicts: the Arab-Israeli conflict, the Israeli-Palestinian conflict and the Western Sahara struggle. They were all deeply convinced that cooperative security was not an effective tool to solve these conflicts and furthermore they were not disposed to accept the idea of shaping a joint Euro-Mediterranean security regime. This idea, together with a rooted idea of instability and insecurity, especially in Southern Lebanon, West Bank, Gaza Strip and Israel, also undermined the achievement of regional cohesion.

Political and, to a certain extent, economical reforms as well, were believed to be too European-oriented and so considered a pernicious interference in the sovereignty of the countries to which the reforms were addressed.

Another cause of the failure of the Euro-Mediterranean Partnership was probably the fact that it was attempting to link the whole Mediterranean region with a unique organisation, without taking into consideration the many peculiarities and differences of each partner. There are differences not only among the Southern countries, but among the EU members as well. Italy and France, for example always followed different paths in promoting the internal stabilisation and integration into the world economic system of those countries which represent a target for their own national interest, such as Morocco and Algeria in the case of France, Libya and Tunisia for Italy.

Italian interest in Tunisia was so deep that it induced the Italian Military Intelligence Service (SISMI) to organise a "constitutional *coup d'Etat*" replacing Habib Bourguiba with a new leader, Zine El-Abidine Ben Ali, in 1987.[19]

The widespread perception of the political failure, pushed the EU to create a new instrument of regional intervention, and in 2004 the European Neighbourhood Policy (ENP) was launched.

Through the ENP, the EU sought to reinforce relations with neighbouring countries, and to achieve its three main goals: prosperity, stability and security at its borders. The main difference with the previous strategies was the regional target. Together with the southern flank, the EU now also wanted to deal with the issues potentially coming from the East. The new countries involved were part of the Caucasus region (Armenia, Azerbaijan and Georgia), Belarus, Republic of Moldova and the Ukraine, the fundamental EU link supplying oil and gas. According to the new policy, the countries concerned could receive financial aid from the EU, on condition that they respected human rights and promoted political and economic reforms.

The ENP priority aim was mainly addressed at the economic and democratic development of the eastern flank, including the potential integration of the institutions of Eastern European countries in the EU framework agreements, to a certain extent neglecting the Mediterranean. How successful this policy was deemed, was affected by several factors: the chronic slowness of the institutional dynamics of the non-EU countries, the high level of corruption still present in some countries, which hampered a coherent and effective cooperation, together with the continuous difficulties in collaborating with the southern Mediterranean countries, already experienced in the past.

To a certain extent the new enlargement of the policy caused an enlargement of the issues, instead of an enlargement of potentialities and security.

---

19   According to the former head of the SISMI, Admiral Fulvio Martini, Bettino Craxi the then Prime Minister and Giulio Andreotti, the then Ministry of Foreign Affairs together with Franco Reviglio, the head of the Italian oil & gas Company ENI, "*in 1985-1987, organized a kind of coup d'Etat in Tunisia, putting president Ben Ali as head of state, replacing Burghuiba, who wanted to escape from the country*". See Commissione Parlamentare Stragi (Italian Parliamentary Commission), October 27, 1999, http://www.parlamento.it/service/ PDF/PDFServer/DF/16671.pdf, and Fulvio Martini, *Nome in codice Ulisse*, Rizzoli, Milano, 1999, pp. 141-142.

The French Grandeur at the Service of the European Union

These missed developments suggested to the Euro-Med partners that they had to find new ways creating new forms of cooperation. Starting from the ENP and on the basis of a French initiative, Nicolas Sarkozy launched a new proposal during the 2007 presidential campaign: the Union for the Mediterranean (UfM). The proposal of a vision of a unified Mediterranean by the presidential candidate was a little bit "unusual", if not "dichotomous and incoherent". On the one hand Sarkozy supported the idea of a union, but on the other hand he strongly opposed the idea of a European future for Turkey. On January 15, 2007, he affirmed that "not all the nations had the vocation to become EU members, starting from Turkey, which has no place in the European Union". Even if the UfM was expected to create a new multilateral architecture which channelled the Turkish aspirations, the formal French closure to Ankara did not help the development of the dialogue.

At the same time, Sarkozy tried to conciliate an EU policy which was seen to be too pro-Arab, with the enhancement of the relations with Israel. The French proposal was brought into an EU framework.

On June 19 and 20, 2008, the European Council, in officially defining the Mediterranean region as "an area of vital strategic importance to the European Union in political, economic and social terms", reasserted the necessity to implement the dialogue: "building on and reinforcing previous successes, the "Barcelona Process: Union for the Mediterranean" will inject further momentum into the Union's relations with the Mediterranean". This because "it will complement ongoing bilateral relations, which will continue within existing policy frameworks". [20]

The EU Council put particular emphasis on the "interlinkages between migration, employment and development as well as the importance of combating the major pull factors of illegal migration, the development of a standardized procedure and a common set of rights for third country nationals". The European Council also highlighted the importance in elaborating a shared strategy for the borders control, through the FRONTEX body, [21] and so through the enhancement of operational coordination. Together with the protection of the EU borders, it also reaffirmed the efforts to fight terrorism. The 2004 Madrid train bombing and the 2005 London attacks reasserted that the EU was in the line of fire of Islamic terrorism. In particular the EU council stated that "in its cooperation with third countries, the Union should usefully contribute to the prevention of recruitment for terrorism, particularly

---

20 See: http://register.consilium.europa.eu/pdf/en/08/st11/st11018-re01.en08.pdf, accessed October 20th, 2011.

21 FRONTEX is an independent body tasked to coordinate the operational cooperation between Member States in the field of border security

through the delivery of technical assistance in the fields of education, human rights, rule of law, civil society and governance".[22]

Besides these strategic approaches, the UfM has a number of key initiatives on its agenda:

1. the de-pollution of the Mediterranean Sea, including coastal and protected marine areas;
2. the establishment of maritime and land highways that connect ports and improve rail connections so as to facilitate movement of people and goods;
3. a joint civil protection programme on prevention, preparation and response to natural and man-made disasters;
4. a Mediterranean solar energy plan that explores opportunities for developing alternative energy sources in the region;
5. a Euro-Mediterranean University (EMUNI), inaugurated in Slovenia in June 2008;
6. the Mediterranean Business Development Initiative, which supports small businesses operating in the region by first assessing their needs and then providing technical assistance and access to finance.

A Disputed Union

The initial French project was subjected to hard criticism and so, under frequent pressure mainly from Germany and Turkey, began to take a different shape. Berlin was afraid to be excluded from the decision making processes, managed by a Mediterranean axe ruled by France, and at the same time did not want to play the role of economic sponsor of the new policy. In this regard Chancellor Angela Merkel declared "it cannot be that some countries establish a Mediterranean Union and fund this with money from EU coffers [...]. This could release explosive forces in the union I would not like".[23]

Sarkozy's opposition to Turkey joining the EU as well as such statements as "The ambitious project which I will propose to Turkey would be its being the backbone of a new alliance, the Mediterranean countries union",[24] attracted much criticism and opposition in Ankara. This is because Turkey perceived UfM as an alternative to its EU membership, a sort of compensation elaborated by EU (or better France), having informally "excluded" Turkey from the enlargement process. After having received assurance by France that the Medi-

---

22 Commission des Communautés Européennes, Secrétariat Général, Conseil Européen, Conclusions de la Présidence – Brussels, 19/20 Juin 2008, point 13.
23 See: http://euobserver.com/9/25284, accessed June 1, 2012
24 See: "Sarkozy: Turkey could be the backbone of a Mediterranean Union", *Turkish Press Review*, February. 28, 2007, http://www.hri.org/news/turkey/trkpr/2007/07-02-08.trkpr. html#05, accessed October 22nd, 2011.

terranean Union was not to be considered as an alternative for Turkey and that the possible participation to UfM would not hamper Turkey's accession negotiations, Foreign Minister Ali Babacan announced Turkish participation the process,[25] even if Turkey, as a Mediterranean country would not to be excluded from the regional cooperation mechanisms, especially for the political weight it could exert in the area. Article 13 of the Paris summit declaration asserted that the UfM "will be independent from the EU enlargement policy, accession negotiations and the pre-accession process"[26]

Slovenia as well criticized the UfM, in assuming the EU presidency in 2008. Slovenian Prime Minister Janez Jansa agreed that EU relations with Mediterranean states should be strengthened, but he was convinced that the Sarkozy's proposal was a "duplication of institutions, or institutions that would compete with EU, institutions that would cover part of the EU and part of the neighbourhood".[27]

Problems and critics came from the southern shore as well. Libya refused to become a member of the Union and refused to attend the 13 July 2008 summit in Paris.

The UfM stemmed from the serious difficulties encountered by the EU approach, based on contractual relations, engagements, norms and regional integration, if not its failure, with the task to replace that approach by going back to an inter-state multilateral approach, based on realism and traditional diplomacy.

A Lack of Dialogue: The Arab Spring and the European Winter

The so-called Arab spring indirectly underlined the failure of the UfM, even if the 2010 and 2011 revolts open new potentialities for Europe.

There was a lack of intelligence in interpreting the many warning signals coming from the Mediterranean countries, especially from Tunisia. Egypt showed, once again, to be out of the EU influence, reasserting a certain role played by Washington. In this case, not a revolution, but a sort of a military coup happened, which brought to an intra-institutional change instead of a real shift.

Libya, above all, showed the inconsistency of a unified EU policy. Once it was Iraq, with the sharp division between interventionists and pacifists for

---

25 "Turkey assured, ready to join Mediterranean Union", *Today's Zaman*, 12 July 2008, http://www.todayszaman.com/newsDetail_getNewsById.action?load=detay&link=14 7343, accessed October 22nd 2011.
26 EU 2008 Council Presidency, www.ue2008fr, accessed October 30th, 2011.
27 "Slovenia criticises French Mediterranean Union proposal", http://euobserver.com/ 9/25470, accessed October 22nd, 2011

the 2003 Iraqi invasion, pushing the then US Defence Secretary Donald Rumsfeld to identify an "Old Europe" (France and Germany, opposing to the war) and a "New Europe", formed by the eastern EU countries, (but also by Spain and UK) supporting the war.[28] In 2011, France and the United Kingdom acted autonomously in order to overthrow Qaddafi regime, and so to start a fruitful economic and political cooperation with a new regime, in a multibillionaire affair.

The French *Realpolitik* towards Libya is to reassert its political and economic influence over southern Mediterranean, after having lost two important bastions of its policy in the area, with Tunisia and Egypt uprising. France also failed in controlling the Mediterranean with the UfM, which had to be co-presided with Hosni Mubarak, but immediately thwarted by Libya.

Political relations between Paris and Tripoli have always been patchy: an initial period of good relations which allowed France to sell Libya a hundred Mirages was followed by a period of a deep crisis (the Chadian–Libyan conflict and the rivalries for the political influence over Northern Africa and particularly the Sahara region). Paris now wants more control over the migratory fluxes, over the Mediterranean shores and so over its national security, especially after the sharp slump in popularity Sarkozy had in the months before the military intervention. Libya represents a fundamental bridge to extend the control over Sub Saharan Africa: who rules over Libya can control part of the continent. That is why in the last years, Libya become a central axis for a new "Great Game" involving part of the EU (France and UK), Africa and China, with its "neo-colonialist policy", as it was defined by US Secretary of State Hillary Rodham Clinton.[29]

According to the first estimations, the business of reconstruction could be worth about 200 billion euro, a treasure which will be split up on the basis of the war efforts: mayor contracts will be assigned to France and the UK (30% of the whole business, 30 billion each), then US (40 bn) and Italy, with a share of 15% of the reconstruction business.

The lessons learned seemed to recall the ancient French adage: *l'argent est le nerf de la guerre.*

On the other side, some countries touched by the Arab spring, hoping with Western support to achieve a regime change, have been completely forgotten by the EU (and US). This is the case of Syria, to which a military

---

28   In January 2003, Donald Rumsfeld declared: "*You are thinking of Europe as Germany and France. I don't. I think that's old Europe ... If you look at the entire NATO Europe today, the center of gravity is shifting to the east. And there are a lot of new members.*" in "The Iraqi crisis: The Path to War", *The Guardian*, March 16th, 2003.

29   "Clinton warns against "new colonialism" in Africa", Reuters, http://www.reuters.com/article/2011/06/11/us-clinton-africa-idUSTRE75A0RI20110611, accessed November 9th, 2011.

option was considered too dangerous and the Western commitment to stop a civilian massacre has been limited to some economic sanctions on Damascus. The same was made by the Arab League in suspending its membership[30]. As NATO Secretary General, Anders Fogh Rasmussen stated, the possibility of a no-fly zone for Syria "is totally ruled out. We have no intention whatsoever to intervene in Syria",[31] adding that the conditions were different to those in Libya. No other reason has been given. But the real explanation is that nobody wants to provoke the breakdown of the Alawi secular regime ruling over the country. The Assad family and the supremacy of the *Ba'th* party are very similar to Saddam Hussein's regime, able to keep together different ethnic, religious and tribal groups. A power vacuum in Syria could worsen the fragile balance of power and stability in the region, threatening Iraq, Turkey and Israel.[32] Two countries, a double standard approach.

The Arab spring or the "awakening", as *The Economist* was titled on February 19th, 2011 will surely give new opportunities to the development for the Arab countries. The southern and eastern Mediterranean are in a unique position to build up new models of democracy, a real political representation, the achievement of human rights, an inclusive development and a sustained growth. The innovative significance of the events characterising the region are that democracy is no more a Western patent, and the change of the Middle East *status quo* is becoming a reality.

---

30   A meaningful precedent was represented by Libya, when its membership was suspended in February 2011, during an emergency meeting held by the Arab League in Cairo to discuss the situation in the country. Decision came in light of violent crackdowns on anti-government protests.

31   See: "NATO chief rules out no fly-zone and intervention in Syria", *Al-Arabiya News*, October 31st, 2011, http://www.alarabiya.net/articles/2011/10/31/174668.html, accessed November 11th, 2011.

32   Iraq is now supporting the Assad regime with oil, after the strong criticism expressed by Saudi King Abdullah II against the situation in the country. In a written statement released via Saudi state television on August 7th, 2011, Abdullah bin Abdul-Aziz declared: "*What is happening there is not accepted by the Kingdom of Saudi Arabia. There is no justification for the bloodshed in Syria, and what is happening has nothing to do with religion or ethics. The Syrian leadership could activate comprehensive reforms quickly.*" (see: "Abdullah's stand on Syria unrest gets wide welcome", *Saudi Gazette*, August 9th, 2011, http://www.saudigazette.com.sa/index.cfm?method=home.regcon&contentID=20110809107021, accessed: November 2nd, 2011). Turkey, trying to preserve Davutoğlu's "zero problems with the neighbours" policy and to implement economic cooperation, which in the past boosted the fortunes of both communities. Ankara is also considering Syria a player through which a solid partnership of political, strategic and economic could be built in order to penetrate the rest of the Arab world, but also to present itself as a mediator, in the eyes of the Western countries. Syria started indirect negotiation with Israel, through Turkey, trying to put an end to the 40-years conflict opposing the two countries. The fall of the Syrian regime could create tensions which could also sweep Israel, especially if Tehran will decide to intervene in filling a potential power vacuum in the region.

The uprising in Tunisia and then in the other part of the Mediterranean ratified the definitive defeat of the Bin Laden model, based on the resurgence of the ancient *Ummah* (the world Islamic community) and the establishment of a new Caliphate, to be realised through the violent downfall of the impious (Arab) regimes. All the people taking part in the revolts called for democracy, respect of human rights, development, job opportunities and not invoking Allah, wielding the Holy Quran and burning the US flags, as the classical stereotyped fundamentalist Muslim protests imposed. This was maybe also due to the political low-profile kept by Washington, abstaining from exploiting the protests.

Protesters also rejected the ruling model of an all-powerful and irreplaceable *Rais*, as once Saddam Hussein, Ben Ali, Hosni Mubarak, Muhammad al Qaddafi and Bashir al-Assad, among others, embodied or still personify.

So the Arab spring, which is becoming an autumn for some Arab countries in the Gulf, could transform itself in a Mediterranean spring. In fact, some positive impacts and potentialities could be also envisaged for the European Union.

And Europe as well could face an important era of change in the relations with the Southern Mediterranean, an era in which it could finally play a more pragmatic role. New regimes will need European help and support in consolidating their change. In addition to the claims of the urban unemployed youth, which have provoked the fall of the regime, now new governments must also address their policies to rural areas. Agricultural processes and development are one of the key aspects in promoting a coherent development of these countries and this issue has also been ignored for a long time by the EU. It must be remembered that in the recent UfM, this aspect was completely absent.

As the revolts started in towns, now the new regimes could be threatened by rural society. Stability of new regimes will depend on the reforms and of the level of the secularism they will put into action, but a response to rural society is needed, otherwise it could take over the reins of the revolution, starting a civil war. That is why Europe should play an active role in supporting a policy of new primary sector regimes.

A new concept of dialogue, based on a unified political willingness, is needed even if it actually seems to be hard because of the European involvement in its own economic and financial crisis.

However, the Arab spring must be transformed into an occasion of economic, social and political development, as a fundamental basis to obtain human security and so regional security and stability. Otherwise our *limites* will be more and more insecure.

We must bring back the Mediterranean to its primal function of "a machine producing civilisation" (Valery, 1945), with the European Union acting as a real political global player. The risk of failure would be to have an Arab spring turn into a European winter.

Bibliography

Alain, Beltran (2010): A Comparative History of National Oil Companies, Brussels: Peter Lang.

Fuller, Graham E./Lesser, Ian O. (1995): A Sense of Siege. The Geopolitics of Islam and the West. Boulder, CO: Westview Press

Keddie, Nikki R. (1983): An Islamic Response to Imperialism, Political and Religious Writings of Sayyid Jamal al-Din al-Afghani. Berkeley: University of California Press.

Kumaraswamy P. R. (2000): Revisiting the Yom Kippur War. London: Routledge.

Rucz, Claude (1978): Les mécanismes de coopération dans le cadre du Dialogue euro-arabe. In: Annuaire français de droit international, vol. 24, pp. 961-976.

Valéry, Paul (1945): Regards sur le monde actuel. Paris: Gallimard.

European Union and African Crises: The Multiple Personalities of an Actor

Marc-André Boisvert

Introduction

Historically, African security has been defined abroad. European powers split the continent into zones of influence during the 1884 Berlin Conference. Subsequently, newly independent African countries called for "African Solutions to African problems", but they have not been able to implement this motto into the field of security despite some recent developments. In spite of several efforts, most strategies for African security are made for foreign imperatives and answer to them.

Europe has always been significant in setting the framework of what African security should be. It has expressed a clear will and taken several initiatives to act in crisis management and conflict prevention in Africa. Scholars have developed a whole curriculum on why the European Union should do so. No one has asked the reverse question.

This chapter attempts to change the perspective and to ask what Africa has to gain from EU crisis prevention and conflict management mechanisms. The EU, in spite of a commitment to human rights and good governance, is also pursuing a tradition of European intervention in Africa, perpetuating the southern continent as a dangerous place that needs to be secured. This chapter will look at the numerous faces of Europe through African eyes and try to understand what kind of actor the EU is, in terms of crisis management and conflict prevention.

This text assumes a differentiation between Sub-Saharan Africa and the Maghreb. The Maghreb countries have been included in the European Neighbourhood Policy, which provides several privileges not offered to other African states. This text concentrates on Sub-Saharan Africa, but it is impossible to clearly delineate between the two regions. The Maghreb countries appear collaterally in this text, but the reader needs to be aware that they hold privileges influencing their relationship with the EU.

A Short Overview of EU's Operations in Africa

For the EU, conflict prevention and crisis management are complementary elements while not being under the supervision of the same organ: conflict prevention is mostly a Commission prerogative while crisis management is a Council one. The nomination of a European Security and Defence Policy (ESDP) representative and the Lisbon Treaty in 2009 aim to bring the two aspects together.

It is difficult to pinpoint the birth of the EU conflict prevention framework as it is based on a variety of measures preceding a clear conflict prevention strategy (Aggestam 2003). The European Union became officially involved in the business of African conflict prevention in the Madrid Summit of 1995, with a first commitment to preventive diplomacy, conflict resolution and peacekeeping in Africa. It became a more coherent policy after the Euro-African Summit of 2000. At first, it incorporated several measures including humanitarian aid, development packages and programs to strengthen the rule of law with clear obligations in regard to the International Court of Justice and other international agreements (Olsen 2004). Those first strategies for conflict prevention focused on using money to ensure the compliance of African states with the EU's vision of what should be done to avert conflict. Since then, the strategy has been constantly redrafted to incorporate more direct conflict prevention tools, notably the 2005 EU Strategy for Africa and the new Joint Africa-EU Strategy adopted in December 2007. It has also become a wide platform that gathered several existing EU strategies, including the Lomé Convention, which regulates trade agreements between certain developing countries and the EU.

Crisis management capabilities were created in February 2001 through Council regulations that implemented rapid-reaction mechanisms. Things moved fast after the adoption of the 2003 European Security Strategy that identifies several African threats to EU's security: terrorism, organized crime, state failure, regional conflicts, and proliferation of weapons of mass destruction (Council 2003). It also identifies historical, geographical and cultural ties with Africa as an asset to build European security on. Moreover, it clarifies European military objectives in Africa, and provides a framework to deploy EU troops abroad.

As of October 2012, the EU has conducted 27 missions abroad: 13 in Africa under the CSDP (see chart). Four African missions are in progress and one has yet to be deployed. Those missions are under the EU Military Committee (EUMC).

EU crisis management contains other tools than just deploying missions abroad. Military-wise, the EU has established cooperation deals to develop African capabilities. In November 2003, the Council created an "African Peace Facility" through the African Union with funding from the European

Development Fund (EDF) (Faria 2004: 36). This initiative led to the hybrid mission in Darfur.

List of ESD Missions

Military Missions:
EUFOR (Chad/Central African Republic): 2008 – 2009
Artemis (Democratic Republic of Congo): 2003
EUFOR (RD Congo): 2006
EUNAVFOR Atalanta (Naval operation along the coast of the Horn of Africa): 2008 –ongoing
EUTM Somalia (Somalia): 2010 – ongoing
EUCAP Nestor (Horn of Africa/ Western Indian Ocean States): December 2010 –ongoing
EUCAP Sahel (Niger): July 2012 – ongoing
EUAVSEC (South Sudan): September 2012 – ongoing
Civilian Missions:
EU SSR (Guinea-Bissau): 2008 – 2010
EUSEC (RD Congo): 2005 – ongoing
EUPOL Kinshasa (RD Congo): 2005 – 2007
EUPOL (RD Congo): 2007 – on going
Hybrid Mission:
Support to AMIS II (Sudan/Darfur): 2005 – 2006

Crisis management includes a comprehensive set of diplomatic measures, targeted sanctions and embargo capabilities. Those means have played a role in several African crises, notably Togo, Cote d'Ivoire and Zimbabwe (Olsen 2009). It also contains the ability to deploy experts to strengthen capabilities of third countries: policing, rule-of-law, civilian administration and security sector reform, humanitarian assistance.

Finally, Frontex, the EU agency responsible for border surveillance of the Schengen area has become an important crisis management tool. The agency was created by Council regulation and began operations in 2005. With resources of its own, including planes, boats and helicopters, it is capable of managing special missions like Operation Hermes, launched during spring 2011, dealing with the massive influx of refugees following the Arab Spring and NATO operations in Libya. With staff located in African airports and heavy patrolling in the Mediterranean Sea, it is definitively part of a "hard security" strategy.

In sum, both conflict prevention and crisis management are various ad-hoc mechanisms: there is no single EU "hot button". It is also a process in progress that changes hastily according to EU developments and contingencies: the means change according to the ends. This provides the EU with the ability to adapt to a situation, but it also makes the EU a highly unpredictable and multi-faceted actor.

The Good Samaritan

EU documents are imprinted with a vision of Brussels being a good global citizen implementing security strategy to help others (Telo 2007, Tüneman 2007). EU strategy papers listed at the core of the strategy, the respect of "human rights", "freedom", "equality", "solidarity", "justice", the "rule of law" and "democracy" (Council 2007). There is a constant reiteration that the EU is a good-hearted actor.

The European Union has contributed to improving African security. Beyond the question on how the comprehensive approach can enhance security, Africa has certainly gained an able actor ready to work on improving the situation. Artemis has been a "controversial deployment that gave rise to nightmare scenarios of ill-informed and unprepared troops caught up in a domestic African conflict that had little to do with European interests" (Martin 2007: 70). This operation, authorized by the UN Security Council's resolution 1484, has succeeded in stabilizing Eastern RDC and even gained a reputation of being more capable than UN forces (Martin 2007: 72, Olsen 2004: 432). Artemis was said to be a military mission "used to promote the long-term well-being of individuals with no ambition to control or defend territory, and to treat them as if they were citizens rather than an alien population" (Martin 2007: 71).

Being a Good Samaritan is not necessarily being unselfish. The EU understands that the best way to ensure a secure neighbourhood is "the spread of the belief that violent conflict is counter-productive" and that "other priorities and values are important" (Smith 2008, Hill 2001: 333).

There are other arguments for a self-interested EU, notably a constructivist one: the EU is still in construction, and it is crucial to build the EU as a global actor on defence (Burgess 2009; Hill 1993). Ventures in Africa become a way of coordinating this actorness and erecting a stronger Europe, as well as providing rehearsals for troops (Gegout 2009). There are numerous other justifications; the EU's motivations are definitively more complex than having a good heart. After all, it is a pragmatic actor (Wood 2011).

But when security comes closer to European frontiers, the EU is definitively less good-hearted. The Arab Spring in 2011 forced the EU to take aggressive means to counter migration with the establishment of a quasi-military mission: Operation Hermes. With a triple-fence around European enclaves and Frontex agents deployed in African airports, there is a counter-narrative being created.

In reality, it is difficult to circumscribe the EU's logic and interests as the organisation is still looking for its own independent vision on security. Decisions may be taken unanimously, but some voices have been stronger to ensure that this unanimity fits national interests.

France has played a prominent role in shaping several EU decisions about Africa. It has influenced decisions and become a "framework nation" for several EU missions, including Artemis in DRC and EUFOR in Chad-Central African Republic (Olsen 2009). Javier Solana has himself acknowledged an "imbalance" between France and others (Gliere 2008: 299). This participation is dubious enough for several critiques eager to label it neo-colonial. France has been accused of pursuing a policy of clientelism through EU interventions, notably in the Chad-CAR mission, where it was perceived as protecting its *protégé*, Chadian President Idriss Deby, against a possible coup (Grunstein 2008, Bayart 2004: 453). For authors like Bruno Charbonneau, it is clear that French leadership in several EU operations is a re-hatted colonial intervention in *Françafrique* (Charbonneau 2009: 552). He concludes that "emerging narratives of EU and UN cooperation in military crisis management are rewriting and re-authorizing European practices of military intervention in Africa (Charbonneau 2009: 545).

The Togo leadership in the 2005 crisis shows exactly that. France and Germany, before that episode, had exhibited signs of cooperation. But their vision of Africa's crisis management turned sour when France renounced its deal with Germany to protect its private relationship with the former President's family. France has also imposed its will against Portugal's in the case of the mission in Guinea-Bissau.

Nevertheless, France's role was possible because nobody else would assume leadership of African security. Several countries, notably several post-communist EU member states that used to have bilateral relationships with African countries, have remained totally muted on African policies. It is also unfair to not acknowledge that France has "europeanized" its policies (Rieker 2006). Moreover, other former colonial powers might have been less militant, but still promote their own agenda at the EU level. The long on-going tensions between the UK and Zimbabwe show that France is not the only power pressing an agenda on its former colonies.

Besides, debates about NATO's no-fly zone to be imposed on Libya in 2011 set Germany against other European members, and revealed a complicated power dynamic. EU policies change fast. The Lisbon Treaty, which came into effect on December 1, 2009, empowered the Common Security and Defence Policy (CSDP). Catherine Ashton, the representative for CSDP has reaffirmed multilateralism and the respect of international law in several speeches (Vasconselos 2010). EU operations in Sudan and on the coast of the Horn of Africa are proof that the EU can be an actor of its own will and follow its own agenda. More importantly, the EU has created its own partnerships with the hybrid mission in Darfur.

The Control Freak

Western countries, after the fall of the Berlin Wall, expressed a certain enthusiasm for intervention in Africa. Failures of the humanitarian intervention
in Somalia then became a cold shower and initiated a withdrawal of foreign
powers in Africa. Since then, from fear of losing control of the agenda, the
international community remained cautious regarding interventions on African soil through the UN (Bellamy 1999: 42).

In other words, the EU Security strategy argues that African insecurity is
a threat to Europe and identifies "strengthening" the United Nations as a priority (Council 2003:10).

Indeed, the EU has an ambiguous role with the UN. The EU follows international law: Missions have been approved by UN mandates and fill a gap
that the UN could not fill itself. But, in many cases, as in the Democratic Republic of Congo or the Chad/Central African Republic (CAR), it is legitimate
to ask the question why the EU member states did not include their contributions directly under UN command. The UN and the international crisis
management have flaws that have commonly resurfaced along with the crises, but at least included Africans in decision-making. Building the EU
capabilities in crisis management is a way of contributing to the correction of
some flaws, but it is also a way to ensure control over missions and putting
EU troops under EU control, while not bearing the stigma of going unilaterally.

There is a gap between what the UN wants and what the EU offers (Giorgis 2010: 80). On that, Gowan and Johnstone argued that while cooperative or
hybrid security arrangements are welcome, they should not provide "license
for any state or organisation with the capacity to do so" (Gowan & Johnstone
2007: 11). The African continent does not lack actors in the domain of the security sectors. Beyond national states, there are several regional, continental
and international actors that are called to play a role in both conflict prevention and crisis management. In this wide spectrum of possibilities, the
European Union is not necessarily the obvious actor to assume those functions. But its presence is possible because others do not commit resources.

EU crisis management and conflict prevention marginalized other international organisations, notably the UN. The EU selects its missions and does
not fill any obligations except the ones it wants to fill; this ad-hoc donor-
driven enterprise leaves little room for developing sustainable mechanisms
based on ascribed rules in the African security architecture. EU crisis management has been about bringing a quick fix to particular problems without
contributing to a strategy that would institutionalize security (Giorgis 2010:
80). ARTEMIS and the likes have meant short-term military responses that
support somebody else's strategy, but that exempt the EU from participating

in a longer-term strategy. Consequently, the EU creates a system of "wait and see" where actions are deferred to times of crisis without obligations. The EU uses European multilateralism to provide a "certain cloak of legitimacy" and a greater degree of credibility to pursue its own agenda (Germond 2008: 175).

The conditionality of certain conflict-prevention tools also reveals the controlling aspect of the EU. Sub-Saharan Africa has been offered a significant amount of trade agreements, which remain the cornerstone of the EU's strategy to bring peace and stability (Smith 2008). The Lomé Convention in 1975 established an agreement between the then European Economic Community and several African, Caribbean and Pacific (ACP) countries to incorporate post-colonial bilateral preferential agreements between those countries and EU member states into the Single European Market. The package was reformed with the Cotonou Agreements in 2000, bringing criticism for the conditionality that it imposes on partners. Signatories had to fulfil criteria in terms of good governance, human rights, sustainable development and democratisation. Article 11 is quite clear:

> [..] in situations of violent conflict, the Parties shall take all suitable action to prevent an intensification of violence. The Parties shall ensure the creation of the necessary links between emergency measures, rehabilitation and development co-operation. (European Commission 2000)

Very few African countries have refused money packages due to conditionality; the rhetoric of equal partners is limited. Even if morally justified, conditionality is inconsistent. The EU, according to its own standards, should have cut financial aid to several African countries that were party in a conflict, notably Uganda, Angola, Burkina Faso and Rwanda. For various reasons, the EU has not sanctioned those countries. Meanwhile, Sudan and Zimbabwe have faced harsh pressure. Conditionality is political.

The European Union has put a lot of energy into building African Union capabilities to lead the security answer. The African Union, born in 2002 from the ashes of the OAU, is a relatively new regional organisation still in search of its soul. Institutionally, there is not much to compare between the two unions. The EU was at first an economic union that gradually integrated other aspects: social, political, military, etc. The build-up in other spheres was progressive with constant reaffirmation of common norms and values. In contrast, the AU has no substantive economic integration processes to compare with the EU, and its organs remain under construction (Toth 2007: 116). More importantly, it is unclear how the AU helps Africans and global governance (Klingebiel 2005). AU norms and values simply do not exist.

The AU is nevertheless a turning point in terms of Africa taking care of its security. It includes the African Peace and Security Architecture, a multi-layered structure allowing the cohabitation under a single union of different regions with different levels of integration (Franke 2008). Moving further than its predecessor, the Organisation of African Unity (OAU), while still protecting the concept of sovereignty, territorial integrity and independence, clearly allows the organisation to intervene in member state affairs in cases of serious crimes, namely war crimes, genocide and crimes against humanity. This has led to the inclusion in the AU Charter of several frameworks in its Article 4, notably human security and the Responsibility to Protect (R2P).

The AU has proactively sought to build-up this architecture, but so far has not imposed itself as a substantive actor in any African crisis. The refusal to invoke Article 4 for intervention in the Sudan has shown an AU unable to fulfil its commitments. There are a lot of inputs in the AU, but so far little outputs and outcomes.

The relationship between the AU and the EU is unbalanced in terms of relative power: the African Union, even if it brings together 54 states, has no leverage to become an equal partner to the EU (Pirozzi 2010: 88). The agenda is donor-driven: the EU decides where it puts the money and the AU acknowledges. This does not mean that the agenda is detrimental to Africans; it simply means that Africans have limited control over the process, and that there is no African agenda for Europe that is being discussed. The AU has never been able to influence the EU agenda on issues that it cares about, such as human mobility and trade partnerships.

Collaboration with the AU is also proof that the EU can disregard its own principles for the sake of security. The AU might have incorporated R2P, human rights and a commitment to democratisation, but expressed a weak commitment to those frameworks. Well-known human rights abusers have been chairman of the organisation, notably Libya's Muammar al-Qaddafi and Equatorial Guinea's Teodoro Obiang Nguema Mbasogo. Military-backed despots rule several countries, participating in capacity-building training and none has been unseated by AU pressure so far. The AU expressed very limited support of the International Criminal Court (ICC). Human security and democratisation seem to matter less in reality in a continent where civilian control of the military does not go smoothly. AU and EU cooperation has not brought the AU closer to its Maastricht Treaty. Furthermore, the AU has a poor score in working on those issues deemed important for conflict prevention by the EU, i.e. development and trade. But the EU still stands by.

Financing the AU is part of an EU strategy to find a sustainable way to ensure African security. As several resources and financial means are being injected in the AU, it is still unsure how long-term funding will be secured. Most of the European contribution to the African Peace Facility, established in 2004, is funded through the European Development Fund. This money can be used to deploy African forces for peacekeeping tasks, but not to cover military preparation or arms expenditures, which still need to be funded by bilateral donors with ethical decisions of their own. It also means that non-ACP countries, like North African countries or South Africa, are not eligible for support. This strategy lacks a long-term vision and sustainable funding other than bilateral aid.

Institutionally, the European Union has stood by the AU in a way to support the African Peace and Security Architecture (APSA). It absorbed the French RECAMP program in 2008, extended strategic-level training to African partners in both military and civilian fields, and contributed to the operationalisation of the African Standby Force (ASF) by 2010. It has also conducted joint military exercises, notably MAPEX in 2009.

In many ways, the EU's crisis management is a way of reaffirming control over a continent, but it is also a blind application of its own rhetoric of norms and values on a totally different place. In the end, it is unclear if Africans gain any more capacity to control their own security. Nevertheless, this control is limited as new players also want to influence African security.

The Competitor

Since the independence from colonial powers, Africa is investigating the meaning of its own motto "African Solutions to African Problems". International actors have often been fast in judging Africa on its incapacity to provide solutions that work. Africa has proven that it can, at times, take the lead to ensure its security. The Economic Community of West African States (ECOWAS) has provided some viable solutions for crisis management and conflict prevention in the last decade, but with several limitations. The 2012 Tuareg rebellion in the succeeding coup in Mali have highlighted the lack of legitimacy and the incapacity to act when there is no clear leadership from a member state.

The European Union and its member states have been proactive in helping their Southern neighbours frame a security policy. In this project, as we have seen in the latest part, there is an EU tendency to project its normative power and promote its own values and agenda in its relationship with the African continent (Pirozzi 2009: 9). But the EU is not the only one doing that.

If security contribution through the UN system appears to have diminished, the number of security actors in Africa has increased significantly in the last decade. The EU, besides the UN and African organisations, must cope with several international organisations trying to influence security, notably the Arab League, the Commonwealth, the Francophonie, etc. Even NATO is now in the business of African security with its operations in Libya.

Although, organisational competition is a fake problem for Europe; it has largely the means to pursue its policies through other organisations. NATO, the EU, the UN or post-colonial organisations have all been channels for the European countries to pursue their vision of security, be it in the name of cultural ties, friendship or effective control. Europe remains the main foreign actor working for Africa security. But the market is opening fast.

The United States of America has increased its presence in Africa in the last decade, notably in strengthening its African Command (AFRICOM) and participating in several military cooperation deals. The USA pursues a narrow vision of African security. Following terrorist attacks on its embassies in Tanzania and Kenya in 1998, the United States government has focused on fighting terrorism in the continent. It has since then participated in several initiatives, notably in the Sahel. A second priority has been securing the oil of the Gulf of Guinea. All those goals are precise and well-targeted (Sarjoh 2008). The Americans are clear: we support what fits US interests. There are several capacity-building initiatives, but the USA has not yet developed a long-term strategy and did not express the will to do so. Crisis management and conflict prevention is not an American priority in Africa.

Brazil, Russia, India, China and South Africa, the BRICS, have established formal relations as emerging global powers, challenging the G8 during a first summit in 2009. The BRICS have emerged as economic partners for Africa. As a group, they have not framed a concrete security policy yet. But unilaterally, the members have a history of African involvement. This involvement has historically proved to be unsteady, but is currently in progression. There is a wide belief that it constitutes an alternative to Europe's vision.

Russia played an important role in African security during the Cold War. Since then, it has receded and remains present mostly through its Security Council permanent seat. Brazil has no interest in African security, although it has expressed a certain will to increase its presence in several other fields, notably business. But China, India and South Africa are significant security actors in Africa.

China is particularly active in African security. Before 1989, China pursued a non-security strategy and has been relatively absent from the security apparatus, even if it holds a UN Security Council seat. China has been clear on where its priorities are: economy first. Security came later when it realized the need to maintain a stable external environment for economic growth and accumulate relative power (Wang 2010). China uses "win-win" partnerships, and has declared its intentions to respect UN rules and international law (Glière 2008). Although, as with the EU, China also uses those interventions as a way of framing itself as an international actor and coordinating its capacities (Gill 2009: 4-5).

The 2008 Chinese White Paper affirmed the Chinese peacekeeping role. In the last decade, China has sent more UN peacekeepers to Africa than Russia, the UK and the USA together (Gill 2009). It increasingly participates in operations with robust mandates and sent three vessels in December 2008 to protect merchant ships on the Somali coast. It has established several training programs and has increased military cooperation with African countries. China, through its efforts, tries to "project a more benign and harmonious image beyond its borders", to reassure neighbours about its peaceful intentions, and to softly balance Western influence while assuming the responsibility of a growing power (Gill 2009). China is also active in developing a soft power approach (Beri 2007: 299, Wang 2010). In Africa, China is slowly, but actively shaping a vision of security.

Likewise, India's involvement is intensifying. The country has historically been a strong troop contributor to UN operations. It has increased its naval presence, especially around the Somali coast, and has developed several military cooperation deals with Indian Ocean area states, notably Madagascar, Mozambique and the Seychelles. India's new military policy toward Africa is motivated by concerns about Chinese expansionism and India's desire to compete with China's growing influence in the region (Volman 2009: 10-11). On the other hand, they have increased communication with China during operations on the Somali coasts. In comparison with China, India is lagging behind in developing a vision for African security or, even ensuring a sustainable role in it.

South Africa has a particular status: It is not included in the Lomé Agreements and its position as the biggest economy in Sub-Saharan African makes it a hegemon. For obvious geographical reasons, African security is also its own and South Africa has been keen on supporting it. It has been involved as a UN troop contributor and in building the APSA. Nelson Mandela and Thabo Mbeki have both made African security a South African priority. South Africa is thus active in all aspects of conflict management and crisis prevention, and a good argument that Africans do care about their security.

Numerous other African countries have tried to influence continental security. Nigeria has led the effort in most ECOWAS operations and has affirmed itself as a regional leader in West Africa. Several African security providers have emerged: Senegal has played a role in several crises in its immediate neighbourhood, as well as Rwanda, Libya, Uganda and Kenya (Jonah 2010). While academics tend to neglect the role of African-led conflict prevention, there is still a wide array of initiatives that have helped to solve and prevent crisis, although in the game of big powers, those efforts are discarded rather than fostered.

Europe faces competition, and knows it: it cannot impose a unilateral vision of African security anymore. The EU has become a platform to make this growing competition efficient. The European Commission and the General Affairs and External Relations Council (GAERC) proposed a triangular dialogue between the EU, China and Africa on the topic in 2008. Through the EU-

RECAMP initiative, the EU is also collaborating with the USA and Canada. In spite of several deficiencies, China, India, the EU and numerous other actors have increased discussions as a way of securing the Somali coasts.

But there are still several clashing visions. As long as it remains the main economic partner of Africa, the EU has incredible leverage to ensure that its vision is stronger than others. It has been able to enforce the International Criminal Court through pressure. But as the EU's role is receding, its pole position is already challenged.

For Africa, new players are opening doors to new visions of security. Europe's critiques have been harsh on China's support of Zimbabwe and the Sudan. But, in the Sudan, China has also contributed to the peace effort, both through diplomacy and by troop contribution. The more other actors are involved in Africa, the more they themselves change. In fact, the EU might not face a challenge, but instead gain vital partners with new tools and ideas. The EU needs to realize this potential and to recognize that a security strategy relying on soft power in a competitive world works if both sides truly embrace those norms and values. Competitors weaken soft power. For Africans, the EU's norms and values on security could become an option, not a forced process. It is an opportunity to break with the past. In no way does this new competition ensure that Africans will gain more control over their security. More competition also means a more complicated and confusing set-up.

The Saviour

EU conflict prevention and crisis management frameworks used several tools as a way of achieving security objectives following Kofi Annan's "Security for Development" framework. Aid and trade agreements are framed as security issues. This ends in migration policies and aid packages promoting security imperatives rather than legal and humanitarian needs (Helly 2010: 52). Undeveloped people are dangerous and are a threat to security. They have to be controlled by "development". Improving their situation is about controlling a situation, not developing a framework based on sustainable development and a frank discussion between the "wretched of the land" and the developed nations. Europe and the USA have all included development in a security framework.

Over the years, a narrative has been built on Africa where risks need to be managed, dangers to be contained and a continent that needs to be secured. Africa has been imagined – or socially constructed – as the site of conflict, crisis, anarchy and disorders which require external intervention (Grovrogui 2001). The Joint Africa-EU Partnership, adopted in Lisbon in December 2007, has set the foundation for a strategic partnership based on a "shared vision and common principles", but listing security as a "first priority" (Council 2007). Relationships with African states are tainted more and more by this security scope.

This new emphasis on security obscures historical relationships between the two continents and undermines more positive exchange (Charbonneau 2009: 551). This narrative sustains a dialogue based on negativism: It serves realistic needs well but does little to change behaviours detrimental to a positive relationship between continents. Western states are the peaceful, law and ordered ones; Africans are chaotic. In this relationship, there is the subtle language that Africa needs foreigners to teach them how to be safe: an "international civilizing process" or an underlying narrative where Africa remains in need of a saviour. African security needs a pragmatic dialogue and cannot be based on submission (Linklater 2005). It justifies foreign intervention and it does not foster African solutions. Crisis management and conflict prevention cannot become the hysterical securitisation of everything if we cannot assume that Africans need to be included in the solution.

Africans have perceived this growing securitisation of narratives. Security took over all aspects of the relationship with Africans: There is no EU-Africa summit without a security agenda, especially border security. The need to securitize every aspect of the relationship has brought short-term hard security quick fixes rather than more complicated and sustainable strategies.

Security and democratisation can lead to counterproductive decisions. The need for a security-sector reform (SSR) brought considerable questions on how this process has strengthened the military in countries desperately looking for effective civilian control of armed forces, notably in Guinea and Guinea-Bissau, where the lack of poverty-reduction strategy nullified the SSR effort (Telatin 1999). For Mpyisi, the EU is simply not doing enough to reward democracies, and securitisation is at the core of the problem (Mpyisi 2009). The real sustainable solution for security is to give tools to emerging democracies to control their security, not to impose security on emerging democracies.

Securitisation also imposes a vision of events based much more on traditional "hard" security rather than the new paradigms developed recently, notably human security. Several long-standing conflicts are now reframed under this framework, and reality is reinterpreted to fit narratives.

Building a saviour means waiting passively for solutions from him/her. But it mostly means not actively seeking local alternatives and accepting foreign solutions. A saviour exists because someone wants to believe in him/her. The problem is not African states or the EU, but the relationship. So far, the EU process has been mostly African states answering to European imperatives. Ending this process necessitates a real commitment to empowerment.

Conclusion

This chapter has listed four different personas of the European Union's conflict prevention and crisis management in Africa. This is not a definitive diagnosis as the EU is polymorphous and adaptive. And there should be no definitive one: The EU is a last-resort security actor, constantly evolving.

Along with this chapter lies a question: what does Africa want from the EU in terms of security? The construction of the African Peace and Security Architecture is the first step in fostering a continental discussion on conflict and crises. It is crucial: Africans need to frame a longer-term vision of their security. So far, African-made solutions have been ad-hoc and reactive rather than organized and preventive. African states have not even been able to create a well-functioning forum to discuss those issues.

This is what makes the EU as well as other foreign actors relevant in African security. Accusing foreigners of subrogating African responsibilities is a false problem as long as Africans will not fully take them on. The real place of the EU in African security needs to be defined by Africans themselves. Not having an interlocutor, it is obvious that the EU will continue to pursue its own vision of what African security should be.

The future has its challenges. Africa has answers to many of them with its uncultivated fertile soils and energy potential. This is sufficient to ensure that foreigners will dictate their vision of security. Africa has enough to become a central security problem for the rest of the world rather than a peripheral one. It is an opportunity as well as a threat. However, no one but Africans can ensure that the process respects their values and views, not even African leaders.

Bibliography

Aggestam, Karin (2003): Conflict Prevention: Old Wine in New Bottles? International Peacekeeping 10 (1): 12-23.

Anderson, Stephanie/Seitz, Thomas R. (2006): European Security and Defence Policy Demystified: Nation-Building and Identity in the EU. Armed Forces and Society 33: 24.

Aning, Kwasi (2007): Africa: confronting complex threats. Coping with Crisis Working Paper Series. New York: International Peace Academy.

Bayart, Jean-Francois (2004): Commentary: Towards A New Start For Africa And Europe. African Affairs 103: 453-458.

Bellamy, Alex J./Williams, Paul (2009): The West and Contemporary Peace Operations. Journal of Peace Research 46 (1): 39-57.

Beri, Ruchita (2007): China's Rising Profile in Africa. China Report (43): 297.

Breuer, Fabian/Vennesson, Pascal/de Franco, Chiara/Schroeder, Ursula C. (2009): Is There a European Way of War? Role Conceptions, Organisational. Armed Forces & Society 35 (4): 628-645.

Burgess, Peter J. (2009): There is No European Security, Only European Securities. Cooperation and Conflict (44): 309.

Charbonneau, Bruno (2009): What is so special about the European Union? EU-UN Cooperation in Crisis Management in Africa. International Peacekeeping 16(4): 546-561.

Council of the European Union (2007): The Africa-EU Strategic Partnership A Joint Africa-EU Strategy. 16344/07. Lisbon: Council of the European Union.

Council of the European Union (2003): A Secure Europe In A Better World. European Security Strategy. Brussels: Council of the European Union

European Commission (2006): The EU and Africa: towards a new strategic partnership. Brussels: European Commission Development.

European Commission (2000): Cotonou Agreements: Partnership Agreement ACP-EU. Luxembourg, Office for Official Publications of the European Communities.

Faria, Fernanda (2004): Crisis Management in sub-Saharan Africa: The Role of the European Union. Paris: ISS.

Fischer, Sabine (2011): The ENP Strategic Review: The EU and Its Neighborhood at a Crossroad. Paris: ISS.

Franke, Benedikt (2008), Africa's Evolving Security Architecture and the Concept of Multilayered Security Communities. Cooperation and Conflict 43 (3): 213-340.

Gill, Bates/ Huang, Chin-Hao (2009): China's Expending Peacekeeping Role: Its Significance and the Policy Implications. Stockholm: SIPRI Policy Brief.

Gebrewold, Belachew (2010): Anatomy of Violence: Understanding the Systems of Conflict and Violence in Africa. London: Ashgate.

Gegout, Catherine (2009): The West, Realism And Intervention In The Democratic Republic Of Congo (1996-2006). International Peacekeeping 16: 231-44.

Germond, Basil (2008): Military Cooperation and its Challenges: The Case of European Naval Operations in the Wider Mediterranean Area. International Relations 22: 173-192.

Giorgis, Andebrhan W. (2010): Coordinating International Support for African Peace and Security Efforts: From the G8 to the EU. The International Spectator 45 (2): 69-83.

Glière, Catherine (2008): EU Security and Defence: Core Documents. Paris: European Union Institute for Security Studies.

Gowan, R./Johnstone I. (2007): New Challenges for Peacekeeping: Protection, Peacebuilding and the War on Terror. Coping with Crisis Working Paper Series. New York: International Peace Academy.

Gray, Christine (2005): Peacekeeping And Enforcement Action In Africa: The Role Of Europe And The Obligations Of Multilateralism. Review of International Studies 31: 207-223.

Grovrogui, Siba (2002): Regimes of Sovereignty: Rethinking International Morality and the African Condition. The European Journal of International Relations 8 (3): 315-38.

Grovrogui, Siba (2001): Come to Africa: A Hermeneutic of Race in International Theory. Alternatives 26 (4): 425-448.

Grunstein, Judah (2008): A Step Forward for European Defence. World Politics Review. URL (consulted on August 30, 2011): http://www.worldpoliticsreview.com/articles/ 1847/ eufor-chad-a-step-forward-for-european-defence.

Hadden, Tom (2009): A Responsibility to Assist. London: Hart Publishing.

Helly, Damien (2010): L'UE et l'Afrique: Les Défis de la Cohérence. Paris: Institut d'Études de Sécurité.

Hill, Christopher (2001): The EU's Capacity for Conflict Prevention. European Foreign Affairs Review 6: 315-333.

Hill, Christopher (1993): The Capability-Expectations Gap, Or Conceptualizing Europe's International Role. The Journal of Common Market Studies 31 (3): 305-25.
Jünemann, A./Knodt, M. (eds.) (2007): European External Democracy Promotion. Baden Baden: Nomos Verlagsgesellschaft.
Klingebiel, Stephan (2005): Africa New Peace and Security Architecture. African Security Review 14(2): 35-45.
Laidi, Zaki (2008): Norms over Force: The Enigma of European Power. Paris: Presses de Science Po.
Linklater, A. (2005): A European civilizing process. In: Hill, Christopher/Smith, Michael (eds.): International Relations and the European Union. Oxford: Oxford University Press.
Martin, Mary (2007): A Force for Good? The European Union and human security in the Democratic Republic of Congo. African Security Review 16 (2): 64-77.
Mpyisi, Kenneth (2009): How EU Support of the African Peace and Security Architecture Impacts Democracy Building and Human Security Enhancement in Africa. Stockholm: International Institute for Democracy and Electoral Assistance.
Nye, Joseph (2004): Soft Power, The Means to Success in World Politics. New York: Public Affairs.
Olsen, Gorm Rye (2009): The EU and Military Conflict Management in Africa: For the Good of Africa or Europe? International Peacekeeping 16 (2): 245–260.
Olsen, Gorm Rye (2004): Challenges to Traditional Policy Options, Opportunities for New Choices: The Africa Policy of the EU. The Round Table 93 (375): 425-436.
Ortega, Martin (2001): Military Intervention and the European Union. Paris: IESS.
Öjendal, Joakim/Stern, Maria (2010): Mapping the Security – Development Nexus: Conflict, Complexity, Cacophony, Convergence? Security Dialogue 41: 5-29.
Othieno, Timothy/Samasuwo, Nhamo (2007): A Critical Analysis Of Africa's Experiments With Hybrid Missions And Security Collaboration. Africa Security Review 16 (3); 25-39.
Pirozzi, Nicoletta (2010): Towards an Effective Africa-EU Partnership on Peace and Security: Rhetoric or Facts. The International Spectator 45 (2): 85–101.
Pirozzi, Nicoletta (2009): EU support to African Security Architecture: funding and training components. Paris: European Union Institute for Security Studies.
Rieker, Pernille (2006): From Common Defence to Comprehensive Security: Towards the Europeanisation of French Foreign and Security Policy? Security Dialogue (37): 509-528.
Smith, Michael (2008): The EU as an International Actor. In: Richardson, Jeremy (ed.): European Union, Power and Policy-Making, 3rd edition. Nottingham: University of Nottingham, 289-310.
Telo, M. (2007): Europe: A Civilian Power? European Union, Global Governance, World Order. New York: Palgrave Macmillan
Toth, Norbert (2007): Historical duty or pragmatic interest? Notes on EU and AU security issues. African Security Review 16 (3): 112-116
Vasconselos, Alvero de (2010): Quelle Défense Européenne en 2020? Paris: European Union Institute for Security Studies.
Victor, Jonah (2010): African Peacekeeping in Africa: Warlord Politics, Defence Economics and State Legitimacy. Journal of Peace Research, Vol. 47, No. 217-229.
Volman, Daniel (2009): China India, Russia and the United States: The Scramble for African Oil and the Militarisation of the Continent. Current African Issues 43. Uppsala: Nordiska Africa Institut.

Williams, MJ (2011): Empire Lite Revisited: NATO, the Comprehensive Approach and State- building in Afghanistan. International Peacekeeping 18 (1): 64–78.

Wang, Yuan-Kang (2010): China's Response to the Unipolar World: The Strategic Logic of Peaceful Development. Journal of Asian and African studies 45: 554-567.

Wood, Steve (2011): Pragmatic Power Europe? Cooperation and Conflict, Vol. 46, No. 242.

EU – Latin America: A Strategic Partnership in the Making?

Franz Kernic

The international system of modern states has changed dramatically over the last hundred years. Several significant reconfigurations of the global political and economic system have occurred and gradually led to the emergence of today's multi-polar world order. In recent decades, a number of new political entities and organisations of both inter-governmental and supra-governmental character have been created. Some of them – most importantly the European Community and later European Union – have managed to gain tremendous political and economic influence and power in international politics. This development is also reflected in a general shift in international relations (IR) theory away from traditional state-centric views and the assumption of a relatively stable modern system of nation states. New theoretical approaches and concepts rather emphasize other aspects and notions such as the role of non-state actors in international politics, the construction and transformation of political identities, the power of norms and rules etc.

Recent debates about the European Union and its foreign policy, i.e. its role as an actor in international politics and as a "global power", are linked to the systemic changes which have occurred in the international system since the end of the Cold War (Bretherton/Vogler 2006). The political, societal and economic reconfiguration processes of the post-Cold War order have been global in nature. They have shaped today's European political landscape as much as they have had an impact on the political, social and economic development of other regions around the globe. They have stimulated regional political integration between states, thus automatically also increasing the importance of inter-regionalism.

The new figuration of the international system has caused certain analytical difficulties within the field of political science, particularly with respect to the classical assumptions and notions of our prevailing IR theories. Therefore, new theoretical approaches have demanded a redefinition of the concept of "actorness" in order to adequately describe and explain the role of various new types of actors in the international realm. This article will follow mostly a neo-realistic perspective when dealing with EU-Latin America relations. It will put an emphasis on both aspects inter-regionalism and traditional state-to-state foreign policy but clearly focus on the development and nature of EU external relations. It will look at the established institutional frameworks for the development of EU-Latin America relations and then analyze recent foreign policy initiatives and trends, primarily from an EU perspective. The analysis will include strategic and geopolitical aspects. It will be based on a short review of historical linkages and common experiences on both sides of the Atlantic. The main focus of the article will be on the "strategic partnership" between the two regions which was proclaimed in 1999. The article intends to examine and evaluate the development and nature of this specific strategic partnership. The key question can be phrased as follows: To what extent have the countries of the European Union and their counterparts in Latin America managed to strengthen and deepen their political and economic relations in the years since the Rio de Janeiro Summit in 1999 when both parties entered into this new strategic partnership?

This article is structured as follows: First, I will give a short account of the historical development of the relationship between Europe and Latin America. Second, I will briefly outline the history of EC/EU relations with Latin America since the 1950s and reconstruct the processes which have led to the creation of new institutional foreign policy frameworks. Third, I will shed light on the strategic partnership between EU and Latin America. I will analyze how this partnership has developed since the Rio Summit and evaluate its political impact, results and prospects. Finally, I will draw some conclusions about the nature of the strategic partnership and its place in global politics and will also try to give a short outlook regarding its future development.

Shadows of the Past: The Historical Dimension of EU-Latin America Relations

Today's relationship between the European Union and Latin America can only be interpreted and understood in the light of its historical past with its multiple variations and forms of political, economic and cultural interaction. The dynamics and complexity of social interaction always contains what one might call "traces of the past", i.e. a wide array of things that are still present in everyday life and communication: collective memories, ideas, values, identities, languages, material objects etc. Those traces can at least in part be brought to light, for example by reconstructing associated narratives that are still present and passed on from one generation to the next – narratives which societies on both sides of the Atlantic share but which also distinguish them from each other: Those narratives deal with stories about discovery and/or conquest, about defeat and/or victory, about good and evil, about one God or another (or multiple Gods), about right and wrong, about white and coloured, about Europe and the other, etc. There can be no doubt that the "encounter of two worlds" (*el encuentro de dos mundos*) about 500 years ago was in fact a historical event of incredible violent nature. The outcome of this "encounter" was in reality some kind of "conquest" and "export" of European values, concepts, traditions etc., thus leading to the creation of a new world (*el mundo nuevo*) which reflects to a very large extent European conditions, dreams and projections. The name "America Latina" can be seen as symbol of this act of violence, i.e. as a European name for something unknown that had to be turned into something familiar.

Therefore, no one can be surprised about the fact that even centuries after the end of the European colonial empires on the American continent people in Europe and Latin America frequently refer to common roots and shared identities and values, and sometimes even stress their closeness to each other. Of course, there are similarities which are not only limited to language, religion, culture, and tradition. European political thinking has also been influential in Latin America and European models of public administration have served as role-models for almost all countries of the "New World". The economic, social and political phenomenon of modernity have shaped all countries of Europe and Latin America but never fully erased the existing huge differences in living standards and wealth. Despite all the similarities and strong ties, the relationship between Europe and Latin America has always been difficult and loaded with tensions and prejudices. This is not limited to aspects of resistance against former "mother countries" or colonial power and aspects of post-colonialism. It is rather a dimension of collective identity formation and transformation and it is frequently tied to strategic and geopolitical perceptions and ambitions, including attitudes towards and perceptions of the other – with all their variations from the 15th century until today's perceptions of the European Union as an emerging global power (Lucarelli/Fioramonti 2009).

Latin America's position and role in global affairs has changed dramatically since the 19th century. From a strategic and geopolitical perspective, one can argue that the US was the dominant power in the region during the entire 20th century. Mostly Central America and the Caribbean were viewed as geopolitically important zones of influence for the United States, i.e. some kind of backyard. The US dominance in this part of the world was never really challenged by European powers after World War I. They limited their own spheres of interest primarily to the few islands in the Caribbean which were European territory. A number of military interventions in this region during the 20th century clearly indicate the United States huge strategic interests in hemispheric foreign politics, i.e. the US desire to maintain its hegemonic power in this region and even in expanding it to the far south of the peninsula (Sicker 2002, Pastor 1992, Hoffmann 1988). After World War II, US foreign policy in Central and South America was mostly concerned with a potential communist threat. During the Cold War, major political developments in this region were seen through the lenses of a bipolar global struggle between liberal democracies and communist-Marxist ideology (Schoultz 1998, Pastor 1992, Blasier 1985, Carothers 1991, Cottam 1994, Dent 1995, Kryzanek 1996, Lowenthal 1990, Martz 1995, Poitras 1990, Wiarda 1992). Western Europe's political involvement in Latin America during this period was very limited due to other political and strategic priorities and the commitment of the major Western European powers to the newly formed security alliance with the United States and Canada in the North Atlantic.

It is worth mentioning that during the Cold War the idea of a "strategic triangle" between United States, Europe and Latin America was promoted at different points in time with different intentions (Whitaker 1951, Reidy 1964, Grabendorff/Roett 1985, Roett 1994, Kaufman Purcell/Simon 1995, Grabendorff 2005). The notion "strategic triangle" derived first from US military plans to establish a comprehensive defence alliance of the free world against the Soviet Union and its allies which were presented and discussed during the first post-World War II decade. During the early 1960s, it referred to the idea of creating a hemispheric defence system in addition to NATO (Reidy 1964, Mason 1963). Later, this concept gradually shifted its focus to joint endeavours to confine socialist ideas and prevent the emergence of new socialist revolutionary movements in the region (Rabe 1988 and 1999, Schwartzberg 2003). According to Rouquié (1987) the main purpose of various US military aid programs for Latin American states during this period was "to convert the armies of the hemispheric defence into forces of internal order mobilized against Communist subversion, thus contributing to the security of 'the free world'" (Rouquié 1987: 137). Finally, the notion "strategic triangle" received a totally new meaning when applied to the post-Cold War order at the turn of the century (Grabendorff 2005, Roett/Paz 2003, Roett 1994 and 1995). This revival of the strategic triangle concept in the 1990s coincided with the foundation of the European Union based on the Maastricht Treaty and the creation of its unique common foreign and security policy. These changes also mark the entrance of the European Union into world politics and the beginning of its distinctive foreign policy.

In this context, it is important to mention that the post-Cold War order has enabled both Europe and Latin America to create and establish new forms of political collaboration between states without getting the dominant world power of the past, the United States, involved. Multi-polarity, the emergence of new regional powers and the formation of new alliances and regional integration have become important characteristics of the post-Cold

War order. The creation of new political entities of both supra- and international nature have radically changed today's global political landscape. In this new international setting and global environment, both the European Union and Latin America appear as important actors in world politics (Atkins 1995, Calvert 1994 Roett/Paz 2003).

In sum, the foundation of the European Union and the creation of a common foreign and security policy in the early 1990s have dramatically changed Europe's traditional state-to-state foreign policy relations with Latin America. European economic integration since the 1950s had already set the stage for the changes that now occurred in the domains of foreign policy, security and defence. The creation of new EU institutions in the mid-1990s, which were established to deal exclusively with foreign and security policy matters, opened the door for a radical renewal of Europe's political relationship with Latin America. Despite the fact that foreign and security policy remained to be inter-governmental (as one of the three central pillars of the Maastricht treaty concept), the European Union managed to gradually take on a huge number of new foreign and security responsibilities (Knodt/Princen 2003, Bretherton/Vogler 2006, Hill/Smith 2000, White 2001, Smith 2004). There can be no doubt that a number of new foreign policy initiatives were launched by the EU during the late 1990s, thus also shaping the Union's profile as a newly emerging actor in global politics. In addition, new institutional frameworks were set up during this time, particularly for the purpose of pursuing a common EU foreign policy.

Institutional Frameworks and Actors

The European integration process and the political and economic success of the European Union during the 1990s was carefully observed in Latin America where new public debates were launched about possible benefits of similar integration processes among the community of Latin American states. References to the strategic triangle US-Europe-Latin America within the context of those debates suddenly took on the meaning of rolling back US hegemony by means of both a closer collaboration with the European Union and a promotion of regional integration à la Europe. The attractiveness of the European Union during this period was linked to an emerging public desire in the region to create a new political and economic equilibrium between North America (US and Canada) on one hand and Central and South America on the other. Latin American states suddenly realized that closer ties with Europe would indirectly strengthen them vis-à-vis the United States. Interestingly, this political phenomenon coincided with a similar trend in Europe to gradually detach the newly emerging European Union from the United States and its "hard power" politics approach, particularly with respect to issues of global crisis and conflict management. Tensions in transatlantic economic relations between the EU and the United States had already reached a new peak in the 1990s (Josling/Taylor 2003). Now they were followed by a political dissent on crucial issues of global politics. A serious crisis in political transatlantic relations occurred a few years later when tensions between the US and major European powers escalated on the Iraq war issue.

These political developments also set the stage for a series of new initiatives in economic and political regional and interregional integration. A comparison of major regional integration processes after World War II between Europe and Latin America shows that while in Europe one integration model – institutionalized in the form of the European Community and later European Union – succeeded, for many decades the American continent has been confronted with a number of different initiatives and integration models. A wide spectrum of competing and overlapping regional integration models still shapes the political landscape of the Americas and makes it difficult for Latin American states to unite in similar terms than the member states of the European Union. The *Organisation of American States* (OAS) has been an important intergovernmental institution for regional integration since its foundation in 1948. But it has always been viewed as a foreign policy tool for the United States (which is not only a member of the organisation but also hosts its headquarters in Washington DC). Another important regional integration forum has been the *Rio-Group* which was founded in 1986. A permanent mechanism of political consultation and coordination was set up. It still serves as the basic institutional framework for its current 19 members. In December 2004, the *South American Community of Nations* was founded in Cuzco, Peru. Its creation was an attempt to intensify collaboration between South American states and to establish a new institutional framework that embraces two smaller regional integration forums: *Mercosur* and the *Andean Community of Nations*. It was modelled on the European Union and quickly became very influential in South America. Four years later, it formally became a "Union" and was renamed into *Union of South American Nations* based on a new constitutional treaty which was signed on 23 May 2008 at the third summit of head of state and government held in Brazil. The treaty entered into force in 2011. The Union includes new member states which had neither been part of the Mercosur nor the Andean Community. A total of twelve member states (Argentina, Bolivia, Brazil, Chile, Guyana, Ecuador, Colombia, Paraguay, Peru, Surinam, Uruguay, and Venezuela) make this Union a new powerful player in international affairs.

In this context, it is important to note that many initiatives to promote regional economic and political integration in Latin America have been launched as an attempt to hamper US plans to expand the *North American*

Free Trade Zone further south and make it an all-American Free Trade zone (*Área de Libre Comercio de las Américas*, ALCA, or *Free Trade Area of the Americas*, FTAA) (Schott 2001). Those plans have found both supporters and enemies among Central and South American states (Weinstein 2005, Weintraub/Prado 2005). This controversy also indicates that there is still a huge political and ideological divide between Latin American states when it comes to economic and political integration plans. US allies in the region, particularly Mexico and Columbia, have tried to keep their doors open for new partnerships and regional integration models in close collaboration with the United States. On the other hand, Venezuela with its initiative to establish a *Bolivarian Alliance for the Peoples of Our America* (with Antigua and Barbuda, Bolivia, Cuba, Dominica, Ecuador, Nicaragua, Saint Vincent and the Grenadines and Venezuela as current member states) has strongly promoted an alternative regional integration model carrying a clear anti-US message.

This wide spectrum of different integration concepts and the existence of a wide variety of sometimes overlapping institutional frameworks have had a strong impact on recent political and economic developments in Latin America and therefore also marked the region's relations with the European Union. From the beginning, the history of EU-Latin American relations shows a clear economic interest of the European Community (EC) to deepen its trade relations with Latin America and the Caribbean. For a number of countries (former French and British colonies, particularly in the Caribbean) the legal framework of the Lomé agreements came into place (ACP group – Africa, Caribbean and Pacific countries), thus providing them with customs preferences and facilitating access to the European market. At the same time funds were made available to stabilize export prices from those countries. In 2000, the Lomé agreements were "upgraded" to "new partnership agreements" (Cotonou Agreements). But for the vast majority of Latin American countries there was no official legal collaboration agreement in place until the 1990s.

Since the early 1990s, EU-Latin American relations have been institutionalized mainly on four different levels: First, an institutional framework for *comprehensive interregional dialogue and collaboration* (EU-LAC) has been established. Second, a number of specialist dialogue forums have been created in order to deal with *specific regions* on the American continent. The most important dialogue forums on this level have been EU-Mercosur, EU-Andean Community, and EU-Central America. Third, several legal frameworks with *individual Latin American countries* were set up (e.g., EU-Chile, EU-Mexico). Finally, a wide variety of collaboration programs were initiated in order to strengthen *civil society actors* across Latin America.

In general, those institutional frameworks cover all three important aspects of EU external relations: economic cooperation, institutionalized political dialogue, and trade relations. Since the 1990s, a number of official agreements on all four levels have been signed between the EU and its partner institutions and states in Latin America. The institutionalisation process of EU-Latin American relations led to the establishment of new mechanisms and a number of dialogue forums which connect different Latin American institutions – ranging from regional integration forums and organisations, states and governmental institutions to various civil society actors – with the established institutions and bodies of the European Union. The entire architecture rests on the following pillars (EU External Relations Website):

- *EU-Latin America and Caribbean*: The institutionalisation process of EU-Latin America and Caribbean relations on bi-regional level started in the early 1990s with an annual dialogue meeting between the EU and the Rio Group. The 1999 Rio de Janeiro Summit of heads of state and government of the European Union, Latin America and the Caribbean (EU-LAC) led to the establishment of a new EU-LAC mechanism of high-level consultations and summits of heads of state and government to be held every second year. The main purpose of those high-level meetings is to discuss important political, economic and social issues in order to deepen the strategic partnership and to explore new possibilities for co-operation and joint action. The EU-LAC summit mechanism needs to be seen in connection with other institutional dialogues such as the EU-Rio Group Ministerial Meetings and the Ibero-American Summits. In addition, it must be mentioned that several bi-regional sectoral policy dialogues have been established and intensified in recent years.

- *EU-Central America*: The San José Dialogue marks the beginning of a closer political collaboration between the European Community and the six Central American countries Costa Rica, El Salvador, Guatemala, Honduras, Nicaragua and Panama in the 1980s. In 1985, an EC-Central America Cooperation Agreement was signed, followed by new cooperation agreements signed in 1993 and 2003. The 2003 document also served as the basic framework for negotiations regarding an Association Agreement which were launched in 2006 and completed in 2010. This Association Agreement covers all three important areas for cooperation: joint political action, cultural relations and trade.

- *EU-South America*: The *Andean Community of Nations* (earlier known as the "Andean Pact") has been a partner for the European Union since the 1980s. The first Cooperation Agreement between the two parties dates back to 1983. It was followed by new Framework Cooperation Agreements signed in 1993 and 2003. Trade nearly doubled in the 1990s and both parties felt encouraged to discuss the possibility of concluding a bi-regional Association Agreement that would create and regulate an extensive free trade area for goods and services in the mid-2000s. But little progress was made. In 2008, the entire negotiating format had to be changed. A thematic and regional split of the negotiations occurred. Therefore, the bi-regional dialogue could be continued. Another important partner for region-to-region dialogue is the *Mercosur*. In 1995, the EU and Mercosur signed an Interregional Framework Cooperation Agreement which came into force on 1 July 1999. Association negotiations were launched between the two blocs in 1999 but no real progress was made in the following years. In 2004 the negotiations came to a dead end. After a six-year break, negotiations were re-launched in May 2010.

- *EU relations with individual countries in Latin America*: The relationship between the European Union and individual Latin American states has been institutionalized in particular with the following three countries: Chile, Mexico and Brazil. Association agreements have been concluded with Chile (2002) and Mexico (1997) and strategic partnerships have been launched with Mexico (2010) and Brazil (2007). The *EU-Mexico Economic Partnership, Political Coordination and Cooperation Agreement* from 1997 (entered into force in 2000) established a regular high-level political dialogue on bilateral and international issues. Both parties adopted an *EU-Mexico Strategic Partnership Joint Executive Plan* in 2010. The EU-Chile relations are based on the *EU-Chile Association Agreement* from 2002 (entered into force in 2005) which is built upon three pillars: political dialogue, trade and development cooperation. The legal basis for EU-Brazil relations is the 1992 *Framework Collaboration Agreement*. The *EU-Brazil Strategic Partnership* was established in July 2007 when the first bilateral summit was held in Lisbon. A three-year *EU-Brazil Joint Action Plan* (2008-11) was adopted at the follow-up summit in Rio de Janeiro in December 2008. This plan is currently under review and negotiations are being held regarding a new document.

- *EU relations with civil society actors in Latin America*: In its Communication to the Council and the European Parliament on The European Union and Latin America: the present situation and prospects for closer partnership 1996-2000 (COM (95) 495 final, 23 October 1995) the European Commission demanded a comprehensive involvement of civil society actors in future partnership and cooperation activities. "Decentralized cooperation" became the keyword for demanding a stronger participation of a wide variety of civil society actors in joint political, social and cultural endeavours. In this respect the report states:

"Civil society in the European Union and Latin America could come to play a more active role in the new partnership on offer. Decentralized cooperation should therefore be encouraged and defined within action programmes governed by clear operating guidelines (e.g. co-financing). Many different agencies (e.g.

town councils, regional administrations, firms, trade associations, universities and NGOs) would thereby be enabled to contribute actively to the process of development cooperation." (COM (95) 495 final; 23 October 1995, p. 17).

Since 1995, a wide network of EU-Latin America civil society relations has been created, including various Civil Society Dialogue Forums. Today, a number of EU programs specifically aim at strengthening civil society actors in Latin America.

The enormous complexity of Latin America's regional integration processes and the continuation of traditional state-to-state relations in this region (mostly following well-established and deeply rooted foreign policy patterns and frequently also linked to specific political ideologies) make it difficult for the European Union and its member states to find its foreign policy role in this relationship and to pursue a coherent foreign policy based on a long-term strategy for interregional collaboration and partnership. Contrary to the United States, the EU is not capable of exercising any kind of cohesive foreign policy power in the region. Thus, exporting European norms, ideas and values seems to be at the heart of EU foreign policy towards Latin America. If there is any form of "hard power" involved from the European side, then it is definitively not military but only economic power. But even this component, particularly in view of today's financial crisis, seems very limited in scope.

The "Strategic Partnership" between the European Union and Latin America: An Analysis and Evaluation

This chapter provides a short analysis of the development and nature of the strategic partnership between the European Union and Latin America which was proclaimed at the Rio Summit of the head of state and government of the European Union, Latin America and Caribbean in 1999. The decision to launch this new *"bi-regional strategic partnership"* was taken when the new political and economic trajectories of the vast majority of Latin American states started to meet Western political expectations and hopes: democracy and human rights, free market economy etc. Its declared main goal was to launch a series of joint actions in the political, social and economic spheres. There can be no doubt that this event marks the beginning of a closer inter-regional collaboration but its long-term impact on EU-Latin America relations still remains largely unclear. What is new in this relationship since the Rio Summit and which direction are both parties heading in political, cultural and economic terms?

Interestingly, EU foreign policy design before the mid-1990s did not put much emphasis on forming such comprehensive strategic partnerships. For example, the European Commission's Communication to the Council and the

European Parliament on *The European Union and Latin America: the present situation and prospects for closer partnership 1996-2000* (COM (95) 495 final, 23 October 1995) did not even mention the word "strategic partnership". It only listed strategic interests of the EU in the region and suggested to re-consider "the content of the Union's future relations with Latin America", particularly with respect to "new opportunities and the challenges facing both sides in the fields of trade, investment and cooperation" (ibid., p. 11). As a matter of fact, the term "strategic partnership" started to infiltrate conceptualisation and design of EU foreign policy in the mid- and late 1990s, thus leading to a series of high-level summits where new long-term strategic partnerships were concluded. When the EU entered into the new millennium, it was on its way to establish a very wide network of such strategic partnerships. One of the Union's key foreign policy goals of this time was to institutionalize political dialogue with basically all major powers and to enter negotiations about comprehensive cooperation agreements which could serve as future policy frameworks. The 1999 Rio Summit and the EU-Latin America strategic partnership must be seen in this broader context of a new EU foreign policy design.

Of course, it is one thing to declare a strategic partnership but it is quite another to properly craft it so that the relationship between the parties can indeed be deepened and new forms of long-term bilateral cooperation can be successfully established. Through a *Joint Declaration* the gathered heads of state and government at the first EU-LAC Summit announced not only their decision to "promote and develop our relations towards a strategic bi-regional partnership" but also indicated the future direction of this endeavour (Rio Declaration, Press Release: Brussels, 29 June 1999):

"The strategic partnership gathers together two important actors on the current international stage. Latin America and the Caribbean is set to be one of the most flourishing regions in the 21st century as a result of important progress made in the political, economic and social spheres in recent years. For this reason, the region is determined to persevere in the advancement of democratic processes, social equality, modernisation efforts, trade liberalisation and broad-based structural reforms. The European Union, in its turn, has advanced towards a historic integration with multiple implications at the global level on political, economic, social, financial and trade matters, which has brought about constant improvement in the living standards of their societies.

This strategic partnership is based on full compliance with International Law, and the purposes and principles contained in the Charter of the United Nations, the principles of non-intervention, respect for sovereignty, equality among States, and self-determination are bases for the relations between our regions.

This partnership is built upon and will contribute to the furthering of common objectives, such as strengthening representative and participatory democracy and individual freedom, the rule of law, good governance, pluralism, international peace and security, political stability and building confidence among nations." (Ibid.)

The 1999 Rio Declaration reads as an ambitious political program that covers political, economic, cultural, educational, scientific, technological, social and human fields. There can be no doubt that the signing parties had to develop a rather comprehensive joint action plan for the years to come in order to add substance to their strategic partnership. But in this respect disappointment quickly started to replace the euphoric mood of the 1999 summit. Despite the fact that the bi-annual summit mechanism came into place, substantial progress with respect to the planned comprehensive joint action plans could not be achieved on a large scale.

The following EU-LAC summits (Madrid 2002, Guadalajara 2004, Vienna 2006, Lima 2008, Madrid 2010) contributed to a deepening of the strategic partnership in selected areas but no real big political success could be achieved. New topics were put on the agenda including questions of how to strengthen state institutions, sustainable development, cultural diversity, poverty and inequality, regional integration and Latin America's economic role in a globalizing world and the new world market. Strategic and geopolitical questions were addressed in a rather broad and general way. Basically no real new initiative to foster foreign and security relations was brought to the table. The European Commission, in one of its documents on the future development of the strategic partnership between EU and Latin America, stressed the Union's main interests with respect to the partnership with the following words (COM 2004, 220 final):

> "The European Union is interested in developing a political partnership with Latin America which promotes global governance and strengthening multilateralism. It is also interested in intensifying the dialogue with the region on the key issues discussed at major UN events and meetings. Latin America's deep commitment to multilateralism was reaffirmed at the last Presidential summit of the Rio Group in Cusco (Peru) which underlined the need to reactivate initiatives related to the reform and update of the United Nations system, especially in collective security matters" (COM 2004; 220 final).

This European Commission Communication signals a certain shift in interest and focus of EU foreign and security policy regarding Latin America. The region was suddenly seen more in the light of a potential ally for global conflict and crisis management than as a genuine partner for bilateral cooperation in a wide spectrum of policy fields. From an international security perspective, the document also shows the Union's interest in having Latin America as a partner because this would potentially strengthen the EU's genuine multi-lateral "soft power" approach towards global security (Carranza 2004: 65-67).

The shortfalls of the strategic partnership became obvious in 2005. No real substantial progress could be reported. The rise of new left-wing regimes in Latin America made the European Union act even more carefully in its foreign relations with Central and South America, particularly in order to avoid further disturbances in its relations with the United States. Disappointment about the little progress that had been made in the first five years of the strategic partnership was wide-spread on both sides of the Atlantic. The European Union even felt a need to go back to the start and initiate a new dialogue on the question of how to build this partnership and strengthen the relationship in the future. New realities in the Latin American political landscape put additional pressure on both sides to reaffirm their common interest in the partnership and to identify at least a few concrete possibilities for improvement.

On 9 December 2005 the European Commission sent a new Communication to the Council and the European Parliament entitled *A stronger partnership between the European Union and Latin America* (COM 2005; 636 final). This document was put together in view of the upcoming EU-LAC Vienna Summit in May 2006. The document provided an analysis of the most important recent changes in the relationship and also listed a number of recommendations on how the strategic partnership could be fostered and enlarged in the near future:

> "The Commission proposes to give a fresh impetus to the EU-Latin America partnership which currently faces a number of challenges. Its objective for the coming years is to:
>
> • establish a strategic partnership through a network of association agreements (including free trade agreements) involving all the countries of the region and liable to contribute to the integration of the region as a whole;
> • have genuine political dialogues which increase the influence of both regions on the international scene;
> • develop effective sectoral dialogues (e.g. on social cohesion or the environment) with a view to the sustainable reduction of inequalities and promoting sustainable development;
> • contribute to the development of a stable and predictable framework to help the Latin American countries attract more European investment, which will eventually contribute to economic development;
> • tailor aid and cooperation more to the needs of the countries concerned;
> • increase mutual understanding through education and culture" (COM 2005; 636 final).

This document also emphasized again the importance of constructing and deepening civil societies and democracies in Latin America. Specific strategies and action plans were proposed in order to achieve this goal in a long-term perspective. Priority was given to projects which could help to strengthen regional integration and sustainable development. This approach also helped the EU in pursuing and strengthening its own unique two-track foreign policy: on the one hand negotiations with Latin American states and governments could be continued, on the other hand a direct dialogue with a wide variety of non-governmental organisations and civil society actors could be conducted.

In sum, a rather vague political agenda marked the pace of the European Union's foreign policy with respect to Latin America during the years 2005-10. This period was also characterized by a general stagnation and an official break in the Union's negotiations with both Mercosur and the Andean Community. The strategic partnership itself suddenly appeared to become "wishful political thinking" that once had been put on paper but which had not been based on solid grounds in order to produce substantial outcome in practice. It was not until the 2010 Madrid EU-LAC Summit that all parties reaffirmed again their commitment to continue promoting and strengthening the bi-regional strategic partnership. Now both sides expressed their will to reinforce the dialogue and cooperation in selected priority areas, particularly in the fields of innovation and technology for sustainable development and social inclusion (compare the Madrid Declaration, Council of the European Union, Brussels, 15 November 2010, 9931/2/10 REV 2). For this purpose, the so-called *EU-LAC Madrid Action Plan* was set up (Council of the European Union, Brussels, 15 November 2010 10449/1/10 REV) which listed specific tasks and projects in the following key areas for closer bi-regional cooperation: 1. Science, research, innovation and technology; 2. Sustainable development; environment; climate change; biodiversity; energy; 3. Regional integration and interconnectivity to promote social inclusion and cohesion; 4. Migration; 5. Education and employment to promote social inclusion and cohesion; 6. The world drug problem. Work toward implementing this plan started shortly after the summit but it still remains an open question whether the identified priority areas for joint action will in fact stimulate closer EU-Latin American political, cultural and economic cooperation in the near future. Thus, the strategic partnership between EU and Latin America still needs to be seen as an idea rather than a program for action despite the fact that bi-regional policy frameworks are in place and the day-to-day business contains a number of smaller projects of political, cultural and economic collaboration between both regions. Therefore, the strategic partnership's impact on international affairs and the global system also remains very limited. At its best, it can be seen as a partnership in the making.

The Strategic Triangle in Today's Multi-Polar World

The shift toward multi-polarity in the international system poses new challenges for EU-Latin America relations. An increasing number of global and regional powers call into question the validity of the notion and concept of a "strategic triangle" between the United States, Latin America and Europe. The United States has become some kind of "lonely superpower" (Huntington 1999) which is increasingly forced to seek new alliances around the globe in order to maintain its dominant status in the international arena. Both the European Union and Latin America have gradually gained power in global affairs and have therefore become much more equal partners to each other than ever before. But at the same time, all major powers and regions have been forced to open their doors for new and more complex political and economic relations with new partners and other rising powers.

One emerging global player with increasing political influence in Latin America is the Republic of China. China has pursued a very active foreign policy and has launched several diplomatic initiatives in the region since the 1990s (Bieritz/Husar 2005, Reiß 2000). Its economic growth has become an important stimulus to foster foreign economic relations between China and Latin America. China's foreign investment has grown and the country's increasing demand for raw material from Latin America (e.g., soya, copper, steal) has become obvious. Chile was among the first Latin American countries to realize the tremendous economic and political potential of playing the "Pacific card" and strengthening trans-Pacific relations with booming Asian nations. In November 2005, Chile and the Republic of China signed a free trade agreement. Other countries (e.g., Peru) have followed the Chilean example and started to negotiate similar agreements with China. In addition, the Asia-Pacific Economic Cooperation (APEC) has become an attractive alternative for strengthening economic cooperation between Latin American and Asian states. Chile, Mexico and Peru joined APEC in the 1990s.

In the field of international security, the above described trends towards a multi-polar international system are closely linked to the emergence of new strategies and security doctrines which emphasize the importance of a multilateral approach to global security and crisis management. The European Security Strategy (ESS) from 2003 must be seen as a key document for this new thinking about security in international relations. This strategy underpins the importance of establishing new bi- and multi-lateral strategic partnerships in order to help maintain international peace and stability. In the trans-American context, the United States and Latin America have drawn similar conclusions regarding the changing global security environment and the emergence of new security threats. The OAS security conference held on 27-28 October 2003 in Mexico City pointed out that the new threat spectrum as well as the new security priorities of the American states increasingly demand multi-lateral and common approaches and joint action (Nolte 2004):

> "The states of the hemisphere recognize different perspectives regarding security threats and priorities. The security architecture in our hemisphere should be flexible and provide for the particular circumstances of each subregion and each state.
>
> The security of states of the hemisphere are affected, in different ways, by traditional threats and the following new threats, concerns, and other challenges of a diverse nature:
>
> - terrorism, transnational organized crime, the global drug problem, corruption, asset laundering, illicit trafficking in weapons, and the connections among them;
> - extreme poverty and social exclusion of broad sectors of the population, which also affect stability and democracy. Extreme poverty erodes social cohesion and undermines the security of states;
> - natural and man-made disasters, HIV/AIDS and other diseases, other health risks, and environmental degradation;
> - human trafficking;
> - attacks to cyber security;
> - the potential for damage to arise in the event of an accident or incident during the maritime transport of potentially hazardous materials, including petroleum and radioactive materials and toxic waste; and
> - the possibility of access, possession, and use of weapons of mass destruction and their means of delivery by terrorists.
>
> It is the responsibility of the specialized fora of the OAS, and inter-American and international fora to develop cooperation mechanisms to address these new threats, concerns, and other challenges, based on applicable instruments and mechanisms" (OAS 2003: II.4,l).

A comparison between the European Security Strategy and the OAS 2003 security conference conclusions shows that there is a common security interest among all three regions – North America, Latin America and Europe. This common security interest is based on shared values regarding international peace and stability, especially through respect for international law and human rights and support of democratic political development. All three regions show a similar attitude towards international security mechanisms and processes as established within the framework of the United Nations. From this perspective, the promotion of new strategic partnerships between regions and communities of states can be interpreted as a reaction to the above described changes in the international system and global security environment. They can be seen as political attempts to meet the new security challenges of today's globalizing world. Strategic partnerships are therefore indirectly also an attempt to overcome major political and social differences and to prevent potential new conflicts among the bigger political and economic powers in the international system. In addition to this international security dimension, they also entail an important domestic security aspect: they aim at stabilizing internal political dynamics and meeting new domestic challenges particularly those stemming from the emergence of new forms of political violence and radicalisation.

This is why the strategic partnership between the EU and Latin America has recently identified an urgent need to develop new strategies and to launch joint political action in order to prevent new political crisis, violence and conflict. Therefore, a number of new partnership projects have been designed to curtail the spread of such developments (e.g., growth of global criminal networks, migration, international drug-trafficking, etc.) and to prevent possible transnational spill-over effects. Those issues are important for both regions in terms of local, regional and global security. They give extra legitimacy to the promotion of civil society and sustainable development in the context of the strategic partnership and go far beyond pure economic interests. The dynamics of a multi-polar and globalizing world has indeed changed politics on both sides of the Atlantic but also simultaneously deepened new connections and interdependencies among all partners. The established forms of cooperation and interaction have been transformed through the changes in the international system and global environment. Consequently, the traditional patterns of EU-Latin America relations have been gradually replaced by a rather open and dynamic new global network of much more complex cultural, political and economic encounters which is not any longer limited to the three poles of the former strategic triangle United States-Europe-Latin America.

Conclusions and Outlook

The above described changes in the global environment and international system have resulted in a general shift in strategic and geopolitical thinking on the side of Latin America: Neither the US nor Europe are the central focus and key partner for Latin American politics any longer. It is rather a combination between maintaining good contacts with traditional allies and a readiness to open doors for new rising powers in world politics that is guiding Latin American foreign policy at the beginning of the 21st century. But this observation is not only true for Latin America. It is also true for both the US and European Union. Both are permanently searching for new partners and allies. The European Security Strategy openly addresses a strong desire for increased multilateral action in today's multi-polar world. The promotion of a series of "strategic partnerships" results from such political thinking regardless of the substance of such a partnership. The strategic advantage of such global networks and partnerships seems to stem rather from flexibility than from permanent interaction, shared experiences and visions, and long-term trust. Of course, this new thinking also leads to some kind of "inflation" of strategic partnerships which are euphorically proclaimed one day and shortly thereafter already start losing importance and political weight. Sometimes they are even built upon very little substance. In short, there is always a certain risk for any political power to lose substance in its external relations when too many strategic partnerships are being built and the new goals one wants to achieve in close collaboration with the selected partner are short-sighted or only focused on short-term strategic advantages.

EU-Latin America relations will always be embedded in the global environment and international system. The nature of the bi-regional relationship will also reflect new trends and changes in international affairs. In the near future, both regions will definitely look much more towards Asia with its tremendous economic and political potential. Transatlantic relations will most likely remain one of the lower political priorities of both the EU and Latin America. However, a much more focused bi-regional dialogue on selected specific political issues of common interest could bring enormous benefits for both regions.

References

Albrow, Martin (1997): The Global Age. State and Society Beyond Modernity. Stanford: Stanford University Press.

Atkins, G. Pope (1995): Latin America in the International Political System. Boulder: Westview, 3rd ed.

Blasier, Cole (1985): The Hovering Giant: U.S. Responses to Revolutionary Change in Latin America, 1910-1985. Pittsburgh, Pa.: University of Pittsburgh Press, 7 Rev. ed.

Bodemer, Klaus/Kurtenbach, Sabine/Menschkat, Klaus (comp.) (2001): Violencia y regulación de conflictos en América Latina. Venezuela: Ed. Nueva Sociedad.

Bretherton, Charlotte/Vogler, John (2006): The European Union as a Global Actor. Cambridge: Routledge, 2nded.

Brown, Seyom (1992): International Relations in a Changing Global System. Boulder: Westview.

Buzan, Barry/Waever, Ole (2003): Regions and Powers: The Structure of International Security. Cambridge: Cambridge University Press.

Calvert, Peter (1994): The International Politics of Latin America. Manchester: Manchester University Press.

Carothers, Thomas (1991): In the Name of Democracy: U.S. Policy Toward Latin America in the Reagan Years. Berkeley: University of California Press.

Carranza, Mario E. (2004): Leaving the Backyard: Latin America's European Option. Internationale Politik und Gesellschaft (IPG) 2/2004.

Cottam, Martha L. (1994): Images and Intervention: U.S. Policies in Latin America. Pittsburgh: University of Pittsburgh Press.

Dent, David (1999): The Legacy of the Monroe Doctrine: A Reference Guide to U.S. Involvement in Latin America and the Caribbean. Westport, Conn.: Greenwood Press.

Ellis, Evan (2012): The United States, Latin America and China: A "Triangular Relationship". Inter-American Dialogue May 2012. Washington.

Frühling, Hugo/Tuchin, Joseph S./Golding, Heather A. (2003):Crime and Violence in Latin America. Citizen Security, Democracy, and the State. Baltimore: The Johns Hopkins University Press.

Grabendorff, Wolf (2005): Triangular Relations in a Unipolar World: North America, South America and the EU. In: Grabendorff, Wolf/Seidelmann, Reimund (eds.): Relations between the European Union and Latin America. Berlin: SWP, Band 57.

Grabendorff, Wolf/Roett, Riordan (eds.) (1985): Latin America, Western Europe, and the US: Reevaluating the Atlantic Triangle. New York: Praeger.

Grabendorff, Wolf/Seidelmann, Reimund (eds.) (2005): Relations between the European Union and Latin America. Berlin: SWP, Band 57.

Held, David/McGrew, Anthony/Goldblatt, David/Perraton, Jonathan (1999): Global Transformations. Politics, Economics and Culture. Stanford: Stanford University Press.

Hellman, Ronald G./Rosenbaum, H. Jon (eds.) (1975): Latin America: The Search for a New International Role. New York: John Wiley & Sons.

Hill, Christopher/Smith, Karen E. (eds.) (2000): European Foreign Policy: Key Documents, London: Routledge.

Hoffmann, Stanley (1988): Orden mundial o primacía. La política exterior norteamericano desde la Guerra Fría. Buenos Aires.

Huntington, Samuel P. (1999): The Lonely Superpower. Foreign Affairs, 78, 2 (March-April).

Josling Timothy E./Taylor, Thomas G. (eds.) (2003): Banana Wars: The Anatomy of a Trade Dispute. Stanford: Institute for International Studies, Stanford University.

Kaufman Purcell, Susan/Simon, Francois (eds.) (1995): Europe and Latin America in the World Economy. Boulder: Lynne Rienner.

Kernic, Franz (2008): Die Außenbeziehungen der Europäischen Union. Eine Einführung. Frankfurt/Main: Peter Lang.

Kernic, Franz/Feichtinger, Walter (eds.) (2006): Transatlantische Beziehungen im Wandel. Sicherheitspolitische Aspekte der Beziehungen zwischen der Europäischen Union und Lateinamerika. Baden-Baden: Nomos.

Knodt, Michele/ Princen, Sebastiaan (2003): Understanding the European Union's External Relations, London: Routledge.

Kryzanek, Michael J. (1996): U.S.-Latin American Relations. Westport, Conn.: Praeger, 3rd ed.

Lowenthal, Abraham F. (1990): Partners in Conflict: The United States and Latin America in the 1990s. Baltimore: Johns Hopkins University Press, 7 Rev. ed.

Lucarelli, Sonia/Fioramonti, Lorenzo (eds) (2009): External Perceptions of the European Union as a Global Actor. New York: Routledge.

Mace, Gordon et al. (1999). The Americas in Transition. The Contours of Regionalism. Boulder: Lynne Rienner.

Martz, John D. (ed.) (1995): United States Policy in Latin America: A Decade of Crisis and Challenge. Lincoln: University of Nebraska Press.

Nolte, Detlef (2004): Neue Bedrohungsszenarien als Grundlage für eine neue Sicherheitsarchitektur in den Amerikas? Brennpunkt Lateinamerika Nr. 7/ 04, 77-88.

OAS (2003), Declaration on Security in the Americas, adopted at the third plenary session of October 28, OEA/Ser.K/XXXVIII, CES/DEC. 1/03 rev.1, Original: Spanish; http://www.oas.org/documents/eng/DeclaracionSecurity_102803.asp

Pastor, Robert A. (1992): Whirlpool: U.S. Foreign Policy Toward Latin America and the Caribbean. Princeton N.J.: Princeton University Press.

Pastor, Robert A. (2001): Exiting the Whirlpool: U.S. Foreign Policy Toward Latin America and the Caribbean. Boulder, Colo.: Westview Press, 2nd ed.

Perry, William/Wehner, Peter (eds.). (1985): The Latin American Policies of US Allies. New York: Praeger.

Poitras, Guy E. (1990): The Ordeal of Hegemony: the United States and Latin America. Boulder: Westview Press.

Rabe, Stephen G. (1988): Eisenhower and Latin America: The Foreign Policy of Anti-communism. Chapel Hill: University of North Carolina Press.

Rabe, Stephen G. (1999): The most dangerous Area in the World: John F. Kennedy confronts Communist revolution in Latin America. Chapel Hill: University of North Carolina Press.

Reidy, Joseph W. (1964): Latin America and the Atlantic Triangle. Orbis: A Quarterly Journal of World Affairs 8, 1 (spring).

Reiß, Stefanie (2000): Die chinesische Lateinamerikapolitik seit 1989. Brennpunkt Lateinamerika Nummer 21 (9. November 2000).

Roett, Riordan (1994): La relación trilateral América Latina, Europa y Estados Unidos. América Latina/Internacional 1, 2 (Otoño–Invierno).

Roett, Riordan (1995): The Trilateral Relations: Europe, Latin America and the United States, in: Kaufman Purcell, Susan/Simon, Françoise (eds.) Europe and Latin America in the World Economy. Boulder: Lynne Rienner.

Roett, Riordan/Paz, Guadalupe (eds.) (2003): Latin America in a Changing Global Environment. Boulder: Lynne Rienner.

Rouquié, Alain (1987): The Military and the State in Latin America. Berkeley-Los Angeles-London: University of California Press.

Ruiz Huélamo/Sánchez Díez, Angeles (2012): Los Acuerdos de Asociación de la Unión Europea con Centroamérica y MERCOSUR: Presente y futuro. Madrid: Fundación Alternativas.

Scheman, L. Ronald (2003): Greater America: A New Partnership for the Americas in the Twenty-first Century. New York: New York University Press.

Schott, Jeffrey J. (2001): Prospects for Free Trade in the Americas. Washington D.C.: Institute of International Economics.

Schoultz, Lars (1998): Beneath the United States: A History of U.S. Policy Toward Latin America. Cambridge, Mass.: Harvard University Press.

Schwartzberg, Steven (2003): Democracy and U.S. Policy in Latin America During the Truman Years. Gainesville: University Press of Florida.

Sicker, Martin (2002): The Geopolitics of Security in the Americas: Hemispheric Denial from Monroe to Clinton. Westport, Conn.: Praeger.

Smith, Hazel (1995): European Union Foreign Policy and Central America. Houndmills: Macmillan.

Smith, Michael E. (2004): Europe's Foreign and Security Policy. The Institutionalization of Cooperation. Cambridge: Cambridge University Press.

Tulchin, Joseph S./Espach, Ralph H. (eds.) (2001): Latin America in the New International System. Boulder: Lynne Rienner, 2001.

Van Klaveren, Alberto (1996): Europa y América Latina en los años noventa. In: Loeventhal, Abraham/Treverton, Gregory (ed.). América Latina en un Nuevo Mundo. Mexico City: Fondode Cultura Económica, pp. 101-128.

Weinstein, Michael A. (2005): Summit of the Americas Fails to Establish Agreement on F.T.A.A. 21. November 2005. Chicago.

Weintraub, Sidney/Prado, Verônica R. (2005): Librecomercio en el hemisferio occidental. Foreign Affairs en Español, April-June.

Whitaker, Arthur P. (1951): The Americas in the Atlantic Triangle. In: Pan American Institute of Geography and History (ed.). Ensayos sobre la Historia del Nuevo Mundo. México, pp. 69-96.

White, Brian (2001): Understanding European Foreign Policy. London: Palgrave.

Whitehead, Laurence (1999): The European Union and the Americas. In: Bulmer-Thomas, Victor/Dunkerley James (eds.) (1999): The United States and Latin America: The New Agenda. London: Institute of Latin American Studies. Chapter 3.

Whitehead, Laurence (2002): Hacia una reconfiguración del Triángulo Atlántico después de la Guerra Fría. In: Bodemer, Klaus/Grabendorff, Wolf/Jung, Winfried/Thesing, Josef (eds.), El Triángulo Atlántico: America Latina, Europa y los Estados Unidos en el sistema internacional cambiante. Sankt Augustin: Konrad-Adenauer-Stiftung, pp. 13-20.

Whitehead, Lawrence (1999): The European Union and the Americas. In: Bulmer-Thomas, Victor/Dunkerley, James (eds.). The United States and Latin America: The New Agenda. Cambridge, Mass: Harvard University Press.

Wiarda, Howard (1992): American Foreign Policy Toward Latin America in the 1980s and 1990s: Issues and Controversies from Reagan to Bush. New York: New York University Press.

Internet (all websites accessed in January and February 2012):

http://eeas.europa.eu/la/index_en.htm
http://eeas.europa.eu/la/docs/index_en.htm
http://ec.europa.eu/trade/creating-opportunities/bilateral-relations/regions/latin-america/
http://trade.ec.europa.eu/doclib/cfm/doclib_section.cfm?sec=150&langId=en
http://www.europarl.europa.eu/intcoop/eurolat/default_en.htm

EU Relations with Turkey

Şebnem Udum

Introduction

EU-Turkey relations have been studied extensively (see Aybet 2006a, 2006b; Müftüler-Baç 1997, 1998, 2008; Emerson and Tocci 2004, Rumelili 2008). This chapter will not repeat the already existing information, but will evaluate the EU's relations with Turkey from the perspective of the former's quest to become a global actor. It argues that Turkey has been an "outsider" and "other" for Europe for centuries; but if the EU seeks to have a global influence, Turkey should be "on board" with Europe – if not "of Europe" – to boost the latter's power in political, economic, military and ideational terms.

The main question is, then, how relations with Turkey would affect the EU's role in global affairs? In this sense, one should first ask whether the EU is indeed a global actor. What does it need to become one? What is the relevance of relations with Turkey to its aspired global role? What has been done so far? What needs to be done and does the EU want to carry out the tasks? Does it feel the need for that? The chapter starts with an assessment of what it takes for an actor to become a global one, by looking at the definition and forms of power in the 21st century. That is, it adopts a Realist approach. To see how relations with Turkey affect the Union's aspiration to become a global actor, it will look at its contribution to the EU's power and influence. To that end, a brief history of relations will be portrayed, followed by the perception of Turkish membership in the EU. To understand Ankara's bid for membership and what it means to Turkey, it will also view this from the Turkish perspective.

This study does not aim to promote Turkey's EU membership, but it seeks to show what Europe will lack without Turkey if it wishes to claim global status, and whether it is justifiable to keep Turkey out. It will not repeat the issue areas between them in detail. In fact, it argues that the main barrier to Turkey's full membership is at the intellectual level, that is, one of "self" vs. "other." This "otherness" has kept Turkey out of Europe for decades (and in fact centuries). Broadly, concerns regarding security (not just military, but also economic and social) and identity push the limits of the capacity to absorb Turkey as a new member. However, globalizing trends pressurize Europe to take Turkey on board in many other areas like economics, energy security and conflict prevention or resolution. On the other hand,

Turkey seems to be losing interest in the EU since the mid-2000s, and has set a new policy direction particularly with Foreign Minister Ahmet Davutoğlu.

The crux of the problem in Turkish-EU relations has to do with the different perceptions of each other in terms of providing security: Europe prefers to keep Turkey both as an ally and a buffer to ensure its security. It believes that this would preserve its European borders, identity, culture, values and norms. On the other hand, Turkey has defined its security within the Western security community: Particularly due to the experience of World War I and its aftermath, the founders of Turkey set development and modernisation (which was equated with Westernisation and Europeanisation) as the two main goals to augment power to deter an external attack. In this sense, "being in the community of Europe" became essential to avoid being seen as a threat or a target by foreign powers. Therefore, for Turkish foreign policy, being out of the European zone is not sustainable, and any arrangement less than membership would be unacceptable.

When one looks through the "global lens," the EU's balance of power – based on the EUs exclusion of Turkey, but contributing to its security – is not sustainable, either. As long as the EU conveys the image that it discriminates the "other," it would lose its soft power. Having its own economic problems, the EU cannot afford to live on the premises of the 20th century. Bridging that divide between Ankara and Brussels is not easy, and the chapter proposes socialisation through international institutions (see Oğuzlu 2003) as a way to develop common identities. Case-by-case cooperation is not enough to change the intellectual barrier of "self vs. other." Continuous cooperation and parallel socialisation of Turkey to the EU norms would transform the identity of Turkey, which could transcend the traditional dichotomy, and identify it as a country "on board." This study argues that cooperation, particularly in energy security, promises to have more significant outcomes than just interdependence.

By definition, global actors have to project power globally. The EU falls behind the United States in military and technological terms. However, it has long enjoyed its "soft power" which is an asset comparable to the powers of the latter, particularly in resolving conflicts or preventing escalation. It is a significant power in the diplomatic table. One of the components of this "soft power" is the ability or willingness to understand the other. Having Turkey on board will significantly raise the EU's soft power capabilities: It will be able to exercise a more effective foreign and security policy in the Middle East and Central Asia, particularly with respect to energy. Ankara is very capable of speaking the same language with regional countries.

Turkey's EU membership prospect is a significant element of stability at home and abroad. It is in the EU's interest to keep this prospect alive. The domestic political climate in key European states has not been conducive to this goal, but the attacks in Norway are likely to reverse the xenophobic trends in EU member states. Turkey already enjoys privileges (through the Customs Union), and proposals like "privileged partnership" are not acceptable to Ankara. Notwithstanding, there are certain dynamics that encourage Turkey to settle for or seek less than membership as such, because of the costs of integration in various fields including security. As a matter of fact, the long sought for European identity is not an end, but a means to ensure security. The historical reasons behind this will be dealt with below.

The EU's Quest for Global "Actorness" and Turkey

Power in the "Global Era"

The traditional definition of state power refers mainly to military capability. The criteria that define power also include the size of the economy, population, geography, natural resources and alliances. Technological superiority and ideational power (image and status) also count. The latter refers to the image of a country which could boost or lower its status in the international community. It also includes the wielding of power through intellect and culture. It establishes acceptance, that is, consent by others to the state's position or status. Another term is "soft power" which is defined in relation to "hard power" that refers to military capability and other tangible forms of power. Soft power has been attributed to the EU, to refer to economic power that plays a significant role in the diplomatic table or addressing conflicts. It determines the reliability and effectiveness of an actor.

Broadly, a global actor should represent four aspects of power: military, economic, technological and cultural (for a detailed discussion of "international actorness", see Bretherton and Vogler 1999: 15-45).[1] Currently, it is the United States which embodies all four of these characteristics. The EU has not attained the military and technological capability of the United States. In fact, for the latter, technological superiority is a vital element of its security culture. In the late 2000s and early 2010s, the EU's economic strength was challenged by the harsh economic crises. What remains is the ability to spread its culture and boost its image in the rest of world.

The European integration project is a case of success, and nowhere else in the world is there a union that has supranational features. The progress of integration after the Cold War is remarkable: It included two new pillars in addition to the economic union. The security and defence pillar is the utmost point of integration, exemplified by successful EU-led peace operations in

---

[1]   Globalness takes being powerful, and the ability to wield that power beyond the neighbourhood.

the region. (The initiative taken by France in the Libya case also signifies the power of the EU in issues that relate to the security of Europe outside its borders.) The EU specified its goal to become a global actor in the Agenda 2000 report of the EU Commission:

> The European project will remain credible only if it ... [finds] more effective ways of building and defending peace, stability and prosperity on the European continent and throughout the world. (...) The Union must increase its influence in world affairs, promote values such as peace and security, democracy and human rights, provide aid to least developed countries, defend its social model, and establish its presence on the world markets...[E]nlargement will have an impact far beyond the new frontiers of an enlarged Europe, because it will increase Europe's weight in the world, [and] give Europe new neighbours (...) Making the EU a global actor: ...[For] an active and effective foreign policy...an integrated approach to external relations must be built. (...) The European Union will increasingly have to acquire the capacity to take foreign policy decisions involving the use of military resources (Agenda 2000, 1997: 33-35).

However, if the EU remains obsessed with its geographical limits, it would continue being a regional actor. The test case for its global actorness could be the accession process of Turkey, whereby the Union can demonstrate its capability to understand the "other" and successfully integrate a former outsider and threat to its community. In fact, the problems it needs to cope with in the new era require improved skills of crisis management, conflict resolution, communication and empathy, particularly in predominantly Muslim countries.

Turkey's Accession and the EU's Global Role

1. A Brief History of EU-Turkey Relations
When Ankara applied for full membership to the European Economic Community (EEC) in 1959, the latter proposed that a partnership agreement be signed until Turkey achieved the compatible development level with the Community. The result was the Ankara Agreement of 1963, which forms the basis of Turkish-EU relations. It is Article 28 of the Agreement that points at full membership as the final target of these relations:

> As soon as the operation of this Agreement has advanced far enough to justify envisaging full acceptance by Turkey of the obligations arising out of the Treaty establishing the Community, the Contracting Parties shall examine the possibility of the accession of Turkey to the Community. (Agreement Establishing an Association Between the European Economic Community and Turkey, 1963).

The accession of Greece to the EEC in 1981 gave new stimulus for membership, but the 1980 coup had stalled the process. Ankara renewed its application for membership in 1987, but the European Commission refused to start negotiations referring to the status of Turkish-Greek relations and the

Cyprus issue. However, on the economic front, the Customs Union between Turkey and the EU entered into force in 1996. Turkey's hopes for membership were not met in the Agenda 2000: Political issues were cited as barriers to its accession. The following period witnessed intense efforts to include Turkey in the enlargement process, and the EU Councils in Vienna (December 1998) and Cologne (June 1999) gave more promising messages. It was in December 1999 at the Helsinki EU Council that Turkey was declared a candidate for membership. However, the conclusions also specified that Ankara first had to meet the political criteria. Since then, Ankara has carried out reforms in several areas *inter alia*, human rights, freedom of thought and expression, democracy, freedom of association, gender equality and freedom and security of the individual. Eventually, the accession negotiations started in October 2005.

Turkey's candidacy has been a challenge for the EU due to numerous reasons. They can be categorized under political, economic, social and intellectual levels, although they are not completely separate from each other. Turkey has a population of more than 70 million, 99% of which is Muslim. Turkey has a young population: As of 2010, half of the population is aged below 30, and those between 15-64 years account for almost 70 % of the total (The Turkish Statistical Institute, 2011a). The high unemployment rate (as of 2011, the unemployment rate for the age range 15-24 is above 17 %; the Turkish Statistical Institute, 2011b) and kinship in several European countries present a potential migration problem on the basis of the free movement of people. This presents political, economic and social problems for the EU.

Identity issue is another important concern: The European culture, values and norms are mainly shaped by a common history and religion. Historically and ideationally, Turkey (and the Ottoman Empire) has been the "other," the "outsider," or the "threat." Historical "separateness" and religious differences put Europe and the Ottomans/Turks on opposite sides. During the stagnation and especially the retreat period, the Ottomans observed the developed Europe and aimed to catch up with it in order to regain the old power. The Westernisation attempts start in the mid 19th century: After the 1856 Crimean War, the Ottoman State was accepted as part of the European state system. However, as it was losing territory by wars or nationalist movements, it became the "sick man of Europe," and turned into the "Eastern Question." For the European powers, it was one of partitioning and re-designing that part of the world to set up a new balance after the empire falls. It was transformed from a "threat" to a "target."

The current status of negotiations faces the dichotomy of "self vs. other" in different forms. The then French President, Nicolas Sarkozy openly stated that Turkey did not belong to Europe ("Sarkozy Snubs Turkey's EU Membership Bid", 2011; "Les priorités du Président de la République"; 2010). He also remarked that Turkey should continue its relations with the EU without accession, because it would not benefit either ("Entretien du Président de la République", 2011). The mood in CDU and CSU-led Germany was not much different. Chancellor Angela Merkel repeatedly stated that Turkey should not become an EU member (McElroy 2009; Bila 2010).

The outstanding problem in EU-Turkey relations is the Cyprus issue. The membership of the Republic of Cyprus[2] before a comprehensive settlement between the Turkish and Greek Cypriot communities on the island exacerbated the issue for Turkish-EU relations. A full member, under the Customs Union, needs to open ports to all members. However, Ankara refuses to open its ports and to recognize Cyprus as long as the political and economic blockade on the Turkish Republic of Northern Cyprus remains. In July 2005, an Adaptation Protocol was signed, extending its Association Agreement to new members. Turkey unilaterally declared that this did not mean the recognition of the "Republic of Cyprus," and Brussels replied that this declaration had no legal effect for Ankara's obligations under the Protocol (Turkey 2005 Progress Report, 2005: 40). In 2006, the EU decided that negotiations on chapters related to Turkey's restrictions to Cyprus should not be opened. In addition, the opening of some chapters is prevented by France and the Republic of Cyprus.

Whether it was a wise decision to accept Cyprus with representation problems and unresolved disputes requires a detailed analysis, but suffice to say it here that, Turkey's membership was made conditional upon the consent of the Greek Cypriots – which turned the tables against Turkish Cypriots and Turkey in the UN-led negotiations on the island. Looking from another perspective, if Turkey were a member of the EU, there would be no Turkish-Greek problem in the Aegean or Mediterranean.[3] In the Aegean and on Cyprus, security is and will likely to be defined by a Realist understanding as long as Turkey remains a non-member of the EU. So, the membership of the Republic of Cyprus before a settlement only complicated and exacerbated the problem.

Other political criteria for membership included the rule of law and respect of human rights and minorities. In this context, two issues were intensely debated: Civil-military relations and the Kurdish issue. They were interpreted differently, mainly due to the different security cultures of Turkey and Europe. The Kurdish issue is a security problem for Turkey, not only due to the irredentist claims of the Kurdish Workers' Party (PKK) which has car-

---

2   Turkey recognizes it as the Greek Cypriot Administration
3   The core of the problem is the Turkish-Greek dispute in the Aegean, and the existence of the Turkish military on the north of the island maintains "strategic stability" in the context of Turkish security policy.

ried out several terrorist attacks since 1984, but also it touches to the sensitive "Sèvres phobia"[4] in Turkish foreign policy.

The process after Helsinki was not smooth. The accession negotiations with Turkey did not start until 2005, and the keyword became "absorption capacity". The next section will deal with the identity question in more detail with a discussion on the perception of the EU on Turkey.

2. The Perception of Turkey in the EU

One of the main barriers to Turkey's accession to the EU is identity, shaped by different values, culture and history, where they placed themselves regarding power balance and justification of war. Therefore, the quotient of Turkey's contribution has usually been much less than the cost (or "threat") it poses. Another concern that is linked to the identity problem is the geographical location and population of Turkey. It straddles both Europe and the Middle East. The prospect of having direct borders with problematic countries worries Europeans due to possible security, political, economic and social risks. The country's geographical identity is also blurred: Thus, as long as Turkey is out of Europe, the Union's borders will clearly remain in the European continent.[5]

Turkey as a full member could pose a problem at the ideational level when we look at the decision-making and voting procedures in the Council. In a qualified majority voting system, the population of the members is taken into account. So, the countries having the most number of votes are Germany, France, Italy and the UK. Particularly in the case of the EU-3 (Germany, France and the UK), it is also the acknowledgement of their status as the leading powers of Europe which is significant. Turkey's population is close to theirs, and in the case of accession, it will receive a close number of votes, hence almost an equal weight in decision-making. Furthermore, with regard to identity, it will be in the same category as the first-tier/big three. A country occupying an equal seat that has been perceived as the "other" and "the enemy" would not be desired by the leading powers.

With concerns over identity, politics, economics and security, Turkey has been challenging the EU, hence "absorption capacity" was pronounced more in the discourse on enlargement. (The term was first mentioned in the 1993 Copenhagen Summit conclusions.):

> The pace of enlargement has to take into consideration the EU's absorption capacity. Enlargement is about sharing a project based on common principles,

---

4   The Sèvres Treaty of 1920 foresaw the partitioning of the Ottoman territories among the victorious powers of World War I. The phobia refers to the fear that foreign powers conspire to weaken and destabilize Turkey.

5   However, it is questionable when judged from the geographical aspect, whether Cyprus is in fact "European".

policies and institutions. The Union has to ensure it can maintain its capacity to act and decide according to a fair balance within its institutions; respect budgetary limits; and implement common policies that function well and achieve their objectives (Enlargement strategy paper 2005: 3).

The EU's absorption capacity, or rather integration capacity, is determined by the development of the EU's policies and institutions, and by the transformation of applicants into well-prepared Member States ... Integration capacity is about whether the EU can take in new members at a given moment or in a given period, without jeopardizing the political and policy objectives established by the Treaties ... The Commission will in the future prepare impact assessments at all key stages of the accession process. Where such assessments are made, the specific characteristics of each country will be taken into account (Enlargement Strategy and Main Challenges 2006-2007, 2006: 17).

Brussels admits that Turkey's accession would be different from previous enlargements (Issues Arising from Turkey's Membership Perspective, 2004: 4-6): It determines that Turkey's population, size, geographical location, economic development level, political system, potential migration, cultural and religious characteristics are points of concern. It is explicit in its expectation that as a country with an overwhelming Muslim population, Turkey adheres to European values and norms (p. 4).

On the benefit/asset side, the EU has a rising interest in the Middle East and Central Asia, especially beginning with the new millennium because of energy security concerns. The EU is interested in having new pipelines to bypass Russia in order not to be affected by disputes between Russia and Ukraine. The Nabucco pipeline project, which includes Turkey, has demonstrated that the country is indispensable to reliable and secure routes for the transportation of fossil fuel.

A second advantage of cooperation with Turkey is image-building, especially after September 11, 2001 terrorist attacks which transformed the perception of Islam in the West. The US administration's discourse equated international terrorism with evil, and which was fed by religious fundamentalism. However, most of the time, the distinction between Islam and international terrorism was not drawn clearly. This had its repercussions in the Islamic world. A rising tension and misperceptions between the West and the East would not be helpful to meet the economic and security interests of the former. Turkey's candidacy and the EU's reaffirmation of this status gave the message to the Islamic world that the EU was not discriminating against Muslims.

3. Turkey's EU Membership: Is it a Choice or Necessity?

Despite the Ankara Agreement which foresees eventual membership for Turkey, there is dissent in the EU. In addition, the process of accession faced a number of stumbling blocks: The procedures of accession negotiations require the consent of member states to open and close the chapters. The Republic of Cyprus could use its membership status as a leverage to gain advantage in the UN-led negotiations on the island. The second is the position of the leading powers of the EU, particularly France and Germany. The Sarkozy and Merkel leaderships challenged the membership prospect. In addition, there is rising xenophobia exemplified by the banning of minarets in Switzerland ("Swiss Voters Back Ban on Minarets", 2009) and the 2011 Norway attacks. Discrimination against "the other" and labelling migrants as social threats were used for political gain in elections.

The EU acknowledges that Turkey is a key country to ensure energy security and strengthening common foreign and security policy. Thus, the best option for the EU turned out to be to keep Turkey on its side, but outside its border: That is, not only as a buffer, but also as an ally. However, what is sustainable for the EU is not necessarily sustainable for Turkey: If Turkey is not a full member, it will lose faith and hence trust in the EU, which is essential for cooperation. Therefore, this equilibrium is not sustainable for Ankara unless Brussels keeps the prospect of membership alive. Turkey, on the other hand, has various reasons to be part of the EU.

For Turkey, the European vocation does not start with the Ankara Agreement: It dates back to the Ottoman period. After 1923, for the new Republic, national security was based on forming alliances for defensive purposes. For the founders, economically and socially, security and stability could be achieved by development and modernisation. Modernisation was equated with Westernisation and Europeanisation in this period. As an important target of the new Republic, the founder, Mustafa Kemal Atatürk, aimed at "reaching the level of contemporary civilisations," which referred to Western nations and Europe in particular. Only at this level, he believed, could Turkey ensure its security and stability.

What rests behind this perception is the "Sèvres syndrome:" The 1920 Sèvres Treaty foresaw the partitioning of the Ottoman territories among the victors of World War I. After the War of Liberation (1919-1922) against occupation, the Lausanne Treaty (1923) was signed that recognized the borders of Turkey. Therefore, in the nation-building period, Lausanne was the antonym of Sèvres, and signified the inviolability of borders and independence. The phobia for the new nation was that these foreign powers would continue to conspire and weaken the country towards implementing Sèvres. Therefore, as long as Turkey remains out of the European/Western community, the "threat of Sèvres" will continue. Thus, becoming an EU member is not the target, but the means to the end.

The Sèvres phobia dominated foreign policymaking for decades, and led Ankara to maintain the status quo in several cases related to foreign and security policy. EU membership has been a state policy, i.e. not one that is subject to change with each new government. It is not conceivable for Turkey to lose its European goal, not only for security, but for also economic and political reasons. EU countries are Turkey's primary trading partners. Being affiliated with Europe raises Turkey's image and has established it as a stable country.

Turkey is a NATO ally and it defines its security policy within the NATO doctrines. Looking from a Realist perspective, alliance with the West is more beneficial in terms of material capabilities. From Ankara's perspective, the Middle East is not a "perfect substitute" for the EU. However, beginning from the mid-2000s economic and political relations with the region received an enormous boost. The new foreign policy led by Foreign Minister Ahmet Davutoğlu, is based on cooperative security: Through economic cooperation and dialogue, it augmented Ankara's power and influence, and raised its image in the region. The drawback of intensified relations with Arab countries was strained relations with Israel, a long-term ally in the Middle East. The next section looks more closely at the "Davutoğlu doctrine".

4. "Davutoğlu doctrine": "Strategic Depth" and "Zero Problems with Neighbours"

The Turkish Foreign Minister (and formerly the foreign policy advisor to the Prime Minister and a professor of International Relations), Ahmet Davutoğlu introduced two concepts – "strategic depth" (Davutoğlu 2001) and "zero problems with neighbours" (Davutoğlu 2008) – as Ankara's new foreign policy direction. The main difference from the traditional foreign policy approach was that it is based on "positive security," that is, one based not on conflict but on economic cooperation and interdependence. It also foresaw extending power and influence through dialogue and intensified relations with the Middle East and Africa that eventually raised Turkey's image. Ankara used the advantage of common cultural and religious values, and demonstrated that it understands regional problems as an insider and speaks the same language. A significant return of these efforts was a temporary seat in the UN Security Council for 2009 and 2010.

When the pace of accession negotiations slowed in the mid-2000s, and particularly due to the French and German positions, the EU lost its appeal and honesty for Turkey. It was in the same period when Ankara was starting to improve relations with the Middle Eastern and African states. This policy signalled to Europe that if the membership prospect was lost, Ankara might have other alternatives. It indicated Turkey's wariness of knocking at the EU's door, and eventual loss of a friend next door. Whether these cooperative relations and agreements can become an alternative to the EU is questionable. However, it is certain that Davutoğlu's policies and the Turkish Prime Minister's stance towards the Arab-Israeli conflict, made the country and its leader quite popular, hence bolstered its soft power in the region.

5. *Is There a Way Out of "Buffer vs. 'All or nothing' "?*

This study has argued that it is not viable either for Brussels or for Ankara to go their own ways – militarily, politically or economically. Thus, one should address the blockage in relations. The problem stems from two related points: Security and identity. The policy to keep Turkey both as a buffer and an ally is no longer sustainable, particularly considering Turkey's increasing influence and power in the MENA (Middle East and North Africa) region.

The EU handles Turkey's accession from a cost-benefit approach, and it is not conducive to a change in Turkey's position or identity. On the other hand, the EU seems content with the costs of Turkey's non-membership; hence it is reluctant to function as a platform to familiarize the candidate with the norms of the community (Oğuzlu, 2003: 253). International organisations could regulate state behaviour (Hasenclever, Mayer and Rittberger, 2000: 3-33). In a firmly institutionalized international system, members would share common political, social and economic values because of the regulative and constraining effects of institutions. They could also socialize states which aspire to join these institutions to share these values and norms (Schimmelfennig 2000: 109-139, cited in Oğuzlu, 2003: 17). Social constructivists assume that in time, this process leads to the formation of collective identities, whereby members would have common understanding for the acceptable behaviour. Under international institutions, security perceptions are transformed, because these collective identities reduce the uncertainty in others' behaviour (Russet and Oneal, 1998: 441-468, cited in Oğuzlu, 2003: 17). For the EU, it is the accession process which is designed for an adaptation, but in the Turkish case, it is not aimed at transforming the candidate's identity. Rather, throughout the accession process, the demands of the EU touch upon sensitive national security concerns, and reinforce the "self" vs. "other" dichotomy, particularly through the Cyprus problem.

Turkey's EU membership prospect is a significant element of stability in the country and beyond. The EU can come to the table with other solutions than "privileged partnership." Turkey already enjoys privileges (like the Customs Union), and proposals less than membership became a matter of honour for Turkey. Privilege in the EU discourse presumes that "*WE* give you something that *YOU* are not in fact entitled to. We are partners, and our interests and policy prescriptions are similar, but *YOU* are not one of us." Thus, "privileged partnership" repeats the same conviction that Turkey should be an ally but also an outsider.

Notwithstanding, some domestic conditions might require Turkey to settle for less than membership status, because of the costs of integration in various fields including security. The main demand of Turkey is to be within the community. As a matter of fact, European identity is not an end, but a means to ensure security. Thus, for Turkey, "privilege" should mean "you are on board with us though not integrated yet." The EU can start arrangements to move from this negative perception of "privilege" to a positive one, through socializing Turkey during the accession process.

Cooperation in energy security could prove to be a positive step. Energy security is a global problem. It affects almost every sector of state power and security. Seeing Turkey as the energy transit route (or hub) would extend the borders of Europe in the minds of its people. Libya can also be a formidable opportunity for socialisation: Cooperation with Turkey is something that the EU will need in the country's reconstruction. It will help understand the values and norms in the Middle East with the help of Turkey – not as an "interpreter" but as a "bilingual friend" in the community. If Turkey loses hope of EU membership, there is a genuine risk of Turkey being dragged into the security zones, where security is still defined in Realist terms.

Prospects and Recommendations

This chapter has argued that both Turkey and the EU need each other: The former needs to ensure security and stability and the latter needs to augment its power to reach beyond its borders. The main issue in Turkish-EU relations is to transform Turkey's identity from an "other" to "friend on board", and it can be done by enhanced cooperation, whereby Turkey will gradually adopt to EU norms and values. The attacks in Norway have proven to be a critical point in re-thinking conservatism. The keywords of the current era are energy and communication. The EU needs Turkey in both. To sustain its military, political and economic power, the EU needs to guarantee its energy security. To have influence and power beyond its borders, it should have the power to communicate with the "other".

The pressing issue in Turkish-EU relations is the Cyprus question: Ankara refuses to recognize the Republic of Cyprus on the basis of its security interests, while the EU has tied Turkey's full membership to this recognition. The inability or unwillingness to address an internal conflict contradicts with the EU's resolve to become a global actor. Brussels can demonstrate its willingness to integrate Turkey with the Union by taking more effective action to overcome this impasse.

Bibliography

Adler, Emanuel/Barnett, Michael (1997): A Framework for the Study of Security Communities. In: Adler, Emanuel/ Barnett, Michael (eds.): Security Communities. Cambridge: Cambridge University Press, pp. 29-65.
Agenda 2000 For a Stronger and Wider Union (1997), European Commission, July 15, 1997.
Agreement Establishing an Association Between the European Economic Community and Turkey, Ankara, September 1, 1963.

Aybet, Gülnur (2006a): Turkey and the EU After the First Year of Negotiations: Reconciling Internal and External Policy Challenges, Security Dialogue, (PRIO, Oslo), Vol. 37, No.4, December 2006, pp 343-361.

Aybet, Gülnur (2006b): Turkey's Long and Winding Road to the EU: Implications for the Balkans. In: Journal of Southern Europe and the Balkans, Vol. 8, No.1, April 2006, pp. 65-84.

BBC (2009): Swiss Voters Back Ban on Minarets. November 29, 2009, <http://news.bbc.co.uk/2/hi/8385069.stm>

Bretherton, Charlotte/Vogler, John (1999): The European Union as a Global Actor. London: Routledge.

Davutoğlu, Ahmet (2001), Stratejik Derinlik ve Türkiye'nin Uluslararası Konumu (Strategic Depth and Turkey's International Position), Istanbul: Küre.

Davutoğlu, Ahmet (2008), Turkey's Foreign Policy Vision: An Assessment of 2007. In: Insight Turkey, Vol. 10, No. 1, pp. 77-96.

Emerson, Michael/Tocci, Nathalie (2004): Turkey as a Bridgehead and Spearhead: Integrating EU and Turkish Foreign Policy, CEPS EU-Turkey Working Papers No. 1, August 1, 2004.

Enlargement Strategy Paper 2005, European Commission, September 11, 2005.

Enlargement Strategy and Main Challenges 2006-2007, European Commission, November 8, 2006.

Entretien du Président de la République avec le quotidien turc Posta (Interview of the President of Republic with the Turkish Daily Posta): February 25, 2011, <http://www.elysee.fr/president/les-actualites/interviews/2011/entretien-du-president-de-la-republique-avec-le.10741.html?search=Turquie&xtmc=Turquie_l_union_europeenne&xcr=1>

European Council Meeting in Copenhagen, June 21-22, 1993, <http://ec.europa.eu/bulgaria/documents/abc/72921_en.pdf>.

Hasenclever, Andreas/Mayer, Peter/Rittberger, Volker (2000): Integrating Theories of International Regimes. In: Review of International Studies, Vol. 26, 2000, pp. 3-33.

Issues Arising From Turkey's Membership Perspective, European Commission, October 6, 2004, <http://ec.europa.eu/enlargement/archives/pdf/key_documents/2004/issues_paper_en.pdf>

Les priorités du Président la République pour l'avenir de l'Union (The Priorities of the President of the Republic for the future of the Union): January 30, 2010, <http://www.elysee.fr/president/les-dossiers/europe/la-politique-europeenne-du-president-de-la-republique/les-priorites-du-president-la-republique-pour.5159.html?search=Union&xtmc=Turquie_l_union_europeenne&xcr=4>,

McElroy, Damien (2009): Angela Merkel Win Ends Turkey's EU Hopes. In: The Telegraph, September 29, 2009, <http://www.telegraph.co.uk/news/worldnews/europe/turkey/6244276/Angela-Merkel-win-ends-Turkeys-EU-hopes.html>;

Müftüler-Baç, Meltem (1997): Turkey's Relations with a Changing Europe. Manchester: Manchester University Press.

Müftüler-Baç, Meltem/Stivachtis, Yannis A. (eds.) (2008): Turkey-European Union Relations: Dilemmas, Opportunities and constraints. Lanham: Lexington.

Müftüler-Baç, Meltem (1998): The Never-Ending Story: Turkey and the European Union. In: Middle Eastern Studies, Vol.34, No.4, pp. 240-258.

Oğuzlu, H. Tarık (2003), The Role of International Institutions in Identity Transformation: The Case of Turkish-Greek Conflict within the European Union and NATO Frameworks. PhD thesis, Ankara, Bilkent.

Rumelili, Bahar (2008): Negotiating Europe: EU-Turkey Relations from an Identity Perspective. In: Insight Turkey, Vol. 10, No. 1, January 2008, pp. 97-110.

Russet, Bruce/Oneal, John R. (1998): The Third Leg of the Kantian Period for Peace: International Organizations and Militarized Disputes, 1950-1985. In: International Organization, Vol. 52, No. 2, 1998, pp. 441-468.

Sarkozy Snubs Turkey's EU Membership Bid on Ankara Visit: RFI, February 25, 2011, <http://www.english.rfi.fr/france/20110225-sarkozy-snubs-turkeys-eu-membership-bid-ankara-visit>

Schimmelfennig, Frank (1999): NATO Enlargement: A Constructivist Explanation. In: Security Studies, Vol.8, No.2-3, pp. 198-234.

Turkey 2005 Progress Report, European Commission, November 9, 2005.

TÜİK (The Turkish Statistical Institute) Press Release (2011a), Address Based Population Registration System Results of 2010, January 28, No. 19.

TÜİK Press Release (2011b). Household Labor Force Survey for the Period of June 2001, 15 August, No: 168.

Utku Bila, Sibel (2010): Merkel Tells Turkey EU Talks 'Open-Ended'. AFP, March 29, 2010, <http://www.google.com/hostednews/afp/article/ALeqM5i9b5IFyo8N6pDutSj6oCTjxDD79>

The EU as a "Target" of Russia's "Energy Foreign Policy"

Martin Malek

Introduction

Energy security, in terms of secure supply and stable prices, is increasingly related to geopolitics and international relations. This has to be taken into consideration by the EU with the world's second largest energy market with 500 million consumers, as crucial players like the Organisation of the Petroleum Exporting Countries (OPEC), the United States, Russia, China, India, and others are more or less determined by geopolitical factors.

The European Commission has addressed energy security in its first Green Paper (adopted in November 2000 and released in 2001), but in the EU's security strategy of 2003, "A Secure Europe in a Better World," only a brief paragraph is devoted to this topic. The energy disputes of early January 2006, when Russia cut off gas supplies to the Ukraine[1] (which transits around 80 percent of Russia's Europe-bound gas), of early 2007 with Belarus due to a price and transit fee conflict and of January 2009, when Moscow halted gas deliveries to the Ukraine and then even shut down the gas pipeline through this country,[2] demonstrated Europe's vulnerability in its dependence on Russian gas to the broader public. These incidents have also illustrated the EU's diminishing power as consumer amid high energy and resource prices and especially its weakness in view of an increasingly assertive Russia. Its role has to be scrutinized in this article for two reasons: Firstly, it is the main actor which the EU has to deal with concerning the rules of the game in the resource-rich Central Asia and Caspian Region (CACR), meaning the post-Soviet republics Georgia, Armenia, Azerbaijan, Kazakhstan, Turkmenistan, Uzbekistan, Kyrgyzstan, and Tajikistan. And secondly, most of the projections for energy consumption indicate that one of the most important energy security challenges facing the EU over the next two decades will be its ability to diversify the sources and modes of transit of its energy imports.

---

1 The reason was that in 2004 the "wrong" candidate, opposition leader Viktor Yushchenko, was elected President of the Ukraine – instead of Kremlin-backed Viktor Yanukovych (who, however, won the elections in 2010).

2 During this gas crisis the EU initially remained passive on the grounds that the dispute between the Ukraine and Russia was "commercial."

Although the EU's 27 member states have ceded some national sovereignty (or competency) to EU institutions in a variety of areas, including economic and trade policy, energy policy remains primarily the responsibility of the member states. However, a fragmented and fractured regional energy market is – and will also be in the future – the best playing field for Russia to "divide and rule" the individual EU member states and their energy companies. As a German energy expert put it, "the still existing lack of coherence of the EU's external energy policy enables Russia to continue the 'bilateralisation' of energy partnerships." According to him, Moscow "is in a powerful position to play off individual European states and their national energy champions against each other" (Umbach 2008).

Thus, several EU member states have pursued bilateral energy deals which will increase their and the EU's dependence on Moscow for many years to come. These states have apparently reconciled themselves to the possibility of a long-term Russian control over their economic well-being and are turning a blind eye to Russia's opaque energy and pipeline deals in order to remain on good terms with the Kremlin. Important examples are the Nord Stream gas pipeline on the seabed between Vyborg, Russia, and Sassnitz in north-east Germany (its construction started in April 2010, and in September 2011 Russian Prime Minister Vladimir Putin pressed the start button to open the pipeline) and the Italian energy giant's Eni important role in the Russian South Stream gas pipeline project (see sub-chapter "Russia's Fight Against Nabucco"). Russia's interests are obvious; however, it is incomprehensible why the EU and/or its member countries promote Moscow's goals.

The EU's Present and Future Oil and Gas Import Dependence

Some General Assumptions

EU dependency on energy imports increased from less than 40 percent of gross energy consumption in the 1980s to 45 percent in 1995 and 54.8 percent in 2008 (with the highest energy dependency rates recorded for crude oil and for natural gas; see the next two sub-chapters). This meant hat more than a half of the EU energy consumption was imported. Malta, Luxembourg, Cyprus, Ireland, Italy, Portugal, Spain, and Belgium had an especially high dependence (more than 75 percent); the only net exporter of energy was Denmark (European Commission – Eurostat 2010). And the EU's total energy economy will become increasingly reliant on imports. According to "business as usual" projections of the International Energy Agency (IEA), this dependence could reach 64 percent in 2020 and 67 in 2030 (International

Energy Agency 2008: 19). EU Energy Commissioner Guenther Oettinger said in May 2011 that it could even get up to 75 percent by 2030.

Eurostat reported the following figures on the EU-27 primary energy production in 2009: Renewables 18.4 percent, hard coal 9.6 percent, lignite 11.6 percent, oil 13.1 percent, natural gas 19.3 percent; and with 28 percent, nuclear energy held the largest share (Keenan 2010: 4). But due to the environmental obligations of the Kyoto Protocol and the phasing-out of nuclear energy programs in several important EU member states (especially after the disaster in the Japanese nuclear power plant Fukushima in March 2011 it will be politically almost impossible to build new plants in most of the EU member states), the EU will become more dependent on oil and gas imports from outside Europe – mostly from unstable countries in the former Soviet Union, the Middle East, and Africa.

The situation is getting even more complicated since the EU, as the European Commission's first Green Paper put it, has "very limited scope" to influence energy supply conditions (European Commission 2001: 11). This especially applies to Russia: Notwithstanding official declarations, there is no real "strategic partnership" between Brussels and Moscow in the sphere of energy politics (Westphal 2004: 48). The EU is de facto powerless to persuade Russia to bend to treaty-backed disciplines Moscow sees as detrimental to its national interests. This has been displayed on numerous occasions. One of them is the fate of the Energy Charter Declaration, an initiative intended to promote energy cooperation and diversify Europe's energy supply.[3] Russia has not ratified the Energy Charter Treaty, because it would entail the obligation to implement the principles of freedom of transit without distinction of the origin, destination or ownership of the energy, and of non-discriminatory pricing. Another initiative is the Energy Dialogue EU – Russia, launched in October 2000 on the occasion of the sixth EU-Russia Summit in Paris. The official goal of this Dialogue is "to enable progress to be made in the definition and arrangements for an EU-Russia Energy Partnership" (European Union 2009). Russia offers only very restricted access for foreign investment in its energy sector, and this is one of the reasons why the Dialogue has so far not produced any tangible results.

---

3   The Declaration, launched in 1991, gave way to the 1994 Energy Charter Treaty that entered into legal force in 1998 and established a framework of rules and agreements to promote international energy cooperation. The Treaty seeks to create a level playing field of rules regarding the promotion of foreign energy investments; free trade in energy materials, products and equipment; freedom of energy transit through pipelines and grids; promoting energy efficiency; and providing mechanisms for addressing disputes. The European Parliament's Foreign Affairs Committee said in a statement on 4 September 2007 that support for Russian accession to the WTO should depend on Moscow's ratification of the Energy Charter Treaty. This condition is reasonable, but will be difficult to implement.

Oil Supply

In 2008 the EU's energy dependence rate for oil amounted to 84.3 percent (compared with 75.8 percent in 1997); and 22 EU member states presented dependency rates over 90 percent. There is only a single net exporter, Denmark (European Commission 2010: 31). As of the end 2010, EU countries possessed only 0.5 percent of the proved world oil reserves (BP 2011: 6). Therefore, the Union is highly dependent on imported oil. And with "business as usual" the EU's reliance on imports of oil will rise to 93 percent in 2030 (Commission of the European Communities 2007: 26).

Figure 1 demonstrates that in 2008, some 29 percent of the EU-27's imports of crude oil were from Russia; this was slightly down on the peak of 30.4 percent recorded in both 2006 and 2007.

Figure 1: EU import of crude oil, by country of origin (in million tons), 2000–2008

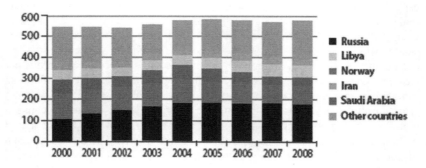

Source: European Commission 2010: 41.

Gas Supply

Over the past four decades, the EU's natural gas consumption has grown much faster than primary energy consumption. EU-27 net imports of natural gas grew by 60 percent from 1997 to 2007. In 2007, the EU-27 energy dependence rate for natural gas was 60.3 percent, in 2008 61.5 and in 2009 63.4 percent (Keenan 2010: 4). And 2010, EU countries had only 1.3 percent of the proved world gas reserves at their disposal (BP 2011: 20).

Between 2000 and 2008 gas imports from Russia presented a slight increase (12 percent). However, the diversification of supply led to a decline of its share compared to 2000 (50 percent). In 2008, 38 percent of EU-27 natural gas imports came from Russia (European Commission 2010: 41).

Figure 2: EU gas import, by country of origin (in Petajoules), 2000–2008

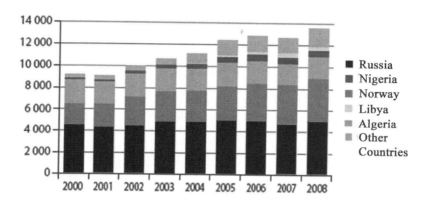

Source: European Commission 2010: 41. – "Petajoule" is a unit of energy equal to 10^{15} joules; one petajoule equals 31.60 million m³ of natural gas.

In the Western EU, markets are large, but diversified. In the Eastern parts of the Union, the markets are smaller, but much more dependent on Russia – sometimes close to 100 percent. The "old" 15 member states (EU-15) account for about 85 percent of the EU's gas consumption. The size of the Western European markets means that slightly more than two thirds of Russian gas consumed in Europe is imported by the EU-15, despite their lesser dependence on Moscow.

The EU's reliance on gas imports could increase to 84 percent by 2030 (Commission of the European Communities 2007: 26), and the European Commission estimated in 2008 that the Russian share will climb to 60 percent of total import (Erixon 2008: 4). Some sources are even afraid of a risk of the EU becoming so dependent on supplies of energy from Moscow that it constrains EU states from criticizing any failings in Russia's record on democracy, human rights, and freedom of the press.

Foundations of Russia's "Energy Foreign Policy"

In the 1990s Russia generally emphasized its intention not to deteriorate to the level of a "raw material appendage to the West". Then, however – and especially in President Putin's second term in office (2004–2008) – Russia began to make a virtue of necessity (Schewzowa 2006: 41). According to the will of the leadership in Moscow, Russia's new claims of being a superpower and global player should not only rely on ostentatiously drawing attention to the military potential, but also on the – unofficial – concept of an "energy superpower": Russia wants to turn as many nations as possible inside and outside the Commonwealth of Independent States, or CIS, into customers of its oil and gas industry, buy shares of companies supplying energy inside and outside the CIS and control the supply chain up to the end users. Other CIS republics, rich in natural resources, such as Azerbaijan, Turkmenistan, Kazakhstan, and Uzbekistan should, according to Moscow's wishes, export their energy exclusively via pipelines running across Russian territory. This entails transit charges and makes both supplier as well as importing countries dependent on the Kremlin, which could easily cut off these pipelines (or at least threaten to do so) whenever required.

Another important fact is that Russia, according to numerous statements, wants to minimize its dependence on "unreliable" transit countries. Thus, Gazprom's former Deputy CEO Alexander Ryazanov said about the Nord Stream gas pipeline project: "It is a rather expensive undertaking, because it is political. But of course, we need this pipeline in order to exert pressure on Byelorussia and Ukraine" (as quoted in Panjuschkin & Sygar 2008: 245). And Viktor Baranov, President of the Russian Union of Independent Gas Producers, took the same line, noting that "even if [the Russians] have to build the thing running across the sky at an even higher cost, they would go for it" (as quoted in RFE/RL 2008).

All these measures are designed to make as many countries as possible dependent on Russian energy suppliers, which under particular framework conditions could be (or already have) turned into political dependencies. The repeated claims of numerous Russian as well as Western politicians, media and pundits that Moscow is an "extremely reliable supplier of energy" are debateable due to other reasons as well. Thus, according to the Defence Research Agency in Stockholm, there have been at least 55 cases (cut-offs, explicit threats, coercive price policy, and certain take-overs), when Moscow actively used the "energy tool" against other states, between 1991 and 2006. Only eleven occurred without any political underpinning (Larsson 2007: 80-81). Moscow has obviously long since begun making policy not only with the *prices* of gas[4] and oil but also with the *supply* of these energy sources *as such*. Mikhail Korchemkin, managing director of East European Gas Analy-

---

4   It is a matter of common knowledge that Moscow regulates its gas price on a political basis: "Loyal" states pay much less that "disloyal". Thus, in 2009 "friendly" Armenia was charged 154 Dollar per 1,000 cubic metres, while the "awkward" Ukrainians (under President Yushchenko) were asked to pay 360 and the average price Gazprom set for EU member states was 390 (Popescu & Wilson 2009: 44). At the beginning of 2010, Germany had to pay 280 Dollar per 1,000 cubic metres – and the Ukraine 305 (Kiselyov 2010). So there are no "market prices" for gas, no matter what Russian senior officials tell their EU counterparts and media outlets.

sis, explained that Russia "just doesn't want to sell gas for a profit but also to control it" (as quoted in Blau 2010).

In its 2003 energy strategy Russia leaves no doubt that it intends to exploit its energy policy for security-related ends (Leijonhielm & Larsson 2004: 11). This document lists the "energy factor" as one of the "principle elements of Russian diplomacy". Among its basic tasks are the "external guarantee of realizing its energy strategy" and "supporting the interests of Russian petrol and energy companies abroad". The document, furthermore, lists "securing Russia's global-political interests" by using its oil companies and "securing Russia's political interests in Europe and the bordering states as well as in the Asian region" with regard to natural gas as "strategic goals" (Minpromtorg Rossii 2003).

As mentioned above, Russia's strategic goals in the sphere of energy policy are also geopolitically motivated. Prime Minister Putin stated that "the role of the country on international energy markets determines, in many ways, its geopolitical influence" (as quoted in Kupchinsky 2009). At a celebration to mark the opening of the oil export terminal in Kozmino in December 2009, he told assembled officials that the new East Siberia–Pacifica Ocean (ESPO) pipeline[5] "is not just a pipe," but rather "a geopolitical project" (as quoted in Henderson 2010). Well-known Moscow-based expert Lilia Shevtsova, senior associate at the Carnegie Endowment for International Peace, spoke about Russian "energy geopolitics" (Ševcova 2007: 37), and Foreign Minister Sergei Lavrov drew a connection between Russia's energy policy and the creation of a "multipolar world": "The emergence of new, global centres of influence and growth and a more even distribution of resources for the development and control of natural resources form the material basis for a multipolar world order" (Lavrov 2007). A publication of the Russian Foreign Ministry's Diplomatic Academy referred to the Russian oil companies as a "further geopolitical weapon" of the Kremlin (Matyash 2004: 111).

Against this background, it is only logical that Gazprom, one of the world's largest energy companies and among the major parties competing for resources in the CACR, plays a key role in Russia's "new energy foreign policy" (Lindner 2007: 1), even beyond the borders of the former USSR. Some Western observers of Russian affairs came to the conclusion that Gazprom's highest business goal was "not profit, but political clout" (Reitschuster 2006: 262), as the company policy is developing in close coordination with the Kremlin.

---

5   Construction of this pipeline started in April 2006. On January 1, 2011 Russia began scheduled oil shipments to China via this pipeline, with the plan to increase the rate up to 300.000 barrels per day in 2011.

Gazprom holds about 25 percent of the global gas reserves and produces 94 percent of Russia's gas and 16 percent of the global output. Production from the three "super-giant" west Siberian gas fields (Urengoy, Yamburg, and Medvezhe) in the Nadym-Pur-Taz region, which account for the bulk of Gazprom's output, is now in decline, while the fourth giant field, Zapolyarnoe, is at its summit. The company's ability to maintain, let alone increase, gas production in the coming decades depends on the development of a new generation of the fields on Yamal Peninsula in northwest Siberia and/or the Shtokman field in the central part of the Russian sector of the Barents Sea.

High prices for crude oil and natural gas not only help the Russian budget, which in 2006, according to the Ministry of Finance, got 52.2 percent of its revenues from export of these two energy sources (Ministerstvo finansov Rossiyskoy Federatisi 2007), but also those pro-Kremlin business elites, which produce and sell them. The well-known Russian foreign policy commentator Andrei Piontkovskiy stated that Russia is de facto ruled by a circle of ten to fifteen persons, who have personal interests in the oil business and are, therefore, interested in keeping oil prices as high as possible (Piontkovskiy 2006). Even the traditionally rather cautious BBC reported that Moscow was interested in an unstable Middle East, as this would likely keep oil and gas prices high (Eggert 2006). Possibly linked to this is the observation of a well-known journal that Russian arms exports are focused on energy-rich regions in Africa and the Middle East (Vatanka & Weitz 2007). Russia was and/or is one of the most important arms suppliers to Muammar al-Gaddafi's Libya, Saddam Hussein's Iraq, Iran, Syria, and Sudan.

European and Russian Interests in Energy Corridors and Pipeline Routes

General "Clashes of Interests" between the EU and Russia

Not only former German Federal Chancellor Gerhard Schroeder, but also many other influential voices in Western Europe turned against even cautious criticism by European politicians as well as European media of Putin's increasingly nationalistic rule or his war in Chechnya, as this would be counter-productive, given the necessity of being supplied with Russian energy sources. At the same time – and occasionally the same voices – deny any "unilateral dependence" of the EU on Russia and claim "mutual dependence," as Moscow is said to depend on its revenues from exports to the EU and rerouting the oil and gas flow to East Asia would be impossible at short notice, due to insufficient pipeline capacities. But this does not answer the question why the Kremlin's self-confidence seemed to be steadily rising with the gas prices, while the EU heads of states and governments – also and especially at meetings with Putin – gave the impression of being undecided, intimidated or, at any rate, divided. The truth is that there is no symmetric "mutual dependence" between the EU and Russia: The EU is, of course, an important customer for Moscow (60 percent of Gazprom's export are delivered to the EU-27), but "while Russia could easily shut down its pipelines to Europe for a few days, [...] Europe cannot do without Russian energy even in the very short-run" (Erixon 2008: 8).

In an angry and often sarcastic speech to top German industry chiefs at a business forum in Berlin in November 2010, Putin lambasted the EU, insisting that Brussels should consult Moscow over planned energy legislation and reminding the EU about its dependence from Russia. At one stage, he mocked the Europeans, saying if they did not want gas or nuclear energy, then they would have to rely on Russian firewood. "How will you heat your houses?" he asked. "You do not want gas, you do not want to develop nuclear energy. Where will you get your heat from then? From firewood? Even for firewood you will need to go to Siberia. You do not even have wood" (as quoted in Dempsey 2010).

Dependence on Russian energy resources would not be a problem if Moscow played by the same rules as other players on the energy markets and European states. What some Foreign Ministries of EU countries are striving for, namely a "rapprochement through entwinement" ("Annäherung durch Verflechtung", as the German Foreign Ministry put it especially under Minister Frank-Walter Steinmeier from 2005 to 2009), also and particularly with regard to energy, implies a logic which is far removed from the present behaviour and mentality of Russia's elite and, furthermore, ignores the principle question about the desirability of an "entwinement" of a union of democratic states (as the EU claims to be) and Russia, a country ruled by an authoritarian regime whose economy is listed in international ratings as highly corrupt.

A report of the European Council on Foreign Relations warned: "While EU leaders believe that peace and stability are built through interdependence, Russia's leaders are working to create a situation where the EU needs Russia more than Russia needs the EU, particularly in the energy sector" (Leonard & Popescu 2007: 1). Russia speaks with one voice, whereas the EU with its 27 members (which have very diverse relations with Moscow as well as interests in the realm of energy policy) faces huge difficulties to find a common course in energy policy. The Kremlin, using his instrument Gazprom, has skilfully exploited divisions among EU member states by striking bilateral deals that undermine Brussels' efforts to forge a common energy policy. Russia is picking off individual EU member states and signing long-term deals which undermine the core principles of the Union's common strategy. Karel Schwarzenberg, Foreign Minister of the Czech Republic, was one of the few EU politicians who saw through Russia's strategy in international energy policy: Moscow, he stated, plays the EU states off against each other (Bota & Nass 2008).

Russian senior officials (starting with Putin) warned Brussels of alternatives to Russian suppliers as well as of creating alleged or real barriers to Russian companies trying to expand on European markets, which could prompt Russia to orient itself towards East Asian markets. European media outlets quoted Gazprom CEO Alexei Miller in 2006 saying that "attempts" to limit his company's "activities in the European market and to politicise questions of gas supplies, which are in fact entirely within the economic sphere, will not produce good results" (as quoted in BBC 2006).

Viewpoint and Interests of the EU in the CACR

The bulk of the world's energy resources, located in Russia, the CACR, the Middle East and North Africa, are all well within geographic reach of the EU: 80 percent of world natural gas supplies are located within a radius of 4,500 kilometres from Central Europe. The CACR's massive potential as an energy supplier is mirrored by the document "The EU and Central Asia: Strategy for a New Partnership," adopted in 2007: "The development of resources in oil and gas has significantly increased the role of Central Asian States as energy producers and transit countries. Increasing oil and gas exploitation will contribute to better world market supplies and will be conducive to diversification. Gas deliveries from the region are of special importance to the EU" (Council of the European Union 2007)[6].

However, nearly two decades after the collapse of the Soviet Union there are still only a few routes for the transit of energy resources from the region to Europe. EU documents point to the facts that, "due to the landlocked nature of the Caspian areas, its reserves are not easily accessible and transportation of crude to the international market will require construction of new oil pipeline(s) as the Turkish straits and the Baku–Tbilisi–Ceyhan pipeline [see sub-chapter "The BTC Pipeline", M.M.] will not be able to transit the future additional oil. If such pipelines are not built, Caspian oil producing countries will look for alternative oil routes for example towards eastern markets" (Commission of the European Communities 2008: 15). In November 2008 the European Commission unveiled a long-term, multidimensional program for energy security, which includes the "development of a Southern Gas Corridor for supply from Caspian and Middle Eastern

---

6   This document does not mention Russia at all, let alone a critical analysis of Moscow's efforts to bar the EU from access to the resources of the CACR without Russian influence and interference.

sources and possibly other countries in the longer term, improving security of supply" (European Commission 2008). And in April 2010 the Foreign Affairs Committee of the European Parliament "recognized" the importance of the South Caucasus for the EU's energy security and supply: It expressed support for the strengthening of EU-South Caucasus cooperation in energy projects, "in particular for the successful realisation of the Nabucco pipeline" (European Parliament – Foreign Affairs Committee, 2010) (see sub-chapter "Russia's Fight Against Nabucco").

Viewpoint and Interests of Russia in the CACR

Numerous statements by Russian officials as well as Moscow's actions do not leave any doubt that it aspires to expand its political, economic, and military[7] presence in the strategically vital CACR. One of the most important objectives of the Kremlin in the CACR is the exclusion of the US, NATO, and EU to the highest possible extent. For this and other purposes, Russia tried to capitalize on the (now "frozen") conflicts on the southern periphery of the former USSR, especially in Moldova (Dnestr Region), Georgia (Abkhazia, South Ossetia), Azerbaijan (Nagorno-Karabakh), and Tajikistan (civil war 1992-97) in order to retain its influence. The EU's passive stance played into Moscow's hands.

While the Central Asian states were mostly underpaid for their gas, Europe is forced to pay a price far above what would be the case if energy was imported directly from the region. For instance, in the early 2000s Russia bought gas from Turkmenistan at the price of 57 Dollar per thousand cubic meters. This gas was then consumed domestically while Russian gas was exported to Europe at a price of 250 US dollars per thousand cubic meters. Therefore "it is no wonder that Russia uses all means necessary to block Europe from engaging directly with the Central Asian states, primarily Kazakhstan and Turkmenistan" (Norling 2007: 10).

Pipelines and Transport Corridors Bypassing Russia

The BTC Pipeline

The 1,760-kilometer-long Baku–Tbilisi–Ceyhan (BTC) oil pipeline, built in 2002 for 3.9 billion US dollars, starts at the Sangachal terminal near Baku in

---

7   Moscow still maintains troops and bases in Georgia (against the will of its government, in particular in the breakaway provinces Abkhazia and South Ossetia), Armenia, Azerbaijan (Gabala radar station), Tajikistan, Kyrgyzstan, and Kazakhstan (space launch facility Baikonur).

Azerbaijan, passes through Georgia and ends at the Ceyhan oil terminal on the Turkish Mediterranean coast. It avoids Russian as well as Iranian territory and the congestion in the Bosporus and therefore provides greater and easier access to world energy markets. The first tanker left the port on June 4, 2006 with about 600,000 barrels of crude oil. This marked the start of export of Azerbaijan's oil via the BTC pipeline.

The BTC pipeline would never have happened without strong US support, because the EU did not actively lobby it – obviously, in order not to "offend" Russia (Meyer 2006: 133, 193, 237). Moscow has tried for several years to thwart the construction of BTC, anticipating that it would lead to a loss of its monopoly on the transportation of West Caspian oil to Europe. But the BTC runs close by the Russian-controlled Georgian provinces Abkhazia and South Ossetia and the Azeri-Armenian ceasefire line around the separatist region Nagorno-Karabakh as well as through the politically insecure Kurdish areas of eastern Turkey. For that reason, the defence of the pipeline even in peace times is one of the greatest security policy challenges facing those countries with an interest in it.

Trans-Caspian Pipelines?

The EU would benefit in a threefold way from a direct pipeline link to Central Asian gas exporters. First, it would be able to buy gas at a lower price than the levels currently set by Russia. Gas could be brought through new pipelines from either Kazakhstan or Turkmenistan across the Caspian Sea along the seabed to Azerbaijan, where it would be pumped into pipelines leading to the Nabucco pipeline, at a lower cost than new Russian fields in Siberia or in the Arctic. Secondly, by diversifying its sources and transit routes, the EU would reduce its dependency on Russian energy. And finally, the Union "would break the neo-colonial dependency situation to Gazprom that Central Asian producers are locked into" (Cornell et al. 2006: 21-22).

However, due to fierce Russian (and Iranian) resistance and disputes between Azerbaijan and Turkmenistan over the ownership of gas fields, Trans-Caspian pipelines are still far from being built. Russian President Putin, whose trip to Tehran in 2007 was the first by a Kremlin leader since World War II, warned that energy pipeline projects crossing the Caspian could only be implemented if all five nations that border the Caspian support them (knowing, obviously, that this will not be the case in the near future). This statement underlined Moscow's strong opposition to efforts to build pipelines to deliver hydrocarbons to the West bypassing Russia (Isachenkov 2007).

Russia's Fight Against Nabucco

The Nabucco pipeline is the EU's flagship project with regard to the CACR. It could bring gas from the Georgian/Turkish and/or Iranian/Turkish border respectively to the Austrian gas hub in Baumgarten, without passing through Russia. Austria's oil and gas company OMV, the Bulgarian Energy Holding, Turkey's Botas, Germany's RWE, Hungary's MOL, and Romania's Transgaz are partners in this project. As initially assumed, it would cost an estimated 8 billion euro; and 3,300 kilometres of pipeline should become operational by 2013 and reach a capacity of 31 billion cubic metres of gas a year by 2020 (which would be 10 percent of EU-27 gas imports in 2005). But then, the initiators of the project hoped to start Nabucco's construction in 2013, so that the first gas could flow in 2017 (Energy, Ecology, Economy 2011). And the projected investment in Nabucco has been revised up to 12-15 billion euro (Coskun 2011).

Moscow does not want Nabucco to be built and is doing its best to derail it. An important initiative in this context is the South Stream pipeline, intended to transport gas from the CACR to Europe. This pipeline with a capacity of 63 billion cubic metres of gas per year is proposed to run from Southern Russia under the Black Sea to Bulgaria, then branch off to the south and to the north. Moscow managed to persuade several Southeast European countries to join the project, and Russian news agency RIA Novosti wrote about a "big victory for Russia and a major blow to Nabucco", when Austria joined the project in April 2010 (Fedyashin 2010). In the same month, Putin labelled Nabucco as "risky" and "dangerous". "What will that pipeline be filled with? Can they show even one supply contract? I cannot see any willing supplier there" (as quoted in Socor 2010). Putin, however, failed to explain why Moscow has neither concluded supply contracts to feed South Stream nor identified willing suppliers for this project. Against this overall background, it is difficult to understand why many politicians and gas industry managers in the EU (with EU's Energy Commissioner Oettinger among them) consider Nabucco and South Stream as "complementary", but not "alternative" projects. "This seems a political-diplomatic response rather than based on economic realities (i.e. new forecasts of the EU's future gas demand)" (Umbach 2011: 68).

The Europeans desperately need supplies from the CACR to make the Nabucco pipeline viable. And the Russians are trying to thwart this. One key battleground is Azerbaijan, which has yet to declare whether it will feed Nabucco with its gas. Senior Russian politicians as well as Gazprom officials have stated on many occasions that they are willing to purchase *all* of Azerbaijan's gas, which would then be exported via Gazprom pipelines to Europe. This, however, would deprive the EU of any possibility to receive gas from Azerbaijan without using Russian transportation infrastructure. In June 2009, during President Dmitri Medvedev's[8] visit to Baku, Gazprom and the State Oil Company of Azerbaijan Republic (SOCAR) signed a deal giving the Russian company first rights to Azeri gas previously seen as reserved for Nabucco. Under the deal, Gazprom agreed to buy 500 million cubic meters of gas from SOCAR in 2010. For Baku, this contract was based on commercial considerations with prices as high as 350 US dollar per 1,000 cubic meters of gas. The volume in question was too small to be a fatal blow by depriving Nabucco of a reliable and vital source, but the Kremlin made clear that it is ready to pay an unprecedented price in order (as a Moscow-based newspaper put it) "to make Nabucco senseless" (Solovyev 2009: 1).

Azerbaijan's gas reserves, even if supplemented by the ongoing expansion of the Shah Deniz field, will not be sufficient to keep Nabucco in business. Other countries in the region must supply Nabucco with gas. Iranian gas has been regarded as a possible option to fill Nabucco second to Azerbaijan, but Tehran currently has only little export capacity as a result of high domestic consumption; and over two-thirds of Iranian natural gas reserves are located in non-associated fields and have not been developed. This will change in the future, especially due to the exploitation of the giant South Pars field. Therefore Moscow was very glad about the signing of a 25-year deal in May 2009 under which Iran aims to export some 110 million cubic meters of gas to Pakistan per day, because this diverts Iranian gas from the European market. And Gazprom immediately claimed its readiness to join the project (Grib & Gabuev 2010: 7).

Owing to its enormous export potential, Turkmenistan is another candidate for the supply of Nabucco, but has yet to decide whether to invest in a Trans-Caspian pipeline linking it to Azerbaijan. Moscow is pushing hard to assure that gas from Turkmenistan will be delivered to Europe via Russia and South Stream, not via Nabucco. At the beginning of 2009 Gazprom bought Turkmen gas at the exorbitant price of 375 Dollar per 1,000 cubic meters. Russia was selling gas to Europe at 280 US dollars at the time, which meant that Gazprom was operating at a loss. Mikhail Krutikhin, a partner in Moscow's RusEnergy Consulting, saw the reason for this in the rivalry with Nabucco: "Gazprom offered Turkmenistan a high price in a desperate attempt to divert its gas from Nabucco" (as quoted in Babich 2009).

Especially since the fall of 2011, prospects for Nabucco appeared to be dwindling due to several reasons. Thus, the amount of non-Russian gas needed to fill Nabucco has not yet materialized. With budgets under severe strain and financing tight, the risk that the pipeline could remain unfilled for years before more gas becomes available looks increasingly unsustainable.

---

8   He is, as former Chairman of Gazprom's Board of Directors, a gas business insider.

Moreover, several alternative projects are under consideration: the Interconnection Turkey–Greece–Italy (ITGI), the Statoil-led Trans–Adriatic Pipeline (TAP), the Azerbaijan–Georgia–Romania Interconnector (AGRI), and a European continuation of the Azerbaijani-Turkish Trans-Anatolia Gas Pipeline (TANAP) project: As TANAP would replace Nabucco on Turkey's territory, a reduced 'Nabucco West' pipeline would link up with TANAP at the Turkish-Bulgarian border, continuing via Romania and Hungary to Austria. In spring 2012, the Nabucco Consortium submitted a proposal for the construction of the 'Nabucco West' pipeline to the Consortium which operates the huge Azerbaijani natural gas field Shah Deniz II.

The Potential Impact of the Turkmenistan-China Pipeline

Gazprom has had a near-monopoly on Turkmenistan's gas since 1991, relying on a mixture of Soviet-era pipeline infrastructures, preferential tariffs, political pressure, and economic support. In December 2009, the 1,833 kilometre-long Turkmenistan-China gas pipeline, which will carry up to 40 billion cubic metres of gas, also traversing Kazakhstan and Uzbekistan before linking into China's network in Xinjiang, was opened. Now Russia can no longer rely on the legacy of the USSR to keep Turkmenistan in its sphere of influence: The Turkmenistan-China pipeline deprived Moscow of its strategic control over large-scale Turkmen gas supplies.

With Russia's own gas production stagnant, the loss of Turkmen volumes can translate into a net loss of Moscow's economic and political leverage in Europe. Without a massive intake of Turkmen and other Central Asian gas, Russia can no longer sustain the geopolitical and business model of its gas trade with European countries. That model enabled Russia to absorb as much as 70 to 80 billion cubic metres per year of Central Asian gas (some two thirds of it from Turkmenistan), creating an aggregate pool under Russia's physical and political control.

Conclusions

The EU should make use of all feasible options of energy saving and diversification of energy sources with special emphasis on an increase in the share of renewable energy (hydro, wind, solar, and bio-mass). But without a significant technology breakthrough, electricity generation will be heavily dependent on gas, and oil will continue to dominate transport even in 2030. Therefore, security of supply of these fuels will continue to be paramount to the EU's economy. The Union and its member states have to take this into account on several levels. As an EU document put it: "Energy must become a central part of all external EU relations; it is crucial to geopolitical security, economic stability, social development and international efforts to combat climate change" (Commission of the European Communities 2007: 18).

More than half of the EU's energy originates from countries outside the Union – and this proportion is rising. Much of this energy comes from Russia, whose disputes with transit countries have disrupted supplies in recent years. The soaring prices of gas and oil have made Russia more powerful, less cooperative and more intransigent. The "Russia first" policy, pursued by the EU for many years, was obviously not sufficient and very likely even counterproductive for its energy security: Although the EU is Russia's energy resources customer, currently Moscow and not Brussels sets the rules of the game. The EU's barriers against Russia using the "energy weapon" are – especially in the short run – low or even nonexistent.

Since 1999 (incidentally the year of Putin's unexpected rise to power in Russia), the oil and gas prices rose steady until mid-2008. That way Russia acquired a strong position to dictate many conditions to its European consumers, not only in terms of pricing issues for natural gas, but also its interest in acquiring distribution networks and downstream assets. Moscow's main tool Gazprom aspires to dominate natural gas supply and distribution networks in Europe. By obtaining control over the infrastructure in transit countries, Russia limits access to markets for other potential suppliers. Without resolute action, the EU sooner or later could find its energy security largely under Russian control, which would give Moscow an undue and possibly dangerous amount of political influence over European decision-making. A "depoliticisation" of the EU-Russian gas relationship is as desirable as it is unlikely, at least in the foreseeable future.

Pipelines now under construction will be still operational several decades from now, and will affect the (geo-)political balance in the Eurasian region. Moscow's behaviour especially since 1999 leaves no doubt that the more pipelines connect the EU and Russia, the more insecure is Europe's oil and gas supply. The Kremlin has shown no willingness to agree to multilaterally binding treaties and agreements. Instead, it prefers a strongly self-interest based energy policy oriented to penetrate and dominate the wider European, Black Sea and CACR energy markets. But the reserves held by the CACR might offer the EU an opportunity to move away from increased dependence on Russian energy sources. Development of CACR's oil and gas reserves via Georgia and the Black Sea, bypassing Russia and Iran, would enhance the EU's energy security.

Bibliography

Babich, Dmitry (2009): Russia, rivals vying for Turkmen gas supplies. RIA Novosti, 15 December. Available from: <http://en.rian.ru/analysis/20091215/157249622.html> [14 September 2011].

BBC (2006): Gazprom warns EU to let it grow. BBC News, 20 April. Available from: <http://news.bbc.co.uk/2/hi/business/4925682.stm> [7 September 2011].

Blau, John (2010): Debate continues as work begins on Baltic Sea pipeline. Deutsche Welle – Energy, 9 April. Available from: <http://www.dw-world.de/dw/article/0,,544 2707,00.html> [15 August 2011].

Bota, Alice/Nass, Matthias (2008): Russland beunruhigt mich. (Interview with Schwarzenberg). Die Zeit, 6 March. Available from: <http://www.zeit.de/2008/11/Interview-Schwarzenberg> [12 September 2011].

BP (2011): BP Statistical Review of World Energy. London. Available from: <http://www.bp.com/assets/bp_internet/globalbp/globalbp_uk_english/reports_and_publicatio ns/statistical_energy_review_2011/STAGING/local_assets/pdf/statistical_review_of_ world_energy_full_report_2011.pdf> [5 September 2011].

Commission of the European Communities (2007): Communication From the Commission to the European Council and the European Parliament: An Energy Policy for Europe, Brussels, 10.1.2007, COM(2007) 1 final, {SEC(2007) 12}. Available from: <http:// eur-lex.europa.eu/LexUriServ/LexUriServ.do?uri=COM:2007:0001:FIN:EN: PDF> [8 September 2011].

Commission of the European Communities (2008): Commission Staff Working Document, accompanying the Green Paper, towards a secure, sustainable and competitive European energy network. Oil infrastructures. An assessment of the existing and planned oil infrastructures within and towards the EU. COM(2008) 782 final, Brussels, 13.11.2008. Available from: <http://eur-lex.europa.eu/LexUriServ/LexUriServ.do?uri =SEC:2008: 2869:FIN:EN:PDF> [12 September 2011].

Council of the European Union (2007): The EU and Central Asia: Strategy for a New Partnership. Brussels, 31 May 2007. Available from: <http://register.consilium.europa. eu/pdf/en/07/st10/st10113.en07.pdf> [26 June 2010].

Cornell, Svante/Jonsson, Anna/Nilsson, Niklas/Häggström, Per (2006): The Wider Black Sea Region: An Emerging Hub in European Security. Central Asian-Caucasus Institute, Silk Road Studies Program, Silk Road Paper.

Coskun, Orhan (2011): Nabucco investment seen at 12-15 bln euros-sources. Reuters, 5 May. Available from: <http://www.reuters.com/article/2011/05/05/nabucco-turkey-idUSIST00770920110505> [11 August 2011].

Dempsey, Judy (2010): Putin Chides E.U. Over Energy Policies, The New York Times, 26 November. Available from: <http://www.nytimes.com/2010/11/27/world/europe/27iht-putin.html> [8 September 2011].

Eggert, Konstantin (2006): Vozvrashchenie ili turpoezdka? BBC Russian Service, 4 August. Available from: <http://news.bbc.co.uk/go/pr/fr/-/hi/russian/russia/newsid_5244 000/5244282.stm> [28 June 2010].

Energy, Ecology, Economy (2011): Reinhard Mitschek: We are confident that the Nabucco construction will start in 2013 and the first gas will flow in 2017. 9 August. Available from: <http://3e-news.net/en/energetika/item/reinhard-mitschek-we-are-confident-that-the-nabucco-construction-will-start-in-2013-and-the-first.html> [11 August 2011].

Erixon, Fredrik (2008): Europe's energy dependency and Russia's commercial assertiveness. European Centre for International Political Economy, ECIPE Policy Briefs, no. 7.

European Commission (2001): Green Paper. Towards a European strategy for the security of energy supply. Luxembourg. Available from: <http://ec.europa.eu/energy/green-paper-energy-supply/doc/green_paper_energy_supply_en.pdf> [11 September 2011].

European Commission (2008): EU Energy Security and Solidarity Action Plan: 2nd Strategic Energy Review. November 13, Brussels. Available from: <http://www.europa-eu-un.org/articles/en/article_8300_en.htm> [26 June 2010].

European Commission (2010): Energy, transport and environment indicators. Eurostat pocketbooks.

European Commission – Eurostat (2010): Energy production and imports. Available from: <http://epp.eurostat.ec.europa.eu/statistics_explained/index.php/Energy_production_an d_imports#Further_Eurostat_information> [8 September 2011].

European Parliament – Foreign Affairs Committee (2010): South Caucasus: EU must play greater role in stabilising the region, say MEPs., 8 April. Available from: <http:// www.europarl.europa.eu/news/expert/infopress_page/030-72203-096-04-15-903-20100406IPR72190-06-04-2010-2010-false/default_en.htm> [19 June 2010].

European Union (2009): EU – Russia Energy Dialogue. MEMO/09/121, Brussels, 19 March. Available from: <http://europa.eu/rapid/pressReleasesAction.do?reference=MEMO/09/121&format=HTML&language=en> [9 September 2011].

Fedyashin, Andrei (2010): Vladimir Putin goes to the land of Strauss and schnitzel. RIA Novosti, 23 April. Available from: <http://en.rian.ru/analysis/20100423/158716228.html> [5 June 2010].

Grib, Natalya/Gabuev, Aleksandr (2009): Rossiya vyvodit iranskiy gaz iz ES v Yuzhnuyu Aziyu, Kommersant 27 May. Available from: <http://www.kommersant.ru/doc/1176982> [26 September 2011].

Henderson, Creela (2010): Reorientation: ESPO points away from the West. Institute for the Study of Conflict, Ideology, and Policy. The ISCIP Analyst (Russia), Volume XVI, No. 7.

Isachenkov, Vladimir (2007): Putin Visits Iran, Sends Warnings to US. AP, 16 October 2007, via: Johnson's Russia List, 2007-#216, 16 October.

International Energy Agency (2008): IEA Energy Policies Review, The European Union. Paris.

Keenan, Rita (2010): Statistical aspects of the energy economy in 2009. Eurostat. Statistics in focus, no. 43.

Kiselyov, Yevgeny (2010): Kharkovskiy razmen. The New Times [Moscow], no. 15. Available from: <http://newtimes.ru/articles/detail/20517/> [12 September 2011].

Kupchinsky, Roman (2009): LNG – Russia's New Energy Blackmail Tool. Eurasia Daily Monitor (The Jamestown Foundation), Volume 6, Issue 77.

Larsson, Robert L. (2007): Nord Stream, Sweden and Baltic Sea Security. Stockholm: Defence Research Agency.

Lavrov, Sergei (2007): Vneshnepoliticheskaya samostoyatelnost Rossii – bezuslovnyy imperative. Moskovskie novosti, no. 1 (19 January). Available from: <http://www.mn.ru/issue.php?2007-1-56> [19 January 2007].

Leijonhielm, Jan/Larsson, Robert L. (2004): Russia's Strategic Commodities: Energy and Metals as Security Levers. Stockholm: Swedish Defence Research Agency.

Leonard, Mark/Popescu, Nicu (2007): A Power Audit of EU-Russia Relations. European Council on Foreign Relations.

Lindner, Rainer (2007): Blockaden der "Freundschaft". Berlin: Stiftung Wissenschaft und Politik, SWP-Aktuell, no. 3.

Matyash, VN (2004): Rossiya – SShA: Neft i geopolitika (Politologicheskiy analiz). Diplomaticheskaya Akademiya MID Rossii / Institut aktualnykh mezhdunarodnykh problem. Moskva.

Meyer, Sebastian (2006): Die Europäische Union im Südkaukasus. Interessen und Institutionen in der Auswärtigen Politikgestaltung. Baden-Baden: Nomos.

Ministerstvo finansov Rossiyskoy Federatisi (2007): Metodologiya formirovaniya neftegazovogo byudzheta Rossii. Available from: <http://www1.minfin.ru/off_inf/1895.htm> [1 April 2007].

Minpromtorg Rossii (2003): Energeticheskaya strategiya Rossii na period do 2020 goda. Utverzhdena rasporyazheniem Pravitelstva Rossiyskoy Federacii ot 28 avgustya 2003. <http://www.minprom.gov.ru/docs/strateg/1/print> [8 September 2011].

Norling, Nicklas (2007): Gazprom's Monopoly and Nabucco's Potentials: Strategic Decisions for Europe. Central Asia-Caucasus Institute and Silk Road Studies Program.

Panjuschkin, Waleri/Sygar, Michail (2008): Gazprom. Das Geschäft mit der Macht. Munich: Drömer.

Piontkovskiy, Andrei (2006): Chuma na oba nashi doma, Grani.ru, 31 August. Available from: <www.grani.ru/politics/world/p.110722.html> [7 June 2010].

Popescu, Nicu/Wilson, Andrew (2009): The Limits of Enlargement-lite: European and Russian Power in the Troubled Neighbourhood. London: European Council on Foreign Relations.

Reitschuster, Boris (2006): Putins Demokratur. Wie der Kreml den Westen das Fürchten lehrt, Berlin: Econ.

RFE/RL (2008): Newsline, Vol. 12, No. 25, Part I, 6 February. Available from: <http://www.rferl.org/content/article/1144046.html> [12 September 2011].

Schewzowa, Lilia (2006): Putins Vermächtnis. Wie die russische Elite die Modernisierung des Landes blockiert. Internationale Politik, vol. 61, no. 7, pp 38-46.

Ševcova, Lilija (2007): Russlands Wille zur Weltmacht. Autokratie, Energie, Ideologie. Osteuropa, no. 4, pp 33-52.

Socor, Vladimir (2010): Austria Joins Gazprom's South Stream Project. Eurasia Daily Monitor (The Jamestown Foundation), Volume 7, Issue 84.

Solovyev, Vladmir (2009): Shiroko kachaet Azerbaydzhan. Ego gaz poydet v Rossiyu po rekordno vysokoy tsene. Kommersant 30 June. Available from: <http://www.kommersant.ru/doc/1195657> [26 September 2011].

Umbach, Frank (2008): Europe's Energy Dependence in Mid-term Perspective. American Institute for Contemporary German Studies at John Hopkins University, 25 February. Available from: <http://www.aicgs.org/documents/advisor/umbach.gmf.pdf> [12 September 2011].

Umbach, Frank (2011): The Black Sea Region and the Great Energy Game in Eurasia. In: Balcer, A. (ed.): The Eastern Partnership in the Black Sea Region: towards a New Strategy. Demos Europa, Centre for European Strategy, Warsaw, pp 55-88.

Vatanka, Alex/Weitz, Richard (2007): Russian roulette. Moscow seeks influence through arms exports. Jane's Intelligence Weekly, no. 1, pp 37–41.

Westphal, Kirsten (2004): Handlungsbedarf. Die Energiepolitik der Europäischen Union. Osteuropa, no. 9-10, pp 39-54.

China and the European Union – Partners in Antagonism

Gerald Brettner-Messler

This article gives a brief overview of the relations between China and the European Union. Guiding sources behind this presentation are selected strategic documents on China by the European Commission as the "defender" of European interests. The article does not take a look at the sum of national China policies but at the approach on the EU level. This approach is manifold, covering an extensive range of topics. The article intends to present these facets without losing sight of the core themes of the relationship like the economy or human rights as well as the defining moments in the historical development.

The history of relations between the People's Republic of China and the European Union is comparatively short. It was not until 1975 that diplomatic relations were established. With individual European countries China has longer ties: The UK set up diplomatic relations as early as 1950. Before 1969, France was the only member of the European Economic Community (EEC) with full diplomatic relations, the UK and the Netherlands had only chargés d'affaires in Beijing (Zhou 2004: 155).

For China the 1970s was a time of transition. The Cultural Revolution was fading away and the rule of the state's founder Mao Zedong was coming to an end. Chairman Mao died in 1976 and one year later Deng Xiaoping took power and inaugurated reforms that in the following decades would change the face of China dramatically. The political isolation of the 1960s ended with the visit of US President Richard Nixon in 1972, eventually resulting in diplomatic relations from 1979.

Political deliberations together with the requirements of trade policy ushered in EEC-China relations. For China the EEC represented an alternative between the Soviet Union and the US. Brussels wanted to introduce a joint trade policy with China, and the Commission presented an outline agreement as a basis for a future trade agreement. The Vice President of the Commission, Sir Christopher Soames, responsible for foreign relations, visited the Chinese capital in May 1975. There was no premeditated outcome, in fact there was not even a program for the visit. The Chinese were only eager to find out which position the EEC representatives took on the Taiwan question. Beijing treated the island as a renegade province and strove for its reunion with mainland China. Soames reassured his hosts that the government in Beijing was recognized as the sole legitimate government. Thus mollified, the Chinese side announced its readiness to establish diplomatic relations with the EEC and its willingness to study the draft agreement.

In September 1975 the first Chinese ambassador to the EEC, Li Lien-Pi, presented his credentials in Brussels. The Trade Agreement between the EEC and the People's Republic of China was signed in April 1978. The intention behind it was to raise the trade with Europe to the same level as with Japan. As a consequence of the agreement a number of high-ranking EEC officials visited China. The Vice-President of the Commission Wilhelm Haferkamp, came with a delegation of representatives of various economic bodies, as well as bankers and businessmen and was received by the Prime Minister and Chairman of the Communist Party, Hua Guofeng, and by Deng Xiaoping. In January 1979 Emilio Colombo, the President of the European Parliament, visited Beijing and also had talks with the political leaders of China. Just a few weeks later, the President of the Commission Roy Jenkins followed suit. On these occasions, the Chinese leaders lauded the endeavours for a strong and united Europe. This positive attitude resulted from China's rivalry with the Soviet Union. Western Europe, as part of NATO, was seen as a possible ally in the competition with the common enemy in Moscow.

The agreement of April 1978 was signed to give the relations between the EEC and China a "new impetus". The aim was to promote and intensify trade. In the agreement both sides guaranteed each other a most favoured nation status and pledged to alleviate market access for the other. A balance of trade was envisaged in the document – an aim that in practice proved to be wishful thinking. From the mid 1980s, the European trade surplus with China turned into a deficit and never reverted again (Europe Information; Zhang: 1; Shambaugh 1997). When China and the European Community established diplomatic relations in 1975, the trade volume was 2.4 billion US dollars, in 2010 the trade volume between China and the European Union reached 479.71 billion. Today, the EU is China's largest trading partner, while China is the second largest for the EU (China's 2010 trade surplus; Facts and figures about China-EU trade; European Commission, Trade, China). In order to facilitate relations a joint committee was set up with the task of managing all matters arising from the agreement but also "to examine means and new opportunities of developing trade". The committee was scheduled to meet once a year (Europe Information: 8). Its last session was held in July 2011 (The 25th Session).

In 1985, the Agreement on Trade and Economic Cooperation between the European Economic Community and the People's Republic of China replaced the agreement of 1978. Even though the title of this document just referred to economics, it turned out to be the main framework paper for the overall relations with China.1 At the same time, it demonstrated that trade remained the core of EU-Chinese relations. The new agreement did not alter the terms of the 1978 agreement, but aimed to intensify the relations by including a chapter on "Economic Cooperation". The main goal was to create a win-win situation by diversifying economic relations, the opening of sources and markets and the improvement of economic and social development. As specific fields of cooperation were named: industry and mining; agriculture, including agro-industry; science and technology; energy; transport and communication; the protection of the environment; cooperation in third countries. The agreement provided for comprehensive economic relations, including joint ventures and production, technology transfers, exchanges between the business communities and investments.

Heavy strain was put on the developing relationship by the rigorous clampdown on the democratisation movement, which found its most expressive manifestation in the rally on Tiananmen Square in 1989. The reforms of the 1980s opened China's politics for a wind of change, a development unforeseen and unintended by the Chinese leadership. Voices for democratisation became louder and in 1986, after student demonstrations, the General Secretary of the Party, Hu Yaobang, was forced to resign after having been blamed for letting the situation get out of control. After his death in 1989, students gathered in mourning on Tiananmen Square in the heart of Beijing. Eventually this gathering turned into a fully fledged democratisation movement. At times, up to one million people filled the square. The leadership let this happen for a few weeks and then decided to strike back without mercy on June 3. The square was cleared by tanks, and between 300 and 3,000 people died. It was exactly the same year in which the iron curtain fell in Eastern Europe and gave way to freedom and democracy. On 27 June the European Council passed a declaration condemning the "brutal repression" and adopting a number of measures against China. The Council demanded that independent observers visit the jails and be present at trials, suspended bilateral ministerial and high level contacts, postponed new cooperation projects, reduced the scientific, technical and cultural programs to a minimum and put requests for credit insurances and new World Bank credits on a waiting list. Military cooperation was interrupted and an embargo on arms trade imposed.

Since then the arms embargo has remained a steady source of friction in the relations between the EU and China. Right from the outset it was more a political statement than a legal barrier against arming China. It neither defined exactly what was forbidden to export nor was it legally binding. The vague formulas gave the member states room for their individual interpretation of the

---

1   In 2007, negotiations for a Partnership and Cooperation Agreement began. This PAC shall supplant the 1985 Agreement. European Commission, Trade, China, http://ec.europa.eu, 18.08.2011

embargo. In fact, lots of items the Chinese military needed were sold by EU countries: aircraft and helicopter components, radar systems, sub-components for missiles, engines for trucks. In December 2004 the European Council declared its readiness to lift the ban. France and Germany in particular had been lobbying intensively for this decision. Opponents of the embargo argue that its only real effect is to cause Beijing's anger about Europe. Moreover, they feel that the remaining instruments like the Code of Conduct would suffice to restrict arms exports. Supporters of the embargo contend that lifting the ban would mean Europe's loss of leverage in the struggle for an improvement of human rights in China and an increase of China's military power, which the US sees primarily directed at itself. This is why the US exerts pressure on European countries to stick to the embargo. However, time is on China's side. Its military is less and less reliant on arms imports. What the Chinese need is high-tech gear for military as well as civil use. To discern to which end goods are purchased is an impossible task, and entirely precluding military use would mean the end for high-tech sector exports to China. Furthermore, an arms embargo is inconsistent with the strategic partnership and shared commitments in international relations, because it implies distrust, which is incompatible with partnership (Hauser/Kernic 2009: 181-188). The discussion has not yet come to an end. Prior to Herman van Rompuy's visit to China in May 2011 the Chinese foreign ministry stressed two points concerning the relations with the EU: The recognition of China as a market economy and removal of the embargo. "We think the two issues involve political discrimination against China", was the brief rationale put forward by the Chinese (China urges EU to lift arms embargo). The reaction of Catherine Ashton, the High Representative of the Union for Foreign Affairs and Security Policy, was in line with Beijing, calling the embargo a "major impediment". She was supported by France, while the UK took the US's side and maintained the embargo (McNamara/Lohman 2011).

A New Beginning after Tiananmen

It did not last long and the economy proved to be a stronger force than any qualms about China's disregard for ethic values. After years of muted contacts, the time had come for normalisation. The former antagonism between the US and the USSR no longer existed, so Brussels had more leeway to conduct its external affairs. The absence of any conflicts with China and the lack of military presence in Asia made the rapprochement relatively easy (Shambaugh et al. 2008: 304-305). With the exception of the arms embargo all restrictions were revoked by 1994 (Zhou 2004: 158). In the same year a new political dialogue between China and Europe was established and ended the stalemate. This was not a return to the status quo ante but the beginning of an unprecedented intensity of contacts. Until 1994 the political dialogue had consisted only of short reunions in the wake of the UN General Assembly meetings. Now high-level visits started. President Jiang Zemin visited France in 1994 and Germany in 1995. To soothe critical voices China proposed a human rights dialogue, which was accepted by the EU. In 1998 the first EU-China summit took place, and has since then been held once a year. In 2000 Prime Minister Zhu Rongji made the first-ever visit of a Chinese leader to the European Commission (Wissenbach: 8; European Parliament Fact Sheets; Barysch et al. 2005: 8; Zhou 2004: 157-158).

In fact there was a need for a closer relationship. The communist regime had proved its stability and no Chinese glasnost or perestroika was to be expected. Instead a huge market with a giant and cheap labour force was waiting to be explored by an expanding European entrepreneurship. Especially export oriented countries longed for normalisation; Germany presented its first China strategy in 1993. At the same time millions of Chinese were striving for a better life and there was a sense in the country that any revolution or unrest would only have a detrimental effect. "Strong man" Deng knew that the reforms had to be carried further to escape the fate of the Soviet Union. In 1992 he travelled to South China ("Southern Expedition") and inaugurated a new wave of economic reforms. "Everyone is becoming a business man/woman" became a popular catch phrase and unleashed a surge of entrepreneurial activity (Gittings 2005: 251-255; Barysch et al. 2005: 6).

This was in the interest of both China and Europe alike. China could not be neglected in international relations any longer and the goal of involving China in the international arena set the tone of the new Communication by the European Commission, *A Long Term Policy for China–Europe Relations*, from 1995, which went along with the restart in relations. Economic data showed that China would one day become the world's strongest economy. Europe did not want to be left out by the US and Japan in the race for the Chinese market. Yet it was not only about the economy, but also political and military power. The Commission clearly realized that it would be "impossible to address the central global issues of the 1990s without particular reference to the impact of China on their evolution and management" (Communication *A Long Term Policy for China – Europe Relation*). Even back then the detrimental effects of China's rise on the environment could be noticed. As a consequence, four points of interest were defined. China should become a responsible stakeholder in international affairs; a demand which referred mainly to nuclear and weapon proliferation, arms sales and human rights, but also inner reforms. The last point reflected the European concern for China's inner stability: A prerequisite for keeping the Chinese at home and foreclosing emigration. Chinese masses drifting to the West was a scenario that raised apprehension in European countries at those times. Protection of the environment and resources, sustainable development and other global issues like health, crime and science/technology formed the second point of the agenda. The further integration of China into the world economy, i.e. through WTO accession, and continued economic growth together with a market access as unrestricted as possible for European companies was the real focus. Data on the recent economic progress was impressive. Between 1979 and 1994 China's total trade rose from 20 billion US dollars to 237 billion US dollars with growth rates above 9%. Nevertheless, the balance of trade with the EU has become negative since the 1980s. Also EU direct investments were far less than those of the US and Japan. The commission acknowledged economic reforms by China but saw much room for improvement. Obstacles like tariff and non-tariff measures, technical barriers, foreign currency controls and the opaque administration hindered exports. To change this for the better the EU pressed for China's WTO accession. The European Union introduced in the negotiations the principle that China would not have to implement some of the commitments of WTO members immediately but only after a certain time because China had raised objections due to its lack of a fully fledged market economy. China saw the membership as part of the reform process and a means to become more competitive on world markets. All in all it was expected to back up the smooth continuation of China's transformation into a market economy. Politically, membership would encourage it to claim the role of a speaker of the developing world (China joins WTO).

In order to facilitate all these goals the contacts between Chinese and EU officials were intensified. This included officers of the People's Liberation Army. The Commission proposed a bilateral dialogue on regional and global security issues, support for a reformed public management system, and a programme for cooperation of law and judiciary. Some aspects of the "constructive engagement" the EU wanted to promote sounded rather overambitious. The conflicts about sovereignty rights in the South China Sea – just as human rights – have never been issues where Beijing accepted any interference by foreign players. Financial shortcomings also put restrictions on the cooperation programmes the Commission wanted to establish. In principle the Commission wanted the cooperation to be as broad as possible but recognized three goals as central in terms of effectiveness and impact: human resources development, economic and social reform and cooperation between private sector actors of both China and the EU. Environmental challenges and scientific and technological cooperation were identified as the two areas with the highest potential for future development. The Commission put special emphasis on the long-term effect of the relationship with China. Only in the long term could the shared goals with China be reached effectively and gain durability. Enhanced cooperation of the EU member states with the Commission and the private sector was considered a prerequisite for a lasting impact of the EU policies on China (Communication *A Long Term Policy for China – Europe Relations*).

A Partnership Develops

How quickly EU-China relations evolved was reflected by the fact that the next Communication on China by the Commission was published only three years after its precursor. In 1998 *Building a Comprehensive Partnership with China* sought stepped-up relations under the term "partnership", the year before Deng died, but his legacy lived on. At the 15th Party Congress in 1997, new reforms were determined, declaring the "non-public-ownership sector ... an important component part of China's socialist economy" (Quoted in: Gittings 2005: 253). Confidence in the Chinese leadership had been raised by the successful and peaceful handover of British Hong Kong to China, in 1997, which guaranteed Hong Kong special rights under Beijing's rule. Furthermore, the Commission worried that some of the structural problems in Asian economies that had been laid open by the economic crisis in 1997 would be a danger for China, too, and so further reforms would be necessary. Change did not happen in China alone. Also the EU entered a new phase in its history. 13 countries had applied for membership, most of them formerly communist-ruled. Thus the biggest enlargement so far was impending – a sea of change for the inner structures of the Union. To be fit for this challenge the Amsterdam Treaty was signed in 1997.

The Commission estimated the integration of China in the international community and the engagement of China's rising power as "one of the most important external policy challenges" (Communication *Building a Comprehensive Partnership with China*: 4). Brussels wanted to engage China internationally through an enhanced political dialogue. Its most important element was to become the EU-China summit, which would lift relations to the same level as with the US, Russia and Japan. China was not seen as a player standing alone but in the context of the wider region. In 1996 the Asia-Europe Meeting with China and EU being part of it had been launched and now the EU argued for a partnership with China on various issues like arms control, non-proliferation, maritime security or combating drug trafficking.

The EU had a broad range of topics it wanted to handle with China, on the list of global issues that were in its own interest, but it did not give a thought to what might be on China's agenda. The Communication included UN reform, commitment against proliferation of weapons of mass destruction – very important because of China's status as a nuclear power – the fight against anti-personnel mines, organized crime and illegal immigration, and the wide field of environmental protection, an ever increasing problem for China's prospering industry.

The EU was aiming for stability in Asia, which could not be secured without China's support, and intended to reach this mainly through the ASEAN Regional Forum. China and the EU alongside the members of the Association of South-East Asian Nations, plus Russia, the USA and the other countries of the region, are partners in this forum on security and stability. Central Asia, as an important provider of oil and gas for both Europe and China, was likewise deemed an issue for talks with China. As the closest ally of communist North Korea, China takes interest in the Korean peninsula and therefore is an indispensable partner for any solution concerning the divided Korean state. The peaceful reunion of Taiwan and mainland China as a question of high importance for Beijing was also not to be omitted from the Communication.

As before the rule of law and human rights played a big role in the 1998 document. It was not all about political rights, the death penalty or enforced labour, but also about a modern law system, which guarantees the citizens their rights and also access to these rights. The Commission saw progress in this field especially because of the human rights dialogue. China had already decided to sign the *UN Covenant on Economic, Social and Cultural Rights* and displayed readiness to sign the *UN Covenant on Civil and Political Rights*. Beijing did as it had said, but the Covenant on Civil and Political Rights is still not ratified – so much for Chinese commitment to human rights. To foster its intentions the EU launched a cooperation program on legal and judicial cooperation[2] and pleaded for initiatives aimed at the strengthening of civil society.

As a logical consequence of its increasing trade with China the EU wanted to integrate China into the world economy, which meant, most of all, China's accession to the WTO. The main reasons for the EU to claim China's WTO accession were more transparency (prompt publication of laws and regulations), the same operational conditions for European and Chinese companies and non-discrimination against EU companies. The EU demanded effective market access, which meant that Chinese tariffs had to be cut back or abolished. And it was also about an open market not only for goods but also for services and the financial sector. The request for a financial and banking system commensurable to those in the West was related to this. Open market meant also better conditions for establishing foreign enterprises in China. In bilateral trade relations the EU proposed to remove the status of non-market economy for China and was ready to give China benefits under the Generalised Scheme of Tariff Preferences – a non-reciprocal arrangement for trade preferences – depending on

---

2   This program started in 2000, 13 million euro was earmarked for it. European Parliament Fact Sheets

China's observing certain labour and environmental standards, and also to lift quantitative restrictions if China did the same. Because of China's need for an influx of fresh money, the EU aimed at better investment regulations in China and intended to set up a European investment strategy. To facilitate trade structural agreements regarding maritime transport, air transport and customs were deemed necessary. Nuclear trade and safety as well as science and technology were also put on the list of further agreements. The Commission took on the 1998 Communication's commitment to support economic and social reform through cooperation and suggested to capitalize on European know-how by restructuring and privatizing state owned enterprises. Financial reform, industrial cooperation (certification, production process, norms/standards etc.) and business dialogue were to facilitate relations with China. Reforms of legal and administrative regulations for the Chinese economy complemented reform suggestions for civic rights. The training of professionals for government and industry was to help develop human resources in China. Cooperation on science/technology and on clean energy represented efforts to pave the way for European companies to Chinese markets. The tackling of environmental problems and regional disparities was also on this very ambitious cooperation agenda (Communication *Building a Comprehensive Partnership with China).*

In 2003 the Commission issued a guidance document called *A maturing partnership – shared interests and challenges in EU-China relations* as an update of the earlier documents. The Commission deemed such an update necessary because of the widening and deepening of EU-China relations. It considered China as a "strategic partner" in managing world affairs. In fact there was a lot of wishful thinking engrained in the document. It said more about how the Commission wanted China to act than it really behaved. A "country that fully embraces democracy, free market principles and the rule of law" reflected only a part of the reality and overestimated Europe as a blueprint for change. Europe was a blueprint for successful economics but not for shaping politics.

Five areas of priority were mentioned. "Shared responsibilities in promoting global governance" referred to China as a stabilizing factor in Asia and as a mediator between the developing and the developed world. Three levels of dialogue were defined: bilateral, regional and global. On the bilateral level the Commission wanted to discuss human rights, Tibet, Taiwan, Hong Kong, Macao, illegal migration and greater cooperation in justice and home affairs. From the Chinese point of view there was and is nothing to discuss about Taiwan or Tibet: both are part of China; Beijing's absolute sovereignty over them is non negotiable. On the regional level, peace and security represented matters of interest as well as cooperation in the ASEAN Regional Forum and the Asia-Europe Meeting. The global level was about cooperation in a rather colourful mix of matters like global governance, counter-terrorism, environment, non-proliferation/disarmament and multilateralism. On all these topics (maybe with the exception of counter-terrorism) differences among EU members and between China and the EU made the chances for a substantial outcome seem very small. In all security related matters an invisible third party sits at the table: the United States. The most important security forum for most European nations is NATO with its leading power, the US (plus Canada and Turkey).

The second priority is the support for China's transition to an open society based upon the rule of law and the respect for human rights. The death penalty, administrative detention, torture and civic and human rights are permanently on the European agenda. This approach, however, is completely one-way oriented. Beijing has no interest, and discussing it is merely a show of good will and has absolutely nothing to do with any ambitions for change. The good will of the Chinese leadership ends where the rule of the Communist Party is threatened. There is no chance to get any concessions from the Chinese leadership that political positions deviating from the official party line will get any representation, neither in the political nor in the public area.

The issue on which a substantial European-Chinese dialogue takes place is "promoting China's economic opening at home and abroad". China had become the EU's second largest trading partner in 2002 (trading volume 115 bn. euro). Increasing economic ties between China and Europe called for due regulations of the terms of trade. Due to its trade deficit with China, the EU wanted an increase in European exports to China and a better protection of intellectual property rights so that the output of European creativity does not help move Chinese conveyor belts. Restricted market access remained despite China's WTO access. A constant dialogue to tackle these problems was seen as necessary (Commission, *A maturing partnership*).

China: Challenge or Chance?

In 2006, only three years after the previous document, a new Communication on China was released: *EU – China: Closer partners, growing responsibilities*. China's rising power in international affairs had become manifest over the years. "What is at stake?" asked the paper right at the beginning and this formulation made it clear that China had become a real challenge for Europe. The wording was now slightly different from that of the 2003 document. China was called "a major power" not only in economic but also in political terms. Brussels had fully realised that a friendly attitude was not enough to gain results. The relations were described as "increasingly mature and realistic" – an implicit confession of naivety and idealism in the past? "An interest in supporting China's reform process" was formulated rather cautiously. Nevertheless, the editors of the document knew that the EU also had something to offer to China: The world's largest market, a global reserve currency, lots of know-how, and its global influence are assets China cannot ignore. The new Communication demanded "to respond effectively to China's renewed strength" and spoke of the mutual responsibilities in a strategic partnership, a reminder for China not only to take but also to give. A "strong and effective multilateral system" was mentioned as a common goal with China. Rebalancing the trade with China ranked as concern number one, and the Commission was very outspoken on that: "Adjusting to the competitive challenge and driving a fair bargain with China will be the central challenge of EU trade policy in the decade to come. This key bilateral challenge provides a litmus test for our partnership." The Commission felt that both sides had an obligation to take the impact of one's own policy on the respective partner into account. A compact analysis of China's driving forces in politics was given: Internal and external stability as prerequisites for economic growth. In the relationship between the EU and China a new Partnership and Cooperation Agreement was to supplant the Trade and Cooperation Agreement and guarantee better market access to China beyond WTO commitments. The Commission lamented the limited efforts on human and civil rights by China and made a commitment to new endeavours. A more focussed and result-oriented, but also flexible dialogue was aspired – thus a formulaic approach without much substance. Intentions for cooperation on sustainable development in the fields of energy supply, environmental protection, climate change and the broad sector of social issues, like health, safety at work and aging population, had far bigger chances of a benign reception by Beijing; the same held for the EU's readiness for cooperation on the sustainable and balanced growth of China's economy to avoid overheating. Still there was the problem of insufficient market access for European companies and the inadequate protection of intellectual property. The Commission strived for solutions by dialogue but stated clearly that it would use trade defence measures if necessary. The strengthening of bilateral cooperation on a wide range of issues formed another part of the agenda. Cooperation in science and technology was considered a priority, while migration, people-to-people links and the structures governing the official relations were deemed improvable. The Commission reminded the member states to speak with one voice. On international relations the Communication contained a commitment of the EU to a multilateral system. Cooperation within the UN framework and regional structures were to foster peace and security. The Communication pleaded for strong relations between China and other major players in East Asia and for continued regional integration. On Taiwan, the EU embraced the policy of "one China", with Taiwan being a province of indivisible China that is represented in the government in Beijing. Therefore the European Union supports a reunion as a result of a dialogue process. China demanded a lift of the EU arms embargo.

The EU took a positive stance on that matter but had to tackle the discrepancy between its unwillingness to arm China and making a concession to China. This question was related to the purported lack of transparency regarding Chinese military expenditure and objectives – an issue mainly raised by the US and probably therefore drawn into the Communication by US allies. Nonproliferation presented a concern for both China and the EU. The EU endorsed China's role in the nuclear conflict with North Korea and hoped for China's support in ending Iran's nuclear program. In both cases China has its own interests. Iran is an important oil provider, North Korea a long-standing ally (Commission, *EU – China*).

One of the problems of the European Union and China is the incoherence of European politics on China. Europe speaks with a multitude of voices. The European Commission and the EU member states all have their own interests and attitudes. For China the European standpoints are often unclear. When Berlin or Paris takes a position, Beijing cannot be sure, if the other member states share it. Beijing has the comparative advantage of a clear agenda set by one government. Business and a strong state are the corner stones. In a giant and fast developing country like China the government cannot control everything, but it knows what to control and foreign relations belong to the affairs that are under the control of the government. In 2003 China released a paper on its EU policy. Apart from the commitment to common endeavours, like counter terrorism, sustainable development, support of the UN, the focus is clearly on the economy. Topics that are dear to the EU include a human rights dialogue or a reference to Tibet, although China only ascertains its rejection of the Dalai Lama and his followers. With the 2003 Paper Beijing reacted to the (never ratified) Constitutional Treaty and demonstrated its recognition of the EU as an entity of special importance. In the course of time, the readiness to perceive the EU as a credible actor was diluted by the awareness of the political limits of European unity. Beijing knows the situation in Europe very well. And it is completely aware of its (economic) power and that the Chinese market is indispensable for Europe (Fox/Godement 2009: 33-34; China's EU Policy Paper; Brettner-Messler 2010: 98). "The EU has the most demands in the relationship but little leverage; China has fewer concrete requests and more power to say no, since it is the EU that believes in the virtue of engagement. So China can dictate the terms of the relationship, turning it on and off as it pleases," (Fox/Godement 2009: 37) two analysts stated. In 2008 the EU-China summit was cancelled after meetings of several European top officials with the Dalai Lama had been announced. Only a few months later, Chinese delegations toured Europe to evoke the impression that a show of good will to China would result in intensified business relations – the old principle of "divide et impera" (Fox/Godement 2009: 35). This policy is not new. Yet in 1996 Prime Minister Li Peng said the Europeans would get more contracts if they were willing to go along po-litically with China (Barysch et al. 2005: 14).

The big problem for the EU is that despite all endeavours China benefits more from the trade with Europe than vice versa. In 2011 136.2 billion euro of goods were exported to China while 292.1 billion euro worth of goods were imported from China, reflecting limited market access for European companies. Reducing this high trade deficit is a constant challenge for Euro-pean politicians. In 2008, a High Level Economic and Trade Dialogue at Vice-Premier level was introduced to tackle these economic problems. Re-sults have been rather meagre so far (European Commission, Trade, China).

China – EU Trade: Fundament of the Relations

The history of China-EU relations is to a large extent a history of commerce. In 1948 China, which was then represented by the Taiwanese government, opted out of the General Agreement on Tariffs and Trade, which preceded today's WTO. Although Beijing never went with this decision, it applied for membership in 1986. The negotiations took 15 years. Much of the work was not done in the WTO Working Party but in bi- and multi-lateral fora where all the individual wishes of the interested states could be discussed. WTO ac-cession in 2001 was an important step for China in the country's reform process aiming at liberalizing and opening markets. With its accession China committed itself to lift trade restrictions and give foreign companies and in-dividuals access to the Chinese market. A transition period till 2013 will give China and the other WTO members time to adjust their legal regulations and markets to WTO requirements (WTO NEWS, Press/243). Beijing described the accession as a "strategic decision … in line with China's reform and opening-up policy" and predicted great chances for foreign enterprises on the huge Chinese market. It would be the end of the beginning of a historic proc-ess, the Chinese chief negotiator said (WTO NEWS, Geneva, 17 September 2001). For China WTO membership indeed marked the beginning of its rec-ognition as a major power. Participation regarding all decisions of the organisation opened the chance to have a say in setting the direction of inter-national trade. Reform-oriented Chinese politicians could argue their decisions with a hint at China's obligations in the WTO (Morrison: 2).

Nevertheless, in 2009 then Commissioner Baroness Catherine Ashton, currently High Representative, had to admit that insufficient market access to China was a constant bone of contention in EU relations with China. "Barri-ers in China not only cost European business, but also deprive the Chinese economy of investment inflows and significant tax revenues", she reiterated. The protection of intellectual property rights and chances for foreign investment were deemed insufficient (EU, Press releases, China: EU calls for less barriers). The European expectations from China's accession were not fulfilled. China lowered its tariffs significantly but non-tariff barriers remained. Impediments like sanitary requirements, product certification and delays in customs clearance made the European export business a hazardous undertaking (EU-China Trade). Complaints by the EU of restricted market access and export restrictions for commodities have been a constant factor in the EU relations with China. Eleven years after its accession China still does not fulfil its obligations.

In May 2011 the Commission imposed the "first ever anti-subsidy tariffs against imports from China.", because, as Trade Commissioner Karel De Gucht put it: "There is a general feeling that economic openness and business climate in China are not improving (...)" (Norris 2011). In July 2011 the WTO decided over a complaint that the EU, the US and Mexico had filed in 2009 because China had restricted exports of some raw materials, like zinc, bauxite or magnesium, the European industry relies on. The complainants had claimed that the restrictions would give the Chinese industry an unfair advantage over their competitors. China had restricted these exports on grounds of environmental protection which the WTO Panel decided as not substantial and therefore passed a judgement in favour of the complainants (European Commission, Press release, Dispute Settlement). The WTO Appellate Body confirmed this ruling in January 2012 (China unfairly limits).

The development of economic relations between China and the EU is impressive in terms of quantity. In terms of quality there are still obstacles to overcome. This cannot hide the fact that the EU and China are very dissimilar partners. The European Union is a transparent system with a lot of players, while China is a centralized state whose structures are not transparent. The Chinese representatives are not answerable to the public, whereas in Europe every politician is under the scrutiny of his/her competitors, the public and the media. So the Chinese leadership can concentrate on what is most important: The economic well-being of the Chinese people. Securing its sales to Europe and protecting its own industries are the priorities. For Europeans, healthy economic developments linked with prosperous relations with China are certainly the main objectives. However, reservations remain due to the authoritarian character of the regime. And if one talks about the EU, the close relationship between the US and a lot of European countries has to be born in mind. Even if the US is not an EU member, it influences decisions in Europe to a great extent.

References

Official Documents

China's EU Policy Paper, October 2003, http://www.fmprc.gov.cn, (16.07.2011).
Communication from the Commission, Brussels, (25.03.1998), COM(1998) 181 final:
  Building a Comprehensive Partnership with China. p. 4, http://eur-lex.europa.eu
Communication of the Commission: *A Long Term Policy for China – Europe Relations*.
  COM(1995) 279/final, p. 3, http://www.eeas.europa.eu
Commission of the European Communities, Brussels, 10.9.2003, COM(2003) 533 final,
  Commission Policy Paper For Transmission to the Council and the European Parlia-
  ment: *A maturing partnership – shared interests and challenges in EU-China relations*
  (Updating the European Commission's Communications on EU-China relations of
  1998 and 2001). http://eur-lex.europa.eu
Commission of the European Communities, Brussels, 24.10.2006, COM(2006) 631 final,
  Communication from the Commission to the Council and the European Parliament:
  EU – China: Closer partners, growing responsibilities. http://eur-lex.europa.eu

Articles, Research Papers, Publications

Barysch, Katinka/Grant, Charles/Leonard, Mark (2005): Embracing the dragon. The EU's
  partnership with China. London: Center for European Reform.
Brettner-Messler, Gerald (2011): Besuch einer Delegation des China Instituts für Internati-
  onale Strategische Studien. In: Bundesministerium für Landesverteidigung und Sport,
  Landesverteidigungsakademie. Jahresbericht 2010, Wien.
China's 2010 trade surplus down 6.4%, http://www.china.org.cn, (10.01.2011).
China joins the WTO – at last, http://www.bbc.co.uk, (11.12.2001).
China unfairly limits raw material exports: WTO, http://www.thehindu.com, (31.01.2012).
China urges EU to lift arms embargo, recognize market economy status, http://www.
  eurochinajob.com, (11.05.2011).
Europe Information, External Relations, 17/79, The People's Republic of China and the
  European Community, pp. 3-8, http://aei.pitt.edu
EU-China Trade: Questions and Answers – Strasbourg, 24 October 2006, http://trade.
  ec.europa.eu/doclib/docs/2006/october/tradoc_130788.pdf
Facts and figures about China-EU trade, http://english.peopledaily.com.cn, (28.04.2008)
Fox, John/Godement, François (2009): A Power Audit of EU-China relations. European
  Council on Foreign Relations, London.
Gittings, John (2005): The Changing Face of China. Oxford: Oxford University Press.
Hauser, Gunther/Kernic, Franz (eds.) (2009): China: The Rising Power. Frankfurt/Main:
  Peter Lang.
McNamara, Sally/Lohman, Walter (2011): EU's Arms Embargo on China: David Cameron
  Must Continue to Back the Ban, http://www.heritage.org, (18.01.2011).
Morrison, Wayne M. (2011): China and the World Trade Organization. CRS Report for
  Congress, http://fpc.state.gov, (20.06.2011).
Norris, Floyd (2011): Europe Frets Over Trade Deficits With China, http://www.
  nytimes.com, (20.05.2011).
Shambaugh, D./Sandschneider, E./Hong, Zhou (2008): From honeymoon to marriage.
  Prospects for the China-Europe relationship. In: Shambaugh, D./Sandschneider, E./

Hong, Zhou (eds.), China-Europe Relations. Perceptions, Policies and Prospects, Abingdon, New York: Routledge.

Shambaugh, David (1997): Europe's Relations with China: Forging Closer Ties. In: Maybaumwisniewski, Susan C./Sommerville, Mary A. (eds.): Blue Horizon: United States-Japan-PRC Tripartite Relations, Part I, Security. Washington, DC: National Defence University Press, http://www.au.af.mil

Wissenbach, Uwe: The EU and China – reconciling interests and values in an age of interdependence. The dilemma between economic interests and human rights, http://library.fes.de/pdf-files/bueros/seoul/06522.pdf

Xiaotong, Zhang: The EU's Trade Relations with China (1975-2008): A Linkage Power at Work? (Presentation on the public defence of PhD thesis on the 20th April in the ULB), http://theses.ulb.ac.be

Yihuang, Zhou (2004): Die Außenpolitik Chinas. Beijing: China Intercontinental Press

Press Releases

European Commission, Press release, Dispute Settlement, Brussels, 5 July 2011, EU welcomes WTO report on China's export restrictions on raw materials, http://trade.ec.europa.eu

EU, Press releases, China: EU calls for less barriers, more IPR protection to boost investment, IP/09/1285, 08/09/2009, http://europa.eu

The 25th Session of China-EU Trade & Economic Joint Committee Held in Beijing, http://english.mofcom.gov.cn, (17.07.2011).

WTO NEWS, Press/243, 17 September 2001, WTO successfully concludes negotiations on China's entry, http://www.wto.org, (20.06.2011).

WTO NEWS, Geneva, 17 September 2001, Meeting of the Working Party on the accession of China, http://wto.org, (18.08.2011).

Internet presentations, Homepages

European Commission, Trade, China, http://ec.europa.eu, (18.08.2011).

European Parliament Fact Sheets, 6.3.11. China, http://www.europarl.europa.eu, (22.02.2001).

The European Union and India
Forming a 'Strategic Partnership'

Heinrich Kreft

Indira Gandhi was right when saying 'A nation's strength ultimately consists in what it can do on its own, and not in what it can borrow from others.' Nevertheless this shall not preclude the fact that in cooperation and unity lies strength. This is understood by both the EU and India, who are not only Unions by themselves (the EU with 27 member states and India with 28 states) but are also forming 'Strategic Partnerships' with each other and other entities.

The EU and India, as the largest democracies in the world, share common values and beliefs that make them natural partners as well as factors of stability in the present world order. Therefore it is a logical step that the EU-India relations have grown over the years from what used to be a purely trade and economic driven relationship to one covering many areas of interaction. In 2004 the landmark Strategic Partnership Agreement between the EU and India was launched. This 'Strategic Partnership' shall lead to cooperation as equal partners and working together in partnership with the world at large.

Historical Overview of Political Relations

India and European countries have always had long-standing relations. After the foundation of the European Economic Community (EEC) following the treaty of Rome in 1957, India in 1962 became not only one of the first countries but also the first developing country to establish diplomatic relations with the then six-member entity. It was understood from the very beginning that this was not going to replace India's relations with individual members of the EEC, in fact India's relations with Germany, France, Italy and the other founding members of the EEC grew steadily. This continued when the EEC was enlarging and when it transformed itself into the European Union (EU after the Single Act of 1987).

Despite this good start, the move towards intensivating the relationship of India and the EEC was marked by a backlash in the beginning. India's initial attempt was to explore the possibility of an Association Agreement with the

EEC similar to those with countries of the Mediterranean basin and later with the African, Caribbean and Pacific countries. But as the European Commission (EC) had then classified all countries in South Asia as 'non-associable', India's effort failed. However, on the part of the EEC the idea of trade preferences for developing countries had arisen at the same time (e.g. Lomé Convention, Generalized System of Preferences). At the 2nd United Nations Conference on Trade and Development in New Delhi in 1968 generalised preferences were established. Although the idea of trade preferences was less based on altruism by the developed countries but more on the reason to reshape their economic ties with one-time colonies, it was the starting point for Commercial Cooperation Agreements (CCA). (Kreft 2005: 79f)

The concept of a CCA acknowledged the sovereign equality between the EEC and India and restructured their relation in a way in which it would not conflict with India's bilateral relations with the EEC member states. The 1st CCA between the EEC and India was signed in 1973. It set up a Joint Commission as the primary forum of all interaction between the two entities.

In 1991 India started its economic liberalisation process. This was regarded by the EU as a welcome development which needed to be strengthened and encouraged. At the same time the EU was transforming due to the fall of the Iron Curtain. Not surprisingly the economic and political relations between the EU and India have intensified considerably since then. For instance, in 1993 the Joint Political Statement was signed which launched a political dialogue with annual ministerial meetings. In 1996 the EU acknowledged with the Enhanced Partnership that India had become an increasingly significant political and economic player on the global stage (Wagner 2009: 115f).

The 1st EU-India Political Summit held in Lisbon in 2000 boosted a regular political dialogue in all areas of common interest and concern. The Joint Summit Declaration set out the path the new partnership was to follow in the years to come. It was decided to hold annual summits alternately in New Delhi and in the capital of the EU Presidency. Since Lisbon, ten summits have been held, the last and 11th in Brussels on 10 December 2010. The summits are considered to be the highest level body in the EU-India relationship. Since the 6th Summit a Business Summit has been held parallel to the Political Summits to give greater relevance to economic, commercial and investment issues.

With the European Security Strategy of 2003 the EU has clarified its security strategy which is aimed at achieving 'a secure Europe in a better world', identifying the threats facing the Union, defining its strategic objectives and setting out the political implications for Europe. There the need for strategic partners was emphasised. Such a partnership is a relationship at a higher level than the normal intercourse between any two entities. The EU has established such a relationship with only six other countries: US, Canada, Japan, Russia, China and Brazil.

At the 5th Summit in The Hague in 2004 the landmark Strategic Partnership Agreement between the EU and India was launched. In 2005, the 6th EU-India Summit in New Delhi approved a Joint Action Plan (JAP) to implement the multi-dimensional EU-India Strategic Partnership. India today has "Strategic Partnerships" with all major powers; it is only its partnership with the EU where a formal document like the JAP has been drawn up. This landmark document commits the EU and India to:

- Strengthening dialogue and consultation mechanisms
- Deepening political dialogue and cooperation in areas such as pluralism and diversity, democracy and human rights, peace-building and post-conflict assistance, regional cooperation, non-proliferation and the fight against terrorism and organised crime.
- Bringing together peoples and cultures through parliamentary, academic and civil society exchanges, including the EU-India Civil Society Round Table, cultural cooperation and dialogues on migration and consular issues.
- Enhancing economic policy dialogue and cooperation through working groups on industrial policy, energy and climate change, the environment, business and development cooperation, clean development, finance and transport.
- Developing trade and investment in the spheres of services, public procurement, intellectual property rights, trade defence instruments in addition to moving forward on World Trade Organisation and Doha Development Agenda negotiations. (European Union – EEAS 2011).

In this context the EU Country Strategy Paper for India (2007-2013) is to be highlighted. It not only forms the basis for the EU's future development cooperation so that India is able to achieve the Millennium Development Goals by 2015 but also concerns the implementation of the JAP (European Commission 2008).

At the 9th Summit in Marseille in 2008, the EU and India identified new activities to complement The Revised Joint Action Plan, with the objective of promoting international peace and security and working together towards achieving economic progress, prosperity and sustainable development. The revised plan also reaffirmed the EU and India's commitments to cooperation on research and technology and 'people to people' cultural exchange (President of the Council of the EU 2008).

The EU-India political partnership is now embedded in a strong institutional architecture. Besides the summits the annual ministerial meetings are the most visible feature of an ongoing political dialogue. Senior officials and experts regularly meet on issues of common concern such as terrorism, human rights, trade and development. Political relations are also strengthened by the regular exchange of visits between EU and Indian parliamentarians and draw on the strengths of the two civil societies.

The launching of an EU-India Round Table of eminent personalities and the creation of an EU-India network of Think Tanks are significant steps towards greater mutual cooperation in all fields as they bring together civil society organisations from the EU and India. In the same spirit, the development of academic and cultural exchanges play an increasing role in broadening the spectrum of EU-India relations.

New formats for dialogue have been created through Indian membership of the Asia-Europe Meeting (ASEM) and the EU's observer status at SAARC summits.

Political Issues

The 'Strategic Partnership' of the EU and India is rooted in shared values and principles: democracy, rule of law, respect for human rights and fundamental freedoms. Therefore both agree on the importance of an effective multilateral system, centred on a strong United Nations (UN), as a key factor in tackling global challenges. Both sides stress the need to pursue the reform of the main UN in order to make the world organisation a central institution for global governance issues.

Nevertheless, the EU and India have a different understanding of effective multilaterism. The EU regards it as a synonym for strengthening international institutions in order to establish a rule-based international order in the long-term perspective. India regards multilateral institutions more as a means to pursue its national interests. It has a keen interest in – the reform of – global institutions that will enhance its international standing. But due to India's strong emphasis on national sovereignty it is difficult to imagine that the Indian government will agree to international agreements that may constrain national sovereignty. This is shown, for example, with regard to the International Criminal Court. In contrast to the EU, India does not support this new institution because of fear of potential interference in its global affairs.

The EU and India have a long tradition in UN peacekeeping operations as well as post-conflict reconstruction. Actually, no other country has lost as many soldiers in international missions as India. Regional conflicts and 'failed' states pose a security threat for both entities as these conflicts are safe havens for terrorist groups. At the 11th Summit in Brussels in 2010, for instance, both sides reiterated their common interest in a stable, peaceful and inclusive Afghanistan free from terrorism, as well as their support to the Kabul Process building upon broad international partnership towards further

Afghan responsibility and ownership in security, governance and development. They also underlined the need for more effective regional cooperation for the stabilisation of Afghanistan and expressed their continued commitment to an ongoing dialogue to this end (Bendiek 2008:153f).

Both entities have suffered from terrorism. In India, the most recent bombing occurred in Mumbai in July 2011. India is mostly affected by militant Islamist groups which use terror attacks for their struggle in Kashmir and to undermine the rapprochement between India and Pakistan. The EU is less affected but the terrorist threat is also very present in Europe. Many attacks have prevailed because of a well operated anti-terror system in the EU and the member states. Nevertheless, the bomb attacks in London and Madrid in 2005 prove that militant Islamistic groups have a global network which needs to be tracked down and dismantled. At the 11th Summit in Brussels in 2010 an EU-India Joint Declaration on International Terrorism was issued. It underlines that cooperation in combating international terrorism, including cross-border terrorism, is one of the key political priorities in the their 'Strategic Partnership'. Both sides put great importance to counter terrorism cooperation in the framework of the UN and share a commitment to universal ratification and full implementation of all UN Counter Terrorism conventions (European Council 2010).

The EU and India have a common commitment to the non-proliferation of weapons of mass destruction. Although India is a – de facto – nuclear power since its nuclear tests in 1974 and 1998, it refuses to sign the Non-Proliferation Treaty. Nevertheless, the EU and India could agree on a common position concerning non-proliferation of weapons of mass destruction as laid down in the JAP. At the 11th Summit in Brussels 2010, for instance, the EU and India reaffirmed their commitment to global and non-discriminatory disarmament and to preventing the proliferation of weapons of mass destruction and their delivery systems. Leaders pledged closer cooperation aimed at providing a robust nuclear non-proliferation regime and, in particular, looked forward to a prompt commencement of negotiations on a Fissile Material Cut-off Treaty in the Conference on Disarmament. They also reaffirmed their commitment to diplomacy to resolve the Iranian nuclear issue and expressed the need for Iran to take constructive and immediate steps to meet its obligations to the International Atomic Energy Agency and the UN Security Council.

The EU and India, as the largest democracies in the world, share a similar understanding of human rights and have a long tradition of democratic governance. The implementation of human rights in India is however still in need of improvement. Especially the human rights situation in Kashmir has led to various controversies with the EU. Not only with regard to the human rights situation in India but also at the global level, it is shown that the EU and India do not always agree on human rights matters, e.g. India, which was elected to the UN Human Rights Council in 2006, has not always been in line with European positions. It can be said that the promotion of democracy is not focused on India's foreign policy even though India has a longer democratic tradition than some EU member states. However, at the 10th Summit in New Delhi in 2009 the EU and India jointly stated their commitment to the respect, the protection and promotion of human rights, fundamental freedoms, and the rule of law. They are also reinforcing cooperation within the UN Human Rights Council, whose creation is considered a major achievement of recent UN reforms.

Cooperation in the Field of Economic and Trade Issues

The EU has together 500 million citizens. Four of the world's seven largest economies are part of the EU. As the EU started as an Economic Community, economic and trade issues play a major part in its relations with other entities. The EU member states have agreed to pool a substantial part of their sovereignty and follow a common policy on international trade: they share a single market, a single external border and a single trade policy. Instead of 27 different sets of trade rules with each of Europe's trading partners there is just one agreement negotiated by the European Commission (EC). Member States' embassies in partner countries are in charge of export promotion and offer a wide range of services to their national operators. The EC also represents the EU member states in the World Trade Organisation (WTO). Therefore it is no surprise that the EU is the world's largest exporter of manufactured goods and services and the biggest export market for more than one hundred countries. Trade can be seen as the engine of Europe's prosperity.

India is one of the rising countries that will reshape the global economy in the twenty-first century. It combines a sizable and growing market of more than 1.2 billion people with a growth rate of 1.4 % a year. India belongs to one of the fastest growing economies in the world. It is estimated that India will be the world's third largest economy behind China and the US by 2050. India's growth also proved to be more resistant to the world economic and financial downturn than most other countries. Although it is far from the closed market that it was twenty years ago before starting the economic liberalisation process, India's trade regime and regulatory environment still remain comparatively restrictive, which hinders trade with the EU. In 2009 the World Bank downgraded India to 165th position – out of 183 economies – from 120th in 2008 in terms of the 'ease of doing business'. In addition to tariff barriers to imports, India also imposes a number of non-tariff barriers in the form of quantitative restrictions, import licensing, mandatory testing and certification for a large number of products, as well as complicated and lengthy customs procedures.

EU-India trade has grown impressively over the years. The EU is India's largest trading partner. In 2010 the EU accounted for 19 % of India's total exports with 29 billion euro (before the US) and 14 % of India's total imports with 35 billion euro (before China). India accounts for a more limited but rapidly growing share of EU trade: 2.6 % of the EU's total exports (almost 35 billion euro) and 2.2 % of the EU's total imports (with 33 billion euro). India ranked 8th in the list of the EU's main trading partners in 2010, up from 15th in 2002. The EU is also India's largest source of foreign direct investment. There is still a huge potential for developing EU and Indian trade and investment.

Although the thrust between the EU and India is today political, the content remains mainly economic. As strategic partners the EU and India have in place an institutional framework, cascading down from the annual Summit held at heads of states and government level, to a senior-official level Joint Committee, to the Sub-Commission on Trade and to working groups on technical issues such as technical barriers to trade, sanitary and phytosanitary measures, agricultural policy or industrial policy. These are the fora where a number of day-to-day issues, such as EU market access problems, are discussed.

Both EU and India are firm supporters of the WTO and key actors in the Doha round of negotiations launched in 2001. A successful conclusion of the Doha round would contribute significantly to a more open and stable environment for trade and investment for both the EU and India. India as a leader of the group of (advanced) developing countries known as the G20, and also as part of G4 (along with the EU, the US and Brazil) is steering the negotiations.

With its combination of rapid growth and relatively high market protection, India was an obvious partner for one of the new generation of EU Free Trade Agreements (FTA) launched as part of the Global Europe strategy in 2006. From India's point of view the EU was a very attractive potential FTA partner because the EU has a market of 500 million affluent consumers– the largest in the world – and forms the first and most important destination for India's goods and services. The parameters for an ambitious and comprehensive FTA, including goods, services, investments and other key aspects, were set out in the report of the EU-India High Level Trade Group in October 2006, which was tasked with assessing the viability of an FTA between the EU and India. Negotiations were launched in June 2007. At the moment the negotiations are in a crucial stage. India is fearing a loss of market and competitiveness because of the EU's demand for lower tariffs for example on automobiles and wine. Differences over services, agriculture, chemicals, intellectual property rights and government procurement are also yet to be resolved. With flexibility on both sides negotiations might be concluded in early 2012 (European Commision 2007a).

To assist India in continuing its efforts to better integrate into the world economy in order to further enhancing bilateral trade and investment ties, the EU is providing trade related technical assistance to India. 13.3 million euro were allocated through the Trade and Investment Development Programme (TIDP) resulting from the Country Strategy Paper (CSP) 2002-2006. This time-restricted programme started in December 2005 and concluded in December 2007. It aimed to assist India in creating an environment that encourages trade and investment. The programme targeted businesses expansion, job creation, and a rise in incomes so that consumers benefit from more choice and lower prices. The 13.3 million euro programme was financed by a 12.7 million euro contribution from the EU and a 0.6 million euro contribution from the government of India. The EU will continue to provide technical assistance to India through the Capacity-building Initiative for Trade Development (CITD) which will address some key areas to further integrate India into the international trade system. It will also aim to enhance India's trade-related regulatory institutions and enforcement systems to meet international standards and requirements while supporting India's trade-related training institutions in strengthening their capacities.

The EU's largest economic cooperation project in India was the EU-India Civil Aviation project (2001-06). This project aimed to improve regulatory links and safety, and facilitate business links while investing in human capital. Furthermore, a Maritime Agreement is currently being negotiated between the EU and India. Formal negotiations were launched at the 4th EU-India Summit in November 2003 and are still ongoing. Such an agreement would improve the conditions and legal framework under which maritime transport operations to and from India are carried out for the benefit of both economies.

Cooperation in the Field of Science and Technology

The EU and India both consider science and technology as a key factor for competitiveness. Therefore cooperation in the fields of science and technology play an important part in EU-India relations. A formal collaboration in science and technology with India started with the signature of the European Community-India Science and Technology Cooperation Agreement on 23 November 2001 which was renewed during the 8th Summit 2007 in New Delhi. The agreement is implemented by the Directorate-General for Research for the European Commission and by the Department of Science and Technology for the government of India. Concerning their 'Strategic Partnership" the JAP contains a number of action points which have important science and technology dimensions.

The India-EU Ministerial Conference on Science in New Delhi on February 7-8, 2007 has set the tone for future cooperation (European Commission 2007b). The 'New Delhi Communiqué', issued at the end of the Ministerial Conference, underlined the importance of a strong science and knowledge base as a major prerequisite for competitiveness, and the strong role of international science and technology collaboration. It confirmed that such a cooperation between the EU and India should be based on the principles of symmetry, reciprocity, mutual benefit and, where appropriate, the co-investment of resources in joint actions. It was recognised that important 'windows of opportunity' existed for a significant increase in the breadth and depth of EU-India science and technology cooperation, especially through the EU's 7th Framework Programme for Research and Technological Development 2007-2013 and India's 11th Five Year Plan.

One new feature of EU-India science and technology relations is the launch of coordinated calls for proposals. At the India-EU Ministerial Science Conference in February 2007, the two sides committed themselves to spending 5 million euro every year on joint research in areas of mutual benefit. Three Coordinated Calls for Proposals have been launched so far. The first such call, launched with the Department of Science and Technology on computation materials science, attracted 25 proposals, of which six have been funded. The second Coordinated Call, launched with the Department of Biotechnology on food, health and well being, again attracted 25 proposals, of which two have been funded. The third Coordinated Call for Proposals launched with the Department of Science and Technology on solar energy systems attracted 23 proposals, of which three have been funded. Currently the call for proposals launched with the Department of Science and Technology on water technology, research and innovation is ongoing.

In addition, India is a valuable partner for the EU in major international projects such as the International Thermonuclear Experimental Reactor (ITER) project, the European Satellite Navigation system GALILEO and the interlinking of India's Education Research Network, ERNET, to its pan-European equivalent GEANT2.

Perhaps the most important dimension in any international cooperation in science and technology are human resources. Researchers are traditionally among the most mobile segments of the population. Researchers leaving for another country do not represent per se a brain drain. On the contrary they remain highly beneficial to their home country, in particular when they communicate and network with scientists at home. European researchers abroad contribute to the vigour, growth and success of European research – as individuals, as organisations and institutes, as commercial companies and as communicators of science and innovation. The EU persistently advocates the benefits of 'brain circulation', both within Europe and at a global level. Each year about 250,000 engineers graduate from Indian universities. Even though not all graduates are qualified according to Western standards, India's human resources offer a huge source of intellectual capacity for European firms. But at present, India's academics are more oriented towards the US which opened its labour market to attract Indian professionals many years ago. Concerning student mobility, Indian students can make use of programmes like Erasmus Mundus and Asia Links when visiting EU universities. Also the EU-wide harmonisation of university degrees to Bachelor and Master will attract Indian students. Nevertheless, the figures on student mobility show that the majority of Indian students still prefer to go to the US or Australia to study, and that the EU countries are not regarded as attractive destinations for Indian students. The EU must therefore intensify its academic ties with India.

Cooperation in the Field of Environment and Energy

The EU treaty is based on the notion of 'sustainable development' and the EU complies with this by integrating environmental requirements into the definition and implementation of other EU policies and activities. The EU can be regarded as the leader in global efforts to protect the environment. The EU, for instance, is a signatory and active participant in the Kyoto Protocol on Climate Change, which entered into force in February 2005. Moreover, the EU participates in a number of international agreements and partnerships, including the UN Framework Convention on Climate Change and the UN Montreal Protocol on Ozone Depletion. Indian governments have consistently emphasised that the per capita CO_2 emissions of the developing world like India are only a small percentage of those of the developed countries. Nevertheless India's emissions will rise sharply in the years to come so that it will be one of the key countries to achieve the reduction of greenhouse gas emissions.

Therefore, the EU supports India's efforts towards sustainable growth and to build mutual understanding on global environmental issues including climate change. The environment is recognised as a strategic area for dialogue in the EU-India partnership. The JAP provides the basis for enhancing cooperation on environment and climate change, e.g. it stipulates that a Joint Working Group on Environment should meet on an annual basis. The launch of an EU-India Environment Forum (e.g. the 2005 Environment Forum focused on hazardous waste management and urban waste management, the 2006 Forum addressed waste minimisation, hazardous waste management and landfill) and the EU-India Initiative on Clean Development and Climate Change are some of the key commitments undertaken to strengthen bilateral cooperation. The EU-India Action Plan Support Facility Programme which provides financial support to policy dialogues in a number of key sectors also includes the environment.

Support for the environment component is towards the creation of a 'pool of expertise' to provide technical assistance, advice and expertise in five priority sectors: waste, water, climate change, air pollution and chemicals.

India's economic achievements since the 1990s and its growth of population made energy security a major issue of its foreign policy. It is already one of the largest consumers of energy in the world and its hunger for energy will further increase. India's energy dependency will increase with regard to all fossil fuels. It is estimated that by 2030 India's import dependency will rise up to 90 % on oil and up to 40 % on gas. The gap between supply and demand will also make it necessary to import more coal even though India's coal reserves are among the largest in the world. After India's nuclear tests in 1974 and 1998 international sanctions were targeted at India and thus limited its nuclear programme. Because of that India's share of nuclear power is today only around 3 % of the total energy production.

The EU with its 500 million citizens is also one of the largest energy markets in the world. Its current emphasis is on the security of energy supply. This includes ways to reduce demand while ensuring diversification of producer and transit routes for the supply of those energy sources that need to be imported, promoting the development and use of alternative sources of energy and increasing the efficient use of energy. The EU is known for its ambitious move towards energy production in the fields of wind energy, biomass, hydro-generated and solar power as well as biofuels from organic matter. Additionally, the EU is de-regulating the electricity and gas sectors through legislation that has already opened up the markets to all participants.

At the 5th EU-India Summit in 2004 the political decision was taken to embark on an energy dialogue. Key priorities for the cooperation are development of clean coal technologies, increasing energy efficiency and savings, promoting environment-friendly energies as well as assisting India in energy market reforms. The EU-India Energy Panel has been created as the formal instrument of EU-India cooperation in the energy sector and its constitutive meeting was held in June 2005. The Panel acts as a platform to analyse the joint and individual progress made in the energy sector, to share experience and knowledge, and to explore areas of cooperation and joint projects. Four working groups were established: Coal and Clean Coal Technologies; Energy Efficiency and Renewable Energy; Fusion Energy/India's participation in the ITER project; Petroleum and Natural Gas. They all meet once a year and report to the Energy Panel. Nevertheless, the field of energy still offers huge opportunities to intensify the cooperation between the EU and India. Especially European energy firms will find attractive investment opportunities in the field of conventional and renewable energy.

Cooperation in the Field of Culture

The EU and India are pluralistic societies – multi-regional, multi-linguistic, multi-cultural and multi-religious. India's experience with Europe was long determined by British colonial rule. Now that the legacies of the colonial period fade, the cultural ties linking Britain (thus more broadly Europe) and India have loosened. The EU which steadily expanded over the years especially by accepting East-European countries is highly preoccupied with its own integration.

However, both sides recognise the importance of their cultural cooperation. For instance, at the 5th EU-India Summit held in The Hague in 2004 the 1st Joint Declaration on Cultural Relations was issued. The document recognizes culture as being instrumental in fostering mutual understanding and close cooperation on both the state and the people-to-people levels, and commits the two sides to enhancing cooperation in areas ranging from education and tourism to media and restoration of works of art and monuments. At the 9th Summit in Marseille in 2008 concerning the JAP it was stated that (The Revised Joint Action Plan):

> "Specific funding has been made available to increase the participation of Indian students in European graduate programmes. The Community Culture Programme has launched a special action for EU-India cultural co-operation for the period 2007-2009. Work continues on promoting civil society exchanges and people-to-people interaction in diverse fields. There is a need for more progress in the area of culture and in the shared ambition of establishing study-centers in both partners' academic institutions. Further effort is needed to facilitate the movement of persons, based on a comprehensive approach to migration issues".

At the 11th Summit in Brussels in 2010 a new Joint Declaration on Culture was signed. Both sides intend to further exploit the potential for cooperation through the development of new policy-oriented activities. They declared that in the light of the 2005 UNESCO Convention on the Protection and Promotion of the Diversity of Cultural Expressions, to which both entities are parties, they will set up a sector policy dialogue covering issues of common interest in the field of culture that will help to protect and promote the diversity of cultural expressions. The sector policy dialogue and cooperation will consist of regular exchanges of best practices, achievements and challenges, and promotion of knowledge building and sharing in relation to commonly identified issues.

Since 2007, the EC has invested 2 million euro through the EU Culture Programme in support of five joint initiatives with India. These included the 'Spice' project which brought together the Attakalari Centre for Movement Arts in Bangalore and art professionals from Europe. The Culture Programme also backed '2050 Cultures of Living', an architecture project where the Darpana Academy of Performing Arts and the Srishti School of Art shared views on design and technology with partners from eight European countries

Conclusion – Strengthening the 'Strategic Partnership'

Relations between the European Union and India have developed positively during the past two decades (Abhyankar 2009: 393f; Wagner 2009: 115f). The cooperation in the field of economy and trade is for both sides the most important. It has intensified enormously since India started its liberation process in the 1990's. But within the framework of the agreed "Strategic Partnership" relations have broadened immensely. The EU-India Joint Action Plan has been the driving force of this development: Relations today cover many different economic, social, financial, scientific and political areas, but there is still lots of room for deepening and improvements: A Free Trade Agreement is under negotiation, but not yet signed. Academic networks and student exchanges are still at a low level, leaving much room for improvement.

There is no doubt that India is not always an easy partner for the EU as its approaches to many security, trade and environmental questions are driven by different foreign policy traditions and ambitions. India wants to become a major power and sees itself already on the way to becoming a world player; therefore it objects for example to any interference in its internal affairs. In this position India is much closer to the foreign policy thinking of the US and China. India takes the EU seriously where the EU is in the driver's seat: in economic and trade issues. However, it barely recognizes the EU in other areas where there is no common EU policy, for example in security matters. More EU integration would no doubt increase the potential for more EU-India cooperation. But even in the absence of breakthroughs to more EU integration in the near future, there is ample room to increase the dialogue on all levels and to broaden and deepen the relations between the European and the Indian Union.

Main references

Abhyankar, Rajendra M. (2009): India and the European Union: a partnership for all reasons. In: India Quarterly (New Delhi), 65 (October-December 2009) 4., pp. 393-404

Aziz Wülbers, Shazia (ed) (2008): EU India relations: a critique. New Delhi: Academic Foundation.

Bendiek, Annegret/Wagner, Christian (2008): Prospects and challenges of EU-India security cooperation. In: Wülbers, Shazia Aziz (ed.): EU India relations: a critique. New Delhi: Academic Foundation, pp. 153-168.

Kreft, Heinrich/Frahm, Ole (2005): Die Europäische und die Indische Union – ein langer Weg zur strategischen Partnerschaft. In: Schucher/Günter/Wagner, Christian (eds.): Indien 2005, Politik, Wirtschaft, Gesellschaft. Hamburg: Institut für Asienkunde, pp. 79-91.

Sachdeva, Gulshan (2009): India and the European Union: Time to de-bureaucratize strategic partnership. In: Strategic Analysis (New Delhi), 33 (March 2009) 2. pp. 202-207.

Salma Bava, Ummu (et al.) (2008): Partnerships for effective multilateralism: EU relations with Brazil, China, India and Russia (Ed. by Giovanni Grevi). Institute for Security Studies – Paris, 05.06.2008, p. 176 (Chaillot Paper; No. 109).

Wagner, Christian (2009): Die Beziehungen zwischen Indien und der Europäischen Union. In: Kramer, Heinz (ed.): Globale Außenpolitik der Europäischen Union: interregionale Beziehungen und „strategische Partnerschaften". Baden-Baden: Nomos, (Internationale Politik und Sicherheit; Bd. 63). pp. 115-127.

Wahlers, Gerhard (ed.) (2007): India and the European Union, Foreword: Vogel, Bernhard. Preface: Merkel, Angela. Konrad-Adenauer-Stiftung, 2nd updated ed. New Delhi (KAS Publication Series; No. 12).

Documents

Council of the European Union (2009): EU-India Summit, New Delhi, 6 November 2009, Joint statement. Brussels, p. 10. http://www.consilium.europa.eu/uedocs/cms_data/docs/pressdata/en/er/110993.pdf

Deutscher Bundestag (2011): EU-Freihandelsabkommen mit Indien stoppen – Verhandlungsmandat in demokratischem Prozess neu festlegen. Drucksachen 17/2420, 17/4616. In: Verhandlungen des Deutschen Bundestages: Stenographischer Bericht (Köln), 17 (10. Februar 2011) 90. pp. 10195B-10200B http://www.bundestag.de/dokumente/protokolle/plenarprotokolle/17090.pdf   http://dip21.bundestag.de/dip21/btd/17/024/1702420.pdf http://dip21.bundestag.de/dip21/btd/17/046/1704616.pdf

European Council (2010): EU-India Summit, Brussels, 10 December 2010: documents. Brussels. http://www.consilium.europa.eu/uedocs/cms_data/docs/pressdata/EN/foraff/118404. pdf http://www.consilium.europa.eu/uedocs/cms_data/docs/pressdata/EN/ foraff/ 118405. pdf http://www.consilium.europa.eu/uedocs/cms_data/docs/pressdata/en/er/118403.pdf

European Commission (2007): Directorate-General External Relations: 8th EU-India Summit, New Delhi, 30 November 2007a. Brussels, getr. Zähl. Enthält: India-EU Joint Statement. P. 9, India-EU Joint Action Plan: Implementation Report. P. 6. http://www. eu2007.pt/NR/rdonlyres/B3930EE0-0E1B-410B-B2E9-D90D864546CD/0/20071130EUIndiaStatement.pdf

European Commission, Directorate-General for Trade (2007b): India: EU bilateral trade and trade with the world. Brussels, p. 12. http://trade.ec.europa.eu/doclib/docs/2006/september/tradoc_113390.pdf

European Commission External Relations Directorate-General (2008): India: Country strategy paper 2007 – 2013. Brussels: European Commission, p 55. graph. Darst., Tab. (Country Strategy Paper 2007-2013) http://ec.europa.eu/external_relations/india/csp/07_13_en.pdf

European Commission External Relations Directorate-General (2008): India: Multiannual indicative programme (2007-2010). Brussels: European Commission, p. 38 (Multiannual Indicative Programme 2007-2010) http://ec.europa.eu/external_relations/india/csp/mip_07_10.pdf

European Parliament (2011): Resolution of 11 May 2011 on the state of play in the EU-India Free Trade Agreement negotiations. European Parliament. In: Texts adopted part II at the sitting of Wednesday, 11 May 2011, Brussels, pp. 212-218.
http://www.europarl.europa.eu/sides/getDoc.do?pubRef=-//EP//NONSGML+TA +20110511+SIT-02+DOC+WORD+V0//EN&language=EN

European Parliament (2009): Resolution of 26 March 2009 on an EU-India free trade agreement (2008/2135(INI)): texts adopted by Parliament, 26 March 2009 – Strasbourg – provisional edition. Brussels. http://www.europarl.europa.eu/sides/get Doc.do?pubRef=-//EP//TEXT+TA+P6-TA-2009-0189+0+DOC+XML+V0//EN& language=EN

European Union – EEAS (European External Action Service): India (2011) http://eeas. europa.eu/india/index_en.htm

President of the Council of the European Union (2008): Main results of the EU-India Summit, Marseille, 2008. Includes: EU-India Joint Press Communique, p. 3; The EU-India Joint Action Plan (JAP), p.5; Joint Work Programme, EU-India Co-Operation on Energy, Clean Development and Climate Change, p. 3. http://www.ue2008.fr/PFUE/lang/ en/accueil/PFUE-09_2008/PFUE-29.09.2008/principaux_resultats_du_sommet_ueinde

Part 3
Current Issues

The Common Foreign and Security Policy of the EU and the Human Rights Issue

Waldemar Hummer

> *„And in all this, human rights are the silver thread that runs through our actions"*
> [Speech of High Representative Catherine Ashton on main aspects and basic choices of the CFSP and the CSDP, European Parliament, 11 May 2011 (A 179/11), p. 3].

> *"Protection and promotion of human rights is a fundamental part of our foreign policy, across the board. Pursuit of our interests must always be combined with promotion of our values".*
> (Annual report from the High Representative of the Union for Foreign Affairs and Security Policy to the European Parliament on the main aspects and basic choices of the CFSP – 2009, June 2010, p. 53).

Introduction

The subject on which the editors of the volume at hand asked me to elaborate on is extraordinarily multifaceted and multi-layered and therefore requires to be operationalised and defined exactly. In simplified terms the complex matter can be allegorised as a set of concentric circles, their centre point being the main topic "human rights in the foreign and security policy relations of the European Union (EU) with third party subjects of international law (nation states, international organisations and international institutions)".

Grouped around this main topic are as a second and third circle, those topics that arise from differentiating the two principal concepts of the main topic – that is *human rights* and *foreign and security policy*. If human rights are perceived as *fundamental freedoms* – as Art. 21 para. 1 subpara. 1 of the Treaty on the European Union (TEU) does – the question arises immediately, if these fundamental freedoms pervade as well in the *Common Foreign and Security Policy (CFSP)* of the Union, and if so to what extent. Such a possible penetration of *CFSP* and *CSDP (Common Security and Defence Policy)* with issues concerning the protection of human rights can be ascribed to the fact, that for the EU the protection of human rights according to Art. 2 TEU is a horizontal value, which is a cross-sectional matter in the internal and external relations of the Union. The EU as an international actor gives priority to the protection of human rights which prevails *inside* the EU so to speak "over" *the outside* and intentionally "contaminates" its external relations too. The same thing happens to the fundamental freedoms, which according to Art. 6 TEU have to be considered by the institutions of the EU in all their configurations in the course of their internal and external activities.

However, when further differentiating the CFSP one obtains the *Common Security and Defence Policy* (CSDP) (Art. 42 TEU), within which it is also necessary to protect human rights. Especially in the CSDP it is necessary to provide for an effective protection of human rights, as military command structures are a major component and therefore so called structural power relations (*strukturelles Gewaltverhältnis*) prevail, within which the issue of the protection of human rights and fundamental freedoms is in any case of a very sensitive nature.

In another circle all further foreign relations have to be taken into account, which is best shown using the former temple model of the EU. Aside from our main focus, the (pure) CFSP and CSDP of the former second pillar, both the other two pillars and the temple itself had foreign relations: In the first pillar these were the external economic relations and in the third pillar these were the external relations in the field of Justice and Home Affairs (JHA), later renamed Police and Judicial Cooperation in criminal Matters (PJC). But even the umbrella – that is the EU itself – has had external (diplomatic) relations through the ius legationis – having the competence to send permanent representatives to third countries as well as to accredit permanent representatives of third countries with the Union itself.

If singling out e.g. the external trade relations of the EC in the former first pillar, one is bound to immediately realise that external trade policy contains an enormous amount of foreign policy. No further explanation is needed to make clear that entering into or suspending business and trade relations with certain states or groups of states is at the same time a highly political matter. This is the case not only in the field of *negative* human rights policy – which sanctions human rights violations e.g. with trade embargos – but even more so in the field of *positive* human rights policy, which creates economic incentives to adhere to and promote the protection of these rights.

As one can easily see with this example, CFSP is regulated in Art. 23 ss. TEU whereas external economic relations are regulated by Art. 205 ss. of the Treaty of the Functioning of the European Union (TFEU). The sole foreign and security policy of the treaties is thus systematically separated from the external economic policy, however the mutual penetration is obvious. There is an intertwining of two types of Union law that are separated both by treaty and legal nature – on the one side the inter-governmentally structured CFSP, on the other side the supra-national external economic policy, with no provisions being taken regarding the frictionless allocation of both spheres of competences except the obligation of both Council and Commission – assisted by the High Representative of the Union for Foreign Affairs and Security Policy – to ensure consistency between the different areas. Art. 21 para. 3 subpara. 2 TEU stipulates in this regard: *"The Union shall ensure consistency between the different areas of its external action and between these and its other policies. The Council and the Commission, assisted by the High Representative of the Union for Foreign Affairs and Security Policy, shall ensure that consistency and shall cooperate to that effect."*

The main topic will hereafter be the focus of analysis, but to give an indication of the whole extent of the topic at hand, certain issues will be explored through separate forays if necessary. Thus it will be possible to present this extraordinarily complex subject at least rudimentarily to greater extent. To begin with, some fundamental observations regarding the new institutional structure of the EU and the legal order of the EU are necessary.

The EU as Legal Successor of the EC, Legal Nature of the Law of the Union, Transitional Provisions

International legal personality, legal capacity and most of all the competence to conclude treaties are necessary prerequisites for a common foreign and security policy. The former EU did not have a legal personality of its own and thus had no international capacity to act. The attempts to assign legal personality and capacity to the former EU through an (alleged) treaty making power in Art. 24 and 38 of the former TEU remained a minority opinion and could not shatter the prevailing legal doctrine (*Schweitzer/Hummer/Obwexer* 2007: 17). With Art. 47 TEU in the version of the Treaty of Lisbon – "The Union shall have legal personality" – legal personality was expressis verbis conferred upon the new Union. Additionally, legal capacity on the basis of treaty making power was attributed by the special provisions of Art. 37 TEU and Art. 216 para. 1 TFEU.

Thus, the Treaty of Lisbon confirms post festum the previously mentioned legal opinion, that the former Union did not have legal personality of its own and hence could not be succeeded. According to Art. 1 para. 3 TEU the new Union is in effect just successor only of the European Community (EC) – "The Union shall replace and succeed the European Community" – but not the old EU, as was previously intended in Art. IV-438 para. 1 of the Constitutional Treaty (2004). The new EU is therefore successor in title solely to the former EC.

The *European Coal and Steel Community (ESCS)* ceased to exist on July 23, 2002 (Hummer 2003: 117) *Euratom* on the other hand was set up under

Art. 4 para. 2 of the Treaty of Lisbon in conjunction with Protocol (Nr. 2) amending the Treaty establishing the European Atomic Energy Community (Euratom-Protocol) (OJ 2007, C 306, 199) as an international organisation in its own right – which constitutes a separate, isolated international organisation independent from the newly created EU.

As *universal successor* to the EC, the EU takes over all internal and external rights and obligations based on the then prevailing primary and secondary Community law. Concerning the external rights and duties this legal succession had to be notified to the international signatories (third countries, international organisations) to come into effect. On November 27, 2009 the Council decided to carry out these around 500 necessary *Notifications* in form of an *impersonalised* verbal note (Doc. 16654/1/09 REV 1 of November 27, 2009; *Beaucillon/ Erlbacher* 2011: 114). With regard to the UNO in this context, the EU notified its new legal personality through a personal letter from the presidents of the Council and the Commission to the Secretary General of the UN on November 30, 2009. Furthermore the EU had the Treaty of Lisbon registered officially according to Art. 102 para. 1 of the Charter of the United Nations on May 11, 2010 with the United Nations Treaty Series.

Part of the (new) law of the Union constitutes the (old) Law of the Union of the two intergovernmental areas, CFSP (*second pillar*) and police and judicial cooperation in criminal matters (PJC) (*third pillar*). However it must be recognised that those legal acts did not adopt the supranational character of the rest of the law of the Union. According to Art. 9 of the *Protocol (Nr. 36) on transitional measures* (OJ 2010, C 83, 322) they keep their *intergovernmental* character "until those acts are repealed, annulled or amended in implementation of the Treaties". Only when these procedures have taken place, will they lose their intergovernmental character and turn into new Union law with its primacy of application.

Following this short presentation of the succession of the EC by the EU, the legal nature of the law of the Union and the transitional provisions concerning the old law of CSFP and CSDP respectively as well as PJC, the next chapters deal with the question of the legal design of the foreign relations of the EU in general and CFSP and CSDP in particular after the entry into force of the Treaty of Lisbon.

The Common Foreign and Security Policy of the EU after the Treaty of Lisbon

At the intergovernmental conference in 2007 to prepare the *Reform Treaty* (renamed on the basis of Art. 7 of the Treaty of Lisbon as *"Lisbon Treaty"*, cf. OJ 2007, C 306, 135) which was opened on July 23, 2007 in Lisbon – the reorganisation of external and foreign relations was one of the most important issues. Relevant literature rightly states that most of the new regulations concerned external relations: No less than 40 per cent of the amendments to the EU constituent treaties that were brought about by the Lisbon Treaty concerned external EU action (Arts 2011: 286).

Systematically seen there is no coherence in the revision of the external relations, as they are separated into two treaties – that is the *Treaty on European Union* (TEU) (OJ 2010, C 83: 13) and the *Treaty on the Functioning of the European Union* (TFEU) (OJ 2010, C 83: 47) – as follows: to obviously accentuate the special (intergovernmental) character of the CSFP it is not part of the *TFEU* – within which the other (miscellaneous) external activities of the Union are enshrined in Art. 205 to 222 TFEU – but is located in the *TEU* (Arts. 23 to 41 TEU).

Due to Art. 2 para. 4 TFEU it is the duty of the Union to design and implement a CFSP, including the progressive implementation of a common defence policy. According to these terms and in relation to Art. 24 para. 1 TEU, the CFSP of the Union is governed differently from the three fundamental ways of distributing competences between member states and the Union (vertical distribution of competences) that usually apply in other policy fields. Usually the distribution of competences between the Union and the Member States moulds in *exclusive competence, shared competence* as well as *actions to support, coordinate or supplement* (Art. 2 para. 1 to 3 in conjunction with Art. 3 to 6 TFEU).

Art. 24 para. 1 subpara. 2 TEU assesses special rules and procedures to CFSP: The European Council and the Council take decisions unanimously, and according to Art. 289 para. 3 in conjunction with Art. 297 TFEU no legislative acts shall be adopted. Decisions taken within the framework of the CFSP are implemented by the High Representative of the Union on the one hand and by the member states of the Union on the other. The member states use both national and Union measures (Art. 26 para. 3 TEU). In doing so the member states abstain from any action that might harm Union interests or *"impair its effectiveness as a cohesive force in international relations"* (Art. 24 para. 3 subpara. 2 TEU). The Council and the High Representative of the Union are responsible for the adherence to these principles (Art. 24 para. 3 subpara. 3 TEU).

In matters concerning the CFSP, the High Representative represents the Union, conducts political dialogue with third parties and represents Union positions in international organisations and international conferences (Art. 27 para. 2 TEU). Aside from the High Representative the President of the European Council can also represent the Union in matters of CFSP, however only on the level of the heads of state or government (Art. 15 para. 6 subpara. 2 TEU).

Another distinctive feature of the CFSP is that the European Parliament is not directly involved in decisions concerning the CFSP, but is heard and informed regularly with regard to the most important aspects of CFSP and its developments (Art. 36 para. 1 TEU). According to Art. 24 para. 1 subpara. 2 TEU in conjunction with Art. 275 para. 1 TFEU no judicial control is exerted through the Court of Justice of the European Union – except concerning the special cases provided for in Art. 40 TEU and in Art. 275 para. 2 TFEU.

Despite this (alleged) intergovernmental character of CFSP (*Calliess* 2011: 72) there is no doubt that this policy area formally constitutes Union law, as it is regulated by the TEU and the previously mentioned declaration (Nr. 17), clarifying any questions regarding the primacy of application of the Union law. Following this line of reasoning, the (factual) *intergovernmental* character of CSFP remains untouched. Though its legislative acts are equipped with primacy of Union law, they usually lack the constituting element that brings about primacy, i.e. *immediate applicability* in the sense of a *self executing* character of a legal act. As legal acts decided upon within the CFSP framework are usually classified as being not immediately executable, doctrine can still qualify CFSP as part of Union law that has primacy, as the primacy only applies hypothetically to those acts. Only if any activity in the framework of CFSP constitutes a thoroughly specified legal act – that is if its provisions are unconditional and sufficiently clear and precise – does legal doctrine meet its limits. This uncertainty – if noticed at all – has not yet been solved in relevant literature. In this context, it is implied that *decisions*, which according to Art. 288 para. 4 TFEU are legally binding in their entirety, if taken in the framework of CFSP might under special circumstances be immediately applicable, in that specific case implying primacy over the law of Member States (*Hellmann* 2009: 76).

Within CFSP and CSDP the typology of their sources of law can be described according to Art. 25 ss. TEU as follows. First the European Council decides on *general guidelines* (Art. 26 TEU) based on which the Council later on takes more specific decisions, either in the form of mandatory *operational actions* (Art. 28 TEU), or as foundations for not binding decisions which shall define the approach of the Union to a particular matter of a geographical or thematic nature and *shall ensure that their national policies conform to the Union positions* (Art. 29 TEU). Furthermore decisions regarding the *implementation* rest within the European Council. According to Art. 22 para. 1 TEU the European Council has to define the *strategic interests and goals* of the Union, based on the general rules for external policy of the Union according to Art. 21 TEU.

As a consequence of the intergovernmental character of the CFSP the European Council as well as the Council take their decisions normally only *unanimously* (Art. 31 para. 1 subpara. 1 TEU). In mere procedural questions the Council decides with absolute *majority* of its members (Art. 31 para. 5 TEU). Additionally a member state may resort to the voting instrument of a *constructive abstention* in the sense of Art. 31 para.1 subpara. 2 TEU.

This short overview of the special status and unique legal nature of CFSP has to be followed by an analysis of the development of the protection of human and fundamental rights in the former EC and the EU respectively, in order to later on display the mutual penetration of both fields.

The Protection of Human Rights and Fundamental Freedoms in the European Communities and the European Union Respectively

The EC and the Former EU on the Basis of the Treaties of Maastricht (1992), Amsterdam (1997) and Nice (2001)

The founding fathers of the European Communities (ECSC 1951, EEC 1957, EAC 1957) refrained from adding a catalogue of fundamental rights to these as those institutions were devised as regional preference areas, being mere associations for the purpose of functional integration (Ipsen 1972: 196). The primary goal of the European Communities was to set up a customs union by technical means (i.e. reduction of tariffs and quotas etc.) followed by a "Common Market". In contrast, the draft of the statute of the *European Political Community* (EPC), that was adopted by the Common Assembly of the European Coal and Steel Community (ECSC) in 1953, provided that the European Convention for the Protection of Human Rights and Fundamental Freedoms (ECHRFF) (1950) constitutes an integral part of it. Obviously the founding fathers were of the opinion that organisations being set up for *technical* harmonisation and integration of economies did not need a catalogue of fundamental rights, whereas *political* organisations, such as the EPC, did.

Deriving from the concept of rule of law, the Court of Justice of the European Communities (ECJ) had to fill the gap and solve this lack of a catalogue of fundamental rights *judicially*. Surprisingly, it took 11 years between the entry into force of the Treaty establishing the European Economic Community (EEC) in 1958 and the first pertinent judgement of the Court being passed in 1969, when the ECJ decided the case Stauder versus City of Ulm (ECJ, Case 29/69, Reports 1969: 419). In order to find a sound reasoning for its judgment, the Court referred to the general principles of law, deriving them on the one hand from the fundamental legal principles as found in the constitutional orders of the Member States, and on the other from the above mentioned European Convention for the Protection of Human Rights and Fundamental Freedoms (1950).

For obvious reasons those decisions of the ECJ regarding fundamental rights happened in a piecemeal fashion, leading to subsequent attempts of systematic codification. In a Memorandum of April 4, 1979 the Commission proposed that the European Communities should accede to the ECHRFF. This proposal gained much attraction in the Parliamentary Assembly of the Council of Europe and consequently in 1981 the Resolution 745/1981 was adopted. Though no further steps were taken, debates about the Resolution and its implementation continued. After fifteen years of discussion, the Council asked the Court of the European Communities to render a legal opinion on the possibility of an eventual accession of the European Community to the ECHRFF. In its Opinion 2/94 (ECJ, Reports 1996, I-1759) the Court argued that the EU lacked the specific competence necessary to adhere to the ECHRFF and that such an accession would mean a profound change of the existing system of the protection of human rights and fundamental freedoms with "utmost constitutional implications".

As a consequence of the Treaty of Maastricht (1992) the European Communities, which used to be focused on mere economic integration, transformed into the European Union (EU). This new entity was enriched by a political component and penetrated two new policy areas, that is the Common Foreign and Security Policy (CFSP) and the Common Security and Defence Policy (CSDP) forming the second pillar, and the Justice and Home Affairs (JHA) as the third pillar, which was redefined and renamed Police and Judicial Cooperation in Criminal Matters (PJC) as a consequence of the Treaty of Amsterdam (1997). Hence the Maastricht Treaty constructed an organisational arrangement, which can be illustrated as a "temple construction", resting on three pillars: the economic integration of the first pillar, CFSP and CSDP as the second pillar, JHA or rather PJC, as the third pillar. Legal personality however only belonged to the three European Communities of the first pillar.

As a consequence of this shift towards a more political and policy oriented Union, the need for an internal democratisation, legitimation and legalisation grew stronger, a development that had happened in a similar fashion during the time of the previously mentioned failed European Political Cooperation (EPC) of the 1950s. To answer this challenge calls for an intensification of the protection of fundamental freedoms and the drafting of a "Charter of Fundamental Rights" emerged.

The then German Federal Foreign Minister, Joschka Fischer, introduced this idea during the European Council, taking place in Cologne on June 4, 1999. This lead to the instalment of a Convention tasked with drafting a *Charter of Fundamental Rights of the European Union* in October 1999. It took the Convention until October 2000 to finalise and adopt a text, which was then forwarded to the European institutions. The European Council in Biarritz unanimously approved the draft and forwarded it to the European Parliament and the Commission, where it received support. The Commission declared its support on December 6, 2000. The first solemn proclamation of the Charter by the presidents of the three institutions: Parliament, Council, Commission, took place on December 7, 2000 in Nice. This proclamation was repeated on December 12, 2007 in Strasbourg (OJ 2007, C 303: 1) ahead of the signing of the Treaty of Lisbon on December 13, 2007 in Lisbon. However, as this proclamation only constituted a mere "Interinstitutional *Declaration*" of the presidents of the EP, the Council and the Commission, it did not constitute an "Interinstitutional *Agreement*" and therefore had no legal implications.

According to para. 6 of the Preamble, the Charter of Fundamental Rights of the EU refers to the European Convention for the Protection of Human Rights and Fundamental Freedoms (1950), the European Social Charter (1961), the Community Charter of Fundamental Social Rights for Workers (1989), the Unions regulations regarding the Citizenship of the Union, the fundamental freedoms of the internal market as well as the regulations regarding the labour and social law.

Only 50 per cent of the substantive law is rooted in the ECHRFF or in the case law of the ECJ. The interpretation of the Charter is therefore complex and byzantine. The *Explanations*, which were composed by the Presidium of the Convention (OJ 2007, C 303: 17), shall be drawn up as a way of providing guidance in the interpretation of this Charter by the courts of the Union and of the Member States and shall be given due regard (Art. 6 para. 1 subpara. 3 TEU in conjunction with Art. 52 para. 7 of the Charter).

A pertinent consequence of the Maastricht Treaty's pillar construction was the extension of the protection of fundamental rights from the area of Community law of the first pillar onto the second and third pillar. The Council, when acting on behalf of the Union within its competences of the second and third pillar was bound to the fundamental freedoms developed in the framework of the first pillar according to the former Art. 6 para. 2 TEU. Regarding the CFSP this was stated explicitly in Art. 11 para. 1 fifth indent of the former TEU. On top of that Art. 6 para 2 of the former TEU declared that the fundamental freedoms that derived from the general principles of law, also apply to the second and third pillars of the EU. These general principles stem from international human rights protection treaties as e.g. the ECHRFF and the constitutional traditions common to the member states as well. Additionally Art. 177 para. 2 and Art. 181a para. 2 TEC obliged the European Community to "respect the human rights and fundamental freedoms" in the areas of development cooperation as well as within the economic, financial and technical cooperation with third countries.

The New European Union

Differentiating between Fundamental Freedoms and Human Rights as two separate legal concepts, the situation post Lisbon Treaty presents itself as follows.

Fundamental Freedoms

In Art. 6 of the new TEU three different sources of law protecting fundamental
freedoms are listed:

(a) the Charter of Fundamental Rights of the European Union (para. 1),
(b) the European Convention on the Protection of Human Rights and Fun-
    damental Freedoms (para. 2) and
(c) the constitutional traditions common to the member states (para. 3).

Ad (a): The Charter did not become a part of the Lisbon Treaty itself, but
Art. 6 para. 1 TEU in conjunction with the Declaration (Nr 1) concerning the
Charter of Fundamental Rights of the European Union (OJ 2010, C 83, 337)
declared the Charter as being part of the primary law of the Union, entailing
the primacy of the Union law. Poland, the United Kingdom and the Czech
Republic abstained from the enactment of the Charter on their territory or
their internal affairs. As stated in Art. 51 of the TEU the Charter applies primarily to the institutions and bodies of the Union and to the Member States
only when they are implementing Union law. Further elaborations are found
in the *"Explanations"* dealing with Art. 51 para. 1 of the Charter (OJ 2007, C
303, 32) as mentioned before.

   Due to this stipulation the member states are bound to the fundamental
freedoms of the Union whenever they act in the field of application of Union
law (*Schima* 2009: 333; *Ranacher* 2003: 96).

Ad (b) The Treaty of Lisbon included – in contrast to its predecessor treaties –
the obligation of the EU to accede to the European Convention for the Protection of Human Rights and Fundamental Freedoms. This obligation is derived
from Protocol Nr. 8 relating to Art. 6 para. 2 TEU and Declaration Nr. 2 relating to Art. 6. para 2. TEU. Initially the ECHRFF was only addressing states as
signatories, however with the change resulting from Art. 17 of the Protocol Nr.
14 (2004) to the ECHRFF, Art. 59 was amended by adding a second paragraph
with the following laconic wording: "The European Union may accede to this
Convention." Other than an Additional Protocol, which is only binding for the
signatories, Protocol Nr. 14, being an Amending Protocol, required the ratification of all members of the ECHRFF, before it took effect.

   After postponing the ratification for some years, Russia signed the Protocol
Nr. 14 in January 2010, being the last of the 47 Member States to do so and
thus finally giving way to the taking effect of the Protocol on June 1, 2010.

The Union is deemed to adhere solely to the ECHRFF, not to the Council of Europe. Neither was the wording of the ECHRFF adapted to reflect the accession of an international organisation, the hitherto terms, based on the presumption that the ECHRFF signatories were states only, were left unchanged.

The complex procedure necessary for the accession of the EU has to be arranged by a special form of an accession treaty on the basis of Art. 218 para. 8 subpara. 2 TFEU (Hummer 2010: 13). This process might be concluded by the middle of 2012, so that the EU as an international organisation submits itself and its public authority (Verbandsgewalt) to the ECHRFF, creating the problem that the stipulations of the ECHRFF have been originally created to shield individuals from the infringement by acts of sovereign states. A similar problem arises in respect of the obligation for the Court of the European Union to adopt the interpretation of the European Convention on the Protection of Human Rights and Fundamental Freedoms (ECHRFF) given by the Court of the ECHRFF in a strict manner.

Ad (c) The constitutional traditions and international obligations common to the Member States form the general principles of law for the protection of human rights and fundamental freedoms and have not been affected by the Treaty of Lisbon.

According to the settled case law of the ECJ those general principles bind the Union's institutions and the member states only in their application of Union law, and also when they intend to differ from the four fundamental freedoms of the Internal Market (Griller 2002: 137). As previously stated, the Charter of Fundamental Rights of the EU covers all cases of application of Union law by the member states, therefore binding them according to Art. 51 para 1 also in the areas of CSFP and CSDP.

The impact of the protection of fundamental rights on the Union's CSFP will subsequently be demonstrated on the basis of the difficulties the Union faces in the adoption and implementation of UN Security Council resolutions, dealing with the fight against terrorism.

Excursus: Protection of Fundamental Freedoms in Counter-Terrorism

The Security Council (SC) created a comprehensive regime of sanctions to aid the fight against terrorism with Resolution 1267 (1999). These *smart sanctions* or *targeted sanctions*, based on Chapter VII of the UN Charter, target individuals and legal entities alike, that are suspected of involvement in terrorist activities. The 1267-Sanctions Committee, lately amended with Resolution 1989 (2011), is tasked with creating a list of persons and entities suspected of aiding terrorist activities, attached to the pertinent Resolution, and to update this list frequently. Currently this consolidated list includes approx 500 persons, having the effect that bank accounts are frozen and travel bans are imposed (http://www.un.org/sc/committees/1267/aq_sanctions_list. shtml).

This procedure caused some problems as some individuals who found themselves included in the list, were logically not informed about this fact as their naming resulted from secret intelligence information, usually forwarded by the home state of the presumed terrorist to the listing committee of the Security Council, therefore depriving the individual of being able to demand diplomatic protection from his or her home state. With SC Resolution 1822 (2008) the procedure was enhanced with an obligation to include summaries of reasons for listing of the person in question. In order to be able to be removed from the list, the presumed terrorists could turn to the Office of the Ombudsperson, established by SC Resolution 1904 (2009), for which Kimberly Prost is the current office bearer. However this institutional arrangement is purely administrative and therefore deprives those persons, suspected of terrorist activities, of their right to appeal to a judicial institution, access to due process, it limits their right to be heard in front of a court (audiatur et altera pars) and tarnishes their right to a fair trial.

As the member states have transferred their national competences in these areas to the Union, the EU is responsible for implementing the embargo resolutions of the Security Council, including the *smart sanctions*, into Union law. Procedurally this is implemented by first adopting a decision according to Art. 29 TEU, taking for example the form of a joint decision, which is then put into legally binding form by adopting an embargo regulation according to Art. 215 para. 2 TFEU which specifies the concrete restrictive actions taken by the Union (blocking of accounts, freezing of funds, seizure of assets). Unlike other acts in the CFSP framework, the legality of those acts can be challenged in front of the European Court of Justice, as Art. 275 para. 2 TFEU allows the affected individuals or entities to seek legal protection in form of an action of annulment according to Art. 263 para. 4 TFEU.

Thus a number of individuals and entities sought legal protection by the court, claiming that their fundamental rights to due process, an effective judicial control and the fundamental right to property were violated. The case of Yassin Abdullah Kadi, for example, demonstrates the problems that arise from the current situation, as he has been continuously blacklisted by the 1267-Sanctions Committee since October 17, 2001, although he twice successfully challenged the legal acts that put him on the list (*Kadi v Commission*, Judgment of the General Court of September 30, 2010, Case T-85/09, OJ 2010 C 317, 29, not yet published in the European Court reports, and *Yassin Abdullah Kadi and Al Barakaat International Foundation v Council of the European Union and Commission of the European Communities*, Judgment of the Court of September 3, 2008, Joined cases C-402/05P and C-415/05P, European Court reports 2008, I-06351ss). The Court followed this reasoning in a further, similar case, thereby confirming his previous judgement (*Faraj Hassan v Council of the European Union, European Commission and Chafiq Ayadi v Council of the European Union*, Judgment of the Court (4th Chamber) of December 3, 2009, Joined Cases C-399/06P and C-403/06P, European Court reports 2009, I-11393ss).

A conflict may thus arise between the protection of fundamental freedoms in the external relations of the Union and the policy of imposing *smart sanctions* by the UN Security Council. The listing, as well as the de-listing procedure, are as mentioned before, both mere administrative procedures, not able to grant any form of effective due process against decisions of the 1267/1989 Committee (*Kadi v Commission*, Judgment of the General Court of September 30, 2010, Case T-85/09, recital 128).

The violation of fundamental freedoms hence happens already within the orbit of the UN and is seamlessly implemented in the Union law, as the Union is obliged to implement binding UN Security Council Resolutions on the basis of Art. 25 of the UN Charter. The legal act transforming those Resolutions into Union law [Council Regulation (EC) No 881/2002; OJ 2002, L 139: 9] is therefore violating fundamental freedoms of the Union, although the Commission is committed to inform the concerned person, who additionally has the right to appeal to the Ombudsperson and the Listing Committee itself.

Consequently the General Court could only rule in favour of the claimant and invalidate the underlying legal act of secondary law, which however in turn would lead to a violation of Arts. 25 and 48 in conjunction with Art. 103 of the United Nations Charter. The reasoning of such a judgement of the General Court is based on two legal assumptions: firstly, the law of the European Union is a *self contained regime*, which as an autonomous legal order is not subjected to an eventual higher ranking of public international law; secondly, the obligations of the Union derived from public international law themselves "cannot, however, be understood to authorise any derogation from the principles of liberty, democracy and respect for human rights and fundamental freedoms enshrined in Art. 6 para. 1 TEU" (*Yassin Abdullah Kadi and Al Barakaat International Foundation v Council of the European Union and Commission of the European Communities*, Judgment of the Court of September 3, 2008, Joined cases C-402/05P and C-415/05P, European Court Reports 2008, Recital 303s).

With this reasoning the Court – as part of the rule of law of the EU – granted priority to the protection of fundamental freedoms and human rights against conflicting obligations derived from public international law and even went so far as to empower itself with judicial review over the legality of those legal acts that implement UN Security Council resolutions (sic) within its domestic legal sphere.

With regard to this judgement, it can be reasonably assumed when future resolutions regarding the 1267 (2001) and 1989 (2011) sanctions are on the agenda of the Security Council, that the two member states of the Union holding permanent seats on the Security Council, i.e. France and Great Britain, are fully aware of the fact, that the UN Charter is the older treaty, imposing therefore in the light of Art. 351 para. 2 TFEU the obligation to "take all appropriate steps to eliminate the incompatibilities" and "assist each other to this end and shall, where appropriate, adopt a common attitude".

Human Rights

The Lisbon Treaty anchored the protection of *human rights* in the TEU, e.g. in Art. 2 declaring that, among others, the respect for human dignity, freedom, equality, and respect for human rights, including the rights of persons belonging to minorities, form the core of essential values of the Union and are therefore an issue that is interdisciplinary and cross sectional. This, together with the obligations resulting from Art. 3 para. 5 TEU, results in the pledge of the Union to reflect these values in its international relations as well. By binding itself strictly to public international law and the principles of the United Nations Charter it thereby strengthened its commitment to human rights.

These general provisions are given form by the more specific stipulations of Art. 21 para 1. subpara. 1 TEU, which are part of the General Provisions on the Union's External Action. These External Actions and the relationships and partnerships with third countries shall be guided by the principles (among other matters) of the universality and indivisibility of human rights and fundamental freedoms and respect for human dignity. It could not be stated more clearly as in Art. 21 para. 2. lit. b TEU, where the Treaty declares that all Union activities shall "consolidate and support democracy, the rule of law, human rights and the principles of international law".

Therefore it is clear that the general provisions establish the framework of the stipulations of Art. 23 ss. TEU regulating the "Specific Provisions on the Common Foreign and Security Policy". The same applies to the Common Security and Defence Policy, which is regulated in Art. 42 ss. TEU, as this policy area is a mere subset of the CFSP.

The Human Rights Issue in the Common Foreign and Security Policy (CFSP)

Following a series of communications regarding the role of human rights and democratisation in the external relations of the EU [COM(1995) 567; COM(1995) 216; COM(1998) 146; COM(1999) 256; COM(2000) 191] the Commission published a communication on May 8, 2001 entitled *"The European Union's role in promoting human rights and democratisation in third countries"* [COM(2001) 252 final]. This communication is up till today the most relevant document, explaining how the EU intends to incorporate this policy into its overall strategic objectives regarding the external relations of the Union. The first implementation of the communication was subject of the Council Regulation (EC) Nr. 975/1999 laying down the requirements for the implementation of development cooperation operations which contribute to the general objective of developing and consolidating democracy and the rule of law and to that of respecting human rights and fundamental freedoms (OJ 1999, L 120: 1, as amended OJ 2003, L 284: 1), which subsequently was amended by Regulation (EC) Nr. 2240/2004 of the EP and of the Council of December 15, 2004 (OJ 2004, L 390: 3).

To ensure a certain degree of effectiveness the issue of human rights and democracy has to be an integral aspect of the foreign policy (so-called "mainstreaming") [*General Secretariat of the Council* (ed.), Mainstreaming Human Rights and gender into European Security and Defence Policy (2008)]. A result of this broad based approach is the necessity to incorporate those policies not only into the CFSP and CSDP (Art. 23-46 TEU) but also in all other fields of the external relations (Art. 205-222 TFEU) by the various actors of the Union. As mentioned before, it is the task of the Council and the Commission – with the support of the High Representative of the Union for Foreign Affairs and Security Policy – to secure the consistency of the respective measures (Art. 21 para. 3 subpara. 2 TEU).

The coordination rests upon the delegated experts on human rights of the members in the Working Party on Human Rights of the Council (COHOM) in coordination with the relevant CFSP geographical working groups of the Council of the EU and the subcommittee on Human Rights and Democratisation under the direction of the European Commission. Since 2005 a personal representative of the High Commissioner is involved in those bodies. At the beginning of 2010 the newly founded *Working Party on Fundamental Rights, Citizens' Rights and Free Movement of Persons* (FREMP) started its operations.

The Personal Representative for Human Rights of the High Representative

During its meeting on December 16-17, 2004 the Council decided to set up a Personal Representative of the Secretary General of the Council/High Representative for Human Rights in the area of CFSP as a contribution to the coherence and continuity of this EU policy. On January 16, 2005 Javier Solana appointed the Danish Diplomat Michael Matthiessen as his first Personal Representative. In February of 2005 another Council meeting formulated his main tasks as the mainstreaming of human rights in the area of the CFSP, implementation of binding guide lines regarding human rights in the Unions operations, participation in the human rights dialogue with third party countries, establishing a dialogue with the European Parliament, pursuing an active communication policy and lobbying towards the general public, etc. As of December 2005 the Council in its role as Council of General Affairs, expanded the mandate by assigning the Personal Representative to support the various committees and panels that deal with the protection of human rights within the EU (8. Bericht 2008: 236).

Matthiessen was succeeded after just two years in office in 2007 by the former Undersecretary for EU affairs at the Ministry for Foreign Affairs of Estonia, Riina Ruth Kionka. Both, Matthiessen and his successor remained relatively unknown to the general public, signalling the perceived insignificance of the position. With the Lisbon Treaty and the appointment of Catherine Ashton as High Representative of the Union for Foreign Affairs and Security Policy, Ms Kionka took over the position as Head of Division for Human Rights Policy Guidelines in the European External Action Service (EAD), organised on the basis of the Decision 2010/427/EU of the Council of July 26 establishing the organisation and running of the European External Action Service (OJ 2010, L 201: 30).

The EU Special Representative for Human Rights

On a proposal by Catherine Ashton, the EU High Representative for Foreign Affairs and Security Policy, the Council appointed *Stavros Lambrinidis* on 25 July 2012 as EU Special Representative for Human Rights (EUSRHR) (OJ 2012, L 200: 21ff.). Mr. Lambrinidis, a former Foreign Affairs Minister of Greece and a former Vice-President of the European Parliament, will take office on 1 September, with an initial mandate running until 30 June 2014. He will be the EU's first thematic Special Representative in the sense of Article 33 TEU. His role will be to enhance the effectiveness and visibility of EU human rights policy. He will have a broad, flexible mandate, giving him the ability to adapt to circumstances, and will work closely with the European External Ac-

tion Service (EAAS), which will provide him with full support (http://eeas.
europa.eu/top_stories/2012/250712_euenvoy_en.htm).

His appointment follows the adoption on 25 June 2012 of the *EU's Strategic Framework and Action Plan on Human Rights and Democracy* (Doc
11855/12). The Framework sets out principles, objectives and priorities, which
are all designed to improve the effectiveness and consistency of EU policy as a
whole in the next ten years. One of the commitments of the Action Plan is that
the EU should give an account of its performance in its Annual Report on Human Rights and Democracy in the World. The Action Plan covers the period
until 31 December 2014.

Application of Human Rights Policy Tools by the EU

The EU has developed a number of tools and instruments for the promotion
of human rights (and democracy) within its CFSP, such as political dialogues, démarches, a financial instrument – the European Instrument for
Democracy and Human Rights (EIDHR) – guidelines, actions at multilateral
fora etc (Council doc. 13288/1/07 REV1, Introduction). The result was a
mixed and complex set of instruments which featured significant differences
in structures and procedures, stemming from different financial sources. For
the new Financial Framework (2007-2013) (Interinstitutional Agreement between the EP, the Council and the Commission on budgetary discipline and
sound financial management; OJ 2006, L 139: 1), the EU therefore fundamentally reformed its instruments for the delivery of external financial assistance. The new framework replaced more than 30 geographic and thematic
regulations and established a new and more simplified architecture for the
EU's external assistance (*Bartelt* 2008: 9).

The following overview does not aim at fully covering the variety of tools
at hand but gives an overview of the most important endeavours as well as
the coherence between them. It draws from the reports on the Human Rights
Policy of the German Federal Government (*Berichte der deutschen Bundesregierung über ihre Menschenrechtspolitik* 7th report of 2006, 8th report of
2008, 9th report of 2010).

At the beginning the relevant activities are divided into two groups, those
taking place in a *multilateral* framework and those happening on a mere *bilateral* basis.

Multilateral: Involvement in Institutionalised Human Rights Fora

General Assembly of the United Nations
As an international organisation the EU is not a member of the UN, which
only includes states as members (Art. 4 UN Charter). Although it has had the
status as an ordinary observer within the UN General Assembly (GA) since

1974, it can only intervene in the GA after the member states have had their say. This led the EU to propose a resolution in September 2010 a resolution to upgrade its participation to that of an enhanced observer status at the Assembly and its subsidiary working groups and UN Conferences. This proposal suffered a setback when a majority voted to defer rather than immediately pass the pertinent resolution. On May 3, 2011 the UN General Assembly voted with an overwhelming majority of 180 votes in favour and only two abstentions (Syria, Zimbabwe) on the resolution "*Strengthening of the UN system. Participation of the EU in the work of the UN*" (A/65/L.64/ Rev.1). This resolution enables EU representatives to present and promote the EU's positions in the UN, as agreed by its Member States. With this resolution, the General Assembly acknowledges that since the Lisbon Treaty went into force, the President of the European Council, Herman Van Rompuy, the High Representative Catherine Ashton, the European Commission and EU Delegations ensure the Union's external representation in accordance with the Treaties (Hummer 2011: 675).

The EU's representatives will face a large number of issues in the UN bodies as the statistics of the 65th United Nations General Assembly of 2010 demonstrate: a total of 56 resolutions on social and human rights issues were negotiated and got mostly adopted on the basis of the so called "consensus procedure". The necessary preparations will be dealt with in the United Nations Working Party (CONUN) and the Working Party on Preparation for large UN Conferences.

Although the actual cooperation between the EU and the United Nations is still increasing, the European Parliament has suggested that the EU could one day become a full member of the United Nations (cf. *Horsak* 2011: 3).

UN Human Rights Council
The UN Human Rights Council (UNHRC) was founded in 2006 as a successor to the Commission on Human Rights (CHR). The most import innovation of this alteration is the system of *Universal Periodic Review* (UPR), which shall ensure that within a four-year period the human rights conditions will be examined once in each country. The members of the UPR mechanism meet at least three times a year, special sessions can be convened by a minimum of 16 members (out of a total of 47). Austria was voted by an overwhelming majority of the GA of the UN into the UPR for the term of 2011-2014 and since then has been responsible for the coordination of the Western European and Others Group (WEOG) with its 28 member states.

Since the EU is more than just a regional group in the UNHRC – like for example the Latin American and Caribbean Group (GRULAC) or the African Group – its actions are also evidently more coordinated, coherent and consistent. Accordingly the pertinent literature recognises that the EU's human rights policy in the UNHRC has proven to be quite effective in practice (*Pradetto* 2010).

International Criminal Court

On July 1, 2002 the Rome Statute of the International Criminal Court (ICC) went into force and, four years after the signing of the treaty in 1998, established the ICC as a permanent independent and impartial criminal court. Until September 2011, 117 states have signed the Rome Statute. The European Union intensively supported the foundation of the ICC by a series of conclusions of the European Council Presidency, Resolutions of the European Parliament (EP) and statements by the High Representative. In 2006 the EU concluded an Agreement with the International Criminal Court on cooperation and assistance (OJ 2006, L 115: 50), in which both parties agreed that they shall cooperate closely with each other and consult each other on matters of mutual interest, establishing appropriate regular contacts between the Court and the EU Focal Point for the Court (Art. 4). Due to Art. 11 the EU undertakes to cooperate especially with the prosecutor in providing additional information held by it that he or she may seek.

The last pertinent initiative of the EP was the discussion in plenary sitting of the Report on EU support for the ICC: facing challenges and overcoming difficulties, of October 20, 2011, introduced by the Rapporteur Kreissl-Dörfler/Committee on Foreign Affairs (A7-0368/2011, RR/881255EN.doc), leading to a Motion for a European Parliament Resolution on this subject (2011/2109(INI)).

Furthermore the EU demonstrated its support for the establishment of an international criminal law judiciary by demarches, seminars, inclusion of pertinent provisions in third party agreements and general support for civil society activities and general furtherance of the *International Criminal Tribunal for the former Yugoslavia* (ICTY), the *International Criminal Tribunal for Rwanda* (ICTR), the *Special Court for Sierra Leone* (SCSL), as well as the *Hariri-Tribunal* (cf. *Hummer/Mayr-Singer* 2011: 226ff). The EU financial support to the ICC made it an important donor. Under EIDHR, since 2007, over 4 million euro has been allocated to the Court itself, while around 11 million euro have been allocated to civil society organisations working on the ratification of other Court-related issues (EP, 2011/2109(INI); A7-0368/2011, PE467.296v02-00, 11/12).

An additional instrument in the quest against impunity is the application of the principle of universal criminal jurisdiction *(Weltstrafrechtsprinzips)*, submitting the human rights to a universal jurisdiction. As a result of the 11th EU Troika Meeting in November 2008 with the African Union it became clear that the non-application of the statue had a negative impact on EU-AU relations and subsequently a working group for tackling the arising questions was established.

Another tool at hand to promote the support for the ICC are the various co-operation agreements between the EU and third countries, as the inclusion of corresponding provisions in the revised *Cotonou Agreement* (2005) shows. In Art. 11 para. 7 of the Cotonou Agreement the Parties commit themselves to take steps towards ratifying and implementing the Rome Statute and related instruments.

Bilateral

Protection of Human Rights as accession criteria
Although the protection of human rights through its application as an accession criterion for third party countries is not an issue directly related to the CFSP, the Union's handling of this matter should be highlighted at this point. According to the *vertical* and *horizontal* principle of homogeneity, the Union is based on those fundamental values laid out in Art 2 TEU: respect for human dignity, freedom, democracy, equality, the rule of law and respect for human rights, including the rights of persons belonging to minorities (*vertical* principle of homogeneity). The fact that those values are applicable in all member states defines the *horizontal* principle of homogeneity (*Schweitzer/Hummer/Obwexer* 2007: 22).

Consequently, as stated in Art. 49 TEU in conjunction with the former Art. 6 para. 1 TEU (actually Art. 2 TEU) the EU demands the compliance of applicant countries with those values, which have been specified for example in the Copenhagen Criteria of 1993 or the Agenda 2000 (Common declaration by the Council and the Commission on November 10, 2000 regarding the European Community's Development Policy). The criteria of the Agenda 2000 demanded that applicant countries have achieved the "stability of institutions guaranteeing democracy, the rule of law, human rights and respect for and protection of minorities".

With Council Regulation (EC) No. 1085/2006 establishing an *Instrument for Pre-Accession Assistance* (IPA) (OJ 2006, L 219, 82ff) the EU tries to support the membership perspective of the actual candidate countries and potential candidate countries. The financial volume of IPA for the seven year period from 2007 to 2013 amounts to 11.468 million euro.

The Fundamental Rights Agency of the Union, located in Vienna (*Hummer* 2007: 103ff), is tasked with monitoring the situation in possible or prospective member states and subsequently reports to the European Council and the Council about ongoing developments. Equally the European Commission is responsible for frequently reporting to the European Council. In case of serious and continuing violations of human rights in a candidate state, a suspension of membership negotiations is possible.

Conclusion of Human Rights Protection Agreements
The previously mentioned granting of legal personality to the European Union (Art. 47 TEU) opens up the possibility that the EU could sign human rights treaties as *Union* itself – even beyond the above mentioned access to the ECHRFF (cf. chapter 4.2.1.lit. b) especially foreseen in Art. 6 para. 2 TEU in conjunction with Art. 218 para. 8 subpara. 2 TFEU. The first example of this newly won power of the EU is the accession of the EU to the *UN Convention on the Rights of Persons with Disabilities* (2007), which was adopted by the General Assembly of the UN on December 13, 2006. It was signed by the EU on March 30, 2007, went into effect on May3, 2008 and hence became ratified by the EU on December 23, 2010. By the end of 2011, 103 ratifications had been registered.

Human Rights Clauses in International Agreements
Although there are no specific provisions in the Lisbon Treaty concerning human rights clauses in international agreements, those provisions have been a standard ingredient of third country agreements of the Union since 1992, as the Council decided in November 1991 that those clauses should be included in all treaties with developing countries going forward (§ 10 of Council Directive regarding "human rights, democracy and development", EG-Bulletin 11-1991, item 2.3.1.). Those standard contract clauses are an integral part of agreements between the Union and third party states and are therefore an *essential element*, which are singular in bilateral treaties under international law [*Hoffmeister* (1998); *Hoffmeister* (2001): 89].

As a result of the vertical "division of powers" between the Union and the member states, these agreements regularly involve member state and Union competences simultaneously and are therefore called *mixed agreements*. Depending on the kind of agreement, these clauses are underpinned by sanctions of various intensity ranging from admonitions, obligatory consultations, referring the matter to tribunals up to automatic suspensions of contractual agreements with the Union and its members.

The *Lomé III Convention* of 1984 introduced the instrument of sanctions following aggravating human rights violations in an ACP state, establishing the possibility of suspension and discontinuation of development aid. With the follow up Protocol *Lome IV* of November 4, 1995 these provisions were extended in Art. 366a para. 2 and para. 3 Lome IV: If one Party considers that another Party has failed to fulfil an obligation in respect of one of the *"essential elements"* of the Lomé IV Agreement, it shall invite the Party concerned to hold consultations. If in spite of all efforts no solution has been found, the Party which invoked the failure to fulfil an obligation may take appropriate steps, including, when necessary, the partial or full suspension of application of the Agreement to the Party concerned.

Equally worded stipulations were included in Art. 96 of the Cotonou Agreement (2000). This agreement went into force on April 1, 2003 and was amended in 2005 (cf. Council Decision 2005/599/EG Council Decision of June 21, 2005 concerning the signing, on behalf of the European Community, of the Agreement amending the Partnership Agreement between the members of the African, Caribbean and Pacific Group of States, on the one hand, and the European Community and its Member States, on the other hand, signed in Cotonou on June 23, 2000 (OJ 2000, L 317, 1 ss., revised OJ 2005, L 209, 26ff). On May 14, 2010 the Council Decision 2010/648/EU amended for the second time the Cotonou Agreement (OJ 2010, L 287: 3ff).

Art. 96 para. 2 of the Cotonou Agreement allows a contractual party of the agreement to take "appropriate measures" against another party if it claims that "essential elements" as defined by para. 2 of Art. 9 of the Cotonou Agreement have been violated and consultations have been unsuccessful. However those measures are bound by international law and must comply with the principle of proportionality. In the selection of these measures, priority must be given to those which least disrupt the application of the agreement. It is understood that suspension would be a measure of last resort.

What is remarkable about Art. 96 of the Cotonou Agreement is the extension of the scope of what is considered to be "*essential elements*" beyond human rights protection. The scope of protection presently also includes the rule of law, democratisation, good governance, support for the emergence of an active and organised civil society as well as a systematic inclusion of women and gender issues in all areas, etc.

Such human rights clauses have also been introduced since the 1990s in bilateral agreements, laying the foundation for consultations on the suspension of development aid and other contractually agreed payments as it was the case with Côte d'Ivoire, Fiji, Guinea-Bissau, Haiti, Cameroon, Comoros, Liberia, Mauretania, Niger, Sierra Leone, Zimbabwe, Togo, etc (9. Bericht 2010: 264).

Human Rights Dialogues
The Lisbon Treaty itself does not include provisions governing the human rights dialogues. Therefore the Councils conclusions of June 25, 2001 welcoming the Commissions Communication COM(2001) 252 quoted above, are the guiding documents.

Stressing the importance of close co-operation between its competent bodies, the Council tasked the Working Party on Human Rights (COHOM) in ensuring an effective, coherent and consistent approach to these issues together with geographical and other relevant working parties. Nowadays this list includes bodies such as the Working Party on Development Cooperation, the Human Rights and Democratisation Unit within the Directorate-General for External Relations of the European Commission, the Sub-Committee on

Human Rights of the Committee on Foreign Affairs of the European Parliament etc. (COM(2001) 252 Annex).

These dialogues represent a fully fledged instrument of the foreign policy of the EU and are organised in the following institutional setting:

(a) structured human rights dialogues/consultations (since 1995 with China),
(b) ad-hoc dialogues
(c) dialogues with the major regional groupings of third countries
(d) expert level meetings with like-minded states preceding large scale events on human rights issues

Human rights issues are tackled as a part of the CFSP in distinct *human rights dialogues* but also in the framework of the more general *political dialogues* between the Union and third countries or group of third countries, e.g. as part of the Barcelona Process within the framework of the Euro-Mediterranean partnership or the European neighbourhood policy for the Eastern and Southern neighbours of the European Union or the Cotonou Agreement (2000/2005/2010) implementation. Within the framework of "Strategic Partnerships" between the EU and third party countries those political dialogues are a constitutive characteristic and are opening an area for specific talks on human rights.

Currently the Union is holding formally *institutionalised human rights dialogues* with the African Union, Belarus, China, Georgia, Kazakhstan, Kyrgyzstan, Tajikistan, Turkmenistan and Uzbekistan. Not institutionalised but frequently taking place *human right dialogues* have been established with Canada, the candidate countries (Croatia, FYROM, Turkey) and Japan, New Zealand, USA as well as with Russia. The number of countries engaged in human rights dialogues with the EU is also growing as a result of the subcommittees that have been established between the EU delegations and public authorities in countries like Cambodia, Bangladesh, Egypt, India, Israel, Jordan, Laos, Lebanon, Morocco, Pakistan, the PLO and Sri Lanka. The first human rights dialogues with countries in Latin America started in 2009 and included Argentine, Brazil, Chile, Columbia and Mexico (9. Bericht 2010: 264).

Regarding their content, those dialogues deal with fundamental issues such as capital punishment, torture, freedom of expression, association or assembly, free exercise of religion, etc. Moreover those dialogues also open a forum for the discussion of issues regarding the signature and ratification of universal and regional human rights conventions and help to establish corporation procedures for the supervision of the implementation of already ratified human rights conventions.

Precondition for the establishment of a human rights dialogue is the positive deliberation on the issue by the COHOM Working Party Group. The final decision rests within the Council. In 2010 the EU had established approximately 30 human rights dialogues, either as stand-alone procedures or as integrated parts of an established general political dialogue.

European Instrument for Democracy and Human Rights (EIDHR)
Since 1994 the EU aggregates its activities regarding human rights, democratisation, election observation and conflict prevention under the umbrella of the *European Initiative for Democracy and Human Rights* (EIDHR I). Two Regulations [Regulations (EC) No. 975/1999 and No. 976/1999 of April 29, 1999; OJ 1999, L 120, 1ff. and 8ff.], that expired at the end of 2006, formed the legal foundation for those co-operations that take place under the leadership of the Commission between the EU and international organisations (IGOs) as well as non-governmental international organisations (INGOs). All in all the Union dedicated a budget of approx. 100 Million euro each year for those projects.

With the approval of the budget plan for 2007-2013 the *"European Initiative for Democratisation and Human Rights"* was renamed and restructured into the *"European Instrument for Democratisation and Human* Rights" (EIDHR II) [Regulation (EC) No. 1889/2006 of the European Parliament and of the Council of December 20, 2006 on establishing a financing instrument for the promotion of democracy and human rights worldwide (OJ 2006, L 386, 1ff]. The European Instrument (EIDHR II), based on Regulation No. 1889/2006, is the successor programme of the European Initiative (EIDHR I) and contains a funding volume for the period 2007-2013 of 1,103 million of euro.

The EIDHR II intervenes as an independent instrument to complement the other tools for implementation of EU policies on democracy and human rights (political dialogue, diplomatic demarches etc). As a global financing instrument, the EIDHR covers all third countries. Community assistance under this instrument is therefore designed to address global, regional, national and local human rights and democratisation incentives in partnership with civil society organisations which are the main beneficiary of the EIDHR II. Specific financing tools are ad hoc measures which allow for the allocation of small grants to human rights defenders in response to urgent protection needs (*Bartelt* 2008: 26).

In the current EIDHR II-Strategy Paper for the period of 2011 to 2013 (http://eeas.europa.eu/human_rights/docs/eidhr_strategy_paper_2011-2013_en.pdf) the following five objectives are listed:

- Enhancing respect for human rights and fundamental freedoms in countries where they are most at risk;
- Strengthening the role of civil society in promoting human rights and democratic reform, in supporting the peaceful conciliation of group interests and consolidating political participation and representation;
- Supporting actions on human rights and democracy issues in areas covered by EU guidelines, including those on human rights dialogues, on

human rights defenders, on the death penalty, on torture, on children and armed conflict, on the rights of the child, on violence against women and girls and combating all forms of discrimination against them, on International Humanitarian Law and on possible future guidelines;

• Supporting and strengthening international and regional frameworks for the protection and promotion of human rights, justice, the rule of law and the promotion of democracy;

• Building confidence in and enhancing the reliability and transparency of democratic electoral processes, in particular through election observation.

Developing EU Guidelines on Human Rights
The EU began to adopt guidelines for specific issues in 1998 with the target of a more effective implementation of human rights in the CFSP. Those guidelines are documents that are adopted by the Council, putting together the activities of the EU towards specific third party countries regarding human rights.

In the years between 1998 and 2010 a total of eight Guidelines were adopted, focusing on the following topics: Death penalty (1998/2008); Torture and other cruel, inhuman or degrading treatment or punishment (2001/2008); Human Rights dialogues with third countries (2001/2009); Children and armed conflict (2004/2008); Human Rights defenders (2004/2008); Promotion and Protection of the Rights of the Child (2007/2008), Violence against women and girls and combating all forms of discrimination against them (2008); Promoting Compliance with International Humanitarian Law (IHL) (2005/2009); (cf. http://eeas.europa.eu/human_rights/guidelines/ index_en.htm).

Each of these guidelines is evaluated regularly and recommendations are taken from these evaluations, which are then incorporated into implementation strategies accordingly.

Demarches and Public Announcements
Import instruments in the world of diplomatic affairs are *demarches*. These are diplomatic contacts, not reaching the intensity of a formal diplomatic protest, which should influence the recipient to take or refrain from an action. If they are transmitted in writing they are referred to as verbal notes but they can also be delivered by personal contacts mostly by the Council Presidency or the Presidency in the formation of the Troika.

The transmission of demarches might take place in secrecy but if a more intense diplomatic pressure is intended they might by accompanied by public announcements. The strongest form of public critic is articulated by unilateral sanctions, which were put into action against Uzbekistan in 2005. The Council decision of February 2010 to temporarily suspend the special trade preferences for Sri Lanka that was extended as part of the GSP+ (Generalised System of Preferences+) for good governance, does not count as such a sanction. In the opinion of the German Federal Government this decision has to be seen as an incentive, as it did not imply an immediate suspension but comes along with a six-month grace period, during which the government would be able to avoid a suspension by complying to the respective human rights conventions (9. Bericht 2010: 76).

The Austrian Federal Ministry for European and International Affairs reports on its homepage that the EU is following 200 cases of endangered individuals that are at risk of imprisonment, torture and condemnation to death trying to protect them with means of diplomatic pressure (http://www.bmeia. gv.at/aussenministerium/aussenpolitik/menschenrechte/menschenrechte-in-der-eu.html).

Inclusion of Human Rights Policy into the Development Cooperation of EC and EU
As part of the foreign development and cooperation assistance programmes of the EU – PHARE, TACIS, ALA, MEDA and CARDS – each year 5 billion euro are dedicated to the ACP countries, on top of the 22.68 billion euro European Development Fund (EDF) that is being invested between 2008 and 2013. But only a small portion of this funding is formally dedicated to supporting human rights, democracy and the rule of law.

Given that since 1999 (EIDHR I) and 2006 (EIDHR II) a special financing instrument for the promotion of democracy and human rights worldwide is still under operation, the new geographic, thematic and horizontal financing instruments of development cooperation abstain to a large extent to provide financial assistance for this special objective. This is true for example in the case of Regulation (EC) No. 1905/2006 of the EP and the Council establishing a financial instrument for development cooperation (DCI) (OJ 2006, L 378: 41ff) which replaced 14 different Regulations (Art. 39 DCI) and introduced an overall funding of 17 billion euro for the period 2007-2013, the largest part of it was allocated to geographic programmes.

The Network of Independent Legal Experts on Human Rights and Fundamental Freedoms
In September 2002 the European Parliament initiated a Network of Independent Legal Experts on human rights and fundamental freedoms, that presented its first report on March 31, 2003 titled "Report on the situation as regards fundamental rights in the European Union (2002)". This report included the summaries of the national reports of the independent experts and recommendations for the EU and the member states (7. Bericht 2006: 226).

Activities regarding the Abolition of the Death Penalty and Torture
The Charter of Fundamental Freedoms clearly outlaws the death penalty in Art. 2 para 2 and states that no one shall be executed. This policy of strict damnation of capital punishment is perused systematically by the Union in the international human rights fora as well as within the political dialogues and human rights dialogues. The first corresponding guideline was adopted back in 1998 (cf. chapter 5.2.2.6.)

Art. 4 of the Charter of Fundamental Freedoms includes a prohibition of torture and inhuman or degrading treatment or punishment. A guideline in this regard was introduced in 2001 (cf. chapter 5.2.2.6.) and the Commission has dedicated financial means for this cause, including means for the rehabilitation of the victims.

Fighting Racism, Xenophobia and Discrimination of Minorities and Indigenous People
Before the Treaty of Lisbon went into effect, Art. 13 of the TEC tasked the Council with taking appropriate action to combat discrimination based on sex, racial or ethnic origin, religion or belief, disability, age or sexual orientation when a unanimous vote of the Council decided to do so. This authorisation was at the heart of two directives of the Union (Directive 2000/43/EC of June 29, 2000 und Directive 2000/78/EC of November 27, 2000; OJ 2000, L 180, 22 ss. and L 303: 16ff), that installed principles of equal treatment, strictly outlawing discrimination, due to e.g. race or ethnic origin. It also created a framework for ensuring the principle of non discrimination on the job.

With the Lisbon Treaty the provisions of Art. 13 former TEC transformed into Art. 19 TFEU telle quelle and form the present legal provisions together with the Art. 20, 21 and 22 of the Charter of Fundamental Rights of the EU, stipulating the general principle of equality of treatment, inhibiting all discrimination and guaranteeing cultural, religious and linguistic diversity (*Hummer* 2011: 81).

These stipulations of bans on discrimination which are enshrined not only in the TFEU but also in the Charter of Fundamental Freedoms and which did not originate in the CFSP itself, naturally apply to the CFSP too.

Annual Report on Human Rights
In 1999 the German Presidency of the Union initiated the Annual Reports on Human Rights, covering the protection of human rights within the Union and its foreign relations. The Human Rights Reports are the result of the collective collaboration of the responsible experts from the 27 member states that form the *Working Group on Human Rights of the Council* (COHOM). Support is given by the European External Action Service (EEAS) under the direction of the High Representative of the EU for the CFSP, Catherine Ashton.

The current 10th report EU annual Report on Human Rights and Democracy in the world of 2010 (http://eeas.europa.eu/human_rights/docs/2010_hr_report_en.pdf) deals in the area of CFSP with the implementation of guidelines on human rights and international humanitarian law, human rights dialogues and consultations, declarations and demarches, human rights clauses in agreements with non EU countries, European Neighbourhood Policy (ENP) (cf. Regulation (EC) No. 1638/2006 of the EP and the Council establishing a European Neighbourhood and Partnership Instrument (ENPI); OJ 2006, L 310: 1ff) and activities funded under the European Instrument for Democracy and Human Rights (EIDHR II).

EU Human Rights Fact sheets
The EU Human Rights Fact sheets result from an initiative of the Austrian Presidency, which aimed to consolidate information about the actual situation on human rights in the specific country in which the EU and its representatives are accredited. By the end of 2011 this instrument should have been converted into country-specific human rights strategies.

The New Democratic Scrutiny Dialogue
On the basis of Declarations No. 4 and 5 attached to the Interinstitutional Agreement between the EP, the Council and the Commission on budgetary discipline and sound financial management (OJ 2006, C 139, 1 ss.) a newly established democratic scrutiny dialogue between the Commission and the European Parliament in the field of development cooperation has been created. Where the basic legislative act was adopted under the co-decision procedure on the basis of Art. 251 TEC – actually Art. 294 TFEU with its ordinary legislative procedure – the new democratic scrutiny dialogue foresees that the Commission sends draft strategy papers to the Parliament and undertakes to enter into a regular dialogue with the EP.

The new democratic scrutiny dialogue is a modus vivendi of political nature between the EP and the Commission to provide the responsible committees of the EP with the necessary information and does not, in any way, replace the official comitology procedures on the basis of the Comitology Decision 1999/468/EC of the Council (OJ 1999, L 184: 23ff as amended by Council Decision 2006/512/EC; OJ 2006, L 200: 11ff). The new dialogue is rather complementary to the comitology procedures and will also not be replaced by the provisions of Art. 290 TFEU dealing with "delegated acts", although Strategy Papers and multi-annual indicative programmes would have to be adopted as "delegated acts" within the meaning of Art. 290 TFEU (*Passos/Gauci* 2008: 156). The very fact that the EP might eventually object on the basis of Art. 290 para. 2 lit. a) TFEU to the Strategy Papers and multiannual indicative programmes, once adopted by the Commission, enhances the importance of an early and constructive dialogue with the Commission, thus showing the increasing demand of the democratic scrutiny dialogue.

Due to the fact that measures of the EU in the field of *development cooperation* can at the same time pursue objectives relating to the *CFSR* – for example on the scope of Art. 208 TFEU dealing with the eradication of poverty – the democratic scrutiny dialogue can also be employed in legislative procedures adopting measures designed to protect human rights and fundamental freedoms.

The EU Strategic Framework and Action Plan on Human Rights and Democracy
With the EU Strategic Framework and Action Plan on Human Rights and Democracy, adopted by the Council on 25 June 2012 (Council, Press 11855/12, 25 June 2012), the EU will step up its efforts to promote human rights, democracy and the rule of law across all aspects of external action. The Strategic Framework provides an agreed basis for a truly collective effort, involving EU Member States as well as the EU institutions. It also includes a commitment to a strategic partnership with civil society. The purpose of the Action Plan is to implement the Strategic Framework with sufficient flexibility so as to respond to new challenges. It builds upon the existing body of EU policy on human rights and democracy in external action, in particular the aforementioned "European Instrument for Democracy and Human Rights" (EIDHR). The recently appointed and also aforementioned "EU Special Representative for Human Rights", Stavros Lambrinidis, shall contribute to the implementation of the Action Plan, in accordance with his mandate.

In the Strategic Framework the EU reaffirms its commitment to the promotion and protection of all human rights, whether civil and political, or economic and cultural. The Joint Communication of the European Commission and EU High Representative for Foreign Affairs and Security Policy to the European Parliament and the Council "Human Rights and Democracy at the heart of EU external action – Towards a more effective approach" (COM(2011) 886 final, 12 December 2011) is a welcome contribution towards the development of an EU human rights strategy to promote these goals through its external action.

Due to the Strategic Framework "the EU will promote human rights in all areas of its external action without exception. In particular, it will integrate the promotion of human rights into trade, investment, technology and telecommunications, internet, energy, environmental issues, corporate social responsibility and development policy as well as into Common Security and Defence Policy and the external dimensions of employment and social policy and the area of freedom, security and justice, including counter-terrorism policy. In the area of development cooperation, a human rights based approach will be used to ensure that the EU strengthens its efforts to assist

partner countries in implementing their international human rights obligations" (Council Press 11855/12, 25 June 2012: 2).

It is with this in mind that the EU will continue to speak out in the United
Nations General Assembly, the UN Human Rights Council and the International Labour Organisation against human rights violations. The EU will also
continue its engagement with the invaluable human rights work of the Council
of Europe and the OSCE. It will work in partnership with regional and other
organisations such as the African Union, ASEAN, SAARC, the Organisation of
American States, the Arab League, the Organisation of Islamic Cooperation
and the Pacific Islands Forum with a view to encouraging the consolidation of
regional human rights mechanisms (*Hummer/Karl*, 2008).

Other Policy Fields

The list of activities and measures of the Union that have been listed above is
not exhaustive and not concluding. The impact of human rights in the CFSP extends further, e.g. into the Council Conclusions on *Gender Mainstreaming*
(Council doc. 14779/06), into the *Implementation of UN Security Council Res.*
1325 (Council doc. 11932/2/05), into the *Generic Standards of Behaviour for*
ESDP Operations (Council doc. 8373/3/05), and the *Protection of Civilians* in
the PSC Working Document (Council doc. 4805/03). It touches upon the cooperation with the Civil Society as the Conclusion on Enhancing Cooperation
with NGOs and CSOs in the framework of EU *civilian crisis management* and
conflict prevention (Council doc. 1555734/1/06) and sets precedents for *Moni-*
toring Missions like the Human Rights Advice on the Aceh Monitoring Mission (Council doc. 11678/1/05).

Other related fields are *Migration and Asylum* (AENEAS-Regulation No.
491/2004/EC of the EP and the Council; OJ 2004, L 80: 1ff), *Food Security*
(Regulation No. 1292/96/EC of the Council; OJ 1996, L 166: 1ff), *Action*
against anti-personnel landmines in third countries other than developing
countries (Regulation (EC) No. 1725/2001 of the Council; OJ 2001, L 234:
6ff), combating the *destabilising accumulation and spread of small arms and*
light weapons (OJ 1999, L 9: 1ff), and the EU *action plan on chemical, bio-*
logical, radiological and nuclear security [COM(2009) 273)].

The impact of human rights in the CFSP forms the foundation for the Decision on *Transitional Justice and ESDP* (Council doc. 10674/06) and is the
reason why the protection of human rights was particularly included in the
mandate of all special envoys of January 2007. This list could be extended in
all directions, as the topic of human rights and fundamental freedoms pene-
trates all policy fields.

Negative Human Rights Implications of EU Development Projects

At least the external accountability of the EU in the field of development co-operation are to be taken into account as regards the accountability vis-à-vis individuals affected by those activities showing harmful effects. EU-financed development projects could infringe fundamental rights safeguarded in Art. 6 TEU and the Charter of Fundamental Freedoms, thus enabling affected individuals contesting the financing decision, the project itself or single implementation procedures as well. They may file claims of annulment of a legal act (Art. 263 para. 4 TFEU) or for compensation of damages on the basis of a non-contractual liability of the EU pursuant to Art. Art. 268 in conjunction with 340 para. 2 TFEU. As regards the judicial accountability in this connection one author hits the nail on the head in saying: "Be that as it may, the path to justice is rocky" (*Schmalenbach* 2008: 178).

The Human Rights Issue and the Common Security and Defence Policy (CSDP)

As mentioned above, the Common Security and Defence Policy (CSDP) forms an integral part of the Common Foreign and Security Policy (CFSP) according to Art. 42 para. 1 TEU. Obviously the protection of human rights plays a fundamental role in the CSDP missions. 24 CSDP missions – military operations or civilian missions – have been launched so far (Horsák 2011: 2).

ESDP Missions and Operations

"Human rights violations are part and parcel of crisis and conflicts. The promotion of human rights, with special emphasis on gender and rights of the child and the rule of law are key to sustainable conflict resolution and to lasting peace and security" (General Secretariat of the Council (2008): 7, Foreword). In June 2001, two years before the EU launched its first European Security and Defence Policy (ESDP) operation, the Council defined four fundamental elements that could help the EU to achieve a more effective human rights and democratisation policy. One of these elements was the effort of mainstreaming human rights into ESDP, as endorsed by the Political and Security Committee (PSC) in September 2006. The PSC published after its meeting on June 1, 2006 the Doc. 10076/06 concerning the mainstreaming of Human Rights across CFSP and other EU policies (cf. Doc. 11936/4/06).

This document, in its section on *ESDP missions and operations,* stated that the protection of human rights should be systematically addressed in all phases of ESDP operations, both during the planning and implementation phase. ESDP missions and operations should have a *human rights advisor or human rights focal points* close to the Operation/Force Commander or Head of Mission, e.g. as it is the case in *Aceh Monitoring Mission* (Doc. 11678/05) – the first time that the EU was sending human rights monitors in the context of a crisis management operation (cf. General Secretariat of the Council (2008): 12).

In 2000, the international community committed itself to take into account the vulnerable situation of women in times of war and to cooperate in involving women at all decision-making levels in peace-building and conflict resolutions operations, as well as in humanitarian efforts. This was the background of UN Security Council Resolution 1325. The EU has made Res. 1325 a guiding principle for ESDP operations and has developed a framework for gender mainstreaming itself.

As part of the implementation of a comprehensive approach towards the implementation of the UN Security Council Res. 1325 and 1820 on women, peace and security the EU developed an integral concept in its CSDP dealing with those issues. In the introductory notes the EU intentions are explained as follows:

> "Women, men, girls and boys experience and take action differently in the context of armed conflict, peacekeeping, peace building and reconstruction. Contemporary conflicts affect civilian populations in particular, in this context women have often become strategic targets, sometimes on a massive scale, as when rape is used as a tactic of warfare and ethnic cleansing" (cf. Doc. 15671/1/08 REV 1).

To ensure the inclusion of gender mainstreaming Doc. 15782/3/08 REV 3 revised the former operational paper and included the new provisions of Resolution 1820.

Humanitarian Public International Law

In addition to the inclusion of human rights as a general principle in the various CSDP missions and operations the Humanitarian Public International Law also plays an important role (cf Doc. 16842/09). All member states of the Union are parties of the four Geneva Conventions for the protection of victims of war (1949) and their additional Protocols (1977).

A key element in this context are the *European Union Guidelines on promoting compliance with international humanitarian law (IHL)* (OJ 2005, C 327:4ff) which oblige the Union to include the principle of *Responsibility to Protect* (R2P) in its foreign policy. Derived from Resolution 60/1 of the General Assembly on October 24, 2005 (2005 World Summit Outcome) the principles of R2P now oblige the Union to take collective action in the framework of the Security Council whenever a states fails to protect its people from genocide, war crimes, ethnic cleansing or crimes against humanity.

This obligation to include the Responsibility to Protect principles is repeated and confirmed by the "*European Consensus on Humanitarian Aid*" of

January 30, 2008, which is based on a joint statement by the Council and the representatives of the governments of the Member States meeting within the Council, the European Parliament and the European Commission (OJ 2008, C 25, 2) declaring in its number 2.2, points 16 and 17:

> "16. The EU will advocate strongly and consistently for the respect of International Law, including International Humanitarian Law, Human Rights Law and Refugee Law. In 2005, the EU adopted Guidelines on promoting compliance with international humanitarian law. The EU is committed to operationalising these Guidelines in its external relations.

> 17. The EU recalls the commitment to the responsibility to protect, in accordance with UN General Assembly Resolution 60/1 of 24 October 2005. Each individual state has the responsibility to protect its populations from genocide, war crimes, ethnic cleansing and crimes against humanity. The international community, through the United Nations, also has the responsibility to protect populations from those crimes. Where national authorities are manifestly failing to meet the responsibility to protect, the international community has confirmed that it is prepared to take collective action through the UN Security Council."

When in 2011 the UN Security Council authorised the member states that have notified the Secretary-General – acting nationally or through regional organisations or arrangements, and acting in cooperation with the Secretary-General – to take all necessary measures, to protect civilians and civilian populated areas under threat, the principle of R2P was put into action for the first time.

As the humanitarian aid of the European Union is based on Art. 214 TFEU which forms part of Part V, Title III ("Cooperation with third countries and humanitarian aid", Arts. 208-214) of the TFEU, humanitarian aid and *development cooperation* (Art. 208 TFEU) are strongly intertwined, whereby the development cooperation still draws its principles and tasks from the 2006 document *"European Consensus on Development"* (Joint Statement by the Council and the representatives of the governments of the Member States meeting within the Council, the European Parliament and the Commission on European Union Development Policy: 'The European Consensus', OJ 2006, C 46: 1ff).

The Abolition of the Former "Third Pillar" and its "Communitarisation"

One of the most important changes brought about by the Lisbon Treaty was that it abolished the former three pillar structure (*temple construction*) by merging the then existing pillars into the present day one pillar construction, which strangely rests on two basic treaties (TEU and TFEU) of equal legal importance. Hence the provisions of the former third pillar, merged with the other provisions in the "freedom, security and justice area" into the "*Area of Freedom, Security and Justice*" (AFSJ) (Arts. 67-89 TFEU).

Although the AFSJ does not constitute a part of the CFSP or CSDP, linkages between human rights issues and the AFSJ are obvious as can be exemplarily shown in the case of FRONTEX, the European Agency for the Management of Operational Cooperation at the External Borders of the Member States of the European Union. When coordinating the measures to control the external (Schengen) borders of the Union, questions of the protection of human rights immediately arise.

Excursus: FRONTEX

The European Agency for the Management of Operational Cooperation at the External Borders of the Member States of the European Union (FRONTEX) was established by the Council Regulation (EC) No. 2007/2004 of October, 26th 2004 (OJ 2004, L 349: 1 ss.) and started its operations in May 2005. The agency carries legal personality and its headquarters are situated in Warsaw. In 2007 the above mentioned Regulation was amended by Regulation (EC) No. 863/2007 of the European Parliament and of the Council of July 11, 2007, establishing a mechanism for the creation of *Rapid Border Intervention Teams* (RABITS) (OJ 2007, L 199, 30 ss.).

Another enlargement of the role of FRONTEX's was the result of the Council Conclusions of 4th and 5th December 2006, when the concept of integrated border control was adopted which resulted in the formation of "*special border protection teams*".

While protecting the external Schengen borders of the Union, the members of these teams are bound to the Union's human rights and fundamental freedoms regulations as stated in Regulation (EC) No. 562/2006 of the European Parliament and of the Council of March, 15th 2006 establishing a Schengen Borders Code (OJ 2006, L 105, 1 ss.). However, it would seem unlikely that in daily practice those rules have never been violated, especially in the context of principles and standards on asylum and refugees. The activities of FRONTEX are subjected to Art. 33 of the United Nations Convention Relating to the Status of Refugees (1951, hereinafter referred as Geneva Convention), therefore the provisions regarding the prohibition of "*non-refoulement*" have to be obliged and an access to the asylum process has to be granted, stipulations that seem to have been violated on several occasions in the past (Europäische Grüne Partei, 10th Session of the Council, March 29, 2009, 6). The parliamentary rapporteur Simon Bussutil (Malta, European People's Party) expressed his doubts in the parliamentarian session on September 8, 2011 when he declared that FRONTEX had so far not met the expressed expectations, irrespective of its good intentions. A similar opinion expressed Birgit Sippe, member of the S&D Group in the European Parliament when she declared that FRONTEX was being frequently criticized for continuing violations of human rights during its operations.

Lately Bill Frelick, director of the refugee program of Human Rights Watch joined the group of critics, especially because of the inhuman conditions in the refugee camps in Greece. The Commission diverted the criticism towards the member states, as FRONTEX can not be blamed for wrongdoings that are not within its legal capacity. However, in reply Frelick claimed that FRONTEX had been a partner in submitting refugees to treatment, although aware of the fact that it violated human rights (Human Rights Watch erhebt schwere Vorwürfe gegen EU-Grenzschützer, The Epoch Times of September 21, 2011).

In order to improve the deplorable situation and to increase the sensibility for human rights in the external relations of the *Area of Freedom, Security and Justice*, in 2010 the Commission put forward a proposal to the EP and the Council [COM(2010) 61], to amend the Council Regulation (EC) No. 2007/2004 that established FRONTEX. Following the ordinary revision procedure the European Parliament took a respective vote with a large majority (431 in favour, 49 against, 48 abstentions) and produced the legislative resolution P7-TA-PROV(2011)0344; A7-0278/2001. Finally on October 25, 2011 the European Parliament and the Council adopted the Regulation (EU) No. 1168/2011 amending Council Regulation (EC) No. 2007/2004 establishing a European Agency for the Management of Operational Cooperation at the External Borders of the Member States of the EU (OJ 2011, L 304, p. 1 ss.).

By the end of 2011 FRONTEX will therefore carry an extended mandate with the following human rights related elements:

- The Agency shall fulfil its tasks in full compliance with the relevant Union law, including the Charter of Fundamental Rights of the European Union ("the Charter of Fundamental Rights"); the relevant international law, including the Convention Relating to the Status of Refugees concluded in Geneva on 28 July 1951 ("the Geneva Convention"); obligations related to access to international protection, in particular the principle of non-refoulement; and fundamental rights, and taking into account the reports of the Consultative Forum referred to in Article 26a of this Regulation (Art. 1 para. 2);
- The Agency shall draw up and further develop a Code of Conduct applicable to all operations coordinated by the Agency. The Code of Conduct shall lay down procedures intended to guarantee the principles of the rule of law and respect for fundamental rights with particular focus on unaccompanied minors and vulnerable persons, as well as on persons seeking

international protection, applicable to all persons participating in the activities of the Agency (Art. 2a para. 1);
- The data protection Regulation (EC) No 45/2001 shall apply to the processing of personal data by the Agency (Art. 11a);
- The establishment of cooperation with third countries shall serve to promote European border management standards, also covering respect for fundamental rights and human dignity (Art. 14 para. 1);
- Developing a Fundamental Rights Strategy on the basis of the following measures (Art. 26a):
  (1) The Agency shall draw up and further develop and implement its Fundamental Rights Strategy. The Agency shall put in place an effective mechanism to monitor the respect for fundamental rights in all the activities of the Agency;
  (2) A Consultative Forum shall be established by the Agency to assist the Executive Director and the Management Board in fundamental rights matters. The Agency shall invite the European Asylum Support Office, the Fundamental Rights Agency, the United Nations High Commissioner for Refugees and other relevant organisations to participate in the Consultative Forum. On a proposal by the Executive Director, the Management Board shall decide on the composition and the working methods of the Consultative Forum and the modalities of the transmission of information to the Consultative Forum. The Consultative Forum shall be consulted on the further development and implementation of the Fundamental Rights Strategy, Code of Conduct and Common Core Curricula. The Consultative Forum shall prepare an annual report of its activities. That report shall be made publically available.
  (3) A Fundamental Rights Officer shall be designated by the Management Board and shall have the necessary qualifications and experience in the field of fundamental rights. He/she shall be independent in the performance of his/her duties as a Fundamental Rights Officer and shall report directly to the Management Board and the Consultative Forum. He/she shall report on a regular basis and as such contribute to the mechanism for monitoring fundamental rights.
  (4) The Fundamental Rights Officer and the Consultative Forum shall have access to all information concerning respect for fundamental rights in relation to all the activities of the Agency.

As a consequence of this, FRONTEX missions can be ended or discontinued if violations of fundamental rights and freedoms occur.

The mandate of the agency extends towards the assistance of member states in cases of humanitarian emergencies and sea rescue operations, as it happened in 2006 with the Joint Operation Hera II, including Spain, Mauretania, Senegal and Cap Verde (*Fischer-Lescano/Tohidipur* 2007: 1219).

Not included are the EU operations at the Horn of Africa, targeted at piracy in the region *EU NAVFOR Somalia* (*Operation Atalanta*), which started in December 2008 and which has been prolonged on a year to year basis since then. Based on a transfer and remittance agreement with Kenya and the Seychelles more than 100 presumed pirates have been handed over to the judicial authorities of those nations to face trial.

Final Considerations

Considering the aforesaid facts it can be concluded that CFSP and CSDP of the European Union include a differentiated and comprehensive human rights policy, which however is not consistent and coherent in all of its aspects.

This is not the result of a structural problem resulting from the integration of human rights in the European model of democracy, market economy and regional integration (cf. Heinz/Liebl 2008: 20), instead this can be attributed to the disagreement among the EU member states as history has shown that member states do not show the necessary commitment to override internal political constraints and conflicting interests. Hence the difficulties in finding a common, coherent and outwardly expressed human rights agenda remain unsolved.

A number of examples can be given demonstrating the Unions shortcomings in finding a consistent position in regards with human rights, most prominently the problematic relations with non-democratic leaders of the Arab world, the middle east conflict, Kosovo, Cuba, Turkey, etc. The splitting of the foreign relations of the EU into a (security) policy titled CFSP and CSDP on the one hand (Art. 23 ss TEC) and all other external (economic) relations on the other hand (Art. 205 ss TFEU) highlight this aggravation.

However the contribution of the EU in strengthening the international protection of human rights has to be held in high esteem, as the necessary compromises leading to a joint commitment could only be reached by overcoming 27 national "egoism" and therefore carry a higher relevance, legitimacy and plausibility in comparison to a pertinent single stance.

Bibliography

Arts, Karin (2011): The European Union, Development Cooperation and Human Rights at a Crossroads, European Yearbook on Human Rights 2011, pp. 283-296.
Aschenbrenner, Jo Beatrix (2000): Menschenrechte in den Außenbeziehungen der Europäischen Union. Gemeinschaftspolitik versus GASP.
Bartelt, Sandra (2008): The legislative architecture of EU external assistance and development cooperation, EuR Beiheft 2/2008, 9ff.

Bericht der (deutschen) Bundesregierung über ihre Menschenrechtspolitik in den auswärtigen Beziehungen und in anderen Politikbereichen: 7. Bericht vom 17. Mai 2006; 8. Bericht vom 8. Oktober 2008, 9. Bericht vom 26. August 2010.

Beaucillon, Charlotte/Erlbacher, Friedrich (2011): „Comme une lettre á la poste". Rechtliche und praktische Aspekte der Rechtsnachfolge von der EG zur EU, in: Eilmansberger, Thomas/Griller, Stefan/Obwexer, Walter (eds.): Rechtsfragen der Implementierung des Vertrags von Lissabon, Wien: Springer, pp. 101-119.

Calliess, Christian (2011): Die Außenpolitik der EU – verderben zu viele Köche den Brei? Hanns Seidel-Stiftung, Argumente und Materialien zum Zeitgeschehen 74.

Fischer-Lescano, Andreas/Tohidipur, Timo (2007): Europäische Grenzkontrollregime. Rechtsrahmen der Europäischen Grenzschutzagentur FRONTEX, ZaöRV 2007, 1219 ss.

General Secretariat of the Council (ed.) (2008): Mainstreaming Human Rights and Gender into European Security and Defence Policy

Griller, Stefan (2002): Der Anwendungsbereich der Grundrechtscharta und das Verhältnis zu sonstigen Gemeinschaftsrechten, Rechten aus der EMRK und zu verfassungsgesetzlich gewährleisteten Rechten, in: Duschanek, Alfred/Griller, Stefan (eds.), Grundrechte für Europa. Die Europäische Union nach Nizza, Wien/New York: Springer.

Heijer, Martin de (2010): Europe beyond its borders: Refugee and human rights protection in exterritorial immigration control, in: Ryan, Bernard/Mitsigelas, Valsamis (eds.), Exterritorial immigration control, Martinus Nijhoff Publishers.

Hoffmeister, Frank (1998): Menschenrechts- und Demokratieklauseln in den vertraglichen Außenbeziehungen der Europäischen Gemeinschaft: Max-Planck-Institut für ausländisches Recht und Völkerrecht. Berlin: Springer Verlag.

Horsák, Vojtěch (2011): The European Parliament and the Common Security and Defence Policy: Does the Parliament Care?, AIES Fokus 2/2011, 1-4;

Hummer, Waldemar (2003): Untergang, „Entkernung" und Funktionsnachfolge Internationaler Organisationen – dargestellt am Beispiel der EGKS und der WEU, in: Zehetner, Franz (ed.), Festschrift für Hans-Ernst Folz, 117ff.

Hummer, Waldemar (2005): Die Union und ihre Nachbarn – Nachbarschaftspolitik vor und nach dem Verfassungsvertrag, in: integration, 233 ss.

Hummer, Waldemar (2007): The European Fundamental Rights Agency, in: Reinisch, August/Kriebaum, Ursula (eds.), The Law of International Relations – Liber amicorum for Hanspeter Neuhold (2007), pp.103-130.

Hummer, Waldemar (2010): Grundrechtsschutz in der EU durch die EMRK, in: Rill, Bernd (ed.), Von Nizza nach Lissabon – neuer Aufschwung für die EU, Argumente und Materialien zum Zeitgeschehen Nr. 69, Akademie für Politik und Zeitgeschehen, 13 ss.

Hummer, Waldemar (2011): Hybride Rechtsstellung der Europäischen Union in der UNO, ecolex, Zeitschrift für Wirtschaftsrecht, Manz'sche Verlags- und Universitätsbuchhandlung, 675ff.

Hummer, Waldemar (2011): Minderheitenschutz im Recht der EU vor und nach dem Inkrafttreten des Vertrages von Lissabon – Vom bloßen Diskriminierungsverbot zu „affirmative actions", EJM Vol. 2-2011, 81ff.

Hummer, Waldemar/Karl, Wolfram (2008): Regionaler Menschenrechtsschutz. Dokumente samt Einführungen, Band I Allgemeiner Schutzbereich, Teilband 1: Europa; Teilband 2: Amerika, Afrika, Islamisch-Arabischer Raum, Asiatisch-Pazifischer Raum.

Hummer, Waldemar/Mayr-Singer, Jelka (2011): Internationale Strafgerichtsbarkeit in: Woyke, Wichard (ed.), Handwörterbuch Internationale Politik, 12. ed., Opladen: Verlag Barbara Budrich, 226ff.

Ipsen, Hans Peter (1972): Europäisches Gemeinschaftsrecht, Tübingen: J.C.B. Mohr (Paul Siebeck).

Lerch, Marika (2004): Menschenrechte und europäische Außenpolitik. Eine konstruktivistische Analyse, Wiesbaden: VS Verlag für Sozialwissenschaften.

Passos, Ricardo/Gauci, Daniela (2008): The European Parliament and development cooperation: Shaping legislation and the new democratic scrutiny dialogue, EuR Beiheft 2/2008, pp. 138-161.

Pradetto, Kajetan (2010): EU Human Rights Policy in the UN Human Rights Council, Europa-Kolleg Hamburg, Study Paper No 3/10;

Ranacher, Christian (2003): Die Bindung der Mitgliedstaaten an die Gemeinschaftsgrundrechte, ZÖR, 21ff.

Schima, Bernhard (2009), Grundrechtsschutz, in: Hummer, Waldemar/Obwexer, Walter (eds.), Der Vertrag von Lissabon, Baden-Baden: Nomos, 325ff.

Schmalenbach, Kirsten (2008), Accountability: Who is judging the European development Cooperation?, EuR Beiheft 2/2008, pp. 162-190;

Schneiders, Benedikt (2010), Die Grundrechte der EU und die EMRK. Das Verhältnis zwischen ungeschriebenen Grundrechten, Grundrechtecharta und Europäischer Menschenrechtskonvention, Baden-Baden: Nomos.

Schweitzer, Michael/Hummer, Waldemar/Obwexer, Walter (2007), Europarecht.

Combating Terrorism in the 21st Century: The European Approach

Olivier Scherlofsky

Introduction

Since the 1970s (at that time within the European Community (EC)), fighting terrorism and linked forms of organised crime has emerged as an EC/EU topic – a topic that has become increasingly prominent in recent years.[1]

As a matter of internal security coping with terrorism, organised crime and linked forms of extremism progressed in the late 1990s under the Treaty of Amsterdam and its Area of Freedom, Security and Justice (AFSJ) and further advanced in the years after the attacks of 9/11, Madrid 2004 and London 2005 – especially in the field of criminal law and on the operational police and intelligence levels, e.g. by installing an EU Anti-terrorism Coordinator. Finally the Treaty of Lisbon that amended both the Treaty on European Union (TEU) and the Treaty on the Functioning of the European Union (TFEU) provided a higher degree of integration concerning the institutional frame and procedural law. Quite noticeably, the aspects of operative interstate cooperation (such as information exchange or even joint operations) gained improvements for the counter terrorist effort thanks to the legal incorporation and expansion of the former third pillar of inner security.

However: globalisation drives global power diffusion and started to change the behaviour of terrorism networks (Nye/Welch 2011: 289-292, 296-310); the nation state is in a long term decline concerning its monopoly of coercive force and its public order power (Hobshawm 2008: 125, 143-151); the disappearance of empires and the Cold War in particular left behind unstable and uncontrolled areas as well as weak states. Furthermore, in terms of international law the UN has started to identify non-state actors (as terrorist groups) as enemies of peace and international security and therefore as potential targets for actions and interventions in the field of foreign politics. So fighting terrorism is no longer an exclusive matter of the civilian and internal authorities. It has become a significant task for foreign policies as well as diplomatic and military operations – provided by the EU as part of the Common Foreign and Security Policy (CFSP) and its Common Security and

---

1 Recent years and that is related to a rising threat potential caused by forms of political and/or religious extremisms.

Defence Policy (CSDP) in close cooperation with NATO and single states, above all the USA. The CFSP and CSDP also made huge advances in EU law with the Treaty of Lisbon. Within CFSP and CSDP matters, concerns about inner European security and global stability, have forced the EU to use foreign policies, foreign services and civilian or military instruments to address the expanding problems of terrorist threats and asymmetric warfare resulting in destabilisation (which is regularly identified legally as terrorist acts and not seen as law of war-privileged partisan résistance).

Therefore a comprehensive, systemic-coherent and synchronised horizontal bringing-together of the AFSJ and the CFSP/CSDP as well as a vertical fitting of EU and member state policies and actions are some of the main critical success factors for the prevention of and battle against terrorism in Europe and abroad. The Treaty of Lisbon provides a new institutional framework, which offers "an unprecedented opportunity to better interlink its different counter terrorism instruments, as well as the internal and external dimension" as the Commission communicated it in 2010 (COM(2010)386 final).

The formal, institutional and procedural *de jure* and above all *de facto* frames of multinational authority cooperation is (in the history of European integration more than elsewhere) subject to a (*de facto*) never ending dynamic transformation (Streinz/Ohler/Herrmann 2010: 167), formed by the "normative power of the factual" and *ad hoc* measurements (have a look at the Euro-crises management). So this area of politics is a dynamic evolution process, changing its concrete forms and details continuously: Hence I will mainly focus on the EU anti-terrorism strategy by analyzing the respective EU law and main strategic documents – discovering the constants of the process. In doing so I will try to identify a European strategic approach of preventing and combating terrorism in Europe and abroad.

Procedural Law and Institutional Frame of Anti-Terrorism Policy within the AFSJ and the CFSP/CSDP

The Institutional Framework

With the coming into force of the Lisbon Treaty on 1 December 2009 the EU was transformed into a single entity of a legal personality, that shows both supranational and intergovernmental traces.

The fields of internal security, foreign affairs and military issues, as sensitive core areas of state sovereignty, are still being handled in an institutional framework of intergovernmental coordination and cooperation rather than by supranational mechanisms of common market policies: The strategic main decisions are predominated by the multilateral organised council-type bodies of the EU, and the operational capacities are still national bodies i.e., courts, police forces, intelligence services and military structures which are national in nature and under immediate national law, directives and orders. Therefore, the EU coordinates, supports and – to a certain degree – leads in ways of indirect rule, while the member states continue to be the immediate executing actors.

However, a few supranational EU structures exist already: In the field of AFSJ are some legal responsibilities and operational capacities of immediate EU nature, especially Europol, Eurojust and Frontex. Furthermore, relevant EU structures exist in the area of CFSP/CSDP: some EU foreign, security and defence bodies (especially the recently established European External Action Service, security/military staff/cooperation/coordination bodies, and the European Defence Agency) as well as operational EU commanders under direct command of the foreign EU bodies in EU foreign military and/or civilian missions.

Legal and Obligation Character of Norms and Documents

The legal norms of the EU treaties are explicit hard international law. Other multilateral European documents and decisions concerning the former second and third pillar (such as EU strategy documents) are either secondary EU law or independent multilateral (international) law (linked to EU topics and aims): In the first case of secondary EU law, decisions have to be seen as mandatory as far as their contents postulate compliance and are not just regarded as a recommendation or similar; in the second case of independent multilateral law, it has to be interpreted case by case whether or not the intention of the parties covers hard or soft law character (Streinz/Ohler/Herrmann 2010: 91-103).

The above mentioned hard law has to be carried out by the Union's member states in an efficient way following the international law principles of pacta sunt servanda and good faith, as well as the EU principles of loyalty and loyal cooperation, which can be seen as the fundamental principles of CFSP/CSDP law, obligating all member states to efficient cooperative behaviour and solidarity. Soft law agreements establish a certain degree of binding powers in a factual-political way, which in the reality of EU politics may de facto create powers of equal strength or of an even stronger nature than formal hard law.

Analyzing the Substantive Law: Identifying the Fundaments and the Core Content of the EU's Anti-Terrorism Strategy

The legal basis and the strategic content of the EU's counter terrorism policy can be outlined in the following way. (In this chapter, the content of the fundamental norms, policies and strategies beyond the concrete anti-terrorism level are reduced to those which are immediately important for counter terrorism politics, policies and strategies).

In its Article 3 the Lisbon Treaty sets as meta-aims of the EU as a whole the promotion of peace, the EU values and the well-being of its peoples. In the same Article it declares that an Area of Freedom, Security and Justice (AFSJ) without internal frontiers shall be offered and crime shall be prevented and combated. Furthermore Article 3 stipulates, that, in foreign affairs the Union's values and interests shall be upheld and promoted, its citizens protected and it shall contribute to global peace, security, sustainable development, free and fair trade, the eradication of poverty and the protection of human rights, as well as the strict observance and development of international law – under the principles of solidarity and mutual respect among peoples.

For the AFSJ article 67 TFEU states as one of its core objectives that a high level of security shall be ensured by preventing and combating crime, racism and xenophobia, by coordination and cooperation measures between authorities. Article 75 TEU calls for a framework for financial measures concerning terrorism and related activities. The articles 82 to 86 TFEU regulate the fundaments of criminal law cooperation. Article 87 and 88 TFEU provide a legal fundament for sophisticated police cooperation and Europol. Furthermore a Standing Committee on Operational Cooperation on Internal Security (COSI) was established to ensure effective cooperation between authorities (Article 71 TFEU). Article 222 TFEU established the solidarity clause, calling for assistance (explicit inclusive military assets) of member states in cases of terrorist attacks.

For the CFSP, Article 42 TEU declares the CSDP as its military and civilian operational structure for security and peace missions outside the Union. It obligates all member states (with the exception of Denmark), including neutral states like Austria (which, in the process of joining the EU, has explicitly devoted itself to fully support the CFSP in an active way), to provide respective and sufficient civilian and military capabilities and to improve its military assets for that purpose (armament clause).

These obligations do not trigger automatic and burden sharing effects in cases of operational needs/decisions, but work as a solidarity obligation in general. This means that a country can vote against measurements and decide on its own if or what it wants to contribute to joint actions under the auspices of CSDP. Article 43 proclaims the so called *Petersberg plus* spectrum as possible types of operations, including peace-making (offensive combat tasks) and fighting terrorism (including the support of third countries in their territories). Such operations may include tasks of combating terrorism as the main mission objective by e.g. fighting terrorist leaders and infrastructure by the use of military special forces and intelligence to support a foreign government. They also may consider anti-terrorism measures as mission defence (e.g. by fighting insurgents threatening peacebuilding efforts) or as pure force protection.

For the AFSJ, the so called *Stockholm Programme* (COM 2009a: 25) provides a roadmap to *inter alia* establish a Europe that protects its citizens and fights organised crime and terrorism, carried by "the spirit of solidarity". Thereby it seeks to follow a comprehensive approach, also taking into consideration the external dimension of EU policy. This comprehensive approach is further defined in the Communication Act of the Commission "*A strategy on the external dimension of the AFSJ*" (COM (2005c) 491): To address threats from terrorism and a growing organised crime, it demands international cooperation in the fields of border management, rule of law abroad, and other cross-border issues. Hereto it recommends to establish geographical priorities, appropriate and tailored strategies, flexibility or partnerships with non-EU countries as well as, regular exchange of information; external action and progress evaluation.

Both the AFSJ and the CFSP have their main strategic documents:
The AFSJ-based Internal Security Strategy (5842/2/10 REV 2) declares security and "the ability to guarantee security and stability in Europe" as one of the main priorities of EU politics. It outlines as a background picture for the situation of security and safety a legally (*Schengen*) and technologically (cross-border) opened society effected by revolutionised modes and speeds of communications, high mobility and instant financial transactions. The strategy seeks to combat terrorism, serious and organised crime, trafficking drugs/humans/arms, cyber-crime, economic crime, corruption and cross-border crime. As enemies to be combated it identifies: terrorists "in any form", actors of "serious and organised crime", actors of "cyber-crime" as a global, anonymous threat, and actors ("often gangs") of significant cross-border crime.

For all of these actors it can be noted that they "adapt extremely quickly to changes in science and technology". For strategies of terrorists it identifies the recruitment "through radicalisation and dissemination of propaganda". For their potential allies in organised crime ("of increasing importance") it analyses their occurrence and development "wherever it can reap the most financial benefit with the least risk, regardless of borders".

The main methodical approach of the Internal Security Strategy concept to tackle those actors can be described as a pro-active, integrated, wide, pragmatic, and realistic global approach, continually adapting to reality. The approach shall be intelligence-led activity in order to anticipate and prevent, with efficient operational and analytical tools (and early-warning systems); protecting people, core values, critical infrastructures (including virtual environments) in a global and opened society; aiming at the effects and the causes; and involving all relevant political, economic, social sectors and state as well as non-state actors. It also stresses integration as a key security factor. Therefore it calls for extended and sophisticated common cooperation of all EU and member state authorities under the principles of solidarity, mutual trust and efficiency to tackle common threats by common means.

In all of the matters a balance is demanded between the needs of security/ protection ("security is in itself a basic right" and freedom needs security) and the other principles and values of the Union, especially the respect for human rights, the rule of law, fundamental freedoms (such as the freedom of expression), democracy and transparency, tolerance, solidarity, maintaining dialogs and taking account of concerns and opinions. The above shall be guaranteed by effective democratic and judicial supervision of security activities.

Concerning the external dimension it wants to address serious crime and terrorism by maintaining a high security standard abroad, in order to protect the rights of EU citizens within the EU ("internal security increasingly depends to a large extent on external security") and EU citizens in third country's territories, but also to promote a general rule of law worldwide ("crucial importance"). Especially weak or failed states have to be prevented from becoming "hubs of organised crime or terrorism". In the long term development is seen as the most effective way to provide security abroad. Therefore a global security approach has to be established in foreign affairs (security as a key factor in foreign relationships) for effective and close international cooperation and support. It consequently calls the CSDP European Security Strategy as an "indispensable complement". Concerning the operational level, it explicitly asks for close cooperation between the EU agencies and CSDP missions.

The main strategic document for CFSP/CSDP is still the *European Security Strategy* (ESS). Adopted by the European Council on 12 December 2003, this document calls for concerted European counter action in the field of terrorism. The ESS sees terrorism caused by complex realities, such as pressures from modernisation, crises of cultural, social and political nature, leading to an alienation of young people in foreign societies.

Furthermore, concerning potentially terrorism-linked crimes it seeks to globally combat organised crime including, in the worst case, supporting states as well as the proliferation of weapons of mass destruction that, linked with terrorism, is declared as the greatest threat to Europe's security). In addition, the 2008 update of the ESS expands to the security issues of threats to energy security (consider e.g. constant terrorist attacks on European energy facilities in Yemen or Central Africa), economic crimes, cyber crimes and piracy. It also seeks to dry up and smoke out the rear hinterland and infrastructural territory for terrorism by supporting fragile states and rebuild failed states by civilian and/or military operations: Civil conflict shall be settled and bad governance, corruption, and abuse of power shall be fought. The ESS also identifies security as a prime precondition for development.

The side effects of globalisation are blamed as the background for all these troubles, which for some people are causing frustration and subjectively felt injustice, often linked to environments of economic failure, political problems and violent conflict. Furthermore, the global potential for turbulence is seen to rise due to the competition for natural resources while Europe is becoming more and more energy dependent. (It has to be noted that the EU primary law as well as the strategic documents such as the ESS are stressing the promotion of globalisation, as a matter of principle, multilateralism, global commitment and a worldwide free trade as desirable main (meta-) tasks in foreign policies – excluding all kinds of isolationism as alternatives. The EU's foreign policy approach has to be seen as global and proactive in general.)

The approach defined for the ESS can be seen as an active and coherent political-strategic culture of addressing threats to Europe and world peace globally, that recognises threats early, reacts rapidly and as robust as necessary. Thereby European civilian and military action abroad shall be carried by effective and law based multilateralism with the US-European relationship as the main axis.

The member states shall build up sufficient military and civilian capabilities for such interventions. On the basis of the legal foundation and the political strategies discussed above the 2005 EU Counter-Terrorism Strategy (14469/4/05 REV 4) and derived implementation plans and recommending analyses, especially the 2010 Counter Terrorism Policy (COM(2010) 386), provide the principle reference framework for EU action in the realm of AFSJ based anti-terrorism policy.

First, these strategies identify, as the backdrop for the evolution of terrorism, a Europe of increasing openness and interdependence as well as an increase due to globalisation in "the ability to put ideas into action [...by] ease of travel, transfer of money and communication [...] easier access to radical ideas and training".

The type of actors the Counter Terrorism Strategy and the Counter Terrorism Policy want to combat are terrorist groups ("Islamist, separatist and anarchist"), ("lone wolves"); and terrorist-linked youth organisations – which are identified as a matter of particular concern.

As offensive forms of terrorist operations are analyzed physical and electronic attacks and kinds of propaganda aimed to make others consider and justify violence (as an important example the paper quotes "propaganda which distorts conflicts around the world as a supposed proof of a clash [...] between the West and Islam").

The Counter Terrorism Policy characterises the strategic attack behaviour of terrorist groups as striking "whenever, wherever and with whatever they think they will have the most [society disruption and self interest] impact". Thereby they are assumed to adapt very well and quickly to counter-terrorist efforts and other changes in their environments "as demonstrated by the 2008 Mumbai attacks".

Their logistic means are communication technologies ("The internet is commonly used by terrorists for propaganda communication, training, indoctrination, recruitment, and fund-raising [...] terrorist organisations also use the internet to plan operations and publicise claimed attacks."), financial assets, weapons and explosives, as well as other logistic goods such as dual use-goods. In this context chemical, biological and radiological weapons are identified as today being relatively inexpensive.

The methodical strategic approach of the Counter Terrorism Strategy and its Counter Terrorism Policy can be characterised as a systematic (less incident-driven), comprehensive and tailored response to the international terrorist threat – keeping in mind the proportionality of means and the balance between security and "letting it overwhelm our daily lives" as well as fundamental rights and the rule of law, which are quoted as being at the heart of the EU's counter terrorism approach.

The EU Counter Terrorism Strategy and its derived policies and plans are based on the following four groups of objectives: to prevent, to protect, to pursue, and to respond.

Prevention aims to keep people from turning to terrorism, which should be achieved by tackling the root causes of radicalisation and recruitment. Priorities are: spotting and tackling problematic behaviour and addressing incitement and recruitment ("limiting the activities of those playing a role in radicalisation, preventing access to terrorist training, establishing a strong legal framework to prevent incitement and recruitment ["in particular in key environments, for example prisons, places of religious training or worship"], and examining ways to impede terrorist recruitment through the internet", implementing legislation for prosecuting and punishing people who try to involve others in terrorist activity or support them to do so); communicate and explain the EU policies; promoting good governance, democracy, education, economic prosperity, integration and targeting inequalities, discrimination, racism and xenophobia; developing intercultural dialogue as well as a non-emotive atmosphere for discussion (working with the civil society, operating public private partnerships, empowering local communities to oppose radicalisation, and cooperate with faith groups that reject terrorist ideas); research for understanding and developing policy responses.

Protection refers to citizens, infrastructure (including cyber infrastructure and supply chains), crowded places and other soft targets, and aims to reduce the vulnerability to terrorist attacks. This includes to identify vulnerabilities domestically and abroad, to develop common standards on civil aviation, port and maritime security and to set priorities in the protection of critical infrastructure and key targets.

Pursuing aims to "pursue and investigate terrorists across our borders and globally; to impede planning, travel, and communications; to disrupt support networks; to cut off funding and access to attack materials and bring terrorists to justice". The key priorities refer to a strengthening of national and EU anti-terrorism capabilities, giving assistance to third countries, and legal cooperation and adaption. They also include operational cooperation between law enforcement agencies and judicial authorities, the denial of access to weapons and explosives, tackling of terrorist financing (e.g. by abusing the non-profit sector) and ensuring "that financial investigation is an integral part of all terrorism investigations".

Response means preparing the EU, its states and its citizens "in the spirit of solidarity, to manage and minimise the consequences of a terrorist attack". Here, the solidarity clause enshrined in Article 222 TFEU provides a legal ground for common reactions.

For all of these matters the member states are called to focus on the security of the Union as a whole when conducting national security tasks and to strengthen their national capabilities and abilities, e.g. the ability of the concerned national authorities to collect and analyze intelligence and the ability to pursue and investigate terrorists.

Concerning the external dimensions, the necessity of global proactive anti-terrorism policies and operations is underlined. It refers to the European Security Strategy and its picture of the EU's role in the world as a contributor to global security and – linked in both directions – development. Therefore, reinforced cooperation with other states, IGOs, NGOs and economic actors, as well as the assistance of third countries in their fight against terrorism (e.g. Afghanistan, Pakistan, Iraq, Yemen, Somalia or the Sahel region) is demanded. Developments in the Middle East and North Africa region will likely boost the need for such assistance, considering the instability that will no doubt follow the regime changes or attempts to change regimes. These efforts shall be supported by dialogues and alliances between cultures, underpinning radicalisation, and shall respect human rights and international law.

The long term success of fighting terrorism and radicalisation within and outside Europe will depend on the effective complexity management of a comprehensive European approach. There is much at stake – but the EU can prove its necessity and fundamental value by providing stability and security to its citizens in Europe and abroad, while promoting wealth, stability, freedom and justice.

References

Bremmer, Ian/Preston, Keat (2010): The Fat Tail[,] The Power of Political Knowledge in an Uncertain World. Oxford: Oxford University Press.

Cragin, Kim/Daly, Sara A. (2004) : The Dynamic Terrorist Threat. Santa Monica: RAND Corporation.

De Baere, Geert (2008): Constitutional Principles of EU External Relations, Oxford: Oxford University Press.

European Union Institute for Security Studies (2009): What ambitions for European defence in 2020? Paris.

European Commission (2008), From early warning to early action? Brussels.

Fearon, James D. (2006): Ethnic Mobilisation and Ethnic Violence. In: Weingast, Barry R./Wittman, Donald A.: The Oxford Handbook of Political Economy. Oxford: Oxford University Press.

Fukuyama, Francis (2004): State-Building, New York: Cornell University Press.

Gropp, Walter/Sinn Arndt (2006), Organisierte Kriminalität und kriminelle Organisation, Baden-Baden: Nomos.

Hobshawm, Eric (2008): Globalisation, Democracy, and Terrorism. London: Abacus.

Leidenmühler, Franz (2008): From Common Market to Common Defence. In: EU Watch (MAY/JUN 2008). Oxfordshire: EU Watch.

Lenz, Carl Otto/Borchardt, Klaus-Dieter/Bitterlich, Joachim (2010): EU-Verträge. Köln: Bundesanzeiger.

Mann, Michael (1994; 1998; 2001): Die Geschichte der Macht 1-3, Frankfurt am Main: Campus.

Matuszek, Krzysztof C. (2007): Der Krieg als autopoietisches System, Wiesbaden: VS Research.

Münkler, Herfried (2004): Die Neuen Kriege, Hamburg: Rowohlt.

Neves, Marcelo (2007): Die Staaten im Zentrum und die Staaten an der Peripherie. In: Neves Marcelo/Voigt, Rüdiger (2007): Die Staaten der Weltgesellschaft, Baden-Baden: Nomos.

Nye, Joseph S./Welch, David A. (2011): Understanding Global Conflict and Cooperation, New York: Longman.

Rehrl, Jochen/Weisserth, Hans-Bernhard (2010): Handbook on CSDP – The Common Security and Defence Policy of the European Union. Vienna: Landesverteidigungsakademie of the Austrian Ministry of Defence.

Shelton, Dinah (2007): Commitment and Compliance, Oxford: Oxford Univ. Press.

Soros, George (2006), The age of fallibility: The consequences of the war on terror. London: Orion.

Streinz, Rudolf/Ohler Christoph/ Christoph, Herrmann (2010), Der Vertrag von Lissabon zur Reform der EU. Munich: Beck.

Wallace, Helen/Pollack, Mark A./Young, Alasdair R. (2010): The new European Union Series: Policy-Making in the European Union. Oxford: Oxford University Press.

Wimmer, Hans (2009): Gewalt und Gewaltmonopol des Staates, Vienna: LIT.

Special online sources for counter terrorism analysis, used for that paper:

http://www.stratfor.com/weekly/burton_and_stewart_on_security
http://www.stratfor.com/weekly/friedman_on_geopolitics

Arab Foreign Fighters in Bosnia – The Roads to Europe

Nico Prucha

"If we extend the focus and if we set out to expand the influence and the perception of the *voice of jihad* in the world, either by governments or the peoples, then we will hear the echoes of this *voice* reverberate from the depth of the world of the disbelievers in Europe and elsewhere."
Abu Yahya al-Libi[1]

"The first defenders of the Arab Mujahideen arrived, coming from Afghanistan, two months after the war broke out in the Balkans."
Of the Stories of the Arab Martyrs in Bosnia-Herzegovina (al-Qatari/al-Madani 2002: 7)

Introduction

The war in the Balkans (1992-95) attracted the attention of Muslim foreign fighters, who had mostly participated in a proclaimed defensive-jihad against communist occupation forces in Afghanistan. The Balkan war became highly appealing when Bosnian territory, defined as Islamic ground, came under attack and the Mujahideen now considered it a divine obligation to rush to aid their fellow Muslims – even when, as it seems, a great deal of combat-ready fighters did not even know where Bosnia was (Hegghammer 2010: 48). With Islamic territory under attack by Christian forces, many jihadists considered the "conflict as a new opportunity to liberate a Muslim population from *infidel* rule" (Calvert 2011: 33) and – most importantly – responded to reports of atrocities committed against Muslim civilians (al-Qatari/al-Madani 2002: 19-25).

The early to mid-nineties are an important and vital episode in the history and the making of al-Qa'ida (AQ) and for other jihadist groups who fought together in Afghanistan and subsequently expanded their networks to new zones of conflict. In 1989 the Mujahideen in Afghanistan, consisting of Arab foreign

---

1   In a video published by al-Sahab after his escape from the US-operated Baghram prison in Afghanistan. Al-Libi is a high-ranking military commander and claims an authoritarian ideological role as well.

fighters as well as local Afghans and Muslim fighters from neighbouring countries defeated the Red Army who withdrew by the end of that year.[2] The victory over the Red Army in Afghanistan unleashed a momentum that allows the jihadists to re-build and recruit for ongoing struggles against defined occupational armies and tyrannical states, even now, ten years after 9/11.[3] In the jihadists' mindset, this defeat consequently led to the dissolution of the Soviet Union shortly after, as the Mujahideen had waged a costly guerilla war of attrition for the Red Army, both in material as well as human terms, and its ungodly communist ideology.[4] With the civil war in Afghanistan in full swing after the Soviet withdrawal and in favour of the advancing Taliban and their allied Arab Mujahideen, many of these combat-hardened veterans were on the lookout for new theatres of jihad. These new theatres unravelled with the demise of Soviet influence over Islamic countries and provinces that were now driving for independence such as Chechnya[5], Kazakhstan[6] or Tajikistan. These new conflicts developed next to already existing ones in the Islamic world such as Palestine,

---

2 Martyr stories, describing the life and deeds of those Mujahideen, who died on the path of God thus ultimately 'confessing' the utmost possible for their belief and God in this world are a fundamental part of jihadist literature. Abdallah Azzam, for example, provided lengthy accounts of martyrs (*shuhada'*) in Afghanistan of the 1980s and nowadays Arabic writings are disseminated via the Internet with similar stories. For a accounts of the shuhada' of the 1980s: Abdallah Azzam, *Ushshaq al-hur*, available online: http://tawhed.ws /dl?i=pwtico4g. For contemporary accounts of Arab and non-Arab Mujahideen who had been killed in the recent years in Afghanistan: Abu Ubayda al-Maqdisi, *Shuhada' fi zaman al-ghurba* (2007); to reference two examples of countless sources.
All referenced Internet sources were accessible as of 08.11.2011.

3 Part of this success story is the highly efficient, proficient, and comprising use of the Internet to disseminate and propagate a specific interpretation of Islam via all means of modern media. This includes materials (filmed and written) ranging from the 1980s to Bosnia and beyond. In short, the jihadists, as an ideology with key ideologues as mediators, attempt to assume authoritarian roles of interpreting historical Arabic religious sources, which are then embedded in an active – mostly militarily or resisting – complex and published as guidance and role models to be re-enacted by individuals and groups – worldwide. Nico Prucha, *Online Territories of Terror – Utilizing the Internet for Jihadist Endeavors,* in: Orient IV/2011 pp. 43-48, available online at: http://www.oiip.ac.at/fileadmin/Unterlagen/Dateien/Publikationen/Article_ORIENT_IV_NicoPrucha.pdf

4 A similar notion is propagated by jihadist online sources nowadays, particularly since the economic crisis.

5 Chechnya remains the most active zone of conflict in the Caucasus as of 2011. According to the many martyr stories, backed by *the Guantanamo Files* released by WikiLeaks, most foreign fighters had a strong desire to enter Chechnya and fight there against the Russians. Bosnia and other conflict zones are often described as alternative destinations that had then been exploited to build Global Jihad Support Networks, as US administrators refer to it according to WikiLeaks. http://wikileaks.ch/gitmo/.

6 http://almanac.afpc.org/Kazakhstan; recently, via the jihadist online forum *shabakat al-shumukh*, an unknown jihadist group "The Soldiers of the Caliphate" (*jund al-khilafa*) claimed bomb attacks in Kazakhstan and threatened further attacks in a video because of the prohibition of the headscarf for Muslimas: http://shamikh1.info/vb/showthread.php?t=132941&highlight=%E4%D2%C7%D1%C8%C7%ED%ED%DD.

Kashmir, the Philippines, Eritrea or Algeria[7], where in the 1990s a bloody civil war unfolded. In Iraq, Muslims suffered under the economic embargo, imposed by the UN after 1991, to punish the regime of Saddam Hussein for invading Kuwait. The suffering of the Iraqi Sunni Muslims composes a narrative exploited by jihadist propaganda after 2003 to justify attacking US soldiers, and is also part of perceiving the United Nations as an alliance by non-Islamic forces.[8]

The reality of mostly Arab foreign fighter veterans in Afghanistan did not offer many options. Most of these Mujahideen could not return to their countries of origin and nevertheless had been seeking to continue fighting elsewhere anyway.

Recruitment was sought on a global level, but Bosnian jihad documents indicate the flow of Arab veterans of war from Afghanistan to Bosnia. Not all of the Arab foreign fighters in Afghanistan could return to their countries of origin. The majority of these Mujahideen were fugitives, wanted by their respective governments (Lia 2007: 106-7). The Mujahideen based in Afghanistan had an existent infrastructure,[9] had been supported financially by some Islamic states and in most cases were disappointed not to have died fighting (Anas 2002: 91). Muhammad al-Habashi, known by his nom de guerre Abu Zubayr al-Madani, a cousin of Osama bin Laden (Kohlmann 2005: 58) fought in Afghanistan since 1984 and then moved onwards to Bosnia. "After the conquest of Kabul and the return of a great number of the supporting Mujahideen to their countries, al-Habashi was ready to go home. But it became clear to him how he saw the Afghan episode. First and foremost, he is entitled to be killed as a martyr, if God wills it, but not in Afghanistan?" (al-Qatari/al-Madani 2002: 71).

---

7 For a personal account of a jihadist fighting in Afghanistan: Abdallah Anas, (2002), *Waladat al-afghan al-arab – sira Abdallah Anas bayna Masud wa-Abdallah Azzam*. According to his autobiography Anas was one of the first Arab fighters in Afghanistan from Algeria and guided by Abdallah Azzam whose writings and religious decrees had inspired him to join. Later, he was embedded as an Arab with the Afghan Northern Alliance leader Ahmad Shah Masud, who would be assassinated by al-Qa'ida prior to 9/11. After the Soviet withdrawal he "found himself in a very difficult position. There was no justification for me [Anas] to remain in Afghanistan. I thought about leaving since 1990. I was not bestowed with the *shahada* [i.e. being killed fighting] and the Mujahideen were in the wake of entering Kabul". In 1990 the Front Islamique du Salut won the elections in Algeria, triggering the civil war after the intervention by the army. Anas "was beginning to be divided between two regions: Algeria and Afghanistan", p. 91.

8 This sentiment triggered the horrific attacks against the UN in Iraq in 2003.

9 The *Maktab al-Khidamat*, founded by Abdallah Azzam, was slowly transferred into a network that would later manifest itself into al-Qaeda. After Azzam was assassinated in 1989 in Peshawar, Pakistan, both Osama bin Laden and Ayman al-Zawahiri extended the network and fuelled money, fighters, ideologues and ideological material into contested areas such as Bosnia or Chechnya among other zones of conflict (Prucha 2010a: 36-8).

Thus some Afghan veterans simply sought a new warzone in the hope of being killed. Others, as Abdallah Azzam wrote, wanted to continue their religious endeavours, consisting of a militant-missionary mixture:

> "From the morning into the middle of the night, and we are like this, if we have liberated Afghanistan tomorrow, what will we work on? (...) Or God will open up a new front for us somewhere in the Islamic world and we will go, wage a jihad there. Or will I finish my *sharia* studies at the Islamic University in Kabul? Yes, a lot of the Mujahideen are thinking about what to work on after the jihad ends in Afghanistan" (Azzam; no year: 85).

Afghanistan served as a unifying front for various jihadists that would be crafted into operational and ideological perfection in Bosnia. For the first time, members of jihadist groups such as the Egyptian al-Gama'a al-Islamiyya, the al-Jihad Organisation, the Libyan Islamic Fighting Group, or the Algerian Groupe Islamique Armé trained and fought together and would later in parts be absorbed by al-Qa'ida and its global agenda. Besides the civil war in Afghanistan, Bosnia subsequently became a new additional conflict to be fought, in addition to the hotspots such as Kashmir, Tajikistan, Somalia or Chechnya (Tuhhan 2007: 401), where above mentioned groups started to join together. This merger was on a much broader international level with new recruits coming from Germany[10], France[11] or Britain[12] to help support their brothers in need in Bosnia under the guidance of primarily Arab ideologues and combat veterans.

The agendas of the jihadists include a wide variety that could be termed as "policy" by "missionary work" (*da'wah*) and implementing a specific interpretation (*ta'wil*) of Islamic sources (Quran and *sunna*). In the jihadists mindset, missionary work and militant jihad are inseparable and oftentimes the arriving foreign fighters wanted to teach the Bosnian Muslims the

---

10   For example: Abu Musa al-Almaani – "the cameraman of the Mujahideen in Bosnia, killed during Operation Miracle, Bosnia, 21 July 1995." http://caravansofmartyrs.atspace.com/html/Abu_Musa_Al-Almaani.htm.
     Another account is the story of Abu Maryam al-Afghani, who was raised in Germany by his father who had fled Afghanistan. Later, Abu Maryam returned to his original country to fight. "After the conquest of Kabul, he went back to his father in Germany and married a German woman, new to Islam. (...) After hearing what was happening to their brothers in Bosnia-Herzegovina, he became active." He was killed when he was hit by shrapnel while engaging Serbian forces (al-Qatari/al-Madani 2002: 99-102).

11   Abu Ali al-Fransawi, a convert from France, joined the Mujahideen in Bosnia together with his friend Abu Said al-Jaza'iri, originally from Algeria but of French citizenship (al-Qatari/al-Madani 2002: 111-114).

12   The account of Dawood "from Britain. Killed during a battle against Croatian forces in Bosnia in 1993. Aged 29." *The Undead Warriors*, compiled by Dar Al Murabiteen Publications, available online at http://www.slideshare.net/hudahashmi/the-undead-warriors, pp. 134-136.

'proper' conduct of Islam as most Bosnians were too liberal and secular (al-Qatari/al-Madani 2002: 16).

Many Islamic charities were created to funnel and utilise money to Bosnia, often disguised as legitimate non-governmental organisations (NGO). A lot of these NGO's had a public façade of providing humanitarian assistance and conducting missionary work, while having operational outlets to equip and fund existent networks of fighters.[13] "Estimates put the number of foreign jihadis at 1,500 to 5,000. Because the foreign fighters did not receive direct financial support from Muslim states, as had been the case during the Afghanistan war, they were forced to rely on private sources of funding, especially Islamic charities" (Calvert 2011: 33). This provided opportunities for recruitment and for introducing a new generation of Mujahideen into the networks with fighters from all over the world. Working for the NGOs also provided convenient cover stories and appears frequently in the interrogation with US agents of captured terrorists in Afghanistan and Pakistan.[14] "Bosnia provided an environment where trained foreign Muslim fighters arriving from Afghanistan could mingle with unsophisticated but eager terrorist recruits from Western Europe, and could form new plans for the future of jihad. No such contacts had ever occurred before for groups like Al-Gama'at al-Islamiyya and Al-Qaida, and it provided these organisations limitless possibilities for development and growth" (Kohlmann 2006: 2).

Ethnic Cleansing in the Balkans – the Propagated "War against Islam"

With the war in the Balkans intensifying and reports of genocide and ethnic cleansing being made public as early as 1992[15], Bosnian-Muslims became part

---

13 Foremost the Saudi High Commission for Muslims for Bosnia-Herzegovina, led by its director Abdullah Almaitrafi, an acquaintance of Osama bin Laden. He was associated with the who's who of what would become the senior leadership of al-Qa'ida, including Abu Zubayr al-Haili – a renowned jihad leader in Bosnia. *Gitmo Files*, published by Wikileaks, case file US9SA-000005DP.
14 As the *Gitmo Files* reveal – for example: The case file US9KU-000065DP – the "detainee", a Kuwaiti, worked for over six years for the Kuwaiti Joint Relief Committee and facilitated the movement and support of Mujahideen in Bosnia and Croatia. He travelled to Afghanistan shortly after 9/11 and was arrested in Pakistan, fleeing Afghanistan. The NGO assisted the "Algerian Six", a group of Algerian Bosnia veterans who had stayed after the war and allegedly planned to assault the US embassy in Sarajevo sometime in October 2001.
15 ITN *Tonight with Trevor McDonald*, claims having been the first to have visited a concentration camp in 1992 where Muslim inmates and Serb guards had been interviewed. In its recent report (15.09.2011) entitled *Bosnia – Unfinished Business*, Season 13 Episode 40, the reporter and her crew who made the discovery in 1992 return to interview – once again

of the comprising problems affecting the Islamic world in terms of suppression and occupation. News footage from Bosnia, the concentration camps and especially from Sarajevo where scores of civilians had been gunned down by snipers during the siege of the city was used for jihadist videos in combination with either sequences taken by the Mujahideen themselves during combat in defence of these victims[16], or by addressing issues of grief as the jihad video "The Catastrophe of Bosnia-Herzegovina in 1992" (*al-Karitha al-Busna wa-l Hirsik*) depicts. As in introduction to the one-hour long film, burning houses and scores of shot-up bodies and wounded are lying in the street, while the viewer hears "Sarajevo, Sarajevo" repeatedly. The video continues with a map of Europe and a narrator explaining the geographical situation of the dissolved former Yugoslav state, as well as Bosnia as part of the Ottoman Empire with its people having been Muslims since. The film implies that the Muslims in Bosnia have been punished for their Islamic faith by both the Orthodox and Catholic neighbours and by the occupation and annexation by the Austrian – Catholic – Habsburg monarchy. It was only during the period of Ottoman rule that security and peace was made possible, while the Christian enemies surrounding Bosnia-Herzegovina were plotting their attacks that appeared in the jihadists' understanding in waves. This includes the tragedies of World War I and the demise of the Ottoman Empire, the abolishment of the Caliphate shortly after, marking the start of misery, and the Second World War.[17] Bosnia had to a great extent been a "no man's land between the Ottoman and Habsburg Empires, which contained Roman Catholic, Orthodox, and Muslim religious and, Croatian, and Serbian, and Muslim populations, had never been a state or even self-governing (…). For thirty years, Bosnia-Herzegovina had been under Turkish suzerainty, Austrian administration, and local autonomy without experiencing a serious challenge to this multinational arrangement" (Kissinger 1994: 195). And with the dissolution of Yugoslavia in the early nineties, "the Christians of the Balkan and their Jewish, former Yugoslavian ruler Tito, slaughtered the Muslims for the sole reason and none other because they are Muslims" (Qutb 1992: 21) – expressing the continuation of the perceived and propagated war against Islam. Muhammad Qutb, the brother of the legendary Egyptian Islamist scholar Sayyid Qutb who was sentenced to death in Cairo in 1966, recalls the account of a Bosnian student at the University Umm al-Qura (Mecca) in 1988,

---

    – victims and their former captors. The episode can be watched online at http://www. videobb.com/watch_video.php?v=0IjBZPcI197G.

16   Videos from Bosnia, depicting combat scenes, military planning, various foreign fighters from all over the world, and ideological sermons are, for example, *Badr al-Busna* part one and two. These films had been 'official' movies by the El-Mudzahidin Brigade, part of the Bosnian Army.

17   The movie *al-Karitha al-Bosna wa-l Hirsik* – produced in a documentary style – shows sequences from early 20th century Sarajevo and other parts of the Ottoman Empire and footage of the two world wars.

"who said that since the withdrawal of the Ottoman Army from the Balkans until today, the Muslims had been slaughtered nine times. And the truth is, the
Western media has been silenced and not reported on it. Under Tito's rule
750,000 Muslims had been killed. And Tito, as is generally known, was a Jew"
(Qutb 1992: 1). Muslims in Bosnia entered the list of trials experienced by the
Islamic world – included as oppressed subjects, suffering severe hardships and
facing extermination due to their Islamic belief, according to radical and extremist propaganda sources. Destroyed mosques and the call by Bosnian leader
Aliya Izetbegovic[18] for support, as, the narrator of the video continues, "Sorry
for saying this, the Bosnians lacked weapons to defend themselves." The help-
less Muslims are thus deprived of their right of self-defence while being
surrounded by Christian-Crusader enemies who saw a ripe opportunity to re-
take Islamic territory at the doorsteps of Europe. This was a key argument for
recruitment intended by movies of jihad such as "The Catastrophe of Bosnia-
Herzegovina." The jihadist writings furthermore, acted as proclaimed theological and ideological authoritative sources and instilled and affected fellow
Muslims worldwide, purporting the misery that the Caliphate has ceased to exist and hence the divided Islamic world is in parts occupied. The root-cause for
this misery is perceived to be in the hands of an unholy alliance – which

> "is repeating the catastrophes for the Muslims over and over again. It is but the
> hand of the Jews and Christians, which is clearly involved [in the fate of the Is-
> lamic world]. And the final confirmation is the dismemberment or the assault of
> the great Islamic State [the Caliphate and its subsequent division] into tiny state-
> entities.[19] These states are so tiny that they hardly can be found on a map. Conse-
> quently, the tyrannical Crusader hostilities began against the Muslim countries of
> Afghanistan and Iraq after Bosnia, the Philippines, Somalia, Sudan and the occu-
> pation of the land of the al-Aqsa Mosque [Palestine] by the Jews in accordance
> with the pledge to their Crusader-brothers [to wage war on Islam].[20] They have
> risen by killing women and children there. And when the Islamic *Sahwa*[21] began

---

18   http://tr-tr.facebook.com/alijaizzetbegovic – a fan-page for online commemoration.
19   Usually this is a reference to the Sykes-Picot arrangement, which led to the creation of the
     modern-day Arabic states, in the jihadists' understanding.
20   A footnote states that "it is well known that the first phase in establishing a Crusader-
     Zionist state in Palestine was the Belfour agreement". Since this historical agreement, al-
     Maajid argues, further phases have come into effect to secure the creation of such a state
     that would manifest the final stage of the assumed war against Islam and Muslims alike.
     Furthermore, the pledge contains "active help and support by the British to the Jews to [first
     of all] proclaim the state of Israel on Palestinian territory and assist to seek recognition of
     this state on an international level."
21   A term describing *awakening* or *recovery of consciousness* – al-Maajid refers to it as the
     beginning and the rise of a militant-jihadist struggle against perceived enemies and vassal
     regimes that developed into a global network. Parallel to active insurgencies and attacks,
     ideological parameters and rulings have been established and disseminated by the Internet.

to become more widely known in the 20th century, they turned against it by any means possible." [22]

The debacle in Bosnia, with Europe standing idly by and the UN not able to intervene, was, according to some, based on the perception of a global conspiracy against Islam with the goal of murdering as many Muslims as possible and in order to de-territorialise Islamic countries. This

> "reality is clear when turning to the Muslims of Bosnia-Herzegovina who suffered under the Christians and the duration of the wars for years. The United Nations of the infidels condemned and denounced [the war] in the United Nation's councils, but without any practical effect. The same happened in the region of Kosovo, while for many years the Serbs were prosecuting Muslims and driving them away from their lands. The West is condemning and disapproving and promising military strikes against the Serbs, but this won't happen" (al-Shu'aybi 1999: 68).

Muhammad Qutb in his writing *Lessons of the Trial of Bosnia-Herzegovina* (1992), claims western media, contrary to journalistic spirit, failed to report that

> "not even one day passed without a man, women or a child being slaughtered or a women being raped" and thus, no wonder, "no one in the West did anything! Certainly not! Rather, they intervened! By banning weapon deliveries to the Bosnians so that they could defend themselves! What is the meaning of this? In clear words: Continue, you Serbs. Go on with the killing, the slaughtering, the raping, the displacement and the destruction" (Qutb 1992: 25).

Qutb neglects the fact that the United Nations imposed an arms embargo, with the US and EC, for all warring parties (sipri 2007: 35), and this is not unusual for members agitating within a specific frame of reference, worldview, or ideological parameters. Unfortunately, and this was rhetorically easily exploited, the imposition of an arms embargo contributed to a misbalance at the costs of the Bosnians. "It implicitly favored those with the best access to existing government stocks (Serb forces) and with the geographical conditions and the means to circumvent the arms embargo (Croatian forces)" (sipri 2007: 57).[23]

The notion carried and furthered was that in Bosnia "women were raped. Even children were slaughtered or ripped out of the bodies of pregnant women. This happened due to the actions of the Crusaders, the Serbs, who had been fighting without any moral constraints" (Itan 2008: 104).[24] In the jihadist mind-

---

22 In an article written by prolific ideologue Abd al-Majiid Abd al-Maajid in the seventh edition of the magazine *Tala'i al-Khurasan*, August 2006, p. 45.
23 This was, according to the sipri report, page 57, the reason why the USA channeled weapons via Iran to bypass the arms embargo and to even the balance with hopes of ending the conflict sooner.
24 Citing an unnamed leader of a jihadist-salafist movement in Lebanon.

set, Bosnia was another zone of occupation, this time by the greatest threat, namely European-Christian armies with the backing of the United Nations ("The United Nations of Gravediggers" – al-Harbi 2010: 311-312), while Islam and Muslims had just been militarily successfully safeguarded and defended by volunteer Mujahideen in Afghanistan. The networks crafted and created there, now effectively served the cause in Bosnia, where Afghan veterans and new recruits started to expand a global jihad support network.

Afghanistan served as a unifying front for many jihad groups and individuals that adhered to the call of repelling a non-Muslim conqueror of an Islamic territory. In Bosnia, the jihadist propaganda materials propagated a consequent genocide of Muslims in the Balkans in order to re-Christianise parts of Yugoslavia that fell into the horrors of "a complex conflict in which religion was arguably more important as an identity marker than a driving force" (Hegghammer 2010:32-33).

Bosnia Enters the Jihadist Perception and Media

The war in the Balkans, the turmoil after the dissolution of Yugoslavia, is embedded in key ideological definitions and a corresponding frame of reference of jihadist propaganda materials, consisting of writings, and most appealing videos. While "the question, however, is always about how 'Weltanschauung' and 'ideologies' translate into individual perception and interpretation, and how the acts of individuals are affected" (Welzer 2011: 19), the agenda of global jihadism is heavily reliant on its media outlets to propagate and advocate proper religious conducts, further its inclusive and niche-covering ideology and provide role models the reader or viewer should re-enact or impose.

The media of *jihad*, fuelled by writings and videos of the war against the Soviets in Afghanistan, quickly developed capacities to recruit and motivate for the new scenario in southern Europe where "Croatian and Serbian Crusaders" were now further enemies. As had been the case during the Afghan-Jihad, magazines, writings, religious sermons and subsequently *jihad* videos showing atrocities committed against Muslims as well as first Mujahideen units fighting in Bosnia emerged, and were disseminated through existent networks established in the 80s.[25] This included English cassettes such as "In the Hearts of Green Birds" (Kohlmann, 2004: 53-69) or "Under the Shades

---

25 http://www.youtube.com/watch?v=th1pk36wb94&feature=related, video excerpts showing the address of the British Mujahideen in English, calling for recruits, money and any possible support. Kohlmann describes the first speaker, Abu Ibrahim, as a "21-year-old third-year medical student at Birmingham University living in Golders Green, London" (Kohlmann 2005: 94).

of Swords"[26] where the biographies of martyrs were portrayed and later enhanced by mostly Arabic writings and films. The portrayed Mujahideen seek either victory (*nasr*) or, more importantly, death (Prucha 2010a: 39). Being killed on the path of God (*fi sabil l-llah*) is accredited to the outmost act of confessing one's conviction and belief (*shahada*) while being recompensed in the afterlife by God (Prucha 2010b: 59-61).[27] Adhering to the propagated individual obligation (*fard ayn*) of fighting and defending not only Muslim civilians but rather seeking the liberation of occupied Islamic territories plays a vital role in the jihadist religious habitus and frame of reference.

Jihadist propaganda materials have various genres, ranging from highly ideological writings to practical military handbooks or bomb-making manuals,[28] and in combination with the *movies of jihad*, practical role models are advertised that are sought for re-enactment. The propaganda depicts presumed theological obligations every Muslim should fulfil. These are portrayed by jihadi scholars who claim authoritative-religious roles and subsequently establish a monopoly of truth over the interpretation (*ta'wil*) over Islamic sources and its history within the written and filmed corpus of jihadist propaganda (Prucha 2011: 44).

The fate of the conflict in Bosnia served as a common denominator to apply grievances and oppression as known in other parts of the Islamic world, foremost Palestine, to southern Europe where the conflict against Islam was now perhaps even more attractive due to the propagated enmity of Christian armies killing, torturing and raping Muslims while ethnically cleansing Islamic territory – with Western European countries standing by and not intervening to end the slaughter of civilians. This enabled a fluent rhetoric for incitement and recruitment.

The frame of reference and the media work of the veterans from Afghanistan was now applied to Bosnia and coming into effect by collecting martyr tales, and shooting videos in the field of operations after the first Arabs arrived in May-June 1992 (al-Qatari/al-Madani 2002: 7).

---

26 http://www.ummah.com/forum/showthread.php?79293-In-the-Hearts-of-Green-Birds (with transcriptions of exemplary martyr stories); http://www.islamicawakening.com/viewarticle.php?articleID=200.
27 As based on the interpretation of Quran 3:169 by jihadists.
28 Bomb-making materials are in great parts written in academic styles, with the introduction usually outlining specific theological degrees, sanctioning attacks. See for example the English-Language jihadist magazine *Inspire* (first edition) that offers its readers a simple recipe to "Make a Bomb in the Kitchen of your Mom" (Inspire 2010: 33-40). The process is embedded in the jihadists' doctrinal frame of reference, which in this magazine is advertised in bright colours and 'easy talk'.

This, again, includes the constant reminder that jihad is not only deemed an individual obligation (*fard ayn*)[29] among other parameters, but the thorough detailing of crimes – unpunished – against Muslim civilians adds a highly emotional fundament.

In a major publication entitled "Of the Stories of the Arab Martyrs in Bosnia-Herzegovina" (*min qissas al-shuhada' al-Arab fi l-Busna wa-l Hirsik*), edited by Majid al-Madani and his colleague Hamd al-Qatari,[30] detailed reports on "crimes committed by the Serbs against the Bosnian Muslims" (pp. 19-25) and a general introduction to the Mujahideen (pp. 6-17) are tied to an action – reaction scheme. While the Serbs killed and humiliated the Muslims of Bosnia, Western states upheld the "charade of The Hague War Crimes Tribunal" disguising atrocities committed against Muslims. The authors ask whether or not "this is a real court" and if so, "what would be the intention of the European Christians to trial their Croat and Serbian brothers?" Women, placed in concentration camps, were subject to systematic rape and torture, while Serbian militias gruesomely slaughtered Muslims, depopulating whole Muslim villages. "The Serbian dogs raped Muslim women without any restrain. The number of raped Muslimas outreached 50,000. Every truth is documented by the witness accounts by the Research and Documentation Center in Sarajevo" (al-Qatari/al-Madani 2002: 19-20). The reaction, a *fard ayn*, to safeguard and protect Muslims began "with the spreading of the news of the slaughtering and the crimes committed by the rotten Serbs and their expanding stench, the first defenders of the Arab Mujahideen arrived, coming from Afghanistan, two months after the war broke out in the Balkans" (al-Qatari/al-Madani 2002: 7).

The Islamic Territory of Bosnia-Herzegovina under Attack

The cases of rape and concentration camps elevated fears and threats of direct warfare against Muslims by campaigns of ethnic cleansing, with the implication of systematically destructing historical Islamic territory, implementing a 'de-Islamisation' by Christian-crusader armies with the alleged

---

29 As defined, set and established by several ideologues, foremost by Abdallah Azzam. Recently, after the death of Osama bin Laden, the theological *fard ayn* concept was recapitulated and propagated by the remaining (as of June 2011) ideologues and commanders, such as Abu Yahya al-Libi, Attiyattullah al-Libi, Ayman al-Zawahiri, or, Azzam al-Amriki. Arguing by the *fard ayn* concept among other theological and historical notions, individual terrorist acts against the West – inside western countries – are stressed and termed as an obligation for any true believer by AQ senior leadership. *La tukallifu ila nafsaka,* as-Sahab Media Productions, June 2011.

30 Available online at: http://www.saaid.net/book/133.zip. The book is introduced by the foreword of Saudi scholar Salman al-Awda.

backing and support of Christian-majority countries in the West. "In regard of the Crusader-Serbs, and all of Crusader-Europe, Islam was indeed on the verge by the hand of the Ottomans" (Qutb 1992: 17) and remains a potent and active threat.[31] The Jihadists' propaganda was quick to perceive such a threat for Muslims in the Balkans with the tactical advantage of Bosnia as an ideal basis to expand into European countries. The "unique geographic position directly between Western Europe and the Middle East was the ideal jumping-off point for organisational expansion of various Muslim extremists movements into the United Kingdom, Italy, France, and even Scandinavia" (Kohlmann 2006: 2).[32]

Ironically described as a shock, and intended as further proof of the religious background of the Balkan war, the stories of foreign fighters, driven by religious motifs, embedded with the Serbs are provided to stress and hasten one's commitment for the 'Islamic cause'. "Christian Orthodox states supported the Serbs. Russia sent 400 railway carriages full of ammunition and there had been plenty of volunteers to fight against Islam and defend Christianity as well. The Christian-Orthodox volunteers only joined ranks with their Serb brothers, including volunteer delegations of fighters from Bulgaria, Hungary, Russia and Cyprus, including Communist mercenaries from Iraq" (al-Qatari/al-Madani 2002: 14).

Since Islam in its specific understanding and interpretation by jihadists is under attack, Islamic territories (*dar al-Islam*) are highly relevant and must be first and foremost protected (Azzam 1983: 10, Holtmann 2009: 33). This protective stance comprises missionary means (*da'wah*), the "true understanding of religion" with the aim of broadening influence of a specific interpretation. Subsequently, propagated ideals and rulings are implemented, and issues of conquest, occupation, neo-colonisation and murder of Muslims worldwide are addressed. In the militant extremist sense, the aim of conducting *da'wah* concludes seeking recruits for a violent *jihad* at the same time with the appeal of changing oneself (mentally and physically) into a *Mujahid* with all its proscribed theological and historical dimensions with the aspired reward of gaining entry into Paradise.

At the start of the war and the dissolution of Yugoslavia,

"the Yugoslav army besieged and destroyed parts of Slovenia, who are Catholics, as well as Christian-Orthodox Serbs. Europe supported the Slovenians until their declaration of independence and immediately recognised [the proclaimed state].

---

31 Qutb then cites Wilfred Cantwell Smith's writing and builds his arguments on Smith's writing, published in 1959. In the hot phase of the Cold War, Communism is a threat and an enemy as much as Islam, for both ideologies are extremely dangerous for the West and must be – ultimately – combated by all means.

32 Evan Kohlmann: "The Afghan-Bosnian Mujahideen Network in Europe", available online at www.aina.org/reports/tabmnie.pdf.

Shortly thereafter, the Croats declared their independence and the Serbs mounted their army, in direction of the Croatian cowards, who received full support by Europe with all its might – as they are Catholics. But when the independence of Bosnia-Herzegovina was declared by the military leader Alija Izetbegovic, the Serbs occupied three zones in Croatia as protection areas for their army and directed armed detachments against Bosnia while both the Croats and the Slovenes facilitated weapons and support" (al-Madani/Qatari 2002: 7).[33]

It seems that Muslims once again, just like in Chechnya and particularly Palestine, fell victim to non-Islamic occupational forces whose strategy included a systematic eradication of Islam from a historical Islamic territory. The ideological parameters were clearly set and combined with reports and video footage, partially taken from international news media outlets, to incite and recruit in order to fulfil the obligation to defend Muslim civilians and to repel Christian armies defined as "Crusaders."

Bosnia in the Contemporary Understanding of Jihadists

Bosnia was included in the jihadi propaganda writings – and subsequently in videos shot in Bosnia by fighters – and is re-emerging and present in contemporary jihadi materials. Despite the setbacks suffered by the Arab foreign fighters after the war ended, many Arab foreign fighters stayed after the Dayton Peace Agreement was signed. The war in the Balkans and the networking it enabled furthered the global jihadi endeavours. The media outlets and the awareness of the conflict in 1980s Afghanistan, crafted by the combination of appealing videos alongside doctrinal writings, serve as a role model of jihadist missionary work to this very day. The means of the internet nowadays facilitate professional propaganda that is consequently conducted and decidedly organised. The victorious Mujahideen of the 1980s and their increasing independent networks learned their lessons and started investing time and proficiency for their media-work, which, after all, is part of the greater understanding of the theological dimensions of "jihad". Bosnia enabled various jihadists groups to build a network that consisted of fighters, ideologues and media-workers that were now channelling money and weapons much more clandestine by using NGOs as frontrunners and who welcomed new recruits into their ranks. Afghanistan was an 'Islamic Cause' – unlike Palestine – where individuals could fight for the defence of occupied Islamic territory. For Bosnia a similar notion was applied with the difference that the Muja-

---

33 The text continues that Izetbegovic made a public radio and TV announcement "declaring to the Bosnian people the start of a guerrilla war as no Bosnian army existed. Every one, in the streets, the provinces and the villages must defend themselves until Muslims will fill their ranks."

hideen community was perhaps much more internationalised and consisted of older veterans who now guided, instructed and indoctrinated a new generation of jihadis. The proximity to Europe and the propagated religious clash between Christians and Muslims was, on a broader scope, highly appealing and inspired young men to join – particularly from Europe. Many former fighters of Arabian origin remain in Bosnia, having married or acquired Bosnian citizenship by other means, such as a reward for having fought with the Bosnian Army. The doctrine and the Islamic interpretations of the mainly Arab foreign fighters introduced by the Mujahideen remains, even if only marginalised. "The Serbian aggression was viewed as a Christian assault on a Muslim population, even though most Bosnian Muslims were highly secularised and did not strongly identify with Islam. A 1985 poll indicated that a mere 17 percent of Bosnia's Muslims considered themselves as believers in Islam" (Calvert 2011: 33). However, small enclaves exist in Bosnia, where the extreme interpretation is valued and, to varying degrees, being implemented. The notion may be increasing of perceiving oneself – the true believer in contrast to the masses who have been led astray – as part of a growing global community of jihadists, who are fighting against the West and its influences. The recent attack on the US Embassy in Sarajevo, when a lone gunman armed with an AK-47 assault rifle opened fire on the embassy building, is embedded and incorporated into the jihadist online propaganda with the aims and hopes of reviving the jihad in the Balkans. Named a "martyrdom seeker" (*istishhadi*) in a posting of the *al-Shumukh* jihad forum, the attacker is cherished accordingly.[34]

Bosnia remains active as a narration of grievances suffered worldwide by Muslims due to various reasons with the uniting element that jihadist propaganda usually point out a global anti-Islamic conspiracy at work. The individual duty consists of abandoning ones perception as a victim and to start striking – within the ideological frame of reference – against the defined enemies and apostates who are ruling contrary to what God commanded.

The jihad in Bosnia in the understanding by contemporary jihadi scholars has been a complete failure. The signing of the Dayton Peace Agreement in 1995 led to the installation of a pro-western, non-Islamic government while most parts of the war took place within a UN-framework. Comparing the Bosnian situation to post-Gaddafi Libya,

"we do not want a recurrence of what happened to the Mujahideen before. Particularly, what occurred in Bosnia-Herzegovina during the battles of liberation against the crusading Serbs, where the Arab and non-Arab Mujahideen joined the fight. In the end, betrayal and treason resulted in the extradition, imprisonment or

---

34 http://shamikh1.info/vb/showthread.php?t=133577

murder of the Mujahideen and the fruits of *their jihad*[35] had been harvested by the installation of a secular government, controlled by the Crusader West – while the firebrand of *jihad* is extinguished, fearing the declaration of an Islamic state led or supported by those Mujahideen" (al-Amili 2011: 6-7).[36]

The jihadi media outlets and their ideologues propagate a 'return home' with the local Arab regimes finally being swept away. In the jihadists understanding – traditionally neglecting anything else but a specific universe of principles of faith – the Arab Spring is comprised of Jihadists and Islamists alike who will now have the power to initiate the rebooting of the Caliphate. An imagined statehood entity that will protect all Muslims and guarantee the 'proper' inter-pretation of Islam is being finally implemented – thus being the ultimate salvation and a restoration of former might.

Bibliography

Al-Amili, Abu Sa'ad (2011): al-Thawrat al-Libiyya (The Libyan Revolution), Part One, Mu'assasat al-Mas'ada li-l-i'lamiyya.

Azzam, Abdallah (1983): al-Difa' an aradi l-Muslimin aham furud al-ay'ian, Minbar al-Tawhid wa-l Jihad.

Azzam, Abdallah (no year): Muqaddima fi l-hijra wa-l idad.

Anas, Abdallah (2002): Waladat al-afghan al-arab – sira Abdallah Anas bayna Masud wa-Abdallah Azzam, Dar al-Saqi.

Calvert, John (2011): Regional Struggle in the Shadow of Pan-Islamic Militancy: Exam-ples from Indonesia and Bosnia, in: ORIENT, IV/2011, pp. 31-35.

Al-Harbi, Abu al-Mundhir (ed.) (2010): Awn al-hakim al-khabir fi l-radd ala kitab "al-burhan al-munir fi dahd shabahat ahl al-takfir wa-l tafjir", Second Edition, Global I-slamic Media Front.

Hegghammer, Thomas (2010): Jihad in Saudi Arabia – Violence and Pan-Islamism since 1979. Cambridge: Cambridge University Press.

Holtmann, Philipp (2009): Abu Mus'ab al-Suri's Jihad Concept. The Moshe Dayan Center.

Itani, Fida (2008): al-Jihadiyyun fi Lubnan – min "Quwat al-Fajr" ila "Fatah al-Islam". Dar al-Saqi.

Kissinger, Henry (1994): Diplomacy. Touchstone.

Kohlmann, Evan (2005): Al-Qaida's Jihad in Europe: The Afghan-Bosnian Network. Ox-ford, New York: Berg.

Kohlmann, Evan (2006): "The Afghan-Bosnian Mujahideen Network in Europe", available online at www.aina.org/reports/tabmnie.pdf.

---

35 i.e. the outcome of war.

36 He concludes: "I believe the scenario in Libya is different than in Bosnia and rather unlikely of being repeated. The situation gravely differs on numerous aspects; regarding the [different] nature of the Libyans and Bosnians, the geography, or the history of these two peoples: Libyans have adopted a number of initial [religious] invulnerabilities; they are [Sunni] Muslims well-kept [in their belief]; their noble jihadist history; the geographical position, next to Algeria and its neighboring countries where the Organisation al-Qa'ida of the Islamic Maghrib (AQIM) is present. For Libya is part of this Islamic Maghreb, as it is known."

Lawrence, Bruce (2005): Messages to the World – the Statements of Osama bin Laden. London, New York: Verso.

Lia, Brynjar (2008): Architect of Global Jihad – The Life of Al-Qaida Strategist Abu Mus'ab al-Suri. New York: Columbia University Press.

Al-Madani, Majid / al-Qatari, Hamd (2002): Min qissas al-shuhada al-Arab fi l-Busna wa-l Hirsik. www.saaid.net

Prucha, Nico (2010b): Notes on the Jihadists' Motivation for Suicide-Operations. In: Journal for Intelligence, Propaganda and Security Studies, Vol. 4, Nr.1, pp. 57-68, http://www.univie.ac.at/jihadism/blog/wp-content/uploads/2011/03/Prucha_1.pdf

Prucha, Nico (2011): Online Territories of Terror. In: ORIENT, IV/2011, pp. 43-48.

Prucha, Nico (2010a): Sawt al-Jihad – die Stimme des Dschihad – al-Qa'idas. In: Erstes Online Magazin, Verlag Dr. Kovac

Qutb, Muhammad (1992): Durus min mihna al-Busna wa-l Hirsik. Minbar al-Tawhid wa-l Jihad, http://tawhed.ws/dl?i=3dgishf4

Al-Shu'aybi, Hamud bin Uqla (1999): al-Qawla al-mukhtar fi hukm al-isti'anat bi-l kuffar. Minbar al-Tawhed wa-l Jihad

Sipri (2007): United Nations Arms Embargoes – Their Impact on Arms Flows and Target Behaviour. Uppsala Universitet, Department of Peace and Conflict Research.

Sorg, Eugen (2011): Die Lust am Bösen – Warum Gewalt nicht heilbar ist. München: Nagel & Kimche im Carl Hanser Verlag.

Tuhhan, Ahmad (2007): al-Harakat al-Islamiyya bayna 'l-fitna wa-l jihad. Dar al-Marefah

Securing the External Borders of the EU – The Role of Frontex

Arnold H. Kammel

Securing and policing the European Union's (EU) external borders, comprising of 42,672 km of sea and 8,826 km of land borders respectively, and coordinating the efforts among Member States to this end are of utmost importance for the EU. Thus, it is not surprising that since the early beginnings of European cooperation in the area of justice and home affairs, there has been the vision of an internal market without internal borders, allowing the free movement of goods, persons, services and capital. In 1985, on an intergovernmental level and outside the existing legal framework, the Schengen Agreement was concluded with the main objective of abolishing the internal border controls on persons (Article 2 of the Schengen Convention). This approach was later reflected on in drafting both the Maastricht and Amsterdam Treaties (Corrado 2006: 184). Subsequently, the so-called Schengen acquis was then incorporated into the EU legal framework with the Treaty of Amsterdam of 1997. However, its application has remained diverse due to different national caveats in Member States such as Ireland, Great Britain and Denmark. Nonetheless, EU membership does not automatically admit a new member state to the Schengen area.

As a consequence of the Schengen acquis, on the one hand, the internal borders of the Schengen area have been abolished, making controls obsolete as a consequence but replacing them by thorough controls at the external borders. On the other hand, the Schengen Borders Code (SBC), substituting the 1985 Schengen Agreement and the 1990 Schengen Implementing Agreement (SIA) was adopted by the European Parliament and the Council in 2006. It sets out the rules governing border controls on persons crossing the external borders of the Member States of the EU. In this context, border control itself is defined as 'activities carried out at a border, in response exclusively to an intention to cross a border, and consisting of border checks and border surveillance' (European Union 2009: 3).

In Article 17 of the SIA, the Member States are authorised to jointly control the EU's external borders and to conclude agreements for that purpose. Thus the Agreement harmonises the conditions under which people can legally enter the EU, but it also lays down the conditions according to which a person can be denied access to the EU territory. However, the SBC goes even further by requiring border guards to 'fully respect human dignity' and not to discriminate against persons (Article 6). Generally, the code can best be described as a set of norms and conditions carefully balanced to promote common rules and work habits, but not to such a degree that the rules would infringe on the authority of Member States (Marenin 2010: 90).

Integrated Border Management (IBM)

Nonetheless, the whole issue of Schengen has to be seen in a much broader context, namely the EU policies related to integrated border management – an issue controversially debated among Member States due to the fact that some of the states are directly at the external borders, and thus have the responsibility of securing them, whereas others remained in the inner circle of the Union without possessing external borders. Integrated Border Management is understood as 'the organisation and supervision of border agency activities to meet the common challenge of facilitating the movement of legitimate people and goods while maintaining secure borders and meeting national legal requirements' (World Bank Group 2005: 1).

It was the merit of the Laeken European Council of December 2001 having sensed these tensions and initiated a discussion on this new topic called 'integrated border management', which would take into account the interests of both members on the external border and others far away from it (Hobbing 2005: 1). The Laeken European Council Conclusions of December 14 and 15, 2001 asked the Council and the Commission to: '[...] work out arrangements for cooperation between services responsible for external border control and to examine the conditions in which a mechanism or common services to control external borders could be created'(European Council 2001: 12). In response, the Commission elaborated and published its 2002 Communication on integrated management of the external borders. In this communication, reference was first made to the establishment of a 'common corpus of legislation' in relation to the management of the common Schengen borders (European Commission 2002: 12). The development of border management policies by the EU and its Member States is – as described above – historically linked with the development of the internal market, and has acquired a security dimension over the years. In order to establish efficient and sustainable border management policies, a comprehensive approach is applied, combining control mechanisms and tools based on the flows of persons into the EU. Having said that, border management cannot be solved at the borders alone, but needs to include the relevant agencies within countries, at the borders and in other countries to meet the basic Schengen and EU standards for granting full border services. Thus, as Marenin points out, control systems must be effective, be adjusted to the specifics of risks and threats faced, and be based on best practices and experiences taken from reforms in prior-accession and candidate countries (Marenin 2010: 68).

With respect to the competences in the area of integrated border management, the Amsterdam Treaty and the end of the transition period on May 1, 2004, stipulated that border management effectively became a shared competence between the EU and its Member States, whereas other aspects related to integrated border management remained under the third pillar, such as police and judicial cooperation in criminal matters in particular (Wolff 2010: 25).

According to the Conclusions of December 4 and 5, 2006 of the Justice and Home Affairs Council (JHA), the framework for an integrated approach of external borders contains the following dimensions:

- Border control (checks and surveillance) including risk analysis and crime intelligence;
- Detecting and investigating "cross-border crime" in cooperation with all the relevant law enforcement authorities;
- The four tier filter access control model, which, as stipulated in the EU Schengen Catalogue of 2002, includes measures in third countries of origin or transit, cooperation with neighbouring countries, measures of border control at the external borders and control measures within the common area of free movement;
- Inter-agency cooperation in border management including border guards, customs officers, police officers, and other national security officers or otherwise relevant authorities; and
- Coordination and coherence at the national and transnational level.

With the entry into force of the Lisbon Treaty on December 1, 2009, the pillar structure was formally abolished and the remaining areas of JHA of the former third pillar were integrated into the supranational community pillar. Even though the Treaty of Lisbon has meant the formal abolition of the pillar divide in the EU's area of freedom, security and justice (ASFJ) and a substantial expansion of the Community method of cooperation, EU agencies like Frontex and Europol have presented several features, practices and political ambitions that bring back the 'third pillar spirit' (European Parliament 2011: 109). Therefore, it seems to be worth taking a closer look at the European border agency Frontex.

History of Frontex and its Tasks and Key Facts

In comparison to the original concept of a European border guard, Frontex may appear a more modest achievement, provided that it foresees no direct operational assignments (Hobbing 2005: 18). The European Agency for the Management of Operational Cooperation at the External Borders of the Member States of the European Union was established by Council Regulation (EC) No. 2007/2004 of October 26, 2004 (Official Journal L 349 of November 25, 2004, henceforth "Frontex Regulation") with regard to the Treaty establishing the European Community aimed at controlling irregular migration especially at the external borders of the EU. Here it is worth citing the basic aim of the agency in full:

> 'While considering that the responsibility for the control and surveillance of external borders lies with the Member States, the Agency shall facilitate and render more effective the application of existing and future Community measures relating to the management of external borders. It shall do so by ensuring the coordination of Member States' actions in the implementation of those measures, thereby contributing to an efficient, high and uniform level of control on persons and surveillance of the external borders of the Member States' (Article 1).

Its tasks are listed in Article 2 of the regulation as follows:

- Coordinate operational cooperation between Member States in the field of management of external borders;
- Assist Member States on training of national border guards, including the establishment of common training standards;
- Carry out risk analysis;
- Follow up on the development of research relevant for the control and surveillance of external borders;
- Assist Member States in circumstances requiring increased technical and operational assistance at external borders;
- Provide Member States with the necessary support in organizing joint return operations.

To ensure EU-wide coherence of operational border management, Frontex has been given the competence over:

- Evaluating the results of joint operations (including the establishment of a comparative analysis in view of enhancing the quality, coherence and efficiency of future operations (Article 3.3);
- Co-financing such operations (Article 3.4);
- Developing and applying a common integrated risk analysis (Article 4);
- Establishing a common core curriculum for border guards' training (Article 5);

- Following the development of research related to control and surveillance equipment and disseminating results to Member States (Article 6);
- Providing organisational and operational assistance to Member States in cases of need and at their request, including the deployment of its experts for support (Article 8); and
- Facilitating operational cooperation with third countries (Article 13).

The Agency's tasks can be described as both 'operational cooperation and coordination' and 'capacity building by training, research and development' (Laitinen 2008: 31).

Warsaw has been determined as the seat of the Agency by Council Decision 2005/358/EC of April 26, 2005.

Lastly, Article 33 requires that the management board 'commissions an independent external evaluation on the implementation of this Regulation' three years after the agency has begun its work and every five years thereafter, to assess 'how effectively the Agency fulfils its mission', and 'the impact of the Agency and its working practices'. This evaluation has been carried out by a Danish company, submitting its report in 2009. However, the report did not examine the agency's compliance with fundamental rights or rule of law. The new Frontex Regulation now includes an explicit requirement in Article 33.2(b) suggesting that the next evaluation of Frontex to be carried out 'shall include a specific analysis on the way the Charter of Fundamental Rights was respected pursuant to the application of the Regulation' (European Parliament 2011a: 25).

In terms of operational productivity, 2010 saw an increase in operational intensity despite a reduced operational budget. According to the Frontex Annual Report 2010 the Agency's overall budget rose in 2010, but the net amount allocated to operational activities (Pilot Projects and Joint operations) fell marginally, from 48.2 million euro to 47.4 million euro. Despite this fact, the number of operational man hours rose by about 27% to 6,411, well over twice the stated objective of an 11% increase in productivity. This heightened efficiency was made possible due to increased commitment of human and technical resources made available by the Member States and Schengen-Associated Countries participating in operational activities, which numbered 28 in all in 2010 (Frontex 2010: 13).

In 2010, the Annual Report 2010 provides that the Agency's budget increased to 92.8 million euro, i.e. by 5.2% compared to 2009. This increase is largely due to additional funding provided by the EU Commission for the RABIT Operation in Greece. Excluding the budget for RABIT, the Agency's budget increase would have been only 1.2%. In a four years' perspective comparing the budgets from 2006 to 2009, it can be noted that the percentage increase in budget amounted to 360%. As the report states, this increase led to consumption challenges, as the Agency's annual financial cycle differs from the operational one. The increase in budget for 2010 by 5.2% was more modest and, due to the concerted approach taken by the different units within the Agency, the utilisation of the funds by December 31, 2010 rose significantly, to 69%, although the final actual utilisation will be much higher since Frontex has the opportunity to make payments on carry-over appropriations until December 31, 2011 (Frontex 2010: 20). The number of staff rose from 43 to 294 at the end of 2010. Currently, 289 staff members are working for the Agency. With regard to equipment, Frontex reported that it possessed 26 helicopters, 22 light aircraft and 113 vessels in February 2010 (Keller et. al. 2011: 7).

The Legal Nature of FRONTEX and Remedy on European Level

Frontex is a semi-supranational body, having its own legal personality and operational as well as budgetary autonomy, but being reliant on Member States for operational mandates, equipment and finances and subject to the national law of the Member State in which the Agency operates (Fiott 2011: 2). Frontex was conceived as an agency of the EU and can therefore be considered a decentralised entity based on European public law with legal personality. In the pre-Lisbon era the agency was based in the first pillar especially on Art. 62 (2) lit a TEC, stipulating the adoption of measures on the crossing of the external borders of the Member States and thereby establishing standards and procedures to be followed by Member States in carrying out checks on persons at such borders, and on Article 66 TEC, enabling the Council to take measures to ensure cooperation between the relevant departments of the administrations of the Member States in Justice and Home Affairs. Despite being based on the principle of subsidiarity, it would still be in the competences of the Member States to implement the rules set out in the Treaties except for the case that the objectives of the measures could better be implemented on the European level.

Following the logic of Article 28 (5) of the Frontex regulation, it is foreseen that any decision or action of the agency may give rise to the lodging of a complaint to the Ombudsman or form the subject of an action before the Court of Justice of the European Communities, under the conditions laid down in Articles 195 and 230 of the Treaty respectively. On a Member State level the exercise of executive powers by the Agency's staff and the Member States' experts acting on the territory of another Member State shall be subject to the national law of that Member State.

A number of new rules for Frontex were finally agreed by the Council on October 10, 2011 as a follow-up of a revision process which began in 2010.

Indeed, after inter-institutional and public consultations, the Member States agreed that the Agency needed to provide a better standard of integrated management of external borders through uniform and high level surveillance and to better protect the fundamental rights of those entering the EU (European Commission 2010: 13). Among these new tasks are the following (Fiott 2011: 2):

- the Council has agreed that Frontex can buy or lease its own equipment such as cars, vessels and helicopters, or to buy such equipment in co-ownership with any single or group of Member States, with the full inventory of equipment registered in a Technical Equipment Pool (TEP);
- there is now the possibility that on the basis of agreement between Frontex and the Member States, the Agency can request border guards and equipment from national authorities;
- the Frontex Agency assumes a co-leading role in joint operations and pilot projects through the deployment of European Border Guard Teams (EBGTs), who will replace the Rapid Border Intervention Teams (RABITs);
- in terms of its operational capacities Frontex is now able to draw up detailed provision plans (i.e. control over the composition of the EBGTs as well as command and control structures) and conduct risk analysis on the capacities of Member States to meet border challenges;
- Frontex can now lead training and research under common core curricula for national border guards and launch technical assistance projects in third-countries.

RABITs and Frontex Operations

In 2007, the Frontex Regulation was amended by the Regulation (EC) No 863/2007 of the European Parliament and of the Council of July 11, 2007 establishing the Rapid Border Intervention Teams (RABIT) for technical and operational assistance to Member States in mass influx situations at the external borders of the Union. Moreover, the powers of guest officers participating in joint operations were regulated. The RABIT were established as specially trained border guards from EU Member States being deployable at short notice in emergency situations. Following the logic of Article 12 of the RABIT regulation, Frontex operations would no longer be restricted to advisory functions but could perform border guard tasks together with host officers, under the command of the border guard authority of the host country. The deployment of RABITs is very much in the hands of the director of the agency as they may send a team of experts to assess the situation in the requesting Member State (Article 8d.1), and shall take into account 'the findings of the Agency's risk analyses as well as other relevant information' provided by the requesting member state.

All operations carried out are planned and executed by the operations unit of the Agency. The Frontex unit responsible for coordinating these actions is divided into four sectors: three sectors dealing with the operational cooperation at the air, land and sea borders respectively and one sector responsible for providing assistance to Member States organizing return operations. Already since the establishment of the agency, the expectations have been especially high regarding the coordination of operations at the southern maritime border.

Within the Frontex Regulation there are three kinds of scenarios that can lead to the decision to engage in a joint operation at sea (Article 3 (1)). The first one is a proposal of the Agency itself based on facts identified in a risk analysis conducted by Frontex. In a situation of 'urgent and exceptional [migratory] pressure' at the borders of a Member State or a country with which Frontex has signed an agreement, the Agency can also deploy the above mentioned RABITs.

The second possibility is that a Member State makes a proposal for a joint operation or a pilot project. It comprises 'joint return operations' (JROs), which have increased considerably in number (1,622 persons returned in 2009, compared with 428 in 2007). Moreover, the Agency's budget for coordinating JRO flights has risen from 0.5 million euro in 2005 to over 7 million euro in 2010. Frontex will evaluate the proposal before it decides whether or not it will co-finance the operation in the form of a grant (Article 3 section 4 Frontex Regulation). Joint operations are proposed by Frontex based on a risk analysis conducted by its staff. Every year, the Risk Analysis Unit of Frontex produces the so-called Annual Risk Assessment (ARA) giving an overview of the irregular migration across the EU and including recommendations and specific conclusions. Once the director approves, a proposal is passed to the relevant Member States, which are invited to a planning meeting; once all agree that a JRO should be launched, an operational plan is developed listing tasks, goals, contributors and needed equipment. A Frontex coordinator is assigned to monitor the implementation of the project, but operational lead stays with the main host country (Marenin 2010: 108).

The last scenario is that a Member State requests an operation, because it faces a particular situation requiring assistance.

In the two latter instances the needs and requirements of the concrete situation are evaluated by Frontex in a risk assessment. The results of this assessment are then discussed with the Member States involved. Other Member States are then requested if they are willing to participate in the operation and asked to specify their offers regarding personnel and material. These offers are evaluated against the background of the concrete identified needs, and

with the input from participating Member States the operational plan is final-
ised.

In late October 2010, Frontex for the first time received a request from a
Member State for a deployment of Rapid Border Intervention Teams (RA-
BITs). This request also marked the litmus test of the agency due to the fact
that despite a number of preparatory exercises to test and enhance the deployment mechanism, the necessary procedures had never been put to the test
in reality. Therefore it has to be noted that already four days after the request
was achieved from the Greek government, the first guest officers arrived in
the crisis area. The subsequent four-month operation led to reduced irregular
migration at the Greek-Turkish land border. In terms of the daily average
numbers of irregular migrants crossing the border, between the first deployments in November 2010 and the end of the operation in March 2011, a
reduction by 76% was recorded. In terms of situational awareness, monitoring and reporting as well as inter-agency cooperation, the first RABIT
deployment can be seen as a full success (Frontex 2010: 26). However, the
success on the border control side was not coupled with favourable results on
the humanitarian one. According to Carrera/Guild 'The presentation of Frontex Operation RABIT 2010 as 'the solution' to the situation at the external
borders of Greece with Turkey illustrates the kind of responses that the EU
prioritises in situations such as those taking place in Greece: more security
(Frontex) and not going at the heart of the issue, which is that of human
rights protection of refugees and undocumented migrants' (see Carrera/Guild
2010: 15). RABIT was taken over by Joint Operation Poseidon which was
active in the area prior to the RABIT deployment and which lasted till the
end of March 2012. Besides Poseidon, the Agency has deployed JO Hermes
since March 1, 2011 to the Mediterranean and as a consequence of the Libyan crisis extended to Malta. Hermes was formed following a request from
Italy for assistance in managing the recent arrivals from Tunisia and migrants
from North Africa on the island of Lampedusa.

Conclusion: Securing Europe's Border or Fortress Europe?

The process of perfecting border management is sometimes seen as an integral part of a repressive strategy to make borders less permeable and
discourage the free movement of people. It is certainly true that IBM helps to
further some aspects of security through the EU-wide introduction of advanced equipment and coordinated communication/database structures
(Hobbing 2005: 22). Borders shall be a greater obstacle to those who are not
wanted inside the territory. Thus it is not surprising that especially the human
rights concern remains at stake. Already starting with the establishment of

the Agency, there have been criticisms voiced by the European Parliament and various NGOs on what they considered to be the fortress Europe. This issue is also very much related to the question of transparency of Frontex' action. As it is stated in a report edited by Green MEPs, 'the best guarantee that fundamental rights will be respected in procedures involving representatives of public authority is the transparency of those procedures. This principle is particularly relevant to FRONTEX operations given the potential for incidents to occur (especially during joint return operations) and the fact that these operations target vulnerable individuals' (Keller et.al. 2011: 44). Therefore some argued that the activities of FRONTEX should be submitted to a full evaluation of their impact on fundamental freedoms and rights, including the responsibility to protect human dignity (Jeandesboz 2008: 18).

These critics have been dealt with in the further development of the agency. On September 13, 2011, the European Parliament (EP) adopted new Frontex rules which were finally adopted by the Council under the co-decision procedure on October 10, 2011. Due to the fact that compliance with international human rights standards was considered one of Parliament's key objectives, the EP achieved the inclusion of new provisions to ensure full respect of human rights in all Frontex actions. One of the innovations is that the agency creates the post of a "fundamental rights officer" and sets up a "consultative forum on fundamental rights" to assist the agency's management board. The consultative forum will include the EU Fundamental Rights and Asylum Support agencies, the UN High Commissioner for Refugees and NGOs specializing in this field. Under the new framework, in the case of a violation of human rights, Frontex missions may be suspended or terminated. In addition, the agency's tasks will be extended and after the adoption include issues such as providing assistance to Member States in situations that may involve humanitarian emergencies and rescue at sea. Frontex will also develop codes of conduct to guarantee compliance with human rights in all its different types of missions, including return operations. This is a special reference to the international law rule that no person may be sent back or handed over to the authorities of a country where his/her life or freedoms could be threatened. Hence, according to the agreed text the agency will respect this principle of "non-refoulement" in all circumstances (European Parliament 2011b).

Securing Europe's external borders is perceived as one of the key tasks for ensuring a functioning internal market. Thus the ambiguous relationship between markets on the one hand and the respective policies to secure the freedom of the markets on the other has evolved. More than 25 years after the conclusion of the Schengen Agreement, the idea of a borderless Europe has produced striking developments, but there still remain significant issues regarding the free movement of third-country nationals, i.e. individuals who are not citizens of EU Member States (Maas 2005: 242). While the integration of Europe has granted freedom of movement inside the Schengen area, it has also hardened and given greater significance to the line between 'integrated Europe' and the rest of the world as the external borders of the Schengen zone have gained greater significance. Securing this region in terms of concrete policy formulation, however, is not only the task of Frontex, but rather lies within the responsibility of the Member States as indicated in the principle of subsidiarity. Therefore, it seems unfair just to blame Frontex for any action, because the agency serves more as a toolbox for securing the EU's external borders than as policy formulator.

However, the human dimension in this conflict between the idea of securing the freedoms of the internal market on the one hand and the concrete action taken at the external borders on the other needs to be examined more thoroughly, as the issue of migration will not disappear but become far more salient in the near future. Consequently, it is not surprising that the tasks and competences of Frontex have been extended, taking into account the various points of criticisms that have been raised with regard to its operations on the ground. But with the new rules to be adopted, further steps might be undertaken to pacify these critics. Nonetheless, these new rules need to be implemented and applied in practice. Finally, answering the overarching question whether the freedoms of the internal market should be either secured by making the EU a fortress or by keeping its border permeable, lies within the responsibility of the EU and its Member States and not within the realm of an agency.

References

Carrera, Sergio (2007): The EU Border Management Strategy. FRONTEX and the Challenges of Irregular Immigration in the Canary Islands, CEPS Working Document No. 261.

Carrera, Sergio/Guild, Elsbeth (2010): 'Joint Operation RABIT 2010' – FRONTEX Assistance to Greece's Border with Turkey: Revealing the Deficiencies of Europe's Dublin Asylum System, CEPS.

Corrado, Laura (2006): Negotiating the EU External Border. In: Balzacq, Thierry/Carrera, Sergio (eds.): Security versus Freedom? A Challenge for Europe's Future. London: Ashgate, pp. 183-203.

COWI (2009): External evaluation of the European Agency for the Management of Operational Cooperation at the External Borders of the Member States of the European Union. Final Report.

Fiott, Daniel (2011): The New Frontex: A Model for the Common Security and Defence Policy?, Madariaga Paper – Vol. 4, No. 11 (Oct., 2011).

European Commission (2010): Proposal for a regulation of the European Parliament and the Council amending Council Regulation (EC) No 2007/2004 establishing a European Agency for the Management of Operational Cooperation at the External Borders of the Member States of the European Union (FRONTEX), COM 2010 61 final (24 February 2010).

European Commission (2002): Commission Communication 'Towards Integrated Management of the External Borders of the Member States of the European Union', COM(2002) 233.

European Council (2001): Presidency Conclusions of the Laeken European Council, 14 and 15 December 2001, Doc. Nr. 00300/1/01.

European Parliament (2011a): Implementation of the EU Charter of Fundamental Rights and its Impact on EU Home Affairs Agencies. Frontex, Europol and the European Asylum Support Office.

European Parliament (2011b): FRONTEX: New human rights watchdog, new powers, Press release, Reference No:20110913IPR26455.

European Union (2009) 'Community code on the rules governing the movement of persons across borders (Schengen Borders Code). Activities of the European Union, summaries of legislation.' Available at http://europa.eu/legislation_summaries/justice_freedom_security/free_movement_of_persons_asylum_immigration/l14514_en.htm [02 November 2011]

Frontex (2010): General Report 2010, Warsaw.

Hobbing, Peter (2005): Integrated Border Management at EU Level. CEPS Working Document No. 225.

Jeandesboz, Julien (2008): Reinforcing the Surveillance of EU Borders. The Future Development of FRONTEX and EUROSUR, Research Paper No. 11.

Keller, Ska/Lunacek, Ulrike/Lochbihler, Barbara/Flautre, Hélène (eds.) (2011): Frontex agency: which guarantees for human rights?, Brussels: Migreurop.

Laitinen, Ilka (2008): Frontex. An Inside View., EIPASCOPE 2008/3, pp. 31-34.

Maas, Willem (2005): Freedom of movement inside 'fortress Europe'. In: Zureik, Elia/Salter, Mark B. (eds.): Global Surveillance and Policing. Borders, Security, Identity. Portland: Willan Publishing, pp. 233-245.

Marenin, Otwin (2010): Challenges for Integrated Border Management in the European Union, Geneva Centre for the Democratic Control of Armed Forces (DCAF), Occasional Paper – №17.

Möllers, Rosalie (2010): Wirksamkeit und Effektivität der Europäschen Agentur FRONTEX, Frankfurt: Verlag für Polizeiwissenschaft.

Wolff, Sarah (2010): EU Integrated Border Management Beyond Lisbon: Contrasting Policies and Practice, pp.23-36.

World Bank Group (2005): Integrated Border Management, GFP Explanatory Notes.

Environmental Protection: Global Challenges for the EU

Klaus Fischer

Introduction: Europe's Environmental Situation – an Overall View

In its report on "The European Environment – State and Outlook 2010" the European Environment Agency (EEA) draws the following picture of Europe's environmental situation:

"Environmental policy in the European Union and its neighbours has delivered substantial improvements to the state of the environment. However, major environmental challenges remain which will have significant consequences for Europe if left unaddressed. What differs in 2010, compared to previous EEA European environment – State and outlook reports, is an enhanced understanding of the links between environmental challenges combined with unprecedented global megatrends. This has allowed a deeper appreciation of the human-made systemic risks and vulnerabilities which threaten ecosystem security, and insight into the shortcomings of governance" (EEA 2010a: 9).

Prospects of further developments are "mixed", the EEA points out, putting forward what it calls 10 key messages which can be summarised as follows:

Europe uses more and more natural resources to meet the demands of its economy and its people, resulting in a "significant environmental footprint in Europe and elsewhere" (EEA 2010a: 9). Then, there is the challenge of what Menne and Ebi call "climate-related impacts" (Menne/Ebi 2006: 2), a term used for the combined effects of natural climate variability patterns and "climate change", i.e. of human contribution to these patterns. The EEA sees keeping average global temperature increases below 2°C which is regarded by the Intergovernmental Panel on Climate Change (IPCC) to be sufficient to avoid irreversible effects of climate-related impacts at risk. It calls for greater efforts in both cutting greenhouse gas emissions (mitigation) and implementing measures to cope with unavoidable effects of climate-related impacts (adaptation). As the EEA points out despite a number of environmental protection programmes being in place as well as a wide-spread net of protected areas, Europe still faces major challenges to nature and biodiversity. A variety of ecosystems is threatened by degradation, leading to a loss of biodiversity. Also, the use of natural resources and methods of waste treatment need to be further improved (EEA 2010a: 9). As all these problems are closely related to each other the EEA calls for an "integrating concept for dealing with environmental pressures from multiple sectors. Spatial planning, resource accounting and coherence among sectoral policies implemented at all scales can help balance the need to preserve natural capital and use it to fuel the economy. A more integrated approach of this sort would also provide a framework for measuring progress more broadly and underpin coherent analyses across multiple policy targets" (EEA 2010a: 9).

The EU Commission, in its communication "A resource-efficient Europe – Flagship initiative under the Europe 2020 Strategy" published on January 26, 2011 draws a similar picture, laying stress on the concept of efficient use of natural resources which it says will bring about both ecological and economic benefits:

"Using resources more efficiently will help us achieve many of the EU's objectives. It will be key in making progress to deal with climate change and to achieve our target of reducing EU greenhouse gas emissions by 80 to 95% by 2050. It is needed to protect valuable ecological assets, the services they provide and the quality of life for present and future generations. It will help us ensure that the agricultural and fisheries sectors are strong and sustainable and reduce food insecurity in developing countries. By reducing reliance on increasingly scarce fuels and materials, boosting resource efficiency can also improve the security of Europe's supply of raw materials and make the EU's economy more resilient to future increases in global energy and commodity prices" (COM(2011) 21: 2).

Based on that the commission calls for "a resource-efficient and low-carbon economy" (COM(2011) 21: 2) which not only focuses on dealing with environmental risks and challenges but also with strengthening the EU's position on global competition. Presenting the communication, European Commission President, José Manuel Barroso stated that continuing current patterns of resource use was no longer an option, putting too much pressure on planet earth and making the EU's economy even more dependent on external supplies than it is already today. According to Barroso:

"… a smarter use of scarce resources is therefore a strategic necessity, but also an economic opportunity. Through more resource-efficiency, clearer long-term policies and joint investments in green innovation, we are strengthening the basis for growth and jobs for our citizens and delivering on our climate and energy objectives" (Barroso 2011a).

In view of this, the overall challenge Europe is facing regarding its environmental situation is to provide a reliable and affordable supply of energy and natural resources to its economy and its citizens without putting the global environment at risk. This goes far beyond the classic approach of environmental protection which originally focused on "end-of-pipe"-technologies and which until recently has been developed towards the life-cycle management of products, aimed at reducing air, water and soil pollution as well as other threats to the environment and risks for human health at all stages from production of goods to their final disposal as waste (Bank 2007: 35ff.). It is – or could be – an approach that also takes into account elements of a comprehensive understanding of security. This especially becomes clear when looking at climate-related impacts. These impacts occur in the form of "climate change" influenced by mankind using fossil primary energy sources like coal, oil, and natural gas especially for transport, production processes as well as heat and power generation. Energy use in oil and natural gas fired power plants is by far the most important source of greenhouse gas emissions within the European Union, accounting for about 3,000 million tons of CO_2 equivalents or 59.8% of the EU's total greenhouse gas emissions (Eurostat 2010: 525). Taking into account that also the greenhouse gas emissions in the transport sector are mainly derived from the use of fossil fuels, an additional amount of 19.5% of greenhouse gas emissions can be attributed to fossil fuels, making them responsible for almost 80% of the EU 27's greenhouse gas emissions (Eurostat 2010: 525). According to the Intergovernmental Panel on Climate Change (IPCC), the share of fossil fuel-based power generation in global greenhouse gas emissions is about 70% (IPCC 2007a: 254). As for their effects on climate, it does not really matter where these energy sources are used; their impact is there and going to affect people worldwide.

The European Union's common approach of dealing with ecological challenges and environmental protection, which at least officially is shared by all member states, is described in Article 191 of the Lisbon Treaty which states:

> "Union policy on the environment shall contribute to the pursuit of the following objectives: preserving, protecting and improving the quality of the environment, protecting human health, prudent and rational utilisation of natural resources, promoting measures at international level to deal with regional or worldwide environmental problems, and in particular combating climate change" (2010/C 83/01: 132).

The article stresses the EU's environmental policy "shall be based on the precautionary principle and on the principles that preventive action should be taken, that environmental damage should as a priority be rectified at source and that the polluter should pay" (2010/C 83/01: 132). Two objectives are quite specifically addressed: the efficient use of natural resources and climate change. In order to deal with climate change among other things, Article 192 allows the Council, after consultations with the European Parliament, the Economic and Social Committee and the Committee of the Regions, to adopt unanimously "measures significantly affecting a member state's choice between different energy sources and the general structure of its energy supply" (2010/C 83/01: 133). This though, according to Article 194, "shall not affect a member state's right to determine the conditions for exploiting its energy resources, its choice between different energy sources and the general structure of its energy supply, without prejudice to Article 192(2)(c)" (2010/C 83/01: 135). In other words, EU member states are still free to decide if and to what extent they wish to use particular primary energy sources, in principal regardless of potential ecological consequences.

This paper will briefly describe the challenges expected for Europe due to climate change and give an outline of the steps taken by the European Union to deal with this challenge. Following that, it will show how the power sector has responded to the EU's efforts before developing some ideas for future EU climate policies.

Climate Change – a Challenge for Europe

Potential environmental challenges, also for Europe, derived from climate change have been extensively described by the Intergovernmental Panel on Climate Change (IPCC) in its Fourth Assessment Report in 2007 (IPCC 2007). Though there were accusations of data mongering regarding this report (the so-called "climate gate" affair), an investigation on behalf of the House of Commons found no evidence that there was the intention to mislead (House of Commons 2010). A similar conclusion concerning the work of Michael Mann, one of the most prominent climate scientists, was drawn by an Investigatory Committee of the Pennsylvania State University (Pennsylvania State University 2010). As for non-intentional errors, the IPCC has repeatedly published corrections on its website and continues to do so. The point is: Whether the IPCC's findings draw a realistic picture of what is going on or not, there is no doubt the majority of actors in climate politics more or less rely on its reports, if not for other reasons then for a lack of reasonable alternatives. The IPCC itself warns there are a lot of uncertainties in climate projections, one of which is the future of the North Atlantic Thermohaline Circulation. Also, global climate models still lack a level of resolution sufficient for regional projections (IPCC 2007: 564).

Taking this into account the 4th Assessment Report states that "climate-related hazards will mostly increase, although changes will vary geographically" (IPCC 2007: 543). According to the IPCC emissions scenarios until the end of the century "Europe undergoes a warming in all seasons" with the greatest temperature rises to be expected in eastern Europe in winter and in western and southern Europe in summer (IPCC 2007: 547). Mean annual precipitation is assumed to increase in northern Europe and to decrease in southern regions, with seasonal and regional precipitation patterns varying strongly (IPCC 2007: 547). Some climate scientists assume this might lead to a more frequent occurrence of heat-waves and droughts, though the IPCC stresses findings pointing in that direction "may be slightly over-estimated" (IPCC 548). The report identifies the 11 key future impacts and vulnerabilities. These are water resources, coastal and marine systems, mountains and sub-arctic regions, forests, scrublands and grasslands, wetlands and aquatic ecosystems, biodiversity, agriculture and fishery, energy and transport, tourism and recreation, property insurance, and human health (IPCC 2007: 542).

As for water resources, the IPCC points out that most of the studies it relies on in its report are "based on global rather than regional climate models" (IPCC 2007: 549). So there might be some incertitude in them. Despite that, it is suggested the risk of floods is likely to increase in northern, central and eastern Europe whereas more droughts could occur in the south, especially Portugal and Spain (IPCC 2007: 550). Dealing with agriculture the IPCC states "the effects of climate change and increased atmospheric CO_2 are expected to lead to overall small increases in European crop productivity" (IPCC 2007: 554), but there may be the need for increasing irrigation in regions more frequently affected by droughts.

With temperatures tending to increase, energy consumption patterns will also undergo changes, the IPCC states. Demand for wintertime heating is assumed to be decreasing while on the other hand an increasing demand for space cooling and air conditioning in summer is expected (IPCC 2007: 556). Hydro power plants currently account for about 19.8% of overall European electricity generation, thus being by far the most important renewable energy source. From about 2070 onwards they could suffer losses of about 6% of their overall potential. Losses could even reach some 50% in the Mediterranean region (IPCC 2007: 556). Electricity generation from thermal power plants might also be negatively affected in regions where droughts will occur more frequently (IPCC 2007: 556). This would also be true for nuclear power plants which rely on cooling water as do conventional thermal plants. The effects of climate-related impacts on power lines remain uncertain, though generally "the distribution of energy is also vulnerable to climate change" (IPCC 2007: 556), the IPCC warns.

In some sectors the IPCC sees only limited possibilities to overcome these challenges by adaptation measures. Even if such possibilities exist they are assumed to be costly. In areas suffering from increased water scarcity for example, "new reservoir construction is being increasingly constrained in Europe by environmental regulations and high investment costs" (IPCC 2007: 559). As for the energy and transport sector, the IPCC takes a much more optimistic view, stating

"... A wide variety of adaptation measures are available in the energy sector ranging from the redesign of the energy supply system to the modification of human behaviour. [...] Over the medium to long term, shifting from fossil fuels to renewable energy use will be an effective adaptive measure" (IPCC 2007: 561).

Another comprehensive assessment of environmental challenges derived from climate-related impacts based on 40 indicators was presented by the European Environment Agency, the European Commission, and the European Chapter of the World Health Organisation (WHO) in 2008 (EEA 2008). The overall picture drawn in that report does not differ very much from that of the IPCC. The EEA states that, compared to what it calls "pre-industrial times" Europe's average temperature already has risen by 1.0-1.2°C, with a further rise of 1.0-5.5°C to be expected by the end of the century (EEA 2008: 11). Correspondingly, especially in southern Europe, drought periods are assumed to become lengthier and more frequent, though there are strong uncertainties on precipitation patterns and extreme weather events (EEA 2008: 12). As for water flows the EEA stresses that

"in general, annual river flows have been observed to increase in the north and decrease in the south, a difference projected to exacerbate. Strong changes in seasonality are projected, with lower flows in summer and higher flows in winter. As a consequence, droughts and water stress will increase, particularly in the south and in summer" (EEA 2008: 13).

Even now, water demand for agricultural purposes, especially irrigation, has already increased by 50-70% with a further increase being likely to occur (EEA 2008: 14). However, the EEA warns that

"anthropogenic interventions in the catchment, such as groundwater abstraction, irrigation, river regulation, land-use changes and urbanisation, have considerably altered river flow regimes in large parts of Europe, confounding climate change detection studies" (EEA 2008: 93).

A Response to Kyoto: A Brief Outline of EU Climate Policies

The European Union has reacted to the challenge of climate change in a comprehensive manner of which only some highlights can be briefly described here.

In order to implement the Kyoto Protocol of 1997, the EU established its so-called European Climate Change Programme (ECCP) in June 2000. According to Annex B of the Kyoto Protocol, the EU as a whole has a common obligation to cut its greenhouse gas emissions by 8% compared to the "base year" 1990 (Kyoto Protocol: 20). It should be mentioned that at that time the EU had 15 member states. Only these have to comply with the common obligation. Ten other member states have individual targets independent of the common one, whereas two member states have no obligations under the Kyoto protocol. The ECCP which at the time of writing is in its second phase ("Second European Climate Change Programme") aims at identifying "the most environmentally and cost-effective EU measures enabling the EU to meet its target under the Kyoto Protocol, namely an 8% reduction in greenhouse gas emissions from 1990 levels by 2008-2012" (ECCP II: 5). At least, 42 cost-effective measures for emission reductions were identified, representing a technical emission reduction potential of some 664–765 million tons of CO_2 equivalents, about twice the amount considered necessary to meet the Kyoto target (ECCP II: 6). One of the most important measures proposed was the EU emissions trading scheme (EU ETS) (ECCP II: 47/48). Other proposals included an Environmental Technology Action Plan (ECCP II: 24), CO_2 storage (ECCP II: 25/26) which is now being implemented by directive 2009/31/EC of April 23, 2009 on the geological storage of carbon dioxide (CCS directive), the directive on the energy performance of buildings (ECCP II: 55), mandatory energy labels (ECCP II: 57), a directive on energy services (ECCP II: 59), and a public awareness campaign (ECCP II: 60).

The emissions trading system finally was introduced on January 1, 2005 based on the Directive 2003/87/EC establishing a scheme for greenhouse gas emission allowance trading within the Community. It is the world's largest "cap & trade" system, putting an emission cap (defined in the so-called "national allocation plans" of the individual member states and approved by the EU Commission) on each of the around 11,500 installations in the energy sector (mainly power generation and mineral oil refining) and the manufacturing industry it covers (Schleicher et al. 2011: 29). Owners of installations whose emissions exceed levels permitted by the national allocation plans have either to curb emissions or to buy emission certificates (EU allowances, EUAs). To a certain extent, also certificates generated under the "Flexible Mechanisms" of the Kyoto Protocol can be used. Aside from all 27 EU member states, Iceland, Liechtenstein and Norway are participating in the ETS. From 2012 onwards, domestic air traffic emissions will be included (Schleicher et al. 2011: 29).

The third period of the ETS (2013-2020) will see major changes in the system. The national allocations plans will be replaced "by an EU-wide cap" (Schleicher et al. 2011: 32) on the number of the EUAs. Already from 2013, an auctioning system for up to 50% of the total amount of the EUAs will be progressively introduced, with the power sector having to buy all its allowances right from the start of the third period (Schleicher et al. 2011: 32). Aside from carbon dioxide, the ETS will also cover nitrous oxide (N2O) and perfluorocarbons (PFCs) and will be extended to the petrochemical, ammonia and aluminium industry as well as aviation, while road transport, shipping as agriculture and forestry will not be included (ibid). Although problems occurred with IT security, resulting in the theft of large amounts of EUA's and a temporary shutdown, the ETS is still seen as one of the pillars of the EU's climate and energy policy, even though its effects in terms of emission reductions have been limited so far. There are hopes this will change with the adaptations described above.

In its communication "An Energy Policy for Europe" of January 10, 2007 (COM(2007) 1) the Commission described the challenges for European energy policy as "threefold: combating climate change, limiting the EU's external vulnerability to imported hydrocarbons, and promoting growth and jobs, thereby providing secure and affordable energy to consumers" (COM (2007)1: 5). Already there it proposed the EU should cut its greenhouse gas emissions by 2020 by 20% compared to the 1990 level in any event and to underpin this by a target of even 30% to be put forward in international climate policy negotiations (COM(2007)1: 5). It also called for reducing the Community's global primary energy use by 20% by 2020, thus referring to its Energy Efficiency Action Plan adopted on October 19, 2006 (COM(2007)1: 12) and for increasing the share of renewable energy "in the EU's overall mix from less than 7% today to 20% by 2020" (COM(2007)1: 14), thereby recalling its Renewable Energy Roadmap (COM(2006) 848). These are the so-called "20:20:20 targets" of the EU which entered force with the climate and energy package of April 2009 (see below) (COM(2007)1) and furthermore demanded a "European Strategic Energy Technology Plan" which would allow the Community to "switch to low carbon in the European energy system" by about 2050 (COM(2007)1: 16).

Finally it demanded comprehensive measures to be taken to make the internal markets for electricity and natural gas work more efficiently and to stimulate competition on those markets (COM(2007)1: 6-10) as well as for a more common approach on the security of natural gas supply (COM(2007)1: 10-11). Many of these proposals resulted in the third legislative package for an internal EU gas and electricity market which at the time of writing is in the implementation phase. (This so-called "third package" cannot be described here. For details see Regulation (EC) No 713/2009 Of The European Parliament and The Council of July 13, 2009 establishing an Agency for the Cooperation of Energy Regulators; Regulation (EC) No 714/2009 of The European Parliament and The Council of July 13, 2009 on conditions for access to the network for cross-border exchanges in electricity and repealing Regulation (EC) No 1228/2003; Regulation (EC) No 715/2009 of The European Parliament and The Council of July 13, 2009 on conditions for access to the natural gas transmission networks and repealing Regulation (EC) No 1775/2005; Directive 2009/72/EC of The European Parliament and The Council of July 13, 2009 concerning common rules for the internal market in electricity and repealing Directive 2003/54/EC; and Directive 2009/73/EC of

The European Parliament and The Council of July 13, 2009 concerning common rules for the internal market in natural gas and repealing Directive 2003/55/EC).

On November 22, 2007 the EU Commission published the Strategic Energy Technology Plan (SET-Plan) which states

> "The EU is leading the world in responding to climate change by adopting targets and putting a price on carbon through the Emissions Trading Scheme, as well as creating a truly internal energy market. We must act with equal determination and ambition on a policy for low carbon technologies. These are the conditions to catalyse a new industrial revolution. In a carbon constrained world, the mastery of technology will increasingly determine prosperity and competitiveness. If we fall behind in the intensifying global race to win low carbon technology markets, we may need to rely on imported technologies to meet our targets, missing out on huge commercial opportunities for EU businesses" (COM(2007)723: 4).

The plan called into existence a "European Community Steering Group on Strategic Energy Technologies" and a "European Energy Technology Information System" (COM(2007)723: 9) as the SET Plan's governance structure. It proposed the establishing of six "European Industrial Initiatives" focusing on wind, solar and biomass energy, CO_2 capture, transport and storage, electricity grids, and nuclear fission (COM(2007)723: 10) and a European Energy Research Alliance (COM(2007)723: 11).

In 2009 the EU took its next strategic step by adapting its "climate and energy package" of April 2009 which consists of at least four legislative acts. Directive 2009/28/EC sets targets for the use of renewable energy to be achieved in 2020. The national targets have to be consistent with a "20% share of energy from renewable sources in the Community's gross final consumption of energy in 2020" (L 140/28). Directive 2009/31/EC obliges the member states to develop national plans concerning carbon capture and storage. Decision 406/2009 gives each Member State an emission reductions target for 2020 which is in line with the national targets under the Kyoto protocol. This corresponds to a common reduction target of 20%, reiterating the Community might extend that target to 30% in case a post-Kyoto agreement can be achieved (L 140/140). Finally, directive 2009/29/EC aims at improving and extending the ETS.

According to the European Environmental Agency (EEA), the EU's efforts to tackle the Kyoto targets are likely to be successful.

> "Despite possible short-term increases in European emissions subsequent to economic recovery, European Commission projections show that over the full commitment period 2008–2012 the EU 15's aggregated emissions will stay well below its Kyoto target with the current policies in place. Nevertheless, further efforts are necessary from member states to guarantee that the EU 15 achieves its commitment under the Kyoto Protocol. The EEA analysis of current emission

levels in the EU 15 shows that shortfalls currently exist in Austria, Denmark and Italy. These three countries therefore need to step up their efforts by achieving further emission reductions in sectors not covered by the EU ETS or by revising upwards their current plans on using flexible mechanisms at government level. Shortfalls can be offset using the flexible mechanisms through transfers from member states that exceed their targets. Such transfers should not be taken for granted, however, because any member state has the right to retain or cancel (i.e. not make available to other EU member states) any surplus compliance unit by the end of the commitment period",

the EEA states in a recent report (EEA 2010: 6/7).

Failure to meet a country's individual Kyoto target has its price. According to the Kyoto protocol, whose "compliance mechanism" is defined by the so-called "Marrakesh Accords" (the compliance system is comprehensively described in the Kyoto Protocol Reference Manual of the United Nations Framework Convention on Climate Change, available at http://unfccc.int/kyoto_protocol/compliance/items/2875.php), a state failing its Kyoto target has to buy additional emission reduction certificates covering a third of the state's total Kyoto-relevant emissions. Moreover, the state will not be allowed to take part in international emissions trading. This will raise the cost for that state. As for Austria, which has one of the most ambitious targets according to the Kyoto protocol, a recent report of the federal environment agency (Umweltbundesamt) describes the situation as follows:

"The economic development observed for 2010 and 2011 is more positive than in 2009. Lower emissions achieved through the implementation of climate strategy measures are partly compensated by increasing economic growth. Therefore an average gap corresponding to the average of 2008 and 2009 is expected, resulting in a total gap of approximately 30 Mt CO_2 equivalents for the period 2008–2012. Additional use of flexible instruments will be necessary to make up for the difference and achieve the Kyoto target. The main reason for this substantial gap is the current insufficient implementation of climate strategy measures. In any case, further effective national measures are necessary to keep the deviation from the Kyoto target (and the financial resources to cover this gap) as small as possible. It is also inevitable to implement further measures in view of compliance with the targets applicable from 2013. Further measures need to be implemented not only without delay, but also with immediate effect if they are to provide any contribution to the achievement of the targets for this period at all. Using economic or fiscal instruments, for example, would be such an effective short-term measure" (Umweltbundesamt 2011: 12).

The federal environment agency estimates the costs for bridging the gap could be as high as 155-180 million euro (Umweltbundesamt 2011: 20). This adds to the 531 million euro Austria already budgeted for buying emissions certificates under the "Flexible Mechanisms" of the Kyoto Protocol (Kommunalkredit 2008: 6).

Whether the EU's common targets set by the 2009 climate and energy package will be met remains to be seen, not least given the EU's rather complicated decision making procedures. The European Commission, the European Parliament, and the European Council all have their say in climate and energy policy. As Fischer/Geden points out, all these actors widely accept in principle "the EU needs a 'common policy'. But in many particular areas their positions often differ considerably" (Fischer/Geden 2008: 37; translated by the author). This is especially true for the European Parliament whose members have different views, depending on their nationality, party membership and various partisanships as well as individual interests (Fischer/Geden 2008: 51). It is also true for the European Council where national governments strive to put forward their very interests in all policy fields.

Last but not least, it is also true for the Commission. In February 2010 the EU Commission established its Directorate-General for Climate Action ("DG CLIMA", http://ec.europa.eu/dgs/clima/mission/index_en.htm), headed by Connie Hedegaard, Denmark's former environment minister who presided over the COP 15 at Copenhagen in December 2009. DG CLIMA at present employs some 160 officials from the commission and external staff. According to its website DG CLIMA sees itself "at the forefront of international efforts to combat climate change" and states it "develops and implements cost effective international and domestic climate change policies and strategies in order for the EU to meet its targets for 2020 and beyond, especially with regard to reducing its greenhouse gas emissions. Its policies also aim at protecting the ozone layer and at ensuring that the climate dimension is appropriately present in all Community policies and that adaptation measures will reduce the European Union's vulnerability to the impacts of climate change" (DG CLIMA 2010). Moreover, it "leads international negotiations on climate, helps the EU to deal with the consequences of climate change and to meet its targets for 2020, as well as develops and implements the EU emissions trading system" (DG CLIMA 2010).

This sounds impressive but hardly describes the situation as a whole. Of course the Commission has its say in climate and energy politics, and so obviously does DG CLIMA, but it is not even the Commission's voice on climate change and is far from being the EU's one and only voice on that topic. As DG CLIMA's policy field is closely connected to energy, it is evident that also Guenther Oettinger, Commissioner for Energy and Transport, has his say. For example in March 2011, he was at loggerheads with Hedegaard when warning of setting emission reduction targets higher than the 20% currently in place would hamper economic development (Spiegel Online 2011). Also there are inconsistencies in the targets of the Commission's directives. On the one hand, the Renewable Energy Directive (Directive 2001/77/EC) calls for increasing the amount of electricity from renewable energy sources. On the other hand, the Water Framework Directive (Directive 2000/60/EC) aims at preventing "further deterioration and protects and enhances the status of aquatic ecosystems and, with regard to their water needs, terrestrial ecosystems and wetlands directly depending on the aquatic ecosystems" (Directive 2000/60/EC: 5). This is hampering efforts to increase electricity generation from hydro power which at present is the most cost-effective way of generating power from renewable energy sources (Kalt-schmitt 2009: 75-94). Also the directive on the conservation of wild birds (Council Directive 79/409/EEC) can lead to conflicts with renewable energy projects aimed at reducing greenhouse gas emissions, as birds – and also bats – can fall prey to collisions with (rotating) wind turbines (Ohl/Monsees 2008:10, Kaltschmitt 2009: 223).

Moreover, as already mentioned, the Commission is not the EU's single decision-making body. Far from being something like a "United States of Europe", the EU is hardly much more than a free-trade association with widened cooperation in a variety of policy fields. This has not substantially changed with the Lisbon Treaty. As has been mentioned, opinions on how to deal with climate change differ within the Commission, between the Commission, the Council and the Parliament, but also within the Council and the Parliament. Concerning the Council, there can be no doubt that it is finally the "national interests" that count since the governments represented in the Council would rather run the risk of failures on the EU level than lose parliamentary elections at home. They have to take into account pressure put on them from various interest groups. For example, the Commission's opinion, that reacting to climate change somehow "automatically" leads to what is called "green growth" and "green jobs" (whatever that means), is being challenged at least by representatives of the European industry. In July 2011 Eurofer, the association of Europe's steel producers, filed a lawsuit at the European Court of Justice against the benchmarking in connection with the third period of the EU emissions trading system, arguing the benchmarks put forward by the Commission are not achievable and would lead to costs of about 5 billion euro by 2020 – in addition to the 6.5 billion euro the steel industry already will have to spend on buying greenhouse gas emission certificates (EUAs) (Luther 2011). An example of the quite different interests between the EU's member states in terms of energy policy is their access towards nuclear energy. While some states after the 2011 Fukushima event decided to withdraw from nuclear energy, others do not even intend to start, as will be described below.

A Case of Negotiations – Copenhagen and its Aftermath

Contrary to its (expected) success in meeting its own Kyoto targets, on a global scale, the EU's efforts – mainly put forward by the Commission – of bringing together an internationally binding agreement as an immediate successor to the Kyoto Protocol have been all but successful so far. A preparatory meeting for the COP 17 in Durban which took place in Bonn from June 6-17, 2011 showed progress in "technical" questions like the adaptation fund for developing countries but did not bring any steps towards a comprehensive post-Kyoto agreement. The situation before the COP17 has been described by the International Institute for Sustainable Development's (IISD) Earth Negotiations Bulletin as follows:

> "... How do you drive a multi-track process forward when some parties already have what they want, others want what is impossible and all imagine different futures? This was the challenge faced by delegates in Bonn as they attempted to negotiate a path towards the UN Climate Change Conference in Durban, South Africa in six months' time" (ENB 2011a: 24).

As the editors pointed out, even to the negotiators it still remained unclear what the outcome of COP 16 in Cancun in December 2010 really means. What seems clear is that if there is a second commitment period of the Kyoto protocol it "would be considerably weaker than the first. Japan, Canada and the Russian Federation have declared that they will not commit to a second commitment period" (ENB 2011a: 24). As the IISD points out there are considerations on a "Kyoto light" or "Kyotino" agreement, including emission reduction commitments from the European Union, Iceland, Norway, and Switzerland (ENB 2011a: 24) although this hardly would make sense in terms of global emission reductions. Therefore it was also considered if "it would be better to bury the Protocol in Durban" (ENB 2011a: 24).

But maybe the Protocol is dead already, following the "Copenhagen Accord" accepted though not formally adopted at the Copenhagen climate conference of December 2009 (COP 15). Summarised in brief, the Copenhagen Accord states that the increase in global average temperature should be kept below 2 degrees Celsius (Copenhagen Accord: 5). Developed countries should commit themselves to further emission reductions, the compliance to which should be monitored internationally. Moreover they should give financial support to developing countries to implement measures for adaptation to climate change (Copenhagen Accord: 6). Developing countries were invited to put forward their own emission reduction targets, the compliance to which would be monitored by themselves (ibid). Finally, the Accord called for establishing a Green Climate Fund for supporting measures of developing countries in connection with climate change, a Technology Mechanism for accelerating the development and transfer of technologies to support emission reduction and adaptation measures (Copenhagen Accord: 7). An assessment of the Accord's implementation was scheduled for 2015 (ibid).

The EU Commission summarised its position on the outcome of Copenhagen in Communication (2010)86 of March 9, 2010. There it stated

"Europe's core goal is to keep the increase in temperature below 2°C, to prevent the worst impacts of climate change, and this is only possible through a coordinated international effort. This is why the EU has always been a strong supporter of the UN process, and why Copenhagen fell well short of our ambitions. Nevertheless, increasing support for the Copenhagen Accord shows that a majority of countries are determined to press ahead with action on climate change now. The task for the EU is to build on this determination, and to help channel it into action" (COM(2010) 86: 2).

This should be achieved by showing leadership in climate policy by becoming "the most climate friendly region in the world" (COM(2010) 86: 8). Therefore the Commission announced to

"outline a pathway for the EU's transition to a low carbon economy by 2050, to achieve the EU agreed objective to reduce emissions by 80-95%, as part of the developed countries' contribution to reducing global emissions by at least 50% below 1990 levels in 2050. [...]The goal is to come with intelligent solutions that benefit not only climate change, but also energy security and job creation in our efforts to decarbonise the economy" (COM(2010)86: 8).

In short the EU decided to stick to its front-runner strategy that already at the time of Copenhagen had proven not to be successful. The EU was moving forward but no-one followed. It should be mentioned in this context the Copenhagen Accord had been negotiated by the US administration with China and other states all during 2009. The EU was neither invited to nor involved in these talks (Spiegel Online 2010).

Schleicher et al. see Copenhagen as a kind of tipping point:

"In many ways, the Copenhagen summit of December 2009 marked an important departure from the practice of multilateral climate cooperation over the previous two decades. The Copenhagen Accord, which was driven by the US and strongly influenced by China and a few other emerging economies, is characterised by a voluntary pledge and review system for emission reductions, and therefore a fundamental change in the current UN based multilateral approach. The Copenhagen Accord reflects the US vision for international climate architecture but is not in line with the EU approach of the continuation of Kyoto-style top-down climate architecture after 2012" (Schleicher et al. 2011: 34).

In vain the EU proposed to reduce its greenhouse gases not only by 20% but even by 30% in case of a legally binding follow-up agreement to Kyoto. As Schleicher et al. state

"The European Union and many developing countries still favour a multilateral science and rules-based approach, or a second commitment period under the existing Kyoto Protocol in combination with a treaty under the convention. The EU hoped to convince several major industrialised countries to join such a Kyoto-style agreement, e.g. Russia and Japan may have interest in a continuation of the Kyoto-mechanism. [...] Neither Japan nor Russia are currently supporting the EU position. The US did not move from their view since Copenhagen and the divergence of views became bigger than ever" (Schleicher et al. 2011: 35).

This was also reflected by the ways in which China and the US described the outcome of the Cancun climate change conference (COP 16) in December 2010, the so-called Cancun Agreement. According to a report from Xinhua news agency, the Chinese delegation called the outcome "positive", stressing its adherence to the United Nations Framework Convention on Climate Change (UNFCCC); the Kyoto Protocol and the "Bali Roadmap" which had been agreed upon at the COP 13 in Bali in 2007 describing the pathway for the negotiations on a post-Kyoto agreement, as well as to the principle of differentiated but common responsibilities. Moreover progress on particular topics like adaptation, technology transfer, finance and capacity building "sends positive signals to the international community", the delegation said (China 2010a).

The United States' view on the outcome of Cancun was quite different, laying more stress on the consistency of the Cancun Agreement with the Copenhagen Accord. In a press briefing in Washington, DC on December 14, 2010, Todd Stern, the United States' Special Envoy for Climate Change stated

"the resulting Cancun agreement advances each of the core elements of the Copenhagen Accord. Specifically, it anchors the accord's mitigation pledges by both developed and developing countries in a parallel manner. It outlines a system of transparency with substantial detail and content, including international consultations and analysis; that was the negotiated phrase from the Copenhagen Accord. And this will provide confidence that a country's pledges are being carried out and help the world keep track of the track that we're on in terms of reducing emissions" (Stern 2010a).

He added

"we (i.e. the United States) are comfortable with however the Kyoto issue gets resolved. But you can understand the hesitance on the part of some countries to want to go into a second period, given that a second Kyoto period would probably only cover 20-something percent of global emissions. It doesn't have the United States in it and you don't have any commitments from the major developing countries. Still, it is, again, a very passionately felt issue on the part of both developing and developed countries. So the issue there is would there be binding caps under Kyoto. But again, Kyoto is not the larger agreement that includes emission commitments from the US, China, India, Brazil, et cetera" (Stern 2010a).

On behalf of the European Union, Commissioner for Climate Action Hede-gaard and Joke Schauvliege, Flemish Minister for Environment, Nature and Culture, who represented the Belgian presidency of the Council of the Euro-pean Union at Cancún, called the Cancun Agreement "a well balanced com-promise between different interests within the United Nations system" (IP/10/1699). They stated that for the first time in a UN document the aim of keeping global warming below 2°C was acknowledged and the "Copenhagen pledges" were anchored in the UN process (IP/10/1699). Nevertheless, He-degaard stressed

> "the EU came to Cancun to get a substantial package of action-oriented decisions and keep the international climate change negotiations on track. We have helped to deliver the successful outcome the world expected and needed. But the two weeks in Cancún have shown once again how slow and difficult the process is. Everyone needs to be aware that we still have a long and challenging journey ahead of us to reach the goal of a legally binding global climate framework" (IP/10/1699).

In other words: The EU succeeded in bringing the results of Copenhagen un-der the umbrella of the UN climate negotiations. But this resulted in a "tactical" problem: The Cancun Agreement doubtlessly is an agreement with-in UN process, and it also includes emission reduction targets – also for developing countries. But neither the Cancun Agreement nor the targets are legally binding, what the EU would have desired most. So if Cancun was a "success" for the EU, it carries some marks of a "Pyrrhic" victory.

The Durban climate conference (COP 17) lasting from November 28 to December 11, 2011 did not change the overall picture although EU Climate Action Commissioner Heedegaard stated that "with the agreement on a roadmap towards a new legal framework by 2015 that will involve all coun-tries in combating climate change, the EU has achieved its key goal for the Durban climate conference" (MEMO/11/895). In fact, little more was agreed upon than continuing the negotiations on a legally binding agreement. The so-called "Durban Package" includes a decision "that the second commit-ment period under the Kyoto Protocol shall begin on January 1, 2013 and end either on December 31, 2017 or December 31, 2020, to be decided by the Ad Hoc Working Group on Further Commitments for Annex I Parties under the Kyoto Protocol at its seventeenth session" (CMP.7 2011: 2). But neither in Durban nor at the Bonn Climate Change Conference (May 14-15, 2012) did it become clear what that means in particular and what the "legal framework" Hedegaard referred to might look like. As the Earth Negotiations Bulletin put it,

> "Bonn demonstrated that, as many have said, Durban was a carefully negotiated package contingent on all elements of the outcome moving forward in tandem.

However, what is clear is that parties have a very different perspective on what the future looks like in terms of, inter alia, the ADP's mandate, how to terminate the AWGs and what to focus on for effectively addressing climate change. As evidenced in Bonn, constructive ambiguity results in uncertainty that can sometimes breed mistrust. This mistrust is often manifested through disputes over procedure and consequently hampers progress. Looking ahead, parties have their work cut out to accomplish tasks they agreed to in Durban. They will need to exercise goodwill, integrity and congeniality in order to deliver on the ultimate objective of meaningful mitigation action for the post-2012 era" (ENB 2012: 25/26).

The US and also China made it quite clear after Durban that their position in the international negotiations on climate change remains unchanged (Stern 2011, China 2011). So did Canada, which on December 15, 2011 formally withdrew from the Kyoto Protocol (Canada 2011) after having stated already in 2006 it would not implement the Protocol. In a statement on December 12, 2011 minister of environment Peter Kent said Kyoto would have cost Canada 14 billion Canadian dollars or "1600 Canadian dollars from every Canadian family -- with no impact on emissions or the environment" (Kent 2011).

Just a few days after the Bonn Conference Christiana Figueres, Executive Secretary of the UNFCCC, said at the Carbon Expo in Cologne

"There is no doubt that we're moving toward low-carbon economies. There is no doubt that mitigation efforts in both industrialised countries and developing countries needs to, not increase, not grow, it needs to exponentially increase. There is no doubt that the only way to optimise the global investment in mitigation is via the markets and there is no doubt that we see signs everywhere of emerging market schemes" (Figueres 2012: 3).

She stressed the question was

"can we create a market system that will attract not just those companies that were specifically created to take advantage of the market, but can we also attract the more mature and long-term investors such as pension funds, sovereign wealth funds, much more seasoned entities that would look at these markets as being mature enough to be able to incorporate them into their well-rounded portfolio of investments. If we get there, ladies and gentlemen, we will have created the market that we need to move toward the level of mitigation that is necessary and urgent" (Figueres 2012: 4).

Given that it remains to be seen if the result arising in 2015 from another four years of negotiations on climate change – if there is any – might be something other than a kind of voluntary international emission trading system leading in fact more to increasing profits for financial investors than to decreasing global CO_2 emissions.

A Possible Solution? Low Carbon Prospects for the European Power Sector

How then to move forward? If, as noted above, the use of fossil energy sources is a major cause of these problems, then obviously the call is for alternatives. On March 8, 2011, the European Commission presented its "Roadmap for moving to a competitive low carbon economy in 2050" (COM (2011) 112/4) which in the corresponding press was called "the cost-effective pathway to reach the EU's objective of cutting greenhouse gas emissions by 80-95% of 1990 levels by 2050" (RAPID 2011: IP/11/272). The Roadmap states this is in line with the IPCC's proposal for keeping "climate change" (i. e. human contribution to climate-related impacts, see above) within the limits of 2°C (COM(2011) 112/4: 3). Should the Roadmap have been put into a legally binding document, the power sector would have to reduce its $CO2$ emissions by 93-99%. The target of the industry would be 83-87%, that of the transport sector (including aviation, but not marine transport) 54-67%, that of the residential and services sector 88-91%, that of agriculture 41-49% and that of other sectors 70-78% (COM(2011) 112/4: 6). In meeting these targets electricity will play a key role, the Commission states, pointing out the share of "low carbon technologies" (i.e. renewable energy sources, carbon capture and storage technologies (CCS), and nuclear energy) in the electricity (generation) mix will have to rise to almost 100% in 2050. (COM (2011) 112/4: 6). A key role of electricity is also seen in the transport sector. Nevertheless,

"In case electrification would not be deployed on a large-scale, biofuels and other alternative fuels would need to play a greater role to achieve the same level of emissions reduction in the transport sector. For biofuels this could lead, directly or indirectly, to a decrease of the net greenhouse gas benefits and increased pressure on bio-diversity, water management and the environment in general. This reinforces the need to advance in 2nd and 3rd generation biofuels and to proceed with the ongoing work on indirect land use change and sustainability",

the Commission states (COM(2011) 112/4: 8). It is also a reminder of the re-cast Directive on energy performance of buildings (Directive 2010/31/EU) according to which "new buildings built from 2021 onwards will have to be nearly zero-energy buildings" (COM(2011) 112/4: 8). Investing in energy-saving building components and equipment will have to be increased by up to 200 billion euro (COM(2011) 112/4: 8).

As for the industrial sector the commission points out that in order to achieve the CO_2 reduction target of 83-87% by 2050 "in addition to the application of more advanced industrial processes and equipment, carbon capture and storage would also need to be deployed on a broad scale after 2035, notably to capture industrial process emissions (e.g. in the cement and steel sector)" (COM(2011) 112/4: 8). As the Commission warns of its own ambitions, this would demand annual investments "of more than 10 billion euro", probably making it even more challenging for European companies to cope with competitors from regions which have no or less stringent emission reduction targets (COM(2011) 112/4: 9).

The Commission leaves little doubt this will require huge sums of investments in the coming 40 years. Public and private investments are estimated to be 270 billion euro annually or 1.5% of the EU's annual GDP (COM(2011) 112/4: 10). In order to stimulate private investments the Commission suggests "setting aside" emission reduction certificates of the EU ETS (EU allowances) from the amount to be auctioned (COM(2011) 112/4: 11). This would reduce the number of EUAs available, thus forcing industrial enterprises to curb their emissions by energy efficiency measures or by switching from more carbon-intensive fuels to less carbon-intensive ones.

The Commission stresses investment costs will be outweighed by far by reduced imports of fossil fuels which "will reduce the EU's average fuel costs by between 175 billion and 320 billion euro per year" (COM(2011) 112/4: 11). Moreover it points out the opportunity of creating about 1.5 million so-called "green jobs" by 2020 in the renewable energy and energy efficiency industry (COM(2011) 112/4: 12). This, though, does not seem very convincing as the Commission neither mentions at what cost these jobs would be created nor how many jobs in other sectors might get lost in turn.

In principle, the electric power industry seems willing to deal with the challenges put forward by such proposals. Already in June 2010, Eurelectric, the union of Europe's electricity industry, published a comprehensive study called "Power Choices – Pathways to Carbon-Neutral Electricity by 2050" (Eurelectric 2010). In his foreword, Lars G. Josefsson, at that time Eurelectric president, stated the power sector was "fully committed to this goal. To achieve it, it must be supported by policy makers and stakeholders and be translated into strong, coherent and urgent action" (Eurelectric 2010: 1). By implementing the measures put forward in the study, the power sector would be able to reduce the EU's overall CO_2 emissions – not only that of the power sector – by 75% from the 1990 level by 2050. Eurelectric stresses this can be

> "delivered entirely domestically, without recourse to credits generated by international carbon offsets. By accessing such credits, the EU could achieve even higher GHG emission reductions, in line with the EU target of 80-95% emission reductions by 2050" (Eurelectric 2010: 64).

Eurelectric experts calculated two scenarios, the "Basic EU Scenario" ("Baseline 2009" scenario) and the "Power Choices Scenario". In the former, it is assumed the EU would stick to its current emissions reduction target of 20%

until 2020 and for the decades to follow maintains its linear CO_2 emissions reduction path, keeping up its energy efficiency targets. Only the sectors covered by the EU emissions trading system ETS have to pay for emitting CO_2. Renewable energy is still subsidised by the existing support mechanisms which are not assumed to be harmonised EU-wide. Germany and Belgium are phasing out their nuclear power plants but no other EU country which currently uses nuclear is doing so. Power lines are expanded in line with current plans. Electricity will not become a major energy supply source for the transport sector, in other words there is no dominant role of e-mobility (Eurelectric 2010: 6). In contrast, the "Power Choices" scenario assumes "Climate Action becomes a priority and the EU sets and reaches a target of cutting via domestic action 75% of its CO_2 emissions from the whole economy versus 1990 levels" (Eurelectric 2010: 6). This, as already mentioned, is widely in line with the EU Commission's plans at the time of writing. Basic assumptions for this scenario aside from the much more ambitious emission reduction targets are described by Eurelectric as follows: All economic sectors have to pay for their CO_2 emissions with CO_2 prices being set on an international – potentially global, although Eurelectric does not say so explicitly – carbon market. As systems for subsidizing renewable energy sources are assumed to be gradually being phased out from 2020-2030, this carbon price is regarded as the main driver for implementing low-carbon technologies. This is a highly market-based approach where politics only sets the framework but does not strongly intervene in mitigation procedures. In other words, the EU would mainly rely on its energy market for mitigation purposes. Another key assumption is that the EU will push energy efficiency, thus limiting the growth of energy demand although it does not actually reduce energy demand. Eurelectric assumes that "all power generation options remain available, including nuclear power in these countries that currently produce it, but envisaged national phase-out policies remain [...] CCS technology is commercially available from 2025" (Eurelectric 2010: 6). Phasing out nuclear energy in the way scheduled at the time of writing would mean losing reactors with an overall generation capacity of about 27 GW whereas only 12 GW of new nuclear generation capacity will go online, meaning a net loss of 15 GW (Eurelectric 2010: 57). That is only little less than Austria's total electricity generation capacity of about 21 GW (Oesterreichs Energie 2011: 7).

    What, then, might the generation mix look like in 2050, and what does that mean for greenhouse gas emissions? In the Baseline Scenario, the EU's overall generation capacity is estimated to be about 1,382.1 GW, of which 628 GW or 45.44% will be renewable energy sources, especially onshore wind (238.3 GW), offshore wind (139.5 GW), and solar power (151.7 GW). The overall capacity of thermal power plants is seen at 570 GW, most of which (406.9 GW) will be gas and oil fired plants without CCS. 184.1 GW will be nuclear (Eurelectric 2010: 62). It is interesting to note that even in this "conservative" scenario, renewable energy surpasses thermal power plants as the major source of the EU's power generation portfolio. Currently, 51% of Europe's installed generation capacity consist of fossil-fired thermal power plants, 30% of renewable generation capacities, 16% of nuclear power plants, and 3% of other energy sources like waste (UBS Investment Research 2011: 60). Even the "Baseline" generation mix would result in cutting the power sector's carbon emissions by 66% from about 1,400 million tons of CO_2 per year to just 750 (Eurelectric 2010: 9). In the "Power Choices" scenario, the results are – not surprisingly – even more striking, as of a total generation capacity of 1,457.8 GW 821 GW or 56.32% will be renewable energy sources, with onshore wind alone reaching a capacity of 340 GW, offshore wind accounting for 173.8 GW, and solar being at level of 199.3 GW. In that scenario, fossil-fired thermal power plants will have an overall capacity of 442 GW, whereas nuclear power plants will be at 196.9 GW (Eurelectric 2010: 62).

The "Power Choices" scenario would result in cutting down the EU's overall emissions of CO_2 equivalents by 75% from 5,195 million tons in 2005 to 1,390 million tons in 2050 (Eurelectric 2010: 64). From 2030-2050, CCS technologies will play a key role in achieving this, accounting for about 32% of emission reductions in that period (Eurelectric 2010: 66). As Eurelectric points out, the changes in the power generation mix will also have their impact on SO_2 emissions which will be at about 10% of the level they were in 2000 (Eurelectric 2010: 67). NOx emissions will decrease 38% of the 2000 level (ibid).

Reaching these targets will not be cheap, though. Eurelectric estimates the overall investments needed to be as high as 3.2 trillion euro between 2010 and 2050, of which 1.75 trillion euro will go into power generation and 1.5 trillion euro will have to be invested in expanding the power grids (Eurelectric 2010: 71).

In order to illustrate the impacts of policy options Eurelectric calculated four variants to its basic "Power Choices" scenario. One is called "Nuclear Facilitated" and deals with the assumption of Belgium and Germany not phasing out their nuclear power plants. Both countries even expand their nuclear capacities if this is economically viable under market conditions (Eurelectric 2010: 75). In the second variant of the "Power Choices" scenario called "CCS Delay", CCS technologies are available for commercially operated power plants not before 2035 (Eurelectric 2010: 76). The third variant, "Lower Wind Onshore" analyzes the effects of a delay of wind power projects due to regional resistance (ibid). Finally, the "No Efficiency" variant examines the effects of not implementing bottom-up policy measures making it attractive to invest in advanced energy efficiency measures for buildings, energy efficient customer devices and in e-mobility projects (Eurelectric 2010: 77).

For the "Nuclear Facilitated" variant, Eurelectric concludes that electricity generation from nuclear power plants will increase by 20% from 2005 to 2050, cutting down emissions by another 0.9% to 1,488 million tons and saving investments of 360 billion euro compared to the original "Power Choices" scenario (Eurelectric 2010: 75).

Delaying CCS post 2035 would raise the investments by 164 billion euro and lead to an increase of CO_2 emissions by 2.3% (Eurelectric 2010: 76). This indicates emissions reductions, as envisaged in a scenario like "Power Choices", might be possible either without nuclear power or without CCS, but hardly without both. The "Lower Wind Onshore" variant does not affect CO_2 emissions but makes the power supply system more expensive by about 119 billion euro compared to "Power Choices" in its original variant (Eurelectric 2020: 76). At least, "No Efficiency Policies" has the least favourable economic consequences as it adds 3,552 billion euro to the costs of the "Power Choices" scenario. In terms of CO_2 emissions, the outcome of "No Efficiency Policies" is less dramatic. Emissions are estimated to be 7.3% lower than in the "Power Choices" scenario (Eurelectric 2010: 77). This is important to note because it raises doubts about the effectiveness of both renewable energy sources and energy efficiency measures for mitigation purposes.

Though for Germany the "Nuclear Facilitated" meanwhile has been frustrated by the government's decision to phase out the country's nuclear power plants (BGB 2011a: 1704), it is still of interest to look at the variants of the "Power Choices" scenario in order to gain an impression of the effects of a specific form of dealing with energy supply under more or less favourable conditions. However, it will be up to politics to lead the way. But politicians will have to take into account what is required to make their preferred model of future energy supply work. This refers to financial support as well as to the legal and regulatory framework, and not forgetting, to creating a public atmosphere allowing it establish the necessary infrastructure.

This is a problem not only for building new power lines but especially for CCS. For example, in Germany's Brandenburg province, a citizens' initiative fiercely fought against CCS pilot projects, as can be seen at the website of "Bürgerinitiative contra Endlager" (http://www.co2bombe.de/joomla/index.php).

The CCS directive states that member states

> "shall retain the right to determine the areas from which storage sites may be selected pursuant to the requirements of this Directive. This includes the right of Member States not to allow for any storage in parts or in the whole of their territory" (L 140/121).

In line with that, some EU member states intend to rule out carbon storage facilities on their territory or have already done so. For example Austria's ministry of economy proposed a bill implementing the EU's CCS directive which would allow storage projects only for research purposes but not for commercial use. The storage volume is limited to 100,000 tons of carbon dioxide. The proposal, though, has been challenged by representatives of Austria's industry as well as the country's utilities. Especially the steel-producing industry says it simply cannot do without coal, making the need for CCS inevitable. The utilities argue, Austria will rely on fossil fired power plants to cover parts of its electricity demand, making CCS a necessity too (Chemiereport 2011).

Going for 2050

On December 15, 2011 the European Commission issued its communication "Energy Roadmap 2050" (Com(2011) 885) aimed at describing the way beyond 2020 in more detail. The "Roadmap" was issued at the Council meeting on energy items on June 15, 2012 as a presidency proposal supported by 26 member states (11135/12: 8). It includes seven scenarios of which the first two were extrapolations of current trends. Three other scenarios depicted pathways of moving towards a more or less "decarbonised" energy system by means of either stressing energy efficiency, diversified supply technologies, strongly supporting renewable energy sources. In addition to these three scenarios, two alternatives were provided, one stressing the role of nuclear energy at the expense of a delay of CCS technologies, and the other one seeing a more important role for CCS at the expense of nuclear power (COM(2011) 885: 4). According to the commission its scenarios show "decarbonising" the energy system is possible at costs which do not differ very much from those occurring if current policy trends continue (COM(2011) 885: 5). To achieve that, energy policy should focus on increasing energy efficiency (COM(2011) 885: 9) and increasing the share of renewable energy sources to about 30% in gross final energy consumption by 2030 (COM(2011) 885: 10).

The Commission stressed using the "full scale of the internal market ... is the best response to the challenge of decarbonisation" (COM(2011) 885: 14) though it admitted that currently markets do not properly address the problem arising from the increasing share of renewable energy sources in electricity generation. This kind of electricity

> "has low or zero marginal costs and as their penetration in the system increases, in the wholesale market spot prices could decrease and remain low for longer time periods. This reduces the revenues for all generators, including those needed to ensure sufficient capacity to meet demand when wind or solar are not available. Unless prices are relatively high at such times, these plants might not be economically vi-

able. This leads to concerns about price volatility and for investors, about their ability to recover capital and fixed operating costs" (COM(2011) 885: 14.

This problem has already been indicated by Georg Erdmann, professor of energy economics at the Technical University of Berlin in a study published in 2011 (Erdmann 2011); see below, Renewable Energy Challenges).

The Commission therefore demands that "flexibility needs to be rewarded in the market. All types of capacity (variable, baseload, flexible) must expect a reasonable return on investment" (COM(2011) 885: 14). The Commission does not say what a mechanism for generating rewards for flexible generation capacities like gas-fired power plants might look like. But it points out that "Carbon pricing can provide an incentive for deployment of efficient, low-carbon technologies across Europe. The ETS is the central pillar of European climate policy" (COM(2011) 885: 14).

In February 2012 Eurelectric published a "Response Paper" to the Energy Roadmap, stating that a call for an increasing role of electricity in future final energy consumption "confirms the trend towards electrification of final energy usage, a necessary change that Eurelectric already identified as a "paradigm shift" in its own modelling exercise, Power Choices, in 2010" Eurelectric 2012: 11). Nevertheless Eurelectric criticised the Commission's estimates of costs for transforming the energy system in its various scenarios. According to Eurelectric the Commission "suggests that the difference between 14.05% of EU GDP – the costs in the delayed CCS scenario – and 14.6% – the costs in the energy efficiency scenario – is negligible. Considering that the cumulative EU GDP in 2010 was 12.3 trillion euro, a 0.50% difference amounts to 61.5 billion euro per year – 60% of the investments that the Commission has estimated are needed up to 2020 just to make Europe's electricity grids fit for the 2020 targets" (Eurelectric 2012: 15/16).

Grid Challenges

As mentioned above, Eurelectric sees a key role for power grids in adapting the electricity supply system to the needs of "low carbon". The importance of having grids able to cope with the new generation mix must not be underestimated. In autumn 2010, Germany's national energy agency (DENA) published a comprehensive examination of what is to be done if Germany sticks to its ambitious program of expanding renewable power generation until 2020 (DENA 2010). According to DENA's estimates, in 2020 about 37 GW of wind power capacities will have been installed onshore and 14 GW offshore. Photovoltaic solar power will have an overall generation capacity of about 17.9 GW (DENA 2010: 9). To cope with that, some 3,600 kilometres of new high-voltage power lines will be necessary, costs are estimated to be at about 9.7 billion euro, including 3.7 billion euro for connecting the off-shore wind parks to the grid (DENA 2010: 363/364).

In its Pilot Ten-Year Network Development Plan (TYNDP 2010) the European Network of Transmission System Operators for Electricity (ENTSO-E) estimates new high-voltage power lines with an overall length of 35,300 kilometres need to be built by 2020 to cope with the challenges posed by the integration of renewable power generation sources. Power lines of another 6,900 kilometres will have to be upgraded. Together, this accounts for about 42,200 kilometres or 14% of ENTSO-E's network of 300,000 kilometres (ENTSO-E 2010: 9). This corresponds to investment costs of 23-28 billion euro (ENTSO-E 2010: 10).

But it is not only transmission grids that will be needed to make the opportunity of energy supply work. Much attention currently is being paid to adapting the distribution network by which electricity is being brought to the customers. In connection with this, there are two basic aims. The first is facilitating distributed generation by renewable energy sources. The second is helping customers to become aware of their overall consumption and their consumption patterns which could lead to a more efficient use of energy, especially electricity. Therefore so-called "Smart Grids" are being developed in many European countries. The EU itself sees smart grids as one of the pillars of its Strategic Energy Technology Plan (SET Plan). An industrial initiative on smart grids under the SET plan has been established, with national platforms in almost all EU member countries.

The basic concept of smart grids is described by the European Technology Platform SmartGrids as follows:

> "It is vital that Europe's electricity networks are able to integrate all low carbon generation technologies as well as to encourage the demand side to play an active part in the supply chain. This must be done by upgrading and evolving the networks efficiently and economically. It will involve network development at all voltage levels. For example, substantial offshore and improved onshore transmission infrastructure will be required in the near term to facilitate the development of wind power across Europe. Distribution networks will need to embrace active network management technologies to efficiently integrate distributed generation (DG), including residential micro generation, on a large scale. There are many other examples but all will require the connectivity that networks provide to achieve the targets for energy security and environmental sustainability" (SmartGrids 2010: 6).

Nuclear Challenges

Following the accident at Japan's Fukushima Daiichi (Fukushima I) nuclear power plant on March 11, 2011, the European Commission announced so-called "stress tests" for all European nuclear power plants. These tests are being carried out on a voluntary basis as the EU has no competencies in the field of nuclear energy. According to Article 194 of the Lisbon Treaty,

> "Union policy on energy shall aim, in a spirit of solidarity between Member States, to: a) ensure the functioning of the energy market; b) ensure security of energy supply in the Union and promote energy efficiency; c) and energy saving and the development of new and renewable forms of energy; and d) promote the interconnection of energy networks" (2010/C 83/01: 134).

Therefore, there is no legal basis for obligatory "stress tests" or for mandatory consequences in case potential risks are being detected.

The procedure of the tests has been designed by the European Nuclear Safety Regulatory Group (ENSREG) and was published on May 25, 2011. Based on this paper, the operators of all nuclear power plants within the EU had to report to the national regulators by October 31. The regulators reviewed these reports and issued their national reports by December 31 (ENSREG 2011: 2). Following the national reports there was a peer review process, including independent experts, which was completed by April 2012 (ENSREG 2011: 3). It must be mentioned that the composition of the peer teams had to be agreed upon by the country which is subject to review (ENSREG 2011: 3), allowing countries operating nuclear power plants to influence which experts take part in the peer reviews.

Technically the "stress tests" focused on initiating circumstances of nuclear accidents, especially earthquakes and flooding which both played a decisive role in the Fukushima disaster (ENSREG 2011: 4), consequences of the loss of safety functions from any initiating circumstance conceivable at the plant site, in particular the loss of electrical power or of the so-called "ultimate heat sink" (UHS, i.e. the core cooling system) or a combination of both, and thirdly severe accident management issues, i.e. means to protect from and to manage the loss of the core cooling function, means to protect from and to manage the loss of the cooling function in the (spent) fuel storage pool, and means to protect from and to manage the loss of the containment's integrity (ENSREG 2011: 4). Plant operators had to identify the means to maintain the three fundamental safety functions (i.e. the control of reactivity, fuel cooling, and confinement of radio-activity) and support functions (power supply and cooling through ultimate heat sink), the possibility to use mobile external means and the conditions of their use, the possibility of using one reactor to help another reactor, and the dependence of one reactor on the functions of other reactors at the same site (ENSREG

2011: 6). Where necessary, plant operators had to identify the time before damage to the fuel becomes unavoidable as well as the time before the water in the
spent fuel pools starts boiling and the time before fuel in the pool becomes
damaged (ENSREG 2011: 6).

Terrorist attacks including aircraft crashes were not covered by the stress
tests

> "hence it is proposed that the Council establishes a specific working group com-
> posed of Member States and associating the European Commission, within their
> respective competences, to deal with those issues" (ENSREG 2011: 1).

On 26 April 2012, the 26 anniversary of the Chernobyl disaster, ENSREG together with the European Commission published its final report on the stress
tests (ENSREG 2012) carried out in the EU member states, Switzerland, and
the Ukraine. In addition, country reports were issued on the nuclear power
plants in all participating countries. The main message of the report was

> "that all countries have taken significant steps to improve the safety of their
> plants, with varying degrees of practical implementation. In spite of differences in
> the national approaches and degree of implementation, the peer review showed an
> overall consistency across Europe in the identification of strong features, weaknesses
> and possible ways to increase plant robustness in light of the preliminary lessons
> learned from the Fukushima disaster. As a result of the stress tests, significant
> measures to increase robustness of plants have already been decided or are con-
> sidered" (ENSREG 2012: 3).

In other words the report found there is potential for further improvements
regarding the safety and security of nuclear plants but there is no need to
immediately shut down a single plant. The report identified "four main areas
of improvement to be considered at the European level" (ENSREG 2012: 3).

First, it recommended the Western European Nuclear Regulators Association (WENRA) should develop guidance on dealing with natural hazards,
especially earthquakes and flooding (ENSREG 2012: 3). Second, ENSREG
should periodically (at least every ten years) bring to mind the importance of
evaluating measures taken to protect nuclear power plants from natural hazards
(ENSREG 2012: 4). Third, national regulators should make sure the integrity of
the containments of the nuclear power plants in their country is being properly
addressed (ENSREG 2012: 4). Finally, national regulators should also be mind-
ful of measures limiting the consequences of accidents arising from natural
hazards (ENSREG 2012: 4).

EU energy commissioner Guenther Oettinger stated the report was a major
element of the EU's stress test. Following it, additional visits would be done to
nuclear power plants in order to analyze some safety aspects in more detail (Oettinger 2012). "EU citizens have the right to know and understand how safe the
nuclear power plants are they live close to", Oettinger added (Oettinger 2012).

Speaking to members of the Austrian parliament on May 30, 2011, Oettinger already had made clear that the tests should neither absolve plant operators of all their responsibilities nor could they lead to an "automatic shutdown" of any plant (OTS_20110530_OTS0274). In December 2011, the European Commission stated in its "Energy Roadmap" communication that

"nuclear energy contributes to lower system costs and electricity prices. As a large scale low-carbon option, nuclear energy will remain in the EU power generation mix. The Commission will continue to further the nuclear safety and security framework, helping to set a level playing field for investments in Member States willing to keep the nuclear option in their energy mix. The highest safety and security standards need to be further ensured in the EU and globally, which can only happen if competence and technology leadership is maintained within the EU. Furthermore, on a 2050 perspective, it will become clearer which role fusion power will be able to play" (COM(2011) 885: 13).

In its "Global Nuclear Power Report" of April 4, 2011 UBS Investment Research described the prospects of nuclear power in Europe as follows:

"We think that to preserve public acceptance of nuclear power governments will be required to take some action. We think these are most likely to be decided on a national level rather than the EU level. In our view, age, any seismic activity in the area, and proximity to borders are issues that will be factors in what are in the end political decisions to close any plants" (UBS Investment Research 2011: 63).

UBS added it estimates

"the capital costs for new nuclear to be US$5,000-6,000/kW in the US and Europe and about US$2,000/kW in China – about two to eight times the cost of new fossil-fuelled capacity. In this situation, we think investor-owned utilities are unlikely to consider nuclear a good risk-reward option. We believe it will mainly be an option only for public or semi-public entities and in particular in systems with regulated cost pass-through regimes" (UBS Investment Research 2011: 5).

Aside from the "stress tests", the WENRA is working on harmonised standards and security levels. In January 2011 WENRA's Reactor Harmonisation Working Group (RHWG) published a study concerning the current state of security regulations and progress in harmonizing them. The issues that were dealt with covered "important aspects of reactor safety where differences in substance between WENRA countries might be expected. They did not seek to cover all topics that could have an impact upon safety or to judge the overall level of safety in existing plants" (WENRA 2011a: 3).

WENRA stated implementing common "Reference Levels" of reactor safety since 2006 had been "a unique international voluntary effort and is a step towards harmonisation of nuclear safety in Europe. The study is also believed to be the most extensive joint international use of the IAEA safety standards" (WENRA 2011a: 6).

Work on further harmonisation is in progress (WENRA 2011a: 7). Germany's decision to opt out of nuclear power doubtlessly will affect the country's efforts to deal with climate change. The federal government stated it is sticking to the target of cutting its CO_2 emissions by 40% by 2020 and by 80% by 2050 (Government 2011). According to a study done by the Prognos institute, achieving the 40% target is possible although CO_2 emissions will be 51 million tons higher than they were if Germany's nuclear power plants remained in service (Prognos 2011: 32). As Germany is the EU 27's largest power generator, accounting for about one-fifth of the EU's electricity generation (Eurostat 2010: 572), changes in its generation like the nuclear phase-out mix will doubtlessly affect its neighbours. By the end of 2022, nuclear power plants with a net generation capacity of almost 20,000 MW will be phased out (BGB 2011a: 1704). Estimates from Austria's energy regulatory body Energie-Control Austria (E-Control) indicate Austria will have to replace electricity imports from Germany by increasing domestic generation in particular from gas-fired power plants, leading to an increase of CO_2 emissions by 6 million tons, compared to average annual emissions of 87 million tons (E-Control 2011: 15).

Moreover, Germany's energy market regulatory body Bundesnetzagentur (BNetzA) warned of problems related to grid stability and the security of supply as a result of the nuclear phase-out (BNetzA 2011). In August 2011, BNetzA asked Austrian utilities if they could provide electric energy in case of a shortage in Germany due to the phase-out in winter 2011/2012 (Kurier 2011).

Aside from Germany, Switzerland decided not to replace its fleet of nuclear power plants (ENSI 2011). Italy will not proceed with the planned revival of nuclear energy in the near future, following a referendum on June 13, 2011 (Le Monde 2011). But especially in the eastern and south eastern parts of Europe, phasing out nuclear power is not an option. Russia has nine reactors under construction; another 14 are in the planning stage (WNA 2011: 9/10). On March 13, 2011 just two days after the Fukushima event, Areva, a state-owned French company which designs and builds nuclear power plants, disclosed an agreement with Bulgarian Energy Holding Company (BEH) on cooperation in the fields of nuclear and renewable energy (Areva 2011). On March 15, 2011 Russia and Belarus agreed to build the first nuclear power plant in Belarus which will have a generation capacity of about 1200 MW. It will be built by Atomstroyexport, an affiliate of Russia's state-owned nuclear power company Rosatom (Atomstroyexport 2011). Finland will complete its Olkiluoto 3 reactor, the world's first European Pressurised Water Reactor (EPR) with a net capacity of 1600 MW (IAEA 2010a: 29). A fourth reactor at the Olkiluoto site is in the licensing process (TVO 2010). The World Nuclear Association sees nuclear power "under serious consideration" in at least twelve European (not only EU) countries that currently do not use it, among them Norway, Poland, Portugal, and Turkey (WNA 2011a: 1).

So there are prospects for nuclear power in Europe even in the aftermath of Fukushima despite a possible rise in investment costs and safety concerns. A report from DG Energy on the "Investment needs for future adaptation measures in EU nuclear power plants and other electricity generation technologies due to effects of climate change" (DG Energy 2011), stated Europe's nuclear power plants "have incorporated climate change risks and formulated long term strategies more than renewable technologies" (DG Energy 2011: 107).

Renewable Energy Challenges

However, laying more stress on renewable energy will not be easy, and it might become costly, a recent study on the situation in Germany illustrates. The study is called "Kosten des Ausbaus der erneuerbaren Energien" and was done by Georg Erdmann, professor of energy economics at the Technical University of Berlin and former president of the International Association for Energy Economics (IAEE). As Erdmann writes, following the Fukushima event Germany's federal government decided to increase the share of renewable energy in covering the demand for electric power from about 17% at present to 35% in 2020, 50% in 2030, 65% in 2040, and at least 80% in 2050 (Erdmann 2011: 3). To achieve these targets, Germany relies on its bill on subsidizing renewable power generation, the "Erneuerbare-Energien-Gesetz" (EEG). The bill grants producers of electricity from renewable energy sources a feed-in tariff as well as privileged access to the power grids. Whenever they generate electric power they have the right to feed it into the grid, regardless of possible technical problems caused by that (Erdmann 2011: 3).

As Erdmann points out there is a broad range of forecasts for the increase of renewable power generation, leading to a high degree of uncertainty. For example Germany's transmission grid operators (TSO)s estimate the country's offshore wind power capacity to be at about 5,260 MW in 2015, Germany's federal energy agency DENA sees it at not less than 7000MW. Solar power capacity (photovoltaic) is estimated to be at 40,000 MW in 2015 by the TSOs and 13,000 MW by DENA, though the latter figure even would mean a shrinking of the current photovoltaic capacity, as Erdmann states (Erdmann 2011: 7).

The overall volume of the EEG subsidies is estimated to be at about 13 billion euro (Erdmann 2011: 19). Taking into account the increase of wind and solar power generation, this figure is likely to triple by 2025, followed by a decrease by 2030 caused by decreasing feed-in tariffs (Erdmann 2011: 19). In total, Erdmann estimates the cumulated EEG costs to be at about 250 billion euro by 2030 (Erdmann 2011: 24). He sees this as a mere "orientation" ("Orientierungsgroesse") but stresses the EEG will cost hundreds of billions of euro if no fundamental changes in terms of politics or the economy occur (Erdmann 2011: 25). To cut the costs he recommends implementing a harmonised EU-wide system for subsidizing renewable power generation, pointing out this would lead to use the various kinds of technology where the highest electricity output can be expected (Erdmann 2011: 34). In this context he criticised the EEG system granting wind power plants located in areas with "bad" wind conditions higher subsidies than plants in areas with more favourable conditions (ibid).

As Erdmann stresses his calculations do take into account the so-called "merit order effect" of renewable power generation. The effect is described as follows: power generation from renewable energy sources has no need for fossil fuel. This in turn limits the costs for fossil fuel, electricity, and CO_2 (Erdmann 2011: 49). Erdmann does not deny the existence of this effect but warns it is likely to fade away in the long term. The reason is that wind and solar power generation capacities cannot produce electricity whenever it is needed as they rely on wind which does not blow all the time and the sun which does not shine 24 hours a day. There is therefore the need for back-up power plants generating electricity when wind and solar plants do not. Such back-up plants will be needed even more as Germany will opt out of nuclear energy by 2022. But new power plants based on the use of fossil fuel only can be built if the market pays the electricity generated by them. This, though, is being challenged by the very merit order effect. So the long-term result of that effect is a shrinking of generation capacities, leading in turn to less supply at the spot market and therefore higher prices, meaning the merit order effect finally outpaces itself (Erdmann 2011: 49).

Challenges for renewable energy are reflected in investment figures. New financial investments in renewable energy in Europe declined by not less than 22% to 35.2 billion US dollars in 2010 compared to the 2009 figures a recent report of the United Nations Environment Programme (UNEP) and Bloomberg New Energy Finance shows (UNEP Global Trends 2011: 10). Though UNEP adds this was "more than made up for by a surge in small-scale project installation, predominantly rooftop solar" (UNEP Global Trends 2011: 10), it also points out that a number of EU member states like Spain, the Czech Republic, and Germany cut down the subsidies for renewable energy or propose this. Although in Germany and Italy this was due to decreased production costs for photovoltaic technology components, there are fears "that governments, facing economic hardship, might go back on previously promised deals for existing projects, damaging returns for equity investors and banks" (UNEP Global Trends 2011: 16).

Concerning financial investments in renewable energy, Europe lost ground as investments in all other major markets went up considerably:

"Asia & Oceania led the field in 2010 with $59.3 billion, up 30% on 2009, followed by Europe with $35.2 billion, down 22%. North America came third with $30.1 billion, up 53%, and South America fourth with $13.1 billion, up 39%. Middle East & Africa lagged in fifth with $5 billion, but this was up 104% on 2009 levels" (UNEP Global Trends 2011: 19).

From the perspective of renewable energy, what should cause even more concern is the fact that Europe is lagging behind in terms of "energy-smart technologies" which according to Bloomberg New Energy Finance include "advanced transportation; the smart grid and digital energy; energy efficiency including lighting and building-integrated techniques; and energy storage including batteries and fuel cells" (UNEP Global Trends 2011: 29). Global investment in these technologies in 2010 was 23.9 billion US dollars or 27% more than in 2009 (UNEP Global Trends 2011: 29): "The financial new investment part – which excludes R&D – rose from $4.2 billion in 2009 to $5 billion in 2010, with North America dominant and Asia & Oceania in second place, well ahead of Europe" (UNEP Global Trends 2011: 29).

Also, government support for research and development (R&D) for renewable energy remained unchanged at about 2 billion US dollars in Europe in 2010 compared to a rise in Asia and Oceania as well as in the US:

"In Asia and Oceania excluding China and India, government R&D support for renewable energy rose sharply to $4.7 billion, on the back of major stimulus packages in Japan, South Korea and Australia, and probably under-reporting in earlier years. The next biggest bloc was Europe, where overall spending was unchanged at just under $2 billion, followed by the US, up 9% at $1.5 billion" (UNEP Global Trends 2011: 31).

In other words: While Europe still has a strong position in the field of renewable energy, it has already lost ground and runs the risk of continuing to do so. This is also true concerning asset finance, the UNEP report states. In 2010, the Asia and Oceania (ASOC) region had a 44% share of that market, taking over the lead position Europe had held in the three years before (UNEP Global Trends 2011: 41). Dwarfing the rest of the world in investments in small-scale solar projects as Germany did in 2010 (UNEP Global Trends 2011: 45) is fine, but what counts in the end are large-scale financial investments in strategically important technologies as well as the development of such technologies and the ability to bring them to the market. In this regard the picture Europe shows is not really convincing.

Last but not least, for that reason on June 6, 2012 the EU Commission issued a communication on "Renewable Energy: a major player in the European energy market" (COM(2012) 217), calling for improved and more harmonised support schemes for renewable energy sources. In particular the Commission announced it "plans to prepare guidance on best practice and experience gained in these matters and, if needed, on support scheme reform, to help ensure greater consistency in national approaches and avoid fragmentation of the internal market" (COM(2012) 217: 5).

The Commission called for facilitating trading with renewable energy (COM(2012) 217: 5) . It reminded of the "Helios" project aiming at financing a 10GW solar power plant in Greece by other EU member states which could invest to meet their renewable energy targets for 2020 derived from the EU's climate and energy package, though details remain opaque at the time of writing (COM(2012) 217:5; for the Helios project see Stuart 2012). The Commission expressed its reluctance towards so-called capacity payments for gas-fired plants which are said to be needed to cope with the problem of highly volatile power generation from renewable energy sources, as these payments were likely to distort the market (COM(2012) 217: 7). It iterated the importance of investing in transmission and distribution grids and recollected its energy infrastructure package (COM(2011) 658) which aims at streamlining licensing procedures (COM(2012) 217: 8f.). Finally, it called for "milestones" for dealing with renewable energy *post 2020* stating such milestones

> "must ensure that renewable energy is part of the European energy market, with limited but effective support where necessary and substantial trade. They must also ensure that Europe maintains its research and industrial leadership globally. Only in this way can we continue to develop our renewable energy resources in a cost effective, indeed, affordable manner and grasp the associated competitiveness, economic and job opportunities. For this reason, the Commission will also launch proposals for a renewable energy policy regime for the post 2020 period" (COM (2012) 217: 13f.).

Summary and Conclusion

For quite a long time, Europe, or rather the European Union, has claimed to be a forerunner in global environmental protection, and it still continues to be such. This is especially the case in terms of climate change where the EU is proud of still sticking to the goal of a legally binding global arrangement in which each state shall have its obligations. This goal, though, seems hardly to be achievable due to a lack of support from other key players in international climate policy. This may be frustrating for climate commissioner Hedegaard and others who claim to be convinced a lack of such an agreement is putting global climate, and, more importantly, the fate of mankind at risk. But no-one can tell if this really is the case. What is certain is that the effects of the existing binding agreement, the Kyoto Protocol, are limited – and so are the effects of the "Copenhagen pledges" to which almost all Annex I states of the Kyoto Protocol have committed themselves under a voluntary basis in the Copenhagen Accord. UNEP estimates the gap between the cumulative effects of the "pledges" and emission levels in 2020, consistent with limiting the increase of the global average temperature to 2° C, is at about five gigatons but could be more than twice as high as well (UNEP 2010: 42/43). Europe, as well as the quite impressive "rest" of the globe, wants economic prosperity. So far, no solution has been found to achieve that without a growth in energy demand which is connected with more greenhouse gas emissions or other effects detrimental to the environment.

"Re-inventing" the energy system will not be at all easy. In the case of electricity, which does not have the largest share in energy demand: Nuclear energy is regarded as not sustainable. In case of an accident there is the risk of releasing radiation affecting the environment and people's health. Also, discussions on how to deal with nuclear waste are still pending, with deep geological repositories (DGRs) being the only, but hardly satisfying, solution available at present. Last but not least there is the problem of public opinion which seems to make an intensified use of nuclear energy quite challenging. Fusion technologies which might help to avoid some of these problems are not available so far, and there are doubts if they will ever be.

Renewable energy technologies like wind and photovoltaic on the other hand deliver only intermittent generation which is not sufficient to cover the demands of a modern industrialised society which needs stable electricity supply 24 hours a day, 365 days a year, in other words, base load. Their capacities are limited and the usual energy yield is poor compared to that of thermal and nuclear power plants. Therefore back-up power plants are needed which raises the question of what kind of plants these might be, and the demand for balancing energy also rises. Moreover, for wind turbine generators rare earths are needed, the supply of which is challenging and poses environmental risks in itself. As for biomass, there is the "food or fuel" problem, especially when it comes to the production of biofuels. Also, electricity and heat generation from most renewable energy sources still need to be subsidised due to high production costs. Hydro power can avoid this and help to cut greenhouse gas emissions – but on the other hand it might put aquatic biodiversity at risk. The case for wind turbines is similar, but they can also have an effect on bird-life. The latter two examples indicate the conflict of aiming at environmental protection on the one hand versus dealing with climate change on the other.

Energy efficiency as a third possible means is fine, but there are doubts if its potential is sufficient. Technologies like carbon capture and storage (CCS), which would allow the building of more or less "carbon-neutral" thermal power plants, are not available on a commercial scale at the time of writing.

There are proposals for so-called "footprint" models for limiting (global) energy demand, giving everyone the right to consume the same amount of energy during a particular time. But this hardly seems convincing. Eventually it would make necessary to scrupulously plan and monitor any energy-related action of any person because even a single kilogram of CO_2 might bring mankind to the "tipping point" leading to a collapse of the climate system. This might well be called a dictatorship on behalf of "saving the planet" (Kronberger 2011: 141-147).

The only reasonable way out is pragmatism and being aware of the limited but nevertheless impressive capabilities of mankind. Research is the key to further expanding these capabilities, and so is international cooperation. The EU will not be able to cope with the challenges of climate change on its own, but it can make substantial contributions not by setting ever more challenging emission reduction targets, but by technologies it develops and implements not only domestically but also internationally. This does not mean fully abandoning its current approach in terms of climate policy; but it means shifting towards more low-hanging fruits than a global post-Kyoto agreement, which in fact none of the EU's prospective partners want.

References

11135/12: Press Release 3175th Council meeting Transport, Telecommunications and Energy Energy items Luxembourg, June 15, 2012.

2010/C 83/01, Consolidated versions of the Treaty on European Union and the Treaty on the Functioning of the European Union (Lisbon Treaty). In: Official Journal of the European Union, Volume 53, March 30, 2010.

Areva (2011), Bulgaria: AREVA and BEH sign cooperation agreement in the field of nuclear power and renewable energy; press release of Areva on March 13, 2011 available at www.areva.com/EN/news-8837/bulgaria-areva-and-beh-sign-cooperation-agreement-in-the-field-of-nuclear-power-and-renewable-energy.html

Atomstroyexport (2011), Russian Federation and Republic of Belarus signed international agreement on first NPP construction; press release by Atomstroyexport, March 15, 2011, available at www.atomstroyexport.ru/show/press/552.

Bank, Matthias (2007): Basiswissen Umwelttechnik. Würzburg: Vogel Buchverlag.

Barroso (2011a), http://europa.eu/rapid/pressReleasesAction.do, Reference: IP/11/63 Date: 26/01/2011.

BGB (2011a), Bundesgesetzblatt Jahrgang 2011, Teil I, Nr. 43, ausgeben zu Bonn am 5. August 2011

BNetzA (2011), Auswirkungen des Kernkraftwerk-Moratoriums auf die Übertragungsnetze und die Versorgungssicherheit – Bericht der Bundesnetzagentur an das Bundesministerium für Wirtschaft und Technologie, 11. April 2011.

Canada (2011): Depositary Notification on Canada's withdrawal from the Kyoto Protocol, available athttp://unfccc.int/kyoto_protocol/background/items/6603.php

China (2010a), Cancun climate talks send "positive" signals: Chinese delegation; Report by Xinhua news agency, available at http://www.ccchina.gov.cn/en/NewsInfo.asp?NewsId=26593

China (2011): Chinese delegation hails progress made at Durban climate conference; Report by Xinhua news agency, available at http://www.ccchina.gov.cn/en/NewsInfo.asp?NewsId=30584

CMP.7 2011: Draft decision -/CMP.7 Outcome of the work of the Ad Hoc Working Group on Further Commitments for Annex I Parties under the Kyoto Protocol at its sixteenth session; available at http://unfccc.int/resource/docs/2011/cmp7/eng/10a01.pdf#page=2

COM(2007)723, Communication from the Commission to the European Parliament, the Council, the European Economic and Social Committee and the Committee of Regions: A European Strategic Energy Technology Plan (SET Plan)

COM(2010) 86, Communication from the Commission to the European Parliament, the Council, the European Economic and Social Committee and the Committee of Regions, 9 March 2010: International climate policy post-Copenhagen: Acting now to reinvigorate global action on climate change; available at http://ec.europa.eu/ commission _20102014/hedegaard/headlines/docs/com86_reinvigorate_global_action_en.pdf

COM(2011) 21, Communication from the Commission to the European Parliament, the Council, the European Economic and Social Committee and the Committee of Regions: A resource-efficient Europe – Flagship initiative under the Europe 2020 Strategy

COM(2011) 112/4, Communication from the Commission to the European Parliament, the Council, the European Economic and Social Committee and the Committee of Regions: Roadmap for moving to a competitive low carbon economy in 2050.

Copenhagen Accord, Report of the Conference of the Parties on its fifteenth session, held in Copenhagen from 7 to 19 December 2009, Addendum – Part Two: Action taken by the Conference of the Parties at its fifteenth session (Copenhagen Accord; available at http://unfccc.int/documentation/documents/advanced_search/items/3594.php?rec=j&pr iref=600005735#beg

Dahrendorf, Ralf (1990), Betrachtungen über die Revolution in Europa. Stuttgart: Deutsche Verlags-Anstalt.

DENA (2010), dena-Netzstudie II. Integration erneuerbarer Energien in die deutsche Stromversorgung im Zeitraum 2015-2020 mit Ausblick 2025, available at DENA's website www.dena.de

DG CLIMA (2010), Website of the EU's Directorate-General for Climate Action, http://ec.europa.eu/dgs/clima/mission/index_en.htm

DG Energy (2011), Investment needs for future adaptation measures in EU nuclear power plants and other electricity generation technologies due to effects of climate change; available at http://ec.europa.eu/energy/nuclear/studies/

Directive 79/409/ECC, Council Directive 79/409/ECC of April 2, 1979 on the conservation of wild birds

Directive 92/43/EEC, Council Directive 92/43/EEC of 21 May 1992 on the conservation of natural habitats and of wild fauna and flora ("Habitats Directive"); available at http://ec.europa.eu/environment/nature/legislation/habitatsdirective/index_en.htm

Directive 2000/60/EC, Directive 2000/60/EC Of The European Parliament and The Council of 23 October 2000 establishing a framework for Community action in the field of water policy ("Water Framework Directive"; available at http://ec.europa.eu/environment/ water/water-framework/index_en.html

EEA (2008), Impacts of Europe's changing climate – 2008 indicator-based assessment, EEA Report No 4/2008 available at http://www.eea.europa.eu/publications/eea_report _2008_4

ECCP II, Second ECCP Progress Report – Can we meet our Kyoto targets?, April 2003, http://ec.europa.eu/clima/documentation/eccp/

E-Control (2011), Preisentwicklungen am Energiemarkt – Wie geht es weiter?; available at www.e-control.at/de/presse/energie-round-tables

ENB 2011a: Earth Negotiations Bulletin, Summary of the Bonn Climate Change Conference: 6-17 June 2011, available at www.iisd.ca/climate/sb34/
ENB 2011b: Earth Negotiations Bulletin, Summary of the Durban Bonn Climate Change
   Conference: 28 November–11 December 2011, available at www.iisd.ca/climate/
   cop17/
ENB 202: Earth Negotiations Bulletin, Summary of the Bonn Climate Change Conference:
   14-25 May 2012, available at www.iisd.ca/climate/sb36/
ENSI (2011), Die Ausserbetriebnahme von Kernkraftwerken; press release of the Eidge-
   nössisches Nuklearsicherheitsinspektorat (ENSI), 28 June 2011, available at http://
   www.ensi.ch/index.php?id=165&L=0&tx_ttnews[pS]=1312843603&tx_ttnews[pointe
   r]=1&tx_ttnews[tt_news]=328&tx_ttnews[backPid]=164&cHash=3288034de79c7f581
   89c1781bcac7b2f
ENSREG (2011), Declaration of ENSREG – EU "Stress Tests" specifications, available at
   www.ensreg.eu/node/286
ENSREG (2012), Peer review report Stress tests performed on European nuclear power
   plants, available at http://www.ensreg.eu/EU-Stress-Tests/EU-level-Reports
Erdmann, Georg (2011), Kosten des Ausbaus der erneuerbaren Energien – Eine Studie der
   Technischen Universität Berlin im Auftrag von vbw – Vereinigung der Bayerischen Wirtschaft e.V., Bayerische Chemieverbände, Verband Bayerischer Papierfabriken, Verband
   der Bayerischen Energie- und Wasserwirtschaft e. V.; available at http://www. vbw-
   bayern.de/agv/vbw-Themen-Wirtschaftspolitik-Energie-Publikationen-vbw_Studie_ Kosten _des_Ausbaus_der_erneuerbaren_Energien-4361,ArticleID__20670. htm
EU Commission 2011, European Council 24/25 March 2011 – Conclusions, Brussels, 25
   March 2011
Government (2011), Energiewende – die einzelnen Maßnahmen im Überblick; press release of the German federal government, 6 June 2011: http://www.bundesregierung.
   de/nn_1021804/Content/DE/Artikel/2011/06/2011-06-06-energiewende-kabinett-wei-
   tere-informationen.html
The Guardian (2010), US goes to Basics over Copenhagen accord tactics WikiLeaks cables
   show how the Basic countries are the object of US diplomatic attention and admiration, http://www.guardian.co.uk/environment/2010/dec/03/us-basics-copenhagen-accord-
   tactics
House of Commons (2010), House of Commons Science and Technology Committee: The
   disclosure of climate data from the Climatic Research Unit at the University of East
   Anglia Eighth Report of Session 2009–10 http://www.publications.parliament.uk/pa/
   cm200910/cmselect/cmsctech/387/387i.pdf
IAEA (2010a), International Atomic Energy Agency (IAEA): Nuclear Power Reactors in
   the World, 2010 Edition; available at www.iaea.org
IP/10/1699, European Union welcomes Cancún Agreement as important step towards
   global framework for climate action; press release of the European Union, available at
   http://europa.eu/rapid/pressReleasesAction.do?reference=IP/10/1699
IPCC (2007), R.E.H. Sims, R.N. Schock, A. Adegbululgbe, J. Fenhann, I. Konstan-
   tinaviciute, W. Moomaw, H.B. Nimir, B. Schlamadinger, J. Torres-Martínez, C.
   Turner, Y. Uchiyama, S.J.V. Vuori, N. Wamukonya, X. Zhang, 2007: Energy supply.
   In Climate Change 2007: Mitigation. Contribution of Working Group III to the Fourth
   Assessment Report of the Intergovernmental Panel on Climate Change [B. Metz, O.R.
   Davidson, P.R. Bosch, R. Dave, L.A. Meyer (eds)], Cambridge, United Kingdom and
   New York, NY, USA: Cambridge University Press.

Kaltschmitt, Martin/Streicher, Wolfgang (eds.) (2009): Regenerative Energien in Öster-reich. Grundlagen, Systemtechnik, Umweltaspekte, Kostenanalysen, Potenziale, Nut-zung. Vieweg+Teubner publishers, Wiesbaden.

Kent (2011): Statement by Canada's environment minister Peter Kent, December 12, 2011, available at www.ec.gc.ca/default.asp?lang=En&n=FFE36B6D-1&news=6B04014B-54FC-4739-B22C-F9CD9A840800

Kommunalkredit (2008), Österreichs JI/CDM-Programm 2008 – Joint-Implementation-/ Clean-Development-Mechanism-Programm; available at http://www.public-consulting. at/blueline/upload/jicdmbericht2008.pdf.

Kronberger, Hans (2011), Geht uns aus der Sonne – Die Zukunft hat begonnen. Vienna: Uranus Publishers.

Kurier (2011), Deutsche "betteln" um Strom aus Österreich; article in the Austrian daily news-paper "Kurier" of August 12, 2011; available at http://kurier.at/wirtschaft/ 4069024.php

Kyoto Protocol, Kyoto Protocol Under The United Nations Framework Convention On Climate Change; available at http://unfccc.int/kyoto_protocol/items/2830.php

Le Monde (2011): Une gifle cinglante pour Silvio Berlusconi; available at www.lemonde. fr/idees/article/2011/06/14/une-gifle-cinglante-pour-silvio-berlusconi_1535807_3232. html#ens_id=1191686

Lenin, Vladimir Ilic (1918), The Next Tasks of Soviet Power. In: Lenin, Works, tome 27. Berlin: Dietz Verlag 1987, pp. 225-268.

MEMO /11/895: Durban conference delivers breakthrough for climate, available at http://europa.eu/rapid/pressReleasesAction.do?reference=MEMO/11/895&format=HT ML&aged=0&language=EN&guiLanguage=en

Oesterreichs Energie (2011), Strom in Österreich; brochure on Austria's electricity supply. Oesterreichs E-Wirtschaft Akademie GmbH, Vienna.

Oettinger (2012), European Commission – Press release of 26th April 2012: EU nuclear Stress tests: Technical report and additional plant visits agreed, available at http:// europa.eu/rapid/pressReleasesAction.do?reference=IP/12/429&format=HTML&aged= 0&language=EN&guiLanguage=en

Ohl, Cornelia / Monsees, Jan (2008), Sustainable Land Use against the Background of a Growing Wind Power Industry; discussion paper of UFZ Helmholtz Centre for Envi-ronmental Research Leipzig, available at https://www.ufz.de/index.php?de=14487

OTS_20110530_OTS0274, Öttinger zu Stresstests: Weder Persilschein noch Abschaltautoma-tismus; press release by the Press Office of Austria's Federal Parliament, available at http://www.ots.at/presseaussendung/OTS_20110530_OTS0274/oettinger-zu-stresstests-weder-persilschein-noch-abschaltautomatismus-eu-kommissar-fuer-europaeisierung-der-energie-und-klimaschutzpolitik (in German).

Pennsylvania State University (2010), RA-1O Final Investigation Report Involving Dr. Michael E. Mann, The Pennsylvania State University, June 4, 2010, available at: http://www.research.psu.edu/news/2010/michael-mann-decision

Prognos (2011), Konsequenzen eines Ausstiegs aus der Kernenergie bis 2022 für Deutsch-land und Bayern; study by Prognos on behalf of vbw – Vereinigung der Bayerischen Wirtschaft e. V., July 2011, available at www.vbw-bayern.de

Rechnungshof (2011), Bericht des Rechnungshofes Reihe Bund 2011/4 (Report on Aus-tria's Federal Accounting Office concering the Federal Climate and Energy Fund).

SmartGrids (2010), European Technology Platform SmartGrids: Strategic Deployment Document for Europe's Electricity Networks of the Future; available at www. smart-grids.eu

Spiegel Online (2010), Kopenhagener Klimagipfel: USA und China verbrüderten sich ge-
    gen Europa; available at www.spiegel.de/wissenschaft/mensch/0,1518,druck-733230
    ,00.html
Spiegel Online (2011), Oettinger warnt vor zu viel Klimaschutz; online edition of the
    German news magazine "Der Spiegel"; available at www.spiegel.de/wissenschaft/
    natur/0,1518,druck-749316,00.html
Stern, Todd (2010a): Briefing on the UN Climate Change Conference in Cancun http://
    www.state.gov/g/oes/rls/remarks/2010/152847.htm
Stern, Todd (2011): United Nations Climate Change Conference in Durban, South Africa –
    Special Briefing via Teleconference December 13, 2011 http://www.state.gov/r/ pa/
    prs/ps/2011/12/178699.htm
Stuart, Becky (2012): Greece: More details emerge for 10 GW Project Helios; www.pv-
    magazine.com/news/details/beitrag/greece--more-details-emerge-for-10-gw-project-
    helios_100005886/#axzz1xI76ZnPW
TVO (2010), TVO is very pleased with Parliament's nuclear decision; press release of
    TVO, 1 July 2010, available at http://www.tvo.fi/www/page/3452/
UBS Investment Research (2011), Global Nuclear Power Report, 4 April 2011; available
    at http://www.scribd.com/doc/54263128/Can-Nuclear-Power-Survive-Fukushima-UBS
    -Q-Series
Umweltbundesamt (2011), Klimaschutzbericht 2011, available at http://www. umweltbundes-
    amt.at/umweltsituation/luft/emissionsinventur/emiberichte/ The report is in German, but
    includes an English summary.
UNEP (2010), The Emissions Gap Report Are the Copenhagen Accord Pledges Sufficient
    to Limit Global Warming to 2° C or 1.5° C? A preliminary assessment; available at
    www.unep.org/publications/ebooks/emissionsgapreport
UNEP Global Trends (2011), Global Trends in Renewable Energy Investment 2011 –
    Analysis of Trends and Issues in the Financing of Renewable Energy; available at
    http://fs-unep-centre.org/
WNA (2011), Nuclear Power in Russia; Fact sheet of the World Nuclear Association, avail-
    able at www.world-nuclear.org/info/default.aspx?id=366&terms=Russia#Extending_
    nuclear_capacity _
WNA (2011a), Emerging Nuclear Energy Countries: Fact sheet of the World Nuclear As-
    sociation; available at http://www.world-nuclear.org/info/inf102.html

The 'European Social Model' – Light-House for the World or *Sick Man of the Bosporus?*

Arno Tausch[1]

Introduction

In this contribution, we look at the trajectory and the efficiency of the *'European social model' (ESM)*. As of April 13, 2011, there were an astonishing 268,000 entries for the exact occurrence of this English language term on the Internet (of these, 12,000 in *'Google books'*, and 8,150 in *'Google Scholar'* alone). Thus, there exist an almost unlimited number of opinions, but also academic studies on the subject, and there is a lack of clear definitions and empirical criteria, as well as a consensus on the existence of this European social model (ESM), and on its trajectory and future.

This lamentable situation is not improved, if we move over to the world media. We just picked out news items on the exact occurrence of this term from *'Google news'*. Coincidence has it that on April 13th at 9:45, the time of the beginning of the final wording of this article, we are in the midst of a real controversy, involving three key players in the drama – the European Commission, European Labour, and European governments. Notably enough, a Chinese, not a European, news dispatch (Xinhua English.news.cn 2011-04-05 21:04:38) is the first in today's list, quoting *'EU President Herman Van Rompuy[2]'* as saying that recent comprehensive economic measures approved by European leaders were necessary to save *'the European social model'*. Item 2, taken from the influential news agency *Euractiv* (http://www.euractiv.com/en/ socialeurope/unions-ensure-noisy-start-eu-summit-news-503451) tells us that thousands of protesters were recently blocking traffic in Brussels as part of their campaign against neo-liberal austerity reforms agreed upon recently by EU leaders. In the name of the very same *'European social model'* they are against the very same proposals, mentioned by Mr. Van Rompuy above, which he in turn justifies by this very same *'European social model' (ESM)*. *Associated Press,* for its part, complicates the picture even further by describing in the third dispatch on the Google news list of April 13, 2011 the

---

1   The author would like to thank Yitzhak Berman, Peter Herrmann and Almas Heshmati for many insights and comments. All websites and statistics were accessed on April 13th, 2011
2   The old enigma, who is in charge in Europe, was already presented by the former US Secretary of State, Henry Kissinger: 'When I want to call Europe, I cannot find a phone number', see Malici, 2008.

positions taken by European Finance Ministers, who, like Mr. Van Rompuy and the Trade Unions, also justify their austerity actions, against which the trade unionists protested so vehemently, in the name of the very same *'European social model'* (http://www.google.com/hostednews/ap/article/ALeqM5iy 86HBj9um8OJ3pdHtOtAbfS2urQ?docId=b3f7ed5a0afb4f7788b62a9c0da 52711).

What is then this EMS, this European social model? Portugal? Sweden? Romania? Italy? Ireland? The arithmetic mean of the performance of the old and/or new member states of the EU-27? The lessons from the best or the worst five states according to Eurostat poverty statistics? In relation to social protection expenditures?

In this article, we will try to shed some light on this subject, which many see as the 'cornerstone of the European life-style'. The European trade unionists define the ESM as follows:

> 'The European Social Model is a vision of society that combines sustainable economic growth with ever-improving living and working conditions. This implies full employment, good quality jobs, equal opportunities, social protection for all, social inclusion, and involving citizens in the decisions that affect them. In the ETUC's [European Trade Union Confederation's] view, social dialogue, collective bargaining and workers' protection are crucial factors in promoting innovation, productivity and competitiveness. This is what distinguishes Europe, where post-war social progress has matched economic growth, from the US model, where small numbers of individuals have benefited at the expense of the majority. Europe must continue to sustain this social model as an example for other countries around the world' (http://www.etuc.org/a/111).

Eurofound, which is an official European agency under the jurisdiction of the EU Commission, defines in turn the ESM in pretty much the same way (http://www.eurofound.europa.eu/areas/industrialrelations/dictionary/definiti ons/EUROPEANSOCIALMODEL.htm).

Looking at the Main Research Results in International Literature

Arguably, the book with the highest global library circulation[3] on the subject, Professor Gøsta Esping-Andersen's work[4], 1990, which achieved 40 editions, published between 1990 and 2010, and which is available in 5 languages, and which is now held by an astonishing 825 global libraries worldwide, making it

---

3   http://www.worldcat.org/identities/lccn-n84-135803
4   Professor Andersen's website contains many useful insights on the debates and controversies under discussion here: http://www.esping-andersen.com/

a real classic of modern social science, maintains that there are three European social models, not a single one, which he calls the liberal/free market regime of the Anglo-Saxon countries, the Nordic/social democratic regimes, and the 'conservative' European continental welfare regimes, linking social benefits to past work experience and social insurance. Since the advantages and disadvantages of this classification, with the possible addition of a fourth category, the Mediterranean member states of the EU or other possible types of democratic welfare regimes, such a 'radical type', which is sometimes used in reference to Australia and New Zealand, were debated at great length in the relevant literature (see Arts and Gelissen, 2002; Herrmann et al., 2009 as indications of the almost unlimited number of quantitative and qualitative studies on the subject), we will not deal any further with the question of social policy typologies. What we are interested in are parameters of efficiency. Many roads may lead to Rome. But just how good are they?

The *Social Science Research Network* in New York, which is the biggest social science research community in the world today (http://www.ssrn.com/), lists in turn two papers, very much opposing one another, as the ones with the highest global download figures on the subject. Olivier Blanchard, 2006, ranked number 17th among the global economists (http://logec.repec.org/scripts/authorstat.pf) thinks that there is indeed a viable European model, based on three legs: *competition* in goods markets, insurance in labour markets, and the active use of macroeconomic policy. Alesina and Angeletos, 2002, (Alesina is ranked 23 among the global economists, see again http://logec.repec.org/scripts/authorstat.pf) maintain by contrast that if a society believes, like the EU, that luck, birth, connections and/or corruption determine wealth, taxes will be higher and more extensive, thus distorting allocations and making these beliefs self-sustained as well.

Using Thomson Reuters Web of Science, the most authoritative index of the social sciences today (http://thomsonreuters.com/products_services/science/science_products/a-z/web_of_science/), we are similarly confronted with a variety of conflicting views. The most influential journal article on the subject, mentioning the ESM in the title, was written by Scharpf, 2002 and maintains that efforts to adopt European social policies are politically impeded by the diversity of national welfare states, differing not only in levels of economic development and hence in their ability to pay for social transfers and services but, even more significantly, in their normative aspirations and institutional structures. Hyman, 2005, even says that there is simply no agreement what 'social Europe' means in the first place, let alone how it should be defended against the challenges inherent in the neoliberal approach to economic integration. Jepsen and Pascual, 2005 are equally sceptical about the subject. They even maintain that the very use of the concept under scrutiny here – the ESM – in the academic and political debate is simply a rhetorical resource intended to legitimise the politically constructed and identity-building project of the EU institutions. Moving down the article impact factor list, we find, among others the similarly pessimistic note by Alber, 2006 who concludes: (1) for most indicators the range of variation within the European Union is bigger than the gap between Europe and the United States; (2) counter to the idea of policy convergence, differences in the developmental trajectories of countries with different institutional arrangements persist; (3) despite having extended welfare states similar to those of continental European countries, Scandinavian nations have performed as well as the Anglo-Saxon countries in terms of employment and growth dynamics. Hence there are not only different social models in Europe but also different pathways to success. Montanari et al., 2008, examine key aspects of the development of the main social insurance programs during the period 1980-2000 in 14 EU Member States. Their results indicate a divergence rather than convergence of social insurance replacement rates in Europe at that time. In terms of institutional models there is no evidence of a common European social model (ESM) in the area of social insurance over the past decades.

Our Own Research Design

Unsatisfactory, as it may be, a large part of the ESM typology and accounting literature left out the important question of globalisation and its effects on the social situation in Western democracies from its horizon. Thus, we will first analyze the development history of the 15 original members of the European Union by comparison with the USA and some other Western democracies since the 1980s according to their paths of globalisation. We compare these with the trajectory of employment, the reduction of inequality, and economic growth. We will carry out this analysis with International Monetary Fund (IMF) data (real GDP per annum), the globalisation time series data of the Swiss Federal Institute of Technology Zurich (ETH), the University of Texas Inequality Project data, based on payment in 21 industrial sectors, and unemployment rates as per cent of the civilian labour force (OECD). The data sources are documented in the Appendix and in Graph 1. Thus we will highlight differences and or similarities between the trajectories of globalisation and social policy outcomes for the entire EU-15 in comparison with the US and some other major western democracies.

With Herrmann et al. 2009, and based on the latest Eurostat and OECD data, we then go on to ask ourselves how efficient social policy is. One question in this context is how large the percentage of the population, lifted out of poverty by social expenditures really is. Another question is then the establishment of efficiency parameters, which are really viable across countries and independent of the amount of poverty existing before social transfers. For a country with 60% poverty rate before social transfers it is easier to reduce poverty by 10% by social expenditures than for a country, which already reduced pre-social transfer poverty to 15%, and which wants to reduce this poverty by a further 10% (i.e. to 5%). If there were anything like a unique *'European social model' (EMS)* in existence, Europe should be different from all other western democracies under investigation, also according to our efficiency criteria. Our approach is based on a statistical analysis of residuals, established in Herrmann et al.

Finally, we present data from a SPSS XVIII principal components reanalysis of the UNICEF report (2007) on child poverty in advanced countries, weighting the five resulting factors according to their contribution in explaining the total variance of the model. We develop from this analysis a new scale of child welfare in advanced countries. We then compare these results with the social expenditure inputs in the OECD region to measure the efficiency of social policy in bringing about child and youth welfare. We finally ask ourselves whether or not our data analysis offers any conclusion for the dramatic financial and global situation in the PIIGS states – i.e. Portugal, Ireland, Italy, Greece and Spain, which currently are at the centre of the financial storm, affecting the Eurozone.

Globalisation and Social Outcomes in Western Democracies

Graph 1 highlights the development history of the 15 original members of the European Union by comparison with the USA and some other Western democracies since the 1980s according to globalisation and the most tangible possible benefits of any 'social model', i.e. employment, the reduction of inequality, and economic growth.

This first approximation yields very clear empirical results, which might provide a new input to the trodden paths of the entire *'European social model'* debate. The USA not only had lower unemployment and higher economic growth rates than the EU-15. Globalisation inflows were smaller than in the EU-15, and – most importantly – the tendency towards sectoral inequality as a proxy for overall inequality was less pronounced than in the EU-15. The average, unweighted performance of the other Western democracies rather resembles the European performance. So the dire fact number one, established in this essay, is that during globalisation, the *'European social model'* is not better than the USA or other Western democracies:

Arno Tausch

Graph 1: Economic globalisation, economic growth and social performance in Europe (EU-15), the USA, and some other Western democracies

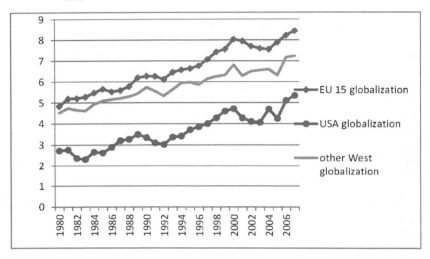

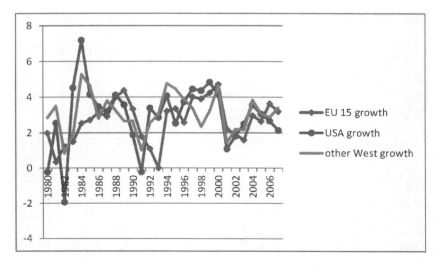

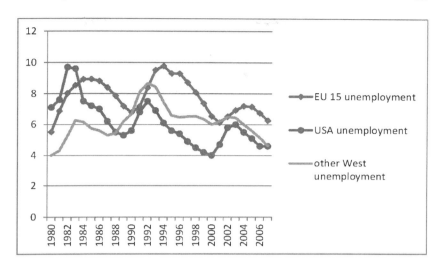

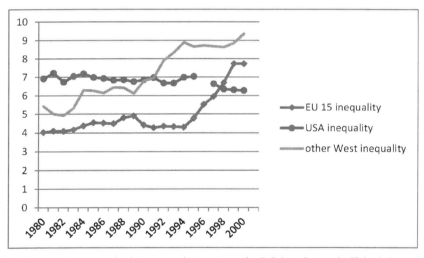

Note: The EU-15 countries in our sample were: Austria, Belgium, Denmark, Finland, France, Germany, Greece, Ireland, Italy, Luxembourg, The Netherlands, Portugal, Spain, Sweden, UK. The other developed Western democracies comprised: Australia, Canada, Israel, Japan, New Zealand, Norway. Economic growth: IMF economic growth data (real GDP per annum) and growth predictions April 2009, http://www.imf.org/external/datamapper/index.php. Globalisation: ETH Zurich globalisation time series data), http://globalisation.kof.ethz.ch/static/rawdata/ globalisation_2010_short.xls The Zurich data, used in this study, refer only to the ETH economic globalisation time series, which covers 'actual flows', combining trade (per cent of GDP), foreign direct investment (flows, per cent of GDP), foreign direct investment (stocks, per cent of GDP), portfolio investment (per cent of GDP), income payments to foreign nationals (per cent of

GDP). Inequality: Theil Index of Inequality, based on payment in 21 industrial sectors; calculated from UNIDO sources in University of Texas Inequality Project, http://utip.gov.utexas.edu/data.html. Unemployment: unemployment as per cent of the civilian labour force: http://stats.oecd.org/Index.aspx. In order to visualise our time series data in a single graph system and on a single easily comprehensible left hand scale, we had to rescale the data by multiplying the University of Texas time series Inequality (Theil Indices of the inequality of wages by sectors) data by a factor of 250 and to divide the ETH globalisation flow data by a factor of 10, to produce scales, which range from 0 to 12.

To Abolish Poverty, Four-Fifths of Total EU-27 GDP Would Be Required

Such phenomena led neo-Keynesian European economists to diagnose that the Euro-area has the lowest growth rate of the industrialised world (Marterbauer/Walterskirchen, 2006). Other euro-sceptical researchers from many different theoretical perspectives (Galtung, 1982; Heshmati and Tausch, 2007; Rothschild, 1999, 2000, 2003, 2009; Seers et al., 1979, 1980; Tausch and Ghymers, 2006; Tausch and Herrmann, 2001; Tausch, 2010) came to the same conclusions. Sluggish economic growth, unemployment and structural blockades on many fronts, including deficiencies in science and research, seem to characterise the trajectory of western Europe ever since the 1970s, to which we have to add the current crisis in Ireland and the European South, long regarded as the number one success stories of the enlarged EU since the 1970s and 1980s[5].

Euro-pessimists would expect a repetition of the Argentina script of the 1970s and 1980s on our side of the Atlantic during the next decade, while Euro-optimists would have to continue to expect that the European Common Agricultural Policy (CAP), the regional and structural policies, the Common Foreign Policy and the European Monetary Union, on all of which we spend an awful lot of money, are and continue to be 'shining paths' for humanity.

Following the methodology, developed in Herrmann et al. 2009, and based on the latest Eurostat data, we first have to recognise that European social policy only lifts 6.8% of the total European population, i.e. 29.44% of the poor population, out of poverty.[6] A very huge amount of money is required for this. Social transfers amount to one quarter of the European GDP

---

5   For current news about the financial crisis affecting Greece, Ireland and Portugal, see http://www.ftd.de/

6   Poverty is defined as corresponding to Eurostat criteria (Persons at-risk-of-poverty after social transfers). The risk-of-poverty threshold is set at 60% of the national median equivalised disposable income. See http://epp.eurostat.ec.europa.eu/tgm/information.do;jsessionid =9ea7971b30dbc963f5167dff4854b205f20cd6cb3681.e34RaNaLaxqRay0Lc3uLbNiNa30Ke0?tab=table&plugin=1&language=en&pcode=t2020_52) .

in 2006. To lift just 1% of the population out of poverty, a staggering 3.66% of the GDP is now needed (Table 1). Tables 2 and 3 show that Sweden, Luxembourg, Finland, Spain, Denmark, Estonia, the Netherlands, Germany, the UK and France currently spend 5% or more of their GDP to lift just 1% of the population out of poverty. In most EU-27 member countries, only one-third or less of the poor population are lifted out of poverty by social transfers. I.e. two-thirds or more of the population are practically not reached by this gigantic machinery EMS, which consumes a quarter of European GDP.

Table 1: The 'European social model' – EMS

	EU-27:% poverty before social transfers	EU-27:% poverty after social transfers	EU-27: social protection expenditure as % of the GDP	EU-27: % of the population lifted out of poverty by social transfers	EU-27: % of the poor population saved by social transfers from poverty	% of the GDP spent to lift 1% of the population out of poverty
2005	26.00	16.40	27.12	9.60	36.92	2.83
2006	25.00	16.50	26.71	8.50	34.00	3.14
2007	24.50	16.70	25.74	7.80	31.84	3.30
2008	23.60	16.40	26.36	7.20	30.51	3.66

Source: our own compilations from Eurostat, http://epp.eurostat.ec.europa.eu/portal/page/portal/product_details/publication?p_product_code=KS-SF-11-017 and http://epp.eurostat.ec.europa.eu/ portal/page/portal/structural_indicators/indicators/social_cohesion

Arno Tausch

Table 2: The (in)efficiency of European social protection: Percentage of the GDP necessary to lift 1 per cent of the population out of poverty

Country	2007	2008
Bulgaria	0.37	0.66
Romania	0.64	0.69
Poland	1.06	1.36
Hungary	1.31	1.44
Latvia	0.76	1.54
Slovakia	1.48	1.65
Lithuania	1.51	2.13
Ireland	3.20	2.70
Czech Republic	3.00	2.97
Cyprus	1.87	3.07
Portugal	3.47	3.24
Greece	3.06	3.25
Slovenia	3.80	3.47
EU-27	3.30	3.66
Malta	3.75	3.85
Italy	4.31	4.21
Austria	5.93	4.55
Belgium	4.19	4.64
Euro 16	4.79	4.91
France	5.16	5.21
UK	5.97	5.27
Germany	5.13	5.67
Norway	4.98	6.23
Netherlands	5.15	6.47
Estonia	4.73	6.55
Denmark	5.65	6.60
Spain	6.18	6.88
Finland	5.77	6.92
Luxembourg	8.05	9.59
Sweden	8.56	10.87
Iceland	7.39	12.96

Source: our own compilations from Eurostat, http://epp.eurostat.ec.europa.eu/portal/ page/portal/ product_details/publication?p_product_code=KS-SF-11-017 and http://epp.eurostat.ec.europa. eu/portal/page/portal/structural_indicators/indicators/social_cohesion

Table 3: Percentage of the poor population, lifted out of poverty by social transfers

Country	2007	2008	2009
Iceland	22.66	14.41	12.07
Switzerland			12.21
Estonia	11.82	10.55	15.81
Luxembourg	15.09	13.55	16.29
Sweden	24.46	18.12	16.35
Spain	14.72	14.41	16.67
Finland	25.29	21.84	18.34
UK	17.11	19.40	21.36
Germany	26.21	24.38	22.50
Norway	27.06	24.00	23.81
Euro 16	25.81	26.17	24.64
Denmark	30.36	27.61	24.71
Malta	25.13	25.13	25.25
Italy	23.75	26.09	25.51
Netherlands	35.03	29.53	26.49
Cyprus	38.49	27.03	27.03
Belgium	29.63	29.33	27.72
Portugal	27.60	28.85	28.11
Greece	28.27	28.47	28.62
Austria	28.14	33.33	29.41
EU-27	31.84	30.51	29.44
France	31.05	31.72	29.89
Lithuania	33.45	27.54	30.17
Latvia	41.11	24.26	31.28
Slovenia	32.75	33.51	33.92
Poland	49.71	44.59	38.49
Czech Republic	39.24	41.18	38.57
Ireland	25.54	34.60	41.63
Slovakia	50.70	47.09	43.88
Romania	45.97	47.06	48.03
Bulgaria	63.76	52.23	52.81
Hungary	58.16	56.03	58.53

Source: our own compilations from Eurostat, http://epp.eurostat.ec.europa.eu/portal/page/portal/product_details/publication?p_product_code=KS-SF-11-017 and http://epp.eurostat.ec.europa.eu/portal/page/portal/structural_indicators/indicators/social_cohesion

In accordance with Herrmann *et al.* 2009, we also analyze the OECD figures on how much it costs to lift 1% of the population out of poverty (Table 4). If there were anything like a unique ESM – *'European social model'*, Europe should be different from all other western democracies under investigation. But clearly, this is not the case.

Neither 'Light-House to the World' nor 'Sick Man' on the Bosporus'

Our analysis reveals that there are only many different single experiences and models of social policy, and these experiences do not confirm stereotypes, typologies or other generalised approaches. Our conclusions from the data suggest that very efficient models, like the Slovak Republic and the Czech Republic, but also Luxembourg, Hungary and Poland, have to be contrasted by the laggards and high-cost models, like Spain and Mexico, but also Finland, Switzerland, New Zealand, and South Korea. The relatively good performance of Greece, Italy and Belgium on this scale is rather a big surprise. The US, *nota bene,* belongs rather to the international laggards on this scale:

Table 4: how much it costs to lift 1% of people out of poverty as a percentage of GDP – OECD countries

Year	2000	2003
Slovak Republic		0.95
Czech Republic	0.91	1.04
Luxembourg		1.05
Hungary	1.11	1.07
Poland		1.09
Greece	1.18	1.13
Italy	1.44	1.35
Belgium	1.11	1.42
Germany	1.32	1.42
France	1.29	1.44
UK	1.49	1.44
Australia	**1.46**	**1.46**
Netherlands	1.38	1.46
Ireland	2.23	1.50
Iceland		**1.51**
Sweden	1.51	1.70
Norway	**1.62**	**1.72**
Japan	**2.33**	**1.75**
Portugal	2.53	1.79
Austria		1.84
Denmark	1.95	2.01
USA	**2.21**	**2.28**
Korea		**2.48**
New Zealand	**1.97**	**2.54**
Switzerland	**2.43**	**2.63**
Finland	2.48	3.13
Mexico	**6.44**	**3.58**
Spain	5.23	5.08

Source: our own calculations from Eurostat and OECD.stats, Microsoft EXCEL and SPSS XVIII

The comparison of the aggregate efficiency parameters would even suggest that there was a convergence of efficiency trends from the mid-1980s onwards across the Atlantic (Table 5). In the EU-15, the cost to lift 1% out of poverty was 2.8% of the GDP, while in the US it was 2.3%:

Table 5: Aggregate social efficiency, EU-15 and USA since the mid 1980s

	1995	2000	2003
EU-15 social transfers in% of GDP	27.6	26.8	27.7
USA social transfers in% of GDP	15.4	14.6	16.2
EU-15 poverty before social transfers	26.0	23.0	25.0
USA poverty before social transfers	31.3	30.3	31.0
EU-15 poverty after social transfers	**17.0**	**15.0**	**15.0**
USA poverty after social transfers	**23.8**	**23.7**	**23.9**
EU-15% of the pop. lifted out of poverty by social transfers	9.0	8.0	10.0
USA% of the pop. lifted out of poverty by social transfers	7.5	6.6	7.1
EU-15% GDP cost to lift 1% of the population out of poverty	3.1	3.4	2.8
USA% GDP cost to lift 1% of the population out of poverty	2.1	2.2	2.3

Source: our own compilations and calculations, based on SPSS XVIII, Innsbruck University, based on Eurostat (http://epp.eurostat.ec.europa.eu/portal/page?_pageid=1090,30070682,1090_33076576 &_dad=portal&_schema=PORTAL) OECD.stats (http://stats.oecd.org/WBOS/index. aspx)

More Sophisticated Methods of Comparison, Based on the Analysis of Regression Residuals

Our more sophisticated approach is based on a statistical analysis of residuals, established in Herrmann et al., 2009. It has been argued in Herrmann *et al.,* 2009 that the simple arithmetic used to calculate the percentage of the GDP necessary to lift 1% of the poor out of poverty is misleading insofar as it is easier for very poor states to be successful than for richer states, whose initial number of poor people before social transfers is smaller. Applying politometric methods, developed in Hermann *et. al.,* 2009, we document our research results for the early mid 2000s on the basis of the OECD data and for 2008, based on the regression residual approach, in the Appendix. It might be sufficient to note that both our data series well document the fact that the PIIGS – i.e. Portugal, Ireland, Italy, Greece and Spain, which currently are at the centre of the financial storm, affecting Europe (Baglioni and Cherubini 2010; Andrade and Chhaochharia 2010; and Zemanek 2010), do not perform well on our refined social protection expenditure effectiveness indicator. The only plausible exception, Ireland in 2008, insofar supports the argument of those who say that the Irish crisis, much more than for the rest of the PIIGS, is a Bank-system driven crisis and was not so much a question of inefficient state expenditures. The five leading countries according to the Eurostat figures for 2008 and our politometric methods, documented in the Appendix, are Hungary, Slovakia, Bulgaria, Czech Republic, and Poland, which are all new member states of the Union. The least efficient social sectors are to be found in Latvia, Estonia, the UK and Greece.

The comparison on the basis of the OECD statistics for the first part of the 2000s reveals the following tendency. The efficiency leaders in poverty reduction were the Czech Republic, the Slovak Republic, Iceland, Hungary, and Luxembourg. The least efficiencies in poverty reduction were to be found in Spain, the US, Portugal, New Zealand and Ireland.

The European Social Model and Future Generations

We also present data from a re-analysis of the UNICEF report (2007) on child poverty in advanced countries. The UNICEF report created a huge international political debate at the time of its publication, and is arguably the best single data-set to compare the well-being of the future generations in the European Union and in other Western democracies. But lamentably enough, its research results were based on simple aggregations of the rankings from more than 40 indicators. Heshmati et al., 2008, already showed the limitations of such an approach and compared the UNICEF results with a model, based on principal components. If Europe's social model were to be the superstar (theory 1) or the villain of this world (theory 2), the data again would have to confirm this (http://news.bbc.co.uk/2/hi/6359363.stm). Based on a renewed standard SPSS XVIII principal component analysis of the UNICEF variables, and weighting the five resulting factors according to their contribution in explaining the total variance of the model (see Appendix), we first arrive at the following scale of child welfare in advanced countries, based on the five factor analytical items, documented in the Appendix. Again, there is no evidence, which would suggest that there is a single European social model, to be distinguished from the rest of other Western countries. Not surprisingly, the Scandinavians and North-west Europeans lead the way: Finland, Sweden, the Netherlands, Switzerland and Denmark. The most lamentable situation of young people according to such criteria as the combined weight of the criteria of education and social empowerment, lifestyle, social cohesion and social-economic status, subjective well-being and peer relationships and a climate of non-violence was to be encountered in the Baltic Republics, the USA and Japan.

Table 6: – child and youth welfare – factor analytical results, based on UNICEF

	Child and youth welfare
Finland	50.98
Sweden	50.88
Netherlands	37.30
Switzerland	**25.94**
Denmark	25.68
Belgium	23.28
Norway	**21.07**
France	17.58
Italy	17.02
Germany	15.83
Spain	10.18
Slovenia	9.42
Iceland	**8.30**
Ireland	2.79
Australia	**2.70**
Czech Republic	2.30
Canada	**-2.16**
Greece	-10.04
Malta	-11.53
Austria	-13.60
Portugal	-13.60
Poland	-14.03
UK	-17.04
Hungary	-18.54
New Zealand	**-19.06**
Japan	**-20.52**
Estonia	-27.96
USA	**-36.49**
Latvia	-55.74
Lithuania	-58.12

Source: our own compilations and calculations, based on SPSS XVIII, Innsbruck University, based on UNICEF data (http://www.unicef-irc.org/cgi-bin/unicef/Lunga.sql?ProductID=445)

It is now legitimate to raise the question of costs again. One might argue for example that the US Federal Government spends a lot less on social expenditures than most European states. Graph 2 plots social expenditures, as documented by OECD, with the social policy outcome for the young generations, as documented in Table 6 above:

Graph 2: social expenditures and child and youth welfare

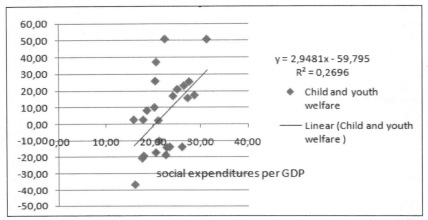

Source: our own compilations and calculations, based on SPSS XVIII, Innsbruck University, based on UNICEF data (http://www.unicef-irc.org/cgi-bin/unicef/Lunga.sql?ProductID=445) and OECD.stats (http://stats.oecd.org/WBOS/index.aspx)

It is now legitimate to compare the 'social policy inputs' (measured by social expenditures per GDP) and the 'social policy output', measured by a social policy outcome variable (i.e. in our case, the data from Table 6). We again apply the regression residual method, introduced by Herrmann et al., 2009. Table 7 documents these efficiency parameters of social expenditures (residuals from the regression line, plotted in Graph 2). Which country was most efficient in using its social expenditures for child and youth welfare? Finland, the Netherlands, Switzerland, Sweden and Ireland were the leaders among the western democracies compared, while Austria, Hungary, the USA, Portugal and Poland were the laggards. The social systems of these countries may have cared well for other groups, like the elderly, but they were not able to respond to the necessities to provide for the needs of future generations.

Table 7: The (in)efficiency of social expenditures to bring about child and youth welfare

	Social expenditures per GDP	Child and youth welfare	Trend value: child and youth welfare, statistically predicted by social expenditures per GDP	(in)efficiency of social spending in providing child and youth welfare
Finland	22,50	50,98	6,54	44,44
Netherlands	20,70	37,30	1,23	36,07
Switzerland	20,50	25,94	0,64	25,30
Sweden	31,30	50,88	32,48	18,40
Ireland	15,90	2,79	-12,92	15,71
Iceland	18,70	8,30	-4,67	12,97
Spain	20,30	10,18	0,05	10,13
Australia	17,90	2,70	-7,02	9,72
Norway	25,10	21,07	14,20	6,87
Italy	24,20	17,02	11,55	5,47
Belgium	26,50	23,28	18,33	4,95
Denmark	27,60	25,68	21,57	4,11
Czech Republic	21,10	2,30	2,41	-0,11
Germany	27,30	15,83	20,69	-4,86
France	28,70	17,58	24,81	-7,23
New Zealand	18,00	-19,06	-6,73	-12,33
Japan	17,70	-20,52	-7,61	-12,91
Greece	21,30	-10,04	3,00	-13,04
UK	20,60	-17,04	0,93	-17,97
Poland	22,90	-14,03	7,72	-21,75
Portugal	23,50	-13,60	9,48	-23,08
USA	16,20	-36,49	-12,04	-24,45
Hungary	22,70	-18,54	7,13	-25,67
Austria	26,10	-13,60	17,15	-30,75

Source: our own compilations and calculations, based on SPSS XVIII, Innsbruck University, based on UNICEF data (http://www.unicef-irc.org/cgi-bin/unicef/Lunga.sql?ProductID=445) and OECD.stats (http://stats.oecd.org/WBOS/index.aspx)

Summary and conclusions

Confronted with the dire fact that neither the European political class, nor the academic community have come up with convincing evidence on the European social model (ESM), we present our own new evidence on the subject. Our approach is efficiency analysis driven and establishes the following facts:

1. The USA not only had lower unemployment and higher economic growth rates than the EU-15. Globalisation inflows were smaller than in the EU-15, and – most importantly – the tendency towards sectoral inequality as a proxy for overall inequality was less pronounced than in the EU-15. The average, unweighted performance of the other Western democracies rather resembles the European performance.

2. We have to recognise that European social policy only lifts 6.80% of the total European population, i.e. 29.44% of the poor population, out of poverty. A very huge amount of money is required for this. Social transfers amount to a quarter of the European GDP in 2006. To lift just 1% of the population out of poverty, a staggering 3.66% of the GDP is now needed.

3. The comparison of the aggregate efficiency parameters would even suggest that there was a convergence of efficiency trends from the mid-1980s onwards across the Atlantic (Table 5).

4. Applying politometric methods, developed in Hermann *et al.*, 2009, we arrive at the conclusion that the five leading countries with a cost efficient poverty reduction system are Hungary, Slovakia, Bulgaria, Czech Republic, and Poland, which are all new member states of the Union. The least efficient social sectors are to be found in Latvia, Estonia, the UK and Greece (based on Eurostat, data for 2008).

5. A comparison on the basis of the OECD statistics for the first part of the 2000s reveals the following tendency. The efficiency leaders in poverty reduction were the Czech Republic, the Slovak Republic, Iceland, Hungary, and Luxembourg. The least efficiencies in poverty reduction were to be found in Spain, the US, Portugal, New Zealand and Ireland.

6. We also present data from a re-analysis of the UNICEF report (2007) on child poverty in advanced countries. Based on a standard SPSS XVIII principal component analysis of the UNICEF variables, and weighting the five resulting factors according to their contribution in explaining the total variance of the model (see Appendix), we arrive at a scale of child welfare in advanced countries (Table 6). The most lamentable situation of young people according to such criteria as the combined weight of the criteria of education and social empowerment; lifestyle, social cohesion and social-economic status; subjective well-being and peer relationships and a climate of non-violence was to be encountered in the Baltic Republics, the USA and Japan.

7. Which country was most efficient in using its social expenditures for child and youth welfare? Finland, the Netherlands, Switzerland, Sweden and Ireland were the leaders among the western democracies compared, while Austria, Hungary, the USA, Portugal and Poland were the laggards. The social systems of these countries may have cared well for other

groups, like the elderly, but they were not able to respond to the necessities to provide for the needs of future generations.

Returning to the basic question of this volume – the EU as a global player – we should finally return to the text, published by Eurofound during the middle of the global financial crisis, on the European Social Model (ESM), already briefly mentioned above (http://www.eurofound.europa.eu/areas/industrialrelations/dictionary/definitions/EUROPEANSOCIALMODEL.htm). Is the ESM an 'exportable product' and a lighthouse to the world? The Commission's 1994 White Paper on social policy (COM (94) 333) described, as Eurofound reminds us, a *'European social model'* in terms of values that include democracy and individual rights, free collective bargaining, the market economy, equal opportunities for all, and social protection and solidarity. Without implying that the ESM, as many neo-liberal critics would suggest, is a *'sick man on the Bosporus'*, we have come to the conclusion in this essay that the ESM, lamentably enough, hardly exists and that at any rate it is not an export product; to which the pressures of globalisation greatly contributed.

Appendix to this Chapter

Statistical sources used in this analysis (accessed on April 13th, 2011):

ECFIN/E3(2007)/REP/50604 and *'Child Poverty and Well-Being in the EU: Current status and way forward"* downloadable at http://www.libertysecurity.org/article1937.html

Eurostat (http://epp.eurostat.ec.europa.eu/portal/page?_pageid=1133,47800773,1133_47 802588&_dad=portal&_schema=PORTAL) and http://epp.eurostat.ec.europa.eu/portal/page/portal/product_details/publication?p_product_code=KS-SF-11-017 and http://epp.eurostat.ec.europa.eu/portal/page/portal/structural_indicators/indicators/social_cohesion

Herrmann, Peter et al. *'Efficiency and Effectiveness of Social Spending"*, IZA DP No. 3482, 2008, available at http://www.iza.org/index_html?lang=de&mainframe=http%3A//www.iza.org/de/webcontent/publications/papers/viewAbstract%3Fdp_id%3D3482 & topSelect=publications&subSelect=papers

OECD.stats (http://stats.oecd.org/WBOS/index.aspx),

UNICEF data (http://www.unicef-irc.org/cgi-bin/unicef/Lunga.sql?ProductID=445).

Arno Tausch

Analytical efficiency parameters of the reduction of poverty – a regression
analytical approach – OECD countries, early 2000s

	Column 1	Column 2	Column 3	Column 4	Column 5	Column 6	Column 7	Column 8	Column 9	Column 10 – efficiency
Czech Republic	21.10	31.70	11.50	20.20	1.04	17.26	-5.76	5.76	0.03	5.73
Slovak Republic	17.30	31.90	13.70	18.20	0.95	17.29	-3.59	3.59	-1.86	5.45
Iceland	18.70	24.70	12.30	12.40	1.51	16.10	-3.80	3.80	-1.16	4.97
Hungary	22.70	33.60	12.30	21.30	1.07	17.57	-5.27	5.27	0.82	4.45
Luxembourg	22.20	34.40	13.20	21.20	1.05	17.70	-4.50	4.50	0.57	3.93
Korea	5.70	23.10	20.80	2.30	2.48	15.84	4.96	-4.96	-7.61	2.65
Netherlands	20.70	28.60	14.40	14.20	1.46	16.75	-2.35	2.35	-0.17	2.52
Norway	25.10	27.00	12.40	14.60	1.72	16.48	-4.08	4.08	2.01	2.07
UK	20.60	29.80	15.50	14.30	1.44	16.94	-1.44	1.44	-0.22	1.67
Switzerland	20.50	23.00	15.20	7.80	2.63	15.82	-0.62	0.62	-0.27	0.90
Denmark	27.60	26.00	12.30	13.70	2.01	16.32	-4.02	4.02	3.25	0.77
Austria	26.10	27.60	13.40	14.20	1.84	16.58	-3.18	3.18	2.51	0.67
Sweden	31.30	29.80	11.40	18.40	1.70	16.94	-5.54	5.54	5.09	0.46
Finland	22.50	22.00	14.80	7.20	3.13	15.66	-0.86	0.86	0.72	0.14
France	28.70	34.10	14.10	20.00	1.44	17.65	-3.55	3.55	3.80	-0.24
Belgium	26.50	34.90	16.20	18.70	1.42	17.79	-1.59	1.59	2.71	-1.12
Australia	17.90	32.60	20.30	12.30	1.46	17.41	2.89	-2.89	-1.56	-1.33
Greece	21.30	38.50	19.60	18.90	1.13	18.38	1.22	-1.22	0.13	-1.35
Mexico	6.80	27.20	25.30	1.90	3.58	16.52	8.78	-8.78	-7.07	-1.72
Japan	17.70	30.90	20.80	10.10	1.75	17.13	3.67	-3.67	-1.66	-2.01
Germany	27.30	36.40	17.20	19.20	1.42	18.03	-0.83	0.83	3.10	-2.27
Poland	22.90	41.90	20.80	21.10	1.09	18.94	1.86	-1.86	0.92	-2.78
Italy	24.20	37.60	19.70	17.90	1.35	18.23	1.47	-1.47	1.56	-3.03
Ireland	15.90	33.90	23.30	10.60	1.50	17.62	5.68	-5.68	-2.55	-3.13
New Zealand	18.00	29.80	22.70	7.10	2.54	16.94	5.76	-5.76	-1.51	-4.24
Portugal	23.50	33.80	20.70	13.10	1.79	17.60	3.10	-3.10	1.22	-4.31
USA	16.20	31.00	23.90	7.10	2.28	17.14	6.76	-6.76	-2.40	-4.35
Spain	20.30	25.00	21.00	4.00	5.08	16.15	4.85	-4.85	-0.37	-4.48

Analytical efficiency parameters of the reduction of poverty – a regression analytical approach –EU-27 countries, 2008

Country	Column 1	Column 2	Column 3	Column 4	Column 5	Column 6	Column 7	Column 8	Column 9	Column 10 – efficiency
Hungary	22.71	28.20	12.40	15.80	1.44	17.95	-5.55	5.55	0.00	**5.55**
Slovakia	16.02	20.60	10.90	9.70	1.65	14.67	-3.77	3.77	-0.16	**3.93**
Bulgaria	15.48	44.80	21.40	23.40	0.66	25.13	-3.73	3.73	-0.18	**3.90**
Czech Republic	18.72	15.30	9.00	6.30	2.97	12.38	-3.38	3.38	-0.10	**3.47**
Poland	18.56	30.50	16.90	13.60	1.36	18.95	-2.05	2.05	-0.10	**2.15**
Romania	14.25	44.20	23.40	20.80	0.69	24.87	-1.47	1.47	-0.20	**1.68**
Netherlands	28.45	14.90	10.50	4.40	6.47	12.21	-1.71	1.71	0.14	**1.56**
Slovenia	21.49	18.50	12.30	6.20	3.47	13.76	-1.46	1.46	-0.03	**1.49**
Austria	28.18	18.60	12.40	6.20	4.55	13.81	-1.41	1.41	0.13	**1.27**
France	30.76	18.60	12.70	5.90	5.21	13.81	-1.11	1.11	0.20	**0.91**
Norway	22.44	15.00	11.40	3.60	6.23	12.25	-0.85	0.85	-0.01	**0.85**
Denmark	29.69	16.30	11.80	4.50	6.60	12.81	-1.01	1.01	0.17	**0.84**
Iceland	22.03	11.80	10.10	1.70	12.96	10.87	-0.77	0.77	-0.02	**0.78**
Ireland	22.12	23.70	15.50	8.20	2.70	16.01	-0.51	0.51	-0.01	**0.52**
Belgium	28.28	20.80	14.70	6.10	4.64	14.76	-0.06	0.06	0.14	**-0.08**
Sweden	29.35	14.90	12.20	2.70	10.87	12.21	-0.01	0.01	0.16	**-0.16**
Malta	18.86	19.50	14.60	4.90	3.85	14.19	0.41	-0.41	-0.09	**-0.31**
Finland	26.31	17.40	13.60	3.80	6.92	13.29	0.31	-0.31	0.09	**-0.40**
EU-27	26.36	23.60	16.40	7.20	3.66	15.97	0.43	-0.43	0.09	**-0.52**
Cyprus	18.42	22.20	16.20	6.00	3.07	15.36	0.84	-0.84	-0.10	**-0.74**
Germany	27.76	20.10	15.20	4.90	5.67	14.45	0.75	-0.75	0.12	**-0.87**
Luxembourg	20.14	15.50	13.40	2.10	9.59	12.47	0.93	-0.93	-0.06	**-0.87**
Euro 16	27.47	21.40	15.80	5.60	4.91	15.02	0.78	-0.78	0.12	**-0.90**
Portugal	24.33	26.00	18.50	7.50	3.24	17.00	1.50	-1.50	0.04	**-1.54**
Italy	27.79	25.30	18.70	6.60	4.21	16.70	2.00	-2.00	0.13	**-2.12**
Lithuania	16.16	27.60	20.00	7.60	2.13	17.70	2.30	-2.30	-0.16	**-2.15**
Greece	25.97	28.10	20.10	8.00	3.25	17.91	2.19	-2.19	0.08	**-2.27**
UK	23.72	23.20	18.70	4.50	5.27	15.79	2.91	-2.91	0.03	**-2.93**
Spain	22.71	22.90	19.60	3.30	6.88	15.66	3.94	-3.94	0.00	**-3.94**
Estonia	15.05	21.80	19.50	2.30	6.55	15.19	4.31	-4.31	-0.19	**-4.13**
Latvia	12.62	33.80	25.60	8.20	1.54	20.38	5.22	-5.22	-0.24	**-4.98**

Column 1	Social expenditures per GDP	OECD stats/Eurostat
Column 2	Poverty rate before social transfers	OECD stats/Eurostat
Column 3	Poverty rate after social transfers	OECD stats/Eurostat
Column 4	Reduction of poverty through social transfers	simple algebraic substraction, based on OECD stats data: Column 2 – Column 3
Column 5	To lift out 1% of people out of poverty, it is necessary to spend …% of GDP	simple algebraic calculation, based on OECD stats: Column 1:Column 4
Column 6	Trend value: poverty after social transfers, as statistically predicted by poverty rates before social transfers	linear trend values EXCEL regression on OECD stats data: poverty before social transfers (x)->poverty after social transfers (y)
Column 7	residual from this regression ('poverty too large in comparison to what one could expect from our knowledge about poverty before social transfers')	subtraction of poverty after social transfers data (Column 3) from predicted value (Column 6)
Column 8	analytical measure of poverty reduction (regression residual * -1)	simple multiplication of column 7 by (-1)
Column 9	Trend value: poverty reduction (social expenditures->analytical measure poverty reduction)	linear trend value EXCEL regression based on OECD stats data: Column 1 -> Column 8
Column 10	efficiency of social spending in poverty reduction	Column 8 minus Column 9

Source: our own calculations from Eurostat and OECD.stats, Microsoft EXCEL and SPSS XVIII

The five extracted factors and their contribution to total variance

Component	Own value Total	% of variance explained by the model	Cumulated% of total variance explained
1	6.627	16.569	16.569
2	5.79	14.475	31.044
3	3.947	9.867	40.911
4	3.231	8.079	48.99
5	2.787	6.968	55.958

Matrix of components

REVERSED FOR THE INTERPRETATION OF THE FACTOR SCORES	Education and social empowerment NO	Lifestyle, social cohesion and social-economic status YES	European youth policy model YES	Subjective well-being and peer relationships YES	Climate of non-violence YES
Percentage of children (0-17) in households with equivalent income less than 50 per cent of the median: most recent data.	-0.502	-0.015	0.525	0.328	0.085
Percentage of children reporting low family affluence, aged 11, 13 and 15: 2001.	-0.586	0.607	-0.222	0.312	-0.065
Percentage of children aged 15 reporting less than six educational possessions: 2003.	-0.375	0.211	-0.152	0.531	0.067
Percentage of children aged 15 reporting less than ten books in the home: 2003.	0.134	-0.12	0.003	-0.116	0.385
Percentage of working-age households with children without an employed parent OECD: most recent data.	-0.052	0.294	-0.047	0.068	-0.355
Infant mortality rate (per 1000 live births): most recent data.	-0.495	0.706	0.141	-0.002	0.018
Low birth rate (percentage of births less than 2500g): most recent data	-0.377	-0.425	0.222	0.352	0.042
Measles: Percentage of children immunised aged 12-23 months: 2003	-0.186	0.405	-0.28	0.061	-0.212
DPT3: Percentage of children immunised aged 12-23 months: 2002.	-0.064	0.336	-0.572	-0.008	-0.356
Polio 3: Percentage of children immunised aged 12-23 months: 2002	-0.005	0.376	-0.659	-0.236	-0.349
Deaths from accidents and injuries per 100,000 under 19 years, average of latest three years available.	-0.62	0.358	0.006	-0.42	0.127
Reading literacy achievement aged 15: 2003	0.757	0.216	0.299	0.003	-0.150

	Education and social empow-erment	Lifestyle, social co-hesion and social-economic status	European youth policy model	Subjec-tive well-being and peer relation-ships	Climate of non-violence
REVERSED FOR THE INTERPRETATION OF THE FACTOR SCORES	NO	YES	YES	YES	YES
Mathematics literacy achievement aged 15: 2003	0.854	0.171	0.091	0.213	0.012
Science literacy achievement aged 15: 2003	0.707	0.191	0.169	0.447	-0.136
Full-time and part-time students in public and private educational insti-tutions aged 15-19 as a percentage of the population of 15-19 year-olds: 2003	0.575	0.154	-0.441	0.25	-0.117
Percentage of 15-19 year-olds not in education or employment: 2003	-0.552	-0.29	0.068	-0.300	0.002
Percentage of pupils aged 15 years aspiring to low skilled work: 2003	0.229	-0.127	-0.124	0.196	0.190
Percentage of young people living in single-parent family structures, aged 11, 13 and 15: 2001	0.285	0.59	0.356	-0.310	0.035
Percentage of young people living in step family structure, aged 11, 13 and 15: 2001	0.504	0.355	0.358	-0.264	-0.058
Percentage of students whose par-ents eat their main meal with them around a table several times a week, aged 15: 2000	0.281	-0.034	-0.654	0.225	0.355
Percentage of students whose par-ents spend time just talking to them several times per week, aged 15: 2000	0.017	0.202	-0.231	0.247	-0.435
Percentage of young people finding their peers 'kind and helpful', aged 11, 13 and 15: 2001	0.334	-0.233	-0.14	-0.447	0.371
Percentage smoking cigarettes at least once per week, aged 11, 13, 15: 2001	0.155	0.296	-0.147	0.121	0.135
Percentage of young people who have been drunk two or more times, aged 11, 13, 15: 2001	0.413	0.592	0.327	-0.22	0.014

REVERSED FOR THE INTERPRETATION OF THE FACTOR SCORES	Education and social empowerment	Lifestyle, social cohesion and socialeconomic status	European youth policy model	Subjective wellbeing and peer relationships	Climate of nonviolence
	NO	YES	YES	YES	YES
Percentage of young people who have used cannabis in the last 12 months, aged 15: 2001	0.304	-0.224	0.307	0.282	-0.04
Adolescent fertility rate, births per 1000 women aged 15-19: 2003.	-0.491	0.55	0.571	-0.078	-0.071
Percentage of young people who have had sexual intercourse, aged 15: 2001	0.487	-0.215	0.407	-0.213	-0.053
Percentage of young people who used a condom during their last sexual intercourse, aged 15: 2001	-0.575	-0.32	-0.082	0.225	0.154
Percentage of young people involved in physical fighting in previous 12 months, aged 11, 13, 15: 2001	-0.444	0.379	0.008	0.357	-0.149
Percentage of young people who were bullied at least once in the last 2 months, aged 11, 13, 15: 2001	-0.245	0.471	0.138	-0.179	0.691
Percentage of young people who eat fruit every day, aged 11, 13, 15 years: 2001	-0.449	-0.568	-0.114	0.173	-0.02
Percentage of young people who eat breakfast every school day, aged 11, 13, 15 years: 2001	0.376	0.378	-0.438	-0.134	0.325
Mean number of days when young people are physically active for one hour or more of the previous /typical week, aged 11, 13, 15: 2001	0.048	0.139	0.581	0.119	-0.202
Percentage of young people who are overweight according to BMI, aged 13 and 15: 2001	-0.126	-0.429	0.488	0.249	-0.288
Percentage of young people rating their health as 'fair or poor', aged 11, 13 and 15: 2001	-0.128	0.731	0.183	0.056	0.310
Percentage of young people with scores above the middle of the life satisfaction scale, aged 11, 13 and	0.275	-0.774	-0.013	-0.146	-0.192

	Education and social empowerment	Lifestyle, social cohesion and social-economic status	European youth policy model	Subjective well-being and peer relationships	Climate of non-violence
REVERSED FOR THE INTERPRETATION OF THE FACTOR SCORES	NO	YES	YES	YES	YES
15: 2001					
Percentage of students who agree with the statement 'I feel like an outsider or left out of things', aged 15: 2003	0.249	0.27	0.169	0.503	-0.183
Percentage of students who agree with the statement 'I feel awkward and out of place', aged 15: 2003	0.341	0.055	-0.019	0.514	0.585
Percentage of students who agree with the statement 'I feel lonely', aged 15: 2003	0.161	0.084	0.039	0.617	0.365
Percentage of young people 'liking school a lot', aged 11, 13, 15: 2001	-0.183	-0.235	0.069	0.041	0.462

Source: our own compilations and calculations, based on SPSS XVIII, Innsbruck University, based on UNICEF data (http://www.unicef-irc.org/cgi-bin/unicef/Lunga.sql?ProductID=445)

Literature

Alber J. (2006), 'The European social model and the United States' European Union Politics, 7, 3: 393-419.

Alber J. (2010), 'What the European and American welfare states have in common and where they differ: facts and fiction in comparisons of the European Social Model and the United States.' Journal of European Social Policy, 20, 2: 102-125.

Alesina, A. F. and Angeletos, G.-M. (1983), 'Fairness and Redistribution: US versus Europe' (January 2003). Harvard Institute Research Working Paper No. 1983; MIT Department of Economics Working Paper No. 02-37. Available at SSRN: http://srn.com/abstract=346545 or doi:10.2139/ssrn.346545

Andrade S. C. and Chhaochharia V. (2010), 'How Costly is Sovereign Default? Evidence from Financial Markets' (November 1, 2010). Available at SSRN: http://ssrn.om/bstract=1706383.

Arts W. and Gelissen J. (2002), 'Three worlds of welfare capitalism or more? A state-of-the-art report'. Journal of European Social Policy, 12, 2: 137-159.

Baglioni A. S. and Cherubini U. (2010), 'Marking-to-Market Government Guarantees to Financial Systems: An Empirical Analysis of Europe' (November 10, 2010). Available at SSRN: http://ssrn.com/abstract=1715405.

Blanchard O. J. (2006), 'Is There a Viable European Social and Economic Model?' (July 11, 2006). MIT Department of Economics Working Paper No. 06-21. Available at SSRN: http://ssrn.com/abstract=916606

Esping-Andersen G. (1990), ,The three worlds of welfare capitalism' Princeton, N.J.: Princeton University Press.

Galtung J. (1982), 'Kapitalistische Großmacht Europa oder Die Gemeinschaft der Konzerne?' Reinbek near Hamburg: Verlag: Rowohlt TB-V.

Guger A., Marterbauer M. and Walterskirchen, E. (2006), Growth Policy in the Spirit of Steindl and Kalecki. Metroeconomica, 57(3), 428-42.

Herrmann P., Heshmati A., Tausch A. and Bajalan C. S. J. (2009), 'Efficiency and Effectiveness of Social Spending. Towards a theoretical and empirical critique of the European Commission's paper 'Efficiency and Effectiveness of Social Spending. Achievements and challenges. Background note for the informal ECOFIN of 4-5 April 2008'' Wirtschaft und Gesellschaft (Vienna), 1, 2009: 13-43.

Heshmati A. and Tausch A. (Eds.) (2007), 'Roadmap to Bangalore? Globalisation, the EU's Lisbon Process and the Structures of Global Inequality', Nova Science Publishers.

Heshmati A., Tausch A. and Bajalan C. (2008), 'Measurement and Analysis of Child Well-Being in Middle and High Income Countries'', European Journal of Comparative Economics 5(2), 227-249.

Heshmati A., Tausch A. and Bajalan, C. S. J. (2010), 'On the Multivariate Analysis of the 'Lisbon Process'' History and Mathematics (Volgograd, Russia), 1, 2010: 92-137.

Hyman R. (2005), 'Trade unions and the politics of the European social model'. Economic and Industrial Democracy, 26, 1: 9-40.

Jepsen M., Pascual A. S. (2005), 'The European Social Model: an exercise in deconstruction' Journal of European Social Policy, 15, 3: 231-245.

Malici A. (2008), 'The Search for a Common European Foreign and Security Policy. Leaders, Cognitions, and Questions of Institutional Viability' Basingstoke and New York: Palgrave Macmillan.

Montanari I., Nelson K., Palme J. (2008), 'Towards a European Social Model? Trends in social insurance among EU countries 1980-2000'. European Societies, 10, 5: 787-810.

Rothschild K. W. (1999), European Integration and Economic Methodology and Research: Questions and Speculations. Atlantic Economic Journal, Vol. 27, num. 3, pp. 243-253.

Rothschild K. W. (2000), Europe and the USA: Comparing What with What? Kyklos, Vol. 53, num. 3, pp. 249-264.

Rothschild K. W. (2003), A Note on European Integration and Fluctuations. Applied Economics Quarterly, Vol. 49, num. 2, pp. 139-148.

Rothschild K. W. (2009), 'Neoliberalism, EU and the Evaluation of Policies. Review of Political Economy, Vol. 21, num. 2, pp. 213-226.

Scharpf F. W. (2002), 'The European social model: Coping with the challenges of diversity' Journal of Common Market Studies, 40, 4: 645-670.

Seers D., Schaffer B. and Kiljunen M.-L. (1979), 'Underdeveloped Europe: studies in core-periphery relations'. Atlantic Highlands, N.J.: Humanities Press.

Seers D., Vaitsos C, with the assistance of Marja-Liisa Kiljunen (1980), 'Integration and unequal development: the experience of the EEC'. London: Macmillan.

SPSS (2007), 'Statistical Package for the Social Sciences, User Guide', Version 14, August 2007.

Tausch A. (2010), 'The European Union's failed 'Lisbon strategy' Society and Economy (Budapest), 32, 1, 2010: 103-121.

Tausch A. and Ghymers Chr. (2006), From the Washington towards a Vienna Consensus? A quantitative analysis on globalisation, development and global governance. Hauppauge NY: Nova Science.

Tausch A. and Herrmann P. (2001), Globalisation and European Integration. Huntington NY: Nova Science.

Tausch A. and Heshmati A. (2010), 'Learning from dependency and world system theory: explaining Europe's failure in the 'Lisbon Process' Alternatives: Turkish Journal of International Relations, Vol.9, No.4, Winter 2010: 3-90, available at: http://www.aternativesjournal.net/new/index.php.

UNICEF (2007), 'Child Poverty in Perspective: An overview of child well-being in rich countries' Innocenti Report Card 7, Firenze: UNICEF.

Zemanek H. (2010), Competitiveness Within the Euro Area: The Problem that Still Needs to be Solved. Economic Affairs, Vol. 30, No. 3, pp. 42-47.

European Union Sanctions as a Foreign Policy Tool: Do They Work?

Clara Portela

Introduction: The "forgotten strand" of EU Foreign Policy

The sanctions regimes recently imposed by the European Union (EU) against the regimes in Syria and Iran have attracted a great deal of public attention towards the collective employment of these measures by the member states of this organisation. Sanctions constitute indeed one of the most frequently used tools by the EU in the framework of its Common Foreign and Security Policy (CFSP).[1] The EU has been imposing sanctions in the absence of a United Nations Security Council (UNSC) mandate since the early 1980s (de Wilde 1998). However, this practice has attracted little scholarly attention (Jones 2007, Brzoska 2006). Previous work has revealed that the autonomous sanctions policy of the EU is not spread uniformly across the globe, but concentrates on certain geographical areas. Also, the nature of the goals the EU intends to advance through the use of sanctions varies from region to region: in Asia and Africa, most sanctions regimes are imposed in response to breaches of human rights and democratic rule; in the Middle East, sanctions have been usually connected with the fight against terrorism – although we have witnessed a departure from that pattern in the aftermath of the Arab spring – while in Eastern Europe, sanctions are imposed for a broader variety of reasons and are triggered by a lower threshold than elsewhere (Portela 2005). A study showed that the relatively infrequent use of sanctions by the EU in response to human rights violations in comparison to US practice can partly be attributed to their decision-making mechanisms: while for the US it is institutionally easier to impose sanctions, the EU can decide on aid more easily than it can wield sanctions (Hazelzet 2001). Criticisms of EU sanctions have pointed to the Council's decision making machinery as a main hin-

---

1   The present contribution is based on the monograph "European Union Sanctions and Foreign Policy", which was published by Routledge in 2010 and awarded the THESEUS Prize for Promising Research on European Integration (*Preis für vielversprechende Forschung in Europäischer Integration*) in 2011. The author would like to thank Pascal Vennesson, Marise Cremona, Michael Brzoska, Thomas Biersteker, Karen Smith, Hadewych Hazelzet, Anthonius de Vries, Tanguy de Wilde d'Estmael, Javier Fernández and Albertus Straver, along with all those EU officials who agreed to an interview, for their valuable help during the research conducted for this work. Interviews for the present study were conducted in Brussels, Berlin, Singapore, Madrid and Canberra from 2005 to 2009.

drance to efficacy: It has been posited that the EU lacks the flexibility to use the instrument of sanctions effectively due to the intergovernmental nature of the CFSP, which obliges it to agree measures at the lowest common denominator and precludes their swift management (de Wilde 2000). However, none of the existing works on the topic has yet attempted to assess their efficacy in compelling the changes for which they are imposed. It is also interesting to note that the traditional debates on European foreign policy have neglected its autonomous sanctions practice. The discussion on the EU as a "civilian power" (Duchêne 1973), the oldest debate attempting to define the character of European foreign policy, centred on the European Community's renunciation of military means, but remained silent on its use of sanctions. Equally, the more recent notion of "normative power Europe" (Manners 2002) has failed to explicitly discuss the role played by sanctions in promoting human rights, democracy and rule of law in the foreign relations of the EU.

The sanctions practice of the EU presents an important peculiarity in comparison with the unilateral practice of other imposers. Since the mid-1990s, the EU has followed a policy of imposing targeted sanctions rather than comprehensive embargoes, although it did not make this policy explicit until the publication of the "Basic Principles on the Use of Restrictive Measures" in 2004, which states that "Sanctions should be targeted in a way that has maximum impact on those whose behaviour we want to influence. Targeting should reduce to the maximum extent possible any adverse humanitarian effects or unintended consequences for persons not targeted" (Council 2004: 3). Indeed, targeted sanctions are measures designed to canalise their effects to the leadership responsible for the objectionable policies the imposer intends to modify rather than to affect the population of the target country as a whole (Tostensen and Bull 2002). Fifteen years after the shift towards targeted sanctions, the impact of this type of measures and in particular their relative efficacy compared to traditional embargoes has not been comprehensively assessed. Thus, the present chapter offers an overview of EU sanctions practice and its effectiveness in an attempt to contribute to a double task. Firstly, it aims at evaluating the efficacy of these measures: Are they effective in compelling the policy changes they aim for in the targets? Also, as the EU's autonomous sanctions practice becomes increasingly frequent and sophisticated, an assessment of the efficacy of these measures can also improve our understanding of the character of the EU as a global actor.

Can EU Sanctions Work?

Under which circumstances do EU sanctions achieve their stated aims? And how can we account for their success and failure? Even though sanctions have a long history as foreign policy tools and have been used as such especially after the First World War (Charron 2011), sanctions research originated in the late 1960s with a seminal article published by Johann Galtung on the impact of the United Nations sanctions on Southern Rhodesia (Galtung 1967). This article inaugurated a pessimistic strand of research which not only concluded that sanctions were failing to achieve their objectives in Southern Rhodesia, but considered them incapable of fulfilling their tasks while ascribing to them perverse effects. This understanding was shared by the first generation of sanctions researchers during the 1970s. Galtung also spelled out the mechanism according to which sanctions were expected to work: The economic pain inflicted by the sanctions was supposed to transform into political pressure that would eventually compel the leadership to comply or face being unseated. A breakthrough in sanctions evaluation occurred when a team of researchers from the Institute for International Economics published a study evaluating the entire international sanctions practice of the twentieth century, which found that sanctions had been at least moderately successful in 33% of the cases in which they were imposed (Hufbauer et al. 1985). Because it affirmed the possibility for sanctions to be successful, the work by Gary Hufbauer, Jeffrey Schott and Kimberly Elliot inaugurated an "optimistic" strand of sanctions research whose aim is to ascertain the circumstances conducive to success (Blanchard and Ripsman 2002). Even though its methodology has been subjected to severe criticism (Pape 1997 and 1998, Drury 1998), it also provided a blueprint for successive researchers in the field. In order to investigate the research question, the present contribution adapts the methodology proposed by Hufbauer et al. and it redefines the explanatory variables in accordance to the nature of the imposer and the measures taken, updating them by incorporating the findings of the most recent sanctions research. In this light, the following hypotheses are formulated:

1/ Sanctions are more likely to be effective if they inflict considerable disutility on the targets;
2/ Sanctions are more likely to be effective if the disutility inflicted is economic in nature;
3/ Sanctions are more likely to be effective if third countries support the EU stance;
4/ Sanctions are more likely to be effective if the EU adjusts its strategy in response to progress or setbacks in the situation it aims to affect;
5/ Sanctions are more likely to be effective if the aims pursued by the EU do not jeopardise the permanence in office of the leadership it aims to influence.

These hypotheses are tested on a dataset featuring the entire autonomous sanctions practice of the EU from the signing of the Treaty of Maastricht in

1991 until 2010, whereby those sanctions which had been agreed previously but were still in force are included.[2] The dataset comprises sanctions regimes imposed by the EU within four different legal frameworks:

- CFSP sanctions, adopted in the intergovernmental framework of the CFSP and reflected in a Common Position. Measures imposed in this framework are referred to as "restrictive measures".
- "Informal sanctions" are sanctions decided jointly by the member states outside the formal framework of the CFSP. They are reflected in Council Conclusions or presidential statements rather than in legally-binding documents.
- "Art 96 sanctions" suspending the application of the Partnership Agreement between the EU and African, Caribbean and Pacific (ACP) states – routinely called Cotonou Agreement – on parties having breached human rights and democratic principles. This entails the suspension of trade preferences and the freezing or redirection of development aid.
- Withdrawal of trade privileges under the Generalised System of Preferences (GSP), technically a trade measure, occurs due to the violation of key labour standards protected by Conventions of the International Labour Organisation (ILO).

Even though this universe is heterogeneous from a legal point of view, all measures fit into the definition of sanctions as restrictive tools imposed in response to undesirable behaviour on the side of the target, and designed to compel the target to rectify its wrongdoing and limit its ability to pursue the objectionable policies. It is noteworthy that certain countries are the target of more than one type of sanction from the above classification: Belarus and Burma/Myanmar are under both CFSP and GSP sanctions, while Zimbabwe and Guinea-Conakry have been subjected to CFSP and Art. 96 sanctions. The sequencing of measures in those rare cases combining two different types also shows a pattern. GSP suspensions have only been imposed on countries after these had been under CFSP measures for several years, while the activation of Art 96 occurred simultaneously with the imposition of CFSP measures on Zimbabwe as this was a legal necessity allowing for the discontinuation of aid.

---

2   For an overview of the dataset, please consult Portela, C. (2010) *European Union Sanctions and Foreign Policy*, Routledge: London

EU Sanctions Efficacy: A Complex Picture

The incidence of positive outcomes, defined as those instances in which sanctions contributed to a successful resolution of the crisis at hand, is generally low. Art 96 suspensions record the highest incidence of positive outcomes. By contrast, the CFSP sanctions display mostly failures, and informal sanctions have an even lower success rate. The GSP suspensions have never been reversed, although this might change soon as the restoration of GSP to Burma/Myanmar is under discussion (Bünte and Portela 2012). However, this group can hardly be regarded as representative, not only because it features only two cases, but also because both suspended beneficiaries – Belarus and Burma/Myanmar – have been simultaneously targets of protracted EU sanctions campaigns. The concentration of most positive outcomes in the Art 96 group seems to confirm hypothesis two, namely that even in the era of targeted measures, sanctions prove more effective if they entail economic disutility for the target, which is normally the case with Art 96 sanctions given that they entail the partial suspension or the redirection of aid. At the same time, Art 96 sanctions are mostly imposed in order to re-establish democratic rule in the target, which was initially considered one of the objectives most unlikely to be achieved. In any case, the number of episodes in which Art 96 sanctions did not lead to success remains high enough to invalidate any assumption of automaticity between their presence and a positive outcome. By contrast, we also find episodes in the CFSP group where sanctions without economic character managed to elicit limited concessions by the target (as in Belarus) that eventually led to the lifting of sanctions (as in Uzbekistan).

A series of insights into EU practice that had not been contemplated previously emerges from contrasting successful and unsuccessful cases. Firstly, in those cases in which the crises were resolved, the lifting of the measures came about after the sender had conducted an intensive diplomatic campaign in which a deal was struck between the sender and the target. Such a deal often emerged from a direct negotiation between both actors and consisted in an exchange in which both sides conceded to some extent. As a result, the final outcome cannot be described as "full compliance by the target", but rather as compliance with a watered-down version of the original demands. In other words, the EU managed to obtain some key concessions from the target, but it settled for outcomes which were inferior to the original aspiration. Uzbekistan – and for some time also Belarus (Portela 2011) – are cases in point, and the same applies to many Art 96 suspension episodes.

Secondly, the assumption that the pain inflicted by the sanctions compels the target to seek accommodation with the imposer is disconfirmed. The reason why targets seek accommodation with the EU is less the desire to be freed from the direct effects of CFSP sanctions, but because they see their prospects for economic growth frustrated by the presence of sanctions. From the target's vantage point, the removal of sanctions opens up the possibility of enhanced investment and trade with the EU, along with the benefits they entail, which are unavailable elsewhere. Again, this expectation of increased wealth was openly expressed by targeted leaders such as Lukaschenko, and remains very present in the calculations of ACP countries. The desire for enhanced relations with the EU is not exclusively motivated by economic considerations, but also by the aspiration for international prestige maintained by countries aiming for regional or global leadership, such as Uzbekistan or China.

Thirdly, an aspect that has often been overlooked in sanctions research is the role of sanctions management, i.e. how the sequence of sanctions is crafted and updated, whether the sender responds to progress and setbacks by the target by easing or tightening the sanctions package. In the absence of any reciprocation of positive steps taken by the target, there is a risk that targeted leaders refrain from meeting demands out of a belief that the senders will not ease sanctions regardless of compliance. There is a wealth of examples in which targeted leaders regard themselves as being demonised, and indeed in certain cases sanctions were not eased in spite of (almost full) compliance by the target (Cortright and Lopez 2000). This danger of demonisation, inevitably conducive to stalemate, appears to be minimised by the presence of a formal process requiring the direct participation of the target, and involving the Commission as a negotiator rather than the member states. In the case of the Art 96 suspensions, the highly structured process facilitates positive outcomes. The suspension of aid can only be decided after high-level consultations have been held with the target. During these consultations, a joint roadmap to rectify the identified breach can be agreed, thereby creating a framework for optimal communication. In addition, the fact that negotiations with the target are conducted by a single interlocutor, namely the Commission, somewhat reduces the possibility that intra-EU disagreements can be exploited by the target. Compliance with the roadmap, once agreed, is directly monitored by the Commission through periodic missions to the targets, which reassures the target of the possibility of lifting. Regrettably, these features are absent from the intergovernmental frameworks of the CFSP and informal sanctions, which are characterised by their opacity and are generally regarded as more politically-ridden processes.

Unexpectedly, the legal framework under which the sanctions are imposed and the incidence of positive outcomes appear to be related. This correlation suggests a relationship between the choice of legal framework and the expected efficacy of the measures: With the ACP countries, the EU entertains a close, longstanding relationship marked by economic asymmetry.

Thus, sanctions have relatively good prospects for success. More difficult sanctions cases such as Sudan, which have a higher international profile and where the relationship is complicated by the presence of other powerful imposers, are dealt with in the CFSP framework, where the expectation of success is much lower. Informal sanctions find themselves at the lowest level of prospects of success: The low degree of unity and political will within the Council is reflected in the lack of formalisation of the measures in a legally-binding Common Position. Finally, the negligible category of GSP suspension, applied against long-standing CFSP targets only, is normally imposed in the absence of any expectation of efficacy.

EU Sanctions as Tools for Democracy Promotion

Any study pertaining to the study of EU sanctions is of particular relevance to the study of the use of sanctions for the promotion of human rights and democracy, as most EU practice can be categorised under such heading. Because the UNSC is empowered to address situations endangering international peace and security, the adoption of mandatory sanctions by this body make it unnecessary for other actors to adopt unilateral measures. As identified by Andrea Charron (2011), UNSC sanctions are typically applied in intra-state conflicts – which constitute the kind of situation the drafters of the Charta had in mind – the condemnation of apartheid, and after the cold war, increasingly intra-state conflicts, the non-proliferation of Weapons of Mass Destruction (WMD) and the fight against terrorism. However, given the lack of consensus among Security Council members on the desirability of promoting democracy and of the relevance of human rights protection to its mission, the Council refrains from action in this field (Brzoska 2006). As a result, it is normally the EU and the US, along with other Western-oriented actors such as Canada, that impose sanctions in response to grave human rights violations, especially when they take the form of government-inspired repression of pro-democracy demonstrations, as in Belarus, China and Burma/Myanmar, or government-tolerated violence against civilians, such as in Indonesia or Sudan before 2004. Since the publication of its programmatic "Basic Principles", it has been the declared policy of the EU to impose sanctions in support of democracy and human rights: "The Council will impose autonomous EU sanctions in support of efforts to fight terrorism and the proliferation of weapons of mass destruction and as a restrictive measure to uphold respect for human rights, democracy, the rule of law and good governance" (Council 2004: 2).

Among these objectives, EU sanctions policy privileges the democratic component. In fact, the sort of human rights violations to which the EU responds with sanctions are often more or less directly linked to the democratic process – harassment of journalists and electoral candidates, disappearances of members of parliaments, restrictions on the freedom of press, association or demonstration, etc. Human rights violations must attain a fairly high degree of international publicity for the EU to respond with sanctions. Conversely, the EU often suspends aid in instances of bloodless *coup d'etats*, notably in Latin America and especially in Sub-Saharan Africa, where the EU wields suspensions more rapidly than in comparable cases in the Pacific or the Caribbean. Illustrative of the EU's particular sensitivity to developments in the Eastern neighbourhood, it has also responded with sanctions to steps obstructive of the democratic process falling short of a *coup d'etat*, such as illegal constitutional changes.

The sample already displays a bias towards sanctions imposed on autocratic regimes, which allows little ground for comparison with cases of sanctions against democracies. In terms of the impact of sanctions, thus, very little differentiation can be made between sanctions imposed for democracy and human rights promotion on the one hand, and for different ends on the other. This is particularly the case in view of EU sanctions dynamics, which display incremental features: the number of regimes in place has been increasing since the inception of the EU's unilateral practice (Jones 2007), and so has the frequency of sanctions imposed for the advancement of human rights and democracy. There is however a tendency for the EU to impose sanctions in response to *coup d'etats* in Sub-Saharan and Latin American countries, while episodes of large-scale repression are among the most frequent justifications of EU sanctions elsewhere, notably in Asia. This can be partly ascribed to the legal configuration of these regimes as well as to relative frequency of *coup-d'états* in Sub-Saharan Africa. Remarkably, two main situations can be identified: those sanctions most directly related to the democratic process tend to be imposed on newly-installed autocratic rulers – precisely in response to their illegal accession to power – and sanctions imposed in reaction to human rights violations, which are normally imposed on autocratic regimes. As found by Laakso et al. in their examination of the application of Art 96 suspensions, the EU tends to react to spiralling degenerations in democratic and human rights conditions, rather than to situations displaying consistently low but stable conditions (Laakso et al. 2007).

Probably one of the most counterintuitive findings of the study concerns the relatively high incidence of positive outcomes in Art 96. This finding needs to be put into perspective, as the success rate of EU sanctions is – generally, also by comparison with the Hufbauer et al. dataset – rather low. Secondly, the aid suspensions managed to compel the authorities to organise elections; however, these often gave way to democratically-elected governments that proved short-lived. Still, this is puzzling because, as has often been claimed, compliance is likely to cost leaders their positions in office. Thus, for the targeted leaderships, the stakes could not be higher; they have every incentive to refrain from accommodating demands (Schimmelfennig and Sedelmeier 2005). The EU's experience with Belarus illustrates how compliance in areas unrelated to democratisation – in particular in the economic policy – can be achieved far more easily (Portela 2011).

The most straightforward explanations for this higher-than-average-success rate can be found in the strong dependence on EU funding of many of these countries. As outlined above, the concentration of most positive outcomes in the Art 96 group seems to confirm the hypothesis that sanctions prove more effective when they produce economic disutility. Certain sub-Saharan countries are hardly economically viable. However, more nuanced explanations advanced by the practitioners consulted in the framework of the present study can help specifying this finding: Some of the *putchistes*, conscious of the political instability prevailing in their countries, accommodated EU demands out of fear that the economic consequences of suspension could provoke unrest and lead to their unseating. This fear clearly connects with Galtung's naive theory of the operation of sanctions. Interestingly, some respondents explained that the perpetrators of coups, having often undergone only military training, are uneducated about the likelihood of aid suspension by donors in case of a coup, and of the severe consequences associated with aid suspension, until the threat has been issued by the donor. Even though EU suspensions never entail the sort of full cut-off of funds that would produce economic deprivation, they still hinder the government's capacity to present itself as a provider of social services of central importance to maintain the support of the population. In some Latin-American countries, members of the democratic opposition highlighted the role that immediate announcements of aid suspension following a *coup d'état* had in compelling the *putchistes* to restore the democratic order.

Conclusions

To some extent, the findings on EU sanctions practice tend to confirm some of the ideas floated already in the field of sanctions research in general: Sanctions with an impact on the functioning of the economy display more coercive power than the timid blacklists featuring individuals who are banned from entering EU territory and holding accounts in European financial institutions. On the other hand, the fact that sanctions imposed in reaction to interruptions of the democratic process are among the most successful in EU practice contradicts much of the conventional wisdom prevailing in current sanctions research – even though this only concerns African cases. This in turn highlights the importance of certain factors that were considered of little relevance before, such as the presence of a single negotiator and of a formal process allowing – and indeed requiring – the direct input of the target.

At the same time, the criticism expressed in the past decade that the present, purely intergovernmental, decision-making process followed by the Council is too unwieldy to allow for the effective management of sanctions, continues to hold today. Finally, due to various reasons, the development of EU sanctions policy has been accompanied by a permanent preoccupation for the avoidance of humanitarian consequences, the protection of human rights, and also by the perennial worry about the compatibility with other obligations incurred by the EU under its international agreements. However, the need to optimise the tools and their design to target those individuals and commodities they aim for, has hardly ever been discussed at EU level. Devoting some effort to improving the design of the measures as well as the means that the EU has at its disposal to monitor their impact would do a great deal to enhance the efficacy of the measures.

Bibliography

Blanchard, Jean-Marc F./Ripsman, Norrin M. (2002): Asking the Right Question: When Do Economic Sanctions Work Best? Security Studies 9, Autumn 1999/Winter 2000: 219-3.

Brzoska, Michael (2006): Sanktionen als Instrument der europäischen Außen- und Sicherheitspolitik. Friedensgutachten 2006, Berlin: LIT Verlag., pp. 247-255.

Bünte, Marco/Portela, Clara (2012): Myanmar: The Beginning of Reforms and the End of Sanctions. GIGA Focus 3/2012.

Charron, Andrea (2011): United Nations Sanctions and Conflict, London: Routledge.

Cortright, David/Lopez, George (2000): The Sanctions Decade. Boulder Co: Lynne Rinner.

Council of the European Union (2004): Basic Principles on the Use of Restrictive Measures (Sanctions). 10198/1/04, Brussels, 7. June 2004.

de Wilde d'Estmael, Tanguy (2000): L'efficacité politique de la coercition économique exercée parl' Union européenne dans les relations internationales. Annuaire Français de Relations Internationales (1): pp. 502-21.

de Wilde d'Estmael, Tanguy (1998): La Dimension Politique des Relations Economiques Extérieures de la Communauté Européenne. Brussels: Bruylant.

Drury, A. Cooper (1998): Revisiting Economic Sanctions Reconsidered. Journal of Peace Research 35: pp. 497-509.

Duchêne, François (1973): Die Rolle Europas im Weltsystem. Von der regionalen zur planetarischen Interdependenz. In Kohnstamm, M./Hager, W. Hager (eds.): Zivilmacht Europa – Supermacht oder Partner? Frankfurt/Main: Suhrkamp, pp. 11-35.

Galtung, J.ohann(1967): On the Effects of International Economic Sanctions, with Examples from the Case of Rhodesia. World Politics 19: pp. 378-416.

Hazelzet, H. (2001): Carrots or Sticks? EU and US Reactions to Human Rights Violations (1989–2000). unpublished thesis, Florence: European University Institute.

Hufbauer, Gary C./Schott, Jeffrey J./Elliot, Kimberly A. (1985): Economic Sanctions Reconsidered. History and Current Policy. Washington, DC: Institute for International Economics

Jones, Seth (2007): The Rise of European Security Co-operation, Cambridge University Press: Cambridge

Laakso, Liisa/Kivimäki, Timo/Seppänen, Maaria (2007): Evaluation of Coordination and Coherence in the Application of Article 96 of the Cotonou Partnership Agreement. Amsterdam: Aksant.

Manners, Ian (2002): Normative Power Europe: A Contradiction in Terms? Journal of Common Market Studies 40(2): pp. 235-258.

Pape, Robert A. (1997): 'Why Economic Sanctions Do Not Work. International Security 22(2): pp. 90-36.

Pape, Robert A. (1998): Why Economic Sanctions Still Do Not Work. International Security 23 (1): pp. 66-7.

Portela, Clara (2005): Where and Why does the European Union Impose Sanctions? Politique Européenne nr 17, autumne/hiver 2005, pp. 83-11.

Portela, Clara (2010): European Union Sanctions and Foreign Policy. London: Routledge.

Portela, Clara (2011): The EU and Belarus: Sanctions and Partnership? Comparative European Politics 9(4/5): pp. 486-505.

Schimmelfennig, Frank/Sedelmeier, Ulrich (eds.) (2005): The Europeanisation of Central and Eastern Europe. Ithaca, NY: Cornell University Press.

Tostensen, Arne/Bull, Beate (2002): Are Smart Sanctions Feasible? World Politics 54 (3): pp. 373-03.

Conclusions and Outlook

Sven Bernhard Gareis/Gunther Hauser/Franz Kernic

Finally we return to the question that guided the analyses presented in this book: "The European Union – A Global Actor?" In their 24 articles the authors give a fairly clear answer: the EU is a major factor in world politics and it acts globally – but there is considerable room and need for using its potential more effectively and in a more determined manner. A glance at the areas of action the Union has been involved in over the last two decades – the Balkans, Middle East, the South Caucasus, Iraq, Libya, Afghanistan, Africa – shows that today's world is hyper-volatile with an extremely high degree of interdependences on the one hand and increasing frictions on the other. In coping with the various challenges of this complex world, Europe is facing an urgent necessity to develop a new strategic culture that can serve "as the balance between and emphasis upon all forms of security engagement ranging from negotiation, international law, trade and commerce, aid and development, alliance and regime building, coercive diplomacy, economic sanctions and military power" (Lindley-French 2011).

The institutionalisation of the EU's Common Foreign and Security Policy (CFSP) over the last two decades has been a remarkable achievement, although the established foreign policy instruments still show significant limitations in practice. CFSP can be seen as an often small common denominator the EU member states can agree upon after having secured their most vital national interests and ambitions. Thus, the so-called "CFSP voice" in world politics never could reach a level of attention comparable to that of real global actors like the US, China or Russia.

The EU is neither a super-state nor a traditional sovereign state, and therefore CFSP can only be understood as a compromise between the EU member states. The institutionalisation of CFSP has also led to the adoption of many common strategies and conclusion of a number of strategic partnerships with states and regions around the globe. But as a "soft power", the EU primarily aims at promoting Western values and exporting norms and ideas to third states and regions. The CFSPs main objectives are all long-term and the available means are primarily civilian and economic. The main goal is to politically and economically stabilise regions and prevent conflicts in the near neighbourhood. As one crucial step towards stabilisation, the EU has always envisaged political, economic, social and security integration of specific states and regions inside and outside Europe. Today the Western Balkans and the Southern Caucasus are generally viewed as such regions. Maintaining good relations with its neighbours has always been a political priority to the European Union and the promise of becoming a more or less integral part of this economically successful realm has always been one of the most important power tools in persuading governments to fulfil European requests related to stability and peace. So when in May 2012 former ultra-nationalist Tomislav Nikolic was elected Serbia's president, EU representatives immediately called upon him to demonstrate "statesmanship" and to keep the country on a pro-European course (Buckley 2012: 4).

It is obvious that the EU has to deal with a number of political troublespots in its near neighbourhood. The South Caucasus is one of them despite the fact that this region is participating in the European Neighbourhood Policy framework (ENP). This troubled area contains a number of different local and regional conflicts which make the European Union face tremendous challenges with respect to its political foreign policy goal of conflict prevention and settlement. The outburst of violence in recent years and the political involvement of Russia in this region have made it nearly impossible for the EU to find its desired role as an accepted political actor and mediator that is in fact capable of contributing to the settlement of those difficult conflicts.

The European dependence on gas and oil from Russia continues to be high and consequently also shows a significant impact on the EU foreign policy with respect to Russia. Attempts to convince Russia to adopt Western human rights standards and Western pluralist-democratic standards show only limited success. Another big challenge for the Union and its Mediterranean Dialogue emerges from recent political developments in the Arab world. It remains an open question whether the "Arab spring" and maybe new political changes in the near future will finally lead to an end of the 50 year-history of autocratic rule in all countries of the region, including Libya, Tunisia, Egypt, Syria and Yemen. It is common wisdom that deep-rooted democratic changes also require comprehensive legal and judicial reforms. The Syrian case is about to become another touchstone with respect to measuring success and efficiency of current EU foreign policy action and preventive diplomacy.

The European Union is also part of the international sanctions regime against Iran. In November 2011 a report from the International Atomic Energy Agency (IAEA) raised new concerns about a "possible military dimension" of Iran's nuclear programme. This report has led to an increased political pressure on the regime in Tehran. Despite the ongoing P5+1 negotiations (the Permanent Members of the UN Security Council United States, Russia, China, France, United Kingdom, and Germany; sometimes also referred to as EU 3+3) with Iran to prevent the country from becoming a nuclear weapon state, new threat scenarios have emerged, reaching from a possible Israeli preventive attack to a potential nuclear arms race in the region sparked by an Iran with the bomb. Unfortunately, the EU still lacks a coherent foreign policy strategy to deal with such important political issues in the extremely unstable Middle East region.

In this context it is also necessary to consider the available power instruments that might back EU policies on the global stage. Up to now the European Union has launched and conducted a total of 24 crisis management missions and operations, all of them appearing as success stories so far. But one also needs to take into account that all EU crisis management operations have required the setup of ad-hoc chains of command due to the fact that the Union still does not have a permanent military strategic command and control structure. At present the EU has mainly only three options to plan and run military crisis management operations: First to rely on NATO assets and capabilities and to use NATO structure according to the Berlin-Plus arrangement; second to rely on member states' assets and capabilities, and third to activate the Operations Centre of the EU Military Staff (EUMS) which was established on 1 January 2007 in order to plan and conduct military operations up to a total strength of 2,000 soldiers. In any case the scope of the available military tool still appears extremely limited.

Summing up, recent developments in global politics indicate that it might get even more difficult for the European Union in the future to pursue an autonomous and coherent foreign policy and to be internationally recognised as a global and powerful actor in world politics. In this regard, the euro and financial crisis contains both new risks and opportunities. Different scenarios about the future development are being discussed in public and academia. The crisis could lead to more solidarity and bring member states to cooperate more closely in the most relevant policy fields – economy, finance but also CFSP and CSDP – in order to tackle the new challenges and risks. This could indeed lead to a stronger, more unified and coordinated Union. On the other hand, if the Europeans fail again to deepen and enhance their integration, this could give way to separation and an increased polarisation among member states, a new divide, and consequently to a further weakening of the Union's capacity as a global actor.

In order to avoid falling apart, the political elite of the European Union is under urgent pressure to develop a new comprehensive overall "Grand Strategy", clarifying the common goals and objectives as well as determining the joint procedures and adequate instruments to reach them. Without such a strategy and without creating an appropriate new culture of collective decision-making the EU as a global actor most probably will be doomed to fail – as the French politician Pierre Lellouche put it once: *"L'Europe sera straté-gique ou ne sera pas."* (Europe will be strategic or it will not be.)

References

Buckley, Neil (2012), Serb president urged to show statesmanship. In: Financial Times, May 22, 2012, p. 4.

Lindley-French, Julian (2011), The future of European Security and Defence Policy: Implications for Member-States, Vienna, 27 June 2011.

Selected Bibliography and Recommended Readings

Bretherton, Charlotte/Vogler, John (1999): The European Union as a Global Actor. London-New York: Routledge.

Carlsnaes, Walter/Sjursen, Helene/White, Brian (eds.) (2004): Contemporary European Foreign Policy. London: Sage.

Cosgrove, Carol/Twitchett, Kenneth J. (eds.) (1970): The New International Actors: The UN and the EEC. London.

Gasteyger, Curt (1996): An Ambiguous Power: The European Union in a Changing World. Strategies for Europe. Gütersloh: Bertelsmann Foundation Publishers.

Ginsberg, Roy (1998): Foreign Policy Actions of the EC: The Politics of Scale. Boulder: Lynne Rienner.

Hauser, Gunther (2010): Europas Sicherheit und Verteidigung. Der zivil-militärische Ansatz. Frankfurt/Main: Peter Lang.

Hill, Christopher/Smith, Michael (eds.) (2005): International Relations of the EU. Oxford: Oxford University Press.

Howorth, Jolyon (2007): Security and Defence Policy in the European Union. Houndmills: Palgrave

Kernic, Franz (2007): Die Außenbeziehungen der Europäischen Union. Frankfurt/Main: Peter Lang.

Kernic, Franz/Hauser, Gunther (eds.) (2006): Handbuch zur europäischen Sicherheit. 2nd edition, Frankfurt/Main: Peter Lang.

Knodt, Michele/Princen, Sebastiaan (2003): Understanding the European Union's External Relations. London: Routledge.

McCormick, John (2002): Understanding the European Union. A Concise Introduction. 2nd ed., Houndmills: Palgrave.

Mkrtchyan, Tigran/Huseynov, Tabib/Gogolashvili, Kakha (2009): The European Union and the South Caucasus. Three Perspectives on the Future of the European Project from the Caucasus. Europe in Dialog 2009/01. Gütersloh: Bertelsmann Stiftung.

Regelsberger, Elfriede/Schoutheete de Tervarent, Philippe de /Wessels, Wolfgang (eds.) (1997): Foreign Policy of the European Union. From EPC to CFSP and Beyond. Boulder: Lynne Rienner.

Regelsberger, Elfriede (2004): Die Gemeinsame Außen- und Sicherheitspolitik der EU (GASP). Baden-Baden: Nomos.

Rosecrance, Richard (1997): Paradoxes of European Foreign Policy: The European Union. A New Type of International Actor. Florence: European University Institute Working Papers 64.

Schumacher, Tobias (2005): Die Europäische Union als internationaler Akteur im südlichen Mittelmeerraum. 'Actor Capability' und EU-Mittelmeerpolitik. Baden-Baden: Nomos.

Sicurelli, Daniela (2010): The European Union´s Africa Policies. Norms, Interests and Impact. Farnham (UK) and Burlington (Vt): Ashgate Publishing.

Sjöstedt, Gunnar (1977): The External Role of the European Community. Westmead.

Terzi, Özlem (2010): The Influence of the European Union on Turkish Foreign Policy. Farnham (UK) and Burlington (Vt): Ashgate Publishing,

Smith, Karen E. (1998): The Instruments of European Union Foreign Policy. In: Zielonka (1998), pp. 67-85.

Smith, Karen E. (1999): The Making of EU Foreign Policy. The Case of Eastern Europe. Basingstoke: MacMillan.

Smith, Karen E. (2003): European Union Foreign Policy in a Changing World. Cambridge: Polity Press.

Smith, Karen E. (2004): The Making of EU Foreign Policy, Houndmills: MacMillan.

Smith, Michael E. (2003): Institutional Moments, Policy Performance, and the Future of EU Security/Defence Policy. EUSA Review 16, 1 (2003), pp. 4-5.

Smith, Michael E. (2004). Europe's Foreign and Security Policy: The Institutionalisation of Cooperation. Cambridge: Cambridge University Press.

White, Brian (2001): Understanding European Foreign Policy. Basingstoke: Palgrave.

Whitman, Richard G. (1998): From Civilian Power to Superpower? The International Identity of the European Union, Basingstoke: Macmillan.

Zielonka, Jan (ed.) (1998): Paradoxes of European Foreign Policy, The Hague: Kluwer.

Index

Authors

Marc-André Boisvert, consultant in African security and freelance journalist based in Abidjan (Côte d'Ivoire)

Gerald Brettner-Messler, National Defence Academy, Vienna (Austria)

Michele Brunelli, Bergamo State University, Bergamo (Italy)

Doris Dialer, University of Innsbruck (Austria), Danube University of Krems (Austria), and Berlin University for Professional Studies (Germany)

Klaus Fischer, Journalist, Vienna (Austria)

Sven Bernhard Gareis, George Marshall European Center for Security Studies, Garmisch-Partenkirchen (Germany), and Westfälische Wilhelms-Universität Münster (Germany)

Bastian Giegerich, Bundeswehr Institute of Social Sciences, Strausberg (Germany)

Gunther Hauser, National Defence Academy Vienna (Austria) and Danube University of Krems (Austria)

Waldemar Hummer, University of Innsbruck (Austria)

Arnold H. Kammel, Austria Institute for European and Security Policy, Maria Enzersdorf (Austria), and University of Applied Sciences Burgenland (Austria)

Lisa Karlborg, Department of Peace and Conflict Research, Uppsala University (Sweden), and Department of Politics, New York University (USA)

Franz Kernic, Swedish National Defence College, Stockholm (Sweden), and University of Innsbruck (Austria)

Heinrich Kreft, Ambassador for Public Diplomacy and Dialogue among Civilisations, Federal Foreign Ministry Berlin (Germany)

Gustav Lindstrom, Geneva Centre for Security Policy, Geneva (Switzerland)

Martin Malek, National Defence Academy, Vienna (Austria)

Anja Opitz, University of Innsbruck (Austria), and Akademie für Politische Bildung, Tutzing (Germany)

Clara Portela, Singapore Management University (Singapore)

Nico Prucha, Austrian Institute for International Affairs (OIIP), and University of Vienna (Austria)

Olivier Scherlofsky, Austrian Armed Forces, Vienna (Austria)

Sebnem Udum, Hacettepe University, Ankara (Turkey)

Arno Tausch, University of Innsbruck (Austria), University of Vienna (Austria), and Corvinus University, Budapest (Hungary)